Classic Cars

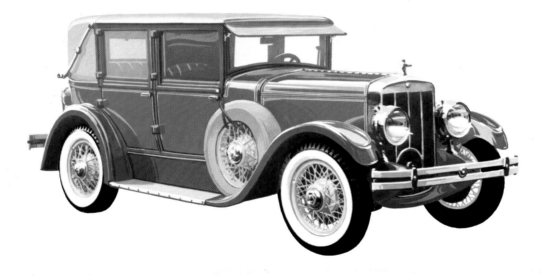

Six-cylinder air-cooled Franklin.

1938 Type 57SC Bugatti Atlantic coupe.

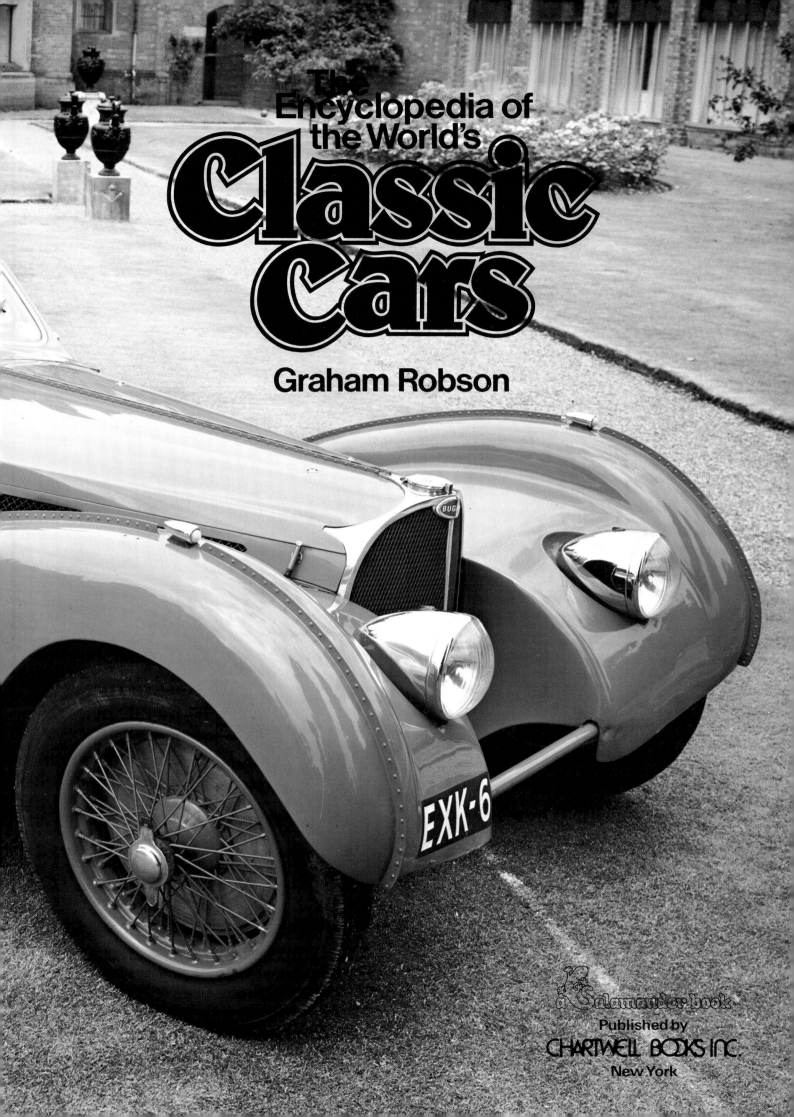

The
Encyclopedia of
the World's
Classic Cars

Graham Robson

a Salamander book

Published by
CHARTWELL BOOKS INC.
New York

EXK-6

A Salamander Book

This edition published in 1977 by
Chartwell Books Inc.
Distributed by
BOOK SALES INC.
110 Enterprise Avenue
Secaucus, N.J.07094
United States of America

ISBN 0-89009-144-7

Library of Congress
Catalog Card Number 77-89590

© **Salamander Books Ltd.**
27 Old Gloucester Street
London WC1N 3AF
United Kingdom

Credits

Editor: Ray Bonds
Designer: Roger Hyde

Color drawings: Gordon Davies,
Ken Rush, James Leech and Terry Hadler
(for full credits see page 248)
Photographic research: Mirco Decet
(for full picture credits, see page 248)

Filmset by SX Composing Ltd.,
Leigh-on-Sea, Essex, England.

Color reproduction by Paramount Litho
Company, 4 Robert Way, Wickford,
Essex, England.

Printed in Belgium by Henri Proost et Cie,
Turnhout.

Lamborghini Miura—transverse mid-engined 4-litre vee-12.

Editor's Acknowledgments

A great many people throughout the world have
helped us to produce this book. They include
fortunate individual owners, museums and private
collections of 'classic cars' where the vehicles are
thankfully well cared for; motor manufacturers
who have scoured their archives on our behalf;
photographers who in many cases have tracked
down a particular car so that its likeness is
permanently recorded; and enthusiasts and
advisers who have so willingly supplied vital facts
and often faded but unique 'snaps' of their favorite
cars. We sincerely thank them all.

We are especially indebted to Gordon Davies, Ken

Rush, James Leech and Terry Hadler, the artists who have permitted us to reproduce their beautiful paintings from their cherished collections. In particular we owe our thanks to Gordon Davies and Ken Rush who so painstakingly researched and studied old and tattered journals and pamphlets in order to bring alive once again in splendid new color illustrations some of the world's most luxurious and interesting cars.

Above all we thank Graham Robson, whose tenacity and unswerving effort have resulted in a magnificent contribution which will delight both the avid enthusiast and the casual reader.

Our 'classic cars' are arranged alphabetically by name of manufacturer–although where the restrictions of such a rigid order threatened to deprive a handsome vehicle of its deserved coverage we rearranged the alphabet! A glossary of terms is presented at the back of the book, together with the index.

Ray Bonds

Rolls-Royce 40-50hp, now known as the 'Silver Ghost'.

Foreword

What is a 'Classic Car', and how can we define one? That was probably the most difficult part of compiling this book. For what is a 'classic' to one enthusiast might be a failure to others. Some cars purposely laid out to become 'classics' fail miserably, and it is not always obvious why this should be. On the other hand, several quite unexpected and apparently mundane machines achieve greatness.

We don't claim that this book is an exhaustive study of the 'Classic Car'. It is, however, a comprehensive survey of the interesting cars—sports or touring, limousine or two-seater, ancient and modern, British, European or American, cheap or expensive—we have seen since that first Benz tricycle puttered out into the streets of Mannheim in 1885.

A car does not need to be exclusive, or even expensive, to merit our accolade, but a moment's thought about the type of car which might evolve in this way suggests that it is more likely. One would expect, surely, to see Rolls-Royce, Ferrari, Mercedes-Benz, Cadillac, Bugatti and Lancia well represented? But a car doesn't have to qualify because of looks, of quality, of road behaviour, or because of high performance.

A 'classic' can also evolve by accident. It might become so outstanding because of its deeds and its contribution to the motoring scene, that its shape and its construction has no bearing. No one, surely, would deny the Mini, the VW Beetle, the Model T Ford, the Fiat Topolino, or the Jeep, its place in our Hall of Fame?

In almost every case, to be sure, the type of car which interests us is out of the ordinary in some

respects. The cars in these pages were all out-standing in one field of motoring, which could embrace high performance, competition prowess, elegant looks, or sheer peripatetic worth. None of them, we hope, could be labelled as dull.

What makes us sad is that many manufacturers of the cars we have chosen no longer exist. Economic depression struck hard at all those cars which were bought more for their status, their sporting value, or for their names, than for their practical uses. The three great world events which are seen to have decimated the ranks were the two World Wars and the economic depression sparked off by the first Wall Street collapse of 1929. And yet it would be unreasonable to expect monstrous and exhibitionis-tic cars like the vee-16 Marmons and Cadillacs, the Grosser Mercedes, or the Phantom III Rolls-Royces to survive today—or would it? What, after all, is the

practical purpose of a car like the Rolls-Royce Camargue, or the Ferrari Berlinetta Boxer, in an increasingly conformist and grey world?

One thing, also, is obvious. Great cars are never designed by committees. Even though, in modern times, it takes a big team to get a major project ready, there is usually one driving force, one visionary, to stamp his character on the new car. Ettore Bugatti was Bugatti, and Ferrari is Ferrari. Equally, Marc Birkigt begat every Hispano, and Dr. Ferdinand Porsche a whole series of cars. Ledwinka, Chapman, Issigonis, Henry Ford and Sir Henry Royce all have their memorials. This book is a permanent tribute to nearly a century of genius.

Graham Robson

AC 'SIX' 2-LITRE

Ace, Acedes, Aceca, Magna, Aero and other versions, built from 1919 to 1956 (data for 1927 Acedes).

Built by: Autocarriers Ltd., then (from 1922) AC Cars Ltd., Britain.

Engine: Six cylinders, in line, in five-bearing, wet-liner, cast-alloy block. Bore and stroke 65mm by 100mm, 1,991cc (2·56 × 3·94in, 121·5cu.in). Cast-iron cylinder head. Two overhead valves per cylinder, operated by single overhead camshaft. Single carburettor. Maximum power about 40bhp.

Transmission: AC plate clutch at rear of engine, cast-aluminium torque tube to gearbox, in unit with back axle. Three forward speeds, without synchromesh, ratios 4·5, 7·00 and 13·2 to 1. Alternative ratios on request. Right-hand gearchange. Overhead-worm-drive back axle.

Chassis: Pressed-steel channel-section side members, with tubular cross members. Front axle suspended on forward-facing quarter-elliptic cantilever leaf springs. Quarter-elliptic leaf springs at rear. Friction-type dampers at front only. Snubbers above back axle. Four-wheel brakes, 12in by 1¾in drums all round. Several variations in coachwork — two/three seat tourer, coachbuilt saloon, or fabric saloon.

Dimensions: Wheelbase 9ft 3in or 9ft 9in (282 or 297cm), tracks (front and rear) 3ft 9in (114cm). Overall length, from 13ft 9in (358cm) — depending on coachwork. Unladen weight, 2320lb (1052kg).

History: The AC 'Six' was not a single, long-lived model, but a progressively improved family of cars. Its engine, in particular, established a record in Great Britain, by being in active production from 1919 until 1963, when it was last used by AC in the Ace sports car.

AC cars were first made in 1913, although there had been tricars before that, and the company always made their products in Thames Ditton, on the south-western outskirts of London. Their first car was a four-cylinder two-seater (the engine being by Fivet, from France) and it had features like the gearbox in unit with the back axle, something which was to be an AC characteristic for so long. There was even an axle disc brake.

The legendary 'Six' was designed by John Weller during World War I, was announced in 1919, and went on sale in 1920. It was quite remarkably advanced by the standards of the day and still looked reasonably up-to-date when being sold in the 1960s. The aluminium-alloy block/crankcase combined with spigoted wet liners, was unusual, as was the fact that a cast-iron cylinder head was specified.

Ex-Napier chief Selwyn Edge joined AC in 1921 and became Governing Director in 1922, whereupon the company's founders, John Weller and John Portwine walked out. Edge then changed the company's name to AC Cars Ltd., by which it is known today.

Success in competition was thought necessary to prove the vehicle, and AC often competed for distance records at the nearby Brooklands track. The Hon. Victor Bruce won the Monte Carlo Rally in 1926 (the first win by a Briton). One production version of the car — the 16/40 'Montlhéry' AC — could exceed 80mph at a time when most cars, including 3-litre Bentleys, were struggling just to approach that speed.

The 'Six' put on weight later in the 1920s, as bodies became heavier and equipment became more complex. AC countered this by tuning up their splendid engine and for 1928 the Acedes was given 56bhp. Half-elliptic front springs and hydraulic brakes appeared before the end of the 1920s, by which time an AC saloon might weigh up to 2,700lb (1,224kg).

When Edge retired in 1929 the company was placed in voluntary liquidation, but it was revived by the Hurlock brothers in 1931. They produced a new design, still relying heavily on the alloy 'six', but with a new chassis, a Moss four-speed gearbox in unit with the engine and a central, remote-control gearshift.

The first 'Ace', perhaps better known in its 1950s guise, appeared in 1935 and was a pretty and light little sports two-seater, ideal for rallies and trials. Acceleration from rest to 60mph in about 18 seconds was fast by any standard and the handling offered by the half-elliptic leaf springs all round was very sporting.

Synchromesh gears, or the option of the British Wilson pre-selector box, came in at about the same time. 80bhp was talked of from the 1,991cc engine, but this was almost certainly optimistic. At one stage, at the end of the 1930s, an Arnott supercharger could be ordered as an extra, and automatic chassis lubrication was standardised in 1937.

After World War II, the existing designs were dropped, and replaced by a single new model, the 2-litre. This was a two-door saloon at first, but a more expensive drop-head convertible also became available. The chassis, although all-new, retained a rigid front axle and half-elliptic springs all round. The company was by no means committed to independent springing at that time. Engine power was now up to a guaranteed 76bhp at 4,500rpm, but needed a triple SU carburettor installation to guarantee this.

AC were always too busy with their other activities (which included making three-wheeler invalid cars under contract to the British Government) to up-date the 2-litre, which eventually went out of production in 1956.

Below: The six-cylinder ACs had an enormously long and successful run, though only the engine was a constant feature. This was a 1925 tourer with disc wheels and the obligatory dickey seat of the 1920s. AC was guided by Selwyn Edge in the 1920s.

Right and below: AC's legendary 'six' was designed during World War I, and built from 1919 to 1956—an astonishing run. The engine's secret was its light-alloy build, and its built-in 'tuneability'. In the first few years it powered neat tourers and saloons like this 1923 model. The radiator design, not unlike that of the 'Bullnose' Morris, stayed with AC through the 1920s. An AC Six won the Monte Carlo Rally for Britain in 1926. One version, the 16/40 'Montlhéry', could exceed 80mph—and that from a relatively modest two litres!

Below: Detail analysis of the 1925 AC six-cylinder Tourer. There was an overhead worm-drive axle, but only a three-speed gearbox. The dickey seat closed up to reveal a sleek shape.

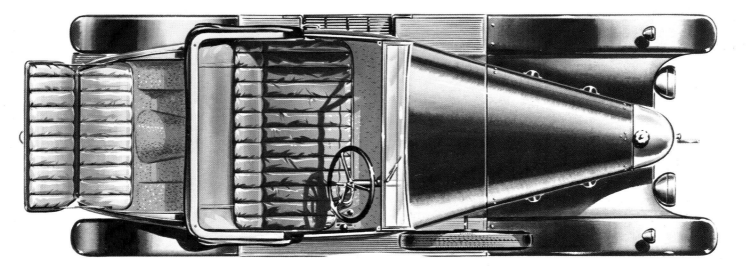

AC ACE

Ace, Aceca, Ace-Bristol, Ace-Zephyr and Greyhound (data for Ace-Bristol).
Built by: AC Cars Ltd., Britain.
Engine: Six cylinders, in line, in four-bearing cast-iron block. Bore and stroke 66mm by 96mm, 1,971cc (2·60 × 3.78in, 120·3cu.in). BMW-inspired pushrod overhead valve operation, two valves per cylinder. Inlet valve directly operated by pushrod and rocker, exhaust valve by pushrod, pivot, cross pushrod and rocker. Single side-mounted camshaft. Aluminium cylinder head with downdraught siamesed inlet ports and three Solex carburettors. In standard tune, maximum power 105bhp at 5,000rpm. In further-modified form, 128bhp at 5,750rpm, and maximum torque 122lb.ft at 4,500rpm.
Transmission: Single-dry-plate clutch and four-speed synchromesh gearbox (with non-synchronised first gear) in unit with engine. Open propeller shaft to chassis-mounted hypoid-bevel final drive. Exposed universally jointed drive shafts to rear wheels.
Chassis: Separate multi-tubular frame, relying on two main tubes for beam and torsional stiffness. Fully independent front and rear suspension, by transverse leaf springs and wishbones. Bishop cam steering. Coil spring suspension, plus rack-and-pinion steering on Greyhound. Telescopic dampers. Drum brakes on all wheels at first, but Girling front discs from 1957.
  Light-alloy coachwork on framework of light

tubes — open two-seat (Ace), closed two-seat (Aceca), or closed 2+2 seater (Greyhound).
Dimensions: Wheelbase 7ft 6in (229cm), tracks 4ft 2in (127cm). Overall length Ace 12ft 8in (386cm), Aceca 13ft 4in (406cm), Greyhound 14ft 7in (444cm). Unladen weight Ace-Bristol sports car 1,850lb (838kg).
History: After years of making nothing but the 2-litre saloon design, AC surprised the world by announcing their new Ace sports car in 1953. Although the Ace retained the distinguished old 1,991cc engine, by now tuned to give 85bhp, the chassis and coachwork were startlingly modern. Inspiration was from John Tojeiro's Bristol-engined sports-racing car which raced in Britain in the early 1950s. Tojeiro, introduced to AC, was asked to productionise this chassis and specify the AC engine. With this superb Ferrari-like styling, the Ace went on sale in 1954. The chassis was rudimentary but strong, with two main tubular longerons suitably attached to transverse leaf springs and lower wishbones. So low were the weight and the centre of gravity, that anti-roll bars were not needed to ensure good handling. Maximum speed was about 105mph in original form.
  The very pretty fastback Aceca soon followed the Ace, and final work on the 40-year-old engine design produced a 105bhp power output. Demands from customers who wanted to race or rally their cars resulted in the BMW-based six-

cylinder Bristol engine being offered. This could (and often was) urged to produce more than 140bhp, and made the Ace very fast indeed. In 128bhp production form a 120mph maximum speed was usual, and roadholding was as well balanced as ever. The AC engine was offered right up to the death of the Ace in the mid-1960s, but the Bristol unit was dropped in 1961, after which a few of the tuned 2·6-litre Ford Zephyr units were offered instead.
  An interesting but unsuccessful diversion at Thames Ditton was that a long-wheelbase 'almost four seater' car, the Greyhound, was sold, but it was both too expensive and too unrefined to be a success. Before time finally caught up with the Ace it was transformed into the Cobra by the transplant of an American V8 engine. Sales of Cobras were so high that AC found they could fill their workshops with no difficulty, and the Ace models had to be discontinued in 1964.

Right: Even prettier than the Ace two-seater was the Aceca coupe—sold with the light-alloy Ace, or with the 2-litre six-cylinder Bristol engine. The styling was all-British, but looked Italian—a compliment to AC's car. Each car was hand-built around a twin-tube steel chassis, with transverse leaf spring all-independent springing. Maximum speed was up to 120mph.

AC COBRA

AC Cobra 260, AC Cobra 289, AC Cobra 427, AC Daytona Cobra (data for Cobra 289)
Built by: AC Cars Ltd., Britain, and Shelby American Inc., USA.
Engine: Eight cylinders, in 90-degree vee-formation, in five-bearing cast-iron block. Bore and stroke 101·6mm by 72·9mm, 4,727cc (4·00 × 2·87in, 289cu.in). Cast-iron cylinder heads. Two overhead valves per cylinder, operated by pushrods and rockers from a single camshaft positioned in the vee of the cylinder block. Single carburettor. Maximum power 195bhp (gross) at 4,400rpm in standard form. Maximum torque 282lb.ft at 2,400rpm. Shelby-modified Mustang-type engines with up to 271bhp (gross) available to special order. Engine based on mass-production Ford of Detroit 4·2/4·7-litre unit.
Transmission: Single-dry-plate clutch, and four-speed all-synchromesh manual gearbox in unit with engine. Open propeller shaft to chassis-

mounted Salisbury limited-slip final drive, with 3·45:1 ratio. Universally jointed exposed drive shafts to rear wheels.
Chassis: Tubular chassis frame, with two main longitudinal tubes and front and rear subframes supporting suspensions. Independent front and rear suspension by transverse leaf springs and lower wishbones (from 1965 by coil springs and unequal length wishbones). Steering by rack and pinion (by worm and sector on first 125 cars built in 1962). Girling disc brakes to all four wheels. Wire wheels with 185 × 15in tyres.
Dimensions: Wheelbase 7ft 6in (229cm), track (front) 4ft 7in (140cm), track (rear) 4ft 6in (137cm). Overall length 13ft (396cm). Unladen weight 2,282lb (1,035kg).
History: American racing driver Carroll Shelby first approached AC Cars Ltd. of Thames Ditton in autumn 1961, proposing that they should supply Ace body/chassis assemblies, for his Los Angeles based company to insert Ford V8 engines

and transmissions. A prototype was completed early in 1962, and production of the first 100 cars began later in the year. Compared with that of the Ace, the chassis was much strengthened, as were the suspension components, and a more robust 4HA Salisbury back axle was fitted. These cars were shipped from Britain to California for American-sourced parts to be fitted. The first 75 cars were equipped with 4·2-litre (260cu.in) engines, and the first 125 with Ace-type worm-

Right: By fitting a massive Ford vee-8 engine, fat wheels, and racing equipment, Shelby turned the stylish Cobra into a brutally efficient racing car. Re-bodied versions were 'Daytonas'.

Left and right: Contrasting shots of the AC Cobra—in road trim, and as prepared for racing by Carroll Shelby's team. The road car was descended from the original AC Ace, but with a stronger chassis, different (coil spring) suspension, and with American engines and transmissions. The 7-litre Cobra, built from 1965 to 1968, was as fast as any Ferrari, if not as sophisticated. The race car shown was driven in the 1964 Targa Florio by Dan Gurney and Gerry Grant. Note the roll-cage and open exhaust.

and-sector steering. From the beginning of 1963 the 4·7-litre (289cu.in) V8 engine, and rack-and-pinion steering became normal.

Shelby raced Cobras with great success, evolving for 1964 the brutal but sensationally fast 'Daytona' coupé body. Thus equipped, the team won the 1964 World GT Championship. There were important changes in 1965. First, a major suspension redesign replaced the transverse leaf springing by a coil-spring and double-wishbone layout. Second, and more important, from mid 1965, all Shelby supplied cars had been fitted with the much bulkier 6,989cc Ford Galaxie-based V8 engine, with 345bhp (gross) at 4,600rpm. At the same time, AC re-designated the smaller version an 'AC 289' and were allowed to sell these cars on the British and other markets. There was always confusion over names. AC insisted that the car was an AC, but Shelby badged it, and marketed it, as a Shelby American Cobra (and it was homologated in sporting form with that name). Later, and even more confusing, the cars became known as Ford Cobras.

Production of Cobras ran out in 1968, but AC themselves produced a long-wheelbase chassis version, called it the AC428, equipped it with stylish and expensive Frua coachwork, and began small scale production in 1967. The last was made in 1973.

ADLER TRUMPF

Trumpf cars, built 1932 to 1939 (data for 1935 Trumpf Junior)
Built by: Adlerwerke vorm. Heinrich Kleyer AG, Germany.
Engine: Four cylinders, in line, in three-bearing cast-iron block/crankcase. Bore and stroke 65mm by 75mm, 995cc (2·56in × 2·95in, 60·7cu.in). Detachable cast-iron cylinder head. Two valves per cylinder, side-mounted in cylinder block and directly operated by single camshaft mounted in side of crankcase. One up-draught single-choke Solex carburettor. Maximum power 30bhp (gross) at 3,800rpm.
Transmission: Front engine and front-wheel-drive. Engine mounted behind gearbox, itself behind final-drive case. All items mounted in unit. Single-dry-plate clutch and four-speed manual gearbox (with synchromesh on top and third gears). Remote-control steering-column gearchange. Spiral-bevel final drive and exposed, universally jointed drive shafts to front wheels.
Chassis: Box-section steel chassis frame, welded up to pressed-steel bodywork (saloon, cabriolet or two-door sports car styles to choice). Independent front suspension by upper and lower transverse leaf springs. Independent rear suspension by leading arms and transverse torsion bars. Lever-arm hydraulic dampers. Rack-and-pinion steering. Four-wheel, rod-operated drum brakes. 17in bolt-on steel-disc wheels. 4·5 × 17in tyres.
Dimensions: Wheelbase 8ft 6·5in (260cm), tracks (front and rear) 3ft 11·2in (120cm). Overall length 12ft 8in (386cm). Unladen weight (four-seater) 1,800lb (816kg).
History: In German, *Adler* means eagle, which symbolises much of Germany's imperial ambitions. There were Adler cars from 1900, and a vast range of cars by 1914. After the war, the company re-introduced some pre-war models, but over the years it moved up market. In 1925, the first Adler six was produced and in 1929 a new eight followed. Adler talked mergers with Chrysler for a time, but Opel fell to General Motors at about the same time and the company's bankers would have nothing more to do with such plans. The German economy was shaky at the beginning of the 1930s, and Adler badly needed new small-engine designs. Hans-Gustav Rohr swept through the design office, turfed out all the old ideas and inspired production of a completely new Trumpf (which means trump in English) for 1932. This had everything which was super-modern — a platform-type chassis, pressed-steel bodywork, front-wheel drive and all-independent suspension. The first car used a 1·5-litre side-valve four, which grew into a 1·7-litre before too long.

By 1935, the company had really broadened its base by offering the Trumpf Junior, with a tiny 995cc engine but all the other modern features. The front-wheel-drive Adler pre-dated the Citroën *traction-avant* by several months and was to be built under licence by Rosengart in France and Imperia in Belgium. At a stroke this brought fine handling and response to vintage-type construction, with acceptable quality and at a series of very reasonable price tags. Later in the decade, the range was widened with the addition of sports models with lowered chassis, aluminium cylinder heads and cycle-type wings. These were all pretty little cars which were not as fast as one might think (because of the limits of the side-valve engines), but their roadholding behaviour was second to none. The front suspension was ingeniously simple, with transverse leaf springs looking after suspension and location, and another good point was rack-and-pinion steering. The Adler factories were destroyed by bombing during the war and the company is now famous for office equipment, typewriters and calculators.

Right: Adler's front-wheel-drive cars were very successful in several sizes. This is a 1935 995cc Trumpf Junior —larger models had 1·7-litre engines.

ALFA ROMEO TYPE RL

Alfa Romeo RLN, RLS, RLSS and RLT, built from 1923 to 1927 (data for RLSS)
Built by: SA Italiana Ing. Nicola Romeo & C., Italy.
Engine: Six cylinders, in line, in cast-iron block with detachable four-bearing light-alloy crankcase. Bore and stroke 76mm by 110mm, 2,994cc (3·0in× 4·33in, 182·7cu.in). Two overhead valves per cylinder, operated by pushrods and rockers by side-mounted camshaft. Cast-iron detachable cylinder head. Dry-sump lubrication, one pressure and one scavenge pump. Twin updraught Solex or Zenith carburettors. Maximum power 83bhp at 3,600rpm.
Transmission: Dry multi-plate clutch, and four-speed manual gearbox, with centre or right-hand gearchange, in unit with engine. Open propeller shaft to spiral bevel 'live' rear axle.
Chassis: Separate steel chassis frame, with channel-section side members, and steel cross braces. Half-elliptic leaf springs front and rear. Forged front axle beam. Mechanically operated footbrake on all four wheels, handbrake on transmission-sited drum. Friction-type dampers. Worm-and-wheel steering. Light-alloy coachwork, various coachbuilders.
Dimensions: Wheelbase 10ft 3in (312cm), tracks (front and rear) 4ft 9·5in (146cm). Overall length (depending on coachwork) about 15ft 0in (457cm). Unladen weight 3,600lb (1,633kg).
History: The RL Series (RL means 'Romeo Series L') stemmed from the design of a car, laid down in 1920, meant to comply with the 3-litre Grand Prix formula. When that formula was changed to a 2-litre limit, for 1922, the project was dropped. The detuned and productionised versions were first shown in Milan in October 1921, but did not properly get into production until 1923. From then until 1927 the various marks of RL Alfas were a mainstay of the Italian company's activities. At first there were two series — the RLN touring car chassis with its 2,916cc engine, and the RLS with a 2,996cc engine. The capacity difference was simply achieved with a one millimetre different cylinder bore.

The 'S' chassis was a foot shorter than the 'N' at 10ft 3in, and the enlarged engine had twin carburettors instead of a single unit. Early cars had rear-wheel brakes only, but a four-wheel system was installed from late 1923. The RLN became the RLT in 1925 and the RLS the RLSS, but the cars continued on with minor improvements only. The engine, with its conventional

Above: The most sporting of all the RL Alfas was the short-chassis RLSS model—this was built in 1927.

pushrod overhead valve gear, was soon to be made obsolete by Alfa's twin ohc units, but of its day it was very powerful; the SS model even had dry sump lubrication.

Racing versions of the S, with shortened (9ft 3in) wheelbases were made and were most successful. Enzo Ferrari, then employed by Alfa, was the team's star driver. Sivocci won the 1923 Targa Florio, and Antonio Ascari failed to repeat this in 1924 only when his engine seized 50 yards from the finish! It was in 1924 that Ferrari won the Coppa Acerbo in a 3·6-litre version, the largest possible in that cylinder block.

Although the chassis was entirely conventional, performance was always high, and the body styles striking. The RLs were dropped not because they had become obsolete, but because Vittorio Jano had become Chief Designer and wanted to see his own ideas put on sale. The famous 6C and 8C models were the result of that resolve. About 2,500 RL Alfas were built, but less than 20 survive today.

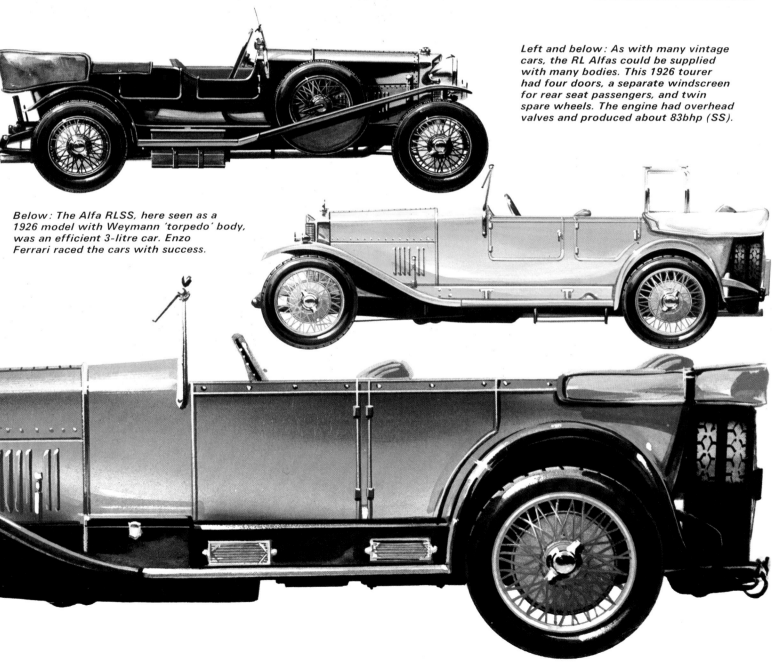

Left and below: As with many vintage
cars, the RL Alfas could be supplied
with many bodies. This 1926 tourer
had four doors, a separate windscreen
for rear seat passengers, and twin
spare wheels. The engine had overhead
valves and produced about 83bhp (SS).

Below: The Alfa RLSS, here seen as a
1926 model with Weymann 'torpedo' body,
was an efficient 3-litre car. Enzo
Ferrari raced the cars with success.

ALFA ROMEO 8C SERIES

8C models built from 1931 to 1939 (data for 8C2300 of 1931 – Spider Corsa version)

Built by: SA Alfa Romeo, Italy.

Engine: Eight cylinders, in line, in two four-cylinder light-alloy blocks bolted up to a ten-bearing light-alloy crankcase. Bore and stroke 65mm by 88mm, 2,336cc (2·56in × 3·46in, 142·5cu.in). Two detachable light-alloy cylinder heads. Two overhead valves per cylinder, opposed to each other at 90 degrees and operated by twin overhead camshafts and tappets screwed on to the valve stems. Single downdraught carburettor and Roots-type supercharger. Dry-sump lubrication. Maximum power 155bhp at 5,200rpm (165/180bhp at 5,400 in 1932/34).

Transmission: Multiple-dry-plate clutch, and four-speed manual gearbox (without synchromesh), all in unit with front-mounted engine. Direct action central gearchange. Propeller shaft enclosed in torque tube to spiral-bevel 'live' rear axle.

Chassis: Separate pressed-steel chassis frame, with tubular and sheet-metal cross-bracing, and channel-section side members. Tubular front axle beam. Front and rear suspensions by half-elliptic leaf springs and friction-type dampers. Four-wheel drum brakes, shaft and cable operated. 29in centre-lock wire wheels. 29 × 5·50 tyres.

Dimensions: Wheelbase 9ft 0·2in (275cm), front track 4ft 6·3in (138cm), rear track 4ft 6·3in (138cm). Overall length 13ft 5in (409cm). Unladen weight 2,205lb (1,000kg).

History: Vittorio Jano joined Alfa Romeo in 1923, and immediately began a design programme which led to the famous P2 Grand Prix cars, and to the use of twin-cam engines in the 6C 1500 and 6C 1750 series of cars. By the end of the 1920s Alfa's sports and racing cars were pre-eminent. To ensure continued domination, Jano then designed the legendary straight-eight twin-cam engine, which was to power the 8C cars throughout the 1930s *and* (in developed form) Alfa's Grand Prix cars for a number of years.

The engine was a constructional masterpiece, with two four-cylinder blocks and two cylinder heads on a common crank and crankcase, with camshaft drive by a train of gears up the centre of the unit. 8C2300 cars were tremendously successful sports cars in the early 1930s, and were speedily developed into the 8C2600 Monza sports-racing machines by the Scuderia Ferrari. The 2300 Monza and B-Type single-seaters had much in common, and the 8C2900 range (with the same basic engine, enlarged and made more powerful — up to 220bhp) kept the government-controlled Milan producers competitive. Production was always low, almost handbuilt, but Mussolini intended the cars as prestige machines, and not profit-makers and if every 1960s and 1970s schoolboy yearns after a Ferrari, in the 1920s and 1930s he wanted an Alfa Romeo. A car needs no better epitaph than that.

Left: The famous 8C Alfa Romeo in 2·6-litre 'Monza' form, used almost always for sports car racing. The link with monoposto racing Alfas is very clear.

ALFA ROMEO MONTREAL

Montreal model built 1970 to 1976

Built by: Alfa Romeo SpA, Italy

Engine: Eight cylinders, in 90-degree vee-formation, in five-bearing light-alloy combined block/crankcase. Bore and stroke 80mm by 64·5mm, 2,593cc (3·15in × 2·54in, 158·2cu.in). Two detachable light-alloy cylinder heads. Two overhead valves per cylinder, inclined to each other and operated by twin overhead camshafts through inverted bucket-type tappets. Spica fuel injection and dry-sump lubrication. Maximum power 200bhp (DIN) at 6,500rpm. Maximum torque 173lb.ft at 4,750rpm.

The engine is a de-tuned and developed version of the Alfa Type 33 racing sports car unit of the late 1960s, raced in 2-litre, 2½-litre and 3-litre form.

Transmission: Single-dry-plate clutch, and five-speed all-synchromesh manual gearbox, all in unit with front-mounted engine. Remote-control central gearchange. Open propeller shaft to hypoid-bevel 'live' rear axle with limited-slip differential.

Chassis: Unitary-construction, pressed-steel, two-door, closed-coupé body shell, based on modern 1750/2000 floor pan. Front suspension by coil springs, wishbones and anti-roll bar. Rear suspension of live axle by coil springs, radius arms and anti-roll bar. Telescopic dampers. Rack-and-pinion steering. Four-wheel ventilated disc brakes with servo assistance. 14in cast-alloy road wheels, 195/70 × 14in tyres.

Dimensions: Wheelbase 7ft 8·5in (235cm), track (front) 4ft 6in (137cm), track (rear) 4ft 3·5in (131cm). Overall length 13ft 0in (422cm). Unladen weight 2,800lb (1,270kg).

History: Alfa Romeo showed a sleek 'styling exercise' at Expo 1967 in Montreal, which nobody took very seriously. The world was much more impressed in 1970 when the same car re-appeared in production form and powered by nothing less than a de-tuned version of the Type 33 racing two-seater's twin-cam V8 engine. The rest of the chassis was fairly ordinary (it was based on the floor pan and suspensions of the 1750/2000 saloon), but the performance was very impressive, with maximum speeds of between 130 and 140mph. Styling was by Bertone, some of whose finest work has been with Alfa-Romeo, and the car was called 'Montreal' after its initial public appearance. It made no concessions to habitability and was a two-seater closed car, pure and simple. A feature was the headlamp positioning, with slatted covers making the lights almost invisible by day, although they were effective in use. The engine had been carefully detuned to take all the temperament out of it, with fuel injection to ensure good behaviour at all times. Never a high-production car, the Montreal was the 'flagship' of the Milan company's range.

Left: The Montreal was a car which started life as a special Motor Show exhibit, but public interest led it to be put into production. The chassis is that of the Alfa 1750 touring car, and the 2·6-litre vee-8 engine is a de-tuned version of the Type 33 racing car unit. Styling was by Bertone, and all those built had left hand drive. The headlamps are partly hidden by slats. Without any doubt this is the fastest production Alfa Romeo ever built, and the racing type of engine is remarkably docile.

ALFA ROMEO GIULIETTA SERIES

Giulietta, built from 1954 to 1964 (data for 1956 Sprint Veloce)
Built by: Alfa Romeo SpA., Italy.
Engine: Four cylinders, in line, in five-bearing light-alloy block/crankcase. Bore and stroke 74mm by 75mm, 1,290cc (2·91in × 2·97in, 78·7cu.in). Detachable light-alloy cylinder head. Two overhead valves per cylinder, opposed to each other at 90 degrees in part-spherical combustion chamber and operated by inverted-bucket tappets from twin overhead camshafts. Two horizontal twin-choke Weber carburettors. Maximum power 90bhp at 6,500rpm. Maximum torque 87lb.ft at 4,500rpm.
Transmission: Single-dry-plate clutch and four-speed, synchromesh manual gearbox, both in unit with front-mounted engine. Remote-control central gearchange. Two-piece open propeller shaft to hypoid-bevel 'live' rear axle.
Chassis: Unitary-construction pressed-steel body/chassis unit, in two-door four-seat coupé style by Bertone. Independent front suspension by coil springs, wishbones and anti-roll bar. Rear suspension by coil springs, radius arms and A-bracket. Telescopic dampers. Worm-and-roller steering. Four-wheel, hydraulically operated drum brakes. 15in pressed-steel bolt-on wheels. 155 × 15in tyres.
Dimensions: Wheelbase 7ft 10in (239cm), track (front) 4ft 2·9in (129cm), track (rear) 4ft 2in (127cm). Overall length 12ft 10·5in (393cm). Unladen weight 1,973lb (895kg).
History: The Giulietta series, born in 1954, was really Alfa's first attempt at mass-production, although the 1900 model had paved the way to this a few years previously. It was laid down specifically to be produced in many versions — four-door saloon, two-door coupé, and open Spider — and each and every one of the cars had a splendid and all-new twin-cam light-alloy engine. Until then, only Jaguar had put a twin-cam into true quantity production, but by the start of the 1960s Alfa-Romeo had overtaken their figures. The 1,290cc engine was only the first of a magnificent pedigree and family of units — since expanded through 1600, 1800 to 2-litre versions, and forming the backbone of middle-size Alfa private car production. The Sprint came about as a result of a *muletto* car built by Bertone, and speedily adopted by Alfa Romeo. For years it was known as the most beautiful of all small GT cars, and was only surpassed by the bigger-engined Giulia GT which followed in the 1960s. Well over 150,000 Giuliettas of all types were built in ten years, which included some really fierce Zagato-bodied competition cars and more than 25,000 Sprint GTs and Veloces. The Giulietta was the car which changed Alfa's public image — before this they had made a few expensive cars, and after it they were to make a lot of middle-class thoroughbreds with world-wide appeal.

Below: One of the most 'classic' sporting shapes yet seen, devised by Bertone for the Giulietta's touring car chassis. The beautiful little Sprints were sold in big quantities for ten years.

ALLARD

Allard J, K, L, M, P, and Palm Beach models built from 1946 to 1959 (data for J1)
Built by: Allard Motor Co. Ltd., Britain
Engine: Ford manufactured, eight cylinders, in 90-degree vee-formation, in five-bearing cast-iron block. Bore and stroke 78·0mm by 95·25mm, 3,622cc (3·07in × 3·75in, 221cu.in). Two cast-iron cylinder heads. Two side valves per cylinder, directly operated from single camshaft mounted in centre of cylinder block vee. Solex downdraught carburettor. Maximum power 85bhp (net) at 3,800rpm.
Transmission: Single-dry-plate clutch, and three-speed manual gearbox (no synchromesh on first gear), with central remote control gearchange. Torque-tube-enclosed propeller shaft to spiral-bevel 'live' rear axle.
Chassis: Separate steel chassis frame, with box section side members, and pressed cross braces. Independent front suspension by swinging half-axles, transverse leaf spring and radius arms. Rear suspension by transverse leaf spring and radius arms. Lever-type hydraulic dampers. Marles steering. Drum brakes, hydraulically operated, with fly-off handbrake. Steel disc road wheels, and 6·25 × 16in tyres.
Open two-seat coachwork with light-alloy panelling on wood framing.
Dimensions: Wheelbase 8ft 10in (269cm), track (front) 4ft 8in (142cm), track (rear) 4ft 4in (132cm). Overall length 14ft (427cm). Unladen weight 2,450lb (1,111kg).
History: Sydney Allard's first special was built in the mid 1930s, from derelict Ford V8 parts and a GP Bugatti body. Between 1936 and 1939 he was persuaded to build and sell half a dozen replicas. Production of Allards on an organised basis began in 1946, most of the cars being intended for export.
The chassis frame was a specially built rigid box section item, and the bodies were built by South London coachbuilders, but almost every other part was British or North American Ford, with or without Allard's own alterations. In the beginning there were touring and competition two-seaters, touring and drop-head coupé four-seaters, and from 1948 these cars were supplemented by a two-door saloon. Engines were either 3·6-litre Ford or 3·9-litre Mercury V8s. By the beginning of the 1950s the lightweight, short-wheelbase Allards were very successful and relatively cheap competition cars. North American exports were often supplied without engines and gearboxes, which the customer then supplied himself.
The 100 inch wheelbase J2X, fitted with Cadillac engines, was particularly fierce. The J2R sports-racing car evolved from the J2X. Transverse-leaf front suspension had given way to coil springs in 1949, but from 1952 a completely new multi-tubular chassis frame was specified. Even so, the day of the big Allards was drawing to a close, and the Palm Beaches built from 1952 to 1959 were smaller, lighter, Austin-Healey/Triumph competitors. Allard sales came to an end in 1959, with just over 1,700 cars sold in all. High selling prices and low production eventually proved too much to sustain.

Below: The Allard evolved from Syd Allard's Special of the 1930s. All but the later Palm Beach cars used the same basic layout, with Ford, Chrysler or Cadillac vee-formation engines, and tubular chassis. There were two-seater and four-seater versions, with sports or touring bodies, and a saloon which won the Monte Carlo Rally in 1952.

ALVIS 12/50

12/50 SA to TJ, built from 1923 to 1932 (data for SA type of 1923)

Built by: Alvis Car and Engineering Co. Ltd., Britain.

Engine: Four cylinders, in line, in three-bearing cast-iron block. Bore and stroke 68mm by 103mm, 1,496cc (2·68 4·06in, 91·3cu.in). Cast-iron cylinder head. Two overhead valves per cylinder, operated by pushrods and rockers from single, side-mounted camshaft. 5·35:1 compression ratio. One Solex carburettor. Engine originally derived from the first side-valve Alvis power unit, introduced in 1920. Power output about 50bhp minimum (each engine power tested before fitting). SC type had 1,598cc (97·5cu.in) engine. TE, TG and TJ types had 1,645cc (100·4cu.in) engine. All other types retained basic engine.

Transmission: Four-speed manual gearbox, without synchromesh, separated from engine by short shaft. Right-hand gearchange. Live spiral-bevel axle, fully floating type.

Chassis: Simple separate chassis, with pressed-steel channel-section side members, and pressed cross members. Half-elliptic front and rear springs. No dampers. Ribbed drum brakes, mounted only on rear wheels. Worm-and-wheel steering, with adjustable steering column. Dash-mounted petrol tank, gravity feed to engine.

Two-seat lightweight sports bodywork normal. Many other options available (including saloon coachwork on later models).

Dimensions: Wheelbase 9ft 0·5in (275cm), track (front and rear) 4ft 2in (127cm). Overall length 12ft 9in (389cm). Unladen weight ???

History: The Alvis car was inspired by T. G. John, who set up his own company in Coventry in 1919. The very first Alvis was dubbed a 10/30 model — which meant 10 British RAC-rating horsepower, and about 30 developed horsepower. Deliveries of this simple, but well-engineered, side-valve car, with its 1,460cc engine, began in 1920. Development, mainly through races and trials, was swift. The 10/30 soon became the 11/40, then the 12/40, and briefly the overhead-valve 10/30hp Super Sports.

The 12/50 Alvis, the first of a famous line of light sporting cars, arrived in 1923 to replace the Super Sports 10/30. Its power unit was a shorter-stroke/larger-bore version of that engine, aimed at giving more power and higher-revving capabilities. The pedigree of this model stretches from 1923 to 1932, when it was finally superseded by more modern designs. Although the chassis received little development in that time, the engine was persistently updated and made more powerful. Cars in factory-sponsored and private hands achieved great success in motor racing of the period.

Over the years there were at least eight basic body types, of which the most famous was undoubtedly the 'duck's back' shell with polished aluminium panelling. In 1931/32 the 12/50 was joined by the 12/60 type, basically the same car but having a more powerful engine with twin SU carburettors, close ratio gears, and more comprehensive equipment.

Below: Everybody loved the boat-tailed Alvis 12/50s, which were typical of the best in vintage sports cars.

ALVIS F-SERIES

FA, FB, FD and FE 4-cyl cars, 8/15 8-cyl cars (data for FA)

Built by: Alvis Car and Engineering Co. Ltd., Britain.

Engine: Four-cylinders, in line, in cast-iron block. Bore and stroke 68mm by 102mm, 1,482cc (2·68 × 4·02in, 90·4cu.in). Two valves per cylinder operated by single overhead camshaft, gears driven from the front of the engine. Available with or without supercharger. 5·1:1 compression ratio with blower (Roots type) or 5·7:1 when fitted with a Solex updraught carburettor. Maximum power about 50bhp in unsupercharged form; 75bhp with supercharger.

Transmission: Gearbox and transaxle ahead of engine; engine therefore turned 'back to front'. Right-hand gearchange and remote linkage. Standard gear ratios 4·5, 6·9, 9·6 and 14·7:1. Lower set also available. Straight bevel differential gear. Exposed universally jointed drive shafts to front wheels.

Chassis: Steel channel-section side members, doubly heavy at the front, to support engine and transmission. Tubular rear cross members, cruciform centre section, and built-up structure around transaxle and front suspension. Independent front suspension by upper and lower leaf springs. Independent rear suspension by quarter-elliptic leaf springs and torque arms. No dampers at first, control being by spring clips. Drum brakes all round, inboard at the front, at each side of the axle casing. Worm-and-wheel steering. Two-seater tourer bodywork normally fitted, although (long-wheelbase) four-seat saloon bodywork was also available.

Dimensions: Wheelbase 8ft 6in (259cm).

History: Interest in front-wheel-drive cars at Alvis stems from 1925 when they built a special four-cylinder sprint car. Chief Engineer W. M. Dunn's search was not so much for roadholding as for lightness. It was the very first European front-wheel-drive racing car. The company then went on to build cars to the 1926/27 Grand Prix racing formula. The first car had a supercharged straight-eight engine, probably developing about 110bhp, and De Dion front suspension. It did not race in 1926; however, a modified version, with independent front suspension, was practised for the 1927 British GP but it blew up.

A high-priced production car, the Type FA, with an overhead-cam, four-cylinder engine distantly related to that of the 12/50, appeared in 1928, and owed much to the Grand Prix car's layout. In effect it had 1925/26 transmission and 1927 front suspension. Cars were built at a low rate and were priced accordingly; the 1929 chassis in supercharged form cost £550 and a body added £150 to that. Works cars had some success in sports-car racing, particularly at Le Mans in 1928 where the unsupercharged 1½-litre cars came in sixth and ninth. Every car which finished in front of the Harvey-Purdy Alvis had at least a 4-litre engine. Later that summer, Leon Cushman's supercharged car took second place in the Tourist Trophy race.

In the 1929–31 period, a handful of special straight-eight sports cars were built (the engine being a modified 1927 Grand Prix type), but these met with little success. Only 155 front-drive Alvis cars were made and the model was dropped early in 1931.

Below: One of the rare front-drive Alvis sports cars, with 4-cyl engine.

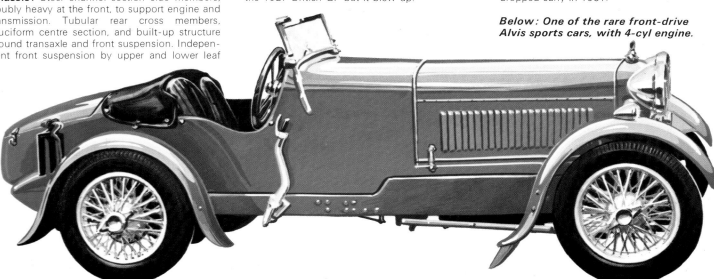

ALVIS TC21/100

TA14, TB14, TA21 and TC21 series (data for TC21/100 of 1953)

Built by: Alvis Ltd., Britain.

Engine: Six cylinders, in line, in four-bearing cast-iron block. Bore and stroke 84 by 90mm, 2,993cc (3·31 × 3·54in, 182·6cu.in). Two overhead valves per cylinder, operated by pushrods and rockers from chain-driven side-mounted camshaft. Twin side-draught SU carburettors. 8:1 compression ratio. Maximum power 104bhp (net) at 4,000rpm. Maximum torque 163lb.ft at 2,000rpm.

Transmission: Single-dry-plate clutch and four-speed synchromesh manual gearbox (no synchromesh on first gear), all in unit with engine. Central gearchange, on extension behind gearbox casing. Open propeller shaft to hypoid-bevel live rear axle.

Chassis: Separate chassis frame with box-section side members. Independent front suspension by coil springs, wishbones, and anti-roll bar. Half-elliptic leaf springs suspending back axle. Recirculating-ball steering. Hydraulically operated drum brakes on all four wheels. Four-door, four-seat saloon coachwork normal, but two-door Tickford convertible coachwork optional. 4½ × 15in centre-lock wire wheels. 6·00 × 15in tyres.

Dimensions: Wheelbase 9ft 3·5in (283cm), track (front) 4ft 6·6in (138·7cm), track (rear) 4ft 6·1in (137·4cm). Overall length 15ft 2·1in (462·5cm). Unladen weight 3,332lb (1,511kg).

History: The first post-World War II Alvis was a revamped 1930s design called the TA14, with a four-cylinder 2-litre engine and traditionally-styled coachwork. The first new Alvis to be announced after the war (as it happened, their only post-war chassis design ever to be put into production) arrived in 1950, and was designated the TA21. The chassis was built on well-tried lines, with the addition of coil-spring independent front suspension. The six-cylinder 2,993cc engine was quite new, and at first produced 85bhp at 4,000rpm. Mulliners of Birmingham built the attractive four-door saloon coachwork, on a wooden framework. In its original form the car had pressed-steel disc wheels and was capable of about 90mph.

In autumn 1953 Alvis turned their TA21 into the TC21/100, and it was given the 'Grey Lady' nickname for which it is now famous. Engine power was boosted to 104bhp by camshaft and carburation changes (the first 3-litres had used a single Solex carburettor) and maximum speed was raised to at least 100mph. Wire spoke wheels and ventilation scoops in the bonnet panels were TC recognition points. General styling was not changed, which made the car difficult to sell in later years. The Alvis solution to this problem was to have the cars rebodied by Graber of Switzerland. Production bodies came first from Willowbrook and later from Park Ward. Thus restyled (and eventually given disc brakes, optional automatic transmission and much more power) the TC became the TD21, then the TE21 and finally the TF21. The last Alvis of all was built in Summer 1967.

Below: Tickford bodied the drop-head version of the classic TC21/100 Alvis, a 100mph car of the 1950s.

ANSALDO TYPE 4A

4A model, built from 1920 to 1928 (data for 1920 model)

Built by: S.A. Ansaldo Automobili, Italy.

Engine: Four cylinders, in line, in three-bearing cast-iron block/crankcase. Bore and stroke 70mm by 120mm, 1,847cc (2·76in × 4·72in, 112·7cu.in). Detachable cast-iron cylinder head. Two overhead valves per cylinder, opposed to each other and operated by rockers from a single overhead camshaft. Single up-draught Zenith carburettor.

Transmission: Single-dry-plate clutch and three-speed manual gearbox (without synchromesh), both in unit with front-mounted engine. Direct-acting central gearchange. Open propeller shaft to spiral-bevel 'live' rear axle.

Chassis: Separate pressed-steel chassis frame, with channel-section side members and pressed and tubular cross bracing. Forged front axle beam. Semi-elliptic leaf springs for front and rear suspension. No dampers. Worm-and-wheel steering. Rear-wheel drum brakes, mechanically operated by foot pedal. Hand lever operating drum brake on transmission, behind gearbox. Bolt-on artillery style road wheels, 760 × 90 tyres.

Dimensions: Wheelbase 9ft (274cm), tracks (front and rear) 4ft 3in (130cm). Unladen weight 2,200lb (998kg).

History: Like several other important aero-engine manufacturers in Europe, Ansaldo turned over their empty factories to motor car production in 1919. Their Type 4A machine was attractive and advanced in engineering, but always rather heavy, and not usually endowed with very attractive styling. The engine, in particular, was a neat little monobloc four-cylinder device, with a single overhead camshaft and opposed valves operated through rockers — one might almost say in modern BMW style. The three-speed gearbox, central 'ball-type' gearchange and artillery-style wheels all gave the Ansaldo a touch of the austere, almost like American family cars of the day. The Type 4A could only reach 55mph, but the rather more sporting 2-litre Type 4CS of 1922 could reach 70mph, which was much more appropriate to that engine. As with other Italian manufacturers, however, Ansaldo of Turin were becoming more and more overshadowed by Fiat, whose products could match their performance and undercut their price. In spite, therefore, of new six-cylinder models and updating of the Type 4 machines, Ansaldo stopped making cars in 1932.

Below: The Ansaldo car was designed to make use of an empty factory in Italy after the First World War, and the well-known Type 4A model was made throughout the Vintage period. The 1·8 litre engine was very advanced, with an overhead camshaft, and was monobloc.

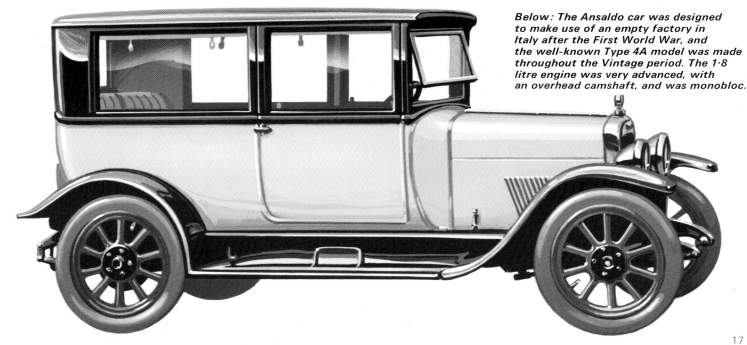

AMILCAR C-SERIES

C-Series cars, built from 1920 to 1929 (data for CGSS model)

Built by: Sté. Nouvelle pour l'Automobile Amilcar, France.

Engine: Four cylinders, in line, in two-bearing cast-iron block/crankcase. Bore and stroke 60mm by 95mm, 1,074cc (2·36in × 3·74in, 65·5cu.in). Detachable light-alloy cylinder head. Two side valves per cylinder, operated by single side-mounted camshaft, via finger placed between stem and camshaft. One updraught Solex carburettor. Maximum power up to 35bhp at 4,500rpm. Optional supercharged version, with 40bhp at 4,500rpm.

Transmission: Multi-plate clutch, running in oil, and three-speed manual gearbox (without synchromesh) all in unit with engine. (Four-speed gearbox on last few built.) Direct-acting central gearchange. Propeller shaft in torque tube to spiral-bevel 'live' rear axle.

Chassis: Separate pressed-steel chassis frame, with channel-section side members, fabricated and tubular cross-bracing. Forged front axle beam. Front suspension by half-elliptic leaf springs. Rear suspension by quarter-elliptic leaf springs. Friction-type dampers. Four-wheel drum brakes, rod and steel-strip operated. 27in centre-lock wire wheels. 27 × 4·00in tyres.

Dimensions: Wheelbase 7ft 7in (231cm), tracks (front and rear) 3ft 7in (109cm). Overall length 12ft (366cm). Unladen weight 1,200lb (544kg).

History: The Amilcar was a typical post-war French *voiturette*, or 'light car', in that it com-

Above: A typically-detailed example of the Amilcar of the 1920s, with its light and functional wings, and the spare wheel fixed to the bonnet side. The body was so narrow that the seats had to be staggered to give elbow room.

Above: Looking quaint with hood up, the 1926 Amilcar Italiana.

bined a tiny engine with minimal chassis and body weight to provide economical and amusing transport for the new motorists who could not afford anything bigger. Many such firms bought all their components from proprietary manufacturers, but Amilcar at least managed to design and build their own four-cylinder water-cooled engines.

The company was set up by Emil Akar and Joseph Lamy, and it is interesting to conjecture how the near-anagram of Amilcar's name

Left: The CGSS model was a more sporting type of Amilcar, which raced and rallied with great success. The engine was small but the car was light. It was nippy and handled well.

evolved from those two people. Design was in the hands of Edmond Moyet, and André Morel worked, tested, and raced for the new firm. Amilcar was really founded from the ruins of the pre-war Le Zèbre firm, for whom Morel and Moyet had worked, and the cars were made in the old factory, near Paris.

The original product, first seen in 1920, was the Type CC, the basis for all four-cylinder cars to come in the 1920s. Its engine was small (903cc) and side-valve, while its rudimentary

chassis had quarter-elliptic leaf springs at front and rear. The original car was so simple that in true 'cycle car' guise it had a straight-bevel final drive, without even a differential; this was later amended. The CC was normally a two-seater and strictly a touring car, weighing not more than 950lb (431kg) complete. From 1922 the range began to expand.

First along was the C4, with a longer chassis and enlarged 1,004cc engine, which could take four-seater bodies, while the CS was a rather more sporting version of the CC, with 985cc. The CS3, on the other hand, was a three-seater, where the third passenger could be accommodated in a dickey seat hanging over the tail. Most cars were built with the Petit Sport body — a narrow two-seat open shell, with a pointed tail and cycle type or combined wings with the running boards.

By 1924 a more sporting Amilcar still had evolved, directly as a result of the events contested by the factory in preceding years. The CGS (GS meaning 'Grand Sport') was a direct development of the CS, but had a bored-out 1,074cc engine, much improved brakes, a strengthened and lengthened chassis, and half-elliptic front springs. Ricardo had redesigned the head, which was now made of aluminium, and even though the CGS was quite a lot heavier than previous Amilcars it could still reach 75mph. Pressure lubrication was a great engine advance (splash lubrication had been normal up to then).

The CGS was good and sold well, but Moyet had even more exciting developments in mind. For 1926 he revealed the CGSS — the 'Surbaissé' model, so named because it had a lowered chassis frame and radiator. The power output had again been increased — to between 30 and 35bhp, and before the end of the model's run it was even given a four-speed gearbox. A few of the cars were built with Cozette superchargers, and such a model won the 1927 Monte Carlo Rally outright. Amilcar's problem, as with most of the other 'light car' builders, was that they were not sufficiently capitalised to change and update their cars frequently. By the end of the 1920s, whatever the increase in performance that had been achieved, they were still very much of an early-vintage design, and indeed a survivor of the 'light car' age which seemed to have all but disappeared. Competition from quantity-production builders (like Citroën, in France, for instance) intensified, and their prices were much lower than Amilcar could manage.

Although their days as *voiturette*-manufacturers were over in 1929, they had already introduced parallel touring-car models. Between 1923 and the mid 1930s, a series of touring cars — the Type Es, Js, Ls, Ms, Gs (almost an alphabet of models) were on offer, some of them with six-cylinder models. Even so, nearly 4,700 of the CGS/CGSS sports cars were built in only five years, and rather more than 6,000 of the touring C-Series four-cylinder cars.

ARMSTRONG SIDDELEY SPECIAL

Armstrong Siddeleys, built from 1919 to 1960 (data for 1933 Siddeley Special)

Built by: Armstrong Siddeley Motors Ltd., Britain.

Engine: Six cylinders, in line, in seven-bearing light-alloy block/crankcase, with cast-iron wet liners pushed in on assembly. Bore and stroke 88·9mm by 133·4mm, 4,960cc (3·5in × 5·25in, 302·6cu.in). Detachable light-alloy cylinder head. Two in-line overhead valves per cylinder, operated by pushrods and rockers from single side-mounted camshaft. Single downdraught Claudel-Hobson carburettor.

Transmission: Armstrong Siddeley 'Wilson-type' preselector four-speed gearbox (with 'clutch' take up, and gear engagement by friction brake bands on appropriate gear trains), in unit with front-mounted engine. No clutch. Pre-selector lever on steering column, under steering wheel. Enclosed torque-tube propeller shaft to spiral-bevel 'live' rear axle.

Chassis: Separate pressed-steel chassis frame, with channel-section side members, pressed, fabricated and tubular cross bracing. Forged front axle beam. Front suspension by half-elliptic leaf springs. Rear suspension by half-elliptic leaf springs, torque tube and radius arms. Hydraulic dampers. Worm-and-nut steering. Four-wheel drum brakes, hydraulically operated (vacuum servo assistance on later models). 19in bolt on wire wheels or steel disc wheels to choice. 6·5 × 19in tyres. Open or closed coachwork to order, from Armstrong Siddeley or from specialists.

Dimensions: Wheelbase 11ft (335cm), track (front) 4ft 8in (142cm), track (rear) 4ft 10in (147cm). Overall length from 16ft 0in (488cm). Unladen weight (depending on body) from 5,000lb (2,268kg).

History: The firm came together by the fusion of Armstrong-Whitworth's car-making activities and Siddeley-Deasy of Coventry, and the cars were henceforth built alongside the planes and aero-engines which were Armstrong's principal products. From 1919 to 1939 the company concentrated on solidly-built, upper-middle-class, family vehicles, built for comfort, ease of driving and high quality rather than performance. The massive vee-profiled radiators and the Sphinx mascots were recognition points, along with the refusal to put styling before interior passenger space.

This readily accepted tradition made the arrival of the beautifully engineered 5-litre Siddeley Special of 1932 a delightful surprise. For the first time the company used its aero-engine knowledge to great effect, for the new six-cylinder unit used hiduminium alloy castings for block/crankcase and cylinder head, and many construction details (for instance the multitude of bolts 'stitching' one casting to its neighbour, and the use of Claudel-Hobson carburettors) were similar. This car had a robust if conventionally engineered chassis, which allowed speeds of well over 80mph even in limousine form, and more than 90mph if open touring coachwork was ordered.

Armstrong Siddeley are famous for introducing the Wilson-type epicyclic self-change gearbox in 1928, and developing the pre-selector facility. The box was heavy, but as it did away with the clutch this nullified the loss, and in the days when the fully-automatic gearbox was still a dream the Wilson-change was startlingly modern. It was taken up by many other car-makers, supplied direct to some, and licence-built by the others.

The Siddeley Special was high-priced — £1,050 bought a good four-seater sports saloon — and only about 140 of these cars were built in four years. There were models for most tastes, and in many engine sizes, and the company's reputation was secure in the 1930s. After the war, times were harder, and in spite of the fine Sapphire model demand dropped and the last car was built in 1960.

Below: Armstrong Siddeley's Special was their finest and most sporting car. Under the impressive coachwork was a powerful 4,960cc straight six-cylinder engine designed up to aero-engine standards. Gears were pre-selected.

AQUILA ITALIANA

15—25hp model, built from 1906 to 1917 (data for 1911 model)

Built by: Fabbrica Italiana d'Automobili Aquila, Italy.

Engine: Four cylinders, in line, in two-bearing monobloc combined cast-iron block/crankcase. Bore and stroke 80mm by 130mm, 2,614cc (3·15in × 5·12in, 159·5cu.in). Cast-iron cylinder head. Two valves per cylinder, inlets overhead and operated by pushrods and rockers, exhausts side-mounted and operated by tappets (all from single camshaft mounted in side of crankcase). Single up-draught carburettor.

Transmission: Engine, clutch and gearbox all supported in common light-alloy casing. Multi-plate clutch in unit with front-mounted engine and shaftdrive to separate three-speed manual gearbox (without synchromesh). Remote-control right-hand gearchange. Propeller shaft, enclosed in torque tube, driving underslung-worm-type 'live' rear axle.

Chassis: Separate pressed-steel chassis frame, with channel-section side members and pressed cross bracing. Forged front axle beam. Front suspension by semi-elliptic leaf springs. Rear suspension by three-quarter-elliptic leaf springs, with torque tube and radius fork location. Worm-type steering. Mechanically operated foot brake acting on externally contracting drum behind gearbox. Hand lever operating, by rod and cross shaft, drums at rear wheels. Artillery-style road wire wheels, or centre-lock wire wheels.

History: The Italian Aquila (which means Eagle) was revealed in 1906 and dropped in 1917. In all that time, the marque remained faithful to the same basic design by Giulio Cesare Cappa. None was made for three of those years, following the death of the company's promoter. The Aquila was quite remarkably advanced for the time, and featured a monobloc cylinder layout — in four-cylinder or six-cylinder alternatives — at a time when blocks of not more than two cylinders were usual. In addition, there was a common support and oil-carrying tray for the engine, clutch and gearbox, which aided alignment. By 1912 there were three models, the largest of which was a 30/45hp six of 4·2 litres; this developed no less than 60bhp at 3,600rpm and made the Aquila a very fast car. An Aquila ran in the 1914 French GP, but did not achieve success. Cappa went on to work for Fiat and for Itala and his Aquila design is remembered for its clean mechanical design and for the features which predated many which were 're-invented' or redeveloped in the Vintage years.

Below: Aquilas were built for 13 years —all to the same basic 'Edwardian' design. This is a 1912/13 two-seater.

ASTON MARTIN DB2

DB2 models built 1950 to 1953, succeeded by DB 2/4 from 1953 to 1957 and DB3 from 1957 to 1959

Built by: Aston Martin Ltd., Britain.

Engine: Six cylinders, in line, in four-bearing cast-iron block/crankcase. Bore and stroke 78mm by 90mm, 2,580cc (3·07in × 3·54in, 157·5cu.in). Detachable light-alloy cylinder head. Two overhead valves per cylinder, inclined to each other at 30 degrees, operated by twin overhead camshafts, through inverted bucket-type tappets. Twin horizontal constant-vacuum SU carburettors. Maximum power 105bhp (net) at 5,000rpm. Maximum torque 125lb.ft at 3,000rpm.

Transmission: Single-dry-plate clutch and four-speed synchromesh manual gearbox (no synchromesh on first gear) both in unit with engine. Steering-column or remote-control central gearchange to choice (column control soon dropped from specification). Open propeller shaft to hypoid-bevel 'live' rear axle.

Chassis: Separate fabricated multi-tube (square-section tubing) chassis frame, with cross and diagonal bracings. Independent front suspension by coil springs, trailing arms and anti-roll bar. Rear suspension by coil springs and twin trailing arms with Panhard rod location. Piston-type hydraulic dampers. Worm-and-roller steering. Four-wheel, hydraulically operated drum brakes of 12in diameter. 16in centre lock wire wheels. 6·00 × 16in tyres.

Light-alloy two-door coupé coachwork by Tickford (like Aston Martin, owned by David Brown Industries).

Dimensions: Wheelbase 8ft 3in (251·5cm), tracks (front and rear) 4ft 6in (137cm). Overall length 13ft 6·5in (412·8cm). Unladen weight 2,500lb (1,134kg).

History: Aston Martin proved their post-war design in the classic manner, by first building prototypes, and subjecting them to the public ordeal of long-distance sports car racing. The DB2 prototypes distinguished themselves in 1949 at the Le Mans and Spa 24-hour events and went into production in 1950. In more and more developed form the cars were then made

until 1959, when they were finally supplanted by the DB4s. The cars were really a very clever amalgam of Aston Martin's post-war multi-tube chassis and Lagonda's Bentley-designed twin-cam engine — industrialist David Brown buying up both firms soon after World War II.

The DB2, too, had sleek good looks and impeccable road behaviour, all allied to an effortless 100mph-plus performance. One feature of the body was that the entire bonnet/wings/nose panel hinged ahead of the wheels and gave unrivalled access to the engine bay. The multi-tube chassis frame was expensive to make and

Above: The DB2 series arrived in 1949, was raced, and went into production in the form shown. The DB2/4 had an opening rear door/window, and later 3-litres. The DB Mk 3 evolved from it.

repair, but as the company only made a handful of cars every week they were prepared for complication. It was, after all, very rigid. Perhaps the best version of this car was the DB2/4, which followed in 1953, with a large opening back window and — eventually — considerably more power, plus a tiny occasional rear seat.

ASTON MARTIN ULSTER

Mk II and Ulster models, built from 1934 to 1936 (data for Ulster)

Built by: Aston Martin Ltd., Britain

Engine: Four cylinders, in line, in three-bearing cast-iron block/crankcase. Bore and stroke 69mm by 99mm, 1,493cc (2·72in × 3·90in, 91·1cu.in). Detachable cast-iron cylinder head. Two overhead valves per cylinder, operated by rockers from single overhead camshaft. Two horizontal constant-vacuum SU carburettors. Maximum power 80bhp at 5,250rpm. Dry-sump lubrication.

Transmission: Single-dry-plate clutch and four-speed manual gearbox (without synchromesh), both in unit with engine. Remote-control central gearchange. Open propeller shaft to spiral-bevel 'live' rear axle.

Chassis: Separate pressed-steel chassis frame, with channel-section side members, tubular and pressed cross bracing members. Forged front axle beam. Half-elliptic leaf springs at front and rear, with Hartford friction-type dampers. Cam-type steering gear. Four-wheel drum brakes, operated by shafts, rods and cables. 18in centre-lock wire wheels. 5·25 × 18in tyres.

Two-seat or four-seat open sports coachwork by Aston Martin.

Dimensions: Wheelbase 8ft 7in (261·6cm), tracks (front and rear) 4ft 4in (132cm). Overall length 12ft 8in (386cm). Unladen weight 2,075lb (941kg).

History: The first Aston Martin cars were built in 1922 and the firm had a chequered financial history for a good many years. Sales were low, because of the car's specialised nature and because the firm was small. There were at least two important changes of management in the first ten years. The well-known single overhead cam arrived in 1927 and was used for the next ten years in one form or another. Bertelli rejuvenated the firm in 1926 and the company made more and more competition entries in the late 1920s and early 1930s. The International and Le Mans models arrived in 1932 and the improved Mark II and Ulster models for 1935. The Ulster was a light, fast and well-mannered car which cost £750 — rather expensive by comparison with

MG and SS equivalents, but nonetheless exclusive. A 2-litre Aston Martin was added in 1936 and a semi-streamlined model followed, but by 1939 the company was again in financial trouble, which not even the fine products could solve. After the war, the company was taken over by David Brown and started to make much larger, more luxurious machines.

Below: The Ulster was one of Britain's best Post-Vintage Thoroughbreds, a road car which raced with success.

ASTON MARTIN DB4, DB5 AND DB6

DB4, DB5, DB6, including DB4GT, built from 1958 to 1971 (data for DB4, 1959 model).

Built by: Aston Martin Lagonda Ltd., Britain.

Engine: Six cylinders, in line, in seven-bearing light-alloy block. Bore and stroke 92mm by 92mm, 3,670cc (3·62in × 3·63in, 223·9cu.in). Light-alloy cylinder head. Two overhead valves per cylinder, inclined to each other, in part-spherical combustion chambers and operated by twin overhead camshafts, through inverted bucket-type tappets. Twin horizontal constant-vacuum SU carburettors. Maximum power 240bhp (net) at 5,500rpm. Maximum torque 240lb.ft at 4,250rpm.

Transmission: Single-dry-plate clutch and four-speed all-synchromesh manual gearbox, both in unit with front mounted engine. Remote-control central gearchange. Open propeller shaft to hypoid-bevel 'live' rear axle.

Chassis: Fabricated steel platform-type chassis frame, with lightweight bodyshell of 'Super-leggera' construction welded to it after assembly. Body has many lightweight forming tubes, light-alloy skin panels and bracing members. Independent front suspension by coil springs, wishbones and anti-roll bar. Rear suspension by coil springs, twin radius arms and Watts linkage. Telescopic dampers. Rack-and-pinion steering. Four-wheel disc brakes, with vacuum servo assistance. 16in centre-lock wire wheels. 6·00 × 16in tyres.

Dimensions: Wheelbase 8ft 2in (249cm), track (front) 4ft 6in (137cm), track (rear) 4ft 5·5in (136cm). Overall length 14ft 8·4in (448cm). Unladen weight 2,900lb (1,315kg).

History: During the 1950s, Aston Martin continued to race their sports cars with great success. In 1957 they produced brand new DBR1 and DBR2 models, both sharing the same basic multi-tube chassis, but whereas the DBR1 had an engine developed from that of the old DB2/DB3 series, the DBR2 used a new and much bulkier 3·7-litre twin-cam unit. It was therefore no real surprise when, in September 1958, a new road car was announced, fitted with a detuned version of this engine. This was the DB4, and it was the first of a family of models which was to carry Aston Martin forward to the end of the 1960s. It was not a direct replacement for the DB2 and 2/4 cars, as it was much larger, heavier and faster, and of rather different construction, but it was not long before it took over the whole of the Newport Pagnell factory. In fact it was the first 'nearly four-seat' Aston Martin for some years, although of course the W.O. Bentley-inspired Lagondas had fulfilled that role for some years in the 1940s and 1950s. The new car was unashamedly styled on Italian lines, by Touring of Milan, and used that firm's patented lightweight method of body construction. The chassis was a complete innovation for Aston Martin, being fabricated, platform style, from sheet steel. The suspension design was also new

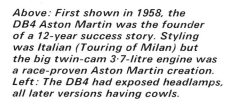

Above: First shown in 1958, the DB4 Aston Martin was the founder of a 12-year success story. Styling was Italian (Touring of Milan) but the big twin-cam 3·7-litre engine was a race-proven Aston Martin creation. Left: The DB4 had exposed headlamps, all later versions having cowls.

— with wishbone independent front suspension replacing the trailing-arm layout of the DB2 family, although the well-located beam rear axle method was retained. Aston Martin found their gearbox within the David Brown organisation. Even in original guise, with an easy 240bhp developed, the DB4 was a very quick car, much better built than some so-called Italian masterpieces, but it was very expensive to build, virtually by hand, for all that.

The first DB4 was sold at the beginning of 1959 and the last of that family — a DB6 Mark II,

Below: The DB4 carried over many well-loved Aston Martin 'trade marks' including the grille shape, and the fast-back theme. Even the mildest versions could nudge 140mph, and the lightweight DB4GTs which followed were race winners when bodied by Zagato.

was delivered early in 1971. In those twelve years the basic design of the car remained unchanged, but there was a persistent updating which led to more and more performance and better and better fittings and equipment. Within months, the prototype DB4GT — a short-chassis version of the DB4, with faired headlamps and rather more power — had been raced successfully by Stirling Moss at Silverstone, and the production version with 314bhp and three twin-choke Weber carburettors was in production by the end of 1959. That led to an even more exciting and very low production version (only 25 were made), with stubby bodies by Zagato of Italy, in which the maximum speed was more than 150mph — and this at a time when anything higher was definitely a racing speed for huge sports cars. More than 1,100 DB4s were made between 1959 and 1963, in standard and Vantage-engine form, before the DB5 appeared. This combined the long wheelbase DB4 body-shell with the DB4GT's faired nose, had a full 4-litre engine and was also to be sold as a smart drop-head convertible. Unlike any other 'DB' Aston Martin, this made its name by being the 'James Bond' car in the film Goldfinger, although Aston Martin resisted all attempts to have them make lethal replicas!

Convertibles became Volantes and the DB5 also became the DB6 in October 1965. This was a more involved change than at first appeared, because the car's wheelbase was slightly lengthened to give more rear seat space, and along with a spoiler on the boot lid the car's

Right: DB4 became DB5 with a 4-litre engine and revised frontal styling, then the DB6 followed in 1965. The DB6's nose was the same as before, but the wheelbase was longer, there was more passenger space, and the boot lid had a spoiler to improve high-speed stability. Many chassis features were carried on to the DBS and DBS-V8 cars still being made. The last of the DB6s was a Mk II, built in 1971.

looks had been altered substantially. By now, too, a five-speed ZF gearbox was standard, or a Borg-Warner automatic gearbox was available at no extra cost.

Aston Martin now turned their attention to a new model, the DBS, which although based on the DB6's basic engineering, was longer and wider and ready to receive a new four-cam V8 engine they were developing. This car was released in October 1967 and meant that the DB6's days were numbered. The DB6 was so popular, however, that it carried on, latterly in

upgraded Mk II guise, until the spring of 1971, by which time it was offered for a time with AE fuel injection, and with various styling touches including flared wheel arches. Even a handful of three-door estate cars were built on the basis of the DB6, but these were even more handbuilt than the usual Aston Martin. It is a sad commentary on the DB4s/5s/6s that although they were beautiful, fast and very roadworthy, they were never really profitable to their makers — a trait common to many other Supercars in Europe in the 1960s.

AUBURN STRAIGHT-EIGHT

Straight-Eights built from 1925 to 1936 (data for 1935 851 Supercharged)

Built by: Auburn Automobile Company Inc., United States.

Engine: Lycoming Type GG. Eight cylinders, in line, in five-bearing cast-iron block. Bore and stroke 77·8mm by 120·6mm, 4,587cc (3·06in × 4·75in, 279·9cu.in). Aluminium cylinder head. Two valves per cylinder operated by single side-mounted camshaft. Stromberg carburettor, in association with Schwitzer-Cummins centrifugal supercharger. Maximum power 150bhp (gross) at 4,000rpm.

Transmission: Single-dry-plate clutch and three-speed manual gearbox without synchromesh, with direct-acting central gearchange. Open propeller shaft to two-speed Columbia 'live' rear axle (ratios 5·00 or 3·47:1); axle speed control by hand lever on steering column, engine-vacuum assisted.

Chassis: Separate steel chassis, with channel-section side members. Pressed-steel front and rear cross members and cruciform bracing under the passenger floor. Half-elliptic springs front and rear. Forged axle beam at front. Hydraulic piston-type dampers. Four-wheel hydraulically operated drum brakes. 16in wire wheels with conventional disc wheel type fastening nuts. 6·50 × 16in tyres.

Two-seater 'Speedster' coachwork, with outside flexible stainless steel exhaust pipes. Fold down hood. No running boards. No rumble seat.

Dimensions: Wheelbase 10ft 7in (323cm), track (front) 4ft 11in (150cm), track (rear) 5ft 2in (157cm). Overall length 16ft 2·4in (494cm). Unladen weight 3,360lb (1,524kg).

History: Auburn's Straight-Eight series of cars, made in steadily developed form between 1925 and 1936, were inspired by the arrival of E. L. Cord as the company's General Manager in 1924. Before Cord, Auburns had been rather ordinary cars; after he arrived they took on considerable style. The chassis of the Straight-Eights was always particularly rigid, and the basic engineering very solid. The engines were always bought from Lycoming in Pennsylvania. Among earlier features were Bijur central chassis lubrication, striking and prolific body options and a great deal of performance. From 1932, the dual-ratio Columbia rear axle was a great feature, but in 1935 and 1936 the much-revised engines were offered with superchargers.

The 851 Speedster was given lines by Gordon Buehrig, who had also shaped the Model 810 Cord, and it made no concessions to the big 127-inch wheelbase. There were only two seats, a vision-restricting hood, and vast shining external exhaust pipes through the side of the bonnet. Ab Jenkins proved that there was performance to go with those looks. At Utah in 1935 his Speedster covered more than 100 miles in each of twelve consecutive hours — a United States stock-car record. For 1936 the 851 was followed by the 852, but by then the American public had turned away from such machines. The last of all Auburns was made in that year; in fact only 500 were made in 1935 and 1936.

Above: Straight-Eight Auburns were built from 1925 to 1936, in many styles. This car was one of the last —a 1935 Type 851 Supercharger with a phaeton body. In this tune the 4·6-litre straight-eight engine produced 150bhp. Right: In 1929 the boat-tail Speedster was one of the most dramatic shapes around. It made no effort to provide more than two seats —not even a dickey. The engines were supplied by Lycoming (who also made aero-engines) and the cars were inspired by E. L. Cord, who ran the Auburn Group.

The Speedster of the early 1930s was popular but expensive. By 1932 it had a dual-ratio rear axle, and visibility from the driving seat was very restricted.

Below: The sort of splendid American car we saw in all the gangster movies —Auburn's 8-100A Speedster, as sold in 1932 with its Lycoming engine.

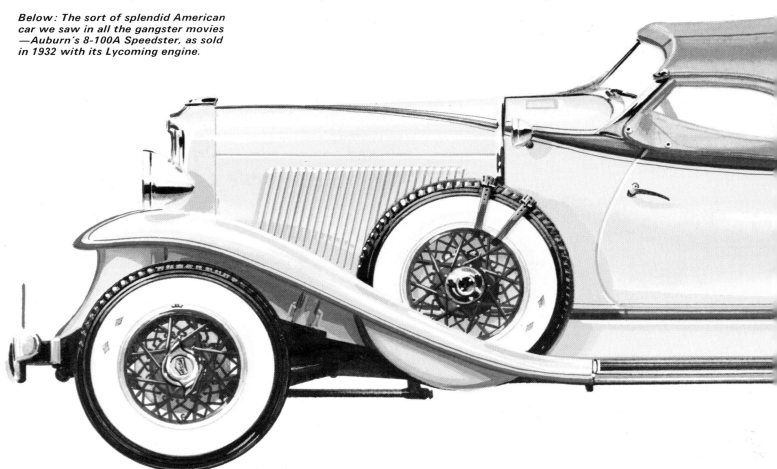

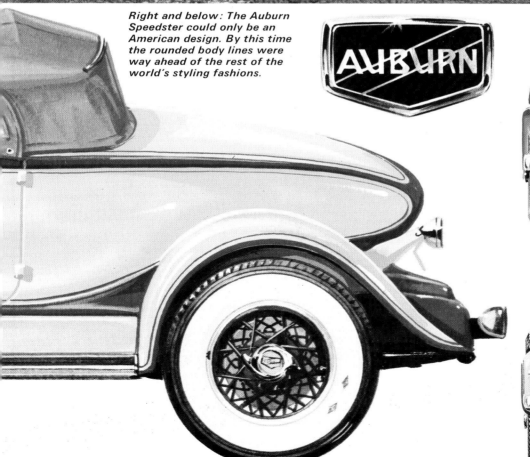

Right and below: The Auburn Speedster could only be an American design. By this time the rounded body lines were way ahead of the rest of the world's styling fashions.

AUSTIN SEVEN

Austin Seven, all models, and Big Seven, 1923 to 1939 (data for 1923 model)

Engine: Four cylinders, in line, in a two-bearing cast-iron block. Bore and stroke 56mm by 76·2mm 747cc (2·2in × 3·0in, 45·6cu.in). Cast-iron cylinder head. Two side valves per cylinder, directly operated by block-mounted camshaft. Single updraught carburettor. Maximum power 10·5bhp at 2,400rpm.

Transmission: Single-dry-plate clutch and three-speed manual gearbox, with direct-acting central gearchange. Forward ratios 4·9, 9·0 and 16·0:1. Open propeller shaft to centre bearing, then torque tube to spiral-bevel 'live' rear axle.

Chassis: Simple separate steel chassis frame, with channel-section side members and minor cross bracing. Front suspension by transverse leaf spring to forged front axle and splayed radius arms. Rear suspension by cantilever splayed quarter-elliptic leaf springs. Worm-and-sector steering. Small four-wheel drum brakes, with handbrake operating on front wheels. No dampers.

Initially only two-door tourer coachwork, but speedily followed by fabric-covered two-door saloons. In later years, every possible variation including vans and two-seater sports cars.

Dimensions: Wheelbase 6ft 3in (190cm), tracks (front and rear) 3ft 4in (102cm). Overall length 8ft 10in (269cm). Unladen weight 800lb (363kg).

History: The Austin Seven was born because of a financial crisis and it made a financial fortune. After World War I, Sir Herbert Austin settled on a 'one-model' policy at Longbridge, but he chose the wrong model — an expensive and stodgy 'Twenty'. With losses mounting up, Austin took one design draughtsman with him to his home and spent months on the all-new 'baby' Austin. Called a 'Seven' because of British fiscal rules, it nonetheless went into production as a 7·8hp car. Its engine, even if it *was* all-new, could only produce about 10 to 11bhp. Fortunately for the customers, the cars' all-up weights were rarely over 800lb (363kg). The Seven, when announced in autumn 1922, was not yet ready for production, and was shown with a 696cc engine even less powerful than the one which went into production the following year. It was, in all respects, tiny and, although four seats were provided, there was really no way that an 800lb car could support and carry the same weight in passengers.

The original asking price in March 1923 was £165, and over the years the cheapest versions of the car (tourers with minimum equipment) were cheapened further. In the mid 1930s a magic £100 car was briefly sold, but a more normal price level in the 1930s was £120–£135. The car was an immediate and heartening success, and by 1924 there was little doubt that

Austin's future was assured. Even though the little car was very crude and small (it soon became the butt of dozens of music-hall jokes) and slow (45mph was a very good maximum speed at first), it was also very reliable — and it was *much* cheaper than almost anything else on the British market, a notable exception being Ford's heavily taxed Model T. Among the car's early vagaries were four wheel brakes which were a bit of a joke, an 'in-out' clutch that was no joke, and fittings which bordered on the primitive. On the other hand, the two-bearing, side-valve engine seemed to stand every abuse and the car itself was small enough and light enough to be taken almost anywhere.

Not only was the Austin Seven a car of its decade, but of the next decade too. In terms of numbers sold it was most popular in the mid 1930s and it only came to a rapid and rather sad end in 1939 when Austin at least began to produce something approaching modern body styling. In all those years the basic chassis and mechanical layout remained unchanged, although the rudimentary frame was stiffened and lengthened and the engine was eventually given a centre crankshaft bearing. Even so, the story of the Austin Seven is one of continuous development within the narrow limits of its layout. The things that should have been changed, if logic had prevailed — like the front and rear suspensions

which put axle location and ride comfort at the back of the development queue — were never touched. However, an electric starter motor was added in 1924, coil ignition in 1927, a stronger crankshaft in 1930, a four-speed gearbox in 1933, synchromesh for that box a year later, second gear synchromesh two years later still and a three-bearing engine in 1937. In the meantime the engine power had been pushed steadily up — to 12bhp at 2,600rpm in 1933, 13·5bhp at 3,000rpm in 1934, and 17bhp at 3,800rpm a couple of years later. Body variations were legion. Specialist body makers like Swallow (William Lyons) and Gordon England made their names by courtesy of the little Austin chassis. Austin themselves offered anything from a stark little two-seat sports car to a 'Top Hat' metal panelled

Below: The little 747cc Austin Seven was a familiar part of the motoring scene between the wars. It was born in 1921/22 to fill a big gap in the Austin range, and designed by Sir Herbert Austin and one young draughtsman. It was simple, rugged, versatile, tiny, light, and very easy to drive. It was Britain's cheapest car for years, and in 16 years about a quarter-million were sold. There was just room for four passengers.

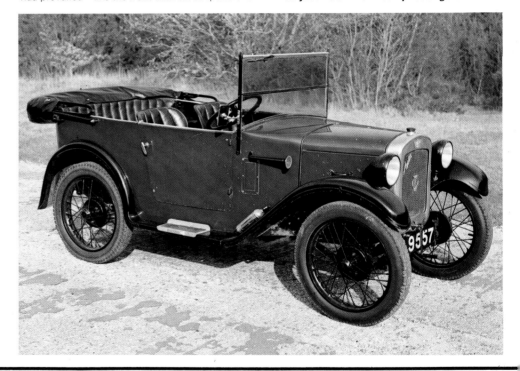

AUSTRO-DAIMLER ADM

ADM models, built from 1923 to 1928 (data for 1924 ADM1 model)

Built by: Österreichische Daimler Motoren A.G., Germany.

Engine: Six cylinders, in line, in four-bearing light-alloy block/crankcase. Bore and stroke 70mm by 110mm, 2,540cc (2·76in × 4·33in, 155cu.in). Detachable cast-iron cylinder head. Two overhead valves per cylinder, opposed to each other and operated by twin overhead camshafts. One up-draught Zenith carburettor.

Transmission: Multi-dry-plate clutch and four-speed manual gearbox, both in unit with front-mounted engine. Direct-acting central gearchange. Propeller shaft, enclosed in torque tube, driving spiral-bevel 'live' rear axle.

Chassis: Separate pressed-steel chassis frame, with channel-section side members and pressed cross-bracings. Forged front axle beam. Front suspension by semi-elliptic leaf springs. Rear suspension by cantilever semi-elliptic leaf springs

and torque tube location, with radius arms. Friction-type dampers. Worm-and-nut steering. Four-wheel, cable-operated drum brakes. Centre-lock wire wheels. 820 × 120mm tyres.

Six-seater bodywork, open touring, saloon and limousine types.

Dimensions: Wheelbase 11ft 3·8in (345cm), tracks (front and rear) 4ft 5·1in (135cm). Overall length 15ft 1·9in (462cm). Unladen weight (chassis only) 2,204lb (1,000kg).

History: Austro-Daimler, having made their name already legendary with the Prince Henry cars, had a formidable reputation to maintain after World War I was over. First of all they produced the six-cylinder AD617 and ADV17/60PS models, both of which had single-over-head-camshaft engines, but by 1923 Dr. Porsche had excelled himself by designing the splendid new ADM cars. Not only did the car look the part and perform accordingly, but when one opened the bonnet the engine was a singularly

pleasing sight. Porsche had given it a light-alloy cylinder block and nothing less than twin overhead camshafts (like the tiny Sascha-type 1,100cc car which preceded it). The engine looked 'all of a piece' with the vertical shaft cam-drive hidden inside castings — which made a nice change from other vintage engines whose bulks were more imposing than their lines.

Over the years the ADM family proliferated and among its number was the 2½-litre ADM1. The radiator style on these cars was more rounded than before, but was still quite unmistakable because of the badging cast into its top and the arrow-shaped motif. ADM1 became ADMII in 1925, when the car was sold in sports form, and after 1926 the engine was bored out to 3 litres and called the ADMIII. By this time the car could achieve more than 100mph, and the engine produced 100bhp at 4,000rpm.

Austro-Daimler, which had progressed a long way from its original German-based parentage, saloon. There were tiny commercial vans and the British Army bought some tourers affectionately called 'prams'. The car was built under licence in Germany as a BMW Dixi, in the United States as a Bantam, and in France as a Rosengart, and it was illegally copied in Japan as a Datsun.

Austin's son-in-law Arthur Waite raced special-bodied Austin Sevens with great success and the engine proved to be so astonishingly tuneable that he sanctioned the building of special single-seater racing cars with supercharged 747cc engines installed. Even when the engine was obsolete at Longbridge, Reliant continued to make and sell replicas for their three-wheelers, and the 750 racing formula insists on engine and basic chassis being used in cars built to its rules.

Production lasted for 16 years, and about a quarter-million of all types were sold. Austin have never made as cheap or as relatively popular a car, before or since. They attempted to revive the name with the A30 and then with the Mini: but there could only be one proper Austin Seven.

Below: One of the earliest of all Austin Sevens was this 1923 Tourer, which sold for £165, and weighed just 800lb. Its maximum speed was 45mph.

was now one of the super-cars of Europe, and undoubtedly Austria's prestige machine. The sports cars were very fast in race-prepared form — taking a team prize in the 1928 Tourist Trophy race, and in Hans Stuck's hands the 19-100 model (as ADM111 was also known) was a formidable hill-climb machine. Porsche's successor, Karl Rabe, designed the ADR, which replaced all the ADMs. This car had a tubular backbone chassis, and independent rear suspension. Austro-Daimler, however, suffered badly in the depression and the big cars disappeared in 1934, after a merger with Steyr.

Right: Austro-Daimler's ADM was the mainstay of the Austrian company's range in the 1920s. Its 2½-litre 'six' had twin overhead camshafts. Dr Porsche was the famous designer.

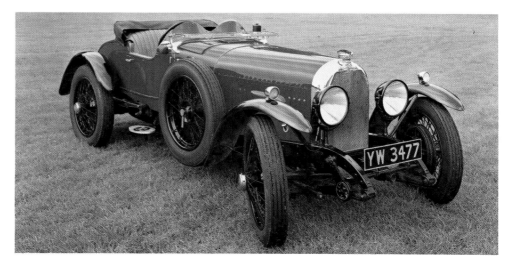

AUBURN V12

M12/160 models, built from 1932 to 1937 (data for 1932 model)
Built by: Auburn Automobile Co., United States.
Engine: Lycoming manufactured. 12 cylinders, in 45-degree vee-formation, in four-bearing cast-iron block/crankcase. Bore and stroke 79·4mm by 108·0mm, 6,409cc (3·12in × 4·25in, 391·6cu.in). Two detachable cast-iron cylinder heads. Two horizontal valves per cylinder, mounted across engine, in cylinder heads, and operated by rockers from single camshaft mounted high in centre of cylinder block 'vee'. Twin single-choke down-draught Stromberg carburettors. Maximum power 160bhp gross.
Transmission: Two-dry-plate clutch and three-speed manual gearbox (with synchromesh on top and second gears), both in unit with front-mounted engine. Free-wheel feature. Direct-acting central gearchange. Open propeller shaft to spiral-bevel 'live' rear axle with two-speed Columbia ratio.
Chassis: Separate pressed-steel chassis frame, with channel-section side members, channel-section cruciform members and pressed and tubular cross bracings. Forged front axle beam. Automatic chassis lubrication. Front and rear suspension by semi-elliptic leaf springs. Lever arm hydraulic dampers. Cam-and-lever steering. Four-wheel hydraulically operated drum brakes, with vacuum-servo assistance. Artillery style, steel-disc or bolt-on-wire wheels. 7·00 × 17in tyres.
Choice of coachwork, closed or open sports and touring.
Dimensions: Wheelbase 11ft 1in (338cm), tracks (front and rear) 4ft 10in (147cm). Overall length 16ft 1in (490cm). Unladen weight, depending on coachwork, from 4,700lb (2,131kg).
History: In 1932, in spite of the gloom of the North American depression, Auburn joined in the trend to really splendid-engined cars. Cadillac had 12s and 16s, Marmon had a 16, and Lincoln had a 12, so Auburn matched them by announcing the M12/160, with its Lycoming-built V12 engine. This was unique for having only a 45-degree angle between cylinder banks (60 degrees was more usual) and for having horizontal valves operated by rockers from a single central camshaft. The combustion chambers were a very odd 'letter-box' shape, with valves to one side and sparking plugs to the other (outside) side. It was a very cheap car — perhaps the only V12 machine ever to sell for less than $1,000, which probably made sure that it was not a profit-maker. The Columbia two-speed axle (vacuum-operated from the cockpit) gave a six-speed gearbox. Most chassis parts were common with those of the eight-cylinder model, but the public was not very interested and Auburn turned in a big loss in 1932. E. L. Cord himself left America for Europe in 1934 and allied attempts to make money from a front-engined Cord flopped, so Auburn, too, were doomed. Perhaps if the M12/160 had cost a lot more, it might have succeeded. Who knows? Even in troubled times, prestige is important.

Below: A splendid boat-tail Speedster body on the 12/160 Auburn chassis.

AUSTIN-HEALEY 3000

3000 models BN7, BT7, BJ7 and BJ8, 1959 to 1967. Also 100-6 models BN4 and BN6, 1956 to 1959 (data for BJ8)
Built by: British Motor Corporation Ltd., Britain.
Engine: Six cylinders, in line, in four-bearing cast-iron block. Bore and stroke 83·3mm by 88·9mm, 2,912cc (3·28in × 3·5in, 177·7cu.in). Cast-iron cylinder head (aluminium on competition cars). Two overhead valves per cylinder, operated by pushrod and rocker from side-mounted camshaft. Two SU carburettors. Maximum power 148bhp (net) at 5,200rpm. Maximum torque 165lb.ft at 3,000rpm.
Transmission: Single-dry-plate clutch, and four-speed synchromesh manual gearbox (without synchromesh on first gear), remote control central gearchange. Optional overdrive on top and third gears. Open propeller shaft to hypoid-bevel 'live' rear axle.
Chassis: Separate steel chassis frame, with box-section side members, box and pressed cross brace and cruciform members. Welded to steel body after manufacture. Independent front suspension by coil springs, wishbones and anti-roll bar. Rear suspension by half-elliptic leaf springs and radius arms. Piston-type hydraulic dampers. Cam-and-peg steering. Disc front brakes and drum rear brakes, hydraulically operated. 15in steel disc or optional centre-lock wire spoke wheels. 5·90 × 15in tyres.
Steel sports car body style, with tiny 'plus 2' seats behind front bucket seats. Optional hardtop. Body/chassis units built by Jensen.
Dimensions: Wheelbase 7ft 7.7in (233cm), track (front) 4ft 0.7in (124cm), track (rear) 4ft 2in (127cm). Overall length 13ft 1.5in (400cm). Unladen weight 2,460lb (1,116kg).
History: Donald Healey's Healey 100 was the result of an unofficial design competition set up by Sir Leonard Lord in 1952. The rules were that mainly BMC components should be used; BMC would sponsor the winner. MG and Jensen

AUSTRO-DAIMLER PRINCE HENRY

Prince Henry models, built from 1910 to 1914 (data for 1911 model)
Built by: Österreichische Daimler Motoren A.G., Austria.
Engine: Four cylinders, in line, in individual cast-iron barrels attached to three-bearing light-alloy crankcase. Bore and stroke 105mm by 165mm, 5,715cc (4·13in × 6·50in, 348·7cu.in). Fixed cylinder heads. Two overhead valves per cylinder, opposed to each other at 90 degrees and operated by fork-type rockers from single overhead camshaft. Single up-draught carburettor. Maximum power about 95bhp.
Transmission: Multi-dry-plate clutch in unit with front-mounted engine. Shaft to separate four-speed manual gearbox (without synchromesh). Remote-control right-hand gearchange. Straight bevel drive unit in gearbox and final drive by countershaft to sprockets and thence by chain to rear wheels.
Chassis: Separate pressed-steel chassis frame, with channel-section side members and tubular and pressed cross-bracings. Forged front axle beam. Front suspension by semi-elliptic leaf springs. Rear suspension by cantilever leaf springs. No dampers. Worm-type steering. Rear wheel drum brakes operated by hand lever. Two foot pedals operating drums, one mounted each side of gearbox, on countershaft. Centre-lock wire wheels. 810×90mm tyres (front) and 815×105mm tyres (rear).
Open four-seater touring bodywork.
Dimensions: Wheelbase 9ft 10in (300cm), tracks (front and rear) 4ft 4in (132cm). Overall length 13ft 6in (411·5cm). Unladen weight (chassis only) 2,125lb (964kg).

History: Austria's most famous car was born when Daimler of Cannstatt established a factory in Vienna to make its own products. At first the Austro-Daimler car was an exact copy of the German parent, but from 1906 it became separately financed, with the young Ferdinand Porsche as technical director. Porsche's first sensational design was the 22/80PS car designed specifically for the 1910 Prince Henry Tour, which it won in a very convincing manner. This was not only powerful — with about 95bhp — but had an advanced engine with a single-overhead-camshaft layout and opposed valves. The use of chain final drive was rather an oddity, but Porsche was not convinced at that stage that shaft drive could do the job. Later on, with the model on public sale, he was convinced and the

design was converted. The 22/80PS also had a smaller relative, the 16/25PS, which gained its spurs in the 1911 Austrian Alpine Tour. Built up to the outbreak of World War I, Austrian—Daimler models (as they were also called) were expensive but excellent prestige cars for their country, and more in the same vein were to be built in vintage years.

Below: The title tells us everything about the car—which was built by the Austrian Daimler company, in Cannstatt. By 1912, when this very impressive Prince Henry car was made, the cars were being designed by Dr Ferdinand Porsche. By 1912 standards the engine was advanced, with an overhead cam.

were losers. The first Austin-Healeys had four-cylinder, 2·6-litre engines, and these were made between 1953 and 1956. Chassis and bodywork were designed by Geoffrey Healey and his father Donald. The car was a great export success, and racing versions (the 100S. — 'S' for Sebring) achieved great things in 1954/5. When supplies of the old 'four' ran out, the car was re-engined as a 'six' with the new BMC 'C' series 2·6-litre unit.

Three years later, in 1959, the engine was enlarged to 2·9-litres, and the Austin-Healey 3000 was born. In the next eight years there were four distinct types of 3000, but illogically enough the last one, with its wind-up windows, walnut facia and most powerful engine, was called the Mk III! If the 3000 had faults they were that it was too low-slung, too coarse and too cramped to be totally successful. It was, however, a real man's sports car and in final tune was capable of over 120mph. The 'big Healey', as it was always affectionately known, was a formidable rally car, winning Alpine and Liège-Sofia-Liège rallies, and it dominated the GT categories for many years. As a racing car it was too standard to be an outright winner, but, properly prepared, it was just about unbreakable. Nearly 43,000 '3000s' were built, and the car was forced off the market at the end of 1967 by United States legislation rendering continued production uneconomic.

Left and right: In the 1950s and 1960s the most exciting of all Austin-Healey 3000s were the 'works' team competition cars, prepared at the MG works at Abingdon. They had light-alloy bodies and powerful (210bhp) tuned engines. They were equally at home in the roughest of rallies (left: Timo Makinen, second in the 1965 RAC Rally) or in long-distance road races (right: Paul Hawkins/Timo Makinen in the Targa Florio). Brute strength and noise were features.

BALLOT RH SERIES EIGHT

RH Eights built 1927 to 1932 – 2·6, 2·8 and 3·0-litre versions (data for 3·0-litre RH3)
Built by: Etablissements Ballot, France.
Engine: Eight cylinders, in line, in cast-iron block, with detachable nine-bearing aluminium crankcase. Bore and stroke 68mm by 105mm, 3,050cc (2·68in × 4·13in, 186cu.in). Light-alloy cylinder head. Two valves per cylinder, operated by single overhead camshaft, driven by skew gears and shaft at rear of engine. Vertical valves in flat faced cylinder head. Single updraught Zenith twin-choke carburettor.
Transmission: Twin-plate clutch in unit with engine. Four-speed manual gearbox without synchromesh, also fixed to engine. Sliding gears at first, constant mesh gears on last batch of cars built. Direct action central gearchange. Open propeller shaft to spiral-bevel 'live' rear axle.
Chassis: Separate steel chassis frame, with channel-section main side members and tubular and pressed cross bracing. Half-elliptic leaf springs at front and rear. Forged front axle. Hydraulic lever arm dampers. Worm-and-nut steering. Rod-operated four-wheel drum brakes, with vacuum-servo assistance. 31in centre-lock wire wheels, fitted with 31 × 5·25in tyres. Several coachwork versions to choice, from Belgian/European specialists.
Dimensions: Wheelbase 10ft 10·5in or 11ft 10in (331cm or 361cm). Tracks (front and rear) 4ft 5in (135cm). Overall length depending on coachwork. Unladen weight (chassis only) 2,520lb (1,143kg).
History: Before 1914, Ballot in Paris specialised in the manufacture of car and stationary engines. From 1918, Edouard Ballot decided to extend his company's prestige by making and selling complete cars. First he engaged Ernest Henry (of 1913/1914 Peugeot fame) to design eight-cylinder and four-cylinder racing cars. The first

Ballot road car was the 2LS, really a slightly civilised racing two-seater, and this was followed in 1923 by the 2LT type. The 2LT introduced Ballot's particular and notable engine/cylinder layout, where the overhead-cam operated in-line valves operated in a flat head with Heron-type bowl-in-piston combustion chambers. The 2LT was supplemented by the 2LTS in 1925, which had more conventional combustion chamber arrangements and rather more performance. In 1927, however, Ballot decided to push up their offerings even more – in specification, performance and price.

Although they catalogued a 2-litre 'six' at the beginning of 1927 this car never went into production. In its place, at the Paris Show of 1927, came the eight-cylinder, 2·6-litre Model RH Ballot. Its chassis followed the 2LT's lines closely, although the wheelbase was considerably lengthened. The engine, more closely

Below: Striking in style and advanced in engineering, the Ballot Type 2LT was a fine vintage car. This body was by Lagache-Glaszmann of France. The car preceded the legendary 'Eights'.

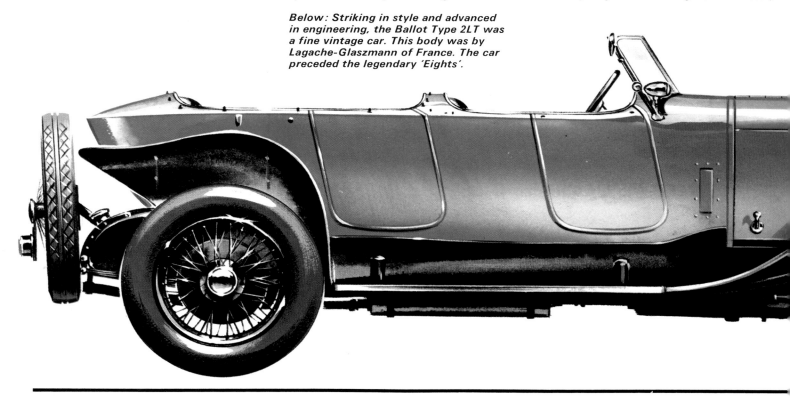

BENTLEY 3-LITRE

3-litre models built 1921 to 1928 (data for short-wheelbase 'Standard')
Built by: Bentley Motors Ltd., Britain.
Engine: Four cylinders, in line, in five-bearing cast-iron cylinder block and light-alloy crankcase. Bore and stroke 80mm by 149mm, 2,996cc (3·15in × 5·87in, 183cu.in). Non-detachable cast-iron cylinder head. Four valves per cylinder, operated by rockers from a single overhead camshaft. Camshaft driven by vertical shaft and gears from nose of crankshaft. Two SU carburettors after 1924, single Smith carburettor up to that date. Maximum power 80 to 85bhp, depending on time.
Transmission: Single-dry-plate, inverted-cone clutch, slightly separated from four-speed unsynchronised gearbox. Remote control right-hand gearchange. Open propeller shaft to spiral-bevel 'live' rear axle.
Chassis: Separate steel chassis frame, with channel-section side members and angled and tubular cross members. Half-elliptic leaf springs for front and rear suspension. Forged front axle beam. Hartford-type friction dampers. Worm-and-wheel steering. Rear-wheel drum brakes (up to 1923), four-wheel drum brakes (after 1923), without servo assistance. Centre-lock wire wheels, several size changes between 1921 and 1928. Initial tyre fitments 820 by 120 type. Coachwork to choice: cars supplied from Bentley

Motors as rolling chassis – sports, touring or saloon styles.
Dimensions: Wheelbase 9ft 9·5in (298cm), tracks (front and rear) 4ft 8in (142cm). Overall length 13ft 3in (404cm). Unladen weight (depending on coachwork), from 2,800lb (1,270kg).
History: W. O. Bentley had already made his name as an importer of French DFP sports cars before World War I, and for his BR air-cooled rotary aero-engine designs during it, when he decided in 1919 to make a car of his own design. The 3-litre, first seen at the 1919 Olympia Motor Show, and first sold in 1921, was the first of his legendary strain. Indeed, it is true to say that the 4½, 6½ and 8-litre cars (if not the unsuccessful 4-litre) are all recognisably descended from the 3-litre. Chassis engineering was conventional in every way. Interest, and praise, was always reserved for the engine. Massively built, tall and elegant in the Edwardian style, it was near-unique in having four-valves per cylinder and gave the bulky cars a sparkling performance.

Even though the firm was always under-capitalised (it was close to bankruptcy at least three times in the 1920s), Bentley himself eventually agreed to a Le Mans racing programme, to speed development and to provide publicity. The three-litre in 'lightweight' open guise won the race in 1924 and 1927. Cars also

raced with distinction in the Tourist Trophy Race (second in 1922) and at the Indianapolis 500 Miles Race (where Hawkes's car averaged 81mph).

Bentley was so confident of his engineering that a five-year guarantee was given on the mechanical items in the car. Three-litres were in production for seven years, in several basic guises and in three wheelbase lengths. The Speed

related to the Heron-headed 2LT 'four' than to the 2LTS 'four', initially had a cylinder bore of 63mm, and a capacity of 2,618cc, but to improve the performance when heavy coachwork was fitted this was twice increased — to 66mm in 1928 and to 68mm for 1930. The RH had a beautifully and flexibly tuned engine, which made the car an aristocrat among French machines, with a rather flexible chassis which sometimes caused grievous harm to the none-too-rigid bodies of the day.

In 1932, like so many other makers of exclusive cars, Ballot ran into financial difficulties, and were soon taken over by Hispano-Suiza. That was really the end of Ballot cars as we know them. A new model produced in Paris and badged as a Ballot HS26 was, in fact, a 4·6-litre small-scale replica of Spanish Hispano models. Even this car reverted to type and became a Hispano-badged machine before long.

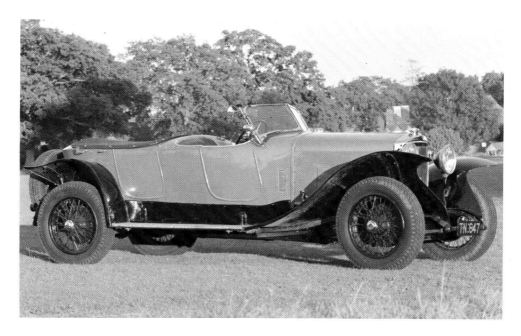

Right: A feature of the RH Eights was its magnificent eight-cylinder engine, with 'Heron' combustion chambers and an overhead camshaft. The long wheelbase encouraged splendid and elegant bodies.

Model, with tuned-up engines, arrived in 1924, and following the development of the 4½-litre Bentley (the engine being an amalgam of 3-litre and 6½-litre 'six' design thought) a number of common parts were specified. There were three distinct sets of gearbox ratios. Chassis price, at first, was £1,100 (usually raised to about £1,400, depending on the coachwork chosen), but by 1924 the long-wheelbase 'Standard' chassis had

been reduced to £895. This long-wheelbase chassis was the most popular — 765 being sold — while 513 of the Speed Model were produced. In total, 1,619 3-litre Bentleys were built. The car was finally replaced by the 4½-litre.

Below: W.O. Bentley's 3-litre was the first of the famous Cricklewood-built cars, many having sports bodywork. 'Old No. 7' was raced by the factory at Le Mans in 1926, then went on to win that event in 1927 after all three team cars were involved in a crash at White House. 'Sammy' Davis and Dr. Benjafield were its drivers. The 4½-litre followed.

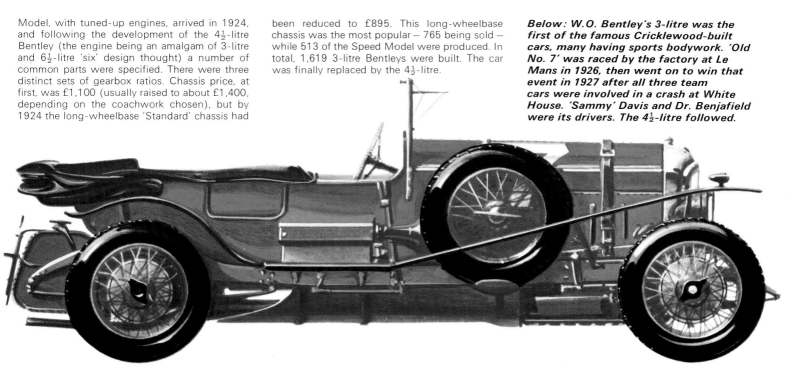

BENTLEY 6½-LITRE 'SPEED SIX'

Speed Six built 1928 to 1930
Built by: Bentley Motors Ltd., Britain.
Engine: Six cylinders, in line, in light-alloy block with non-detachable cylinder head. Bore and stroke 100mm by 140mm, 6,597cc (3·94in × 5·51in, 402·5cu.in). Four-valves per cylinder, operated by bifurcated rocker (inlet valves) or individual rockers (exhaust side) from single overhead camshaft. Three-throw coupling-rod drive and gear from nose of crankshaft. Twin plugs, one each side of cylinder head, under the manifolding; ignition by twin magnetos (coil and magneto supply in tandem later fitted). Twin horizontal SU carburettors. Compression ratio 5·3:1. Maximum power 180bhp at 3,500rpm with 'single port' block.
Transmission: Single shaft-operated dry-plate clutch. Four-speed unsynchronised gearbox, separately mounted, with right-hand gear-change. Open Hardy Spicer propeller shaft to spiral-bevel rear axle, of optional 3·54 or 3·85:1 ratio. Either 'C' Type or straight-cut gear 'D' Type gearboxes fitted.
Chassis: Channel-section side members in steel, liberally cross braced, conventionally overslung at rear. Half-elliptic leaf springs front and rear, with worm-and-sector steering. Cable-operated self-wrapping drum brakes. Outside handbrake, sports car bodies only. Coachwork to choice — saloon, coupé, or open sports.
Dimensions: Wheelbase 11ft 8·5in (357cm), 12ft 8·5in (387cm), or 11ft (335cm) to choice (short wheelbase on Le Mans version only). Front and rear track 4ft 8in (142cm). Overall length 15ft 1in to 16ft 7in (460cm to 505cm) depending on wheelbase length and coachwork. Unladen weight between 4,480lb and 5,040lb (2,031 and 2,286kg).
History: The 'Speed Six' is probably the most famous of all W.O.'s Bentleys. In factory drivers' hands, these cars won twice at Le Mans (in 1929 and 1930 — with Chairman Woolf Barnato in the winning car on each occasion), at Brooklands and in minor races elsewhere. Their domination of sports car racing was so complete that entries from other teams declined sharply.

Bentley's advanced six-cylinder engine, developed from but by no means the same as the original 'four' in design, was conceived in 1924,

and the standard 6½-litre Bentley was put on sale at the end of 1925. Originally it had been a 4¼-litre 'six', but it was found to be lacking in power and torque.

The 'Speed Six', with a chassis intended for sporting use if necessary, followed in 1928, and was produced until 1930, when it was replaced by the magnificent Bentley 8-litre. 545 6½-litre cars were built in all, of which an exclusive 182 were 'Speed Sixes'.

Like others of the period, the car was massively strong and heavy. Even with the 180bhp engine, the Speed Six's normal maximum speed was no more than 92—95mph.

Below: 6½-litre Speed Six Bentleys came in most shapes and sizes. This example has rakish two-seater styling and looks lower than in fact it is.

The engine's overhead camshaft drive was complex and unique, with triple eccentric coupling rod operation, thought by 'W.O.' to be more reliable than either chain or gear-drive systems. The cylinder head, as with all such Bentleys, was non-detachable and in unit with the cylinder block.

Built almost regardless of cost (the new car price, depending on coachwork, was between £2,300 and £2,500), the engineering was painstakingly thorough. There was a vast petrol tank (up to 43 gallons — 195 litres — on the race cars), and even the electron alloy oil sump held more than five gallons.

Although the car was magnificent in build and in durable performance, the company which made it was always financially insecure. Perhaps Bentley had the worst of bad luck when they chose the depths of the depression to upgrade the car to the very exclusive 8-litre; within a year of this launch the company was in liquidation.

Above: Two entirely different and attractive ways of bodying a Speed Six Bentley chassis. At the top is a 1930 fixed-head coupe by H. J. Mulliner, and the 'fast-back' saloon was built for Captain Woolf Barnato by Gurney Nutting in 1930, as low as possible.

Below: Built in 1929, this Speed Six had a touring body by Vanden Plas, who used to build Le Mans coachwork for the Bentley factory. This car had four separate doors, and a windscreen for the rear seat passengers, which could still be used with the hood erect.

BENTLEY 3½-AND 4¼-LITRE

3½-litre and 4¼-litre models, 1933 to 1939 (data for 4¼-litre)

Built by: Rolls-Royce Ltd., Britain.

Engine: Six cylinders, in line, in seven-bearing cast-iron cylinder block. Bore and stroke 88·9mm by 114·3mm, 4,257cc (3·5in × 4·5in, 260cu.in). Cast-iron cylinder head. Two overhead valves per cylinder, operated by pushrods and rockers from side-mounted camshaft. Twin SU carburettors. Power output never officially stated by Rolls-Royce, probably about 125bhp.

Transmission: Single-dry-plate clutch and four-speed manual transmission (synchromesh on top and third gears), in unit with engine. Right-hand gearchange. Open propeller shaft to spiral-bevel 'live' rear axle. 1938 and 1939 models had 'overdrive' gear ratios — in which third gear was direct, and fourth was a geared-up ratio.

Chassis: Separate steel chassis, with channel-section side members and pressed-steel and tubular cross members. Half-elliptic leaf springs at front and rear. Forged front axle beam. Hydraulic Rolls-Royce dampers; additional ride control governing hydraulic pressure, aided by gearbox-driven pump. Rod-operated drum brakes, boosted by gearbox-driven mechanical servo motor. Worm-and-nut steering. Car normally sold as rolling chassis. Wide choice of saloon, coupé and cabriolet coachwork from approved coachbuilders.

Dimensions: Wheelbase 10ft 6in (320cm), tracks (front and rear) 4ft 8in (142cm). Overall length (varied slightly depending on coachbuilder) 14ft 6in (442cm). Unladen weight, chassis only, 2,560lb (1,161kg). Typical weight with saloon body, 3,920lb (1,778kg).

History: Bentley Motors ran into financial trouble at the start of the 1930s, and were finally bankrupted in 1931. The company's trade marks and assets were taken over by Rolls-Royce soon afterwards and manufacture of 'W.O.' cars ceased at once. Although Bentley himself worked for Rolls-Royce until 1935, he had little to do with new designs. Rolls-Royce decided to make a new model called a Bentley, even though they had no intention of using existing components. Even the famous radiator design would be modified. Only the badging would be carried forward. Their first intention was to productionise their 'Peregrine' experi-

Right: Every Derby-built Bentley had a coachbuilt body—saloon, sporting or touring. The green racing version is that raced by Eddie Hall in the TTs —unofficially backed by Rolls-Royce.

mental car, which had a 2·3-litre six-cylinder engine, and to supercharge that engine, as they saw no need to make the 'Bentley' as quiet and dignified as existing Rolls-Royce cars. Development was difficult and at the end of 1932 it was decided to substitute a much-modified Rolls-Royce 20/25 six-cylinder engine for the 'Peregrine' unit. Thus a new concept of Bentley, the 'Silent Sports Car' as adverts would call it, was born. Public release was in October 1933, and deliveries began during the winter.

As originally launched, the car had a 3,669cc engine, with twin SU carburettors. In their usual way, Rolls-Royce never released any maximum power figures, but the engine was thought to produce about 110bhp. The gearbox and right-hand gearchange were based on those of the Rolls-Royce 20/25 models. The car used a beam front axle with half-elliptic leaf springs, no less than was normal in those days. By 1939, though, other makes had begun to fit independent front suspension, which left the Bentley's ride and handling at a competitive disadvantage. The mechanically operated brakes and the gearbox-driven servo motor were Rolls-Royce idiosyncrasies which worked very well, though they did not represent modern thinking. The cars were always sold from Derby as complete rolling chassis with the restyled and very distinctive radiator shell in place. Usually the customer had

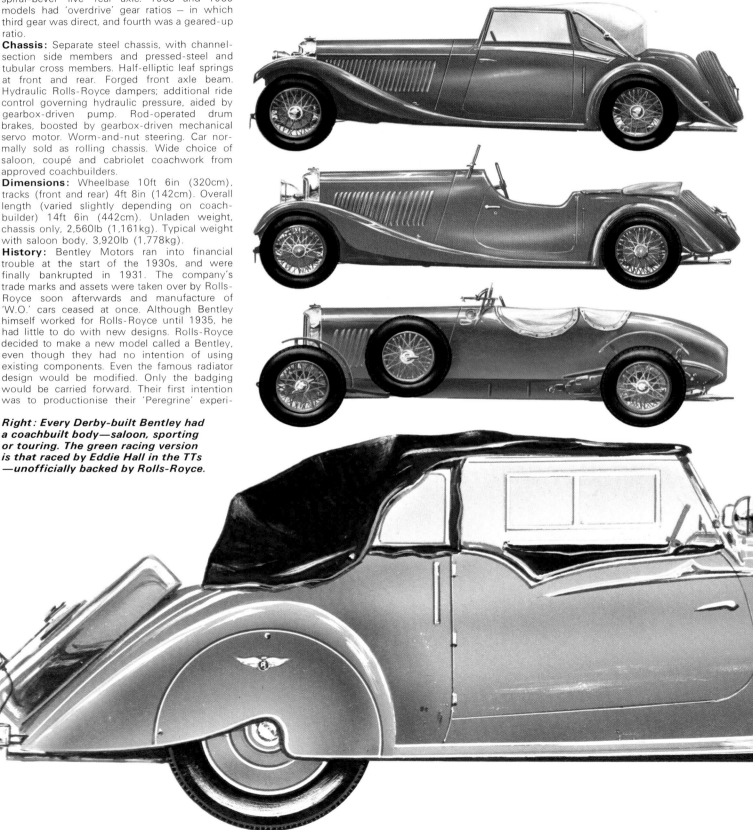

specified a coachbuilder and body style required, and cars took up to three months to be completed. Park Ward, on the other hand, were very close to Rolls-Royce, and offered what amounted to standard styles, which cut down the waiting period considerably.

The problem with most quality British cars of the period was that they carried heavy bodywork, as a chassis price of £1,100 and a typical all-up price of £1,460 indicate. Maximum speeds of over 90mph were common, but year by year acceleration and fuel consumption suffered as weights continued to creep up. Rolls-Royce's solution was to enlarge the engine from 3,669cc to 4,257cc, without any other major change. Slightly more power and considerably more torque did the trick.

In 1938, which meant that the cars would only be available for two selling seasons, the 4¼-litre car was given 'overdrive' gearing, a

misnomer in that no separate overdrive was fitted. In fact the axle ratio was slightly changed and third gear in the box became the direct drive, while fourth was a geared-up cruising ratio. The effect was to make the car more long-legged and even more refined. An increase in tyre section helped this transformation.

The 'Derby' Bentleys, as the cars were soon nicknamed, soon made themselves an excellent reputation and they were in truth much better all-round performers than the old 'W.O.' models had been. Between 1933 and 1940, nearly 2,500 examples were built, slightly more than half of them being 4¼-litre cars; 200 of these were 'overdrive' models. But for the outbreak of war Rolls-Royce would probably have replaced the car for 1940 with the new Mark V Bentley, with a new chassis frame plus coil-sprung independent front suspension. Existing engine, gearbox and other transmission parts would have been speci-

Above: The lightest 'Derbys' were the early 3½-litre models; later cars put on weight. This is a beautiful 1935 saloon, which combined 90mph pace with the best quality coachwork.

fied and — as usual — all bodies would be supplied by outside coachbuilding specialists. In the event, eleven such Mark Vs were completed, of 19 chassis laid down, before the start of hostilities, and several survive. The Mark V, with its 4¼-litre engine, was a precursor of the postwar Bentley (the Mark VI) — although this later car was to have the inlet-over-exhaust cylinder head layout. That engine, a final derivation of the Rolls-Royce 20/25 layout, was last used in 1959, by which time it had grown to 4,887cc. All postwar Bentleys have been built at Crewe, while Derby has concentrated on aero-engine manufacture.

Below: In everything other than name the 3½-litre and 4¼-litre Bentleys were sporting Rolls-Royces. Dubbed the 'Silent Sports Car', they brought high performance to Rolls-Royce, and a new refinement to fast motoring. There was no connection with previous Bentleys.

BENZ 1880s TRICYCLE

¾hp model, built from 1885, replicas sold up to 1890
Built by: Benz and Co., Germany.
Engine: Single cylinder, horizontally mounted fore-and-aft in frame, with exposed vertical crankshaft and flywheel. Water cooled. Bore and stroke 116mm by 160mm, 1,691cc (4·56in × 6·30in, 103·2cu.in). Two valves, single cam operating exhaust valve by rockers and levers and offset pin in cam end face operating inlet slide valve. Benz surface carburettor. Maximum power about 1·5bhp at 250/300rpm.
Transmission: Belt drive from flywheel to differential and cross-shaft, all in unit with engine. Final drive to rear wheels by chain. Release of direct drive (no step-down gears provided) by pulling belt-control arm to neutral position. Engine mounted behind seats and in front of driven rear axle.
Chassis: Separate tubular chassis frame. Three wheels, single front wheel mounted and controlled bicycle fashion. Cog-and-twin-rack steering, between vertical steering posts of front wheel and vertical steering column, via drag links. Front wheel suspended by full-elliptic spring and radius arms. Rear suspension by full-elliptic leaf springs. No dampers. Rear wheel transmission brakes, operated by belt-control lever. Centre lock wire wheels and solid tyres.
Dimensions: Wheelbase 4ft 9·1in (145cm). Unladen weight 585lb (265kg).
History: Lenoir's early gas engine inspired Nikolaus Otto to develop the first practical four-stroke petrol engine. His applications for patents on the very principle of four-stroke internal combustion were turned down, which left the two pioneers – Gottlieb Daimler and Karl Benz – to race towards the building of the first petrol-powered car. Benz had been operating a machine shop in Mannheim since 1871 and had had his first two-stroke engine running in 1879; he started to build a four-stroke machine in 1884 as soon as the patent-application was thrown out. The Benz tricycle which ran in 1885 was the very first practical car – even though it beat Daimler's

invention only by a matter of months. It was a tricycle because Benz could not solve the problems of lightweight twin steered front wheels, and it had a tubular chassis frame because bicycles were built like that. The engine produced only 1½bhp at not more than 250rpm and it was very crude with an exposed crankshaft; nevertheless it was a practical and neat little mechanical package of which several

replicas were sold in the next few years. A good cruising speed was 10mph, but seven or eight mpg was thought to be satisfactory. Benz was nevertheless *the* pioneer, and legendary for all that.

Below: A historic machine—the very first petrol-driven 'car' to be used on the road—by Karl Benz in 1885.

BERLIET

80hp model, built from 1903 to 1908 (data for 1906 model)
Built by: Automobiles M. Berliet, France.
Engine: Four cylinders, in line, in two cast-iron blocks, with three-bearing light-alloy crankcase. Bore and stroke 160mm by 140mm, 11,259cc (6·30in × 5·52in, 687cu.in). Non-detachable cast-iron cylinder heads. Two side valves per cylinder, in 'T-head' layout, with valve stems exposed. Single up-draught carburettor. Maximum power about 80bhp at 1,200rpm.
Transmission: Cone clutch working in oil, mounted in unit with front-mounted engine. Shaft drive to separate four-speed manual gearbox (without synchromesh). Remote-control right-hand gearchange. Straight-bevel differential, in tail of gearbox, and countershaft with sprockets. Final drive to rear wheels by chain.
Chassis: Separate pressed-steel chassis frame, with channel-section side members and tubular and pressed cross bracings. Forged front axle beam. Front suspension by semi-elliptic leaf springs. Rear suspension by semi-elliptic leaf springs with radius arms. No dampers. Worm-and-sector steering. Two externally contracting drum brakes on transmission countershaft operated by foot pedal. Rear wheel drums operated by hand lever. Artillery-style road wheels. 870 × 90mm tyres (front) and 920 × 120mm tyres (rear). Choice of coachwork, open or closed.
Dimensions: Wheelbase 9ft 10in or 10ft 6in (300cm or 320cm), tracks (front and rear) 4ft 7in (140cm). Overall length 13ft 5·4in or 13ft 9·4in (410cm or 420cm). Unladen weight (chassis only) 2,470lb or 2,480lb (1,120kg or 1,125kg).
History: Marius Berliet started modestly in a

Lyons workshop, building cars from 1895, but by 1901 he had the services of Audibert-Lavirotte, and began to market a big range of conventional but dignified cars. From 1902 the Berliet developed on the new and effective Mercédès lines and by 1906 there was a range of big four-cylinder machines from 22hp to 80hp. This last was a veritable monster, with a 160mm (6·30in) cylinder bore which one might expect to find on a racing engine, but not on a road car. Naturally the 80 was expensive – no less than £1,300 in chassis form in Britain – but the engineering was such that a Berliet took second place in the 1906 Tourist Trophy race, and an

American company (Alco) made them under licence. Six cylinder cars followed and future Berliets tended to be dull and conventional. Their heyday was undoubtedly in the early 1900s, when the cars were fast (well over 60mph being normal) and looked impressive. The last Berliet car was built in 1939 and the company is now famous for its splendid large trucks (and is controlled by Citroën-Peugeot).

Below: Berliet are now famous for making excellent trucks. Between 1903 and 1908 they made big sporting cars—this is the 1908 Targa Bologna car.

BIGNAN

12·1hp and variants, built from 1922 to 1930 (data for 1922 model)

Built by: Automobiles Bignan, France

Engine: Four cylinders, in line, in cast-iron block with two-bearing light-alloy crankcase. Bore and stroke 70mm by 110mm, 1,693cc (2·76in × 4·33in, 103·3cu.in). Detachable cast-iron cylinder head. Two overhead valves per cylinder, operated by rockers from single overhead camshaft. Single side-draught Zenith carburettor. Maximum power about 50bhp.

Transmission: Single-dry-plate clutch and four-speed manual gearbox (without synchromesh), both in unit with front-mounted engine. Direct-acting central gearchange. Open propeller shaft to spiral-bevel 'live' rear axle.

Chassis: Separate pressed-steel chassis frame, with channel-section side members and tubular and pressed cross bracings. Forged front axle beam. Front and rear suspension by semi-elliptic leaf-springs. No dampers on original model. Three mechanically operated brakes — two drum brakes on front wheels and one on transmission behind gearbox. Transmission drum incorporates friction servo assistance, applicable to all brakes. No rear brakes. Centre-lock wire wheels. 765 × 105mm tyres.

Open touring, sporting or closed bodywork.

Dimensions: Wheelbase 10ft (305cm), tracks (front and rear) 4ft 3in (129·5cm). Overall length 14ft (427cm). Unladen weight (chassis only) 1,625lb (737kg).

History: Bignan cars neatly spanned the vintage era — the first being built in 1918 and the last in 1930. At first, Bignan cars were built in 'borrowed' territory — the first in the Grégoire works — and with many proprietary components. The company's mainstay, from its Courbevoie factory near Paris, was the 11CV car, built in touring and sports-racing form. The basic machine, revealed in 1922, was interesting because it used front brakes but no rear brakes (this was at a time when the reverse was normal) and because it had a neat single-cam engine, which was soon further modified for racing. Racing versions used a unique type of desmodromic valve gear — in which cam, slide and roller operation both opened *and* closed the valves, without the need of springs. This, in fact, was not a reliable success, and by 1924 the engines had reverted to conventional single-overhead-camshaft layouts, with four valves per cylinder. Such a Bignan won the Monte Carlo Rally in 1924. Later in the decade there were six-cylinder cars and supercharged racing machines, but the firm had to close down in 1930.

Below: Bignan's 12hp tourers were built near Paris throughout the 1920s. This 1925 model, like the others, had front but no rear wheel brakes.

BMW 501 SERIES

501 family, built from 1952 to 1960 — including 502, 503, 505, 507 (data for six-cylinder 501 model)

Built by: Bayerische Motoren Werke A.G., West Germany

Engine: Six cylinders, in line, in four-bearing cast-iron block. Bore and stroke 66mm by 96mm, 1,971cc (2·60in × 3·78in, 120·3cu.in). Detachable light-alloy cylinder head. Two overhead valves per cylinder, operated by pushrods and rockers from single camshaft mounted in side of cylinder block. Single down-draught twin-choke Solex carburettor. Maximum power 65bhp (net) at 4,400rpm.

Transmission: Single-dry-plate clutch in unit with front-mounted engine. Shaft to separately positioned four-speed, synchromesh manual gearbox. Remote-control steering-column gearchange. Open propeller shaft to spiral-bevel 'live' rear axle.

Chassis: Separate pressed-steel chassis frame, with box-section side members and tubular cross bracing. Independent front suspension by torsion bars and wishbones. Rear suspension by longitudinal torsion bars, radius arms and triangulated A-bracket. Telescopic dampers. Pinion-and-sector steering. Four-wheel, hydraulically operated drum brakes. 16in pressed-steel-disc wheels. 5·50 × 16in tyres. Four-door six-window coachwork.

Dimensions: Wheelbase 9ft 3·5in (283·5cm), track (front) 4ft 6in (137cm), track (rear) 4ft 8in (142cm). Overall length 15ft 9in (480cm). Unladen weight 2,800lb (1,270kg).

History: As a result of World War II and the resultant fact that Eisenach now found itself in East Germany, behind the Iron Curtain, BMW had to concentrate on making motor cycles in Munich for some time, but finally returned to making cars in 1952. The 501 series itself was structurally new, but was borrowed from the pre-war Type 326 design in many ways. The engine, based on the pre-war six-cylinder unit, reverted to the conventional pushrod operation of pre-328 engines and the all-new body showed a distinct resemblance to pre-war BMWs and slight likenesses to the latest in Bristols. The car was big, heavy, underpowered and expensive, so it was given a more powerful 2·1-litre engine on the one hand, and a brand-new 2·6-litre V8 engine on the other. The V8 unit was an impressive piece of engineering and endowed the Munich product with a 100mph maximum speed and about 20mpg fuel consumption, but the car was still an expensive product. By the beginning of the 1960s BMW were already changing their marketing approach, having successfully launched a bubble car and followed this with the 600/700 mini-car series, and finally the classic overhead-cam 1500/1600/1800/2000 range.

Below: The big and impressive BMW 501 —made in the 1950s—had a 2-litre six-cylinder engine. Other variants had a modern 2·6-litre vee-8 unit.

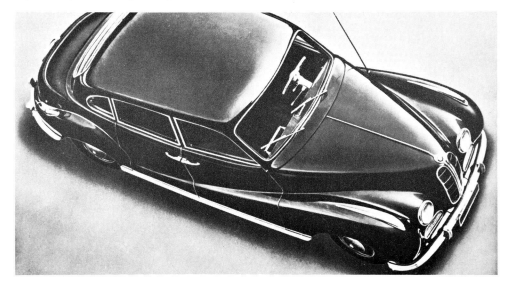

BMW 328

BMW 328 and Frazer Nash-BMW (data applies to both cars).
Built by: Bayerische Motoren Werke AG., Germany.
Engine: Six cylinders, in line, in four-bearing cast-iron cylinder block. Bore and stroke 66mm by 96mm, 1,971cc (2·60in × 3·78in, 120·3cu.in). Two overhead valves per cylinder, with inclined operation in part-spherical combustion chambers. Unique pushrod valve operation: inlet valve directly operated by pushrod and rocker, exhaust valve by pushrod, pivot, cross pushrod and rocker. Single side mounted camshaft. Aluminium cylinder head with downdraught siamesed inlet ports and three Solex carburettors. Maximum power 80bhp (DIN) at 4,500rpm.
Transmission: Single-dry-plate clutch and four-speed manual gearbox (synchromesh on top and third gears), with direct control central gearchange, in unit with engine. Open propeller shaft to spiral-bevel 'live' rear axle.
Chassis: Separate frame, of ladder-type construction, main members of steel tubing, and cross members of box or tubular sections. Independent front suspension by transverse leaf spring and lower wishbones. Rear suspension by half-elliptic leaf springs. Hydraulic dampers all round. Rack-and-pinion steering. Four-wheel hydraulically operated drum brakes. 16in pressed-steel disc wheels, with four-pin drive and centre-lock fixings. 5·50×16in tyres. Two-seat sports bodywork of alloy panelling on ash frame in nearly every case. Cabriolet version, with fold-down hood, also available.
Dimensions: Wheelbase 7ft 10·5in (240cm), track (front) 3ft 9·4in (115cm), track (rear) 4ft (122cm). Overall length 12ft 9·5in (390cm).

Unladen weight (sports body) 1,700lb (771kg).
History: The BMW 328 was the final flowering of a series of designs initiated in 1933. Kernel of the family of cars was a splendidly detailed six-cylinder engine (which was later fitted with unusual valve gear), a rigid tubular chassis, quite unlike most European designs of the 1930s, and independent front suspension, at a time when this was considered expensive and unpredictable. The engine first appeared as a 1¼-litre unit, then in the Type 315 and 319 cars in 1½-litre form.

The Type 328 was a sports car pure and simple,

designed to be smooth, look smooth, and have impeccable road manners — this, at a time when sports cars were normally harsh, crudely equipped and rather spartan. Body styling included faired-in headlamps and flowing integrated lines, which were all ahead of their time. BMW developments from this car undoubtedly inspired William Lyons's thinking on car shapes for his Jaguars of the 1940s.

The Type 328 was announced in 1936, and was distinguished by its unique cylinder head and valve gear. A part-spherical combustion chamber

BMW 507

507 model, built from 1955 to 1959
Built by: Bayerische Motoren Werke A.G., West Germany.
Engine: Eight cylinders, in 90-degree vee-formation, in five-bearing light-alloy block. Bore and stroke 82mm by 75mm, 3,168cc (3·23in × 2·95in, 193·3cu.in). Two detachable light alloy cylinder heads. Two overhead valves per cylinder, operated by pushrods and rockers from single camshaft mounted in centre of cylinder block 'vee'. Two down-draught twin-choke Solex carburettors. Maximum power 150bhp (net) at 4,800rpm. Maximum torque 127lb.ft at 2,500 rpm.
Transmission: Single-dry-plate clutch and five-speed, synchromesh manual gearbox (without synchromesh on first gear) both in unit with front-mounted engine. Central gearchange. Open propeller shaft to hypoid-bevel 'live' rear axle, with optional limited-slip differential.

Chassis: Separate pressed-steel chassis frame, with box-section side members and tubular cross-bracing. Independent front suspension by torsion bars and wishbones. Rear suspension by torsion bars, radius arms and Panhard rod. Telescopic dampers. Pinion-and-sector steering. Four-wheel, hydraulically operated drum brakes. 16in bolt-on or centre-lock pressed-steel-disc wheels. 6·00 × 16in tyres.
Two-seat open sports or hardtop coachwork.
Dimensions: Wheelbase 8ft 1·5in (248cm), track (front) 4ft 8·7in (144cm), track (rear) 4ft 8in (142cm). Overall length 14ft 5in (439·4cm). Unladen weight 2,530lb (1,147kg).
History: As a logical development of their 501 saloon car series, BMW married a shortened version of that chassis with the developed 3·2-litre V8 engine, which had become optional, and clothed the result in an outstandingly attractive two-seater sports car body style. Under the skin,

the separate four-speed gearbox of the saloons had given way to a new five-speed box in unit with the engine and the rear suspension was both revised and improved. Overall design is attributed to Dr. Fiedler, who takes credit for the pre-war Type 328, and apart from its high price the Type 507 was a worthy successor. Maximum speed was between 135 and 140mph, with acceleration and stability to match. Although the 507 looked ideal for use as a competition car, the factory never entered it in any events, and private owners were too impressed by its looks and its high standard of finish and equipment to abuse it in this way.

Below and right: Perhaps the loveliest of all BMWs—pre-war or post-war—was the 507 of the 1950s. It had a 3·2-litre vee-8 engine, and could reach 140mph.

and good breathing were considered essential, but Dr. Fiedler, the designer, was ordered to stick with one side-mounted camshaft. He solved the restriction brilliantly by inventing the extra cross-pushrod arrangement to operate the inclined exhaust valves, and he arranged for the inlet port to enter the cylinder head from the top of the engine, with the carburettors atop that. The only disadvantage was that the engine, in total, was quite tall. BMW styling, however, could easily accommodate this.

Apart from its striking styling, the car was also equipped with a full undertray to improve aerodynamics. Original cars had a hidden spare wheel, but most have the familiar part-recessed spare on the tail panel. The British BMW concessionaires, AFN Ltd., imported the car as the Frazer Nash-BMW, and proved its worth with a 101 miles in a one-hour run at Brooklands in 1937. The last production cars were built in 1940, before German war production caused all private car building to cease. 462 328s were built in all and the engine was adopted in post-war years by Bristol for their 400 to 406 models.

Left, above, and right: The classic BMW 328 sports car, which started a revolution in sports car styling and engineering. The engine had a clever form of valve gear invented by Dr Fiedler, and the unit was used in developed form in post-war Bristols and Frazer Nash cars. The shape also affected Jaguar's thinking with the XK120. This 1938 two-seater is Miss Betty Haig's car, and both the bonnet strap and centre-lock wheels are clear.

BMW SIX-CYLINDER COUPES

BMW 2800CS, 3·0CS, 3·0CSi and 3·0CSL (data for 3·0CSL, 1973 model).

Built by: Bayerische Motoren Werke AG., West Germany.

Engine: Six cylinders, in line, in seven-bearing cast-iron block. Bore and stroke 89·25mm by 80mm, 3,003cc (3·51in × 3·15in, 183cu.in). Light-alloy cylinder head. Two overhead valves per cylinder, inclined to each other in poly-spherical combustion chambers and operated by rockers from single overhead camshaft. Bosch fuel injection, with nozzles in inlet ports. Maximum power 200bhp (DIN) at 5,500rpm. Maximum torque 200lb.ft at 4,300rpm.

Transmission: Single-dry-plate clutch and four-speed synchromesh manual gearbox, in unit with front-mounted engine. Open propeller shaft to chassis-mounted hypoid-bevel final-drive unit, with optional limited-slip differential. Exposed, universally jointed drive shafts to rear wheels.

Chassis: Unitary-construction pressed-steel body/chassis unit, in two-door 2+2 coupé layout. Light-alloy skin panels (some 1974 models fitted with large boot lid aerofoil spoiler, and scoop at rear of roof. All independent suspension, front by coil springs, MacPherson struts and anti-roll bar, rear by coil springs, semi-trailing wishbones and anti-roll bar. Telescopic dampers. Ball-and-nut steering, optionally power assisted. Four-wheel servo-assisted disc brakes. 14in bolt-on cast-alloy road wheels. 195/70VR14 tyres.

Dimensions: Wheelbase 8ft 7·3in (262cm), track (front) 4ft 8.9in (144cm), track (rear) 4ft 7·1in (140cm). Overall length 15ft 3·4in (466cm). Unladen weight 2,600lb (1,180kg).

History: In spite of producing fine post-war cars, BMW were in financial trouble by the end of the 1950s. Not even sales of the little Isetta 'bubble' cars, or the nice little 700cc car could help. The firm was revived very rapidly at the start of the 1960s by the first of an entire series of modern designs, all of which have used the

same family of overhead-camshaft engines. At first there was merely a 'four', originally of 1500cc, then 1600cc, then 1800cc and finally 2000cc. The car which rescued BMW was the 1600 and 1800 saloon (which was later enlarged to become the 2000).

In 1965, however, BMW also announced a sleek two-door coupé, styled and engineered by Karmann, fitted with the 2000's mechanicals. This, the 2000CS coupé, in fuel-injection form, was the first of a very successful line. This car had distinctive styling with vast and wide headlamps.

In 1968, with BMW well and truly in the forefront of executive and sporting car production, the first of the six-cylinder cars was shown. This had all-new structures, but the engine was really a six-cylinder version of the established overhead-cam 'four' and shared many common components. At the same time, by a rather drastic piece of mechanical surgery, the new six-cylinder engine was also persuaded to fit the Karmann-built coupé shell. This had a revised nose, with twin circular headlamps, and was called the 2800CS.

By 1971, with the largest of the six-cylinder engines enlarged from 2·8-litre to 3·0-litre, the coupé was thoroughly re-engineered under the skin, to have the backward-sloping MacPherson strut front suspension of the big saloons. It was also given the full 3-litre engine and became the 3·0CS. A year later, with fuel injection at least offered on the big 'six', the coupé became the 3·0CSi, and had 140mph performance to match its very impressive looks. The car then carried on until 1975, basically unchanged, but eventually in two versions — a carburettor-engined car, with automatic transmission as standard, and the injection-engined car available only with the four-speed manual gearbox.

By 1972, however, BMW's interest in racing had intensified. Up to then they had been happy to enter four-cylinder BMWs (sometimes in turbocharged form) in touring-car events, and

often succeeded in winning outright. Now they turned their attention to the big six-cylinder coupés, which could be homologated as 'touring cars'. Even with their normal engines, they could be super-tuned to give more than 300bhp, but the Karmann-styled car had certain aerodynamic deficiencies. Thus it was that BMW announced a lightweight car. The 3·0CSL (the 'L' standing for 'Lightweight' in most languages!) was effectively a 3·0CSi, but with drastically lightened trim and furnishings, light-alloy skin panels and doors and an engine marginally bored out to take it over the 3-litre class limit. The factory CSLs, therefore, were often entered as 3½-litre cars, and had more than 350bhp, especially after the 24-valve cylinder heads had been developed. The aerodynamic stability problems were solved a year later, in the autumn of 1973, when the CSL was modified to include a slim air-flow aligning wing across the top of the rear window, tiny strakes on the front wings and a vast inverted aerofoil section fixed to the boot lid. Thus equipped, and immediately nick-named the 'Batmobiles', the factory cars could match anything Ford, with their Capris, could field, but the cars were so specialised and costly that they killed all opposition except Ford, and the racing series for which they were evolved died because of lack of entries! There was great controversy over these less-than-practical road cars, and the aerodynamic fittings were actually banned from road use in West Germany, but the cars were sensationally fast.

Private owners could have their cars without the special fittings, and even — if they insisted — with steel instead of light-alloy panelling. The CSL managed to overshadow the more mundane, but still very desirable, CSAs and CSis, which continued to sell well until 1975, when they were all withdrawn in favour of the new 633CSi coupés. No more outrageously shaped nor dramatic 'saloon' car has yet been seen on the world's tracks. Turbocharged versions are, incidentally, still raced by the BMW factory.

Below: With a shape like this, wasn't it inevitable that the be-finned 3·0 CSLs should be called 'Batmobiles'? The wing, the rear roof slot, and the front wing strakes, were all to make the racing versions more stable. It worked so well in 1974 that other cars withdrew in disgust, unable to match their performance. Underneath, the engine, transmission and chassis is all based on a production coupe.

Above: Compare the original 3·0CSL with the 'Batmobile' (below left) which was developed from it—as a road car the Karmann-styled car is very handsome with the extra wind-cheating aids. 140mph performance is matched by all-independent suspension, four seats, and a silky overhead cam 3-litre six-cylinder engine.

Below: The very first coupe from which the classic line was developed was the 2000CS of 1965, but this became the 2800CS (illustrated here) at the end of 1968. The basic lines were not changed, but six-cylinder cars had twinned headlamps, a revised interior, air outlets behind the front wheels, and other visual details.

Bottom: It is difficult to look at the BMW 3-litre coupe, and see that it is based on more mundane saloon car engineering. The floor pan, and all the chassis items, however, are shared with the 3-litre four-door saloons. The neat and integrated coupes are the shortest of the family, which also includes long-wheelbase limousines.

BRASIER 24HP

24hp model, typical of Brasier practice, from 1905 to 1912 (data for 1912 model)

Built by: Société des Automobiles Brasier, France.

Engine: Six cylinders, in line, in two three-cylinder cast-iron blocks with three-bearing light-alloy crankcase. Bore and stroke 90mm by 140mm, 5,340cc (3·54in × 5·51in, 326cu.in). Fixed cast-iron cylinder heads. Two side valves per cylinder, in T-head layout (inlet valves on one side of engine, exhaust valves on other side), operated by tappets from two camshafts mounted in sides of crankcase. Single up-draught Brasier carburettor.

Transmission: Cone clutch in unit with front-mounted engine. Shaft drive to separate four-speed manual gearbox (without synchromesh). Remote-control right-hand gearchange. Propeller shaft, enclosed in torque tube, driving straight-bevel 'live' rear axle.

Chassis: Separate pressed-steel chassis frame, with channel-section side members, stiffened by wood inserts' and tubular and pressed-steel cross-bracings. Forged front axle beam. Front suspension by semi-elliptic leaf springs. Rear suspension by three-quarter-elliptic leaf springs. Truffaut lever-arm dampers. Worm-and-sector steering. Transmission drum brake, foot operated, and two rear wheel drum brakes, hand-lever operated. Artillery-style road wheels. 880 × 120mm tyres.
Open or closed coachwork to choice.

Dimensions: Wheelbase 10ft 10·5in (331·5 cm), tracks (front and rear) 4ft 7in (140cm). Overall length 15ft 2in (462cm). Unladen weight (chassis only) 2,575lb (1,168kg).

History: Georges Richard began building cars

in 1897, but these were copies of the Benz; in 1902, however, he was joined by the engineer Henri Brasier and the cars became Richard-Brasiers. These were Panhard-style cars. 9·9-litre cars won the 1904 Gordon Bennett race, and in enlarged form won again in 1905. In the meantime Richard left (to found Unic) and the cars became plain Brasiers. A wide range developed, at first with chain drive and later with the more modern torque-tube type of shaft drive. The cars were all quite typical of modern Edwardian practice, without being forward-looking, and at one time or another everything from a 10hp twin to a big 50hp six-cylinder car were on offer. The car detailed was one of the last of this family, as from the end of 1912 the engines were redesigned with monobloc cylinders and enclosed valves (the torque-tube transmission, cone clutch and other items had been

progressively introduced earlier). The cars were undoubtedly very handsome, but things were allowed to slide after World War I, when old designs were carried on for too long. The cars became Chaigneau-Brasiers in 1926 and tried to become too technically advanced all at once; the result was that the company folded up in 1930.

Below: Not to be confused with early Richard-Brasiers (built up to 1905 before Georges Richard left to found the Unic company), these cars were sold in many versions. This was a 1910 tourer, typical of pre-war styling, with a big five-seat body, side-mounted spare, and driver access from the other side of the car. The 24hp car had a 5·3-litre engine.

BRISTOL 400

Bristol 400 model built 1947 to 1950

Built by: Bristol Aeroplane Co. Ltd., Britain.

Engine: Six-cylinder, in line, in four-bearing cast-iron cylinder block. Bore and stroke 66mm by 96mm, 1,971cc (2·60in × 3·78in, 120·3cu.in). BMW-inspired pushrod valve operation, two overhead valves per cylinder. Inlet valve directly operated by pushrod and rocker, exhaust valve by pushrod, pivot, cross pushrod and rocker. Single side-mounted camshaft. Aluminium cylinder head with downdraught siamesed inlet ports and three Solex carburettors. Maximum power 85bhp (net) at 4,500rpm. Maximum torque 107lb.ft at 3,500rpm (very early models with three downdraught SU carburettors produced 80bhp at 4,200rpm).

Transmission: Single-dry-plate clutch and four-speed manual synchromesh gearbox (without synchromesh on first gear), in unit with engine. Direct action central gearchange. Open

propeller shaft to spiral-bevel 'live' rear axle.

Chassis: Separate steel chassis, with box-section side members, and strong box and pressed cross bracing members. Independent front suspension by transverse leaf spring and upper wishbones. Rear suspension by longitudinal torsion bars, radius arms and A-bracket. Bristol-made telescopic dampers. Rack-and-pinion steering. Four-wheel hydraulically operated 11in drum brakes, with fly-off cable handbrake. 16in disc wheels with 5·50 × 16in tyres. Steel body produced by Bristol, with aluminium skin panels.

Dimensions: Wheelbase 9ft 6in (290cm), track (front) 4ft 4in (132cm), track (rear) 4ft 6in (137cm). Overall length 15ft 3in (465cm). Unladen weight 2,537lb (1,151kg).

History: The Bristol Aeroplane Company, aided and abetted by the Aldington family (who imported BMW cars in the late 1930s) took over

the obsolete designs of the BMW concern after the war had been won, amalgamated the basis of the 326 chassis frame, the high-performance 328 engine and the styling of the 327 body, to come up with the unexpectedly integrated Bristol 400 design. From that day to this, Bristol cars have been assembled at Bristol airfield (since 1960 under separate management) in small numbers, magnificently detailed and constructed, and sold at high prices.

The BMW-inspired engine was not super-seded until 1961, when the 407 model adopted a Chrysler V8, and the chassis, or rather repeated modifications of it, are still being made. The 400, of which just 700 were made in three years, was an attractive if none-too-rapid Grand Touring car and was only ever available in two-door coupé/saloon guise. Later, the 401 saloon, the 402 convertible, the 403 which evolved from the 401, the 404/405/406 replacements all

BRISTOL 450

Bristol 450, closed and open versions. built 1953 to 1955 (data for 1953)

Built by: Bristol Aeroplane Co. Ltd., Britain.

Engine: Six cylinders, in line, in four-bearing cast-iron cylinder block. Bore and stroke 66mm by 96mm, 1,971cc (2·60in × 3·78in, 120·3cu.in). BMW-inspired pushrod valve operation, two overhead valves per cylinder. Inlet valve directly operated by pushrod and rocker, exhaust valve by pushrod, pivot, cross pushrod and rocker. Single side-mounted camshaft. Aluminium cylinder head with downdraught siamesed inlet ports and three Solex carburettors. Maximum power 142bhp at 5,750rpm. Maximum torque 135lb.ft at 4,750rpm.

Transmission: Single-dry-plate clutch and four-speed manual synchromesh gearbox (without synchromesh on first gear) in unit with chassis-mounted spiral-bevel differential. Short open propeller shaft from engine to clutch. Exposed, universally jointed drive shafts from differential to rear wheels.

Chassis: Separate tubular-steel chassis frame. Main tubular side members, cross members and braces. Independent front suspension by wishbones, coil springs and anti-roll bar. De Dion rear suspension, with coil springs, trailing arms, A-bracket and anti-roll bar. Telescopic dampers all round. Rack-and-pinion steering. Four-wheel hydraulically operated 12in drum brakes, with fly-off cable handbrake. 15in light-alloy road wheels with fixed spiders and detachable rims. 15in racing tyres Closed two-seat coupés in 1953 and 1954, but open cars with 'single-seat' wrap-round screens in 1955.

Dimensions: Wheelbase 8ft 0in (245cm), tracks (front and rear) 4ft 3in (130cm).

History: With nothing more than publicity and the 'will to win' in mind, Bristol decided to go motor racing in the early 1950s. With the Le Mans 24-hour and Rheims 12-hour races in mind, they decided on a high-geared wind-cheating coupé using their own mechanical parts. The chassis and suspension design was that of the erstwhile G-Type ERA Formula Two car, while the engine and transmission were their own and the bodywork a product of Bristol's own aerodynamicists. The tubular chassis had a rudimentary transaxle arrangement, whereby the existing Bristol 401/403 clutch and gearbox were separated from the engine and grafted on to a Ford commercial vehicle axle casing, the whole being fixed to the chassis as De Dion rear suspension was used.

The car had minimal accommodation and was described by its drivers as being like a fighter pilot's cockpit. For 1953 the car's nose was surprisingly untidy, with protruding headlamps, but for 1954 the nose was thoroughly cleaned up with the headlamps behind perspex panels. A year later, to save weight and cut frontal area, the cars were rebodied as open cars, with the driver's position backed by a stabilising fin. At Le Mans the cars could approach 150mph. In 1953 the Bristols retired from Le Mans with engine failure, but one car won its class at Rheims. In 1954 the cars finished 7th, 8th and 9th in team order, while in 1955 (with considerably more power than before) the same result was achieved, at nearly 95mph (a 100mph running average was possible). The cars never raced again, and only one example of the four built survives in factory hands.

Below: Sleek, purposeful and fast— the Bristol 450s took the first three places in their class at Le Mans 1954.

followed on logically from the 400, retaining the traditions and pushing up the performance. The engine was also used by AC, and by Frazer Nash in sports cars, and proved to be surprisingly tuneable for sports car racing and Formula Two.

The early Bristols, as would be expected from an aircraft company, were aerodynamically efficient. Later Bristols have become less slippery and more like high-priced flagships.

Below and right: Showing obvious styling links with the pre-war BMW 326 and 328 models, the Bristol 400 used chassis and engines developed from the German cars. Only a close-coupled 2-door 4-seater was sold. The aerodynamics were excellent, the 400 was a good rally car, with 700 cars built from 1947 to 1950.

BRITISH LEYLAND MINI

Austin and Morris Minis, built from 1959 to 1969 and Minis, built from 1969 to date (data for 850 version)

Built by: (Originally) British Motor Corporation Ltd., Britain. (From 1968 to 1975) British Leyland Motor Corporation Ltd., Britain. (From 1975 to date) British Leyland Ltd., Britain.

Engine: Four cylinders, in line, three-bearing in cast-iron block. Bore and stroke 62·9mm by 68·3mm, 848cc (2·48 × 2·69in, 51·7cu.in). Cast-iron cylinder head. Two overhead valves per cylinder, operated by pushrods and rockers from single camshaft side-mounted in the block. Engine itself transversely mounted in nose of car, on top of and in unit with transmission. Single semi-down-draught SU carburettor. Maximum power 33bhp (DIN) at 5,300rpm. Maximum torque 40lb.ft at 2,500rpm.
Other versions (including Cooper and Cooper S models) have had 970cc, 997cc, 998cc, 1,071cc, 1,098cc and 1,275cc displacement and Coopers and Cooper Ss had twin SU carburettors.

Transmission: Single-dry-plate clutch and four-speed, synchromesh manual gearbox (all-synchro since 1968, before that with unsynchronised first gear) mounted in case immediately underneath engine. Direct or extension gearchange on floor between seats. Drive on right of engine through overhung clutch and drop gears. Spur-gear final drive with differential mounted behind transmission. Exposed drive shafts to front wheels, with Rzeppa-type outboard, constant-velocity joints. Transmission shares lubricating oil with engine.
AP four-speed automatic transmission (with manual override) optional from 1965, mounted in same way under engine. Only available on some versions of the car.

Chassis: Unitary-construction pressed-steel body structure, several coachwork variations. Most are two-door saloons, but longer-wheelbase estates, vans and pick-ups also sold. Riley and Wolseley 'Minis' had extended tails with bigger boots. Mini Clubman series has longer nose and different style.
All-independent suspension, mounted on pressed-steel subframes, by wishbones (front) and trailing arms (rear). Suspension by rubber cone springs, except 1964 to 1969 when by interconnected Hydrolastic suspension. Hydraulic drum brakes on most versions — Cooper, Cooper S and 1275GT versions have front discs with servo assistance. 145 × 12in Dunlop 'run-flat Denovo wheels/tyres on 1275GT. 10in pressed-steel-disc wheels and 5·20 × 10in or 145 × 10in tyres on other versions.

Dimensions: Wheelbase 6ft 8in (204cm), track (front) 3ft 11·4in (120cm), track (rear) 3ft 9·8in (116cm). Overall length 10ft 0·25in (305cm). Unladen weight 1,398lb (635kg).

History: In the aftermath of the first Suez war of 1956, the BMC Mini was Alec Issigonis's brilliant concept of what a new generation of tiny economy cars should be like. Transverse engines with front drive were not entirely new, but the Issigonis layout, with a conventional four-cylinder water-cooled engine was unique. His principle has since been copied by car makers all round the world.
As remarkable as the power plant installation were the car's very small size, its space utilisation and the suspension system chosen. Developed in collaboration with Alex Moulton, it brought rubber compression units back into the limelight. Geometry, apart from the reversed rubber cone actuation at the rear (to save space), was conventional. Between 1964 and 1969 BMC's later Hydrolastic system, where road shocks and suspension displacements were signalled from front to rear wheels through interconnecting high-pressure water/alcohol pipes, was more expensive but did not achieve a great advance in ride.
Front-drive, splendid balance, and sensitive

Since 1959 there have been many different Minis. Above: The original version, sold as Austin or Morris. Left: The Mini 1000, this one a 1974 model. Below left: The perky 1275GT with bigger engine and lengthened nose. Below: A specially developed private venture with lowered body— the Mini-Sprint. All shared the same transverse engine and tiny cabin.

Right: Most famous, if not most numerous, of all the Minis, was the Mini Cooper S, built from 1963 to 1971. Three versions—970S, 1071S and 1275S—all won races and rallies. A powerful engine, disc front brakes, and remarkable handling all helped.

steering combined to give startling handling and roadholding. Apart from being everybody's idea of a cheap and practical runabout the Mini soon became an important competition car. Minis began winning races at once and Cooper versions were followed by the very formidable Cooper S competition cars. Apart from winning the Monte Carlo rally on three occasions (and being spectacularly disqualified from a fourth), the Cooper S won British and European touring car race championships, international rallies, ice races — in fact any kind of motoring event.

The first million Minis were built by spring 1965 and the four millionth arrived in the winter of 1976/7. Since 1969, rationalisation has eliminated many specialised versions like the long-tail Riley/Wolseley Minis and — alas — all the Coopers after nearly 150,000 had been delivered. One ultra-special variant — the stark and almost non-bodied Mini Moke — was withdrawn after hoped-for military contracts did not materialise.

Certain Mini features, like the ingenious installation of the Automotive Products automatic transmission, have never been matched by the competition. Neither (except by the Fiat 126) has its small size. Apart from being a true 'Classic Car', the Mini is also Britain's best-selling car of all time.

Above: The most finely-tuned Minis of all were the 'works' cars from Abingdon. This was a 1275S rally car, with more than 100bhp, a special gear-box, and masses of extra fittings, in the 1968 Swedish Rally. Minis won the Monte Carlo Rally three times, and dozens of other events round the globe.

BUGATTI TYPE 13 'BRESCIA'

Type 13 built from 1910 to 1926 (data for 1921 Brescia)
Built by: Automobiles E. Bugatti, France
Engine: Four cylinders, in line, in cast-iron block with three-bearing light-alloy crankcase bolted to it. Bore and stroke 69mm by 100mm, 1,496cc (2·72in × 3·94in, 91·3cu.in). Fixed cylinder head. Four overhead valves per cylinder, vertically mounted and operated by curved valve tappets from single overhead camshaft. Single Zenith updraught carburettor.
Transmission: Multi-disc clutch, running in oil, in unit with engine, connected to separate four-speed manual gearbox, without synchromesh. Remote-control right-hand gearchange. Open propeller shaft to straight-bevel 'live' rear axle.
Chassis: Separate pressed-steel chassis frame, with channel-section side members and tubular and fabricated cross bracing. Forged front axle

beam. Front suspension by half-elliptic springs. Rear suspension by reversed cantilever quarter-elliptic leaf springs and a tubular torque rod from axle to frame. Friction-type dampers. Worm-and-nut steering. Transmission foot brake and rear wheel brakes operated by handbrake. Centre-lock wire wheels. 710× 90mm tyres.
Open two-seat coachwork by Bugatti.
Dimensions: Wheelbase 6ft 6·7in (200cm), tracks (front and rear) 3ft 9·3in (115cm). Overall length 9ft 0in (274cm). Unladen weight 1,547lb (701kg).
History: Ettore Bugatti had been in the business of designing cars since 1900 and produced one-offs for himself and contracted designs for other people in profusion. His first true 'Bugatti' production cars, by general agreement, were the Type 13 four-cylinder machines which first appeared in 1910. These, even in original form,

established the Bugatti tradition by having overhead-camshaft operation and fixed cylinder heads — something which was not to waver in the next thirty years. Pre-war Type 13s had two valves per cylinder, but the post-war cars had four valves per cylinder, operated in that unique manner by banana-shaped tappets running in the cylinder head. The cars were raced with great success at Le Mans, but it was the 1921 Brescia race which gave the sports versions their now-legendary name. In the meantime the engine had grown from 1,327 to 1,496cc, by being bored out. The 100mm stroke, a Bugatti trade mark along with the 88mm of several racing engines, was established on this engine.

The Type 13 also grew up into the Types 22 and 23, but these were mechanically the same cars with lengthened wheelbases and different coachwork. In one form or another they remained

Above, left and below: The 'Brescia' Bugatti was so named after the Type 13's success in the 1921 Brescia race. Like other early Bugattis, it had four valves per cylinder, operated by curved tappets from an overhead cam. To the left is a young Raymond Mays in his Brescia 'Cordon Rouge', a very fast sprint car of the early 1920s.

in production until 1926, and about 2,000 were built — just about a quarter of all Bugattis. The Brescia's looks are unmistakable, although the radiator shape had not at that stage become the classic Bugatti-horseshoe taken up by cars built to follow its success.

It typified Bugatti's approach to design, in that he paid less attention to the chassis and suspensions than to the mechanical engineering. The suspension — by half-elliptic front springs and reversed quarter-elliptic leaf rear springs, was no more than up-to-date in 1919, but it was carried over to every other Bugatti except for the front-wheel-drive racing car. Steering was precise, but not helped by a flexible frame. Coachwork, profiled like the radiator, was simple but attractive, and the car's appeal was in the manner of its going. Some say it has never since been matched.

BUGATTI TYPE 41 'ROYALE'

Type 41s, built individually between 1927 and 1933 — only six built
Built by: Automobiles E. Bugatti, France
Engine: Eight cylinders, in line, in nine-bearing cast-iron block. Bore and stroke 125mm by 130mm, 12,763cc (4·92in × 5·2in, 778·8cu.in). Fixed cylinder head. Three overhead valves per cylinder (two inlet and one exhaust). Exhaust valves in line, inlet valves in line and parallel to exhaust valves. Operation by adjustable rockers from single overhead camshaft. Single updraught Bugatti carburettor. Dry-sump lubrication. Maximum power about 300bhp at 2,000rpm.
Transmission: Multi-disc clutch, running in oil, connected to engine through two fabric universal joints. Open propeller shaft to three-speed manual gearbox (without synchromesh) mounted in unit with straight-bevel 'life' rear axle. Remote control central gearchange.
Chassis: Separate pressed-steel chassis frame, with channel-section side members and pressed and tubular cross members. Forged front axle beam, machine bored through its centre. Front suspension by half-elliptic leaf springs. Rear suspension by two sets of quarter-elliptic leaf springs — one set cantilevered forward and in use always, another set cantilevered back and only coming into play for heavy loads. Friction type dampers. Four-wheel cable-operated drum brakes, without servo assistance. Cast-alloy road wheels. 6·75×36in tyres.
Individual coachwork by specialists (some cars rebodied several times).
Dimensions: Wheelbase 14ft 2in (432cm), tracks (front and rear) 5ft 3in (160cm). Overall length, depending on coachwork, from 22ft 0in (671cm). Unladen weight, depending on coachwork, from about 5,600lb (2,540kg).
History: The 'Royale' or 'Golden Bugatti' as it has also been named, was a car for kings, and that was how Bugatti himself wanted to see it sold. This vast car, with its engine intended for use (and very successful) in French aeroplanes, was the biggest, the heaviest, probably the

fastest, and certainly the most expensive 'production' car in the world. It is little wonder that, although it was a real masterpiece, with a maximum speed of more than 100 mph, and a three-speed gearbox in unit with the back axle (second was direct and top was very much of *Grand Routes* overdrive), only six cars were ever completed. Bugatti himself had always been sanguine about the car's success, and had laid down a series of 25. The prototype was built in 1926/27 with an even bigger engine, of 14,726cc, than eventually was sold.

In spite of its name, no 'Royale' was ever sold to any of the world's monarchs, although several visited Molsheim to inspect the prototype. Only three cars were ever sold when new — one to France, one to Germany and one to Captain Foster in Britain. Three other machines were built and run by the Bugatti family. It is quite amazing that all six cars survive to this day, all in possible running condition. One at least of these was saved from the scrap business in New York during World War II and one was reputedly hidden down a sewer in Paris during the German occupation to ensure its survival. The car, incidentally, was so exclusive and expensive that in Britain it was listed at £5,250 for the rolling chassis at a time when a Rolls-Royce Phantom II cost a mere £1,900. A Frenchman would have had to pay half a million Francs for the pleasure. Everything was on a grand scale, including fuel consumption which could never have been better than about 6 to 8mpg. Yet in spite of its immense size, and a traditional Bugatti radiator to suit, the proportions are so good that this is not obvious. The engines later found a good home in French high-speed railcars, which were used until the 1950s.

Below: Two views of one of the six enormous, and very expensive Type 41 Bugatti 'Royale' cars. The engine was a 12·8-litre straight eight, and the cars could easily exceed 100mph.

BUGATTI TYPE 49

Type 49 models, built from 1930 to 1934
Built by: Automobiles E. Bugatti, France
Engine: Eight cylinders, in line, in cast-iron block, with nine-bearing light-alloy crankcase bolted to it. Bore and stroke 72mm by 100mm, 3,257cc (2·83in × 3·94in, 198·7cu.in). Fixed cylinder head. Three overhead valves per cylinder (two inlet and one exhaust). Exhaust valves in line, inlet valves in line and parallel to exhaust valves. Operation by adjustable rockers from single overhead camshaft. Crankshaft in two pieces, with camshaft drive bevel bolted to centre. Single updraught Schebler carburettor.
Transmission: Dry-plate clutch and four-speed manual gearbox (without synchromesh) in unit with engine. Central direct acting gearchange. Open propeller shaft to spiral-bevel 'live' rear axle.
Chassis: Separate pressed-steel chassis frame. Channel-section side members, tubular and fabricated cross bracing. Forged front axle beam, drilled through for lightness. Front suspension by half-elliptic leaf springs. Rear suspension by reversed-cantilever quarter-elliptic leaf springs and torque rod from axle to frame. Friction-type dampers. Worm-and-nut steering. Four-wheel drum brakes, rod and cable operated. Cast-alloy road wheels. 5·25 × 28in tyres.
Dimensions: Wheelbase 10ft 7in (323cm), tracks (front and rear) 4ft 2in (127cm). Overall length 13ft 9in (419cm). Unladen weight (chassis only) 2,150lb (975kg).
History: The Type 49 touring Bugatti was the last of a line and therefore the most highly developed of that line. It was an amalgam of design experience and actual components stretching back several years and is really notable as being the very last single-overhead-camshaft Bugatti. The general engine layout was very much the same as in previous machines, but in this instance the camshaft drive was taken up the centre of the engine and the crankshaft was built up from two pieces.

The first eight-cylinder Bugatti dated from 1921 (a six-cylinder engine was never built, nor reputedly ever contemplated), but the first production 'eight' — the Type 30 — followed in 1922. Type 38 replaced it in 1926 and the chassis from this car was used in the Types 40, 43, 44 and 49 cars. The 49's single-cam engine stemmed from the new unit of 2,991cc first seen in Type 44, and was related in many ways to the Type 35 (unsupercharged) family. Elsewhere in the specification were the 'dry' clutch and the central ball-change gear lever, both new. Even so, the Type 49 exhibited many splendid examples of the art of producing Bugattis, among which the delicately styled coachwork, the magnificently sculptured engine, and the unmistakable combination of mechanical noises were the most obvious. The engine's smoothness was noteworthy and had been expected, as the crankshaft ran in nine bearings.

Front and rear suspension was in the traditional style — the front springs passing through the axle beam in the Bugatti racing-car fashion. There was no nonsense with silent gearboxes, or a soft ride, neither of which were thought necessary by Bugatti himself, and the car itself was capable of rather more than 80mph, without showing any signs of temperament. It was always a positive pleasure to look at the carefully profiled cast-alloy road wheels, the engine-turned cylinder head covers, the bunch-of-bananas exhaust manifolds and the general layout of the car. It was not so much of a pleasure, we are told, to contemplate servicing the engine, for the cylinder head could not be removed, and even valve grinding involved removing the unit from the chassis and taking out the crankshaft. But Bugattis were works of art, and nobody seemed to mind that!

Below: Type 49 Bugattis, with their single-cam 3·3-litre engines, came in all shapes and varieties. The Weymann saloon is competing in a speed trial; the sports tourer was a popular type.

BUGATTI TYPE 57

Types 57, 57C, 57S and 75SC (data for Type 57S)
Built by: Automobiles E. Bugatti, France.
Engine: Eight cylinders, in line, in six-bearing block, with cast-alloy crankcase bolted to it. Bore and stroke 72mm by 100mm, 3,257cc (2·83in × 3·94in, 198·7cu.in). Fixed cylinder head. Two overhead valves per cylinder, opposed to each other at 90 degrees included angle in part-spherical combustion chamber and operated by finger-type rockers from twin overhead camshafts. Single updraught Zenith carburettor. Maximum power about 175bhp at 5,500rpm.
Transmission: Twin-dry-plate clutch and four-speed manual gearbox (without synchromesh) both in unit with engine. Direct-acting central gearchange. Open propeller shaft to spiral-bevel 'live' rear axle.
Chassis: Separate steel chassis frame. Pressed-steel channel-section side members, with tubular and fabricated cross bracings. Forged front axle beam, drilled through for lightness. Front suspension by half-elliptic leaf springs. Rear suspension by reversed-cantilever quarter-elliptic leaf springs and torque rod from axle to frame. Worm-and-nut steering. Friction-type dampers. Four-wheel drum brakes, rod and cable operated. Centre-lock wire wheels, 5·50 × 18in tyres (front), 6·00 × 18in (rear). Variety of Bugatti-supplied coachwork, open or closed, or from coachbuilders.
Dimensions: Wheelbase 9ft 9·5in (298·5cm), tracks (front and rear) 4ft 5in (135cm). Overall length 13ft 3in (404cm). Unladen weight (chassis only) 2,100lb (952kg).
History: There is little doubt that although the 'Royale' is the most famous of all Bugattis, the Type 57 series is the most popular. And very deservedly so. Introduced in 1934 and running through until the outbreak of war in 1939, in all its forms it sold to the tune of 710 cars. It was designed almost entirely by Jean Bugatti (son of Ettore), and was almost entirely new. Even the twin-cam engine, with bore and stroke of the single-cam Type 49, was quite unlike earlier twin-cam 'eights' (as used in the Type 50s and 51s), because its cams were driven by a train of gears at the tail of the crankshaft and cylinder block. The gearbox had constant-mesh gears, and at first it was even intended to give the front axle a measure of independence between its wheels, although Ettore Bugatti himself forbade that.

There were several variations. The original Type 58 was in production until 1936, and was followed in 1937 by the Series 2 cars with engine improvements including rubber mountings. The Series 3 cars arrived at the end of 1938 with hydraulic brakes and telescopic dampers as the major changes.

The Type 57S ('S' for Sport) was announced in 1935, had a tuned engine, with dry-sump lubrication, and a modified chassis frame, lowered to allow sleeker bodywork to be offered. The 57C version had a supercharged engine producing at least 200bhp, and the combination of this engine and the 57S chassis gave rise to the 57SC the peak (in most people's opinions) of Bugatti's excellence. Cars with this engine and sports or coupé bodywork could beat 100mph by a wide margin — a good one might touch more than 120mph. Both cars were withdrawn in 1939 as they were becoming too expensive to manufacture, although the 57 and 57C continued to sell well.

Perhaps more sensational even than the chassis was the type and nature of coachwork fitted, some Bugatti-made, and some by outside specialists. The Atlantic coupé, a true fast-back car with pronounced dorsal fin, was the most bizarre of all, and was both rare and effective. The chassis was long enough for four-door saloons to be built (almost impossible on other Bugattis) which makes the 57 chassis very versatile indeed. It was the last of all production cars from Molsheim, as production never got under way again after the war.

Above: Bugatti's Type 57 chassis, with its straight-eight twin-cam 3·3-litre engine, was probably the finest Molsheim car of all. The British drop-head coachwork contrasts sharply with the famous Bugatti radiator. The car had a very simple chassis, hard sprung.

Below: One of the most extraordinary of many exotic Bugattis was the Type 57SC Atlantic coupe. Few were made at Molsheim, and only three are now in existence. The supercharged engine produces well over 150bhp, and top speed is at least 110mph.

CADILLAC V8

Type 51 V8, built from 1914 to – for Series 314 – 1927 (data for 1914 Type 51)
Built by: Cadillac Motor Car Co., United States.
Engine: Eight cylinders, in 90-degree vee-formation, in two four-cylinder blocks, with three-bearing light-alloy crankcase. Bore and stroke 79·4mm by 130·2mm, 5,157cc (3·12in × 5·12in, 314cu.in). Fixed cylinder heads. Two side valves per cylinder, operated by fingers from single camshaft mounted in crankcase. One single up-draught Cadillac carburettor. Maximum power 70bhp (gross) at 2,400rpm.
Transmission: Multi-dry-plate clutch and three-speed manual gearbox (without synchromesh), both in unit with front-mounted engine. Direct-acting central gearchange. Open propeller shaft to spiral-bevel 'live' rear axle.
Chassis: Separate pressed-steel chassis frame, with channel-section side members and tubular and pressed cross bracing. Forged front axle beam. Front suspension by semi-elliptic leaf springs. Rear suspension by semi-elliptic leaf springs, supported on a transverse leaf spring bolted centrally to chassis frame, with torque rod from axle forward to chassis frame. No dampers. Worm-and-sector steering. Rear-wheel cable-operated drum brakes. 36in bolt-on artillery-type road wheels. 36 × 4·5in tyres.
Dimensions: Wheelbase 10ft 2in (310cm), tracks (front and rear) 4ft 8in (142cm). Overall length 15ft 5in (470cm).

History: Cadillac cars were the inspiration originally of Henry M. Leland and were modest little single-cylinder machines at first, while the Model A Cadillac was very similar to the very first Fords in many ways. This car established the Cadillac tradition of interchangeability (at a time when hand-building and hand-fitting -was normal). Cadillac was formed into the new General Motors group in 1909, and soon became the prestige-leader of that group of manufacturers. The V8-engined car of 1914 was a hallmark in modern American design, as it had been

designed to be technically advanced and very reliable. It was, without any doubt, the world's first commercially successful V8. It was so good a unit that in developed form it carried on as the mainstay of Cadillac's products until 1927, when the even more outstanding 341 unit replaced it. The engine's progenitor was D. McCall White, a Briton who had already worked for Napier and Daimler in England before joining Cadillac in 1914; its design had been laid down before then, however. Other features about the car, apart from its engine, were the high quality of its equip-

---

CADILLAC V12

V12 models, built from 1930 to 1937 (data for 1930/31 model)
Built by: Cadillac Motor Car Co., United States.
Engine: Twelve cylinders, in 45-degree vee-formation, in two cast-iron blocks, with five-bearing light-alloy crankcase. Bore and stroke 79·4mm by 101·6mm, 5,676cc (3·12in × 4·0in, 368cu.in). Two detachable cast-iron cylinder heads. Two overhead valves per cylinder, operated by pushrods and rockers from single camshaft mounted in centre of crankcase 'vee'. Two up-draught Cadillac carburettors. Maximum power 135bhp (gross) at 3,400rpm. Maximum torque 284lb.ft at 1,200rpm.
Transmission: Twin-dry-plate clutch and three-speed, synchromesh manual gearbox (without synchromesh on first gear), both in unit with front-mounted engine. Direct-acting central gearchange. Propeller shaft, enclosed in torque tube, driving spiral-bevel 'live' rear axle.
Chassis: Separate pressed-steel chassis frame, with channel-section side members and tubular and channel-section cross bracing. Forged front axle beam. Front and rear suspension by semi-elliptic leaf springs. Lever-arm hydraulic dampers. Worm-and-sector steering. Four-wheel, mechanically operated drum brakes with vacuum-servo assistance. 18in or 19in bolt-on wire wheels. 7·00 × 19in or 7·50 × 18in tyres.
Dimensions: Wheelbase 11ft 11in (358cm), tracks (front and rear) 4ft 11in (150cm). Overall length 17ft 10in (544cm). Unladen weight 4,400lb (1,995kg).
History: Not content merely with launching a near-unique V16 car at the beginning of 1930, Cadillac then surprised everyone by announcing a V12 car only months later, in time for the 1931 season to begin! Having, however, launched the V16 at the beginning of the year, the V12 was not so much of an effort. All chassis and even coachwork parts were shared, and the V12 engine was a very cleverly productionised 'three-quarters' of a V16. Externally one had to count the sparking plugs to be sure which unit it was, as effectively it merely had four cylinders chopped off from one end of the assembly. For 1931, the Cadillac range therefore include a V8, a V12 and a V16 car, along with the Cadillac-built La Salle V8, with a great deal of cross-fertilisation of parts.

The V12, like the V16, was remarkably refined, silent and reliable and gave Cadillac that 'magic

carpet' performance which set them apart from all rivals for a time. The only criticism possibly aimed at the V12 was that it undoubtedly took sales away from the V16 car — and in a market where tycoons and playboys had already suffered financial shock in the Wall Street crash this was unwise. Not that Cadillac cared, as there was very little more complication in having two engines and two models sharing much of the same tooling and assembly processes. Between 1930 and 1940, indeed, total sales of all Cadillac V12 and V16 cars (including the side-valve V16

of 1937–40) were just over 15,000, of which the original V16 accounted for nearly 3,900 cars and the V12 for nearly 11,000. If we consider the level of sales achieved by any other of the 'top hat' brigade, that is a remarkable record of success for a period when the North American buyers were hardly in a buoyant mood. It emphasises just what a high reputation Cadillac held in its own market at the time and it was probably a source of relief to the rivals, world-wide, that Cadillac never seriously thought about exports.

ment, the rigidity of its chassis frame and for its great attention to detail in all respects. GM make no secret of the fact that a De Dion V8 engine was purchased for study, but they were adamant that their own effort was more modern in all respects. One surprisingly backward-looking feature was the rear suspension, where the half-elliptic leaf springs on the axle were separated from the chassis by a further transverse platform spring — something found unnecessary in Europe before this, but retained by Cadillac into the 1920s. Cadillac V8 cars were used in great numbers for high-ranking staff officers' transport during World War I. The Type 51 was followed by Types 53, 55, 57, 59, 61 and V63 before finally giving way to the Type 314 models in July 1925. More than 13,000 cars were built in the 1915 model years and more than 26,000 in the best-yet year of 1922.

Left and right: Cadillac did not make the first vee-8 engined car in the world, but in 1914 their car was the best one. The machines were superbly tooled, with all-interchangeable parts. At this time many cars were still hand-constructed. The tourer (Left) is one of the first 1914 models, the later model (Right) a 1917 example. The new vee-8 engine was used, in developed form, until 1927.

Below: Cadillac's vee-12 model, built in small numbers (11,000 in eight years) was a closely-related sister to the even more magnificent vee-16. The unit produced about 135bhp.

CADILLAC ELDORADO

Eldorado models (front-wheel-drive) introduced 1966 (data for 1967 model)

Built by: Cadillac Motor Co. (GM Corporation), United States.

Engine: Eight cylinders, in 90-degree vee formation, in five-bearing cast-iron cylinder block. Bore and stroke 104·9mm by 101·6mm, 7,031cc (4·13in × 4·0in, 429cu.in). Detachable cast-iron cylinder heads. Two overhead valves per cylinder, in line, operated by pushrods and rockers from single camshaft mounted in cylinder block 'vee'. Downdraught Rochester carburettor. Maximum power 340bhp (gross) at 4,600rpm. Maximum torque 480lb.ft at 3,000rpm.

Transmission: Front-wheel-drive power pack. Engine longitudinally-mounted above line of front wheels, gearbox behind line. Torque converter and chain drive to three-speed automatic gearbox, connected direct to hypoid-bevel final drive. Remote, steering-column-mounted gearchange. Exposed, universally jointed drive shafts to front wheels.

Chassis: Separate box-section steel chassis frame, with box and pressed cross braces. Independent front suspension by wishbones, longitudinal torsion bars and anti-roll bar. Rear suspension by 'dead' beam axle and half-elliptic leaf springs. Telescopic dampers. Power-assisted recirculating-ball steering. Four-wheel hydraulically operated 11in drum brakes, servo-assisted. 15in pressed-steel disc wheels. 9·00 × 15in tyres.

Dimensions: Wheelbase 10ft 0in (305cm), track (front) 5ft 5·3in (166cm), track (rear) 5ft 3in (160cm). Overall length 18ft 5in (561cm). Unladen weight 4,730lb (2,142kg).

History: After World War II, Cadillacs became more and more integrated into the General Motors scheme of things and by the 1960s they had unique body styling with mechanical engineering shared largely with the Oldsmobile range. Consequently, after Oldsmobile had announced their front-wheel-drive Toronado model in 1965, it was only to be expected that

Cadillac would follow suit. The Eldorado was mechanically similar to the Toronado, but had a marginally different engine size and rather 'sharper' body lines. The concept of a two-door close-coupled (by North American standards, at least) car, in saloon or convertible form, was retained.

Surprisingly, General Motors made no attempt to spread the use of this expensive tooling to other models, which ensured that the cars were always exclusive and expensive. In spite of the onset of more and more restrictive North American legislation, the GM front-wheel-drive cars carried on successfully into the mid 1970s.

Above and right: Along with the Oldsmobile Toronado (a sister car) Cadillac's Eldorado is the only front-wheel-drive American car of modern times. All Eldorados are two-door cars —those shown above being 1967 models, that on the right a recent 1976 car. The engine is a big 7-litre vee-8.

Among the interesting features were the 'silent' chain drive from the torque converter output shaft to the transmission input shaft, the self-levelling suspension and the ingenious packaging of the power pack to save space.

CADILLAC V16

V16 (ohv series), built from 1930 to 1937 (data for 1930/31 model)

Built by: Cadillac Motor Car Co., United States.

Engine: 16 cylinders, in 45-degree vee-formation, in two cast-iron blocks, with five-bearing light-alloy crankcase. Bore and stroke 76·2mm by 101·6mm, 7,413cc (3·0in × 4·0in, 452cu.in). Two detachable cast-iron cylinder heads. Two overhead valves per cylinder, operated by pushrods and rockers from single camshaft mounted in centre of crankcase 'vee'. Two up-draught Cadillac carburettors. 165bhp (gross) at 3,400 rpm. Maximum torque 320lb.ft at 1,500rpm.

Transmission: Twin-dry-plate clutch and three-speed, synchromesh manual gearbox (without synchromesh on first gear), both in unit with front-mounted engine. Direct-acting central gearchange. Propeller shaft, enclosed in torque tube, driving spiral-bevel 'live' rear axle.

Chassis: Separate pressed-steel chassis frame, with channel-section side members and tubular and channel-section cross bracing. Forged front axle beam. Front and rear suspension by semi-elliptic leaf springs. Lever-arm hydraulic dampers. Worm-and-sector steering. Four-wheel, mechanically operated drum brakes, with vacuum-servo assistance. 19in bolt-on wire wheels. 7·50 × 19in tyres.

Dimensions: Wheelbase 12ft 4in (376cm), tracks (front and rear) 4ft 11in (150cm). Overall length 18ft 6in (564cm). Unladen weight 5,000lb (2,268kg).

History: Hindsight tells us that nearly every luxury car launched during the depression suffered badly, but Cadillac's magnificent individualistic V16 car survived because of its own excellence, because of the resilience of Cadillac themselves and because of the huge backing from the parent, General Motors. The engine had been conceived in 1927, but took

more than two years to perfect and was not leaked to the dealers until the last days of 1929, just after the whirlwind days of the Wall Street crash had shattered the business community. Cadillac's aims were, quite simply, to produce the smoothest possible power plant which should, at the same time, upstage the products of Packard and Duesenberg, not to mention Rolls-Royce and other imported cars. They had, for years, disclaimed interest in straight-eight engines when all around were adopting them. This engine went two stages better — it had a vee-layout, with two banks of eight cylinders! In mechanical detail it was otherwise identical: it had detachable heads and cast-iron cylinder blocks on a cast-alloy crankcase, with the valve gear operated conventionally from a single camshaft in the crook of the crankcase's 'vee'. Yet in spite of its magnificent looks, it was certainly not as powerful as the Duesenberg engine and the heavy cars themselves could reach only about 90mph. Cadillac did not mind this, as they were interested in prestige rather

than performance. Sales were never expected to be high and many mechanical components were in any case shared with the chassis of the V8-engined cars. Whatever the economic prospects, the Cadillac V16 and its 'smaller sister' the V12, caused rivals to react. From America (Packard, Lincoln and Pierce), from Germany (Maybach), from France (Hispano-Suiza) and from Britain (Rolls-Royce), came a phalanx of V12 units, and Marmon even produced a V16 of their own. Cadillac sold more than 3,000 V16 cars in 1930 and 1931, but less than 300 in 1932 and 125 in 1933, then only about 50 a year until 1937. This car, along with the V12, was supplanted by a new 135-degree side-valve V16 unit, which was also refined, but was somehow cheaper and nastier than the thoroughbred original.

Below: Cadillac's vee-16 model of 1930/37 was a true 'classic'. This two-seater (with dickey) was built in 1932. The complexity was worth it.

CHADWICK 'GREAT SIX'

'Great Six' model, built from 1907 to 1916 (data for 1910 model)

Built by: Chadwick Engineering Works, United States.

Engine: Six cylinders, in line, in three cast-iron blocks, with four-bearing light-alloy crankcase. Bore and stroke 127mm by 152·4mm, 11,583cc (5·0in×6·0in, 707cu.in). Non-detachable cylinder heads. Two side valves per cylinder, in T-head layout with exposed valve stems, operated by tappets from two camshafts mounted in crankcase. Single side-draught Chadwick carburettor. Maximum power 95bhp at 1,450rpm. Optional supercharger, and 120bhp at 1,450rpm.

Transmission: Expanding drum clutch in unit with front-mounted engine. Shaft drive to separate four-speed manual gearbox (without synchromesh). Remote-control quadrant-type right-hand gearchange. Straight-bevel differential in tail of gearbox and countershaft to sprockets. Final drive to rear wheels by chain in chain case.

Chassis: Separate pressed-steel chassis frame, with channel-section side members, additional circular-section tension bars for added rigidity and pressed and tubular cross bracing. Forged front axle beam. Front suspension by semi-elliptic leaf springs. Rear suspension by semi-elliptics leaf springs, with additional transverse 'platform' leaf spring, fixed to rear of semi-elliptics, and radius arm axle location combined in chain case. Friction-type dampers. Worm-and-nut steering. Mechanically operated foot brake, by contracting band on countershaft drum, near gearbox. Hand brake operating on rear wheel drums. Artillery-style road wheels. 36 × 4in tyres (front) and 37 × 5in tyres (rear). Choice of coachwork.

Dimensions: Wheelbase 9ft 4·2in (285cm), tracks (front and rear) 4ft 8in (142cm). Unladen

weight, depending on coachwork, from 4,080lb to 4,850lb (1,850kg to 2,200kg).

History: The Chadwick's claim to fame is that it was America's very first high-performance car to reach volume production. The first Chadwicks had four-cylinder engines, but from 1907 the 'Great Six' (it was 'great' in size, in performance and eventually in reputation) took over. The Type 19 engine introduced in 1911 had overhead inlet valves, but for several years (and in the 'Black Bess' competition cars of 1908 and 1909) a conventional T-head layout was used. The engine was 'classic North American' in this respect, with twin-cylinder blocks sitting atop a common crankcase and with all valve stems exposed. The supercharged cars which appeared in the 1908 Vanderbilt Cup and Savannah Grand

Above: Chadwick's 'Great Six' was aptly named. This 1907 tourer had an 11·6-litre engine. Supercharged cars were raced in 1908—a world 'first'.

Prix employed superchargers, the first recorded instance of a supercharger being used in a motor car, but this feature was not normally offered on production Chadwicks. The whole car was massive and impressive and for production cars the conventional semi-elliptic springs at the rear were augmented by a transverse-leaf 'platform' spring, which had been abandoned in Europe some years earlier, by all apart from Delaunay-Belleville. Chadwick's last car was built in 1916, but the name made an appearance in the 1940s on a golf trolley!

53

CHENARD-WALCKER 3-LITRE

3-litre model, built from 1922 to 1927 (data for 1922–3 model)
Built by: S.A. des Anciens Etablissements Chenard et Walcker, France.
Engine: Four cylinders, in line, in cast-iron block, with three-bearing light-alloy crankcase. Bore and stroke 79·5mm by 150mm, 2,978cc (3·13in × 5·91in, 181·7cu.in). Detachable cast-iron cylinder head. Two overhead valves per cylinder, opposed to each other and operated by rockers from single overhead camshaft. Dry-sump lubrication — separate oil tank to side of normal engine sump chamber. Single Solex carburettor. Maximum power about 90bhp.
Transmission: Single-dry-plate clutch in unit with front-mounted engine. Separate four-speed manual gearbox (without synchromesh) mounted in separate subframe. Direct-acting central gearchange. Propeller shaft, enclosed in torque tube, driving spiral-bevel 'live' rear axle. Reduction gear (bevel to internally toothed drum) at outer end of half-shafts.

Chassis: Separate pressed-steel chassis frame, with channel-section side members and tubular cross-bracings. Forged front axle beam. Front and rear suspension by semi-elliptic leaf springs, with torque-tube location at rear. Friction-type dampers. Worm-type steering. Foot-operated front drum brakes at wheels and transmission drum brake behind gearbox, with Hallot centrifugal servo-assistance (servo in transmission brake); no rear brakes. Handbrake operating on front wheels, by rods and levers. Centre-lock wire wheels. 135×895mm tyres.
Dimensions: Wheelbase 10ft 1in (307cm), tracks (front and rear) 4ft 8in (142cm).
History: The 3-litre Chenard-Walcker of 1922–3 instantly became famous because two examples finished first and second in the very first Le Mans 24-hour race. The design, however, owed its origins to pre-war cars, as the company had been in existence since 1901 and the car's designer Monsieur Touté had been at Chenard-Walcker since the war. The rear axle had reduction

gearing in the hubs — something characteristic of all the cars built since 1901, and another oddity (shared with Bignan) was that front brakes but no rear brakes, were fitted, along with servo assistance which became inoperative when the wheels stopped moving (an early anti-skid feature). The overhead-camshaft engine was advanced in detail and was very powerful for the period. In 1921, a 2-litre version arrived, but the 3-litre followed in 1922. Both these cars were big fours and were joined for 1923 by a straight-eight car, which was really two 2-litre engines joined back to back. These cars carried on until 1927 and ran alongside more ordinary touring machines with side-valve engines.

Right: This Chenard-Walcker, looking very sleek, was a Torpille made in 1927, and intended for use in sports car racing. Chenard-Walcker cars won at Le Mans in 1923, to the joy of France.

CHEVROLET CAMARO

Camaro, introduced in 1966 (data for 1967/68 350SS model)
Built by: Chevrolet Motor Co. (Division of General Motors), United States.
Many different mechanical specifications, from 3·8-litre six-cylinder engine to 6·5-litre V8 engine in Camaros. The following is a typical sporting version.
Engine: Eight cylinders, in 90-degree vee-formation, in five-bearing cast-iron block. Bore and stroke 101·6mm by 88·4mm, 5,733cc (4·0in × 3·48in, 350cu.in). Two detachable cast-iron cylinder heads. Two overhead valves per cylinder, operated by pushrods and rockers from single camshaft mounted in centre of cylinder block 'vee'. One downdraught four-choke Rochester carburettor. Maximum power 300bhp (gross) at 4,800rpm. Maximum torque 380lb.ft at 3,200rpm.
Transmission: Single-dry-plate clutch and four-speed all-synchromesh manual gearbox, in unit with front-mounted engine. Direct-acting central gearchange. Open propeller shaft to hypoid-bevel 'live' rear axle with limited-slip

differential. Optional transmissions include three-speed manual and three-speed fully automatic with torque converter.
Chassis: Unitary-construction, pressed-steel body/chassis structure, in two-door four-seater coupé form. Front suspension by coil springs, wishbones and anti-roll bar. Rear suspension by half-elliptic leaf springs. Telescopic dampers. Recirculating-ball steering, with optional power assistance. Four-wheel drum brakes, with vacuum servo assistance (optional front disc brakes). 14in press-steel disc wheels. F70 × 14in tyres.
Dimensions: Wheelbase 9ft 0in (274cm), front track 4ft 11in (150cm), rear track 4ft 10·9in (150cm). Overall length 15ft 5in (470cm). Unladen weight 3,300lb (1,497kg).
History: The Camaro was conceived by General Motors for Chevrolet to sell in direct compeition to Ford's successful Mustang. Not only that, but it would also be sold, with different mechanical permutations and a face-change, as the Pontiac Firebird. It was a carefully researched answer to an already-successful formula, with a two-door

body shell, 'almost-four' seats and a whole variety of engines, power outputs, transmissions and optional equipment.
The Camaro could be had as a 140bhp, six-cylinder car with drum brakes and three-speed gearbox, while on the other hand it might be a 6·5-litre V8 with 330bhp, automatic transmission and power-assisted everything else. Amid all this the 350SS was the most sporting and had handling improvements to match.
Much restyled, much modified and much-attacked by safety and pollution limits, the Camaros are still made and have been a great and lasting success for General Motors. For a period they were also very successful racing 'saloon' cars in America and in Europe.

Below: By 1972 the Camaro (and its sister car, the Pontiac Firebird) had been re-styled several times. It was sold only as a four-seater coupe, with a choice of vee-8 engines. Race-tuned Camaros were very fast indeed. In shape it was most un-American.

CHEVROLET CORVETTE

Corvettes, built from 1953 to date (data for 1963 Stingray)

Built by: Chevrolet Motor Co., United States. Four engines — 250, 300, 340 and 360bhp versions — available for 1963. The following is typical of the 360hp tune.

Engine: Eight cylinders, in 90-degree vee-formation, in five-bearing cast-iron block/crankcase. Bore and stroke 101·6mm by 83·5mm, 5,363cc (4·00in × 3·25in, 327cu.in). Two detachable cast-iron cylinder heads. Two overhead valves per cylinder, operated by pushrods and rockers from single camshaft mounted in centre of cylinder block 'vee'. Rochester fuel injection. Maximum power 360bhp (gross) at 6,000rpm. Maximum torque 352lb.ft at 4,000rpm.

Transmission: Single-dry-plate clutch and four-speed, synchromesh manual gearbox, both in unit with front-mounted engine. Remote-control central gearchange. Open propeller shaft to hypoid-bevel final-drive unit with limited-slip differential. Exposed fixed-length drive shafts to rear wheels. Optional torque converter and three-speed Chevrolet automatic transmission.

Chassis: Separate pressed-steel chassis frame with box-section side members and boxed cross bracing. Independent front suspension by coil springs, wishbones and anti-roll bar. Independent rear suspension by transverse leaf spring, lower wishbones and fixed length drive shafts. Telescopic dampers. Recirculating-ball steering. Four-wheel, hydraulically operated drum brakes, with vacuum-servo assistance. 15in centre-lock cast-alloy disc wheels. 7·10/7·60 15in tyres. Open or closed glassfibre bodywork.

Dimensions: Wheelbase 8ft 2in (249cm), track (front) 4ft 8·3in (143cm), track (rear) 4ft 9in (145cm). Overall length 14ft 7·3in (445cm). Unladen weight 3,250lb (1,474kg).

History: Chevrolet's interest in two-seater sports car motoring in modern times dates from 1951, when styling chief Harley Earl was

Right: Chevrolet's Corvette has been Detroit's only two-seater car for many years. There have been three distinct pedigrees, of which this—the most European in shape—was introduced in 1967, and is still made. The Stingray, with all-independent suspension, set trends in 1962, which the latest cars continue. There are coupés and open versions, and a confusing variety of engines. Headlamps are hidden behind panels in the bonnet until needed. The wheels on this 1972 model are special, but the choice of options is enormous. Ever since 1953, Corvettes have been made with glass-fibre body shells. The fastest road cars could reach 150mph.

beginning to think about such machines; the first mock-up of a new two-seater car to be called 'Corvette' was completed in 1952. General Motors rushed it into production at the beginning of 1953 and it has been a cult-car, North America's only domestic two-seater sports car, except for the less rorty Thunderbirds of the mid 1950s, ever since. In 1953, apart from its short wheelbase and generally sporting looks, its only technical innovation was the glassfibre body-shell — used mainly to save time in tooling between the decision to go ahead and first deliveries. Since 1953, however, there have been three basic styles of Corvettes — the first rather bulbous machines of 1953 to 1962, the Stingray machines of 1962 to 1967, and the even-more Europeanised cars of 1967 to date. There have been persistent rumours of a new mid-engined Corvette to replace the last of the classic front-engined cars, but this has not yet progressed beyond the status of a motor show 'special' as far as the public is concerned.

The first Corvettes had in-line six-cylinder 'Blue Flame' engines, but the first V8 engine option arrived in 1955. This was speedily followed by fuel injection in 1957, four-speed transmission and limited-slip differential and yet other engine tunes — all optional. The Stingray had a dramatically shaped fastback option, with all-independent suspension (the rear certainly inspired both by the Arkus-Duntov racing 'specials' *and* the Jaguar E-type suspension); four-wheel disc brakes were available from 1965. Bigger and better engines culminated in the 7-litre unit of 1966 (in later years the engines were enlarged and softened at the same time to look after exhaust-emission limitations). Although the latest cars have probably been the most popular, it was the Stingrays which gained most plaudits, and nearly 118,000 cars were built in its production run, rather less than half of these being the coupés. In its most powerful guise, the maximum speed was way over 150mph. Sales have risen steadily for nearly a quarter century, with almost 40,000 a year sold on several occasions.

CHEVROLET INTERNATIONAL SIX

International Six, introduced for 1929
Built by: Chevrolet Motor Co. (Division of General Motors), United States.
Engine: Six cylinders, in line, in three-bearing cast iron block/crankcase. Bore and stroke 84·1mm by 95·25mm, 3,175cc (3·31in × 3·75in, 194cu.in). Detachable cast-iron cylinder head. Two overhead valves per cylinder, operated by pushrods and rockers from single camshaft side-mounted in cylinder block. Single up-draught Carter carburettor. Maximum power 46bhp (gross) at 2,600rpm.
Transmission: Single-dry-plate clutch, and three-speed manual gearbox (without synchromesh), both in unit with front-mounted engine. Direct-acting central gearchange. Propeller shaft, enclosed in torque tube, driving spiral-bevel 'live' rear axle.
Chassis: Separate pressed-steel chassis frame, with channel-section side members and pressed and tubular cross bracing. Forged front axle beam. Front and rear suspension by semi-elliptic leaf springs, rear location by torque tube. Lever-arm hydraulic shock dampers. Worm-and-sector steering. Four-wheel, rod-and-shaft-operated drum brakes. 20in pressed-steel-disc wheels. 4·50 20in tyres.
Variety of open and closed coachwork.
Dimensions: Wheelbase 8ft 11in (272cm), tracks (front and rear) 4ft 8in (142cm). Overall length 13ft (396cm). Unladen weight 2,400lb (1,088kg).
History: Chevrolet's Classic Six was followed by a whole series of four-cylinder cars, but after the complete integration of General Motors, it was decided that Chevrolet should have a new

six-cylinder engine. First thoughts on this date from 1925, but it was not until the end of 1928 that the International Six was ready for sale to the public. The new engine, which had only three crankshaft bearings, and retained cast-iron pistons at a time when almost all modern trends were towards light-alloy pistons, became known very affectionately as the 'Stovebelt Six' after its use, all over the engine, of quarter-inch bolts of a type identical to those found in domestic appliances. Although the International was a very homely car, it was nevertheless twice as powerful as the model it replaced and was more than a match for Ford's new Model A.

Chevrolet had won first place in USA car sales in 1927, when Ford Model T production closed down, and had lost it again in 1929–30, but they took back world leadership firmly thereafter, and have rarely been pipped by Ford.

The International Six, all in all, was designed to give trouble-free motoring without gimmicks and the depression-torn American public loved it for that. It was also a much more relaxed-riding car than the deadly rival Ford, with semi-elliptic springs. The fact that it rarely achieved more than 20mpg fuel consumption was not a sales handicap, for petrol prices in America were very cheap indeed. Internationals became

CHRYSLER AIRFLOW

Airflow models, built from 1934 to 1937 (data for 1934 8-cylinder model)
Built by: Chrysler Corporation, United States.
Engine: Eight cylinders, in line, in five-bearing cast-iron block/crankcase. Bore and stroke 82·5mm by 114·3mm, 4,893cc (3·25in × 4·5in, 298·6cu.in). Detachable cast-iron cylinder head. Two side valves per cylinder, operated directly by single camshaft mounted in cylinder block. Single down-draught carburettor. Maximum power 130bhp (gross) at 3,400rpm.
Transmission: Single-dry-plate clutch, three-speed manual gearbox (without synchromesh) and free-wheel, all in unit with front-mounted engine. Direct-acting central gearchange. Open propeller shaft to spiral-bevel 'live' rear axle. Optional automatic overdrive from 1935.
Chassis: Pressed-steel unitary-construction body/chassis unit, with boxed structural members integral with body framing. Tubular front axle beam. Front and rear suspension by semi-

elliptic leaf springs. Lever-arm hydraulic dampers. Worm-and-wheel steering. Four-wheel hydraulically operated drum brakes. 16in pressed-steel disc wheels. 7·00 × 16in tyres.
Closed four-door six-window coachwork.
Dimensions: Wheelbase 10ft 3in (312cm), track (front) 4ft 8·7in (144cm), track (rear) 4ft 9in (144·8cm). Overall length 17ft 4in (528cm). Unladen weight 4,150lb (1,882kg).
History: The streamlined, unitary-construction 'Airflow' model must go down in history as one of the great pioneering 'flops' of all time, even though it did not sell as badly as rivals would have us believe. The concept was of a conventionally engineered Detroit car, which would take advantage of the latest in unitary-construction techniques to save cost and weight and would introduce full-width styling at a time when such things were becoming fashionable. The public, while admiring Chrysler's products at the time, were not taken by the style, which was to

be tackled with more sympathy by Ford (with the Lincoln Zephyr) less than two years later. Although it continued until 1937, a conventionally styled version – the Airstream – was both more cautious and more successful. The pity of it all was that, apart from its unconventional looks, the Airflow was a fine car. It was in every way a trendsetter for the future, never acknowledged by its business rivals. There was a six-cylinder version, as well as two straight-eight versions. In later models an automatically engaged overdrive was a popular fitting.

Below and right: Chrysler's Airflow concept was a brave attempt to change the shape of modern cars. North America in 1934 was not ready for the full-width styles (some say they were clumsily done), and the model failed. The advance of unit-construction body work was almost ignored at the time.

Left and above: Chevrolet's legendary international model, with its very simple in-line six-cylinder engine, made the company a front-runner in sales in the 1930s. The whole car, and especially the 'stove-bolt' engine, was simple and rugged. The engine, changed in many ways, survived to the 1950s.

Masters and Standards in 1933 and thereafter Chevrolet cars gradually but firmly began to be modernised. They were given 'knee-action independent' front suspension in 1934, but it is interesting to know that a buyer could still have a beam front axle, if he insisted, right up until 1940. There were no more cabriolets after 1935. The 'Stovebolt' engine was much modified in 1937, becoming the 'Blue Flame' unit with four-bearing crank and 85bhp from 3·55-litres. The engine itself ran on and on and on — the cast-iron pistons and splash lubrication lasting until 1953, and there are still six-cylinder engines with a vague descendancy at Chevrolet today. Indeed, Chevrolet's first V8 engine was not introduced until 1955.

CHITTY-BANG-BANG

Chittys I, II, and III (data for Chitty I)
Built by: Count Zborowski, Britain.
Engine: World War I-type Maybach aero-engine. Six-cylinders, in line, (six separate cylinders on cast-iron crankcase). Four overhead valves per cylinder, operated by exposed push-rods and rockers. Bore and stroke 165mm by 180mm, 23,092cc (6·50in × 7·09in, 1,409cu.in). Compression ratio 5·95:1. Originally one horizontal Maybach carburettor, later progressively modified to triple Claudel-Hobsons on separate manifolds. Dry-sump lubrication developed by Zborowski. Maximum power 305bhp at 1,500 rpm. Maximum speed at least 115mph.
Transmission: Mercédès scroll clutch and four-speed gearbox, with output drive to externally mounted sprockets. Final drive to rear axle by exposed chain. Starting of engine by means of crowbar attached to nose of crankshaft.
Chassis: Lengthened 1907 Mercédès 75hp type, with straight channel-section side members. Half elliptic front and rear springs. No dampers originally, but Hartford units in final form. Chassis side members stiffened with flitch plates. Rear wheel and transmission brakes, no front brakes. Centre-lock wire-wheels. 895 × 135 tyres.
Originally two-seat 'sports' type of coachwork by Blythe of Canterbury, including radiator cowl and swept 'boat type' tail in Brooklands racing form. Up to 800lb (363kg) of sand carried behind driving seats to help driving wheel adhesion.
History: The three Chitty-Bang-Bang cars were all exciting and outrageous 'one-off' designs built for Count Louis Zborowski, an English/American who lived in a stately home — Higham — in Kent. His main interest was motor sport, and these cars were intended to give him the fastest and most impressive transport in the world. In each case, the theory was that a simply (even crudely) engineered chassis, would have a vast aeroplane engine installed, would be geared up accordingly, and would have simple touring or sporting bodies appropriate to the purpose. Chitty I was purely a Brooklands racing car,

Chitty II another racing four-seater which also earned its keep as a fast touring car, while Chitty III was originally intended as a racing machine, but was also used for touring. Chitty IV, a much more advanced car, was only partly-built when Zborowski was killed in a factory-owned Mercédès racing car at Monza in 1924, and was never completed. It was to have been a saloon car Chitty.

The idea of Chitty I was born due to the enormous surplus of allied and enemy aeroplane engines immediately after World War I. Zborowski purchased a 23-litre, six-cylinder Maybach engine from the British Disposals Board (it had evidently been used in a German Gotha bomber), took it back to Higham and asked his engineering

consultant Clive Gallop to build a car. The chassis frame, a lengthened 1907 75hp Mercédès type, kept its original transmission and radiator. Final drive by chain was normal for Edwardian if not Vintage cars (but the Mercédès was an Edwardian chassis). Gallop had to devise dry-sump lubrication to get sufficient ground clearance. Blythe Bros. of Canterbury (owned by Zborowski) built the crude but brutal body, and the car first raced in Easter 1921. At Brooklands, Chitty won several races, and proved that it could approach 120mph, in spite of having poor road-holding and negligible brakes! However, even before the end of 1921, the Count had decided that he wanted an improved car. Chitty I was 'retired' and Chitty II was born.

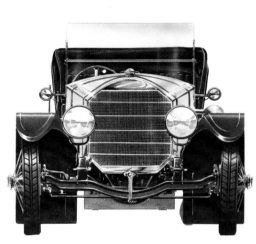 

Above: There was an obvious link with Mercedes in every Chitty—as can be seen from the radiator style fitted to Chitty-Bang-Bang II in 1922.

Above and right: Function and speed were more important than comfort in Chitty II—the hood was more for show than for weather protection.

The second car was built on similar lines. The chassis, as before, was from a pre-war Mercédès, but with a rather shorter wheelbase. The engine, an aero-engine in the same philosophy, was an 18,882cc six-cylinder Benz unit with a nominal 230bhp. Chitty II was intended more as a high-speed touring car, and was given a splendid four-seat touring body by Blythe Bros. It only raced once at Brooklands, in the autumn of 1921, lapping at 108·27mph, but it did not win its race.

Chitty III, built in 1922, was a much-modified Mercédès 28/95 chassis, imported originally as a complete car with a rudimentary test body. The 7¼-litre Mercédès engine was removed and a 14,778cc six-cylinder Mercédès aero-engine, of 160 nominal horsepower, installed. The Mercédès transmission was retained, so this was the only Chitty with propeller-shaft drive to a 'live' axle. During 1924, Chitty III won races at Brooklands, and could lap at more than 112mph, almost as quickly as the original Chitty I. The first car, incidentally, raced at Brooklands again in 1922, but nearly killed Zborowski in an enormous high-speed accident when a front tyre burst on the steep banking. The car finished up in the infield, but was scarcely damaged and was eventually rebuilt.

After Zborowski's death, Chitty I was bought by the Conan-Doyle brothers, neglected for some years, finally abandoned at Brooklands and later cut up. Chitty II, which had been sold to make room for Chitty III at Higham, was sold and resold and eventually restored, and it is now in the United States. Chitty III, raced at Brooklands as recently as 1939, was sold for road use then broken up. Chitty II is therefore the only such legendary aero-engined car still in existence today.

One other car built by Gallop for Zborowski in the same period, *not* called a Chitty but unmistakeably related to them, was the Higham Special Brooklands car. This car, with its 27-litre American Liberty V12 engine, was sold to Parry Thomas, renamed 'Babs' and improved. It took the World Land Speed Record, then killed its owner in a crash on Pendine Sands in Wales. It was buried there, but was exhumed in 1969, and it is now being restored by Owen Wyn Owen in North Wales.

Left and above: Count Louis Zborowski had the money and the enthusiasm to have the fastest possible Brooklands special built. There were three Chitty-Bang-Bang models, all with vast aeroplane engines used in World War One. Chitty II (shown here) had an 18·9-litre six-cylinder Benz engine producing at least 230bhp. Chitty I had a 305bhp 23-litre Maybach 'six', and Chitty III a 14·8 litre Mercedes 'six'. All had lengthened and stiffened Mercedes frames, that of this Chitty thought to be from an Edwardian Mercedes 60 model. In this guise it lapped the Brooklands oval at 108·27mph, but Chitty I was fastest of all—113·45mph at Brooklands, and a top speed of about 125mph. Chain drive was a feature on Chitties I and II, with rear wheel brakes, and an enormous exposed exhaust system.

CHRYSLER 70-72

70 range, introduced 1924 (the original Chrysler motor car)

Built by: Chrysler Corporation, United States.

Engine: Six cylinders, in line, in seven-bearing combined block/crankcase in cast-iron. Bore and stroke 79·4mm by 120·6mm, 3,580cc (3·12in × 4·75in, 218cu.in). Detachable cast-iron cylinder head. Two side valves per cylinder, operated by tappets from single camshaft mounted in side of crankcase. Single up-draught Zenith carburettor. Maximum power 68bhp.

Transmission: Multiple dry-plate clutch (later changed to single-plate type) and three-speed manual gearbox (without synchromesh), both in unit with front-mounted engine. Direct-acting central gearchange. Open propeller shaft drive to spiral-bevel 'live' rear axle.

Chassis: Separate pressed-steel chassis frame, with channel-section side members and pressed and tubular cross bracing. Tubular front axle beam. Front and rear suspension by semi-elliptic leaf springs. Lever-arm hydraulic dampers. Worm-and-sector steering. Four-wheel, hydraulically operated brakes. Hand brake working contracting band on transmission drum behind gearbox. Artillery-style road wheels. 30 × 5·75in tyres.

Choice of coachwork, open or closed.

Dimensions: Wheelbase 9ft 4·7in (286cm), tracks (front and rear) 4ft 8in (142cm). Overall length 13ft 6·5in (413cm). Unladen weight, depending on coachwork, from 2,845lb to 3,160lb (1,290kg to 1,433kg).

History: Before Walter Chrysler sponsored his own make of car in 1924, he had already earned himself a formidable reputation (and a lot of money) as what was effectively the first well-known 'company doctor'. His efforts with General Motors (1912 onwards), Willys-Overland and Maxwell were legendary, which made a good public reception for his new six-cylinder Chrysler 70 almost certain. This was an absolutely conventional Detroit car, except that it embraced hydraulic braking (when this was a very new concept), and its engine breathing arrangements owed a lot to Ricardo ideas.

70mph was easily attained, and no fewer than 32,000 of the cars were sold in 1924 through existing Maxwell dealers (Chrysler had taken over Maxwell in 1923). Walter Chrysler capped this with 43,000 sales in 1925 and the inexorable rise of the Chrysler Corporation to a position in the 1930s where it could challenge Ford for second place (behind General Motors) was under way.

By 1927 total sales had zoomed to 200,000 a year, but this figure was helped enormously by two extra models. One was the frugal and value-for-money 58 model, which succeeded the Maxwell, but the other was the luxurious and rather faster Imperial Six. Not only that, but Chrysler was also thinking of breaking into the lower priced market (good Chevrolet territory) and was planning the De Soto. The 58 and the 70/72 models, however, were the cars on which Chrysler's fortunes were founded, and it was not until Chrysler took over Dodge in 1928 that the next great expansion could develop. The Model 70's hydraulic brakes, incidentally, were of the contracting 'band-brake' type — the more conventional (by our standards) type not being adopted until 1928 for the 1929 models.

Above: Chrysler's 70 range was very conventional, but sold in huge numbers because of Walter Chrysler's splendid reputation. His first 'own name' car was sold through existing Maxwell dealerships—Chrysler himself having taken over that company in 1923. This smart five-seater tourer was built in 1924, the first year of production, when 43,000 examples were sold.
Right: The 70 range's engineering might have been ordinary, but some of the body styles were very dashing indeed. This tourer, registered and still used in Britain, had side-mount spare tyre and a dickey seat behind the hood in the best USA tradition.

Below: In the 1920s, the 'vintage' years, cars were thoroughly reliable, and a joy to drive. Even this Model 70 Chrysler, built in huge quantities, looked dashing, was smartly finished, and was a cut above the ordinary steel-bodied saloon car built in Detroit. It had a 3·6-litre engine and a three-speed 'crash' gearbox.

CHRYSLER 300

300 models, built from 1955 to 1964 (data for 1955 model)

Built by: Chrysler Corporation, United States.

Engine: Eight cylinders, in 90-degree vee-formation, in five-bearing cast-iron block/crankcase. Bore and stroke 97mm by 92·07mm, 5,430cc (3·82in × 3·62in, 331cu.in). Two detachable cast-iron cylinder heads. Two overhead valves per cylinder, opposed to each other in part-spherical combustion chambers and operated by pushrods and rockers (reversed rockers for inlet valves) from single camshaft mounted in centre of cylinder block 'vee'. Twin downdraught four-choke Carter carburettors. Maximum power 300bhp (gross) at 5,000rpm.

Transmission: Torque converter and three-speed PowerFlite automatic gearbox, both in unit with front-mounted engine. Remote-control steering-column gearchange. Open propeller shaft to hypoid-bevel 'live' rear axle.

Chassis: Separate pressed-steel box-section chassis frame. Independent front suspension by coil springs, wishbones and anti-roll bar. Rear suspension by semi-elliptic leaf springs. Telescopic dampers. Optional power-assisted steering. Four-wheel drum brakes, with optional servo assistance. 15in bolt-on pressed-steel-disc or wire wheels. 8·00 × 15in tyres.

Two-door pressed-steel coupé bodywork by Chrysler.

Dimensions: Wheelbase 10ft 6in (320cm), track (front) 5ft 0·2in (153cm), track (rear) 4ft 11·6in (151·4cm). Overall length 18ft 2·6in (555cm). Unladen weight 4,005lb (1,816kg).

Right: Chrysler's 300 series ran for ten years. All were very fast and distinctive. This 1961 Type 300G shows off Chrysler's smooth styling.

History: The arrival of Chrysler's 300 model, in February 1955, was a great and pleasurable surprise to the average North American customer and a rude shock to the competition in Detroit. Although the famous 'hemi' engine, launched in 1951, had shown itself to be both powerful and at the same time economical and had already been used with distinction by Cunningham and others in racing sports cars, it was a shock to find Chrysler suddenly committed to selling out-and-out performance saloons. The 300, for instance, had a top speed of at least 130mph as delivered, which put it way ahead of *any* other car on the American market. Although the 300 was never a uniquely styled car — the 1955 model, in effect, had a hardtop New Yorker bodyshell with an Imperial front end and grille — it was always distinctive enough for it to carry a special aura. It was the first of Detroit's true supercars and a very hot competitor for the new Thunderbird, even though it was a full-sized car. Apart from the tiny-production Plymouth Superbirds of the late 1960s, the 300 series — which became less and less specialised as its ten-year life progressed — was to the forefront of Chrysler's 'engineering-first' image.

CITROEN TYPE A

Type A models, built from 1919 to 1922 (data for 1919 model)

Built by: S.A. André Citroën, France.

Engine: Four cylinders, in line, in cast-iron block, with two-bearing light-alloy crankcase. Bore and stroke 65mm by 100mm, 1,327cc (2·56in × 3·94in, 81·0cu.in). Detachable cast-iron cylinder head. Two side valves per cylinder, operated by tappets from single camshaft, mounted in cylinder block. Single Solex carburettor. Maximum power 18bhp at 2,100rpm.

Transmission: Cone clutch and three-speed manual gearbox (without synchromesh), both in unit with front-mounted engine Direct-acting central gearchange. Open propeller shaft to spiral-bevel 'live' rear axle.

Chassis: Separate pressed-steel chassis frame, with channel-section side members and tubular cross bracing. Forged front axle beam. Front suspension by leading quarter-elliptic leaf springs. Rear suspension by upper and lower trailing quarter-elliptic leaf springs. No dampers. Foot brake acting on transmission drum behind gearbox. Hand-operated brake on rear wheel drums. Bolt-on steel-disc wheels. 710 × 90 tyres.

Dimensions: Wheelbase 9ft 6in (290cm), tracks (front and rear) 3ft 11·2in (120cm). Overall length 13ft (396cm). Unladen weight (chassis only) 990lb (449kg).

History: André Citroën, Managing Director of Mors and the inventor of double-bevel 'herringbone' gearing, built a factory in Paris in 1917 and in the spring of 1919 launched the first of a long line of famous Citroëns — the Type A. It was really to be the first mass-produced French car, and was completely equipped with all-weather and electrical equipment as standard. It was cheap, it was available and it was helped by a strike at the Renault factory at about the time of its launch.

Technically, the Type A was almost completely conventional, but 30,000 orders were taken before deliveries began. Sales were soon aided by a flourishing dealer network and the gimmick of taking over the Paris taxi fleet helped enormously. Within two years the side-valve Type A had been joined by the enlarged and improved Type B2 and shortly after that by an overhead-valve conversion on the same basic engine. Alongside it came the legendary 855cc 5CV, which included the three-seater 'Clover Leaf' style. The Type A had been the first quantity-built French car the public could afford and it was the best possible start for Citroën.

Left and right: Citroen's Type A built only for a few years, established André Citroen as a leading maker of 'peoples' cars' in France. Up to then he had made his name as the chief executive of Mors, who made more costly cars, and had invented the double-bevel 'silent' gear wheel. The Type A was France's first true mass-production car, and post-war buyers queued up to take delivery. Mechanically, the Type A was very simple, and typically 'vintage', with various oddities. The cone clutch was old fashioned, but the unit gearbox advanced. More than 30,000 were ordered before deliveries began, and Citroen never looked back. Even Renault, the acknowledged leaders in France, were very worried. Left: The original 1919 style in open tourer form — this is said to be the very first car. Right: A 1922 model, visually the same with those characteristic disc wheels and the noteworthy radiator shape.

CISITALIA 1100

1100 sports car, built from 1946 to 1948 (data for 1947 model)

Built by: Cisitalia SpA., Italy.

Engine: Fiat manufactured. Four cylinders, in line, in three-bearing cast-iron block/crankcase. Bore and stroke 68mm by 75mm, 1,089cc (2·68in × 2·95in, 66·5cu.in). Detachable light-alloy cylinder head. Two overhead valves per cylinder, operated by pushrods and rockers from single camshaft mounted in side of crankcase. One single-choke down-draught Zenith carburettor. Maximum power 51bhp (gross) at 5,200rpm.

Transmission: Single-dry-plate clutch and four-speed manual gearbox (with synchromesh on top and third gears), both in unit with front-mounted engine. Direct-acting central gearchange. Open propeller shaft to spiral-bevel 'live' rear axle.

Chassis: Separate multi-tubular chassis frames. Independent front suspension by transverse leaf spring and wishbones. Rear suspension by semi-elliptic leaf springs. Lever-arm hydraulic dampers. Worm-and-wheel steering. Bolt-on pressed-steel-disc wheels. Two-door fastback Pininfarina bodywork, or open two-seat sports car.

History: Cisitalia cars were the brainchild of Piero Dusio of Turin, who used his war-earned fortune to make cars based on Fiats in the same way as Gordini leaned on Simca. The Type 202 used Fiat 1100 (508S) mechanicals in an individually designed multi-tube frame, usually clothed with Pininfarina bodies. The cars were neat, tiny, light and modern, and went astonishingly fast considering their very humble parentage. Tazio Nuvolari did wonders for the marque's name, leading the 1947 Mille Miglia most of the way until soaked electrics forced him to retire. Nuvolari had also driven the single-seater racing versions and Piero Taruffi won the Italian championship of that year. A twin-carburettor engine, which boosted power to 70bhp, was made available for 1948, but interest in this class of sports-car racing was waning. In the meantime an advanced four-wheel-drive car was being evolved by Porsche and Abarth for Cisitalia to race; this took up most of Dusio's attention and the little production cars faded from the scene. Cisitalia operations were transferred to Argentina for a time and after they returned to Italy, in 1950, production of the 1100 was restored for a time, but the design was never updated. Its heyday was undoubtedly in those three post-war years.

Right: Cisitalia cars, like others before and since, were low-production specials with mass-produced (in this case Fiat) mechanicals. The car shown was a 1946 model, with sleek Italian coachbuilder's coupe styling.

CITROEN 'TRACTION AVANT'

11CV and 15CV models, built 1934 to 1955 (data for 11CV – post-war types)

Built by: S.A. André Citroën, France.

Engine: Four cylinders, in line, in three-bearing cast-iron cylinder block. Bore and stroke 78mm by 100mm, 1,911cc (3·07in × 3·94in, 116·6 cu.in). Detachable cylinder barrels, wet liners. Cast-iron cylinder head. Two overhead valves per cylinder, operated by pushrods and rockers from side-mounted camshaft. Single down-draught Solex carburettor. Maximum power 56bhp (net) at 4,250rpm.

Transmission: Front-wheel-drive power pack. Engine longitudinally mounted behind line of front axle, gearbox ahead of it. Single-dry-plate clutch and three speed manual gearbox (synchromesh on top and second gears). Spiral-bevel differential. Exposed, universally jointed drive shafts to front wheels.

Chassis: Pressed-steel unitary-construction body shell, with four passenger doors. Power pack bolts on to front of shell and can be wheeled away for major maintenance. Independent front suspension by wishbones and longitudinal torsion bars. 'Dead' rear axle beam (tubular), radius arms and transverse torsion bars. Hydraulic lever-type dampers. Rack-and-pinion steering. Four-wheel hydraulically operated drum brakes. Pressed-steel disc wheels. 185–400mm tyres.

Dimensions: Wheelbase (6-seater) 10ft 1·5in (309cm), (8-seater) 10ft 9in (328cm). Tracks (front and rear) 4ft 8in (142cm). Overall length 14ft 9·5in or 15ft 5·5in (451 or 471cm). Unladen weight 2,465lb or 2,604lb (1,118kg or 1,181kg).

History: Before 1933, Citroën's cars had been relatively conventional, although they had already adopted Budd-type pressed-steel bodies. Then came their great technical breakthrough – the announcement of the all-new front-wheel-drive 7CV. This car would have been complex enough and troublesome enough to bankrupt Citroën had it not been for timely help from the Michelin (tyre) family. Not only did the new car have front-wheel drive, but a unit-construction body/chassis at a time when such things were almost unknown. The styling, although related to currently accepted standards, was low and relatively wind-cheating. The engine, although new, was of only 1,300cc and it soon became clear that it lacked power. Within a year, the bore and stroke had both been increased. The 7CV disposed of 1,628cc and the '7S' 1,911cc. With that engine size the new '11CV' car soldiered on very successfully until 1957 — more than 700,000 were built in the 24 years, which included the war-time years.

From 1938, a six-cylinder version of the car, the 15CV (or Big Six as it was known in Britain), was added to the range. Eventually there were alternative wheelbases — the long-wheelbase cars having extra occasional seats in the lengthened rear compartment, which made them very popular for taxi and hire car use. In the 1930s,

Right and above: One of the most attractive types of traction avant Citroen was the two-seater open tourer, built only in the 1930s. The mechanical features were like those of the saloons.

too, there were higher-priced convertibles (with double dickey seat) and fixed-head coupé cars, but these were not re-introduced in 1945 when production resumed following the war.

The 'traction avant' (front-wheel drive) as it was always affectionately known among motorists, set new standards for roadholding and response, even though its performance was never startling, and its refinement not too obvious. Front-drive was most responsible for this, but the wide wheel tracks and low-slung construction must have helped. One immensely clever practical feature was that after 90 minutes of work in an agency the entire engine/transmission/front suspension power pack could be removed from the body — and this made major work easy to perform. Even when time caught up with the 'traction' the main elements of its design were carried forward to the futuristic DS19 of 1955. The Big Six had already tested hydropneumatic suspension by then.

Above and left: The legendary saloon 'traction avant' Citroen was built from 1934 to 1955 without a break (apart from war years). There were four-cylinder and (from 1938) six-cylinder cars. The 'traction' now lives on as a 'Maigret' police car.

Above and left: Recognition points of all 'traction avant' Citroens included the chevron marks on the radiator grille, the long low lines quite out of the ordinary for the 1930s, the front-drive shafts seen behind the bumper, and the unmistakeable shape of the front wings. Power pack layout was such that the entire engine and transmission could be unbolted from the unit-construction body shell within 90 minutes, for major repairs.

CITROEN 2CV

2CV model, built from 1948 to date (data for original 375cc model)

Built by: S.A. André Citroën (Citroën S.A. since 1968), France.

Engine: Two cylinders, air-cooled, in horizontally opposed layout, in cast-iron cylinder barrels, bolted to two-piece two-bearing light-alloy crankcase. Bore and stroke 62mm by 62mm, 375cc (2·44in × 2·44in, 22·9cu.in). Light-alloy cylinder heads. Two overhead valves per cylinder, inclined to each other in part-spherical combustion chambers and operated by pushrods and rockers from camshaft mounted in the crankcase underneath the crankshaft. Single downdraught Solex carburettor. Power limited to 9bhp (DIN) at 3,500rpm. Maximum torque 17lb.ft at 1,800 rpm.

Transmission: Front-wheel-drive power pack. Horizontally opposed engine ahead of the front wheel line and four-speed all-synchromesh gearbox behind that line. Single-dry-plate clutch, gearbox and transaxle all in unit with engine. Engine drives gearbox by shaft over top of final drive, gearbox is all-indirect and output shaft is directly linked to spiral-bevel final drive unit. Central, remote-control gearchange, with lever protruding through centre of facia. Exposed, universally joined drive shafts to front wheels.

Chassis: Simple pressed, welded, and fabricated platform chassis, carrying all stresses, with rudimentary and very simple body shell welded to it. All-independent suspension, front by leading arms, and rear by trailing arms, interconnected by chassis-mounted coil springs under the centre floor. Inertia dampers, on all wheels, with cast weights and coil springs inside damper body. Rack-and-pinion steering. Four-wheel drum brakes, inboard at front. Bolt-on pressed steel disc wheels. 125 × 400mm Michelin tyres.

Dimensions: Wheelbase 7ft 9·3in (237cm), tracks (front and rear) 4ft 1·6in (126cm). Overall length 12ft 4·7in (378cm). Unladen weight 1,100lb (499kg).

History: Preliminary work began on Citroën's new 'peoples' car' at the end of the 1930s, and prototypes were built in the final form during the German occupation of France, but the 2CV was not actually announced until 1948. It was designed by M. Boulanger, also much credited with the 'traction avant' layout, and followed that car's philosophy of not aligning itself to any fashions. Designed specifically as a bridge between the horse-and-cart trade and the motor car business, the 2CV was meant to operate under all conditions of abuse, on and off the roads, and was deliberately underpowered to restrict the payload possibilities.

The front-drive power pack, with a simple but very strong air-cooled flat-twin engine, was the most complicated part of the car. The interconnected coil-spring suspension (both front and rear springs were housed in the same under-floor chamber and reacted against each other in certain wheel movement conditions) was simple but effective. The rest of the car was simplicity itself, with styling that owed much to French commercial vehicles (and the use of very simple steel pressings), instantly removable doors and seats, and roll-back canvas roofs and boot covers. Even the headlamps were adjustable for vertical alignment via a very simple driver-controlled linkage. Not even the 2CV, however, could resist the demands of progress. Over the years its engine size crept up — first to 425cc and finally to 602cc — as did the power, and even the standard of the fittings.

The 2CV was joined by the much more civilised but mechanically almost identical Ami 6 at the beginning of the 1960s, and by the different but similar Dyane later in that decade. The basic 2CV, however, refused to die, and the 1973/74 energy crisis gave it a boost which continues to this day.

Above and right: When introduced the Citroen 2CV looked extraordinary, and no amount of minor updating has made much difference. The 1959 example (above) retains the tiny round headlamps whose attitude could be adjusted from the driving seat, has the corrugated panel work which was a 2CV 'trade mark' for so long, and the familiar roll-back canvas roof. The modernised version from the 1970s (right) has smoothed-out panels and rectangular headlamps. Under the skin the air-cooled flat-twin engine, the front-wheel-drive, and the interconnected suspension carries on.

CITROEN DS/ID SERIES

Citroën DS and ID19, 21, and 23 family, built 1955 to 1975 (data for DS19)
Built by: S.A. André Citroën, France.
Engine: Four cylinders, in line, in three-bearing cast-iron cylinder block. Bore and stroke 78mm by 100mm, 1,911cc (3·07in × 3·94in, 116·6 cu.in). Detachable cylinder barrels, wet liners. Light-alloy cylinder head. Two overhead valves per cylinder, inclined in part-spherical combustion chamber, operated by pushrods and rockers from single side-mounted camshaft. Twin-choke, downdraught Weber carburettor. Maximum power 75bhp (gross) at 4,500rpm. Maximum torque 101lb.ft at 3,000rpm.
Transmission: Front-wheel-drive power pack. Engine longitudinally mounted behind line of front wheels, gearbox ahead of it. Single-dry-plate clutch and four-speed manual synchromesh gearbox (without synchromesh on first gear). Automatic hydraulic control of clutch and gear-change. Gear lever in facia behind steering wheel. Spiral-bevel final drive. Exposed, universally jointed drive shafts to front wheels.
Chassis: Pressed-steel unitary-construction body/chassis unit, of punt-type design, with detachable skin panels. Self-levelling independent suspension all round, with high-pressure hydro-pneumatic springs; leading arms and anti-roll bar at front, trailing arms at rear. Dampers incorporated in hydro-pneumatic suspension. Power-operated rack-and-pinion steering. Power-operated brakes, disc front (inboard) and drum rear. Pressed-steel disc wheels, 165—400mm front tyres and 155—400mm rear tyres. Four-door saloon bodywork by Citroën. Later models had a long-wheelbase five-door estate car option.
Dimensions: Wheelbase 10ft 3in (312cm),

track (front) 4ft 11in (150cm), track (rear) 4ft 3·2in (130cm). Overall length 15ft 9in (480cm). Unladen weight 2,500lb (1,134kg).

History: To replace their long running 'traction avant' models, Citroën were expected to produce something startling. Their DS19 model did not disappoint anyone. Styled for the 1960s, and engineered for even further ahead, it was technically very advanced, compared with any of the opposition.

The layout was much as before, with a front-drive power pack in which the engine was behind the transaxle, but everything else was new. Everything possible was power-assisted or power-operated. The all-independent suspension had high-pressure hydro-pneumatic units, automatically self-levelling according to load, and a driver's control allowed the car to be raised even further for crossing rough ground. A wheel could be changed by putting the suspension on 'high', inserting an axle stand where appropriate, then 'lowering' the suspension, which allowed the offending wheel to lift itself into the air. The car's shape was shark-like and very sleek, with a low drag coefficient. Even with an ageing engine (rather modified from the unit of the traction) the DS19 had a surprisingly high maximum speed and fuel economy possibilities. Although gears were shifted manually, the gear lever merely signalled the driver's intentions to a hydraulic mechanism which looked after clutch control and gear selectors. This was only the start. The DS19 was soon followed by the mechanically simpler ID19, and shortly by the long-wheelbase 'Safari' estate cars.

Over the years the car was made faster, better equipped, and even more sophisticated. Engines were enlarged in 1965 (and redesigned) to

2·1 litres, and again in 1972 to 2·3-litres. A four-headlamp layout with lamps connected to the steering (and swivelling with the front wheels) arrived in 1967 and a fuel-injected engine option in 1970 (along with a five-speed gearbox). A fully-automatic gearbox was available after 1971. The cars were finally deposed by the transverse-engined CX models in 1975.

CITROEN SM

SM coupé, built 1970 to 1975 (data for 1970 version)
Built by: Citroën S.A., France, and latterly by Automobiles Ligier, France.
Engine: Maserati-manufactured, six cylinders, in 90-degree vee formation, in four-bearing light-alloy cylinder block. Bore and stroke 87mm by 75mm, 2,670cc (3·42in × 2·95in, 163cu.in). Two aluminium cylinder heads. Two overhead valves per cylinder, inclined in part-spherical combustion chamber, operated by two overhead camshafts per cylinder bank, via inverted bucket tappets. Three twin-choke, downdraught Weber carburettors. Maximum power 170bhp (DIN) at 5,500rpm. Maximum torque 170lb.ft at 4,000rpm. Later models had Bosch fuel injection and 178bhp.
Transmission: Front-wheel-drive power pack. Engine behind front wheel centre line and gearbox ahead of it. Single-dry-plate clutch and five-speed all-synchromesh gearbox. Remote control, central gearchange. Hypoid-bevel final drive.

Exposed, universally jointed drive shafts to front wheels.
Chassis: Pressed-steel unitary-construction body/chassis unit. Self-levelling independent suspension all round, with high-pressure hydro-pneumatic springs; wishbone linkage at front, trailing arms at rear. Dampers incorporated in hydropneumatic suspension. Power-operated, variable-ratio rack-and-pinion steering. Power-operated brakes, all-round discs (inboard at front). 15in pressed-steel road wheels. 195/70VR15 tyres.
Three-door coupé coachwork by Citroën. No alternatives.
Dimensions: Wheelbase 9ft 8in (295cm), track (front) 5ft (152cm), track (rear) 4ft 4·2in (132cm). Overall length 16ft 0·6in (489cm). Unladen weight 3,200lb (1,451kg).
History: Citroën formed a liaison with Maserati at the end of the 1960s, and although it was disbanded in 1973 there was time for some joint work to be completed. The most exciting result,

without doubt, was the Citroën SM coupé — although Maserati also benefited from Citroën's expertise in their Bora/Merak series. The SM was unashamedly a very fast, very expensive, prestige Citroën — larger than the DS saloons, but with rather less passenger space. It used every DS technical feature and more, and was driven by a Maserati V6 engine. The engine itself was unusual in that it used a wide, 90-degree, angle between cylinder banks, which was because it was derived from Maserati's existing V8 unit.

Below and right: The eccentric Citroen SM coupe is perhaps the most complex of all modern cars. Front-wheel-drive, hydro-pneumatic springing and a powerful 2·7-litre vee-6 engine are no more than expected from this French concern, but in addition the full power steering is very direct, with variable ratio. In spite of its bulk, the SM has only two doors.

Left: When announced in 1955, the DS19 caused a sensation. Its layout was ultra-modern, its suspension unique, and its styling years ahead of its competition. Suspension height could be varied manually, and most mechanicals—brakes and gearchange— were powered. There was also the Safari.

The transaxle was by ZF, and was not fitted with Citroën hydraulic controls. The rack-and-pinion steering, completely power-operated was special in that it had a variable response ratio, to give easy parking without the usual accompaniment of vague straight-line feel. In the straight-ahead position, the steering felt very direct indeed.

Citroën never found another use for the splendid 2·7-litre V6 engine in production cars (although a few very special V6 DS saloons were made for VIPs). Maserati picked it up for their mid-engined Meraks, and Ligier for their limited-production GT cars. Fuel injection replaced the triple-carburettor installation in 1972, with a small power boost and better low-speed pick-up. Another option in France was the Borg-Warner automatic version, for which the engine was enlarged to a full 3-litres.

The SM was never meant to sell in large quantities and it was something of an embarrassment to Citroën production planners. In the last years of its life, therefore, final assembly was contracted out to Guy Ligier's little factory in Vichy, where the last SM was built in 1975. This, incidentally, was after the Citroën–Peugeot merger had been agreed, and the SM (as a loss maker) was in any case due to be dropped. Apart from the latest Rolls-Royces and the modern Mercedes-Benz executive cars, probably no more mechanically advanced car has ever been sold to the public. It was a car of which André Citroën, founder of the company, would have been proud.

CLEMENT-BAYARD 30

Clément-Bayard 30 of 1914
Built by: S.A. des Etablissements Clément-Bayard, France.
Engine: Four cylinders, in line, in three-bearing light-alloy block/crankcase. Bore and stroke 110mm by 180mm, 6,842cc (4·33in × 7·09in, 417·5cu.in). Fixed cylinder head. Two side valves per cylinder, operated by single camshaft mounted in side of crankcase. Single up-draught Zenith carburettor.
Transmission: Cone clutch in unit with engine. Shaft to separately mounted four-speed manual gearbox (without synchromesh). Remote-control right-hand gearchange. Open propeller shaft to straight-bevel 'live' rear axle.
Chassis: Separate pressed-steel chassis frame, with channel-section side members and pressed-steel cross members. Forged front axle beam. Front suspension by semi-elliptic leaf springs. Rear suspension by cantilever semi-elliptic leaf springs. No dampers. Worm-and-nut steering. Rear-wheel, cable-operated drum brakes. Radiator mounted behind engine, fixed to dashboard.
Dimensions: Wheelbase 12ft 0·9in (368cm), tracks (front and rear) 4ft 9·1in (145cm). Overall length 16ft 4·9in (500cm). Unladen weight (chassis only) 2,645lb (1,200kg).
History: Clément-Bayard cars were the creation of Adolphe Clément, a company promoter who had already involved himself in Gladiators, Clément-Gladiators, Cléments, Clément-Panhards and Clément-Stirlings before the first definitive car was built in 1903. The Bayard connection arose from the 16th-century saviour of the French town of Mezières, where Clément had a factory. The new cars were sold in Britain through the Talbot business in London (and therefore known as Clément-Talbots). Production was prolific, with cars from 7hp up to 30bhp made before World War I. A few very special cars raced — one taking third in the French GP of 1906. The 30hp four detailed is typical of the 1911–14 range. Before this period the cars had favoured chain drive, but shaft drive, a radiator behind the engine, and monobloc cylinder construction were all common to these cars. No less than twelve different models were being made in 1914, along with a great variety of coachwork. Clément, who added the Bayard suffix to his name before the end, retired in 1914, and the company was sold to the S.T.D. combine after the war.

Below: The last Clement-Bayard model was this 30hp machine—here seen in 1913 guise as a close-coupled tourer. In Britain they were sold by Talbot.

COLE AERO EIGHT

Eight-cylinder Cole cars, built from 1915 to 1925 (data for 1920 model)
Built by: Cole Motor Car Co., United States.
Engine: Eight cylinders, in 90-degree vee-formation, in three-bearing cast-iron block/crankcase; crankcase split vertically, with complete four-cylinder block and half crankcase in each piece. Bore and stroke 88·9mm by 114·3mm, 5,676cc (3·5in × 4·5in, 346cu.in). Two detachable cast-iron cylinder heads. Two side valves per cylinder, operated by tappets from single camshaft mounted in centre of engine 'vee'. Single side-draught Stromberg carburettor.
Transmission: Cone clutch and three-speed manual gearbox (without synchromesh), both in unit with front-mounted engine. Direct-acting central gearchange. Open propeller shaft to spiral-bevel 'live' rear axle.
Chassis: Separate pressed-steel chassis frame, with channel-section side members and tubular and pressed-steel cross bracing. Forged front axle beam. Front and rear suspension by semi-elliptic leaf springs. Friction-type Hartford dampers. Worm-type steering. Rear-wheel drum brakes, mechanically operated from foot or hand lever (one set of shoes internally expanding and one set externally contracting for each drum.) Fixed artillery-style wheels with detachable rims. 33 × 5in tyres.
Dimensions: Wheelbase 10ft 7in (322cm), tracks (front and rear) 4ft 8in (142cm). Unladen weight 3,585lb (1,626kg).
History: Cole was another of the various firms which set up shop in Indianapolis at the beginning of the century and made the North American industry such an exciting and varied business. For at least the first ten years of the company's life, Cole cars were conventional by American standards, but with the arrival of their V8 engine, provided by the Northway concern, they took a step out of the ordinary. For one thing, the V8 engine was still a production-car rarity in *any* country in the world (Cadillac, with their famous and original design, announced a V8 in the same year) and for another thing the details of the Cole design were interesting and unique. By normal standards of the day, a V8 would have a light-alloy crankcase with two cast-iron cylinder blocks; the Cole had a two-piece cast-iron combined block and crankcase, split vertically, but with crankshaft and camshaft bearings contained entirely in one casting. Cole also chose to specify fork and blade connecting rods, therefore idealising the stresses on the crankpins; the side-by-side conventional connecting rods followed later on other designs.
The Cole V8 car, called the 'Aero Eight', was a mixture of modern and old fashioned. To the end of its days the car had only rear-wheel brakes and it retained a cone clutch lined with leather. On the other hand the V8 was a modern advance and the company claimed to have pioneered 'balloon' tyres. Cole's problem was that it was always a small company, capable of making only a small number of cars. This meant that the price asked for an Aero Eight had to be high and this in turn meant that customers were few and far between. The car was marketed briefly in Britain after the end of World War I and in 1920 was price-listed at £1,350, at which very high price the spare wheel was an extra! Some of the Cole bodies of the early 1920s carried unusual styling details, such as octagonal rear quarter windows. The last Aero Eight, which had been the company's only product after 1917, was made in 1925 and it was not followed by any other new Cole car.

Right: Cole's Aero Eight was a limited production machine, built before and after the First World War. The vee-eight engine was unusual, with a two-piece block split vertically. Styling was typical of higher-class American cars, but there was much classic engineering under the skin. A cone clutch was used to the end, in 1925.

CLYNO 10.8HP

10·8hp Clynos, built from 1922 to 1929 (data for 1922 model)

Built by: Clyno Engineering Co. (1922) Ltd., Britain.

Engine: Coventry Climax manufactured. Four cylinders, in line, in two-bearing cast-iron block/crankcase. Bore and stroke 66mm by 100mm, 1,368cc (2·60in × 3·94in, 83·5cu.in). Detachable cast-iron cylinder head. Two side valves per cylinder, operated directly by camshaft mounted in side of cylinder block. Single up-draught Solex carburettor. Maximum power about 20bhp.

Transmission: Cone clutch in unit with front-mounted engine. Universally jointed shaft to separate three-speed manual gearbox (without synchromesh). Direct-acting gearchange. Propeller shaft, enclosed in torque tube, driving spiral-bevel 'live' rear axle, without differential. Gearbox pivoted on cross member of chassis.

Chassis: Separate pressed-steel chassis frame, with channel-section side members and tubular cross members. Tubular front axle beam. Front suspension by quarter-elliptic leaf springs. Rear suspension by trailing quarter-elliptic leaf springs. No dampers. Worm-and-nut steering. Rear-wheel drum brakes — one set worked by foot brake, the other by the hand brake. Bolt-on artillery-style wheels. 710 × 85 tyres.

Dimensions: Wheelbase 8ft 6in (259cm), tracks (front and rear) 3ft 10in (117cm). Overall length 11ft 4in (345cm). Unladen weight 1,500lb (680kg).

History: For a time in the 1920s, up to 1926, Clyno were the third-biggest British car makers, behind Morris and Austin, but by 1930 they were out of business. Their one single mistake was to try to match Morris's prices, penny for penny, and there was no way that they could match the profitability of his burgeoning operation. The Smith cousins started by building motor cycles in Wolverhampton and even ran to building aero-engines during World War I. A prototype car was designed in 1918 but shelved; it was then revived with a Coventry Climax engine for release in 1922. The 10·8hp model was work-a-day and nicely built, with the pivoting gearbox as a novelty. Only 623 cars were built in the first year, but sales then soared. Bigger models were added and sales peaked in 1926. The 10·8hp model was up-dated with roller main engine bearings and semi-elliptic front springs, along with the standardisation of four-wheel brakes. More than 11,000 examples were produced in 1926. Clyno opened a big new factory in 1928, then announced a cheap 'Eight' to counter Morris's new Minor. It failed and so did Clyno with it. Thoughtless marketing policies had killed off some good cars.

Below: Clyno's 10·8hp model made a strong bid to rival Morris and Austin, but could not match their low prices. The cars were made in Wolverhampton, and many thousands were built. Now the Clynos are nearly forgotten, and rare.

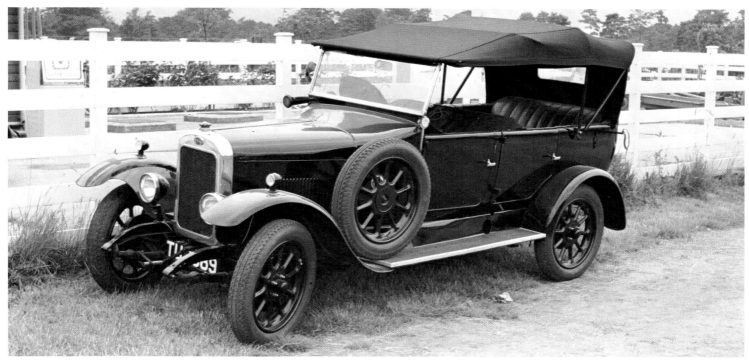

CORD L-29

L-29 front-wheel-drive car, built from 1929 to 1932 (data for 1929 model)

Built by: Auburn Automobile Co., United States.

Engine: Lycoming manufactured. Eight cylinders, in line, in cast-iron block, with five-bearing light-alloy crankcase. Bore and stroke 85·7mm by 114·3mm, 5,275cc (3·37in × 4·5in, 322cu.in). Detachable cast-iron cylinder head. Two side valves per cylinder, operated directly by single camshaft mounted in side of crankcase. Single twin-choke up-draught Schebler carburettor. Maximum power 125bhp (gross) at 3,600rpm.

Transmission: Single-dry-plate clutch and three-speed manual gearbox (without synchromesh), both in unit with front-mounted engine and final-drive unit. Engine mounted behind transmission and transmission behind line of front wheels. Remote-control facia-mounted gearchange. Direct connection to hypoid-bevel final drive. Exposed, universally jointed drive shafts to front wheels.

Chassis: Separate pressed-steel chassis frame, with channel-section side members, tubular and pressed cross-bracings and cruciform. De Dion front suspension, with tube ahead of transmission, by upper and lower forward-facing quarter-elliptic leaf springs. Rear suspension by forged axle beam and semi-elliptic leaf springs. Lever-arm dampers. Worm-and-roller steering. Four-wheel, hydraulically operated drum brakes. 18in centre-lock wire wheels. 7·00 × 18in tyres.

Dimensions: Wheelbase 11ft 5·5in (349cm), track (front) 4ft 10in (147cm), track (rear) 5ft (152·4cm). Overall length 17ft 1·5in (521cm).

Unladen weight 4,620lb (2,095kg).

History: Errett Lobban Cord took control of Auburn in 1924, when they were a stumbling little concern in Indiana, turned round their fortunes very rapidly and decided to launch a new car bearing his own name. By 1928 he controlled assets worth more than $11 million and as the United States was in the grip of an economic boom he decided to market a car with advanced engineering features. The Cord L-29, with front-wheel drive designed by racing genius Harry Miller, was the result. Cord's opinion was that the advanced engineering would sell his cars and he assumed that reliability would follow in the footsteps of his genius design. The L-29, however, was not all new — it's front-drive package involved taking an existing Lycoming straight-eight engine (Lycoming was another Cord-owned company) and a conventional three-speed gearbox, fixed directly to a hypoid-bevel differential. This, of course, had to be chassis mounted, so the L-29, perforce, had to have independent or De Dion suspension. Miller chose the latter system, as his racing cars were also built like that.

The L-29's advantage, because it had no conventional transmission, was that it could be built up to 10in (25cm) lower than its competitors, which gave it a very 'racy' look. Like some other American cars, however, the L-29 was launched, by accident, at exactly the wrong time. It first went into the showrooms at the end of 1929, the launch almost coinciding with the first panics on the Wall Street financial market. Priced at more than $3,000 in 1930 (although reduced, in a panic, to $2,395 a year later) it was too expensive to attract enough custom and was therefore a real marketing albatross around Auburn's and Cord's necks. Production staggered on until the middle of 1932, by which time 5,600 cars had been built. The car itself was excitingly engineered and always looked low and sleek, but it was still unproven when launched and soon had a bad name for reliability. It was, nevertheless, *the* first North American car to be quantity built with front-wheel drive. Cord was not daunted by this failure and tried again in 1934 with the Cord 810.

Right: Errett Lobban Cord's first and quite magnificent folly was the front-wheel-drive L-29 Cord, built for only three years in the depths of the North American depression. Cord had taken control of Auburn in 1924, and by 1928 had built it up strongly. He then wanted to sell an advanced car with radical engineering features. Racing car personality Harry Miller designed one, and the L-29 was the result. The in-line Lycoming straight-eight drove forward to the transmission through a conventional gearbox. Miller also chose to use De Dion front suspension (his racing cars used such a system), and the result was a very low car with wonderfully racy lines. A high price and the depression killed the car.

CORD MODELS 810 AND 812

810 and 812 models, built from 1935 to 1937 (data for supercharged Model 812)

Built by: Auburn Automobile Co., United States.

Engine: Lycoming-manufactured. Eight cylinder in 90-degree vee-formation, in three-bearing cast-iron block. Bore and stroke 88·9mm by 95·25mm, 4,729cc (3·5in × 3·75in, 288·6 cu.in). Two detachable cast-alloy cylinder heads. Two valves per cylinder, operated by rollers, with horizontally positioned intake and exhaust ports. Single down-draught carburettor, and Schwitzer-Cummins supercharger, driven by ring gear from centre bearing of camshaft. Maximum power 195bhp (gross) at 4,200rpm.

Transmission: Front-wheel-drive power pack. Engine behind line of front wheels, driving over differential to gearbox mounted ahead of front wheels. Single-dry-plate clutch, semi-automatic, in unit with engine. Four-speed synchromesh manual gearbox (no synchromesh on first gear). Gear selection by small lever and gate on right of steering column. Actual gearchanging by pressing clutch pedal, helped by electro-vacuum mechanism. Spiral-bevel differential. Exposed, ball-jointed drive shafts to driven front wheels.

Chassis: Front-wheel-drive power pack in the nose, mounted on front portion of chassis/body (including scuttle) and all bolted-up to unitary-construction pressed-steel body/chassis unit. Independent front suspension by trailing arms, and transverse leaf spring. 'Dead' rear axle beam, with half-elliptic leaf springs. Hydraulic lever

Below: Cord's splendidly individual Model 810/812 was a last desperate attempt to keep the Auburn-Duesenberg-Cord empire afloat. First conceived as a Duesenberg in 1933, it was dropped, then quickly re-vamped by Gordon Buehrig and his team in 1935 and announced in the same year. Under the skin was a Lycoming vee-8 engine and front-wheel-drive, but the styling was always the talking point. The later, 812, models could be had with blown engines. Left, the 1936 Model 810 Westchester sedan, and right, the 1937 Model 812 Sportsman, were just two variety of styles sold in two years.

arm dampers. Gemmer steering. Four-wheel drum brakes, hydraulically operated. 16in pressed-steel bolt-on disc wheels. 6·50 × 16in tyres.
Cord (Auburn manufactured) coachwork in various touring and saloon styles, with hidden headlamps; two or four doors.
Dimensions: Wheelbase 10ft 5in (317cm), track (front) 4ft 8in (142cm), track (rear) 5ft 1in (155cm). Overall length 16ft 3·5in (497cm). Unladen weight 3,650lb (1,655kg).
History: The L29 Cord having died in 1932, the front-wheel-drive car was first conceived by Auburn in 1933 as a Duesenberg, then discarded. It was revived, and hurriedly revamped by Gordon Buehrig and his engineers in 1935. Not

only was it remarkable for a very complex transmission, but for some really advanced and attractive styling, which put the Cord at least 10, if not 20, years ahead of its time.
Disappearing headlamps, front wing mounted, were a feature, as was the instantly recognisable horizontal fluting of nose and bonnet sides. The engine was specially designed for the Cord by Lycoming, also part of the Auburn combine. The transmission, perhaps of necessity because of its remoteness from the driver, was controlled by a combination of preselection, electro-vacuum operation and a tiny lever and gate on the steering column. The four-speed transmission had very much of an 'overdrive' top gear, although even third gear was high by comparison with almost

any other contemporary North American car.
Release in the autumn of 1935 was premature, and many sales were lost because production could not immediately begin. Indeed, the first 100 of these beautiful cars were more or less handbuilt, which hit the company's finances very hard. The model 810 was expensive and unusual-looking, which partly explains the reluctance of possible buyers, and even the addition of a very powerful super-charged Model 812 for 1937 could not save the day. The late-model 812s with their external flexible exhaust pipes were striking cars, but all in all only 2,320 810s and 812s were sold in two selling seasons. The last was built in August 1937, but happily a great proportion of these cars survive.

COTTIN-DESGOUTTES

Sans Secousse models, built from 1926 to 1931 (data for 1926 model)

Built by: Cottin et Desgouttes, France.

Engine: Four cylinders, in line, in cast-iron block, with five-bearing light-alloy crankcase. Bore and stroke 80mm by 130mm, 2,614cc (3·15in × 5·12in, 159·5cu.in). Detachable cast-iron cylinder head. Three overhead valves per cylinder (two inlet and one exhaust), operated by pushrods and rockers from single camshaft mounted in side of crankcase (rocker shafts across cylinder head and rockers aligned along the head). Single Zenith carburettor.

Transmission: Single-dry-plate clutch and four-speed manual gearbox (without synchro-mesh), both in unit with front-mounted engine. Open propeller shaft to chassis-mounted spiral-bevel final drive. Exposed, universally jointed drive shafts to rear wheels.

Chassis: Separate pressed-steel chassis frame, with box-section side members, built-up steel propeller-shaft tunnel and welded-on sheet-steel floor pan. Independent front suspension by transverse leaf spring and vertical sliding pillars. Independent rear suspension by four transverse leaf springs (two upper, two lower, effectively forming wishbones). Lever-arm hydraulic dampers. Worm-type steering. Four-wheel drum brakes, cable operated from foot-pedal, with rear brakes mounted inboard, on each side of final drive. Bolt-on wire wheels. Four-door saloon bodywork.

Dimensions: Wheelbase 13ft 4in (406cm), tracks (front and rear) 4ft 11in (150cm). Overall length 16ft 8in (508cm).

History: For many years after its inception in 1905, a Cottin-Desgouttes car was typically Lyonnais — fast, expensive, and beautifully made. The 12CV, which arrived in 1923, was unusual for its three-valve engine, with conventional pushrod overhead valves operated by rockers at 90 degrees to their accepted layout. The 3-litre GP version of the 12CV made its name in touring car races. The car which really startled the motoring business, however, was the Sans Secousse 12CV (which means, in English, 'without shock'). This car had an advanced chassis frame of immense wheelbase (13ft 4in, or 406cm), with independent front and rear suspensions by transverse leaf springs. Many features were startlingly modern, including the inboard rear brakes, and the well-stiffened chassis frame. Cottin-Desgouttes were faithful to this layout for some years, in spite of the disadvantages of size and weight, such that by 1931, when production ran out due to the depression, all the models in the range used this chassis with a six-cylinder version of the engine. It was a well-planned car, for which even the French were probably not ready. Its inventors must have looked at later (even post-war) models and known that their theories had been justified.

Below and right: Cottin-Desgouttes made attractive vintage cars for years, but it was the all-independent 'San Secousse' model of 1926 which excited the world. This had a very long wheelbase and inboard brakes. The 2·6-litre 'four' had to work hard as the chassis was solid and heavy.

CROSSLEY-BURNEY

Crossley-Burney rear-engined car, announced 1933

Built by: Crossley Motors Ltd., Britain.

Engine: Six cylinders, in line, in four-bearing cast-iron block. Bore and stroke 65mm by 100mm, 1,990cc (2·56in × 3·94in, 121·4cu.in). Detachable cast-iron cylinder head. Two overhead valves per cylinder, operated by pushrods and rockers from single camshaft positioned in side of cylinder block. Single up-draught Zenith carburettor. Maximum power 61bhp at 4,000rpm.

Transmission: No separate clutch. Four-speed preselector epicyclic gearbox and transaxle, both in unit with rear-mounted engine. Engine behind line of rear wheels, gearbox ahead of it. Drive over transaxle to gearbox, then back to spiral-bevel final-drive unit by shaft under gearbox. Exposed, universally jointed drive shafts to rear wheels.

Chassis: Separate pressed-steel chassis frame, with channel-section side members and pressed and tubular cross bracing. Independent front suspension by upper transverse leaf spring and tubular wishbones. Independent rear suspension by trailing arms and semi-elliptic leaf springs. Lever-arm hydraulic dampers. Cam and lever steering. Four-wheel, shaft-and-cable-operated drum brakes. Bolt on wire wheels.

Dimensions: Wheelbase 9ft 7in (292cm), track (front) 4ft 8in (142cm). Overall length 15ft 5in (470cm).

History: Crossley made many good but strictly orthodox cars in Manchester from 1904 to 1937 and even assembled a few Brescia-type Bugattis in 1921, but they are now well-known for an unsuccessful attempt to productionise Sir Dennistoun Burney's rear-engined 'streamline' car. These had been made in minute quantities from a factory in Maidenhead by the airship designer, but Crossley altered the design, shortened the wheelbase, and grafted one of their own 15·7hp six-cylinder engines and a Wilson-type preselector gearbox into the tail in place of the Beverley straight-eight favoured by Burney himself. The rear-engine layout was one problem, but Crossley also had to face learning about independent front and rear suspensions and the problems of cooling a rear engine with a front radiator. The car also turned out to be quite heavy, with a massive chassis — it even had the spare wheel in one of the doors — so performance as well as handling suffered. The price was £750, at which only about two dozen were built, but it was a very brave attempt to make an advanced design in the very conventional Britain of the 1930s. One only, at Britain's National Motor Museum, now survives.

Right and below: Crossley's brave but unsuccessful attempt to sell a rear-engined car, used Burney's layout. This 1934 model is all that remains.

CUNNINGHAM C-SERIES

Cunningham C-series sports cars, built from 1951 to 1955 (data for C4R of 1952)
Built by: B. S. Cunningham Co., United States.
Engine: Chrysler-manufactured. Eight cylinders, in 90-degree vee-formation, in five-bearing cast-iron block/crankcase. Bore and stroke 96·8mm by 92·1mm, 5,425cc (3·81in × 3·63in, 331cu.in). Two detachable cast-iron cylinder heads. Two overhead valves per cylinder, opposed to each other in part-spherical combustion chambers and operated by pushrods and long and short rockers from single camshaft mounted in centre of cylinder block 'vee'. Four downdraught single-choke Zenith carburetters. Maximum power 300bhp (gross) at 5,200rpm. Maximum torque 312lb.ft at 2,000rpm.
Transmission: Single-dry-plate clutch and five-speed synchromesh manual gearbox, both in unit with front-mounted engine. Open propeller shaft to hypoid-bevel 'live' rear axle. Direct-acting central gearchange.
Chassis: Separate tubular-steel chassis frame, with large-diameter tubular side members, small-diameter cross members and bracing, and built-on body framework supports. Front suspension independent by coil springs, wishbones and anti-roll bar. Rear suspension by coil springs and radius arms. Piston-type hydraulic dampers. Worm-and-roller steering. Four-wheel hydraulically operated, ventilated drum brakes. 16in centre-lock cast-alloy road wheels. 7·00 × 16in tyres.

Right: In the 1950s Briggs Cunningham financed the construction of a few fast road cars, and a handful of exciting racing sports cars. The C4Rs performed with distinction at Le Mans and in America, with Chrysler vee-8 engines. Only Ferrari and Jaguar beat them.

Two-seat open coachwork, intended for sports-racing purposes, and minimal weather protection.
Dimensions: Wheelbase 8ft 4in (254cm), tracks (front and rear) 4ft 6in (137cm). Overall length 12ft 11in (394cm). Unladen weight 2,410lb (1,093kg).
History: In 1950, Briggs Cunningham, millionaire American yachtsman and car collector, entered two Cadillacs for the Le Mans 24-hour race, one with the standard body and one with an ugly two-seater body. For 1951, he produced two special two-seater machines with tubular chassis frames and Chrysler engines. These were the C2R machines, which had de Dion rear suspension and Ferrari-style coachwork.

A year later came the C4Rs, refined and improved versions of these cars, which were offered for sale in limited numbers with a live

rear axle and coil spring suspension. One car finished fourth overall at Le Mans, averaging 88mph.

In between C2s and C4s was the C3, much more of a road car, with a Vignale-bodied coupé style by Michelotti. Very few C4Rs were sold, either for road or track use, but Cunningham himself persevered at Le Mans, with the improved C5s in 1953 (3rd) and C4Rs in 1954 (3rd and 5th).

The final car was the C6, with an Indy-type Offenhauser engine, but this was not as quick, nor as successful as earlier Cunninghams. The cars failed because, at that time, sports car design in Europe was well ahead of North American thinking, and the Cunningham's were not competitive with cars like the Ferraris or D-type Jaguars.

DAIMLER 4HP

4hp car, built from 1896 to 1903 (data for 1896 model)
Built by: Daimler Motoren-Gesellschaft, Germany, and by Daimler Motor Syndicate Ltd., Britain.
Engine: Two cylinders, in line, in cast-iron blocks, with two-bearing light-alloy crankcase. Bore and stroke 90mm by 120mm, 1,527cc (3·54in × 4·72in, 93·2cu.in). Fixed cast-iron cylinder heads. Two valves per cylinder: automatic (atmospheric) inlet valves, mounted overhead; side-mounted exhaust valves, operated by tappets from camshaft in side of crankcase. Spray-type carburettor. Max. power 4·5bhp.
Transmission: Clutch in unit with front-mounted engine and shaft to separate four-speed manual gearbox (without synchromesh), all mounted in chassis subframe. Straight-bevel differential in tail of gearbox. Countershaft from differential, with sprockets. Final drive to rear wheels by chain. Remote-control gear-change in passenger compartment, on dashboard.
Chassis: Chassis frame of wood with steel-plate reinforcements. Forged front axle beam. Front and rear suspension by full-elliptic leaf springs. No dampers. Tiller steering (wheel steering by 1900). Foot brake by band contracting round drum on gearbox counter-shaft. Hand brake operating bands on rear-wheel drum. Third, spoon, brake on tyres, hand operated. Fixed artillery-style wheels, smaller at front than back, with solid tyres. Choice of open coachwork.
History: Gottlieb Daimler was involved in internal combustion rengine research from the beginning of the 1880s and he built the world's first motor cycle in 1885 (which he never

Right: The very early Daimlers were historically important, but both crude and frail. Note the method of steering, the engine under the floor, the solid tyres, and the fragile chassis.

duplicated). His original car was built in 1886, having road trials in Cannstatt. Although Daimler soon became proprietary suppliers of engines, they did not make complete cars for some years. The company was set up in 1890, but Daimler left it for a while from 1893 to 1895. The first production Daimlers were built in 1896 and the Phönix (Panhard-like with its front engine) soon followed it. This 4hp twin-cylinder machine was also built in Coventry, under licence to one of Harry Lawson's companies. Ironically,

the last Daimler machine in its native Germany was built in 1902, but the British marque became one of *the* most famous of all. Like other pioneering designs, the original 4hp Daimler was startlingly crude, with almost ineffective brakes, very casual cooling (the radiator was out at the back, where it could get liberally plastered with filth) and tiller steering. In those days, too, the struggle was not to make a car go well, but to keep it going at all. The Daimlers did this far better than most.

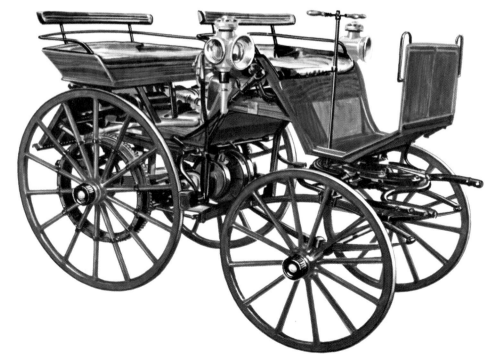

DAIMLER SLEEVE-VALVE MODELS

Sleeve-valve models, built from 1908 to 1934 (data for 1909 38hp car)
Built by: The Daimler Co. Ltd., Britain.
Engine: Four cylinders, in line, in two pairs of cast-iron blocks, with five-bearing light-alloy crankcase. Bore and stroke 124mm by 130mm, 6,280cc (4·88in × 5·12in, 383·2cu.in). Two detachable cast-iron cylinder heads. Two sleeve valves, in cast-iron, running concentrically between cylinder walls and pistons. Operation by connecting rods to operating shaft (equivalent of camshaft) mounted in side of crankcase, running at half engine speed. Single up-draught carburettor. Maximum power about 40bhp.
Transmission: Leather-cone clutch in unit with front mounted engine. Separate four-speed manual gearbox (without synchromesh). Remote-control right-hand gearchange. Open propeller shaft to straight-bevel 'live' rear axle. Lanchester-type worm-gear rear axle from 1910 onwards.
Chassis: Separate pressed-steel chassis frame, with channel-section side members and tubular and steel cross bracing. Forged front axle beam. Front and rear suspension by semi-elliptic leaf springs. Worm-and-nut steering. Rear drum brakes only, rod and cable operated. Centre-lock wire wheels. 920 × 120 tyres.
Dimensions: Wheelbase 10ft 6in (320cm), tracks (front and rear) 4ft 7in (139·7cm). Overall length 15ft 5in (470cm). Unladen weight (chassis only) 2,350lb (1,066kg).
History: By Edwardian times, Daimler had survived all manner of managerial and financial crises and were well-established in the top-class car business, numbering royalty among their customers. Their cars were robust and conventional, so it was a surprise when they announced in 1909 that they would soon be offering cars fitted with the new-fangled sleeve-valve engines. Charles Y. Knight, in the United States, had already demonstrated that his invention, which did way with noisy valve gear, was practical and efficient. Daimler, who needed refinement to keep abreast of Rolls-Royce and Lanchester, after much experiment (which included submitting engines to rigorous RAC testing) announced the sleeve-valve 15hp car in 1909. The sleeves, incidentally, were interposed between cylinder wall and piston, moved up and down and rotated relatively to each other, covering and uncovering inlet and exhaust ports at appropriate times. They worked well enough, although engine speeds were limited by the high inertia of the layout, and it became a characteristic of sleeve-valve units to proceed in slight hazes of blue (oil) smoke.

The first sleeve-valve four-cylinder Daimler was soon joined by six-cylinder derivatives and the company had turned over completely to such engines within a couple of years. From 1910/11 until the early 1930s a Daimler always had a sleeve-valve engine of the 'Silent Knight type' — in sizes varying from just over one litre to a mighty 9·4 litres. The only major change to the basic design was that much slimmer steel sleeves were eventually substituted for the original cast-iron items, which allowed engine capacity to be increased without boring out the cylinder block casting itself; these date from 1923. By the 1920s Daimler policy had settled right down, with the accent firmly on the supply of middle-class and upper-class transport. Even then there was a considerable degree of cross-fertilisation of parts. Bodies were made to very high standards by a variety of coachbuilders. Performance was never a priority until the Double-Six came along later in the 1920s.

Right: For more than a generation, sleeve-valve engines dominated Daimler thinking. The first was sold in 1909, the whole range was given over to Knight-engined cars by 1911, and the last was built in 1934. The rest of the cars' engineering was conservative and the bodies usually high and very stately. The sleeve-valve engines usually left behind them a haze of blue oil smoke as a 'trade mark', but were impressively quiet and refined. Daimler's radiator, with the well-known ribbed top tank, was a very efficient coolant as well as instantly recognisable. The model shown was a 16/20, built in 1931. By this time conventional poppet-valve engines were being developed, whose advantage was lower cost and easier servicing.

DAIMLER DOUBLE-SIX

Double-Six 50, 30, 40/50 and 30/40 models, built from 1926 to 1937 (data for 50)
Built by: Daimler Co. Ltd., Britain.
Engine: Twelve cylinders, in 60-degree vee-formation, based on seven-bearing light-alloy crankcase. Six cylinders per bank, in sets of three-cylinder cast-iron blocks. Bore and stroke 81·5mm by 114mm, 7,136cc (3·21in 4·49in, 435·4cu.in). Detachable cast-iron cylinder heads. Double sleeve-valve system, with sleeves, made from steel, oscillating inside each other and inside cylinders. Sleeve valves operated by chain-driven eccentric shafts. Two Daimler carburettors (one to each cylinder bank). Maximum power 150bhp (net) at 2,480rpm.
Transmission: Single-dry-plate clutch, in unit with engine, and separate four-speed manual gearbox (without synchromesh), with direct-acting central gearchange. Open propeller shaft to underslung worm-drive rear axle.
Chassis: Separate steel chassis frame. Channel-section side members with tubular and pressed cross bracing. Forged front axle beam. Front and rear suspension by half-elliptic leaf springs. Lever-type hydraulic dampers. Worm-and-sector steering. Four-wheel, rod-operated drum brakes, vacuum-servo assisted. Push-on handbrake. Centre-lock wire wheels. Tyres from 6·75 × 33in, depending on wheelbase and body style chosen. Coachwork by specialist builders; many styles and types.
Dimensions: Wheelbase 12ft 11·5in or 13ft 7in (365 or 414cm), tracks (front and rear) 4ft 9in or 5ft (145 or 152cm). Overall length, according to coachwork and wheelbase, from 18ft 7in (566cm). Unladen weight, according to coachwork, from 6,200lb (2,812kg).
History: Daimler's sleeve-valve engine tradition was well established before Laurence Pomeroy (senior) joined the company, but the six-cylinder cars were being left behind in the luxury field by Rolls-Royce, in spite of continual Royal patronage. Pomeroy therefore settled upon the inspired solution of providing a V12-engined Daimler motor car, while using many existing parts. His Double-Six (so named because of the layout, and because in many ways, such as carburation and ignition, it *was* a double-six) comprised, effectively, two sets of cylinder blocks and components from the six-cylinder 25/85 Daimler sleeve-valve engine, placed at 60 degrees to each other on a new light-alloy crankcase. This disposed of 7,136cc, and gave a splendid 150bhp power output and all the flexibility for which Daimler town carriages were famous. Each bank retained its own carburettor, water pump cooling and ignition system. Inlet manifolding was on the outside of the engines and exhaust manifolding neatly in the centre of the 'vee'.

The rest of the chassis, although vast and carefully detailed, was conventional. Coachwork, of course, was by specialist builders approved by Daimler themselves. A typical five-seat saloon of 1926 would cost about £2,500 — rather less than the princely sum of £2,800 or there-

Below: Startling and sleek but quite unlike a Daimler was the low chassis 1931 Double-Six by Corsica of London.

abouts asked for a handsome 40/50 Rolls-Royce.

To look after less affluent (relatively-speaking, that is) customers, the 50 was joined in 1928 by the 30, a similarly-conceived V12, but this time using two sets of 16/55 components and having a 3·7-litre capacity. The lowered-chassis specials, produced by Thomson and Taylor at Brooklands, duced by Thomson and Taylor at Brooklands, were striking sporting versions of the 50. In 1930, the two cars were redesigned to become 40/50 and 30/40 models respectively, with the important addition of the fluid flywheel and Wilson preselector gearbox which was to be standardised on all future Daimlers.

However, with the world depression intensifying, sales of the twelve-cylinder-engined Daimlers were understandably low, and the models were dropped in favour of poppet-valve straight-eight engined cars in 1934. In 1937, for a very brief period, a hybrid 'Double-Six' was sold — having 40/50 cylinder dimensions, but poppet-valve breathing arrangements.

Above: The special Corsica sports body on the Double-Six 50 had special chassis by Thomson and Taylor of Brooklands. The 7·1-litre engine produced about 150bhp in silence.

Below: This stately Double-Six limousine, with greater-than-normal headroom, could only be one of the Hooper-bodied Royal fleet. Radiators on King George V's cars were black.

DARRACQ 6.5HP

6·5hp model, built from 1901 to 1905 (data for 1901 model)
Built by: Société A. Darracq, France.
Engine: Single cylinder, in cast-iron block, vertically mounted, with cast-alloy crankcase. Engine capacity 785cc (47·9cu.in). Non-detachable cylinder head. Automatic (atmospheric) overhead inlet valve and side exhaust valve, operated by tappet from single cam in side of crankcase. Single spray-type carburettor. Maximum power about 6·5bhp.
Transmission: Cone clutch, in unit with front-mounted engine, and separate three-speed manual gearbox (without synchromesh). Remote-control gearchange, mounted on steering column. Open propeller shaft to straight-bevel 'live' rear axle.
Chassis: Separate tubular-steel chassis frame, with tubular side members and tubular cross bracing. Forged front axle beam. Front and rear suspension by semi-elliptic leaf springs. No dampers. Simple pivot-and-linkage steering. Mechanically operated band brake behind gearbox, with foot pedal. Hand lever operating band brake in rear axle. Fixed wire wheels. Four-seat open coachwork, or two/three seat to choice.
Dimensions: Weight, depending on coachwork, 780lb to 900lb (354kg to 408kg).

Right: Darracq's famous 6·5hp model was built from 1901 to 1905, on Panhard lines. For its day, it was advanced, with shaft drive. The chassis was of tubular steel, with conventional half-elliptic springs. The gearbox was under the floor, and the change lever on the steering column.

History: Alexandre Darracq was an engineer whose training lay in an arsenal, then in a sewing machine factory. His financial manoeuvrings led him to make bicycles, then to become involved with Adolphe Clément and later to take up a licence to manufacture the unsuccessful four-wheeler Bollée. Darracq's first own-design car was the handsome 6·5hp single-cylinder light car, laid out on the fashionable 'Panhard' lines This meant that it had already adopted the now-normal layout of a front engine, a gearbox under

the seats and shaft drive to the rear wheels. This, mind you, was at a time when final drive by chain was more normal. This car was intended for quantity production and was licence-built in Germany by Opel, but it was never sold in the numbers Darracq had hoped. Even so, it established his reputation in France, alongside those of Panhard, Peugeot and others, and a range of twin-cylinder and four-cylinder cars followed by 1903. An interesting footnote is that Darracq himself never learned to drive a car!

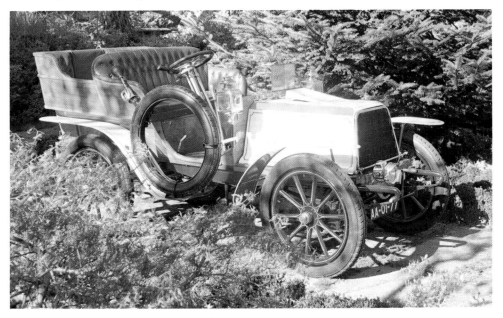

DATSUN 240Z

Datsun 240Z, 260Z and 280Z models, built from 1969 to date (data for 240Z)
Built by: Nissan Motor Co. Ltd., Japan.
Engine: Six cylinders, in line, in seven-bearing cast-iron block. Bore and stroke 83mm by 73·7mm, 2,393cc (3·27in × 2·90in, 146cu.in). Cast-iron cylinder head. Two overhead valves per cylinder, operated by single overhead camshaft. Twin side-draught constant-vacuum SU carburettors. Maximum power 151bhp (gross) at 5,600rpm. Maximum torque 146lb.ft at 4,400rpm.
Transmission: Single-dry-plate clutch and five-speed all-synchromesh manual gearbox, in unit with front-mounted engine. Central, remote-control gearchange. Open propeller shaft to chassis-mounted hypoid-bevel final drive. Exposed, universally jointed drive shafts to rear wheels.
Chassis: Unitary-construction pressed-steel body/chassis unit, in single fixed-head three-door body-style. Independent front suspension by MacPherson struts and an anti-roll bar. Independent rear suspension by MacPherson struts and lower wishbones. Rack-and-pinion steering. Servo-assisted brakes, front discs and rear drums. 14in pressed-steel disc wheels. 175 × 14in tyres.
Dimensions: Wheelbase 7ft 6·5in (230cm), track (front) 4ft 5·5in (136cm), track rear 4ft 5in (135cm). Overall length 13ft 7in (414cm). Unladen weight 2,300lb (1,043kg).
History: Datsun, like other Japanese car makers, have prospered mightily since 1945.

Right: Datsun's 240Z sports coupe family is a long-running success story. Still sold in huge numbers after eight years (and in 2·8-litre form in the USA) the Datsun is a he-man's car. The straight-six makes exciting noises and the performance is vivid. This is Tony Fall driving a Castrol-sponsored version on the 1972 RAC Rally.

With the accent firmly on export, they eventually developed a series of attractive sporting cars. The Datsun Fairlady, with its rigid back axle and MGB-like styling, was successful enough, but in 1969 Datsun's successor to it, the 240Z, was unveiled. It combined striking good looks (reminiscent, some say, of Jaguar's E-Type), with typical Japanese-car reliability, and good performance. In a way, in American eyes it effectively replaced the Austin-Healey 3000. Whereas the big Healey had been killed by USA legislation, the 240Z was designed to meet and beat the same rules.

It began to sell well at once, being sold as a

Nissan in some markets and as a Datsun in others. The factory launched it into a competition programme, and its successes included a win in the East African Safari in 1971. Later, in the modern idiom, its engine, which, incidentally was not at all special to the model, being shared with other Nissan/Datsun saloons, was enlarged, and other versions were developed. The 240Z became the 260Z, and subsequently — for the North American market in particular — the 280Z was developed. The closed two-seater coupé was later joined by a longer-wheelbase 2+2 version. Both cars are still in production in 1977, and have sold in huge numbers.

DE DIETRICH 24/28HP

24/28hp models, built from 1903 to 1905
Built by: De Dietrich et Cie., France.
Engine: Four cylinders, in line, in two pairs of cast-iron blocks with light-alloy water jackets and two-bearing light-alloy crankcase. Bore and stroke 114mm by 130mm, 5,308cc (4·49in × 5·12in, 324cu.in). Fixed cylinder head. Two overhead valves per cylinder, inlets in one line and exhausts in another, operated by pullrods and rockers from two camshafts mounted in crankcase. Single up-draught carburettor. Maximum power about 30bhp.
Transmission: Cone clutch in unit with front-mounted engine. Separate mid-positioned four-speed manual gearbox (without synchromesh). Remote-control right-hand gearchange. Final drive by chain, from sprockets on transmission cross shaft to sprockets at rear wheel hubs. Bevel differential inside rear of transmission case.
Chassis: Separate chassis frame, with wood/steel side members (steel applied as flitch plates) and tubular cross members. Forged front axle beam. Front and rear suspension by semi-elliptic leaf springs. No dampers. Worm-and-nut steering. Foot brake acting on drum mounted on sprocket cross shaft at side of transmission. Hand brake by brake bands on drums at rear wheels. Bolt-on artillery-style road wheels.
Dimensions: Wheelbase 7ft 8·3in (234·5cm), tracks (front and rear) 4ft (122cm). Overall length 11ft 0·3in (336cm).
History: This manufacturer of railway rolling

stock first built cars in 1897 which were licence-built Bollees. From 1902 De Dietrich began to build more conventionally laid out machines, with water-cooled four-cylinder engines of Turcat-Méry design. In the same year he employed the 19-year-old Ettore Bugatti to design the well-known 24/28 De Dietrich. This car was similar in layout to the Turcat-Mérys, but had a new type of engine where the valves were all overhead and the cylinder head was integral with the block (always a Bugatti hall-

mark). Valve operation was by pullrods rather than by pushrods. The transmission layout — a cone clutch, a massive separate gearbox, cross-shaft final drive and chain drive by sprocket to the back wheels, was absolutely typical of the period, and it needed Renault and other influences to convince the firm they should adopt shaft drive later. Bugatti left De Dietrich in 1904 and a year later the cars were renamed Lorraine-Dietrichs to emphasise their French ancestry. The last Lorraine car of all was built in 1934.

Right: Even in stripped 1903 racing guise, the De Dietrich looks massive and impressive. The car was designed by a youthful Ettore Bugatti.

DE DION BOUTON 'SINGLE CYLINDER'

De Dion Boutons, 3½ to 12hp, built from 1900 to 1913 (data for 1900 3½hp)
Built by: De Dion, Bouton et Cie., France.
Engine: Single cylinder, vertically mounted in chassis, water-cooled, with cast-iron cylinder block. Bore and stroke 80mm by 80mm, 402cc (3·15in × 3·15in, 24·5cu.in). Two valves. Automatic (atmospheric) inlet valve, inverted over camshaft-operated side valve, mounted below it. Splash lubrication. Replenishment through steel measuring cup needed every 20 miles. Single De Dion carburettor. About 3·5bhp at 1,500rpm.
Transmission: Two-speed constant-mesh gearbox, in unit with engine, engaged by expanding clutches, controlled from steering column. No reverse gear as standard, but epicyclic reverse train optional. Spur gear drive to differential carrier, mounted on chassis. Exposed, universally jointed drive shafts.
Chassis: Tubular chassis frame, separate from choice of bodies. Tubular front axle beam. Front suspension by half-elliptic leaf springs themselves suspended at their trailing shackles by a transverse leaf spring. Rear suspension by three-quarter elliptic leaf springs, patent De Dion axle with chassis-mounted differential and tube connecting wheels running behind the differential/final drive housing. No dampers. Brakes (early models) operated by foot pedal contracting shoes on to the transmission. Later, handbrake on steering column operated shoes on rear wheel drums. 700—80mm tyres.
Dimensions: Wheelbase 5ft 1·5in (156cm), tracks front and rear 3ft 8in (112cm). Overall length 7ft 8in (234cm).
History: Comte Albert de Dion and Messrs Trepardoux and Bouton began building light steam-powered pleasure carriages in the 1880s. Eventually they became fascinated by the Daimler experiments and Bouton designed his first petrol engine in 1893. Trepardoux, for his part, believed only in steam and left in a huff. Single-cylinder petrol-engined tricycles went on sale in 1895, and logic made it certain that small 'voiturette'

four-wheelers would follow — which they did in 1900.
De Dion engines were of the 'high-speed' variety — 1,500rpm being normal compared with the 500rpm of the Benz — but more significant was the advanced chassis design. The engine/transmission units were rear-mounted at first, fixed up to the chassis, and drove the rear wheels through exposed drive shafts; the wheels were connected by a beam. Thus the world-famous De Dion suspension was born.
The 3½hp model was first, but was rapidly supplemented and supplanted by other 'singles' of up to 12hp, the last being built in 1913.

'Fashion' shortly took hold of De Dion and dummy bonnets were followed, in 1904, by the engines becoming front-mounted in what we now call the 'conventional' manner.
Early transmissions were splendidly detailed, with constant-mesh gears being — literally — clutched to their shafts by expanding friction clutches. Steering, at first, was by hand lever, but a wheel followed in 1904.

Below: One of the most famous and most numerous of all veteran cars—the 3½hp De Dion Bouton. This is a 1903 model.

DELAGE SERIES D1 AND GRAND PRIX CARS

D1 models, all forms, built from 1923 to 1928 (data for 1928 model)

Built by: Automobiles Delage, France.

Engine: Four cylinders, in line, in cast-iron cylinder block with five-bearing light-alloy crankcase. Bore and stroke 75mm by 120mm, 2,121cc (2·95in × 4·72in, 129·4cu.in). Detachable cast-iron cylinder head. Two overhead valves per cylinder, operated by pushrods and rockers from single camshaft mounted in side of crankcase. Single up-draught Zenith carburettor. Maximum power 38bhp (gross) at 2,400rpm.

Transmission: Multi-dry-plate clutch and four-speed manual gearbox (without synchromesh), both in unit with front-mounted engine. Direct-acting central gearchange. Open propeller shaft to spiral-bevel 'live' rear axle.

Chassis: Separate pressed-steel chassis frame, with channel-section side members and tubular and pressed cross bracing. Forged front axle beam. Front and rear suspension by semi-elliptic leaf springs. Worm-and-nut steering. Four-wheel, shaft-and-cable operated drum brakes. Centre-lock wire wheels. 820 × 120mm tyres. Open touring, sporting or saloon car coachwork to choice.

Dimensions: Wheelbase 10ft 6in (320cm), tracks (front and rear) 4ft 5in (135cm). Overall length 13ft 10in (422cm). Unladen weight 2,100lb (952kg).

History: The first Delages were runabouts with conventional shaft drive and a single cylinder 6½-horsepower engine supplied by De Dion. Delage soon became interested in motor sport and second place in the French Coupes des Voiturettes in 1906 was followed by an outright win in 1908. With the racing 'bug' well and truly established, he was to be building Grand Prix cars even before World War I, and all-conquering machines in the 1920s. By then he had engaged the noted designer Lory to design first an impressive 2-litre V12 engine and later a very successful 1½-litre straight eight. His cars also held the Land Speed Record for a short time.

At the beginning of the 1920s there were big six-cylinder Delages, but the company's mainstay — neither as visually exciting, not as fast, as the luxury cars or the racing cars — was the D1 series. This car was laid out on more practical and more simple lines, but it was not made spindly or weak in the process. Indeed, a car built around the D1's frame was used in hill-climbs and sprints with nothing less than a 5·1-litre Type CO engine! The D1, as announced, was a gentle and reliable four-cylinder car, with a 2·1:litre engine and such mechanical niceties as overhead valves (side-valve layouts were still 'conventional' for cheaper machines), a four-speed gearbox and four-wheel brakes. Cruising speed might have been no more than 50mph and maximum speed between 65 and 70mph, but the cars exhibited impeccable handling, great reliability and of course used the noble radiator design which classed them as relatives (even if they were considerably cheaper) of the luxurious 'sixes', and even of the racing Delages.

Delage was quite unable to leave a production car alone if it was not sporting enough for him, so the D1S of 1924/25 evolved. The 'S' was for Sporting ('Sportif' in French) and the cars, built near Paris, backed up this title to some extent. They were given a much shorter wheelbase (9ft 9in in place of 10ft 6in), which did wonders for the handling and the weight, centre-lock 'Rudge' wire wheels, different gearbox ratios, bigger valves and an altered camshaft for the engine and a narrow and distinctive radiator. That was still not enough for Delage, however. Next along, in 1925, was the D1SS model, with the SS in this case denoting Super Sports. This had all the D1S features, with a lowered and lightened chassis, close-ratio gears, from 1926, and other details. Even so, a look at production figures shows that the basic D1 was much the most popular, with more than 9,000 sold in five years, whereas only 983 D1S/D1SS cars were built over the same period. There were other variants too — the D1C being a 'high-chassis'

device intended for 'Colonial' conditions (442 sold) — and between 1926 and 1929 there were the DM/DMS/DMN cars, all of which were based on D1 engineering and fitted with six-cylinder 3·2-litre engines, very closely related to the four used in the D1s. The D1's engine was eminently tunable, as the 50bhp boasted by the D1SS proved, and if it had not been for Delage's predilection for ever-larger and more luxurious machines, sporting or ceremonial, that pedigree would have served the French company well into the 1930s, perhaps even ensuring survival.

Above and top right: Mainstay of the Delage range in the 1920s was the versatile D1 series. The original D1 was a gentle little 2·1-litre touring car, but successive D1S and D1SS types were fiercer and more sporting. Logically enough the first 'S' was for Sports, and the second 'S' for Super. The D1SS is the car most people admire —and (above) examples are still raced in vintage events. Top right: The 1924 D1SS Tourer was an impressive machine.

THE DELAGE GRAND PRIX CARS — 1926/27

In the 1920s Albert Lory designed two wonderfully complex and successful racing Delages. The vee-12 cars of 1923/25 were a miracle of effective complication — by 1925 they were developing 195bhp at 7,000rpm, in supercharged form from two litres. The next series, built especially for the short-lived 1½-litre 'formula', had simpler, but still very powerful 1,488cc straight-eight engines. The first chassis frames were too flexible, and road-holding was not a strong point, and although the team won the 1926 British GP at Brooklands, and took second place at San Sebastian, they had one glaring fault — the hot exhaust pipe was carried past the driver's elbow and effectively 'cooked' him during a long race. For 1927 the engines were re-designed, with the exhaust system on the left, and in this guise Robert Benoist won five major events that year. With twin blowers and two Zenith carburettors, the engines produced a phenomenal 170bhp at 7,000rpm — the best yet achieved in terms of specific output. There were four of these cars, one of which was bought, developed and raced with great success by Dick Seaman in 1936. Even in the 1940s the engines were used in other racing cars.

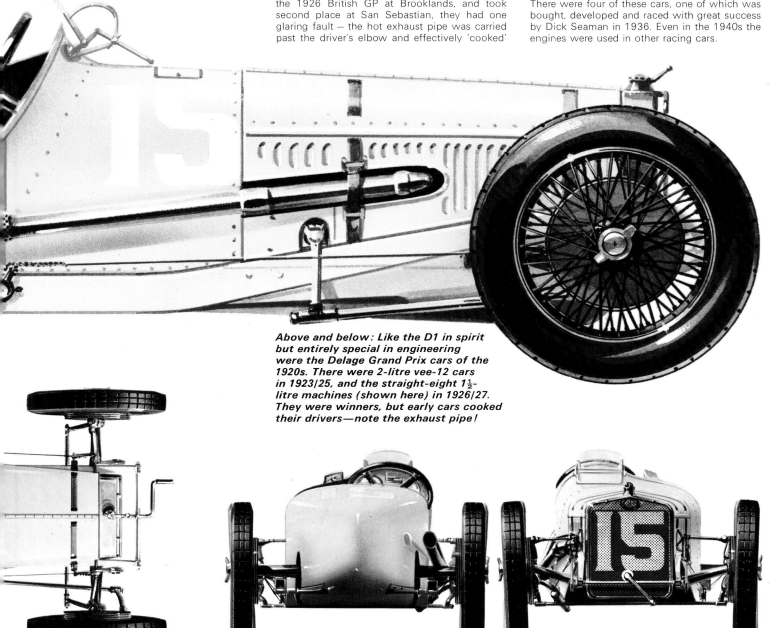

Above and below: Like the D1 in spirit but entirely special in engineering were the Delage Grand Prix cars of the 1920s. There were 2-litre vee-12 cars in 1923/25, and the straight-eight 1½-litre machines (shown here) in 1926/27. They were winners, but early cars cooked their drivers—note the exhaust pipe!

DELAGE SERIES D8

D8 models, built from 1930 to 1935 (data for original 1930 model)

Built by: Automobiles Delage, France.

Engine: Eight cylinders, in line, in cast-iron block, bolted to five-bearing cast-alloy crankcase. Bore and stroke 77mm by 109mm, 4,050cc (3·03in × 4·29in, 247·1cu.in). Detachable cast-iron cylinder head. Two overhead valves per cylinder, operated by pushrods and rockers from single camshaft mounted in side of crankcase. Single Smith Barraquand five-jet carburettor. Maximum power 120bhp at 4,000rpm.

Transmission: Single-dry-plate clutch and four-speed manual gearbox (without synchromesh), both in unit with front-mounted engine. Direct-acting central gearchange. Open propeller shaft to spiral-bevel 'live' rear axle.

Chassis: Separate pressed-steel chassis frame, with channel-section side members and pressed and tubular cross bracing. Forged front axle beam. Front suspension by half-elliptic leaf springs (long torque rods added on later high-power models). Rear suspension by half-elliptic leaf springs. Friction type or hydraulic dampers. Four-wheel, shaft and cable-operated drum brakes, with assistance from Clayton Dewandre vacuum servo mounted to side of gearbox. 18in steel disc wheels. 7·00 × 18in tyres.
Coachwork to choice — two-door and four-door saloons, two-door coupés and open cars, usually by Figoni and Falaschi.

Dimensions: Wheelbase 10ft 10in or 11ft 11in (330cm to 363cm), tracks (front and rear) 4ft 8in (142cm). Overall length depending on body, from 16ft (488cm). Unladen weight, from 4,400lb (1,995kg).

History: If the Delage D1s were the company's mainstay in the last half of the 1920s, and the Grand Prix cars the most beautifully engineered, there is little doubt that the eight-cylinder D8 models were the most magnificent of all Delage machines. From 1930 to 1935 (when Delage sold out to their deadly rivals, Delahaye), the D8 series in all its glory was one of the most desirable high-performance cars being built in France, or perhaps in the whole of Europe. History has now blurred the originator of that famous aphorism: 'One drives, of course, an Alfa Romeo, one is driven in a Rolls, but one gives only a Delage to one's favourite mistress'.

The D8 was a very glamorous car, and it sold well to customers who wanted their friends and business acquaintances to know that they were affluent. The 1930s, for those millionaires whose fortunes were not decimated in the Depression, were halcyon days and motoring conditions, particularly in Europe, were ideal. There were still not too many cars on the roads and the high-performance of a Delage could be used repeatedly.

The D8's chassis, at first, was relatively conventional, with half-elliptic springing all round and cable-controlled brakes, but the all-new eight-cylinder engine combined the best of vintage engineering with a thoroughly up-to-date power output and an ability to turn over fast. Delage's radiator, of course, was very imposing and reminded many people of a Hispano-Suiza (which pleased Louis Delage very much, even though his design had been maturing for an equally long time) and the coachwork which was added to that imposing chassis and prow was never modest and never undramatic.

The original design was soon followed by more sporting variants like the D8 Grand Sport. Front axle location on all D8s was improved with long radius arms to isolate braking torque and to improve steering stability at high speeds. The Grand Sport was not quite a 100mph car, due to the bluff nose and large frontal area, but it had flashing acceleration by the standards of the day and got by on a fuel consumption of about 14mpg, but such would be of no interest to the average D8's owner. Delage himself still hankered after a motor sporting involvement, and sent a special-bodied D8 Grand Sport to attack long-distance records at Montlhéry, where the car achieved nearly 110mph for 24 hours.

Between 1932 and 1935, further D8 improvements were made and the D8S and D8SS models were introduced. These models had a chassis frame dropped by more than three inches, an engine increased in power output from 120 to 145bhp and raised overall gearing. The D8SS also was offered with a shortened, 10ft 2in (310cm), wheelbase, but these were extremely

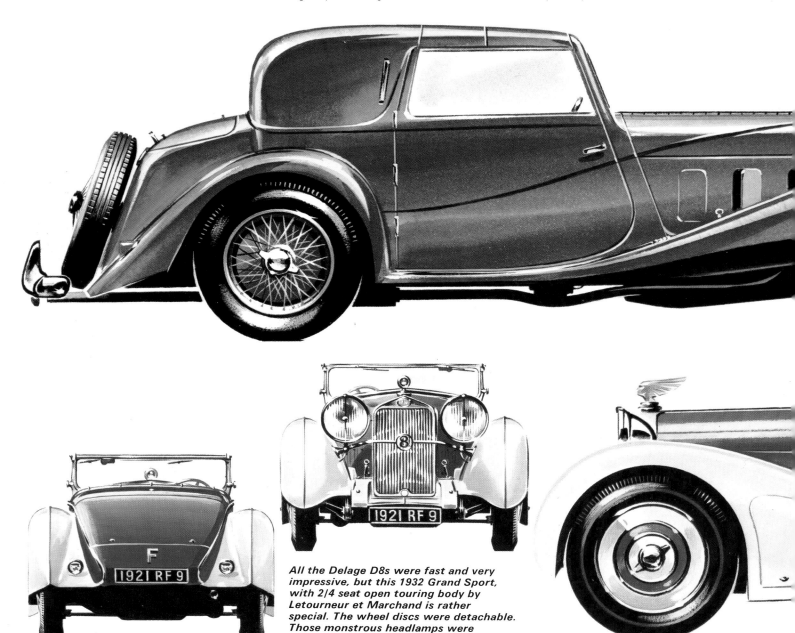

All the Delage D8s were fast and very impressive, but this 1932 Grand Sport, with 2/4 seat open touring body by Letourneur et Marchand is rather special. The wheel discs were detachable. Those monstrous headlamps were powerful, to match the 100mph speeds.

rare. Only two-seater bodies could be fitted to this chassis and the top speed was now well over 100mph. Early D8s had grouped chassis lubrication points, but the D8S and SS cars were endowed with a Rolls-Royce type of centralised chassis lubrication system. Centre-lock wire wheels were standardised, whereas the original D8 had been given steel disc wheels. It was once said that to introduce an eight-cylinder engine in Depression or post-Depression years was a sure guarantee of eventual commercial disaster and in Delage's case there was some truth in the saying.

Although the D8 was a splendid car, well-engineered, often beautifully styled and rather 'sexy' in the modern idiom, it was always an expensive car and sales were never high. Louis Delage himself was reluctant to change the face of his company to suit it more closely to economic conditions and he soon quarrelled with his directors. He therefore left the company that bore his name in 1935 and the firm shortly merged with Delahaye. There had been companion four-cylinder and small six-cylinder and eight-cylinder Delages for some years. By 1935 the cars had acquired synchromesh gears and hydraulic brakes, along with transverse-leaf independent front suspension, but only the D8 120 (a Delahaye creation), with differently dimensioned engine, inherited these, along with the Cotal electro-magnetic gearbox. This, the last of the straight-eight 'Delages', died with the outbreak of war in 1939.

Above: This is an early D8, a 1930 D8C coupe. Hidden behind the upright radiator is a straight-eight engine. Delage supplied most D8s to coach-builders for special treatment.

Left and right: Fastest of all the Delages were the D8SS models, with dropped frames and 145bhp 4-litre engines. This 1933 Sedanca had a British body style by Gurney Nutting.

DELAHAYE TYPE 135 SPORTS/SALOON

Type 135 models, built from 1935 to 1950 (data for 1935 model)

Built by: Automobiles Delahaye, France.

Engine: Six cylinders, in line, in four-bearing cast-iron cylinder block. Bore and stroke 80mm by 107mm, 3,237cc (3·15in × 4·21in, 197·5cu.in); competition model available with engine of 84mm by 107mm, 3,557cc (3·31in × 4·21in, 217cu.in). Detachable cast-iron cylinder head. Two overhead valves per cylinder, operated by pushrods and rockers from single side-mounted camshaft. Three downdraught Solex carburettors. Power output 130bhp at 3,850rpm (Superlux and Coupe des Alpes models), or 160bhp at 4,200rpm (Competition).

Transmission: Single-dry-plate clutch and four-speed synchromesh manual gearbox (no synchromesh on first gear), both in unit with front-mounted engine. Optional Cotal electro-magnetic gearbox. Open propeller shaft to spiral-bevel 'live' rear axle.

Chassis: Seperate pressed-steel chassis frame, with box-section side members and pressed and tubular cross bracing. Independent front suspension by transverse leaf springs and wishbones. Rear suspension by half-elliptic leaf springs. Hydraulic piston-type dampers. Four-wheel drum brakes, with Bendix mechanical servo. Centre-lock wire wheels and 6·00 × 17in tyres. Variety of coachwork: open sports, touring or saloon.

Dimensions: Wheelbase 9ft 8in (295cm), track (front) 4ft 7in (140cm), track (rear) 4ft 10in (147cm). Overall length 15ft (457cm). Unladen weight, depending on coachwork, from 2,750lb (1,247kg).

History: The origins of Delahaye lie in a company set up as long ago as 1845 to produce brick-making machinery. One of the descendants of the founders, Emile Delahaye, was at first a railway engineer, who designed rolling stock for French and Belgian railroads, but he produced his first car, of German Daimler type, in 1895, and two years later he moved his company from Tours to Paris, settling down to a variety of engineering projects.

The first shaft-driven cars arrived in 1907 and a V6 project (remarkably early in the history of the motor car) in 1912. During World War I, the company produced a great variety of items for the war effort, including vast quantities of rifles, stationary engines, gun parts and aircraft components. After the war, the company settled down to build dull and dependable cars, usually of rather backward design.

It was necessary to modernise the car line in a big way and, with the current range selling rather badly, the new design was first shown in 1933 at the Paris Show. Not only did it have a light and modern chassis layout, with independent front suspension, but there was a choice of a 3·3-litre, six-cylinder engine or a related 2·1-litre 'four', backed by the Cotal electro-magnetic gearbox or a synchromesh change to choice. The short cut was made possible without enormous investment because these engines were directly developed from units already in production for the company's commercial vehicles. Not only this, but for the first time in years, the Delahaye car had coachwork with distinct eye-appeal.

The larger six-cylinder car, effectively, was the prototype of the famous '135' series which was to serve Delahaye so well until the end of the 1940s. This design would probably not have done the job on its own, but this is uncertain because, in 1935, Delahaye took over the financially ailing Delage concern, where there was already an established clientele. Delage's elegance was therefore handed on to Delahaye,

Above and below: Different themes on the same Delahaye Type 135 chassis. The stark sports car was developed to race—Arthur Dobson winning the celebrated Brooklands 'Fastest Road Car' event in 1939. The drop head (below) was a fast road version.

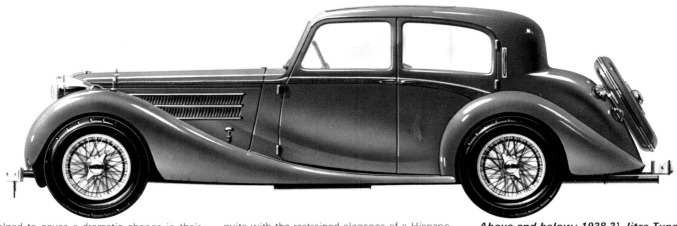

and helped to cause a dramatic change in their fortunes. A Superluxe six-cylinder car soon went to Monthléry to take 18 world and international class records, and when the same car later won an Alpine Coupe in the rally of that name, the Coupe des Alpes variant was born.

More important, though, in 1936, was the 'Competition' Type 135, with its enlarged 3½-litre engine. This car had a rather stark two-seater open body, with cycle-type wings, and a power output of no less than 160bhp (which was already up to Jaguar XK120 standards of more than ten years later). In the French GP of that year, a sports car race, the new cars finished 2nd, 3rd, 4th and 5th behind the winning Bugatti. A 3·2-litre car had already finished 5th at Le Mans in 1935, and one of the cars won the Monte Carlo Rally in 1937. In 1938, however, came the crowning glory of outright victory at Le Mans in the 24-hour race, which completely set the seal on the worth of the Type 135. By comparison with Delage, too, Delahaye was very much the dominant part of the business and they introduced a V12-engined car for competition use in France, which produced no less than 250bhp.

The Type 135 was not, however, solely a competition car. Many were supplied with lusciously appointed coachwork, perhaps not quite with the restrained elegance of a Hispano-Suiza or a Rolls-Royce, but certainly fit to be used (as they often were) in the smart areas of Paris and on the Riviera. They usually looked, as they were, very fast, and always seemed to offer a great deal of comfort and refinement. When the six-cylinder engine's lorry origins are considered, this is remarkable. The chassis and roadholding were advanced, especially by previous Delahaye standards and especially when compared with many of the expensive competitive limousines. The car went out of production after France joined the fighting in 1939, but after concentrating on truck production during the war (at the behest of the Germans) the company came back in 1946 with up-dated Type 135s. They were now even more expensive, relatively speaking, than before, and the market for such cars in a post-war France was small.

The Type 175S model was introduced in 1948 (with a larger seven-bearing, 4½-litre engine); the chassis included De Dion rear suspension. This car was nevertheless dropped in 1951 in favour of the Type 235, which was effectively a 1938-type 135 chassis with an up-rated, 152bhp, engine and more modern Charbonneux-styled coachwork. Delahaye were taken over by Hotchkiss in 1954, after which car production ceased in favour of trucks.

Above and below: 1938 3½-litre Type 135M Delahaye, with Carlton Carriage Co. saloon body, reminiscent in some ways of the late-1930s SS-Jaguars.

DELAUNAY-BELLEVILLE 'SIXES'

Type H models, built from 1908 to 1910, and Type HB, built from 1911 to 1914 (data for Type HB)

Built by: S.A. des Automobiles Delaunay–Belleville, France.

Engine: Six cylinders, in line, on three-bearing light-alloy crankcase, topped by two pairs of three-cylinder cast-iron blocks. Bore and stroke 85mm by 130mm, 4,426cc (3·35in × 5·12in, 270cu.in). Fixed cylinder heads. Two side valves per cylinder, directly operated from single camshaft mounted in side of crankcase. Single Delaunay–Belleville carburettor. Rated at 15–20CV French taxation class. Actual power output about 30bhp.

Transmission: Leather-cone clutch attached to engine. Separate four-speed manual gearbox (without synchromesh), with remote-control right-hand gearchange. Propeller shaft with spring buffers, to relieve torque reaction, and straight-bevel 'live' rear axle.

Chassis: Separate pressed-steel chassis frame, with channel-section side members, channel and tubular cross bracing. Forged front axle beam. Front suspension by half-elliptic leaf springs. Rear suspension by half-elliptic leaf springs, along with transverse 'helper' leaf spring. Worm-and-nut steering. Footbrake acting on transmission drum behind gearbox. Handbrake acting on drums fixed to rear wheels. Fixed artillery-style wooden wheels (detachable rims from 1913). 880×120mm tyres.

Dimensions: Wheelbase 10ft 6in (320cm), tracks (front and rear) 4ft 7·5in (141cm). Overall length, depending on coachwork, from 14ft 10in (452cm). Unladen weight (chassis only) 2,000lb (907kg).

History: Delaunay–Belleville made their first cars in 1904 and soon developed them into exclusive landaulettes and limousines, intended for the carriage trade and for chauffeur-driven transport. Like most other makers of the period, they started by building four-cylinder engines, but as the multi-cylinder craze spread across Europe they were not slow to join in that particular race. In many ways, Delaunay–Belleville had similar fortunes to those of Napier, although their cars were never as sporting; they soldiered on in production until 1950, but towards the end they were merely building tiny numbers of 1930s designs suitably updated.

The very first six-cylinder car from Delaunay–Belleville at St Denis, near Paris, was an 8-litre monster, with separate cylinders, but at least it had a seven-bearing crankshaft and simple 'L-head' valve gear arrangements. It was also chain-driven — another Edwardian 'standard' which was shortly to go out of fashion. All this was in 1908, by which time the Delaunay–Belleville marque was beginning to be talked of as the finest car in France, if not in the whole of Europe.

By 1909 there were no fewer than five six-cylinder models in the line-up, of which the mainstay engine was the H-series. This was built right up to the outbreak of war in 1914, as the H (or, as restrospectively known, the HA) until 1910 and the HB thereafter. Like the British Napier or Rolls-Royce 'sixes', with which there were certain similarities of basic layout, it had its cylinder. blocks cast in groups — in this case in two groups of three cylinders each. The French car, however, did not trust the properties of existing cylinder head gaskets, and used integrally-cast cylinder heads.

Valve gear, as with the pioneering Model-C 'six', used a simple 'L-head' layout, which meant that valves had to be withdrawn through detachable compression caps in the fixed cylinder head for attention. Surprisingly enough, the crankshaft was provided with only three main bearings, even less than a normally expected four-bearing layout, which indicates how understressed and slow-revving the unit was. The rest of the car, mechanically, was conventional enough, with a leather-cone clutch and a massive separate gearbox with the usual right-hand change. Delaunay–Belleville, after all, were offering comfort, reliability, and dignified grace, with the accent on smooth motoring in the finest possible

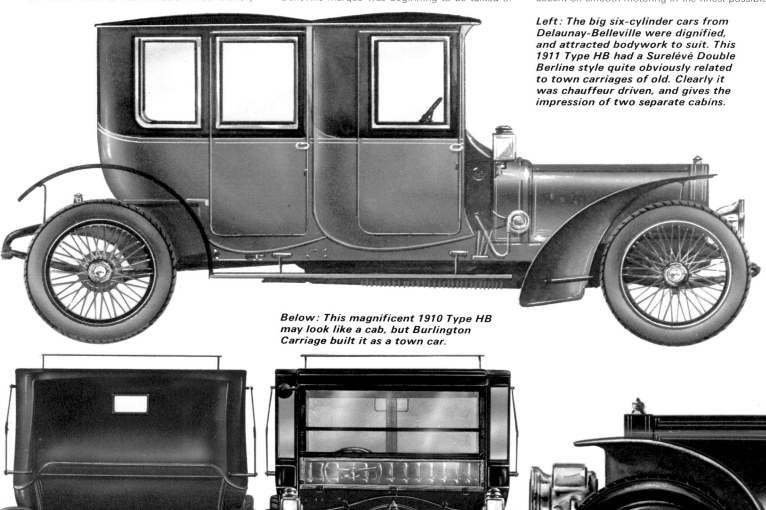

Left: The big six-cylinder cars from Delaunay-Belleville were dignified, and attracted bodywork to suit. This 1911 Type HB had a Surelévé Double Berline style quite obviously related to town carriages of old. Clearly it was chauffeur driven, and gives the impression of two separate cabins.

Below: This magnificent 1910 Type HB may look like a cab, but Burlington Carriage built it as a town car.

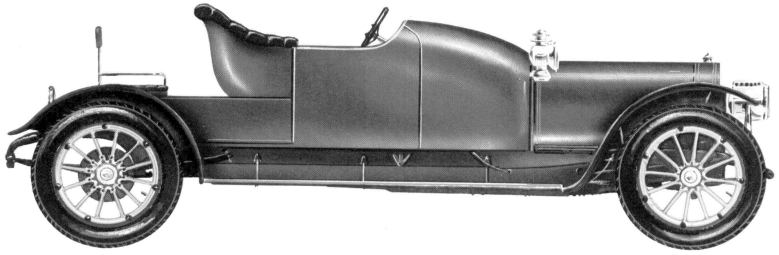

coachwork. The circular radiator was an obvious D-V trademark and many of the cars were distinguished by their high and handsome coachwork. There were 'colonial' models with raised ground clearance, and 'light' models with shorter wheelbases and less passenger space.

In the period from 1908 to 1914, no fewer than 2,227 examples of the H-series cars were built and sold. In spite of this search for a 'best car' reputation, the British price of £600 or French price of 15,000 francs (both for the chassis only) were substantially under those quoted by Rolls-Royce and others. Fittings like wheels fixed to their axles (without even detachable wheel rims until 1913) would have irritated the owner-driver, but D-V expected every owner to have a chauffeur to do that sort of job for him, and to drive the car. Very few of the bodies added to the H-series chassis had completely closed bodies

and a few were clothed in very racy-looking open tourers. The 'Torpedo de Luxe' had two seats behind that massively-long bonnet and a swelling scuttle, and contrived to look the image of a Mercer.

Among the distinguished customers were Czar Nicholas II of Russia, who specified a Barbey compressed-air starter, which was an optional extra. The cars were so tough and reliable that they found favour as staff cars and ambulances during World War I, and such conversions as the fire engine used in Britain in the 1920s were not unexpected. As with Napier in Britain, however, Delaunay—Belleville cars did not generate their own (Rolls-Royce-type) legends, and began a long and slow decline in the 1920s from which they never really recovered. Their great days, the H-series days, were from 1910 to 1914.

Above and below: Two contrasting body styles on Delaunay-Belleville chassis show that not every customer wanted his expensive French car for formal purposes. The red sports car was made in 1911, with a Torpedo style, fixed bucket seats, and a perch behind them for occasional (and unlucky!) extra travellers. The impressive Type HB car by the British Burlington Carriage company was obviously used by the type of person who might also buy a Napier or a Rolls-Royce. The owner travelled in enclosed comfort, with a landaulette hood to be dropped if the weather permitted. The chauffeur had to sit out in the open behind a big screen. The car had a six-cylinder $4\frac{1}{2}$-litre engine.

DE TOMASO PANTERA

Pantera models, built from 1970 to date (data for Pantera with 5.7 litre engine)
Built by: Automobili de Tomaso SpA., Italy.
Engine: Ford (USA) manufactured. Eight cylinders, in 90-degree vee-formation, in five-bearing cast-iron block. Bore and stroke 101·6mm by 88·9mm, 5,763cc (4·00in × 3·50in, 351cu.in). Two detachable cast-iron cylinder heads. Two overhead valves per cylinder, operated by pushrods and rockers from single camshaft positioned in centre of cylinder block 'vee'. One downdraught four-choke Ford (Auto-lite) carburettor. Maximum power 330bhp (gross) at 5,400rpm. Maximum torque 325lb.ft at 3,600rpm.
Transmission: Single-dry-plate clutch, five-speed, all-synchromesh manual ZF gearbox and hypoid-bevel transaxle (with limited-slip differential), all in unit with mid-mounted engine. Engine ahead of line of rear wheels, and gearbox behind it. Remote-control central gearchange. Exposed, universally-joined drive shafts to rear wheels.
Chassis: Unitary-construction pressed and fabricated steel body/chassis unit. Two-seater coupé shape, with engine mounted behind seats but ahead of axle. Independent suspension to all four wheels, by coil springs, wishbones and anti-roll bars. Telescopic dampers. Rack-and-pinion steering. Four-wheel ventilated disc brakes with vacuum servo assistance. 15in bolt-on cast-alloy road wheels. 185/70VR15in tyres on 7in front rims, 215/70VR15in tyres on 8in rear rims.
Dimensions: Wheelbase 8ft 3in (251cm), front track 4ft 9·5in (146cm), rear track 4ft 9in (145cm). Overall length 13ft 11·5in (425cm). Unladen weight 3,100lb (1,406kg).
History: Alejandro de Tomaso, an Argentinian racing driver turned supercar builder, has been selling mid-engined machines since the 1960s. He started by offering the Vallelunga and Pampero, and having bought the Italian coach-building firm of Ghia in 1967 he next marketed the Mangusta (in English this means Mongoose), with styling by Ghia. When Ford took an interest in Ghia they began to market the Mangusta in North America and this was soon followed, in 1970, by the newly designed Pantera. By then the structure and layout were almost 'standard Italian super-car', with a big Ford V8 engine providing the power and a proprietary all-indirect ZF transaxle looking after the transmission, with all-independent suspension, and a Ghia-styled body. The aerodynamic studies were carried out by Ford in their Detroit wind-tunnel.

The Pantera was the first of the truly civilised de Tomaso cars, which also now include the Deauville, a very exclusive front-engined four-door saloon car. The Pantera's maximum speed is nearly 160mph, even in standard tune, while the GTS is quicker and the Silhouette version very fierce indeed. De Tomaso have also controlled Maserati since 1976 and some of their models are being rationalised.

Below: De Tomaso's Pantera—this is a 1973 GTS model—used a normal vee-8 production car from Ford of Detroit, but had all-independent suspension, Ghia styling, and a maximum speed of more than 170mph. It only has two seats.

DOBLE STEAM CAR

Four-cylinder Model E, built from 1923 to 1932 (data for 1923 model)
Built by: Doble Steam Motors Corporation, United States.
Engine: Four cylinder, double-acting, balanced-compound steam engine, with pairs of cast-iron cylinders (one high-pressure, one low-pressure) and one valve chest per block. Blocks fixed to four-bearing light-alloy crankcase, itself integral with rear axle. Bore and stroke (high-pressure cylinder) 66·7mm by 127mm (2·62in × 5·0in), and (low-pressure cylinder) 114·3mm by 127mm (4·5in × 5·0in). Total swept volume 3,494cc (213·2cu.in). Stephenson-link valve gear and piston-type valves. Seamless steel steam generator, 575·7ft (175·5m) long, of forced-circulation, water-tube type.
Transmission: No clutch and no variable-transmission gearbox. Engine in horizontal position, under rear seats, pointing forward, and crankshaft directly linked to 'live' rear axle. No gearchange. Remote-control steam cut-off mechanism, on steering column.
Chassis: Separate pressed-steel chassis frame, with channel-section side members tubular and pressed cross bracing. Forged front axle beam. Steam generator under 'bonnet', engine under rear seats. Front and rear suspension by semi-elliptic leaf springs. Lever-arm hydraulic dampers. Worm-and-wheel steering. Rear-wheel drum brakes; foot operation and hand operation (both mechanical) side by side and independent. Bolt-on steel disc or bolt-on wire wheels. 6·20in section tyres. Choice of open or closed, touring or limousine coachwork.
Dimensions: Wheelbase 11ft 10in (361cm), tracks (front and rear) 4ft 9in (145cm). Unladen weight, depending on bodywork chosen, 3,900lb to 4,550lb (1,769kg to 2,063kg).
History: Abner Doble was the grandson of a Scot who arrived in San Francisco in 1850. The family fortune was made in manufacturing mining tools, but Abner Doble built his first steam car in 1905. In 1914 he drove a prototype 'condenser' Doble to Detroit and found some backing for his project. The first car, a twin-cylinder steamer, was offered for sale in 1917. About 80 cars of the Doble Detroit series were sold before he returned to San Francisco, joined with his three brothers, and offered the well-developed Series E and Series F four-cylinder cars from 1923. As steam cars go, it was very advanced, raised steam very rapidly from cold and had lots of performance and dignity to match its silence, but it was very expensive. Doble modelled his Emeryville factory on the Rolls-Royce operations at Springfield and since his selling prices were between $8,000 and $11,000 few cars were made and the market was restricted to the rich, the famous and the pleasure-seeking. No less a person than Howard Hughes bought a couple of them. In spite of early claims to be ready to make 1,000 cars a year, not more than 42 of the fine four-cylinder Dobles were ever built.

The company finally collapsed in 1931, never having made a profit on its car sales. Doble himself remained faithful to steam for the rest of his life, as a consultant to many companies making non-automotive steam engines.

Left: If ever a car deserves to be called exclusive, a Doble steam car is one such. Only about 42 Dobles were built between 1923 and 1932, though Abner Doble once said he was ready to make 1,000 cars every year. This 1925 tourer emulated the Springfield-built Rolls-Royces in every way but ultimate quality, and was impressively silent.

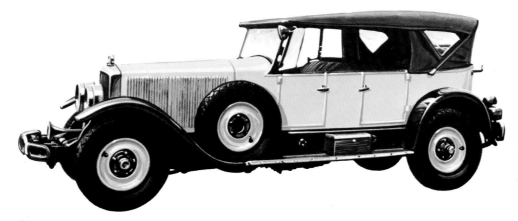

DUESENBERG MODEL A

Model A, built from 1921 to 1927

Built by: Duesenberg Motor Co., United States.

Engine: Eight cylinders, in line, in three-bearing cast-iron cylinder block. Bore and stroke 73·0mm by 127·0mm, 4,261cc (2·875in × 5·00in, 260 cu.in). Detachable cast-iron cylinder head. Two overhead valves per cylinder, opposed to each other in part-spherical combustion chamber, and operated by rockers from single overhead camshaft. Single updraught Stromberg carburettor (later cars had Schebler unit). Maximum power 90bhp at 3,600rpm. Maximum torque 170lb.ft at 1,500rpm.

Transmission: Single-dry-plate clutch and three-speed manual gearbox (without synchromesh), both in unit with front-mounted engine. Direct-acting central gearchange. Propeller shaft enclosed in torque tube to spiral-bevel 'live' rear axle.

Chassis: Separate pressed-steel chassis frame, with channel-section side members, fabricated and tubular cross bracings. Tubular front axle beam. Front and rear suspension by half-elliptic leaf springs; rear axle located by radius arms. Watson Stabilator dampers at front and rear. Four-wheel, hydraulically operated, drum brakes. Handbrake acting on drum fixed to transmission shaft behind gearbox. Centre lock wire wheels, with 5in × 33in tyres.

Open touring, sporting and closed coachwork to choice.

Dimensions: Wheelbase 11ft 2in (340cm), front and rear tracks 4ft 8in (142cm). Overall length depending on coachwork, from 15ft 11·5in (486cm).

History: The Duesenberg brothers first made their names as racing car designers, but decided to make road cars just a year after their 'straight eight' machine won its first big event. The road car was intended to have engines with horizontal valve gear, but 1920 race engines were so successful that their single-overhead-camshaft layout was adopted for road use, in a much bigger unit altogether. This was odd in that it only had three main bearings (which is theoretically undesirable), but was reliable in service.

The Duesenberg Eight (the 'A' followed years later, as a bastardisation of 'Eight' and was never an official title), pandered to the richest and most sporting North Americans, who wanted a lot of passenger space, and refused to use more than three gears. Therefore a splendidly detailed chassis was provided, and some extremely attractive American-vintage coachwork was conceived to suit. There were many racing-inspired details in chassis layout. Duesenbergs were used in all manner of long-distance and record attempts, and got involved very successfully in stock car racing. Supercharged versions were tried by the factory, but never sold. The company was taken over by E. L. Cord in 1926, who then prepared for a bigger, better and even more magnificent Duesenberg, the Model J.

Below: The Duesenberg brothers' first production car was the 'Eight' (which later became known as the 'A'), with a 4·3-litre straight-eight engine. Only the richest and most sporting of North Americans bought one, to enjoy the overhead camshaft engine's performance —this tourer body is by Springfield.

DUESENBERG J AND SJ

J and SJ models, built from 1928 to 1938 (data for Model J)

Built by: Duesenberg Motor Co., United States.

Engine: Eight cylinders, in line, in five-bearing cast-iron block/crankcase. Bore and stroke 95·25mm by 120·6mm, 6,882cc (3·75in × 4·75in, 420cu.in). Detachable cast-iron cylinder head. Four overhead valves per cylinder (two inlet and two exhaust), opposed to each other at 70 degrees in part-spherical combustion chambers and operated by twin overhead camshafts. Single updraught twin-choke Schebler carburettor (from 1932, downdraught twin-choke Stromberg carburettor). Maximum power 265bhp (gross) at 4,250rpm.

Transmission: Double-dry-plate clutch and three-speed manual gearbox (without synchromesh), both in unit with front-mounted engine. Direct-acting central gearchange. Propeller shaft, enclosed in torque tube, to hypoid-bevel 'live' rear axle.

Chassis: Separate pressed-steel chassis frame, with channel-section side members, and tubular cross members. Forged front axle beam. Front suspension by half-elliptic leaf springs. Rear suspension by half-elliptic leaf springs and radius arms. Lever-type hydraulic dampers. Cam-and-lever steering. Four-wheel, hydraulically-operated drum brakes (with vacuum servo assistance from 1930 models). Drum transmission handbrake. 19in centre-lock wire wheels, (17in optional from 1935).

Open or closed coachwork to choice.

Dimensions: Wheelbase 11ft 10·5in or 12ft 9·5in (362cm or 390cm), tracks (front and rear) 4ft 8in (142cm). Overall length depending on coachwork 16ft 8in (508cm). Unladen weight from 5,000lb (2,268kg).

History: After his purchase of Duesenberg, E. L. Cord asked his engineers to produce an all-new car. This was revealed in December 1928, at the height of the American economic 'boom', and was advertised as 'The World's Finest Motor Car'. The Model J was magnificently engineered without an eye to cost, with a beautiful twin-cam engine, modern features, and some of the most sumptuous body styling America had yet seen.

The chassis price in 1929 was $8,500, which rose to $9,500 by 1932, and Cord intended it to be as good as the Bugatti Royale and as well-thought-of as a Rolls-Royce. To boost the performance even more (production cars could beat 110mph without much difficulty), the SJ arrived in 1932, where 'S' stood for 'supercharged', and the power output was boosted to an astonishing claimed 320bhp at 4,750rpm. Even if we take this as an exaggeration, the SJ was probably the world's most powerful production car. Two very special SSJ cars (Short Supercharged J models) were made — for Clark Gable and Gary Cooper.

Js and particularly SJs were sometimes stripped out for record attempts with great success, Ab Jenkins taking international class records at Utah at 152mph in 1935. The Cord Corporation collapsed in 1937, taking the J/SJ cars with it, which was tough justice after the car had survived the Great Depression. Rather less than 500 examples were built in all.

Below: Perhaps the most desirable of all American vintage cars was the Duesenberg Model J, with twin-cam 6·9-litre engines. SJs were supercharged.

EXCELSIOR ADEX

Adex overhead-cam range, built from 1920 to 1929 (data for 1922 Albert Premier model)

Built by: S.A. des Automobiles Excelsior, Belgium.

Engine: Six cylinders, in line, in cast-iron block, with seven-bearing light-alloy crankcase. Bore and stroke 90mm by 140mm, 5,344cc (3·54in × 5·51in, 326cu.in). Detachable cast-iron cylinder head. Two overhead valves per cylinder, operated by cam follower from single overhead camshaft. Three side-draught single-choke Zenith carburettors.

Transmission: Cone clutch, in unit with front-mounted engine, and shaft drive to separate four-speed manual gearbox (without synchromesh). Gearbox, propeller shaft enclosed in torque tube and spiral-bevel 'live' rear axle all assembled as one unit, pivoting from front of gearbox casing. Direct-acting central gearchange.

Chassis: Separate pressed-steel chassis frame, with channel-section side members and pressed-steel cross bracing. Forged front axle beam. Front suspension by semi-elliptic leaf springs. Rear suspension by cantilever leaf springs, with torque tube location, and 'axle centralising device' (links from chassis frame to axle casing). Cam-and-lever steering. Four-wheel, mechanically operated drum brakes, diagonally compensated. Centre-lock wire wheels. 895 × 135mm tyres. Choice of coachwork.

Dimensions: Wheelbase 12ft 6in (381cm), tracks (front and rear) 4ft 10in (147cm). Overall length 16ft 6in (503cm).

History: Along with the Minerva, the Excelsior was one of Belgium's two most celebrated motor cars. Minerva, perhaps, were more sporting more often, but Excelsior probably made the finest luxury machines. Their first car was sold in 1903 and their first-ever six-cylinder car followed in 1907. This latter was of a conventional design, but it was large enough and tunable enough for the company to build Grand Prix cars in 1912 (a car taking sixth place in the French GP that year). After the war came the completely redesigned Adex B range, central to which was the splendid new overhead-camshaft six-cylinder

engine. That was good enough, but the magnificent sporting Albert Premier model of 1922 (so named because the first was delivered to the King of Belgium) surpassed it. Prosaically named the Adex C series, this chassis used a complex anti-roll bar and axle location device to the rear suspension, which was probably the first time such a feature figured on a touring car. The Albert Premier was updated in 1926, with even more power, and carried on until the company was taken over by Imperia in 1928. The last true production year was 1929, although

Above: Excelsior's Albert Premier sports car was named after the King of Belgium, who took the first car built in 1922. The Adex range, of which it was a part, spanned the vintage years —this car was built in 1925.

a few cars were later assembled from existing parts. It was a sad end to a car which certainly rivalled Bentley and Hispano-Suiza at its best and was certainly their equal in engineering design.

FERRARI 250GT BERLINETTA

250GT series, built from 1953 to 1964 (data for 1959 Berlinetta)

Built by: SEFAC Ferrari, Maranello, Italy.

Engine: 12 cylinders, in 60-degree vee-formation, in seven-bearing light-alloy block/crankcase. Bore and stroke 73mm by 58·8mm, 2,953cc (2·87in × 2·31in, 180·2cu.in). Two detachable light-alloy cylinder heads. Two overhead valves per cylinder, opposed to each other in part-spherical combustion chambers and operated by rockers from single overhead camshaft per cylinder head. Three down-draught twin-choke Weber carburettors. Maximum power 260bhp (net) at 7,000rpm.

Transmission: Twin-dry-plate clutch and four-speed, synchromesh manual gearbox, both in unit with front-mounted engine. Remote-control central gearchange. Open propeller shaft to hypoid-bevel 'live' rear axle.

Chassis: Separate multi-tubular chassis frame, with large-section side members and tubular cross bracing. Independent front suspension by coil springs, wishbones and anti-roll bar. Rear suspension by half-elliptic leaf springs and radius arms. Lever-arm hydraulic dampers. Worm-and-wheel steering. Four-wheel hydraulically opera-

ted disc brakes. Centre-lock wire wheels. 175 × 400 tyres.

Dimensions: Wheelbase 7ft 10·5in (240cm), track (front) 4ft 5·3in (135·4cm), track (rear) 4ft 5·1in (135cm). Overall length 13ft 7·5in (415cm). Unladen weight 2,400lb (1,088kg).

History: Ferrari's first attempt at building a

Gran Turismo car was the 250 Europa of 1953, but unlike all its descendants this model was powered by the large Lampredi-designed V12. The 250GT, which followed in 1954, reverted to the original Colombo V12. The chassis was Ferrari-conventional, being built up of large-diameter tubing, and there was a front-mounted

Right: Simply styled but brutally attractive short-wheelbase Ferrari 250GT Berlinetta, bodied by Scaglietti —made 1959 to 1963.

Far right: Inevitably the 250GT range was stretched—the original 250GT 2 + 2 was a Farina-styled 1960 model.

FACEL VEGA

Facel Vega models HK500 and Facel II (data for HK500)

Built by: Facel S.A., France

Engine: Chrysler-manufactured. Eight cylinders, in 90-degree vee-formation, in five-bearing cast-iron block. Bore and stroke 107·95mm by 85·85mm, 6,286cc (4·25in × 3·37in, 384cu.in). Cast-iron cylinder heads. Two overhead valves per cylinder, operated by pushrods and rockers from single camshaft positioned in centre of cylinder block 'vee'. Two four-choke Carter carburettors. Maximum power 360bhp (gross) at 5,200rpm.

Transmission: Single-dry-plate clutch and four-speed all-synchromesh Pont-à-Mousson manual gearbox. Central gearchange (optional three-speed Chrysler automatic transmission, with facia push-button selection). Open propeller shaft to hypoid-bevel 'live' rear axle.

Chassis: Separate steel chassis frame, with tubular main side members, and lateral and diagonal bracing by tubular and channel cross members. Steel body welded to chassis frame on assembly. Independent front suspension by coil springs, wishbones and anti-roll bar. Rear suspension by half-elliptic leaf springs. Telescopic dampers. Cam-and-roller steering, optionally power assisted. Four-wheel, hydraulically operated disc brakes, vacuum servo assisted. 15in pressed disc wheels. 6·70 × 15in tyres.

Facel-built coachwork, two-door coupé or convertible styles.

Dimensions: Wheelbase 8ft 9in (267cm), front track (front) 4ft 7·5in (141cm), track (rear) 4ft 9·5in (146cm). Overall length 15ft 1in (460cm). Unladen weight 4,030lb (1,828kg).

History: *Forges et Ateliers de Construction d'Eure et de Loire*, founded in the 1930s, produced pressed metal items embracing kitchen equipment, gas-turbine engine parts, tools and dies before they started making car bodies in the 1940s. The decision to make their own Facel cars came after they had lost a particularly factory-filling Panhard contract. From 1954, when announced, to 1964, when the company went into liquidation, a series of big and impressive Chrysler-V8-engined coupés were built. They were very fast, very expensive, and beautifully finished. The problem, as with similar imitators, was that there were not enough customers to appreciate such excellence.

Even though the HK500 was succeeded by the improved Facel II for 1962, the company needed volume to sustain it. The little Facellia, with its home-produced twin-cam engine, looked good and sounded good, but there were far too many service problems, and it was this car, rather than the 130/140mph flagships, which killed off Facel S.A. From the original FVS to the last Facel II the design pedigree was retained — big torquey Chrysler engine, Pont-à-Mousson gearbox, and Facel-designed tubular chassis — and while the cars were by no means nimble handlers, they were effortless high-speed highway cruisers.

The Facel was France's largest and most expensive car by a large margin while it was being built. Only the still-born Monica project has tried to emulate it; that, too, failed to make the grade.

Above: There were Facel Vega cars for ten years (1954-64), but few more impressive than the HK500 four-seater, with its 6·3-litre Chrysler vee-8 engine.

all-synchromesh gearbox and a live rear axle located by leaf springs and radius arms. The Berlinetta cars (much lighter than production two-seater coupés) began to appear in the mid 1950s and were intended for competition purposes. The name has been applied indiscriminately to *all* 250GTs, particularly those with short wheelbases, although the true Berlinettas, which became famous in GT racing, were built from 1959 to 1963, with that distinctive body by Scaglietti. Steel-bodied versions of these cars, rightly, became legendary and about 250 were made all in all. Out of the Berlinetta, of course, came the 250GTO, which was a pure competition car, and the 250GT Lusso, which was a pure road car. Successor to all of them, of course, was the smooth 275GTB, with its axle-mounted gearbox and 'rope-drive' propeller shaft. The 250GT cars, however, are those which truly signify Ferrari's change from being a racing car maker to being a production car maker.

FERRARI TYPE 340/375 SPORTS CARS

340 and 375 models, built from 1951 to 1954 (data for 1954 Le Mans car)

Built by: Auto Costruzione Ferrari, Italy.

Engine: 12 cylinders, in 60-degree vee-formation, in seven-bearing cast-alloy block/crankcase. Bore and stroke 84mm by 74·5mm, 4,954cc (3·31in × 2·93in, 302·3cu.in). Two detachable light-alloy cylinder heads, complete (when assembled) with screwed-in cylinder liners. Two overhead valves per cylinder, opposed to each other at 60 degrees in part-spherical combustion chambers and operated by rockers from single overhead camshaft per cylinder head. Three down-draught twin-choke Weber carburettors. Maximum power 344bhp (net) at 6,500rpm.

Transmission: Multi-dry-plate clutch in unit with engine. Open propeller shaft to four-speed manual gearbox in unit with chassis-mounted spiral-bevel final drive, with limited-slip differential. Remote-control central gearchange. Exposed, universally jointed drive shafts to rear wheels.

Chassis: Separate tubular-steel frame, with large elliptic-section side members and tubular cross-bracing. Independent front suspension by transverse leaf spring, wishbones and rubber blocks. Rear suspension De Dion, by transverse leaf spring and radius arms. Lever-arm hydraulic dampers. Worm-and-wheel steering. Four-wheel, hydraulically operated drum brakes. 16in centre-lock wire wheels. 6·50 × 16in (front) and 7·50 × 16in (rear) tyres.

Dimensions: Wheelbase 8ft 6·5in (260cm), track (front) 4ft 2in (127cm), track ·(rear) 4ft 2·5in (128cm). Overall length 13ft 7·5in (415·5cm). Unladen weight 2,204lb (1,000kg).

History: This very successful, impressive and at times brutally fast series of sports-racing cars evolved directly from the fact that Ferrari had developed a powerful and very reliable new V12 engine for Grand Prix racing. Whereas the Colombo-designed Type 125 V12 started life at 1½-litres and grew eventually to well over 3 litres, the new unit by Lampredi was always laid out with a 4½-litre GP capacity in mind and proved capable of even further stretching. In sports-racing, or even in production-car form, it was produced in 3·3-litre, 4·1-litre, 4·5-litre and in two 4·9-litre forms, usually with a combination of twin-choke Weber carburettors and always with the classic single-overhead-camshaft cylinder heads to which non-GP Ferraris were faithful for so long. The GP cars of 1950 and 1951, which used the basic 'building block' of this engine, were fitted with twin-cam cylinder heads. Apart from the fact that the engine was physically larger (and was therefore stronger with some built-in stretch), it was also distinguished by the fact that the wet cylinder liners were screwed into the cylinder heads, thereby ensuring a water-tight and gas-tight head/cylinder joint. Especially with his supercharged V12s, Colombo had experienced trouble with gasket failures, which this new design very effectively overcame.

The Type 275S car was not a success, because the transmission to deal with massive increases in torque and power was not ready, but the Type 340/342 cars which followed in 1951 were much improved. The chassis, used by racing cars and production America models alike, was based on elliptic-section tubing, with transverse-leaf-spring front suspension. The gearbox was front mounted at first, but for the 1954–6 375 Plus and 410 Plus models a four-speed unit, placed together with the differential of the De Dion rear axle was fitted, being a direct crib from the old Grand Prix car thinking. The Type 340MM (Mille Miglia) won its first event — appropriately enough the Mille Miglia of 1953, but the Type 340 Mexico had already won the Panamerica Road Race in Mexico in 1951. After that Italian success the cars' engines were enlarged to 4·5-litres and given extremely attractive closed Pininfarina bodies. They had no success at Le Mans, but won several other long-distance sports car races that year. For 1954 the ultimate 375 Plus car appeared, with a low-revving 4·9-litre engine and the back-axle-mounted gearbox. It was really the ultimate in brute-force machines, very powerful, very noisy and rather unwieldy, but it was geared for something like 180mph at Le Mans and other fast circuits and seemed to have a completely unburstable engine which, after all, was considerably derated

Right: Mike Hawthorn driving a 340MM sports-racing Ferrari at Silverstone in 1953. It had a 4·1-litre vee-12 engine and the body is by Touring of Milan. He won the sports car race outright.

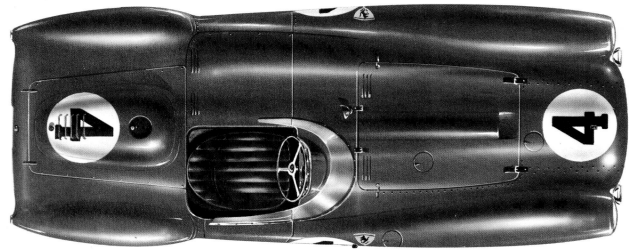

from the Grand Prix units. In the event the Gonzales/Trintignant car won the 1954 Le Mans outright from the first of the D-type Jaguars, but it was not the easy victory which had been prophesied, as the car suffered various electrical problems. The same model of car was good enough to win the Carrera Panamerica again and also to take the Buenos Aires 1,000km sports car race, before Ferrari were ready to supersede it with a new family of straight-six-engined cars. The last cars, however, were phenomenally powerful — their outright output of 380bhp was not to be beaten until the more-developed rear-engined 330P racing sports cars arrived at the beginning of the 1960s — but even shortened wheelbases and attention to suspen-sion could not solve their brutish handling. The series had been developed specifically to attack so-called 'sports car' races, but were so obviously related to the 4½-litre Formula One cars that it brought this class of racing into disrepute. The only Ferrari production cars to benefit from their experiences were the small-production Americas and Superfasts.

Above and below: The nose was typical of early-1950s Ferraris, and on this car most of the tail was filled by the vast fuel tank. The gearbox was fixed to the differential, and the car could reach 180mph in a straight line.

Above: The sleek lines and the usual Ferrari badging do nothing to hide the brutal menace of Gonzales' 1954 Le Mans 375S model. Its 4·9-litre engine produced a dead-reliable 344bhp.

FERRARI TYPE 375 AMERICA

America models, built from 1951 to 1959 (data for 375 model of 1953)

Built by: SEFAC Ferrari, Maranello, Italy.

Engine: 12 cylinders, in 60-degree vee-formation, in seven-bearing light-alloy block/crankcase. Bore and stroke 84mm by 68mm, 4,522cc (3·31in × 2·68in, 276cu.in). Two detachable light-alloy cylinder heads, complete (when assembled) with screwed-in cylinder liners. Two overhead valves per cylinder, opposed to each other at 60 degrees in part-spherical combustion chambers and operated by rockers from single overhead camshaft per cylinder head. Camshaft drive by chain from nose of crankshaft. Hairpin valve springs. Three down-draught twin-choke Weber carburettors. Maximum power 300bhp (net) at 6,000rpm.

Transmission: Multi-dry-plate clutch and four-speed, synchromesh manual gearbox, both in unit with front-mounted engine. Remote-control central gearchange. Open propeller shaft to hypoid-bevel 'live' rear axle.

Chassis: Separate multi-tubular chassis frame, with elliptic-section-tubing side members and tubular cross bracing. Independent front suspension by transverse leaf spring, wishbone and integral rubber block. Rear suspension by semi-elliptic leaf springs and twin radius arms. Lever-arm hydraulic dampers. Worm-and-wheel steering. Four-wheel, hydraulically operated drum brakes. 15in centre-lock wire wheels. 7·10 × 15in tyres.

Dimensions: Wheelbase 9ft 2·7in (280cm), track (front) 4ft 2in (132·5cm), track (rear) 4ft

3in (132cm). Unladen weight 2,205lb (1,000kg).

History: To add to the limited appeal of the 166s, 195s and 212 Inters, Ferrari introduced a much bigger car specifically for the North American market, the first being the Type 342 America of 1951. Much of the chassis engineering was based on Ferrari's racing sports cars and the engine was a detuned Lampredi-type V12, as used in the 4½-litre Grand Prix cars. The 375 America followed, with 4,522cc in place of 4,101cc and 300bhp instead of 220bhp, which made it more attractive to the customers. Once the big 4·9-litre engine had proved itself at Le Mans and in other road races, it was adopted (in detuned form) for the Type 410 Superamerica,

Above: Ferrari Americas evolved into Superamericas—this was a 1956 model.

which carried on in small-scale and exclusive production until 1959. The cars' charm was in their exquisite engines and in their parentage. Body styles varied, according to customer taste, but those magnificent and sensuous-sounding V12 engines persisted. Enormously fast two-seater cars could not possibly be very practical, but they were *the* most glamorous form of transport. Out of the Americas came the Type 410 Superfast, the even more rare Type 500 Superfast and — eventually — the more modern Type 365GT 2+2 cars. All these were the largest, the fastest and the most desired of Ferrari's road cars.

FERRARI DINO

Dino 206GT and 246GT, built from 1967 to 1973 (data for 246GT).

Built by: SEFAC Ferrari Maranello, Italy.

Engine: Six cylinders, in 65-degree vee-formation, in four-bearing cast-iron block, transversely mounted behind driving compartment. Bore and stroke 92·5mm by 60mm, 2,418cc (3·64in × 2·36in, 147·5cu.in). Light-alloy cylinder heads. Two valves per cylinder, inclined to each other, in part-spherical combustion chambers and operated by inverted-bucket tappets from twin overhead camshafts per bank. Three down-draught twin-choke Weber carburettors. Maximum power 195bhp (DIN) at 7,600rpm. Maximum torque 166lb.ft at 5,500rpm.

Transmission: Single-dry-plate clutch and train of transfer gears to five-speed, all-synchromesh manual gearbox, mounted in unit with, but behind and below, the cylinder block. Remote-control central gearchange. Hypoid-bevel final drive unit, with limited-slip differential at rear of gearbox. Exposed, universally jointed drive shafts to rear wheels.

Chassis: Fabricated tubular and sheet steel load-bearing chassis frame, with steel and light-alloy body welded to it on assembly. Light-alloy skin panels, in two-seat coupé or spider construction. Engine/transmission unit behind driving compartment. All-independent suspension, by coil springs, wishbones, anti-roll bars and telescopic dampers. Rack-and-pinion steering. Four-wheel, hydraulically operated disc brakes, with vacuum servo assistance. 14in bolt-on cast-alloy road wheels. 205VR14in tyres.

Dimensions: Wheelbase 7ft 8·2in (234cm), track (front) 4ft 8·1in (142cm), track (rear) 4ft 7·1in (140cm). Overall length 13ft 9in (420cm). Unladen weight 2,400lb (1,088kg).

History: Ferrari's first mid-engined road car came about because of a desire to go racing in the 1967 Formula Two (which meant that engines had to be 'production' based), and because they were already committed to supplying such engines to Fiat for the same validation

purpose. Mid-engined Dinos, entirely different from the road cars, were raced in 1965 to 1967, but the first true prototype was shown in 1967.

Styled by Pininfarina, the original car had a longitudinally-mounted engine, but all production cars had the now-familiar transverse engine location shared by the Lancia Stratos. The first batch of Ferrari Dinos used 2-litre engines with cast-alloy cylinder blocks, but from the end of 1969 this was replaced by a cast-iron block unit of 2,418cc. Incidentally, the cylinder dimensions are identical to those of Grand Prix Ferraris of the late 1950s, the engines being very closely re-

lated. Apart from the engine, the rest of the Dino was all new, and the luscious styling was startlingly unique.

In spite of its racing origins the Dino was a thoroughly practical road car, fast enough (about 140mph maximum speed) for almost everybody, and had remarkable roadholding powers. It was replaced in 1974 by the new and larger 308GTB car, with a new V8 engine.

Right: The lines effectively hide the mid-mounted engine position. The car is small, with impeccable road manners.

Right: The classic lines of the Ferrari Dino, by Pininfarina. Coupe or Spider versions were built. First cars had mid-mounted 2-litres, later 2·4-litres.

FERRARI 330GT 2+2

250GT 2+2 and 330GT 2+2 series, built from 1960 to 1967 (data for 1965 330GT)
Built by: SEFAC Ferrari, Maranello, Italy.
Engine: 12 cylinders, in 60-degree vee-formation, in seven-bearing light-alloy block/crankcase. Bore and stroke 77mm by 71mm, 3,967cc (3·04in × 2·80in, 242cu.in). Two detachable light-alloy cylinder heads. Two overhead valves per cylinder, opposed to each other in part-spherical combustion chambers and operated by rockers from single overhead camshaft per cylinder head. Three down-draught twin-choke Weber carburettors. Maximum power 300bhp (net) at 6,600rpm. Maximum torque 288lb.ft at 5,000rpm.
Transmission: Multi-dry-plate clutch and four-speed, synchromesh manual gearbox, with Laycock overdrive unit operating on top gear, all in unit with front-mounted engine. Remote-control central gearchange. Open propeller shaft to hypoid-bevel 'live' rear axle.
Chassis: Separate multi-tubular chassis frame, with large-section side members and tubular cross bracing. Independent front suspension by coil springs, wishbones and anti-roll bar. Rear suspension by semi-elliptic leaf springs, auxiliary coil springs and radius arms. Telescopic dampers. Worm-and-wheel steering. Four-wheel, hydraulically operated disc brakes. 15in centre-lock wire wheels. 205 × 15in tyres.
Dimensions: Wheelbase 8ft 8·2in (265cm), track (front) 4ft 7in (139·7cm), track (rear) 4ft 6·5in (139cm). Overall length 15ft 9in (484cm). Unladen weight 3,180lb (1,420kg).

History: Before 1960, Ferrari had never sold a touring car with more than two seats, but export demand in particular forced him to produce the 250GT 2+2 in 1960. Styled by Pininfarina, at first with single headlamps, but later with paired units, the 250GT 2+2 used almost entirely standard 250GT coupé mechanicals, although the front seats and steering gear were moved forward and the passenger cabin was lengthened by 12 inches, all on the same 250GT coupé wheelbase. The rear seats were not quite spacious enough for fully grown passengers, but for most purposes the cars were practical four-seaters. In due course, the car was re-engined, with a 4-litre V12 unit and thereafter became the 330GT 2+2. Ferrari's type numbering has often indicated the capacity of one cylinder in cubic centimetres and this was the case here. A Laycock overdrive was an interesting fitting on these cars — but on succeeding models a change to a newly designed five-speed gearbox was made. Descendants of these cars were the bigger and even more luxurious 365GT 2+2, which also had links with the superseded Type 410 and Type 500 Superfast cars.

Below: The 330GT 2 + 2 Ferrari evolved from earlier 250GTs, with 300bhp vee-12 4-litre engine, and 140mph performance.

FERRARI 365GTB4 DAYTONA

Daytona model, built from 1968 to 1974.
Built by: SEFAC Ferrari Maranello, Italy.
Engine: Twelve cylinders, in 60-degree vee-formation, in seven-bearing cast-alloy block/crankcase. Bore and stroke 81mm by 71mm, 4,390cc (3·19in × 2·79in, 268cu.in). Two detachable light-alloy cylinder heads. Two overhead valves per cylinder, inclined to each other in part-spherical combustion chambers and operated by inverted-bucket tappets from twin overhead camshafts per cylinder head. Six down-draught twin-choke Weber carburettors. Maximum power 352bhp (DIN) at 7,500rpm. Maximum torque 318lb.ft at 5,500rpm.
Transmission: Single-dry-plate clutch in unit with front-mounted engine. Torque tube and enclosed propeller shaft to combined gearbox/differential transaxle. Five-speed, all-indirect, all-synchromesh manual gearbox, and hypoid-bevel differential with limited-slip device, all chassis mounted. Exposed, universally jointed drive shafts to rear wheels.
Chassis: Separate multi-tubular steel chassis frame, with light-alloy closed two-seater coupé coachwork by Scaglietti. All independent suspension by coil springs, wishbones and anti-roll bars, with telescopic dampers. Worm-and-nut steering. Four-wheel, hydraulically operated ventilated disc brakes, with vacuum servo assistance. 15in centre-lock cast-alloy road wheels. 215/70VR15in tyres.
Dimensions: Wheelbase 7ft 10·5in (240cm), track (front) 4ft 8·5in (143·5cm), track (rear) 4ft 8in (142cm). Overall length 14ft 6in (442cm). Unladen weight 3,530lb (1,600kg).
History: To replace the long-running 250GT production cars, with their conventional mechanical layout and obligatory V12 engines, Ferrari launched the 275GTB in 1964. This was improved to become the 275GTB4 in 1966. Although it remained true to the traditions, with front-mounted V12 engine and two-door two-seater coupé body, it had a multi-tubular chassis frame, all-independent coil-spring suspension and the five-speed gearbox in unit with the chassis-mounted differential.

There was little doubt that the four-cam 275GTB4 (with the final stretch of the original Colombo-type engine) was one of the fastest cars in the world, but Ferrari was not satisfied. In the autumn of 1968, his engineers had produced the delectable 365GTB4 Daytona car, which did everything that the now obsolete 275GTB4 could have done, but also had the massively powerful four-cam 4·4-litre engine and dramatically styled body (by Pininfarina) constructed as usual by Scaglietti. The 275GTB4's basic chassis and mechanical layout were retained, including the rear-positioned gearbox. However, the front and rear wheel tracks were wider and the shovel-nosed shape, with its hidden headlamps, was more shapely even than before. With all that power, the Daytona was tremendously fast. Its maximum speed was between 175 and 180mph, it could break almost any speed limit in the world in its 86mph second gear, and beat 140mph in fourth! Without any doubt it was the world's fastest production car, faster even than the Lamborghini Miura, in the six years it was on sale. Yet the whole business of going fast was carried out in exemplary Ferrari manner, with refinement to suit the high price, and the most amazingly flexible engine, as one had come to expect from the Maranello-built products.

The only way for the car to be significantly improved would be to make it faster, or even more docile, but Ferrari was not interested in half-measures. He had decided that the Daytona should be the last of his front-engined super-car two-seaters and from 1974 it was deposed by the wickedly attractive mid-engined Berlinetta Boxer, with a new flat-12 power unit, also of 4·4-litres. To drive a Daytona was a truly memorable and exciting experience.

Right: Without any doubt, Ferrari's Daytona was one of the fastest and most glamorous cars in the world until replaced by the Boxer (see below). It combined a 170mph maximum speed with fierce Scaglietti coachwork, the unique Ferrari 4·4-litre vee-12 engine and immaculate road manners. Anyone could learn to drive a Daytona fast, but few could find the money to buy one. The Daytona was the last and finest of the front-engined coupes.

FERRARI BOXER

Boxer 365GT/BB and 512GT/BB – 1971 to date (data for 365GT/BB)
Built by: SEFAC Ferrari Maranello, Italy.
Engine: Twelve cylinders, in horizontally opposed formation, based on seven-bearing light-alloy crankcase and cylinder blocks. Bore and stroke 81mm by 71mm, 4,390cc (3·19in × 2·79in, 267cu.in). Two light-alloy cylinder heads. Two valves per cylinder, inclined in part-spherical combustion chambers and operated by inverted bucket tappets from twin overhead camshafts per bank. Four triple-choke Weber carburettors. Maximum power 380bhp (DIN) at 7,700rpm. Maximum torque 318lb.ft at 3,900rpm.
Transmission: Mid-engine layout, with engine above and ahead of line of rear wheels. Single-dry-plate clutch behind transaxle and five-speed, all-synchromesh manual gearbox in unit with, and under, engine. Spiral-bevel final drive unit

Right: The latest Ferrari Boxer, with its mid-mounted 5-litre flat-12 engine is good for nearly 200mph. Styling, engineering, and Ferrari mystique all combine to make this the most desirable of all Italian 'supercars'.

with limited-slip differential at rear of gearbox. Exposed, universally jointed drive shafts to rear wheels.

Chassis: Separate multi-tube steel chassis frame, mainly square-section tubes, with box and sheet cross bracing. Independent front suspension by coil springs, wishbones and anti-roll bar. Independent rear suspension by double coil springs, wishbones and anti-roll bar. Telescopic dampers. Rack-and-pinion steering. Four-wheel, hydraulically operated disc brakes with vacuum servo assistance. 15in cast-alloy, centre-lock road wheels. 215VR15in tyres.

Dimensions: Wheelbase 8ft 2·5in (250cm), track (front) 4ft 11in (150cm), track (rear) 5ft (152cm). Overall length 14ft 3·7in (436cm). Unladen weight 2,480lb (1,123kg).

History: Having developed, and made a success of, the mid-engined Dino, Ferrari next turned

their attention to a really fast and brutal supercar. The result, first shown as a prototype in 1971, was the Berlinetta Boxer, which probably had more performance than any other car in the world. Only Lamborghini, with the Countach, would argue with that claim. Now, with a five-litre engine in the Boxer (since the autumn of 1976) Lamborghini's claim goes by default.

The engine itself was derived from that of the Grand Prix 3-litre unit, but had — sensibly — the same bore and stroke as the front-engined Ferraris. Unlike the smaller Dino, however, the engine/transmission layout was entirely different. Although the flat-12 sat in front of and above the final drive, its clutch was behind the centre line, and drop gears transferred the drive to a shaft into the gearbox which was below the engine and also ahead of the final drive. By comparison, the rest of the car was conventional Ferrari, with

a multi-square-tube chassis frame, all-independent coil-spring suspension and a sleekly-styled (by Pininfarina) body made in light alloy at the Scaglietti works near Maranello.

The secret of the car is not in the specification, nor in the looks, but in the manner of its performance. With a maximum speed of more than 170mph, Ferrari-like acceleration, and the noise that no other car in the world can match, the Boxer has to be the sexiest of all expensive GT cars. As a Ferrari, it has roadholding, aerodynamics and stability to match the colossal performance, and (if any car with this performance can be safe) it is immensely safe. Yet, for all that, it suffers from the mid-engined car's habitual disadvantage of having just two seats and very little stowage space. But the queuing customers for this superfast beauty seem not to care about this for a second.

Right: Shaped by Pininfarina, with the four-cam flat-12 engine related to Ferrari's Grand prix unit, the Boxer is exquisite, and exclusive.

FIAT 500 'TOPOLINO'

Type 500, models built from 1936 to 1955 (data for 1936 model)

Built by: Fiat SpA., Italy.

Engine: Four cylinders, in line, in two-bearing cast-iron block. Bore and stroke 52mm by 67mm, 569cc (2·05in × 2·64in, 34·7cu.in). Detachable cast-iron cylinder head. Two sidevalves per cylinder, operated directly from single camshaft in cylinder block. Single side-draught Solex carburettor. Maximum power 13bhp (net) at 4,000rpm.

Transmission: Single-dry-plate clutch and four-speed manual gearbox (with synchromesh on top and third gears), all in unit with front-mounted engine. Direct-acting central gearchange. Open propeller shaft to spiral-bevel 'live' rear axle.

Chassis: Separate pressed-steel chassis frame, with channel-section side members, liberally pierced with holes for lightness, tubular and pressed cross-bracing. Independent front suspension by transverse-leaf spring and wishbones. Rear suspension by quarter-elliptic cantilever leaf springs and radius arms. Hydraulic piston-type dampers. Four-wheel, hydraulically operated drum brakes. 15in bolt-on pressed-steel wheels. 4·00 × 15in tyres.

Two-door saloon coachwork by Fiat themselves, with two seats and large luggage/occasional seating space behind seats, in pressed steel.

Dimensions: Wheelbase 6ft 6·7in (200cm), track (front) 3ft 7·5in (110·5cm), track (rear) 3ft 6·5in (108cm). Overall length 10ft 8·5in (326cm). Unladen weight 1,185lb (537kg).

History: Fiat's tiny little 'Topolino' ('little mouse') 500 model was the first of that company's really small cars, for which they are now justly famous. They had toyed with a small 'peoples' car in 1919, and even published catalogues, but never sold any cars. The 500 was designed in 1934 to slot into a Fiat range of which the 1-litre Balilla was then the smallest. It was new from end to end and caused as much of a sensation in Italy as the Austin Seven had done in Britain more than a decade earlier. It was, in every way, an 'ordinary' car in miniature, with no compromises or crudities due to the small size. Fiat never attempted to give it four seats, which was wise, as it had a small 78·5in (200cm) wheelbase and a conventionally mounted front engine. The independent front suspension was advanced by its rivals' standards and it had a very cheerful and cheeky character. It was a huge success, if slow but sure, right from the start, but inevitably, like the Austin Seven, it began to grow up.

In 1939 the frame was lengthened so that conventional half elliptic springs could be added and a rear seat provided. The car therefore put on weight and, after the war, the original side-valve engine was displaced by a 16·5bhp overhead-valve conversion, which raised the maximum speed to something approaching a creditable 60mph. An aluminium cylinder head arrived in 1949, at the same time as the half-timbered Giardiniera estate car. Minor restyling gave it a recessed-headlamp nose, but the car carried on basically unchanged until 1955, when it was discontinued in favour of the brand-new rear-engined 600 model. More than 120,000 500s were built between 1936 and 1948 and these were followed by 376,000 of the overhead-valve 500Cs. Apart from being reliable and incredibly versatile, the 'Topolino' really scored because it looked like, sounded like and behaved like a much bigger car. More than any other Italian car of the period, it was an ideal machine for the new motorist, or for the ex-motor cycle customers. Like later mini-Fiats, it was meant to take the place of the horse-and-cart in areas which were not used to cars, and it succeeded admirably.

Right: In its way Fiat's Topolino was as popular and versatile as the Austin Seven or the Model T Ford. The first was sold in 1936, and half a million were built up to 1955, with a break during the war years. Though tiny, its engineering was conventional, with a four cylinder engine in the nose, and rear wheel drive. It was always sold as a two-seater, with open or closed body work. It was really indestructible.

FIAT 508 BALILLA

Type 508 and 508S, side-valve and overhead-valve, built from 1932 to 1937 (data for 508S overhead-valve)

Built by: Fiat SpA., Italy.

Engine: Four cylinders, in line, in three-bearing cast-iron block. Bore and stroke 65mm by 75mm, 995cc (2·56in × 2·95in, 60·7cu.in). Cast-iron cylinder head. Two overhead valves per cylinder, operated by pushrods and rockers from single side-mounted camshaft. Zenith downdraught carburettor. Maximum power 36bhp at 4,400rpm.

Transmission: Single-dry-plate clutch and four-speed manual gearbox (synchromesh on top and third gears), both in unit with engine. Central direct-acting gearchange. Open propeller shaft to spiral-bevel 'live' rear axle.

Chassis: Separate steel chassis frame, with channel-section side members, and cruciform bracing. Forged front axle beam. Half-elliptic leaf springs at front and rear and friction type dampers (hydraulic on earlier 508 models). Worm-and-wheel steering. Four-wheel, hydraulically operated drum brakes. Separate drum handbrake on transmission, behind gearbox. 17in bolt-on wire wheels. 4·00 × 17in tyres.

Coachwork to choice, on 508, but 508S built as two-seat sports car.

Dimensions: Wheelbase 7ft 6·5in (230cm), tracks (front and rear) 3ft 10in (117cm). Overall length (depending on coachwork) about 12ft 10·8in (368cm). Unladen weight 1,300lb (590kg).

History: Fiat's all-new Balilla model was launched in 1932, at the very depth of the depression years. Fiat were well-protected against economic disaster (with 90 per cent of the Italian market), but could not afford to make another bad car after the Type 514, which had failed. The 508 was typical in most ways of the small family machine developed to expand the European market in the 1930s, with a one-litre engine, strictly conventional mechanical layout and lightweight construction. Fiat, better than most, engineered their car well, made it reliable and somehow ensured that it was interesting to drive. The original 508 had a marginally shorter wheelbase than the later 508S and a side-valve engine, but otherwise the specification remained mainly settled for five years. 'Balilla', incidentally, means 'plucky little one' and had rather sinister

Above: Fiat's Balilla sports car was a real advance over the heavy type of 'vintage' car—small, light, and with up-to-date engineering. In five years the styling was improved and the engine converted from side to overhead valves. This car had British-built bodywork.

connotations with a Mussolini/fascist youth movement.

The 508S, built first as a side-valve car, but from 1934 with an overhead-valve conversion of the same basic 995cc engine, arrived in 1933 and eventually made its name in trials, rallies, and even in endurance racing. Class for class it was very competitive, although it was overshadowed by such exotic machinery as the supercharged MG Magnettes. Cars sold in Britain were usually given British two-seater bodywork, of which a recognition point was usually the pronounced tail-fin behind the cockpit. One very desirable version of the car was the *berlinetta aerodinamica*, a fastback coupé with attractive flowing lines; maximum speed was raised, but the car was not much faster overall than open versions. A bald look at the specification tells us little about a Balilla's charm, except that it had an unusually 'short stroke' and small-capacity engine for the period. Somehow it was much more of a small car than a scaled down battle cruiser, and handled accordingly. All in all, about 2,000 508Ss were built, and a few were licence-made by Simca in France and by NSU in Germany.

Right and below: Because it had a separate chassis, the Balilla was sold with several different body styles. On the right is one of the original 1932 Roadsters (a 'Spider Lusso') with twin exposed spare wheels and rather upright lines. By 1935 the car was a 508S, with overhead valves, and the fast back coupe competed with honour in the Mille Miglia. The large illustration shows the typical two-seater open sports car style which went well with the final engine. The pronounced tail fin was a 1930s fashion. Although only 2,000 508S models were made, a few being licence-built in France and Germany, they were loved.

FIAT 8V

8V model, built from 1952 to 1954.
Built by: Fiat SpA., Italy.
Engine: Eight cylinders, in 70-degree vee-formation, in three-bearing light-alloy block/crankcase with cast iron cylinder liners. Bore and stroke 72mm by 61·3mm, 1,996cc (2·83in × 2·41in, 121·8cu.in). Detachable light-alloy cylinder heads. Two overhead valves per cylinder, operated by pushrods and rockers from single camshaft mounted in centre of cylinder block 'vee'. Two downdraught twin-choke Weber carburettors. Maximum power 105bhp or 115bhp (net) at 6,000rpm. Maximum torque with 115bhp engine, 107lb.ft at 4,600rpm.
Transmission: Single-dry-plate clutch and four-speed, all-synchromesh manual gearbox, both in unit with front-mounted engine. Direct-acting central gearchange. Open propeller shaft to chassis-mounted hypoid-bevel final drive. Exposed, universally jointed drive shafts to rear wheels.
Chassis: Tubular-steel chassis frame, with sheet-steel floor and reinforcements, and steel bodywork all welded up into a unitary-construction structure. Independent front suspension by coil springs, wishbones and anti-roll bar. Independent rear suspension by coil springs, wishbones and anti-roll bar. Two-piece track rod steering. Four-wheel, hydraulically operated drum brakes. Centre-lock wire wheels. 165 × 400mm tyres.
Two-seat closed coupé coachwork by Fiat, with passenger's seat set back to give driver more elbow room.

Dimensions: Wheelbase 7ft 10·5in (240cm), tracks (front and rear) 4ft 2·7in (129cm). Overall length 13ft 2·6in (403cm). Unladen weight 2,340lb (1,061kg).
History: Fiat were such a vast company by the 1950s that they could indulge themselves in a sporting whim when it took their fancy. The 8V coupé, of which not more than 114 examples were ever made, was such a fancy. It pandered to the rich Italian sportsmen who wanted a competition car, but would not pay out for a very exclusive Alfa Romeo or wildly impractical Ferrari or Maserati. The 8V's engine itself was entirely special and was never shared with another model. Its 70-degree vee engine was specifically designed to fit under narrow bonnets, which explains the unique included angle. The body made no compromises to comfort and convenience: the passenger/co-driver seating position was set back by at least a foot to give the driver's elbows room to operate and there were only two seats.

The combined multi-tube/sheet-steel shell could only ever be made in small quantities. Under the skin, however, the front and rear suspension components were lifted from Fiat's popular 1100 saloon, while the axle and drive shafts were *front* components from the Campagnola cross-country car. The gearbox was all-synchromesh, at a time when such things were rare and the body had actually been wind-tunnel tested at a time when many competition cars were shaped by eye and by personal preference. It was a car once described as 'Fiat engineers

thinking aloud' — in other words the sort of engineering they would like to see adopted on a large scale if only their masters would agree. As a potential competition car, the 8V was well-designed, although the overhead-valve engine could not be tuned much above 130bhp. The cars won the Italian 2-litre GT championship in 1954, and Ghia and Zagato both produced unique-looking and very purposeful machines, Ghias with a five-speed gearbox. The last series of production cars were given a 'Chinese' slant-eye four-headlamp system, which predated Triumph by several years.

Fiat's only gas-turbine-powered car, which ran in 1954, used an 8V's chassis and suspensions as its base. The last of the 8Vs were built in 1954 and there were no other sporting Fiats until the beginning of the 1960s.

Right: Fiat's 8V model is unique in several respects. It is the only vee-8 Fiat car sold to the public, and was the only model in which the engineers' whims triumphed over sales requirements. 8Vs were sold in tiny numbers—only 114 were built in three years—and it was intended mainly for competition use. There were only two seats, that of the passenger being set back to give more elbow room to the hard-working driver! Bodies were usually by Ghia or Zagato, and made few concessions to comfort or silence. The 8V was a very successful sports car of its day.

FORD MODEL A

Model A, built from 1903 to 1906 (data for original 1903 model)
Built by: Ford Motor Co., United States
Engine: Two cylinders, horizontally opposed, in two cast-iron cylinders, with two-bearing cast-iron crankcase. Bore and stroke 107·9mm by 101·6mm, 1,860cc (4·25in × 4·00in, 113·5 cu.in). Two fixed cylinder heads. Two side valves per cylinder, directly operated by single camshaft mounted in base of crankcase. Single horizontal carburettor, mounted ahead of one cylinder, with one very short and one very long inlet manifold. Maximum power about 9bhp at 800rpm.
Transmission: Engine and transmission mounted in unit, under seats of car. Engine to left of car, with cylinders pointing forward and back, driving across to transmission. No separate clutch. Two-speed epicyclic gearbox, with friction bands and friction discs. Remote-control right-hand gearchange. Final drive to differential by chain.
Chassis: Separate pressed-steel chassis frame, with channel-section side members and channel-section cross bracing. Forged front axle beam. Front suspension by full-elliptic springs. Rear suspension by full-elliptic springs with radius arms. No dampers. Lever-type steering. Single rear brake, in axle casing and surrounding differential, cable operated from hand lever. 28in artillery-style road wheels. 28 × 3in tyres.
Dimensions: Wheelbase 6ft (183cm), tracks (front and rear) 4ft 7·5in (141cm). Overall length 8ft 3in (251·5cm). Unladen weight 1,250lb (567kg).
History: Henry Ford's world-wide fame was founded on the ubiquitous Model T, but he had been in the motor car business for a decade before this car appeared. The first-ever Ford was built in 1896 and the second in 1898. However it was not until the beginning of the 20th century that Ford left his employment with the Detroit Automobile Co. and set up his own business. The Model A, not to be confused with the late-vintage mass-production Model A, followed some of Leland's design details, learned by Ford at the Detroit company. It is notable for having an underfloor flat-twin engine, a two-speed epi-

cyclic transmission, alongside that engine, and chain drive. The chassis was flimsy in the extreme, and there was a type of rear-entrance tonneau bodywork. It was very high off the ground and, in spite of having 1·8-litres, it could only produce 9bhp. Even so, it sold for $850 (more, in those days, than a Cadillac!) and more than 1,700 were sold in the first year. He followed this success with the Model C (based on the A, but with different coachwork), and the Model B, which had the first four-cylinder Ford engine.

The Model K (a six) and the Model N followed, but all of these were mere scene-setters for the legendary Model T, which replaced them all at one fell swoop.

Below: Ford's Model A was the first of many enormously successful models which Henry Ford sponsored. It was the spiritual ancestor of the Model T, but with an entirely different layout. The two cylinder engine was under the seats.

FORD V-8 1930s

V8 cars, built from 1932 to 1941 (data for 1932 model 18)

Built by: Ford Motor Co., United States

Engine: Eight cylinders, in 90-degree vee-formation, in three-bearing cast-iron block/crankcase. Bore and stroke 77·8mm by 95·25mm, 3,622cc (3·06in × 3·75in, 221cu.in). Two detachable cast-iron cylinder heads. Two side valves per cylinder, operated directly from single camshaft positioned in centre of cylinder block 'vee'. One single-choke down-draught Detroit Lubricator carburettor. Maximum power 65bhp (gross) at 3,400rpm.

Transmission: Single-dry-plate clutch and three-speed manual gearbox (without synchromesh on first gear), both in unit with front-mounted engine. Direct-acting central gearchange. Propeller shaft, enclosed in torque tube, driving spiral-bevel 'live' rear axle.

Chassis: Separate pressed-steel chassis frame, with channel section side members and tubular cross bracing. Forged front axle beam. Front suspension by transvers leaf spring and radius arms. Rear suspension by transverse leaf spring and radius arms. Lever-arm hydraulic dampers. Four-wheel, rod operated drum brakes. 18in bolt-on wire spoke wheels. 5·25 × 18in tyres.

Dimensions: Wheelbase 8ft 10in (269cm), track (front) 4ft 7·2in (140cm), track (rear) 4ft 8·7in (144cm). Overall length 13ft 9·5in (420cm). Unladen weight 2,580lb (1,170kg).

History: To replace the obsolete Model T, Ford developed the new Model A at the end of the 1920s and from the beginning of 1932 they further improved their range by slotting the first of the now-legendary side-valve V8 engines into the Model A's chassis and body styles. There was nothing remarkably new about the V8 engine in the United States, but at the time the straight-8 configuration was fashionable and it was the first real sign Ford had given of being interested in making powerful cars. The V8s were always quick, for they combined lusty torque with light weight. In Europe, where modified versions were built in several countries (in Britain, for instance, from 1935 onwards) the V8 soon became a recognised rally car and one won the Monte Carlo Rally in 1936. The V8 was

always hampered by its crude suspension (transverse leaf springs at front and rear) and its eventual development was always to be hindered by the side-valve layout with exhaust gases being led out across the cylinder block casting, but it formed the backbone of Ford's world-wide power-plant engineering until the beginning of the 1950s. There were several changes in body style which transformed the V8 from an upright saloon to a much smoother machine by the outbreak of World War II. After

an initial period the engines soon got their reputation for being dead reliable and the cars always offered extremely good value. The engine was the symbol of Ford's modernisation at the end of the 1920s.

Below: In the United States, and all over the world, Ford's vee-8 car was a low-priced sensation. It was a very successful rally car too—this car is on a Scottish Rally of the 1930s.

FORD MODEL T

Model T, built from 1908 to 1927
Built by: Ford Motor Co. Ltd., United States.
Engine: Four cylinders, in line, in three-bearing cast-iron block/crankcase. Bore and stroke 95·2mm by 101·6mm, 2,896cc (3·75in × 4·0in, 176·7cu.in). Cast-iron cylinder head. Two side valves per cylinder, directly operated by camshaft in cylinder block. Single Holley or Kingston carburettor. Splash lubrication. Maximum power 20bhp.
Transmission: Epicyclic transmission, two forward speeds and reverse, incorporating take-up clutches, in unit with engine, and running in engine oil. Contracting bands applied to epicyclic drums for low gear and reverse, as appropriate; direct drive top gear with multi-disc clutch fixed to engine. Propeller shaft in torque tube to straight-bevel 'live' axle (overhead worm gear on light commercials).
Chassis: Very simple separate steel chassis frame, with channel-section side members, and minimal cross bracing. Forged front axle beam. Front and rear suspension by transverse leaf springs. No dampers. Epicyclic reduction gear steering in steering wheel boss; direct connection from column to drag link by drop arm. Foot brake by contracting band on to direct-drive transmission clutch. Handbrake mechanically connected to drums on rear wheel hubs. 30in artillery-type wheels. 30×3in or 30×3·5in tyres. Coachwork: many Ford-sourced choices, from two-seat tourers to five-seat four-door saloons. All on same basic chassis and mechanicals.

Right: Ford's legendary Model T looked spidery and fragile when new, but soon made a wonderful reputation for town and country use. Even if it broke down sometimes, it was simple to repair, and spare parts were available everywhere. More than 15 million were sold.

Dimensions: Wheelbase 8ft 4in (254cm), tracks (front and rear) 4ft 8in, or (late models) 5ft (142cm or 152cm). Overall length slightly dependent on coachwork, from 11ft 4in (345cm). Unladen weight from 1,450lb (658kg).
History: Before the VW Beetle came along, the Model T Ford could be described in one sentence – it was the world's highest selling car. Between 1908, when production began at Highland Park in Detroit, and 1927 when the last Model T was built, 15,007,033 examples were sold. The car, which started modestly enough at 10,000 units in 1909, came to dominate the American market with just over two *million* sales in 1923. It was also assembled at several overseas Ford plants,

not least at Trafford Park, Manchester, in Great Britain. Even so the Model T had two basic faults – in almost every way it was unimproved between 1908 and 1927, and Henry Ford hung on to it for far too long, before replacing it by the new Model A. The hiatus this caused – the Model A having to be developed in a rush and the factory having to be closed down for re-equipment – set back Ford very seriously, and it was not until after World War II that stability was really achieved.

Although the Model T was not the first ever Ford to be put into production (that was the original Model A, of course), it was the first ever mass-production Ford. Indeed, it was really the

world's first mass-produced car and, in spite of its mechanical crudities, the facilities and production techniques developed to assemble it very easily and quickly were advanced and modern. Ford, for instance, undoubtedly 'invented' the moving production line, where cars were moved on from one specific assembly station to the next.

Henry Ford's theory was that the great mass of the American people wanted reliable and basic transportation, not necessarily modern styling and complex mechanical equipment, and with the Model T he set out to give this to them. By developing the Ford service network all over the world, and by making the Model T very simple to strip down and repair, he kept the whole concept as cheap as possible. The fact that the Model T was by no means as reliable nor as simple as other cars made no difference. The time it spent off the road was minimal.

The chassis was not at all rigid; it was very simple and had the most rudimentary of transverse-leaf suspensions. Bodies, more and more variations of which became available over the years, were light and also simple. It was a long time before weather protection and enclosed cabins became the norm for Ford customers. The engine, too, was as basic as Ford could make it. Of nearly 2·9-litres, it nevertheless had very undeveloped manifolding, and produced about 20bhp. The only real mechanical complication was in the transmission, which had two forward gears and one reverse, relying heavily on epicyclic gearing. Not only that, but the 'clutch' pedal was really a gearchange pedal. In its mid position, held by applying the handbrake, the transmission was in neutral; when pressed right down, the epicyclic low gear was engaged and when released completely the direct-drive top gear was in use. There was no foot accelerator pedal, and engine speed changes were effected by hand levers under the steering wheel which controlled throttle opening and spark advance.

In addition to the T's reputation for low running costs Henry Ford had an affinity for regularly cutting selling prices. The five-seat tourer cost $850 in 1909, and $950 in 1910, but thereafter the price-cutting began. By mechanising more and more of the production process, Ford was able to cut that same car's price to $360 by 1916. In Britain, for instance, where the Model T had a larger engine than many cars (and an RAC horsepower rating absurdly high for its performance) it was by far the cheapest car on the market. The only thing which could kill the T in its home country was complete and absolute obsolescence. Sales began to fall after the record year of 1923 and by the time it was discontinued in 1927 the T was on its last legs. Not only had the opposition advanced too much technically, but their cars were reliable, cheap *and* smart. The new Model A would have to match them, in a way that the T could not.

Left: Between 1913 (model on facing page) and 1919 (this page) only the body styles had been noticeably updated —there were no mechanical innovations. The lazy 2·9-litre four-cylinder engine and two-speed epicyclic transmission were kept for 20 years.

Above (both pages): Details of the Model T's evolution. Above far left is a 1909 Phaeton; Left a 1911 Runabout; Above one of the last, a 1927 Tourer. Top left is a 1909/16 radiator, and top right the 1917/27 radiator shell. Minor changes were legion through the years.

FORD GALAXIE

Galaxie, introduced 1959 (data for 1960 model)
Built by: Ford Motor Co., United States.
Engine: Eight cylinders, in 90-degree vee-formation, in five-bearing cast-iron block/crankcase. Bore and stroke 101·6mm by 83·7mm, 5,441cc (4·0in × 3·30in, 332cu.in). Two detachable cast-iron cylinder heads. Two overhead valves per cylinder, operated by pushrods and rockers from single camshaft mounted in centre of cylinder block 'vee'. Single downdraught four-choke Ford (Autolite) carburettor. Maximum power 225bhp (gross) at 4,400rpm.

Maximum torque 324lb.ft at 2,200rpm.
Transmission: Torque converter and three-speed fully automatic gearbox, both in unit with front-mounted engine. Remote-control steering-column-positioned gearchange. Optional three-speed all-synchromesh manual gearbox. Open propeller shaft to hypoid-bevel 'life' rear axle.
Chassis: Separate pressed-steel chassis frame, with box-section side members, and pressed cross members and bracings. Pressed-steel bodywork in several forms — principally four-door saloon. Front suspension on subframe, independent by coil springs, wishbones and anti-roll bar.

Rear suspension by half-elliptic leaf springs. Telescopic dampers. Recirculating-ball steering, power assisted. Four-wheel, hydraulically operated drum brakes, vacuum-servo assisted. 14in pressed-steel disc wheels. 8·00 × 14in tyres.
Dimensions: Wheelbase 9ft 11in (302cm), track (front) 5ft 1in (155cm), track (rear) 5ft (152cm). Overall length 17ft 9·7in (543cm). Unladen weight 4,050lb (1,837kg).
History: Ford's Galaxie series is a classic merely because it is so typical of a class of machine — large, easy to drive, and mechanically undistinguished — which the North American public

FORD THUNDERBIRD

Thunderbird two-seater cars built from 1955 to 1957 (data for 1956 model)
Built by: Ford Motor Co., United States
Engine: Eight cylinders, in 90-degree vee-formation, in five-bearing cast-iron block. Bore and stroke 96·5mm by 87·4mm, 5,113cc (3·80in × 3·44in, 312cu.in). Two detachable cast-iron cylinder heads. Two overhead valves per cylinder, operated by pushrods and rockers from single camshaft mounted in centre of cylinder block 'vee'. Single down-draught four-choke Ford carburettor. Maximum power 225bhp (gross) at 4,600rpm. Maximum torque 324lb.ft at 2,600rpm.
Transmission: Single-dry-plate clutch and three-speed, all-synchromesh manual gearbox, both in unit with front-mounted engine. Direct-acting central gearchange. Optional three-speed automatic transmission, with torque converter. Open propeller shaft to hypoid-bevel 'live' rear axle.
Chassis: Separate pressed-steel chassis frame, with box-section side members, and pressed cross bracing. Independent front suspension by coil springs, wishbones and anti-roll bar. Rear suspension by half-elliptic leaf springs. Telescopic dampers all round. Four wheel, hydraulically operated drum brakes, with vacuum-servo assistance. 15in pressed-steel road wheels. 6·70 × 15in tyres.
Two-seat sporting bodywork by Ford, supplied with folding hood or detachable hardtop.
Dimensions: Wheelbase 8ft 6in (259cm), tracks (front and rear) 4ft 8in (142cm). Overall length 15ft 5·2in (470·5cm). Unladen weight 3,450lb (1,565kg).
History: The Thunderbird took shape in 1953, and was publicly launched in 1954, as the first true 'sporting' two-seater Ford for many years. Although a multitude of normal saloon car parts were used under the skin, the styling was fresh, youthful in its appeal and unique to this model. The importance of the early T-Birds was that their appeal was not compromised by other commercial considerations. Although Ford were already looking ahead to a more sporting future in the early 1950s, the arrival of the deadly rival

from Chevrolet, the first of the Corvettes, was a great spur to their ambitions. Even though the T-Bird was — by North American standards — a sports car, it was by no means small. The first cars had 4·8-litre V8 engines and weighed in at around 3,500lb (1,587kg), which put them a full size class ahead of the Jaguars even though they were no more expensive in their native North America. Styling of the first two-seaters was crisp and clean, certainly by Detroit's saloon car styling standards, and the first cars in particular had virtually no extraneous decoration to spoil the overall effect. The windscreen was well swept, as were all such cars from Detroit, and the lines were very low, with a height of only 4ft 5in (135cm). Either manual transmission

or Ford-o-Matic automatic transmission was available. Unlike the rival Corvette, and this was thought to be a great selling point, every T-Bird was equipped with a V8 engine; there was no 'cheap' six-cylinder option. A feature of 1956 and later models was the optional external mounting of the spare wheel, atop the back bumper, to give a 'continental' look. There was an extensive retouching of the style for 1957, which included portholes in the optional hardtop, but the car's whole character was lost for 1958 when it was rebodied into a much less sporting four-seater. After that the T-Bird became just another Ford, and it was not until 1964 and the arrival of the Mustang that sporting motoring really came back to Ford's ranks.

flocked to buy in millions in the 1950s and 1960s. A classic does not have to be the fastest, the most beautiful, the rarest, or even the most quirky. It has to be something which is recognisable as a worthy type. The Galaxie was just one of the Detroit breed which most observers disdain. Like other full-size cars from Chevrolet or Chrysler, Galaxies were built to a formula. They all had around a 10ft (305cm) wheelbase, and were over 6ft (183cm) wide. They could all carry six people, along with a mountain of luggage, without too much of a squeeze and for long distances, without needing attention. Petrol consumption was usually high — 14 to 16mpg was normal — but fuel was very cheap. The cars were all fast — more than 100mph maximum speed without much effort — even though they were meant to be driven on speed-limited North American highways. Technically, the advances were in cost-control, and in clever production-engineering of castings and body assemblies.

Surprisingly, the manufacturers were slow to relinquish a separate chassis frame and drum brakes. Galaxies, for instance, had separate frames well into the 1960s, and although front disc brakes were optional by mid 1960s they were not standardised until the end of the decade. Once established as a breed, they remained popular, and not even the threats of petrol rationing in 1973/74 killed off their appeal. Size for size they were at their fastest and (arguably) their most enjoyable at the end of the 1960s. Thereafter, safety and anti-pollution legislation meant added weight and drastically reduced performance. Even so, if you don't mind a soft ride, there is good engineering, fine brakes and long-life components in the modern North American car. The appeal is in the long life and the easy service.

Left and right: Archetypal American car of the 1950s and 1960s was Ford's big Galaxie range, introduced in 1959. It is classic because of its typical layout, its big, lazy, powerful and utterly reliable cast-iron vee-8 engine, and because of the evidence that Detroit's bosses put annual style changes and long-term reliability ahead of high-cost mechanical innovation and exclusive detailing. Detroit cars of the period still used separate chassis frames, and sophisticated production techniques made a whole variety of alternative bodies possible. On the Galaxie, as on competing models, there were four-door saloons, convertibles, rakish coupes, and vast estate cars. By the 1960s just about everything possible was power-assisted. Detroit put the removal of driver effort above that of mechanical advances.

Facing page and below: Only in the first three years of its long life was the Ford Thunderbird a true sporting two-seater. It persisted in growing up, and from 1958 became a close-coupled four-seater 'personal car' in advertising parlance. Conceived in 1953 the Thunderbird was Ford's first sporty two-seater for many years, and aimed to beat Chevrolet's new Corvette. The T-Bird used mainly standard Ford touring parts under a sleek pressed-steel skin, had optional automatic transmission, and a big selling point was that every car had a vee-8 engine. More than 53,000 were built in three seasons.

FORD MUSTANG

Mustang, built from 1964 to 1968, six-cyl and V8 models (data for 289cu.in).

Built by: Ford Motor Co., United States.

Engine: Eight cylinders, in 90-degree vee-formation, in cast-iron cylinder block. Bore and stroke 101·6mm by 72·9mm, 4,727cc (4·0in × 2·87in, 289cu.in). Two cast-iron cylinder heads. Two overhead valves per cylinder, operated by pushrods and rockers from single camshaft mounted in cylinder block 'vee'. Downdraught four-choke Ford carburettor. Maximum power 271bhp (gross) at 6,000rpm. Maximum torque 312lb.ft at 3,400rpm.

Transmission: Single-dry-plate clutch and four-speed, all-synchromesh manual gearbox, both in unit with engine. Central remote-control gearchange. Open propeller shaft to hypoid-bevel 'live' axle. Optional limited-slip differential. Optional three-speed Ford automatic transmission with torque converter.

Chassis: Unitary-construction pressed-steel body/chassis unit, sold as open tourer four-seater, closed two-door coupé, or with fastback closed coupé style. Independent front suspension by coil springs, wishbones and anti-roll bar. Rear suspension by half-elliptic leaf springs. Recirculating-ball steering with power assistance optional. Four-wheel, hydraulically operated and servo-assisted drum brakes, with optional front discs. 14in pressed-steel disc wheels.

Dimensions: Wheelbase 9ft (274cm), track (front) 4ft 8in (142cm), track (rear) 4ft 8in (142cm). Overall length 15ft 1·6in (461cm). Unladen weight from 2,925lb (1,327kg) depending on equipment and bodyshell.

History: Ford's Mustang can probably thank the first very sporting Thunderbirds for its birth. The T-Bird, a two-seater at first, soon grew up and became a much larger car. By the early 1960s, with compact cars popular and sporting motoring again important to Ford, a place for a 'small' sporting machine developed. By European standards, of course, the Mustang has never been small — in original production form it was more than 15ft long, which is Aston Martin size, and bulkier than any sporting Jaguar. By Detroit standards, however, it was a very neat little package.

The production car was launched in April 1964, but had already been trailered by other prototype 'Mustangs' for the company to gauge reaction. The mid-engined car (the engine being a German V4) made public in 1962, was far too sophisticated for Ford to build in quantity and was made purely as a 'taster'. Mustang II, revealed at the US Grand Prix in the autumn of 1963, was still a non-production car, but since it was closely based on a prototype Mustang and redecorated lightly, its impact on the public was important. The public liked it and Ford went ahead to build the cars.

Chief of the Mustang project was Lee Iacocca, who was no innovative designer, but was sporting minded and already had the successful development of the compact Ford Falcon to his credit. It was therefore no surprise that the Mustang was such an enjoyable car to drive. It was more of a surprise that it could be persuaded to become a winner on the race tracks, but this was mostly because of the very imaginative list of high-performance options made available. The car used many Falcon components, including the basic engines and transmissions, and in true Detroit style there was a vast range of choice right from the start. One option much discussed, and even pictured in 1964, was an independent rear suspension for racing, but this was never proceeded with, and all Mustangs had to rely on the very basic half-elliptic leaf spring layout for location.

Engines ranged from the cheapest and least powerful straight six of 2,781cc to the highest-performance V8 of 4,727cc. The difference in power was from 101bhp to 271bhp, and shows the spread of owners' preferences for which Ford was aiming. By 1966, indeed, two tunes of sixes and five tunes of eights had already been listed, and as the years went by this choice widened. Cars could have manual or automatic transmission, drum or disc brakes, manual or power-assisted steering, soft or hard-tops, 13in or 14in wheels, extra instruments, special colour schemes and many other options.

Mustangs were successful in factory-sponsored teams almost at once, and their biggest early win was in the 1964 Tour de France where two cars prepared in Britain finished first and second overall, the winning car being driven by Peter Procter. As a racing 'saloon' car (for the Mustang was ideally dimensioned to satisfy international regulations), it was only ever beaten by other and even more special Fords, usually the lightweight Falcons. No young man, or young-at-heart man in North America could live until he had owned a Mustang, with the result that 400,000 were sold within twelve months, and the first million sales were notched up in 1966. Engine tuners like Carroll Shelby hurried to market their own special Mustangs (Shelby's was the GT350 and was very fierce indeed), while the 'add-on' accessory suppliers made a good living with special customising kits. The Mustang was an aggressively marketed runaway success in North America and (because of its reasonable size) was well-received in other countries. So much so, in fact, that Ford did not need to go for an important restyling operation until 1968. With that move, the Mustang, like the Thunderbird before it, began to move 'up-market' and to put on weight and bulk. Apart from the 5-litre 'Boss' of the late 1960s, it became less of a sporting car and more of a virility symbol. It was completely redesigned in the early 1970s and Mustang II is a much smaller, simpler and slower car.

Below: The original version of the fabulously successful Ford Mustang. This convertible has the optional 289cu.in high-performance vee-8 engine, special wheels and tyres. Softer versions had six-cylinder engines and rather less performance. More than a million Mustangs sold in the first three years.

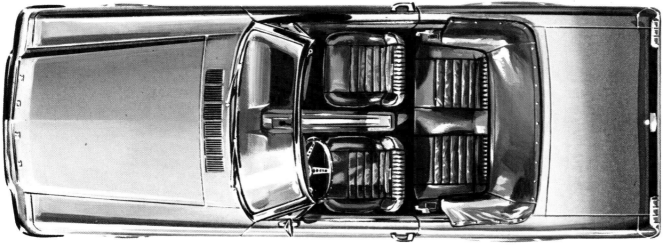

Above: Two views of the Mustang show that the original cars had striking styling, but still found space for four full-size passengers. The car was a 'tourer' in every way, and was raced and rallied in the standard saloon car categories. Mustangs won the Tour de France in 1964, hundreds of races all over the world, and were a virility symbol to American youth of the 1960s. Through the years it grew up gradually but recent cars are smaller and slower, with European power trains.

FORD GT40

GT40 I, to III (data for Mk I)
Built by: Ford Advanced Vehicles Ltd., Britain.
Engine: Eight cylinders in 90-degree vee-formation, in cast-iron block. Bore and stroke 101·6mm by 72·9mm, 4,727cc (4·00 × 2·87in, 289cu.in). Cast-iron cylinder heads. Two overhead valves per cylinder, operated by pushrods and rockers from a single camshaft positioned in the vee of the cylinder block. Four downdraught, 48mm, dual-choke Weber carburettors. Fabricated tubular exhaust manifolds, with silencers positioned above the transmission.

Wet-sump lubrication system. Maximum power 390bhp at 7,000rpm in 'production' form. Maximum torque 325lb.ft at 5,000rpm. Engine derived from quantity-production Mustang/Cobra design, and built by Ford in Detroit.
Transmission: Transaxle and five-speed ZF gearbox mounted integrally behind mid-positioned engine. No propeller shaft. Gear ratios and final drive gearing depended on racing application; many alternatives available. Limited-slip differential standard. Engine mounted ahead of axle and drive shafts, gearbox behind it. Exposed

drive shafts with two universal joints. Maximum speed, depending on overall gearing, could be between 140mph and 200mph.
Chassis: Sheet-steel monocoque, with integral roll hoop and cockpit supports. Glassfibre skin panels. Doors cut high into the roof, also made of glassfibre. All-independent suspension by coil springs and wishbones; rear suspension pivoted direct from the transaxle. Four-wheel ventilated disc brakes, outboard all round. Cast-alloy 15in road wheels with centre-lock 'knock-off' nuts, originally with 6in front rims, 9in rears. Tyre size

FORD ESCORT RS1600

Escorts — Twin-Cam, RS1600 and RS1800 (data for RS1600)
Built by: Ford Motor Co. Ltd., Britain.
Engine: Four cylinders, in line, in five-bearing light-alloy block (1970/72 models with cast-iron cylinder block). Bore and stroke 80·97mm by 77·62mm, 1,601cc (3·19 × 3·06in, 97·7cu.in). Light-alloy cylinder head. Four overhead valves per cylinder, operated by inverted-bucket tappets from twin overhead camshafts. Twin sidedraught dual-choke Weber carburettors. Maximum power 120bhp (DIN) at 6,500rpm. Maximum torque 112lb.ft at 4,000rpm.
Transmission: Single-dry-plate clutch and four-speed, all-synchromesh manual gearbox, both in unit with front-mounted engine. Remote-control central gearchange. Open propeller shaft to hypoid-bevel 'live' rear axle.
Chassis: Unitary-construction pressed-steel two-door saloon body/chassis unit. Front suspension independent by MacPherson struts and anti-roll bar. Rear suspension by half-elliptic leaf springs with radius arms and telescopic dampers. Rack-and-pinion steering. Hydraulically operated and servo-assisted front wheel disc brakes, and rear wheel drums. Cable-operated handbrake to rear wheels. 13in pressed-steel disc wheels. 165 × 13in tyres.
Dimensions: Wheelbase 7ft 10·5in (240cm), track (front) 4ft 3·7in (131cm), track (rear) 4ft 4in (132cm). Overall length 13ft 0·6in (398cm). Unladen weight 1,920lb (870kg).
History: The Ford Escort, announced in 1968, was the latest in a long line of conventional small family saloons from Ford. One version of it – the Escort Twin-Cam – was a very special, limited-production car intended for use in touring car racing and rallying. This car used Lotus-Cortina mechanicals, including the twin-overhead-cam engine. It was extremely successful, but the two-valves-per-cylinder engine was obsolescent.

In 1970, it was replaced by the RS1600, almost identical to the Twin-Cam except for its magnificently conceived four-valves-per-cylinder Ford-Cosworth BDA engine. This was a twin-overhead-cam conversion of the pushrod 1,600cc Cortina unit, with belt-driven overhead camshafts. It was also, in effect, a productionised variant of the wildly successful Cosworth FVA Formula 2 racing engine. Thus equipped, and with all manner of tuning gear added, an Escort could have up to 280bhp in enlarged (2-litre) racing guise, and could win rough rallies all over the world. The first RSs had cast-iron cylinder blocks, which could only safely be bored out to 1,800cc; the aluminium block, adopted in 1972, allowed boring to give the full 'capacity limit' of 2-litres.

In 1975, when the Escort's styling was changed, the RS1600 became the RS1800, with a larger but more simply carburated engine. All previous competition extras could be fitted. Other popular Escorts for sporting purposes have been the 1,600cc Mexico and the 2,000cc RS2000, neither with the special Cosworth engines.

Below: Without any doubt, Ford Escorts are the world's most successful rally car of all time. The factory have been using them for ten years in Twin-Cam, RS1600 (the model shown), and RS1800 form. More recent cars have a 2-litre 16-valve Cosworth BDA engine producing 245bhp. The performance is shattering.

according to racing requirements; racing tyres obligatory.

Dimensions: Wheelbase 7ft 11in (241cm), track (front) 4ft 6in (137cm), track (rear) 4ft 6in (137cm). Overall length 13ft 8·6in (418cm). Unladen weight 1,835lb (832kg).

History: In 1963, Ford of Detroit turned to high performance and motor sport in a big way. Apart from their Indianapolis engine projects, their main effort went into an assault on the Le Mans 24-hour race. Their original Ford GTs were partly based on Eric Broadley's Lola GT and they raced without success in 1964 with light-alloy 4·2-litre engines and Colotti transmissions. For 1965, the race cars, further developed by Carroll Shelby's team in California, won the World Championship event at Daytona.

Production cars, called GT40 because 40in was the height of the machine, were built to the 1965 design, in the FAV Ltd. factory in Slough, Bucks. Fifty had to be sold for the car to qualify as a 'Production Sports Car' in racing circles, but demand was such that a total of 107 were constructed before 1968, when the FAV Ltd. business was closed down. Almost every GT40 built was sold specifically for competition use, but 31 were converted for road use and seven detuned, silenced and better-trimmed Mark IIIs were specially built for the road. The price of a Mk III, in 1967, was £7,254 in Britain.

Ford of Detroit rapidly developed the original car into a Mk II version, which first ran at Le Mans in 1965, with the larger and heavier 7-litre V8 engine and a Kar-Kraft transmission utilising Ford Galaxie internals. Also in this special GT40-based (but factory-only) Mk II was a dry-sump

Left: Among the 107 GT40s built were seven de-tuned road cars like this 1966 model. Right: A GT40 Mk II won the Le Mans 24 Hour race in 1966, but not this car. Ford also won in 67/68/69.

lubrication system and minor aerodynamic changes to the glassfibre bodywork. Mk IIs in this form could easily top 200mph with Le Mans gearing and they dominated most events in 1966. Ford's first Le Mans win came in that year, with the winning car driven by Bruce McLaren and Chris Amon.

For 1967, Ford built a few very special Mk IV Ford GTs, which used Mk II mechanicals in entirely new monocoque chassis with light-alloy honeycomb structural members. The company took their second Le Mans victory at a record

135·48mph (218kph) average speed. Immediately after this race they retired from racing.

GT40s, further refined and developed by JW Automotive (whose chief, John Wyer, had been Managing Director of FAV Ltd.) went on to win many more races in 1968 and 1969, including the Le Mans 24-hour event each year. Latterly their engines were enlarged from 4·7 litres to the full 5-litre limit, and fitted with Gurney–Weslake cylinder heads. JWA also raced the Ford Mirage, which was really a GT40 fitted with a non-standard engine and more streamlined bodywork.

FRANKLIN AIR-COOLED MODEL IIB SIX

Six-cylinder Franklins, built from 1905 to 1934 (data for 1927 model)

Built by: Franklin Automobile Co., United States.

Engine: Six cylinders, in line, in individual finned (air-cooled), cast-iron blocks, with seven-bearing light-alloy crankcase. Bore and stroke 82·55mm by 101·6mm, 3,263cc (3·25in × 4·0in, 199cu.in). Detachable cast-iron cylinder heads. Two overhead valves per cylinder, operated by pushrods and rockers from single camshaft mounted in side of crankcase. Exposed valve gear. Air impeller at front of engine, blowing air across cylinder head and down radially finned cylinders. Single up-draught carburettor.

Transmission: Single-dry-plate clutch and three-speed manual gearbox (without synchromesh), both in unit with front-mounted engine. Direct-acting central gearchange. Open propeller shaft to spiral-bevel 'live' rear axle.

Chassis: Separate chassis frame, with laminated ash wood side members, reinforced by steel plates and tubular and pressed cross bracing. Forged front axle beam. Front and rear suspension by full-elliptic leaf springs. Worm-and-gear steering. Mechanically operated foot brake on transmission drum and hand brake on rear-wheel drums. Artillery-style wheels, fixed to hubs. 32 × 4in tyres.

Dimensions: Wheelbase 9ft 11in (302cm), tracks (front and rear) 4ft 8in (142cm). Overall length 14ft 8in (447cm). Unladen weight 3,255lb (1,476kg).

History: Franklin's claim to fame in the history books is that they were America's most successful makers of air-cooled cars. In more than 30 years of manufacture they never made a water-cooled machine and sold more than 150,000 cars in all. At their peak, with the final development of the six-cylinder engines, they

sold 14,000 in 1929. Not only this, but until 1927, even with the big cars of the vintage years, they stayed loyal to a chassis frame with wooden side members and used full-elliptic springs to give the best possible ride (not losing out all that much on precision of steering or handling).

Externally, a vintage Franklin looked conventional, with a dummy 'radiator' grille hiding the big engine-driven fan; this impelled air along the top of the engine, where ducts channelled this down the finned sides of the individually cast cylinders. The rest of the chassis and layout was entirely conventional and none the worse for that. Before the end of the decade Franklin had espoused four-wheel hydraulic brakes and he

finally adopted a pressed-steel chassis. By 1932, indeed, synchromesh had been fitted. Also Franklin announced their splendid 'white elephant' in 1932 — a 6·8-litre supercharged V12, still with air-cooling.

The United States depression caught out Franklin, as it did most of the other independents. The technology carried on, however, in aero-engines.

Below: The most successful maker of air-cooled cars was Franklin. This late vintage six-cylinder machine had a 3·3 litre engine and a wooden chassis frame but in 1932 Franklin even tried a V12! Franklin sold 14,000 cars in 1929.

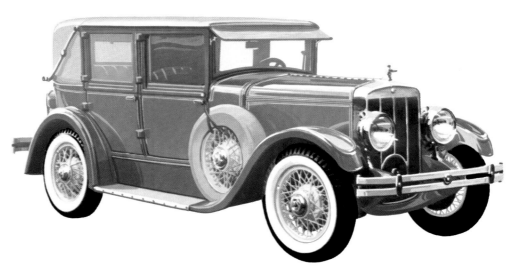

FRAZER NASH 'CHAIN GANG'

'Chain gang' models, built from 1924 to 1939 (data for TT Replica model)

Built by: A.F.N. Ltd., Britain.

Engine:. Meadows manufactured. Four cylinders, in three-bearing cast-iron block/crankcase. Bore and stroke 69mm by 100mm, 1,496cc (2·72in × 3·94in, 91·3cu.in). Cast-iron detachable cylinder head, modified by Frazer Nash. Two overhead valves per cylinder, operated by pushrods and rockers from single block-mounted camshaft. Twin horizontal constant-vacuum SU carburettors. Maximum power dependent on state of tune, but normally 62bhp at 4,500rpm.

Transmission: Single-dry-plate clutch in unit with engine. Open propeller shaft to bevel box. Four-speed-and-reverse transmission by chain drive, from cross shaft, with dog engagement. Chains exposed, and no differential. Remote-control right-hand gearchange.

Chassis: Separate pressed-steel chassis frame, with channel-section side members, tubular and fabricated cross bracing. Tubular front axle beam. Front suspension by cantilever semi-elliptic springs and radius arms. Rear suspension by cantilever quarter-elliptic springs and radius arms. Hartford-type adjustable friction dampers. Rack-and-pinion steering with fore-and-aft drag link. Four-wheel, cable operated drum brakes. 19in centre-lock wire wheels. 4·50 × 19in tyres.
Two-seater open sports coachwork of light-alloy on ash frame.

Dimensions: Wheelbase 8ft 6in (259cm), track (front) 4ft (122cm), track (rear) 3ft 6in (106·7cm). Overall length 12ft 6·3in (351cm). Unladen weight 1,800lb (816kg).

History: After Archie Frazer-Nash left the defunct GN concern, he set up in business on his own to make two-seat sports cars carrying his own name. It is not surprising, therefore, to see several design points from the GN in the earliest Frazer Nash cars, including the extremely simple but effective chain-drive transmission. Even the first cars, however, were much more 'grown-up' than the GN had ever been, as they had a proper channel-section chassis frame and always used water-cooled four-cylinder or six-cylinder engines. In spite of his engineering prowess, however, Frazer-Nash himself was not always a prudent business man and his company was taken over by H. J. Aldington in 1929. The Aldington family controlled the destinies of Frazer Nash, through AFN Ltd., until the cars were finally taken out of production in the 1950s. Production, albeit on a very limited scale, was moved from Kingston-on-Thames to Isleworth in 1926, where it settled permanently. Even so, cars were hand-built at a very low rate. Between 1924 and 1939, no more than 350 'chain gang' cars were built and production of these cars, now legendary, had been reduced to the merest trickle after about 1936, when the Aldingtons were more interested in building up their British concession to sell the Fiedler-designed BMW cars.

The GN ancestry showed up in the Frazer Nash (as it did in the HRG car which was masterminded by GN's other partner, Godfrey). The chassis was very simple and easy to repair, with cantilever springs fore and aft to keep the frame short and the wheels well under control. The suspension was very hard, which was exactly

what the sporting-minded Frazer Nash customers wanted, and weather protection minimal. The chain-drive transmission was so simple that critics often used to disbelieve its efficiency. If, however, the chains were cleaned and oiled regularly — about every 500 miles was best — they operated well, and the consequences of a snapped chain were not so serious as those of smashed gear wheels. There was no torque-splitting differential, because of the (literally) solid rear axle, which explains the fact that all 'chain gangs' had very narrow wheel tracks and extremely sensitive handling characteristics. Traction in all conditions, of course, was superb.

The main changes over the years centred around engines. The original cars were built with Plus Power four-cylinder engines, but after that firm closed down (with only 16 engines delivered) British Anzani engines were used for the next six years. In the early 1930s, a whole series of units were tried, including the Meadows overhead-valve engine sold in the first batch of TT Replica cars. These progressively became more of Frazer Nash and less of Meadows as their designer (Gough) developed special components. As a more refined alternative to the sporting Gough-Meadows, Aldington then began to fit the six-cylinder, 1½-litre Blackburne units, redesigned to have twin overhead camshafts. However, even at the same time, the company were developing their own single-overhead cam 'Gough' engine, which was entirely special but rather under-developed.

Many of the car's variants were named after the races or circuits where competition success had been gained, which explains the naming of the 'Shelsley' and 'Boulogne' cars. TT Replicas, first built in 1931, as prototypes, were named after the cars which ran in the British Tourist Trophy races of 1931, 1932 and 1934, and the first 'production' car was sold in the spring of 1932. Because of its no-nonsense specification, it became the most popular of all 'chain gangs', a total of 85 being manufactured between 1932 and 1938; 54 of the cars were equipped with the Meadows engine (complete with 'Gough' improvements). Only a few had the splendid twin-cam Blackburne engine, which in racing form (and supercharged) could be persuaded to give more than 150bhp.

It might be fair to say that the Aldingtons had new ideas for improved models, but that they did not need to introduce them because the basically vintage 'chain gang' was popular as long as they needed to make it. Their ideas for post-war Frazer Nash cars, in the 1940s, were as interesting and advanced as the 'chain gangs' had been twenty years earlier.

Right: The 'chain gang' cars are so special and so well-loved that most have survived to this day. This TT Replica model was built in 1935, one of 85 production models. It had a Meadows engine and a crude but effective type of chain-drive transmission.

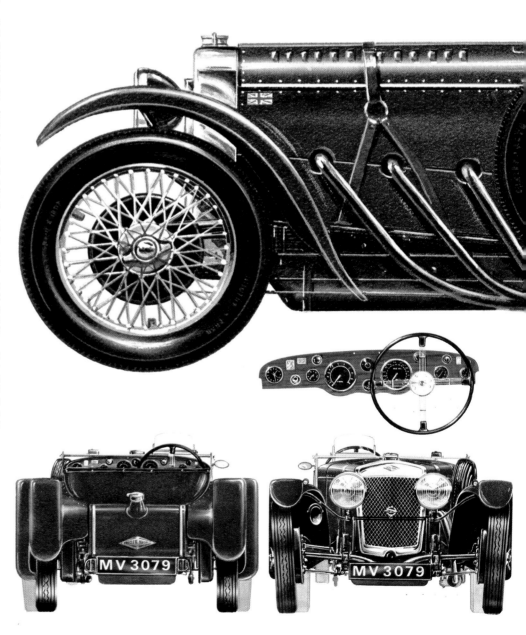

Right: Full and glorious detail of the TT Replica 'chain gang', so called as cars had run successfully in the Tourist Trophy of the early 1930s. Not more than 350 'chain gang' cars, all of the same general design, were built in fifteen years. There were several different engines, but all used the unique transmission, with a separate and exposed chain and sprockets for each gear. This needed regular greasing, but put up with a lot of abuse. The cars' ride was very hard, the steering direct, and creature comforts very few. Owners loved them!

FRAZER NASH POST-WAR MODELS

Post-war cars, built from 1946 to 1956 (data for Le Mans Replica).

Built by: A.F.N. Ltd., Britain.

Engine: Bristol manufactured. Six cylinders, in line, in four-bearing cast-iron block. Bore and stroke 66mm by 96mm, 1,971cc (2·60in × 3·78in, 120·3cu.in). Aluminium cylinder head. Two overhead valves per cylinder, with BMW-inspired pushrod operation: inlet valve directly operated by pushrod and rocker and exhaust valve operated by pushrod, pivot, cross pushrod and rocker from single side-mounted camshaft. Three Solex carburettors and downdraught siamesed inlet ports. Maximum power 110bhp at 5,250rpm (8·5:1 compression ratio) or 120bhp at 5,500rpm (9·5:1). Maximum torque with high-power engine 125lb.ft at 4,500rpm.

Transmission: Single-dry-plate clutch and four-speed, synchromesh manual gearbox (no synchromesh on first gear), both in unit with engine. Direct-acting central gearchange. Two-piece open propeller shaft to spiral-bevel 'live' rear axle.

Chassis: Separate tubular-steel chassis frame, ladder type with large-diameter side members, and tubular cross members. Independent front suspension by transverse leaf spring and lower wishbones. Rear suspension by longitudinal torsion bars and A-bracket location. Telescopic hydraulic dampers. Rack-and-pinion steering. Four-wheel, hydraulically operated drum brakes. 16in centre-lock steel disc wheels, with four-pin drive. 5·25 × 16in tyres. Minimum open two-seater bodywork by Frazer Nash, with cycle-type wings.

Dimensions: Wheelbase 8ft (244cm), tracks (front and rear) 4ft (122cm). Overall length 11ft 9in (358cm). Unladen weight 1,500lb (680kg).

History: Plans for the post-war cars were laid in 1945 and 1946, after the Aldingtons had arranged for BMW's Dr Fiedler and his 328 engine design to come to Britain. Bristol (touring cars) and Frazer Nash (sports cars) were to share the same engine and transmission and the same basic layout of suspension. The Frazer Nash two-seater was first shown in 1946, when it looked very like a 1940 full-width BMW 328,

but the production car, shown at the 1948 Earls Court show, was a purposeful and very stark two-seater with minimal bodywork and cycle-type wings. This, the High Speed model, was the first of a proliferating range, but after one had competed at Le Mans in 1949, finishing a magnificent third overall, the High Speed or Continental two-seater became the Le Mans Replica. Demand intensified, and a total of 60 (substantial by Frazer Nash standards) were built.

The same chassis, in one or more engine tunes, was also applied to full-width two-seaters, the cheapest of which was the Fast Roadster, and a more exclusive (with de Dion rear suspension) one which was called the Sebring. The Sebring name came about because a Le Mans Replica had been taken by two private owners to the American 12-hour race in 1952 where it won outright. Engine power was squeezed up on competition cars every time Bristol themselves could provide it, but the only important chassis change came in 1952 when the Mk II Le Mans Replica was announced. De Dion rear suspension was an option, and attention was paid to weight saving and a lower frontal area with cut-down scuttle. These cars also raced as 'Formula Two' cars by dint of removing wings and electrical equipment, but were valiant overweights for that class of racing. The last Le Mans Replica model was built in 1953, but the other more civilised versions were made in tiny numbers for another two or three years.

As in the late 1930s, the Aldingtons were also busy importers — they now took up the Porsche concession — and they also wanted to make cars based on the existing chassis frame but with BMW V8 engines. However, only a handful of these were made. As with the pre-war cars, the post-war Frazer Nashes scored as much on handling and reliability as on all-out performance.

Below: Post-war Frazer Nash cars used Bristol engines and transmissions. Each car was handbuilt, and there were several different body styles. There are obvious links with BMW 328 design in this example—the Aldingtons used to import BMWs in the 1930s.

GN

GN models, built from 1911 to 1925 (data for 1913 vee-twin models).

Built by: G.N. Ltd., Britain.

Engine: JAP manufactured. Two air-cooled cylinders, in 90-degree vee-formation in cast-iron cylinder barrels on light-alloy crankcase. Bore and stroke 84mm by 98mm, 1,086cc (3·31in × 3·86in, 66·3cu.in). Detachable cylinder heads. Two valves per cylinder; overhead inlets operated by pushrods and rockers, side exhausts operated direct from crankcase-mounted camshaft. Single B&B carburettor. Maximum power about 12bhp at 2,400rpm.

Transmission: Clutch on rear of engine crankcase, mounted in nose of car. Open propeller shaft drive to bevel box driving countershaft. Two-speed dog-and-chain transmission to counter shaft and final drive to solid rear axle by side-mounted belts. Remote-control right-hand gearchange.

Chassis: Separate ash chassis frame with tubu-

lar cross bracing. Tubular front axle. Front suspension by quarter-elliptic leaf springs, cantilevered forward, and lower radius arms. Rear suspension by quarter-elliptic leaf springs. No dampers. Wire-and-bobbin steering. Belt-rim brakes on rear wheels only, footbrake working on inside of rims and handbrake on outside of rims. Centre-lock wire wheels. 650 × 65 tyres. Rudimentary two-seat open coachwork by GN.

Dimensions: Wheelbase 8ft (244cm), tracks (front and rear) 3ft 6in (106·7cm). Overall length 11ft (335cm). Unladen weight 670lb (304kg).

History: Viewed from the 1970s the GN is a joke, but of its day it was a popular and effective little cycle car. This type of machine was an ultra-cheap half-way house between motor cycles and light cars and most owners graduated to them from motor cycles, when they found sidecar progress too tedious. GN was founded by H. R. Godfrey and Archie Frazer-Nash in 1910 and the first cars were sold a year later. To keep the price down to around 100 guineas (the cheapest of all, in 1915, sold for 88 guineas) the cars had to be as light and simple as possible. This no doubt explains the use of a wooden (ash) chassis frame, steering by wires which passed round strategically placed bobbins, and a two-speed chain-and-belt transmission, which was open to attack by the elements.

All the early models used proprietary vee-twin JAP motor cycle engines, which kept the passengers' feet warm as they were set right up against the toe board. Bodywork was minimal, in line with the rest of the specification, so an early GN built in 1911 or 1912 (before the inevitable refinement process set in) weighed no more than about 400lb (181kg). In many ways a GN was crude, but it was also practical and very easy to repair when it went wrong. Almost everything in the design was simple, accessible, and with an obvious function, and the steering and (within reason) the performance were most satisfactory.

GN made very few machines before World War I (perhaps less than 200 in all), but in a post-war factory, production rose to the dizzy heights of 50 cars a week in the cycle-car boom, even though the price of the vee-twin-engined machine had risen to £275 or even £315. Engines were modified persistently at the start of the 1920s and right at the end an attempt was made to upgrade the car with an imported Chapuis-Dornier engine with four-cylinders and water-cooling.

In fact it was a vain hope; the GN was not only being beaten by its own price, but by the fact that the customers were demanding more weather protection and by the fact that the mass-produced Austin Seven became available in 1923 for not more than £165. Both Godfrey (with HRG) and Frazer-Nash (with cars bearing his own name) went on to build more modern and even better 'classic' cars.

Above and below: The GN's charm lay in its light weight, its simplicity and in its sporting potential. This two-seater was built in 1922. The radiator was a dummy as the JAP vee-twin engine was air-cooled. Final drive was by chain and there were only two forward gears. From 1923 the Austin Seven killed GN.

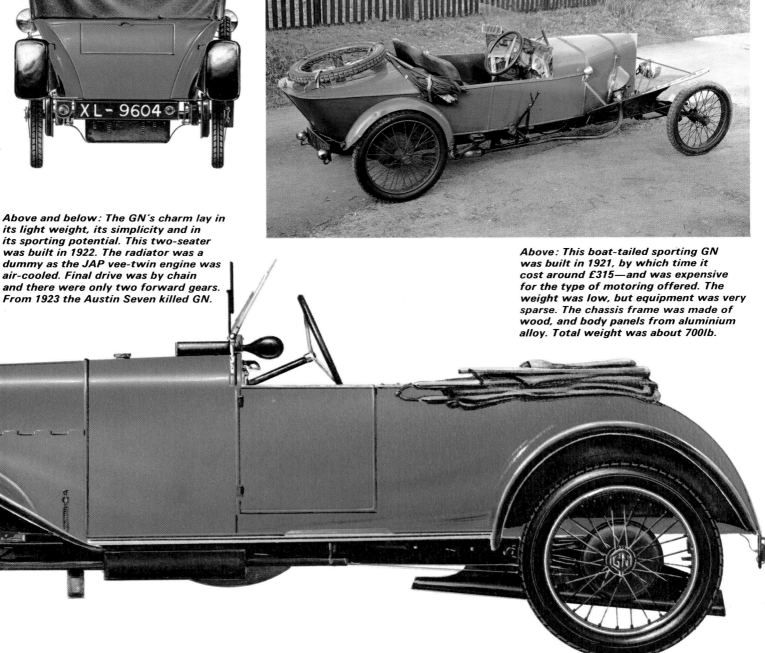

Above: This boat-tailed sporting GN was built in 1921, by which time it cost around £315—and was expensive for the type of motoring offered. The weight was low, but equipment was very sparse. The chassis frame was made of wood, and body panels from aluminium alloy. Total weight was about 700lb.

GOBRON-BRILLIE 100MPH CAR

110hp racing Gobron-Brilliés built in 1903 and 1904 (data for 1903 car)

Built by: Sté. Gobron-Brillé, France.

Engine: 'Double four cylinder', actually four cylinders, in line, but with two pistons moving in each cylinder. Two cast-iron blocks, with three-bearing light-alloy crankcase. Upper and lower pistons with common bore, one piston operating conventionally from crankshaft, with other piston above it, operated by eccentric shaft. Bore and (combined) strokes 140mm by 220mm, 13,547cc (5·51in × 8·66in, 827cu.in). No cylinder heads, combustion chamber formed between opposed piston crowns. Two valves per cylinder, side mounted (with respect to conventional piston and cylinder) and operated by tappets from single camshaft in side of crankcase. Single Gobron up-draught carburettor. Maximum power 110bhp.

Transmission: Cone clutch, in unit with front-mounted engine and separate four-speed manual gearbox (without synchromesh). Remote-control right-hand gearchange. Straight-bevel differential in tail of gearbox and countershaft to sprockets. Final drive to rear wheels by exposed chain.

Chassis: Separate tubular-steel chassis frame, with upper and lower longitudinal small-diameter-tube side members and tubular cross bracing. Forged front axle beam. Front and rear suspension by semi-elliptic leaf springs. No dampers. Worm-type steering. Mechanically-operated foot brake on countershaft drum. Hand brake on rear-wheel drums — externally contracting. Fixed wooden artillery-style wheels.

Dimensions: Wheelbase 9ft 10·5in (300cm). Overall length 13ft 2·5in (403cm). Unladen weight 2,185lb (991kg).

History: Gobron-Brillié made cars between 1898 and 1930, but they are really noted for two things — for their engines, with an ungainly opposed-piston design used for more than twenty years, and for the car which first took the Land Speed Record at more than 100mph in 1904.

Each cylinder had a conventional piston and connecting rod, along with a further opposed piston operated by long connecting rods and cross-head beams external to the cylinders. The combustion chamber, such as it was, was sandwiched between the two piston crowns as they approached each other and the combustion space and valves were squeezed out of the side of the cylinders, half way up the block! This unlikely arrangement worked very well.

The Paris—Madrid racing cars, built in 1903, also boasted multi-tubular chassis frames and although they achieved little in that ill-starred race, their record-breaking abilities became legendary. Between July 1903 and July 1904 a Gobron-Brillié based on the road racing cars took the record on four occasions, the last time (at Ostend in the height of summer and driven by M. Rigolly) at no less than 103·55mph.

Below: The first ever attempt at wind-cheating? This was how the first 100mph Gobron-Brillié was shaped in 1904.

GRAF UND STIFT SP8

SP8 model, built from 1930 to 1938 (data for 1936 model)

Built by: Wiener Automobilfabrik A.G. vorm. Graf und Stift, Austria.

Engine: Eight cylinders, in line, in nine-bearing cast-alloy block/crankcase. Bore and stroke 85mm by 132mm, 5,923cc (3·35in × 5·20in, 361·4cu.in). Detachable cast-iron cylinder head. Two overhead valves per cylinder, operated by single overhead camshaft. One down-draught twin-choke Zenith carburettor. Maximum power 125bhp at 3,000rpm.

Transmission: Multiple-dry-plate clutch and four-speed, synchromesh manual gearbox (without synchromesh on first and second gears), both in unit with front-mounted engine. Remote-control steering-column gearchange, with vacuum-servo assistance. Open propeller shaft to worm-drive 'live' rear axle.

Chassis: Separate pressed-steel chassis frame, with pressed-steel side members and cross bracing. Forged front axle beam. Front and rear suspension by semi-elliptic leaf springs. Lever-arm hydraulic dampers. Worm-type steering. Four-wheel, hydraulically operated drum brakes, with vacuum-servo assistance. 18in pressed-steel-disc wheels. 7·50 × 18in tyres. Choice of prestige coachwork, open touring or saloon/limousine.

Dimensions: Wheelbase 12ft 4in (376cm), track (front) 4ft 10·3in (148cm), track (rear) 4ft 11in (150cm). Unladen weight (limousine) 5,512lb (2,500kg).

History: Three Graf brothers joined with Willy Stift in 1902, to make cars, and the first product bearing their name was sold in 1907. Within a few years, this Austrian company had established itself with large and luxurious machines, with a 5·8-litre 28/32hp achieving notoriety in 1914 as the vehicle in which the Archduke Franz Ferdinand was assassinated. With the exception of the 2-litre VK model, all between-wars Graf und Stift cars were large-engined, luxurious and dignified machines. The SR4 was a 7·7-litre, overhead-valve six, the SP5 was a 4·9-litre, overhead-camshaft unit developed (through racing) from it and last, and most magnificent of all, was the 5·9-litre SP8, whose engine was really an eight-cylinder version of the SP5. Built only to individual order and then only for acceptable customers, and SP8 was dubbed the 'Rolls-Royce of Austria' and became the accepted mode of transport for the country's leaders. Technical details included a vacuum-servo-assisted gearchange, a worm-drive back axle, and 'overdrive' transmission (Bentley style), but the chassis layout was entirely conventional. The company, however, could not sustain itself on the sales of this increasingly Teutonic colossus and the last was built in 1938, after which the factory's mainstay became commercial vehicles.

Above: The Graf und Stift SP8 rivalled Mercedes and Horch as a vast and heavy machine for politicians and military men to use in the 1930s. This car weighed more than 5,500lb.

GREGOIRE 16/24

16/24 model, built from 1911 to 1914
Built by: S.A. des Automobiles Grégoire, France.
Engine: Four cylinders, in line, in monobloc casting, with three-bearing light-alloy crankcase. Bore and stroke 80mm by 160mm, 3,217cc (3·15in × 6·30in, 196·3cu.in). Integral cylinder head. Two side valves per cylinder, operated by tappets from camshaft in side of crankcase. Single up-draught Zenith carburettor.
Transmission: Leather-cone clutch, in unit with front-mounted engine, and shaft to separate four-speed manual gearbox (without synchromesh) mounted on chassis subframe. Remote-control right-hand gearchange. Propeller shaft, enclosed in torque tube, driving straight-bevel 'live' axle.
Chassis: Separate pressed-steel chassis frame, with channel-section side members and pressed cross bracing. Forged front axle beam. Front suspension by semi-elliptic leaf springs. Rear suspension by three-quarter-elliptic leaf springs, torque tube and radius arm. No dampers. Worm-type steering. Foot brake operating by shaft on internally expanding drum at rear of gearbox. Hand brake operating by cable on twin drum brakes in rear wheel hubs. Choice of centre lock or artillery-style wheels. 875 × 105mm tyres.
Dimensions: Wheelbase 10ft 6in (320cm), tracks (front and rear) 4ft 7in (140cm). Overall length 14ft 6in (442cm). Unladen weight (chassis only) 1,900lb (862kg).
History: In France, Grégoire is a legendary name in motor industry history, but there were two such heroes. The one connected with Tracta, Amilcar, Hotchkiss and Dyna-Panhard is no relation of the original pioneer. The pioneering Grégoire cars arrived in 1903 and established a

tradition for conventional but well-engineered machinery. Twins and fours were announced at first, but the fours became the company's mainstay and their pedigree was advanced through racing. An overhead-camshaft engine was developed in 1911, but did not race. A conventional side-valve version, however, competed in the Coupe de l'Auto event.

The most celebrated Grégoire was the sporting 16/24 model, technically advanced because of its monobloc engine layout and showing traces of Coupe de l'Auto parentage because of its small-bore/long-stroke configuration. It is interesting to note that aluminium pistons (developed by Professor A. M. Low) were first

fitted in a British 16/24, effectively predating anything W. O. Bentley had in mind. One extraordinary version of the 16/24 offered for sale was the Triple Berlina, looking for all the world like three tiny stage coaches linked together. This was, in effect, an early attempt at making a motor caravan. The car was outdated after World War I and therefore had a production run of only three years. It was probably the high-point of the company's fame and the last Grégoire of all was built in 1924.

Below: The distinctive 16/24 model Grégoire, with notable radiator shape, and (hidden) an advanced engine.

GUY 20HP

20hp models, built from 1919 to 1921 (data for 1919 model)
Built by: Guy Motors Ltd., Britain.
Engine: Eight cylinders, in 90-degree vee-formation, in two cast-iron blocks, with three-bearing light-alloy crankcase. Bore and stroke 72mm by 125mm, 4,072cc (2·83in × 4·92in, 248·5cu.in). Two detachable cast-iron cylinder heads. Two valves per cylinder, in semi-side-valve layout (actually disposed horizontally across the engine), mounted in the top of the cylinder blocks and driven directly by a single camshaft mounted high in the crankcase 'vee'. Twin Zenith carburettors.
Transmission: External cone clutch and four-speed manual gearbox (without synchromesh), both in unit with front-mounted engine. Remote-control gearchange, offset from centre of car towards driver. Engine and transmission mounted on separate pressed-steel subframe attached to main chassis. Open propeller shaft to spiral-bevel 'live' rear axle.
Chassis: Separate pressed-steel chassis frame, with channel-section side members, pressed and tubular cross bracing and three-point suspension for engine/transmission subframe. Forged front axle beam. Front and rear suspension by semi-elliptic leaf springs. No dampers. Worm-and-wheel steering. Rear-wheel drum brakes, and transmission brake, wheel drums operated by hand lever and transmission drum by foot pedal. Automatic chassis lubrication from central reservoir. Centre-lock wire wheels. 820 × 120mm tyres. Five-seater open tourer bodywork.
Dimensions: Wheelbase 10ft 10in (330cm), tracks (front and rear) 4ft 8in (142cm). Overall length 15ft 1in (459·7cm).
History: Sidney Guy founded his vehicle manufacturing business in 1914, building a new

factory in Wolverhampton, where Guy commercial vehicles are still produced. The first Guy was a 25-hundredweight payload truck, and the luxurious (and expensive — £1,475 complete) V8 20hp car followed immediately after the war in 1919. The engine of this car was almost unique in Britain (the only other V8 was the Vulcan) and the inclined-side-valve engine layout was special to Guy. Automatic chassis lubrication was very strange in a car which

would be looked after by a chauffeur. Only 150 of these splendid machines were built, in not more than two years, before Guy moved on to smaller four-cylinder cars which were even less successful. Demand for Guy trucks, on the other hand, was so buoyant that they took precedence over the cars and the last Guy private car was built in 1925. The removable engine/transmission subframe was very effective and was characteristic of the commercial vehicles.

Right: Guy are now known as famous makers of lorries, but they built a few vee-eight engined 20hp cars just after the First World War. It was a fine car but too costly. Guy cars died in 1925.

H.E. 11.9HP

H.E. cars, built from 1919 to 1931 (data for original 11·9hp model)
Built by: Herbert Engineering Co Ltd., Britain.
Engine: Four cylinders, in line, in cast-iron block with three-bearing light-alloy crankcase. Bore and stroke 69mm by 120mm, 1,795cc (2·72in × 4·72in, 109·5cu.in). Detachable cast-iron cylinder head. Two side valves per cylinder, operated by roller-type tappets and interposed rockers from single, side-mounted camshaft. Single side-draught Zenith carburettor.
Transmission: Multi-dry-plate clutch in unit with front mounted engine. Separate four-speed manual gearbox (without synchromesh). Remote-control right-hand gearchange. Propeller shaft, enclosed in torque tube, driving overhead-worm-gear final drive.

Chassis: Separate pressed-steel chassis frame, with channel-section side members and tubular cross bracings. Forged front axle beam. Front suspension by semi-elliptic leaf springs. Rear suspension by three-quarter-elliptic leaf springs, with long member underslung. No dampers. Worm-and-nut steering. Rear wheel drum brakes, with separate sets of brake shoes for foot brake and for hand brake. Bolt-on artillery-style wheels. 760 × 90mm tyres. Open two-seater sporting bodywork.
Dimensions: Wheelbase 9ft 6in (290cm), tracks (front and rear) 4ft 2in (127cm). Overall length 13ft 6in (411·5cm). Unladen weight (chassis only) 1,570lb (712kg).
History: The H.E. was a classic vintage car. It was born immediately after the end of World War I, and the last of all the H.E.s were built during the depression at the start of the 1930s. The first H.E., the 11·9hp sporting model, was typical of the make, and altogether typical of the fine and simple cars offered to British sportsmen by several companies of the day. The mechanical layout was simple, with a proprietary four-cylinder engine, separate gearbox and right-hand gearchange. The overhead-worm final drive was more of a novelty and the brake drums, which shared separate sets of shoes for foot and hand brakes, were not entirely usual arrangements. The H.E.'s radiator was a most elegant 'horse-collar' design, as distinctive in its way as that of the Bugatti. By current standards, the H.E. was light, well-built and fast, but it suffered due to coming from new manufacturers without established distribution outlets. The price, too, at £700 complete, was much too high to guarantee large sales and this in turn meant that the Reading-based company could not afford to lay down expensive cost-reducing machinery. Technically, however, the H.E. was a reliable and enjoyable experience, which some owners enjoy even to this day.

Left: The H.E. was a classic British vintage car which disappeared in 1931. This smart fixed-head coupe four-seater, with a fabric body, was more rakish than most H.E.s, and hid a conventional chassis layout. The car's radiator was elegant and horse-shoe profiled, in the Bugatti style. H.E.s were made in Reading—not a 'motor town'—and were rather costly.

HISPANO-SUIZA ALPHONSO

Alphonso model – short and long chassis, built from 1911 to 1914
Built by: S.A. Hispano-Suiza, Spain.
Engine: Four cylinders, in line, running in four-bearing light-alloy crankcase and detachable cast-iron block. Bore and stroke 80mm by 180mm, 3,620cc (3·15in × 7·09in, 220·9cu.in). Non-detachable cast-iron cylinder head. T-head valve arrangement, side inlet valves directly operated by offside camshaft, side exhaust valves by nearside camshaft. Single Hispano-Suiza carburettor, directly bolted to block/head. Maximum power 64bhp (net) at 2,300rpm.
Transmission: Multi-dry-plate clutch on short-chassis cars, cone clutch on long-chassis cars, and three-speed gearbox, without synchromesh (early versions), or four-speed gearbox (later versions), both in unit with engine. Right-hand gearchange. Open propeller shaft to bevel 'live' rear axle.
Chassis: Separate steel chassis frame, with channel-section side members. Forged front axle beam. Half-elliptic leaf springs at front and rear; later cars had three-quarter-elliptic leaf springs at the rear. Transmission drum footbrake, aided by rear wheel drum handbrake. Worm-and-sector steering. Centre-lock wire wheels. 815×105mm or 820×120mm tyres.
Variety of sports two-seat or four-seat coachwork.
Dimensions: Wheelbase 8ft 8in or 9ft 10in (264cm or 300cm), tracks (front and rear, short chassis cars) 4ft (122cm), tracks (front and rear, long chassis cars) 4ft 3in (130cm). Overall length (short chassis) 12ft 9in (389cm). Unladen weight, chassis only (short) 1,450lb (658kg), chassis only (long) 1,680lb (762kg).
History: Every Hispano-Suiza car designed between 1904 and 1934 was the work of Marc Birkigt, who also designed the first Spanish car of all, the La Cuadra. This company, along with Birkigt, was taken over by Hispano. Like many other Edwardian companies, Hispano used motor sport for publicity and were encouraged by the Spanish monarch King Alfonso XIII when he put up a cup for a voiturette race at Sitges in 1909. A team of Hispano-Suiza cars looked to be possible winners, and led at one stage, but all succumbed to troubles. The team fared better at the *Coupe de l'Auto* races at Boulogne, the best car finishing fifth overall. A year later the revised cars took third place at Sitges, but won outright at Boulogne. It was but a short step for Birkigt to decide that his customers should be able to buy near replicas. He enlarged the engine from 2·6-litres to 3·6-litres, but the basic chassis and mechanical layout was the same.

He named his car in honour of the Spanish monarch. The Alphonso XIII, probably, was one of *the* first 'production sports cars', as opposed to pensioned-off Grand Prix cars, or vast open-bodied tourers. By our modern standards the Alphonso was not a small nor delicate car, but it was thought very advanced for 1911. By Edwardian standards it was adequately fast, with a maximum speed probably of about 80mhp — this at a time when anything approaching 100mph was almost Grand Prix car pace. It was renowned for its ease of control, and the very long-stroke engine made it a very easy car to drive in give-and-take country. Among its features were the engine/clutch/gearbox in unit — most cars still placed their gearboxes in isolation in the centre of the chassis — and the centre-lock wire wheels when the artillery type was more usual.

In spite of its engine size the Alphonso was not a very large car. Most Hispanos succeeding it were mechanically more complex, larger and much more expensive.

Left: Looking rather frail and spidery, the Hispano-Suiza Alphonso was a very rugged little sports car. Like all other Hispanos, it was the work of Marc Birkigt, and this model had a light-alloy 3·6-litre engine. The Alphonso raced with distinction —the name was from King Alphonso XIII.

HEALEY

Healey Warwick, Elliott, Duncan, Sports-
mobile, Silverstone, Tickford, Abbott,
Nash-Healey and Alvis-Healey, built from
1946 to 1954 (data for Healey Silverstone)
Built by: Donald Healey Motor Co. Ltd., Britain.
Engine: Riley manufacture. Four cylinders, in
line, in three-bearing cast-iron block. Bore and
stroke 80·5mm by 120mm, 2,443cc (3·17in ×
4·72in, 149·1cu.in). Cast-iron cylinder head.
Two overhead valves per cylinder, inclined in
part-spherical combustion chambers, with inlet
valves operated by one side-mounted camshaft,
pushrods and rockers, and all exhaust valves
operated by similar means but by a second
camshaft, mounted on other side of cylinder
block. Twin side-draught constant-vacuum SU
carburettors. Maximum power 104bhp (net) at
4,500rpm.
Transmission: Single-dry-plate clutch and
Riley four-speed synchromesh manual gearbox
(without synchromesh on first gear), both in
unit with engine. Central gearchange. Propeller
shaft, in torque tube, to spiral-bevel 'live' rear
axle. Many alternative final-drive ratios.
Chassis: Separate steel chassis frame, with box-
section side members, box, pressed and tubular
cross braces. Independent front suspension by
coil springs and trailing links, with piston-type
hydraulic dampers, plus anti-roll bar. Rear
suspension by coil springs and a Panhard rod,
with telescopic dampers. Four-wheel, hydraulically operated drum brakes. 15in bolt-on steel
disc wheels. 5·50 × 15in tyres.
Light-alloy stressed-skin two-seater bodywork.
Cycle-type wings.
Dimensions: Wheelbase 8ft 6in (259cm), track
(front) 4ft 6in (137cm), track (rear) 4ft 5in

(135cm). Overall length 14ft (426cm). Unladen
weight 2,070lb (940kg).
History: After years as technical director of
Triumph in the 1930s, Donald Healey decided to
build his own cars after the war. The first was
announced in 1946 and the last built in 1954, by
which time his latest design (the Healey 100)
had been adopted by BMC for large-scale production. All Warwick-built Healeys shared the
same chassis frame, designed by Geoff Healey,
Donald's son. Bodies, saloon and sporting, were
usually built by coachbuilders.

Healey was always tiny and under financed,
therefore many 2½-litre Riley components —
including engines and transmissions — were
specified. The exception was the export-only
Nash-Healey, with an American Nash power
train, and the last series of Alvis-Healeys, which
shared the Nash's body. The cars were always

*Above: The Healey Silverstone, with
Riley engine in special chassis.*

carefully shaped, light weight and had very high
performance. Most famous of all, because of
their no-nonsense appearance, and because of
their racing successes, were the Silverstone
Healeys, where driver comfort took second place
to function. One interesting feature in those cars
was that the tail-mounted spare tyre also doubled
as a bumper in emergencies.

By standards of the day, the Healey was
technically advanced, and attractively styled. If
BMC had not taken over production of the
Healey 100, it would have added to the Warwick
firm's reputation. In later years, too, there were
the little Austin-Healey Sprites (and MG Midget)
and the Jensen-Healeys, all from the prolific
brain of the Healey family.

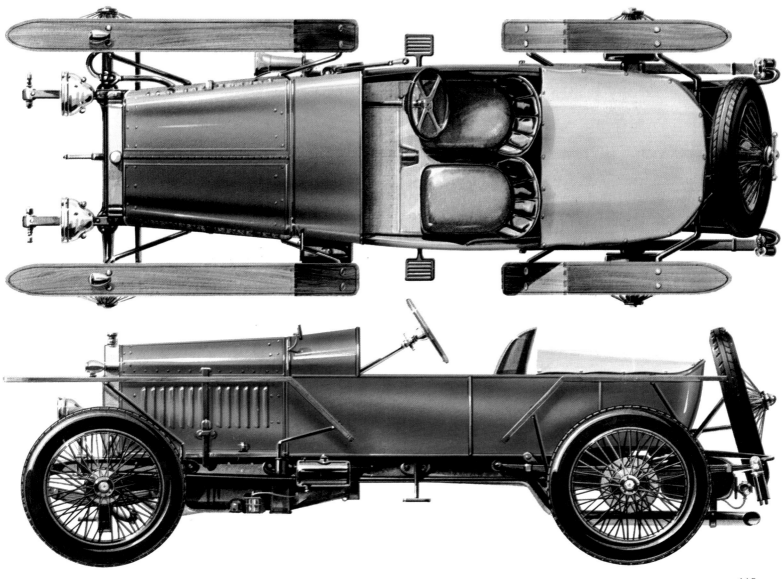

HISPANO-SUIZA H6B

H6B models, built from 1919 to 1938 (data for 1919 model)
Built by: S.A. Hispano-Suiza, Spain
Engine: Six cylinders, in line, in light-alloy block, with seven-bearing light-alloy crankcase. Bore and stroke 100mm by 140mm, 6,597cc (3·94in × 5·52in, 402·5cu.in). Non-detachable cylinder head. Two overhead valves per cylinder, operated by disc-type tappets from single overhead camshaft. Single up-draught Hispano-Suiza carburettor. Maximum power approx 135bhp at 3,000rpm.
Transmission: Multi-dry-plate clutch and three-speed manual gearbox (without synchromesh), both in unit with front-mounted engine. Remote-control right-hand gearchange. Two-piece propeller shaft, front half open, and rear half enclosed in torque tube, connected to spiral-bevel 'live' rear axle.
Chassis: Separate pressed-steel chassis frame, with channel-section side members and pressed and tubular cross bracings. Forged front axle beam. Front and rear suspension by semi-elliptic leaf springs. No dampers (friction-type dampers added to later models). Four-wheel mechanically operated drum brakes, with Hispano-type mechanical servo assistance, driven from side of gearbox. Centre-lock wire wheels. 935 × 135 tyres.
Dimensions: Wheelbase 12ft 1in (368cm), tracks (front and rear) 4ft 8in (142cm). Overall length 15ft 10in (482·6cm). Unladen weight 3,360lb (1,524kg).
History: After the great success of Hispano-Suiza aero-engines during World War I, motoring enthusiasts looked forward with great anticipation to seeing Marc Birkigt's post-war private car design. They were not disappointed. The H6B, revealed at the 1919 Paris show, was technically in advance of any other car in the world. Its six cylinder engine was conventional enough if one had studied the famous aeroplane engines (indeed, it was at once simpler and more effective), but there was also the question of servo-assisted four-wheel brakes, with a mechanically driven servo invented by Birkigt, the sheer quality of the chassis, the magnificent stability and performance and the matchless coachwork styles which the specialists felt inspired to produce for this car. It was without any doubt the last word in advanced motor engineering for the very rich, and if you had to ask the price you could not afford it! Not surprisingly, Hispano pursued what was effectively a 'one-model' policy for some years — with all H6Bs and H6Cs made in the Paris factory. From the H6B, itself at a pinnacle of achievement, Birkigt then developed the H6C cars — Sport or Boulogne models — in 1924. These used the same basic chassis, but had an engine enlarged to nearly eight litres. The 'Boulogne' title was earned because modified H6Bs had won the Coupe Boillot at the Boulogne racing circuit in 1921, 1922 and 1923. One exceptionally beautiful Boulogne was built for the 1924 Targa and Coppa Florio races, with a wooden body shell, and in this guise probably

HISPANO-SUIZA V12

V12 models, built from 1931 to 1938 (data for 1931 Model 68).
Built by: Société Française Hispano-Suiza, France.
Engine: Twelve cylinders, in 60-degree vee-formation, in seven bearing crankcase, in combined light-alloy blocks and heads, with seven-bearing crankcase. Bore and stroke 100mm by 100mm, 9,424cc (3·94in × 3·94in, 575cu.in). Two overhead valves per cylinder, operated by pushrods and rockers from single camshaft mounted in centre of engine 'vee'. Two down-draught twin-choke Hispano-Suiza carburettors. Maximum power (on 5·0:1 compression ratio) 190bhp at 3,000rpm; (on 6·0:1 compression ratio) 220bhp at 3,000rpm.
Transmission: Multi-plate clutch and three-speed, synchromesh manual gearbox (without synchromesh on first gear), both in unit with front-mounted engine. Direct-acting central gearchange. Propeller shaft, enclosed in torque tube, to spiral-bevel 'live' rear axle.
Chassis: Separate pressed-steel chassis frame, with channel-section side members and pressed and tubular cross-bracing. Forged front axle beam. Semi-elliptic leaf springs at front and rear. Hydraulic dampers. Four-wheel, mechanically operated drum brakes, with Hispano-type mechanical-servo assistance. Centre-lock wire wheels. 17 × 50 tyres.
Coachwork in many styles by European specialist builders.
Dimensions: Wheelbase 11ft 3in, 12ft 2in, 12ft 6in or 13ft 2in (343cm, 371cm, 381cm or 401cm). Tracks (front and rear) 4ft 11in (150cm). Overall length, depending on wheelbase and coachbuilder, from 16ft (488cm). Weight, depending on wheelbase and coachwork, from 4,900lb (2,222kg).
History: Having built some of the world's finest cars between 1904 and 1930, Hispano-Suiza were not prepared to face the depression with

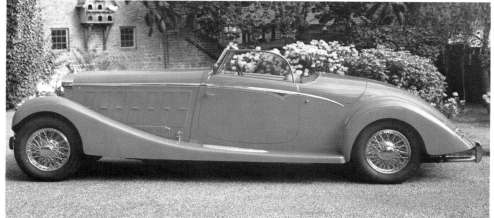

produced about 200bhp, with a maximum speed getting on for 120mph. It was the detail in the building of an H6B which made it so remarkable, like the machining of the massive crankshaft from a steel billet originally weighing 770lb and the way the steel (later cast-iron) cylinder sleeves were individually screwed into the light-alloy cylinder block from below. The mechanical servo-assistance to the brakes (where friction clutches driven from the transmission helped increase braking effort) was so good that it was eventually adopted by Rolls-Royce for their own cars. This was the final compliment which Birkigt richly deserved. Even the best were willing to copy the best. An H6B deserved that title.

Right: In the 1920s there is little doubt that the H6B Hispano-Suiza was the best car in the world, though Rolls-Royce disagreed. The model was built for nearly twenty years, to 1938.

mundane machinery. Instead, Marc Birkigt decided to replace the company's splendid six-cylinder machines with an even finer V12 Hispano, drawing on all his company's aero-engine experience in the designing of it. The company's V8 aero-engine had been built in several Allied countries during World War I and details of its valve gear and general layout were to filter down to many other makes.

The new Type 68 engine, displacing an impressive 9·4-litres, was really a comprehensive up-date of a V12 aero-engine Birkigt had designed in the war, but to achieve quieter running the famous single-overhead-camshaft design was abandoned in favour of a conventional pushrod system. The car, announced in the autumn of 1931, was magnificently built and magnificently priced (it was certainly the most expensive French car if one discounts the 'white elephant' Bugatti Royale). It was probably the fastest saloon/limousine in the world and, in terms of mechanical excellence, could only be matched by such marvels as the 16-cylinder Cadillacs. Although the chassis was truly 'vintage' in concept, there were advanced features like the gearbox-driven brake servo and, of course, the engine was very powerful (190bhp or 220bhp to choice).

The Type 68 sold in small numbers, as one would expect, but the makers then added an even more impressive option, the 68-Bis, with nothing less than an 11·3-litre V12 engine. This produced more than 250bhp and left all the opposition gasping. Hispano had, in the meantime, taken over Ballot, and for a short time made a 'small' six-cylinder car of only 4·9 or 4·6 litres. It is worth noting that the massive and overbodied Hispanos could reach 100mph without trouble, and there were very few out-and-out sports cars in the world which could approach these magic figures. The last of the cars were made in 1938.

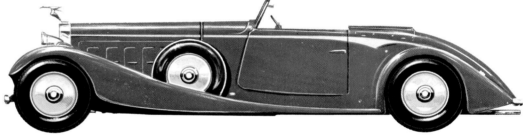

Above: Every one of Saoutchick's body creations was startlingly beautiful, like this four-seater drop-head on the Hispano-Suiza vee-12 chassis. Exposed side-mounted spare wheels were a 1930s fashion. The wheels were very heavy.

Below: With a 12ft 1in wheelbase, it was easy to make all special bodies look long and sleek, even with that imposing Hispano-Suiza radiator. The grey saloon is by Letourner et Marchand and the gold De Ville by Binder.

Left and above: Marc Birkigt's masterpiece, the best of all his splendid creations, was the splendid vee-12 Hispano-Suiza. Much of his experience with successful World War One aeroplane engines went into the vee-12, which was a 9·4-litre with conventional pushrod overhead valves. At least 220bhp was produced on the high compression, and a vee-12 could reach 100mph with great ease, and in complete serenity. Any vee-12 was enormously expensive, especially the later 11·3-litre examples like this with a Saoutchick two-seater touring body. The elegant stork radiator mascot would be dismissed as dangerous these days, but was a symbol of wealth and mechanical good taste in the 1930s.

HORCH TYPE 850

Type 850 straight-eight, built from 1935 to 1939 (data for 1936 model)

Built by: A. Horch & Co., Motorwagenwerke A.G., Germany.

Engine: Eight cylinders, in line, in ten-bearing cast-iron combined block/crankcase. Bore and stroke 87mm by 104mm, 4,946cc (3·43in × 4·09in, 301·8cu.in). Detachable cast-iron cylinder head. Two overhead valves per cylinder, operated by single overhead camshaft. One twin-choke down-draught Solex carburettor. Maximum power 100bhp at 3,200rpm.

Transmission: Single-dry-plate clutch and four-speed, synchromesh manual gearbox (without synchromesh on first gear), both in unit with front-mounted engine. Direct-acting central gearchange. Open propeller shaft to worm-drive 'live' rear axle.

Chassis: Separate pressed-steel chassis frame, with box-section side members and pressed and cruciform cross bracing. Independent front suspension by two transverse leaf springs and radius arms. De Dion rear suspension by semi-elliptic leaf springs. Lever-arm hydraulic dampers. Worm-and-wheel steering. Four-wheel, hydraulically operated drum brakes, with servo assistance. Centralised chassis lubrication. 17in bolt-on wire wheels, or bolt-on steel-disc wheels. 7·00 × 17in tyres.

Open touring and sporting roadster coachwork.

Dimensions: Wheelbase 11ft 6in (350cm), tracks (front) 4ft 11in (150cm), track (rear) 5ft 0in (152cm). Overall length 17ft 6in (533cm). Unladen weight 5,070lb (2,300kg).

History: August Horch was one of the motor industry pioneers in Germany, selling his own cars from 1900, after working for Benz for three years. The company's reputation for making prestige models was founded in the 1920s, beginning with the 33/80PS 8·4-litre car. In the meantime, however, Horch himself had quarrelled with his fellow directors and had gone off to found the Audi marque. Paul Daimler (son of Gottlieb) joined Horch in 1923 and began to develop even more splendid machines. Overhead-cam fours and sixes were already under development, but his first designs were the straight-eights of 1926 and onwards, with twin-camshaft engines. This range grew and grew and before Daimler himself left the company, in 1930, he had also supervised the design of the Type 450 single-cam straight-eights and that of the splendid 6-litre V12 engine, which followed in 1931. That car, splendid and dignified as it was, was just too much for the impoverished times and in 1933 the basic chassis was relaunched with a 3·5-litre V8.

By this time Horch had joined with Wanderer and by 1938 cars were being tested with the Singer overhead-camshaft engine in its place. This link with the Coventry firm also led to another HRG — the 1100 — being sold. The engine in this case was the famous 1,074cc Singer 'Nine' unit. Post-war designs were not basically different from the 1930s models, although 30 of the distinctive full-width 'Aerodynamic' HRGs were built.

The general shortage of cars all over the world and Audi to form the 'Auto Union', and it was here at Zwickau that the legendary 16-cylinder Grand Prix cars were built. After the end of 1933, small-engined versions of the eight were dropped and the 5-litre became the company's prestige model. It was sold in a confusing number of versions, really as a second-division Mercedes (especially to the Nazi heirarchy), some with rigid axles, some with independent front suspension and some (like the Type 850 and the 951 models) with a De Dion type of rear suspension.

The V8 and the straight-eight models continued right up to the outbreak of war — the single-cam eight, therefore, had had a life of nearly ten years — and many were put to good use by high-ranking German staff officers during the war. Production could not be resumed in 1945 as the factory had been over-run by the Russian forces and found itself in East Germany. The depressing two-stroke Trabants are now made at this once-famous factory.

Right: Horch was one of the four German marques which combined to make up the Auto-Union. The Type 850 model, with 5-litre straight-eight engine, was splendid, and individually made.

HRG

HRG 1½-litre, 1100 and 1500 (data for HRG 1500)

Built by: H.R.G. Engineering Co. Ltd., Britain.

Engine: Singer manufactured, four-cylinders, in line, in three-bearing cast-iron block. Bore and stroke 68mm by 103mm, 1,496cc (2·68in × 4·06in, 91·3cu.in). Two overhead valves per cylinder, operated by single overhead camshaft. Twin constant-vacuum SU carburettors. Maximum power 61bhp (net) at 4,800rpm.

Transmission: Single-dry-plate clutch, and four-speed, synchromesh manual gearbox (without synchromesh on first gear), both in unit with engine. Remote-control central gearchange. Open propeller shaft to hypoid-bevel 'live' rear axle.

Chassis: Separate steel chassis frame, simply built with channel-section side members, tube and pressed cross-brace members. Front suspension of tubular axle beam by leading quarter-elliptic leaf springs. Rear suspension by half-elliptic leaf springs. Friction-type front dampers, friction and/or hydraulic piston-type rear dampers. Four-wheel cable operated drum brakes. 16in centre-lock wire wheels. 5·50 × 16in tyres. Light-alloy two-seat sports bodywork in wood framework.

Dimensions: Wheelbase 8ft 7·5in (263cm), track (front) 4ft (122cm), track (rear) 3ft 9in (114cm). Overall length 12ft 2in (371cm). Unladen weight 1,625lb (736kg).

History: Messrs Halford, Robins and Godfrey came together in 1935, set up in business in Surrey and decided to make a few exclusive and responsive two-seater sports cars. The result was the individualistic HRG. All were renowned motoring enthusiasts. Godfrey had been the 'G' in the GN car, Robins had been associated with Trojan car manufacture, while Halford was an engineer and Brooklands racing enthusiast. There was much GN influence in the HRG's design, but it was by no means as spartan. At first there was only the 1½-litre model, which used a 4ED Meadows unit, linked to a Moss gearbox. The engine was set well back in the chassis and the forward facing quarter-elliptic front springs were a feature. The roadholding was superb on good surfaces, but the ride is best described as *very* firm.

Production began from the Tolworth works in 1936 and continued there until the 1950s. Output was tiny — less than 20 cars a year was usual — but every car was substantially handbuilt. The Meadows engine was near the end of its competitive life (as Frazer Nash also found)

led to more than 60 HRGs being built at Tolworth in 1946 and 1947 — flat-out building by HRG standards. Even so, it normally took five months to complete a car — three months for the chassis and two more for the body, which was erected by coachbuilders nearby. Performance, considering the light weight of the HRG sports car, was only average. The Singer-engined 1500 model reached 84mph, while the 1100 could only boast of 78mph. In spite of the marque's

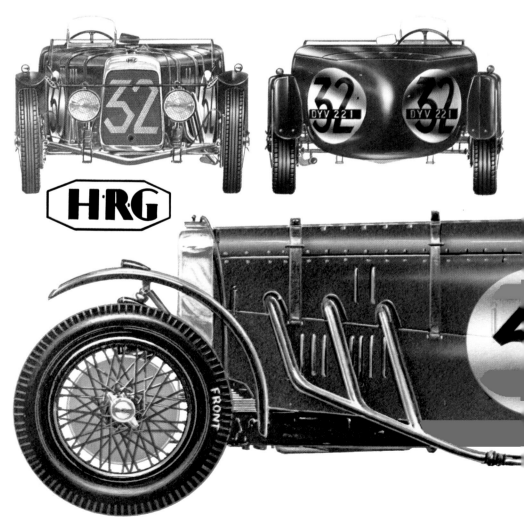

splendid competition record — particularly in the rough and fast post-war European rallies — the HRG was too expensive and too spartan to be very popular. Only 14 cars were built in 1949, and by 1950 production was very much on a hand-building process. Just before the end, in 1956, hydraulic brakes replaced cable operation, and a few Singer 'SM' engined cars were sold. Probably not more than 240 HRGs in all were ever built.

Below: Every HRG was lovingly hand-built, the numbers built were tiny, and the cars were ultra-sporting. It needed little work to convert a road car to competition use. For example, the 1937 1½-litre HRG won its class in the Le Mans 24 Hour Race and was mechanically nearly standard. HRGs had few creature comforts.

HOTCHKISS SIX-CYLINDER CARS

Six-cylinder cars, built from 1929 to 1954 (data for Type 686 – Grand Sport)

Built by: Hotchkiss et Cie. (Automobiles Hotchkiss from 1935), France.

Engine: Six cylinders, in line, in seven-bearing cast-iron block/crankcase. Bore and stroke 86mm by 100mm, 3,485cc (3·39in × 3·94in, 212·6cu.in). Detachable cast-iron cylinder head. Two overhead valves per cylinder, operated by pushrods and rockers from single camshaft mounted in side of cylinder block. Twin down-draught Stromberg carburettors; alternatively one downdraught twin-choke Stromberg. Maximum power 125bhp at 4,000rpm.

Transmission: Single-dry-plate clutch and four-speed, synchromesh manual gearbox (without synchromesh on first gear), both in unit with front-mounted engine. Direct-acting central gearchange. Open propeller shaft to spiral-bevel 'live' rear axle.

Chassis: Separate pressed-steel chassis frame, with channel-section side members, and pressed and tubular cross bracings, with cruciform. Forged front axle beam. Front and rear suspension by semi-elliptic leaf springs. Lever-type hydraulic dampers. Worm-and-nut steering. 16in pressed-steel bolt-on disc wheels. 6·00 × 16in tyres. Variety of coachwork, open or closed.

Dimensions: Wheelbase 9ft 2in (279cm), tracks (front and rear) 4ft 8in (142cm). Overall length depending on coachwork, from 14ft 7in (444cm). Unladen weight 3,050lb (1,383kg).

History: Harry Ainsworth led the French Hotchkiss fortunes through most of the inter-war years and in many ways the well-known six-cylinder cars ignored current Gallic trends. The first, the AM80, was revealed at the 1928 Paris salon, and was seen to have a conventional but efficient 3-litre pushrod engine, but used several features well proven in the pushrod AM2 four-cylinder car. Over the years the design improved logically, with lowered and stiffened chassis frames, hydraulic instead of cable brakes and synchromesh gears in place of 'crash' gearing.

Rallying was always a Hotchkiss strong point, with outright Monte wins in 1932, 1933 and 1934. After a gap, and some near misses, Trevoux's Grand Sport model tied for first place in 1939 and a pre-war model won again in 1950.

Smaller-engined versions were tried in countries where taxation demanded them, but the classic 3,485cc unit arrived in 1933. The Grand Sport in particular, with its short wheelbase, was very fast (up to 110mph was claimed) and cost about £825 in France.

The French luxury cars lost their market after World War II, but even a Detroit-style full-width facelift could not save the big Hotchkiss. No important mechanical redesign was attempted and the last were made in 1954.

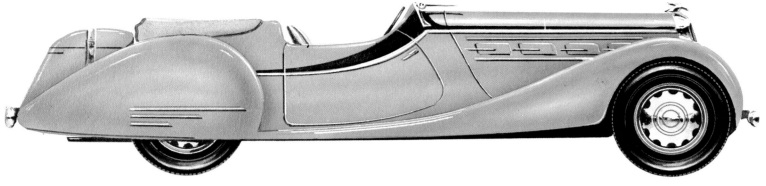

Above: An exciting Type 686 Hotchkiss Grand Prix 3½-litre, with a Le Mans Sports body. The chassis was a rally-winner; this body was well-equipped.

Left: The epitome of the fast and very glamorous French Grand Touring car of the 1930s—the Hotchkiss Model 686 Grand Sport with its drop head body by Henri Chapron. Along with Delahaye and Delage, Hotchkiss provide a clear statement of French fashion of the period. There were four full-size seats and a snug convertible hood. The chassis was conventional, but the push-rod 3½-litre engine pushed out 125bhp. 100mph was possible.

Right: Smart and sober saloon version of the original Model AM80 Hotchkiss, built in 1930 with a 3-litre engine. Harry Ainsworth inspired the design.

Below: The Hotchkiss badge shows that the company did not always build cars. Those are crossed gun barrels—guns were supplied in huge numbers.

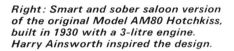

INVICTA

Invicta 1½-litre, 2½-litre, 3-litre and 4½-litre, built from 1925 to 1933 (data for 4½-litre S)
Built by: Invicta Cars, Britain.
Engine: Meadows-manufactured. Six-cylinder, in line, in cast-iron block or detachable five-bearing light-alloy crankcase. Bore and stroke 88·5mm by 120·6mm, 4,467cc (3·46in × 4·75in, 272·5cu.in). Cast-iron cylinder head. Two overhead valves per cylinder, operated by pushrods and rockers from single side-mounted camshaft. Two SU constant-vacuum carburettors. Maximum power in excess of 115bhp.
Transmission: Single-dry-plate clutch and Meadows four-speed manual gearbox (without synchromesh), both in unit with engine. Right-hand gearchange. Open propeller shaft to hypoid-bevel 'live' rear axle.
Chassis: Separate steel chassis frame, with channel-section side members, tubular and channel-section cross-bracing members. Forged front axle beam. Front and rear suspension by half-elliptic leaf springs. Hydraulic piston-type dampers, with Hartford friction dampers in over-riding control. Rod-operated drum brakes. Coachwork to choice from nominated coach-builders, including Invicta's own two-seat light-alloy sports body on ash framing.
Dimensions: Wheelbase 9ft 10in (300cm), tracks (front and rear) 4ft 8in (142cm). Overall length 13ft 6in (411cm). Unladen weight 2,800lb (1,270kg).
History: Noel Macklin got together with Oliver Lyle (of the sugar-making family) in 1924 to produce cars of a type new to the British market — cars that would combine British standards of quality and roadholding with American standards of performance and engine flexibility. To do this, as their company was to be very small, they had to be skilful assemblers of proprietary parts and 'bought-out' components. The first Invicta 'factory', indeed, was the three-car garage of Macklin's own home at Cobham, Surrey, south-west of London.

The first three cars, with 2½-litre six-cylinder Coventry-Climax engines did not match Macklin's high standards, so for future production he turned to Henry Meadows of Wolverhampton, who were already producing engines for various uses. From 1925, all Invictas, with the exception of the 1½-litre model announced in 1932, used Meadows 'sixes'. Macklin's designer was W. G. Watson, later renowned for his post-war twin-camshaft Invicta Black Prince, and in the eight years of what are now thought of as 'vintage' Invictas he was loyal to one basic chassis layout. The 2½-litre Meadows model was succeeded a year later by the enlarged-bore 3-litre, but by 1928 the big six-cylinder unit had been further stretched to give a powerful and reliable 4½-litres. Mechanically the Invictas' performance was way ahead of their brakes, and indeed of their styling. Before the end of the decade there was nothing very striking about the cars' lines, even though the radiator was simple and noble, and the bonnet rivets aped those of Rolls-Royce to a very obvious degree.

The 4½-litre NLC Invicta, often with a body as expensive and individually produced as those for Rolls-Royce, was the company's most expensive car of all; its chassis price of £1,050 was only £50 under that of the contemporary 20/25 Rolls. Unlike the Rolls, however, the Invicta had an engine not noted for smoothness or silence, even if it *was* powerful. An 85mph maximum speed was normal for this car — far better than the average.

By 1930, the 4½-litre chassis was being supplied in two forms — the 'high' A-Type, and an entirely different lowered S-Type. The latter, usually supplied with lightweight sporting coachwork, formed the basis of really sensationally effective competition cars. Though colloquially known as the '100mph' Invicta, the production car was really capable of a 90-plus maximum. Nevertheless, Invicta, who only sold 77 of these scarce sports cars, did nothing to discourage the unofficial title, as it could only be good for sales. The chassis was reputedly inspired by that of the

successful Delage Grand Prix cars, was very rigid, and was passed underneath the back axle. This rather limited wheel movement, and may have contributed to the rather knife-edge road-holding for which the 'flat iron' Invicta was later renowned. One lurid accident involving 'Sammy' Davis of *The Autocar*, which happened in front of thousands of spectators at Brooklands, did nothing to help.

During the production run, really a misnomer as all cars were hand-built at Cobham, engine power was increased and the last cars probably boasted 140bhp at 3,600rpm. The maximum of this bluff-fronted machine would undoubtedly have been over 100mph by then. It is worth recalling that Meadows also sold this engine to Lagonda for their 4½-litre machines, and that W. O. Bentley joined Lagonda in 1935, refined

the installation and ensured the engine's life right up to 1939.

No attempt was ever made by Invicta to prove their products on the race track, but they were keen on competition in long-distance trials of various types. In 1930 several top events in Europe were tackled with great success, and in 1931 Donald Healey astonished the motoring world by winning the Monte Carlo Rally outright. A year later the same car and driver took second overall, but as before were fastest of all on the tests where performance was at a premium. The world depression had the same effect on Invicta as on other luxury-car makers, and an entirely different 1½-litre Blackburne-engined car was briefly sold. The company stopped making cars in 1933 and Macklin turned to Railtons in their place.

Above right: A Cadogan-bodied 4½-litre Invicta of 1929, with normal 'high' frame and four-seater layout. The chassis cost £1,050, body another £300.

Above and below: Perhaps the most famous of all Invictas, the 'flat iron' 4½-litre of 1931. Donald Healey won the Monte Carlo Rally in one, and up to 100mph was possible. Only 77 of these cars were built, and they were as fierce as any Bentley or Bugatti, though without the glamour. The rivetted bonnet was a trademark, carried on to the Railton.

Right: This was the simple but very charming 3-litre Invicta of 1927. All the six-cylinder Invictas built from 1925 used Meadows engines, which were powerful, reliable, and rugged. The Invicta was never built in large quantities, being the brainchild of Noel Macklin, and was never intended to be other than a bespoke sporting and touring car. From 1926 to 1933 there were 2½-litre, 3-litre and 4½-litre cars, all using the same basic parts. Railtons succeeded Invictas after 1933.

ISO GRIFO

Grifo model, introduced 1963, discontinued 1974 (data for GL365, 1966 car)

Built by: Iso S.p.A., Italy.

Engine: Chevrolet manufactured. Eight cylinders, in 90-degree vee-formation, in five-bearing cast-iron block. Bore and stroke 101·6mm by 82·6mm, 5,359cc (4·0in × 3·25in, 327cu.in). Two detachable cast-iron cylinder heads. Two overhead valves per cylinder, operated by pushrods and rockers from single camshaft positioned in centre of cylinder block 'vee'. Single fourchoke downdraught Holley carburettor. Maximum power 365bhp (gross) at 6,200rpm. Maximum torque 360lb.ft at 4,000rpm.

Transmission: Single-dry-plate clutch and four-speed, all-synchromesh gearbox, both in unit with front-mounted engine. Remotecontrol central gearchange. Open propeller shaft to hypoid-bevel final drive with limited-slip differential. Exposed, universally jointed drive shafts to rear wheels.

Chassis: Platform-type pressed and fabricated-steel frame, with Bertone-styled two-door two-seat coupé body. Independent front suspension by coil springs, wishbones and anti-roll bar. De Dion rear suspension, with coil springs, longitudinal and transverse links. Telescopic dampers. Recirculating-ball steering. Four-wheel hydraulically operated disc brakes, with vacuum-servo assistance. 15in centre-lock cast-alloy road wheels. 205 × 15in tyres.

Dimensions: Wheelbase 8ft 2·5in (250cm), tracks (front and rear) 4ft 7·5in (141cm). Overall length 14ft 6·75in (444cm). Unladen weight 3,100lb (1,406kg).

History: Iso's Grifo and Rivolta cars were their second attempt to break into the car market, their first having been with the little Isetta bubble cars of the mid 1950s. The second attempted design could not have been more different, as these cars were true Italian-American 'mongrels', with enormously high performance. The chassis was designed by Bizzarrini, a platform structure, topped by Bertone-styled and constructed coachwork. The Grifo was a dramatically styled two-seater coupé while the Rivolta was a more conservative (but still very fast) four-seater car. Both were made near Milan and should not be confused with the Bizzarrini coupés which looked remarkably like the Grifos (and mechanically, too, there were resemblances).

Iso were never completely financially stable, but even so in 1968 they were able to market the Fidia (a four-seater car replacing the Rivolta), with four doors, and the Lele, which was more of a 2+2 and effectively replaced the Grifo. Engines were from Chevrolet until 1973 and from Ford of Detroit thereafter, but Iso never recovered from the energy crisis and economic downturn of 1973–4 and have now closed down.

Below: The Iso Grifo (this is a 1966 model) used elegant Bertone styling to hide powerful Chevrolet engines. The fastest had 7-litres, and beat 170mph.

ISOTTA FRASCHINI TIPO 8 SERIES

Tipo 8 models, built from 1919 to 1935 (data for 1919 model)

Built by: Fabbrica Automobili Isotta Fraschini, Italy.

Engine: Eight cylinders, in line, in light-alloy block with nine-bearing light-alloy crankcase attached. Bore and stroke 85mm by 130mm, 5,902cc (3·35in × 5·12in, 360cu.in). Fixed cylinder head. Two overhead valves per cylinder, operated by pushrods and rockers from single side-mounted camshaft. Two side-draught Zenith carburettors. Maximum power 80bhp at 2,200rpm.

Transmission: Multi-dry-plate clutch and three-speed manual gearbox (without synchromesh), both in unit with front-mounted engine. Direct-acting central gearchange. Enclosed propeller shaft, to spiral-bevel 'live' rear axle.

Chassis: Separate pressed-steel chassis frame, with channel-section side members and fabricated and tubular cross bracing. Forged front axle beam. Front and rear suspension by semi-elliptic leaf springs, and friction-type dampers. Four-wheel drum brakes, foot pedal or hand operated. 895×135mm tyres.

Open or closed four/five seater coachwork.

Dimensions: Wheelbase 12ft 1in (368cm), front and rear tracks 4ft 8in (142cm). Overall length depending on coachwork, from 16ft 3in (495cm). Unladen weight (chassis only) 3,100lb (1,406kg).

History: Before the end of World War I, Isotta Fraschini already had a fine reputation, not only for making cars, but also for making military machines, marine engines and aero engines. During the war, prototypes of a new eight-cylinder car, designed by Giustino Cattaneo, were on the road and these went on sale in 1919. The Tipo 8, as it became known, was the world's first quantity-production 'eight', and was intended to provide the ultimate in luxurious motoring for the rich — particularly in the United States, where Isotta's sales efforts were very strong.

The Tipo 8 was very American in some ways, particularly in the flexibility of its 6-litre engine, and was renowned for impeccable roadholding and a great deal of solid engineering. It was by no means as refined as either Rolls-Royce or Hispano-Suiza cars, but this did not harm its image at first. Cars were sold to Rudolph Valentino, Clara Bow, Jack Dempsey and William Randolph Hearst, which did wonders for its image. The Tipo 8A arrived in 1924, with 7·4-litre engine and more performance, and the 8ASS (Super Spinto) cars were offered to counter Hispano's claims. After the luxury car market collapsed at the end of the 1920s, Isotta turned more to aero engines, and sold only a handful of 8Bs (further improved Tipo 8s) before closing down car production in 1935. The car had been truly 'vintage' but did not advance with the rest of the industry.

Left: The straight-eight Isotta-Fraschini range—the Tipo 8—was meant to be one of the world's best cars, and had a splendid reputation for more than ten years. It was the first quantity-production straight-eight in the world, and sold very well in North America. Like Rolls-Royce or Hispano-Suiza cars, it was built without regard to cost, and was almost the ultimate in prestige machines, with customers among the tycoons and film stars of the day. The concept was 'vintage' in every way, and as the Tipo 8 was not improved in the 1930s it was eventually eclipsed by its prestigious opposition.

ITALA 12.9-LITRE

Itala sixes, built from 1908 to 1915 (data for 1908 model)

Built by: Fabbrica Automobili Itala S.A., Italy.

Engine: Six cylinders, in line, in three cast-iron blocks, with three-bearing light-alloy crankcase. Bore and stroke 140mm by 140mm, 12,930cc (5·51in × 5·51in, 789cu.in). Non-detachable cylinder heads. Two side valves per cylinder, in T-head layout with exposed valve stems and springs, operated by tappets from two camshafts, mounted each side of crankcase. Single up-draught carburettor. Maximum power about 75bhp.

Transmission: Multiple-dry-plate clutch, in unit with front-mounted engine, and shaft drive to separate four-speed manual gearbox (without synchromesh). Remote-control right-hand gear-change. Open propeller shaft to straight-bevel 'live' rear axle.

Chassis: Separate pressed-steel chassis frame, with pressed and tubular cross bracings. Forged front axle beam. Front and rear suspension by semi-elliptic leaf springs. No dampers. Worm-type steering. Two foot brakes — one operating on transmission drum behind gearbox by contracting band, and one operating on twin rear drums. Hand lever also operating on rear drums (later models were modified to single brake pedal). Artillery-style road wheels. 880 × 120mm tyres (front) and 895 × 135mm tyres (rear).

History: Itala, like the S.P.A. concern and the Ceirano company, were inspired by Matteo Ceirano himself. He had abandoned his own-name concern to found Itala in 1904, but stayed only two years. All the early Italas were disciples of the sensational new Mercedes type of design, with big T-headed engines and rakish open bodywork. Performance was everything. Although the first-ever Itala had 4·6-litres, this figure was soon left behind. A 15·3-litre monster won the Coppa Florio (this, incidentally, was the first-ever race win by a shaft-driven car), while Prince Scipio Borghese won that incredible Peking-Paris marathon in 1907 in a 35/45 model of 7·4 litres. Big six-cylinder cars followed, using the same engine parts and dimensions. By 1908, the smallest Itala was a modest little 2·6-litre four, but the two magnificent sixes were of no less than 11·1-litres and 12·9-litres. The latter was the biggest 'production' Itala — as engines became more sophisticated and at the same time smaller in displacement in subsequent years. The cars were both sporting (in behaviour and on the racing circuits) and prestigious. so it was reasonable that they should command a very high price indeed. This majestic motor car, of which the Italians were very proud, was only really killed off by World War I; the 'vintage' Italas were very different.

Below: The vast Edwardian Italas were inspired by the genius of Matteo Ceirano, with overtones of Mercedes layouts. A 35/45 model won the Peking-Paris marathon in 1907.

ITALA 61

61 models, built from 1924 to 1931 (data for 1926 model)

Built by: Fabbrica Automobili Itala S.A., Italy.

Engine: Six cylinders, in line, in seven-bearing light-alloy combined block and crankcase. Bore and stroke 65mm by 100mm, 1,991cc (2·56in × 3·94in, 121·5cu.in). Detachable cast-iron cylinder head. Two overhead valves per cylinder, operated by pushrods and rockers from single camshaft mounted in side of cylinder block. Single horizontal Zenith carburettor.

Transmission: Two-plate clutch, running in engine oil, and four-speed manual gearbox (without synchromesh), both in unit with front-mounted engine. Direct-acting central gear-change. Propeller shaft, enclosed in torque tube, driving spiral-bevel 'live' rear axle.

Chassis: Separate pressed-steel chassis frame, with channel-section side members and pressed cross members, under and overslung at rear on later Type 65 (axle effectively in hole in much-deepened side member). Forged front axle beam. Front and rear suspension by semi-elliptic leaf springs, with rear location by torque tube and ball joint. Friction-type dampers. Worm-and-wheel steering. Four-wheel mechanically operated drum brakes, with friction-clutch servo-assistance (servo positioned inside gearbox). Centre-lock wire wheels. 30 × 5·25in tyres. Saloon or touring coachwork.

Dimensions: Wheelbase 9ft 10in or 10ft 6in (300cm or 320cm), tracks (front and rear) 4ft 7in (139·7cm). Overall length 13ft 1in or 13ft 9in (399cm or 419cm). Unladen weight 2,778lb or 2,933lb (1,260kg or 1,330kg).

History: After the series of huge and magnificent Edwardian cars, Itala graduated to smaller and rather conventionally designed machines. Unsuccessful attempts to build Hispano aero-engines during World War I had cost Itala dear and they were never financially secure in the 1920s. However G. C. Cappa joined Itala from Fiat and it was he who designed the successful and long-running Type 61 machine, which first appeared in 1924. It was notable for having a light-alloy cylinder block and four-wheel brakes right from the start. The four-speed gearbox, which embraced a brake servo followed on in 1926. The Type 61 was a handsome if rather 'vertical' car in the best vintage Italian tradition, but did not spark off enough interest to save Itala. Even though they developed a twin-cam 2-litre engine to up-date the car into the Type 65, it was not enough, and the company stopped trading in the early 1930s.

Below: The Type 61 Itala, a 2-litre Italian 'vintage' car with a light-alloy engine and four-wheel brakes. Final versions had twin-cam engines.

JAGUAR SS100

Previously known as SS100. SS90, SS100 2½-litre and 3½-litre (data for 3½-litre)
Built by: SS Cars Ltd., Britain.
Engine: Six cylinders, in line, in seven-bearing cast-iron block. Bore and stroke 82mm by 110mm, 3,485cc (3·23in × 4·33in, 213cu.in). Cast-iron cylinder head. Two overhead valves per cylinder, operated by pushrods and rockers from camshaft mounted in side of cylinder block. Compression ratio 7:1. Twin constant-vacuum SU carburettors. Maximum power 125bhp (gross) at 4,250rpm.
Transmission: Single-dry-plate clutch and four-speed, synchromesh manual gearbox (without synchromesh on first gear), both in unit with engine. Central remote-control gearchange. Open propeller shaft to spiral-bevel 'live' rear axle.
Chassis: Separate steel chassis, with channel-section side members, and pressed-steel cross-bracing members. Forged front axle beam. Half-elliptic leaf springs front and rear. Hydraulic piston and extra friction dampers at front, hydraulic piston-type dampers at rear. Four-wheel, rod-operated drum brakes to all four wheels. Fly-off handbrake. Worm-and-nut steering. 18in knock-off wire-spoke wheels. 5·50 × 18in tyres.
Two-seater open sports coachwork fitted, of alloy panels on ash framing. No alternatives.
Dimensions: Wheelbase 8ft 8in (264cm), track (front) 4ft 4·5in (133cm), track (rear) 4ft 6in (137cm). Overall length 12ft 9in (389cm). Unladen weight 2,680lb (1,215kg).
History: William Lyons entered the motor industry in the 1920s as a designer and builder of special coachwork for ordinary cars like the Austin Seven and the Standard Nine as well as for sidecars. His 'Swallow' car designs, like his sidecars, were soon famous. His first SS car, the SS1, was launched in 1931 and built in Coventry. The first SS sports car, the SS90, was an attractive short-wheelbase mechanical version of the 20hp SS1 with a side-valve 2½-litre engine. The SS100, which was born in 1935, used the same

SS1 type of chassis, but with suspensions and other details from the also-new SS-Jaguar saloon cars. The engine was a Heynes-designed overhead-valve conversion of the original side-valve 2,663cc Standard six-cylinder unit.

The first SS100 was sensational enough, but the 3½-litre version, announced in 1937, was even more so. The 3,485cc engine, although keeping some Standard parentage, was largely new, and very powerful. The car, priced at a mere £445 in Britain, could achieve just over 100mph and had the looks usually associated with Italian-designed thoroughbreds. The SS100s, in 2½-litre and 3½-litre form, did much for the SS company's prestige up to the outbreak of World War II.

The car made few concessions to comfort. Style and function was considered all-important, with performance a great selling point. One has to remember that in those days a 100mph maximum speed was rare, as rare as a 150mph maximum is in the late 1970s. The new engine was found to be very tuneable and a Jaguar development car eventually lapped the Brooklands oval at 125mph in tests. Only 23 of the SS90 side-valve cars were made, but SS sold 190 2½-litre SS100s and 118 3½-litres. Only one car was built up (from a partly-completed war-time state) in post-war years. In Ian Appleyard's hands it was a remarkably competitive rally car. One fixed-head coupé SS100 was built and exhibited at the 1938 Earls Court Motor Show; this car still exists.

Below: Styled by William Lyons, the SS100 sports car was sensationally fast and attractive. There were 2½-litre and 3½-litre versions, 1935/39.

JAGUAR D-TYPE

D-types, 3·4-litre and 3·8-litre (data for 3·4-litre)
Built by: Jaguar Cars Ltd., Britain.
Engine: Six cylinder, in line, in seven-bearing cast-iron block. Bore and stroke 83mm by 106mm, 3,442cc (3·27in × 4·17in, 210cu.in). Aluminium cylinder head. Two overhead valves per cylinder, in part-spherical combustion chambers, directly operated by inverted-bucket tappets from twin overhead camshafts. Dry-sump lubrication system, with oil tank alongside engine in engine bay. Three Weber twin-choke carburettors. Maximum power 250bhp (net) at 6,000rpm. Maximum torque 248lb.ft at 4,500 rpm.
Transmission: Triple-dry-plate clutch and four-speed, all-synchromesh manual gearbox, both in unit with engine. Central remote-control gearchange. Short open propeller shaft to hypoid-bevel 'live' rear axle. Several alternative final-drive ratios.
Chassis: Front section a multi-tube 'space frame', bolted to centre-section steel monocoque tub. Front suspension by wishbones, longitudinal torsion bars and anti-roll bar. Rear suspension by trailing arms and 'A' bracket, with transverse torsion bars. Telescopic dampers. Rack-and-pinion steering. Four-wheel multi-pot disc brakes, without servo. 16in centre-lock light-alloy disc wheels. 6·50 × 16in racing tyres. Almost-two-seat open sports-racing coachwork, with minimal screen and no hood.
Dimensions: Wheelbase 7ft 6·6in (230cm), track (front) 4ft 2in (127cm), track (rear) 4ft (122cm). Overall length (short nose) 12ft 10in (391cm). Unladen weight 1,900lb (862kg).
History: Jaguar's distinguished racing history began with an XK120's appearance at Le Mans

in 1950. The first 'specialised' racing Jaguars were the streamlined 150mph C-types, used between 1951 and 1953, which won the Le Mans 24-hour race outright twice. To replace them, both for factory and private owners' use, Jaguar designed the D-type. The new car appeared in 1954, narrowly failed to win at Le Mans on its maiden appearance and won the Rheims 12-hour race only weeks later. Shaped, as was the C-type, by aerodynamicist Malcolm Sayer, the car was a very efficient wind-cheater and could reach 180mph in wrap-round windscreen trim.

Many components — including the basic engine, front suspension and axle — were production based, making the D-type *the* least exotic of all 1950s racing two-seaters. Not content with winning races themselves, the factory laid down a short production line. Between 1955 and 1957 a total of 45 production cars were sold. 'Works' specials totalled 17 cars. Although the car was designed specifically to

JAGUAR XK SERIES

**XK120, XK140, XK150 and XK150S models
(data for XK120)**
Built by: Jaguar Cars Ltd., Britain.
Engine: Six-cylinders, in line, in seven-bearing cast-iron block. Bore and stroke 83mm by 106mm, 3,442cc (3·27in × 4·17in, 210cu.in). Aluminium cylinder head. Two overhead valves per cylinder, in part-spherical combustion chambers, directly operated by inverted-bucket tappets from twin overhead camshafts. Twin SU constant-vacuum carburettors. Maximum power 160bhp (gross) at 5,000rpm. Maximum torque 195lb.ft at 2,500rpm.
Transmission: Single-dry-plate clutch and four-speed, synchromesh manual gearbox (without synchromesh on first gear), both in unit with engine. Open propeller shaft to hypoid-bevel 'live' rear axle.
Chassis: Separate steel frame, with box-section side members, braced by pressed cruciform members and pressed and tubular cross members. Independent front suspension by wishbones and longitudinal torsion bars, with anti-roll bar. Rear suspension by semi-elliptic leaf springs. Telescopic dampers at front, piston-type at rear. Recirculating-ball steering. Four-wheel, hydraulically operated drum brakes and fly-off handbrake. 16in centre-lock wire wheels. 6·00 × 16in tyres.
Coachwork (first 200 cars), in light alloy on ash frame base; (all other cars) pressed-steel bodywork in two-seat drop-head, and two-seat fixed-head versions.
Dimensions: Wheelbase 8ft 6in (259cm), track (front) 4ft 3in (129cm), track (rear) 4ft 2in (127cm). Overall length 14ft 5in (439cm). Unladen weight (drop-head version) 2,920lb (1,324kg).
History: The XK Jaguars are, rightly, legendary. Announced in 1948, they combined smooth and ultra-modern styling with fine engineering and were powered by an advanced twin-overhead-camshaft engine. This last, incidentally, was the first quantity-production 'twin cam' in the world.

The XK's success was all rather accidental. The engine and a longer-wheelbase version of the chassis were intended for Jaguar's new Mark VII saloon car and William Lyons planned his XK sports car as a small-production publicity project. The customers thought otherwise. In six years, more than 12,000 XK120s were sold. The XK140 (9,000 sold) and the XK150 (9,400 sold) all added to the reputation. XK140s had better steering and more power. XK150s had revised styling, even more power and four-wheel disc brakes. The last versions also had 3·8-litre engines. Apart from looking beautiful, the XKs were always very good value for money and

Above: The legendary XK120 sports car, powered by the twin-cam 3,442cc engine. It could reach 120mph at a time when most cars struggled to 80.

very fast. The twin-cam engine, although quite an oil-slinger, lasted for ever.

XKs were great rally cars and successful race cars, although they were really too heavy to take on the specialised French and Italian machines. Production eventually ceased in 1961, 13 years after launch. The XK's successor – the E-type – made as much of a stir as its ancestor.

---

win at Le Mans (which it did in 1955, 1956 and 1957) it won races all over the world, including the Sebring 12-hour event in Florida. D-types could be, and were, used on the open road, being docile and surprisingly economical. For 1957, inspired by a private conversion, the factory made a few road-equipped cars with proper screen and hood, called the XK-SS. Only 16 were sold before a disastrous fire destroyed assembly fixtures and caused policy changes. The E-type, none the less, was directly descended from the philosophy of the XK-SS.

Left: The Jaguar D-Type, used by the factory from 1954 to 1956. The final 1956 cars like this had fuel injection

Above: The fastest D-Types had wrap-round single-seat screens. Le Mans rules in 1956 enforced this version.

JAGUAR E-TYPE

E-type 3·8-litre, 4·2-litre, and Series III V12 (data for V12 car)
Built by: Jaguar Cars Ltd. (later British Leyland Motor Corporation Ltd.) Britain.
Engine: Twelve cylinders, in 60-degree vee-formation, in seven-bearing cast-aluminium block. Bore and stroke 90mm by 70mm, 5,343cc (3·54 × 2·76in, 326cu.in). Aluminium-alloy cylinder heads. Two overhead valves per cylinder opening into 'bowl in piston' combustion chambers and operated by inverted-bucket tappets from single overhead cam per bank. Four constant-vacuum SU carburettors, positioned at the outside of the engine, feeding through vertical inlet ports. Maximum power 272bhp (DIN) at 5,850rpm. Maximum torque 304lb.ft at 3,600rpm. Exhaust emission restrictions caused both figures to drop slightly during the model's production run.
Transmission: Single-dry-plate clutch and four-speed, all-synchromesh gearbox, both in unit with engine. Remote-control central gearchange. Open propeller shaft to subframe-mounted hypoid-bevel final drive. Limited slip differential standard. Exposed, universally jointed drive shafts to rear wheels. Optional Borg Warner automatic transmission.
Chassis: Front section a multi-tube 'space frame', bolted to centre/tail section steel monocoque tub, with rear subframe for suspension and final drive. Independent front suspension by wishbones, longitudinal torsion bars and anti-roll bar. Independent rear suspension by lower wishbones, fixed-length drive shafts, radius arms and double coil springs to each wheel. Telescopic dampers. Four-wheel hydraulically operated disc brakes, with vacuum-servo assistance, inboard at the rear. Rack-and-pinion steering, power assisted 15in steel-disc wheels. ER70VR15in tyres.
Open two-seater or closed coupé 2+2 seater bodies to choice, plus optional hard-top.
Dimensions: Wheelbase 8ft 9in (267cm), track (front) 4ft 6·3in (138cm), track (rear) 4ft 5·3in (135cm). Overall length 15ft 4·4in (468cm). Unladen weight 3,230lb (1,453kg).
History: The E-type Jaguars, even more successful than the XK series they replaced, were — like the XKs — popular by chance. The first E-type, designed in 1956, was a racing sports car to replace the D-type. Only after Jaguar retired from racing was the order given to 'productionise' the car. It was, in all major design respects, a direct descendent of the D-type/XK-SS family, but with one major difference. It was a completely refined, docile, and roadworthy machine. It was also unbelievably cheap and used very few sophisticated special parts.

Like the D-type, the basis of the E-type (or XKE as the North Americans called it) was a combined monocoque/multi-tube chassis, covered by a sleek, aerodynamically tested bodyshell in which the headlamps were faired into the long nose, and in which the air-intake was as small as possible. All-independent suspension was new from Jaguar. The rear suspension, hung with its differential and inboard brakes from a separate steel subframe, set a pattern followed by every other Jaguar from that day to this. The fixed-length drive shaft effectively formed an upper wishbone, and to keep stresses in check there were *two* combined coil-spring/damper units controlling each rear wheel — one at each side of the drive shaft. The famous six-cylinder XK engine was used, in 3·8-litre 'S' tune, and specially prepared road test cars, running on Dunlop racing tyres, beat 150mph in otherwise standard form, when tested in 1961.

The racing E-type project had been for an open car, but for production a sleek fast-back coupé with what we would now call a 'third door', was offered. This, the afterthought, was by far the more popular version. The first *public* appearance of a prototype was at Le Mans in 1960, when the Cunningham racing team were asked to run a works-built light-alloy version. This, although fast, did not finish the race.

The early cars were none-too-large inside,

Above: Just two variants of the big family of E-Type Jaguars. Both are vee-12 Series III cars, which can be recognised by the flared wheel arches and the disc wheels. The closed 2 + 2 coupe was otherwise like its six-cylinder predecessors, but the hard-top model (top) was on the long wheel-base chassis when fitted with the vee-12 engine. The hardtop was detachable, and the basic car was supplied with a convertible hood (see right). The structure combined a multi-tube front section and a monocoque centre and rear, there was all-independent suspension, and optional automatic.

and had poor ventilation. The United States market also found that they overheated too rapidly in heavy traffic and summer conditions. These, and other minor problems, were all rectified. In 1964, the engine was enlarged to 4,235cc and the first of the all-synchromesh gearboxes was fitted. Over the years the engine power dropped a little (due to having to meet US exhaust emission limits), the headlamp cowls were discarded and the interior was revised. Disc wheels supplanted wire-spoke 'knock-ons', and power steering was made optional.

The big change, however, was in 1971, when the six-cylinder E-type was dropped and replaced by a brutal and very rapid V12 car! This, like the XK engine, was a quantity-production 'first' in the whole world, at least of any V12 that could be called modern and technically advanced. Jaguar intended the V12, also, for their saloon cars, and for their long-term future. The rest of the E-type, basically unchanged, was extensively redeveloped to cope with the V12's power. Fatter wheels and tyres from the XJ6 were fitted, which meant that the bodywork had to be altered to suit. Early cars had a 96in (244cm) wheelbase, supplemented by a 105in wheelbase (267cm) for the 2+2 coupé announced in 1966. For the Series III cars, the longer wheelbase was standardised, which made the open version that much more spacious. A six-cylinder version of the Series III was announced, but none was ever produced. The last of the V12s were produced in the winter of 1974/75 (the last fifty were painted black, and specially plaqued) and the E-type has been replaced by the XJ-S. A total of 72,507 were made in all, more than 15,000 of them being V12s.

Right: From any angle, the E-Type Jaguar was slinky and beautiful. The original lines were settled in a wind tunnel, as in the beginning the car was to have raced at Le Mans.

*Above: One of the final batches of
E-Types, with the vee-12 5·3-litre
engine. Early 'sixes' had short
wheelbases and less passenger space.
Headlamps were exposed after 1968,
partly to improve lighting at night,
but this marginally spoiled the sleek
lines. The vast majority of all
E-types were exported, many to the USA.*

JENSEN FF

Jensen FF I, II and III (data for FF Mk I).
Built by: Jensen Motors Ltd., Britain.
Engine: Chrysler manufactured. Eight cylinders, in 90-degree vee-formation, in five-bearing cast-iron block. Bore and stroke 108mm by 86mm, 6,276cc (4·25in × 3·38in, 383cu.in). Detachable cast-iron cylinder heads. Two overhead valves per cylinder, operated by pushrods and rockers from single camshaft mounted in centre of cylinder block 'vee'. One down-draught four-choke Carter carburettor. Maximum power

325bhp (gross) at 4,600rpm. Maximum torque 425lb.ft at 2,800rpm.
Transmission: Four-wheel-drive layout, comprising Chrysler Torqueflite torque convertor and automatic three-speed gearbox, and central torque-splitting gearbox (Ferguson Formula), all in unit with front-mounted engine. Steering-column mounted gear shift. Open propeller shaft to hypoid-bevel 'live' rear axle. Transverse chain drive from central gearbox, then exposed propeller shaft to front chassis-mounted hypoid-

bevel final drive. Exposed, universally jointed drive shafts to front wheels.
Chassis: Fabricated chassis frame, with tubular-steel side members and pressed-steel floor, scuttle and cross-bracing members. Steel/light-alloy three-door coupé bodyshell welded to chassis after assembly. Independent front suspension by double coil-spring/telescopic damper units, wishbones and anti-roll bar. Rear suspension by semi-elliptic leaf springs, Panhard rod and telescopic dampers. Power-assisted rack-

JOWETT JAVELIN AND JUPITER

Javelins, built from 1947 to 1954, Jupiters, built from 1950 to 1953 (data for Jupiter).
Built by: Jowett Cars Ltd., Britain.
Engine: Four cylinders, in horizontally opposed layout, in three-bearing cast-aluminium block. Bore and stroke 72·5mm by 90mm, 1,486cc (2·85in × 3·54in, 90·7cu.in). Two cast-iron cylinder heads. Two overhead valves per cylinder, operated by pushrods and rockers from single centrally positioned camshaft. Two down-draught Zenith carburettors. Maximum power 60bhp (net) at 4,750rpm.
Transmission: Single-dry-plate clutch and four-speed, synchromesh manual gearbox (no synchromesh on first gear). Steering-column-located gearchange. Open split propeller shaft to hypoid-bevel 'live' rear axle.
Chassis: Separate multi-tubular steel chassis frame. Tubular side members with tubular cruci-form bracing and built up structures near front and rear suspensions. Independent front suspension by wishbones and longitudinal torsion bars. Rear suspension by radius arms, Panhard rod and transverse torsion bars. Telescopic dampers. Rack-and-pinion steering. Four-wheel, hydraulically operated drum brakes. 16in pressed-steel-disc wheels. 5·50 × 16in tyres. Telescopic dampers.
Two-seater sports bodywork, mainly in steel, with build-up hood.
Dimensions: Wheelbase 7ft 9in (236cm), track (front) 4ft 4in (132cm), track (rear) 4ft 2·5in (128cm). Overall length 14ft (427cm). Unladen weight 1,900lb (862kg).
History: The post-war Jowett production cars were entirely different from those of the 1920s and 1930s. No common parts survived. The five-seater Javelin, a streamlined saloon bearing some resemblance to late-model American cars, was designed during the war and went into production in 1947. Apart from its neat, small and efficient little 1½-litre flat-four engine (whose forward location ensured a lot of passenger space in an 8ft 6in (259cm) wheelbase), it also had clean wind-cheating lines and very good road-holding by any standards. Only the steering-column gearchange (wanted, no doubt, for export markets) was unsatisfactory. The car was sporting enough to be entered in the 1949 Spa

24-hour race, where it won the 2-litre touring-car class.

For 1950, the Javelin was joined by a sports car, the Jowett Jupiter. This had originally been called an ERA-Javelin, as ERA designer Eberan von Eberhorst had used Javelin parts to complete his multi-tubular chassis frame. Jowett adopted the car, improved it — particularly the chassis stiffness — and sold it alongside the Javelin. The Jupiter had attractive lines, but was not really powerful enough. The engines showed teething troubles and it was not until the early 1950s that they were reliable enough to be race-tuned. Cars entered by the factory won the 1½-

Above: The Jowett Javelin saloon and the two-seater Jupiter sports car shared the same mechanicals, but different chassis and bodies. Engines had 1½-litres and were 'flat fours'.

litre class three times in succession at the Le Mans 24-hour race (1950/51/52) and were also successful in rallies.

A successor to the Jupiter, the R4 Jupiter, with laminated plastic body and much less weight to carry, was planned for 1954. Jowett failed financially at the end of 1953 and car production stopped at once.

and-pinion steering. Four-wheel, hydraulically operated disc brakes, with vacuum-servo assistance and with 'Maxaret' anti-skid sensor connected to central gearbox. 15in disc road wheels. 6·70 × 15in tyres.

Dimensions: Wheelbase 9ft 1in (277cm), tracks (front and rear) 4ft 8·9in (145cm). Overall length 15ft 11in (485cm). Unladen weight 4,000lb (1,814kg).

History: In the 1960s, Jensen of West Bromwich got together with Harry Ferguson Research of Coventry to develop a practical four-wheel-drive private car. Ferguson had tried, and failed, to get their own car project adopted by the British motor industry. Now they were happy to sell their expertise and components to a customer in the normal way. Jensen first built a prototype in 1964/65 on the basis of the CV8, which was a 6·3-litre V8-engined GT car with glassfibre coachwork. To accommodate the chassis-mounted front final drive of the Ferguson Formula, the chassis had to be lengthened. The mechanically similar FF went into production at the end of 1966, but this carried the striking Vignale light-alloy coachwork shared with the new Interceptor.

Left: The four-wheel-drive Jensen FF—a unique private car, with Ferguson transmission and a 6·3-litre Chrysler vee-8 engine. Right: The Interceptor convertible had two-wheel-drive, but many similar components.

The four-wheel-drive system was much more sophisticated than that of a Land-Rover or Jeep 4 × 4, and incorporated Ferguson's patented central torque-splitting gearbox, which dramatically cut down any tendency for lightly loaded wheels to spin. In addition, the Dunlop 'Maxaret' anti-skid device was added to the braking system; this was connected to the transmission and sensed a sudden deceleration of a drive shaft (ie if a wheel locked up), whereupon brake line pressure to those wheels would be released.

Thus equipped, the FF was probably the safest car in the world to drive on slippery surfaces. Handling and roadholding were excellent, and the FF system's reliability adequate for a pilot scheme. On the other hand every car had to be adjusted individually before delivery and this helped to make the first cost very high indeed — £6,000 in 1968. The last FF was built at the end of 1971 — 318 were built in all. The Interceptor on which the FF was based carried on until Jensen closed down in 1976.

KISSEL 6-55 GOLDBUG SPEEDSTER

6-38, 6-45 and 6-55 family, built from 1915 to 1928 (data for 1925 model)

Built by: Kissel Motor Co., United States.

Engine: Six cylinders, in line, in cast-iron block, with four-bearing cast-alloy crankcase. Bore and stroke 84·1mm by 130·2mm, 4,340cc (3·31in × 5·12in, 265cu.in). Detachable cast-iron cylinder head. Two side valves per cylinder, operated by tappets from single camshaft mounted in side of crankcase. Single horizontal Stromberg carburettor. Maximum power about 61bhp.

Transmission: Multiple-dry-plate clutch and three-speed manual gearbox (without synchromesh), both in unit with front-mounted engine. Direct-acting central gearchange. Open propeller shaft to spiral-bevel 'live' rear axle.

Chassis: Separate pressed-steel chassis frame, with pressed and tubular cross bracing. Forged front axle beam. Front and rear suspension by

semi-elliptic leaf springs. Lever-arm hydraulic dampers. Cam-and-lever steering. Four-wheel, hydraulically operated (externally contracting band) drum brakes. Hand brake by externally contracting band on transmission drum behind gearbox. Centre-lock wire wheels. 33 × 6in tyres.

Choice of coachwork — Speedster had two-seat sporting body.

Dimensions: Wheelbase 10ft 1in (307cm), tracks (front and rear) 4ft 8·5in (143·5cm).

History: Kissel first built agricultural equipment then turned to stationary gas engines. Their first car came from the Hartford, Wisconsin, factory in 1906 and was rather cutely named the Kissel Kar. The first of the company's sixes arrived in 1909, but a much more modern six — the 6-38 — arrived in 1915. This was to be a very important member of the Kissel family for well over a

decade, as it was developed and redeveloped along with the rest of the car. A big change in image, to more sporting machines, began in 1917 when the Silver Special Speedster was unveiled (its designer was C. T. Silver). The model was further developed and from 1919, when one of the company's popular colours — chrome yellow — was standardised, the speedsters became known unofficially as Gold Bugs. The engines had side valves, but at 4·3 litres they gave plenty of torque (and when later enlarged to 4·7-litres they made the Gold Bugs very quick cars). The cars themselves developed along with North American fashion, and in 1924 the Kissel became one of the first cars to be fitted with four-wheel, externally contracting hydraulic brakes. At about the same time a splendid eight-cylinder Kissel car (with engine made by Lycoming) appeared, but the last of the true Kissels was built in 1930.

Below: Kissel's Gold Bug Speedster, so called because that was the popular colour. It was built from 1915 to 1928.

LAGONDA V12

V12 model, built from 1937 to 1939
Built by: Lagonda Ltd., Britain.
Mechanical specification as for Lagonda LG45 six-cylinder model, except for the following.
Engine: Twelve cylinders, in 60-degree vee-formation, in four-bearing cast-iron block/crankcase. Bore and stroke 75mm by 84·5mm, 4,480cc (2·95in × 3·33in, 273cu.in). Detachable light-alloy cylinder heads. Two overhead valves per cylinder, operated by adjustable tappets from single overhead camshaft per cylinder head. Two vertical single-choke Solex carburettors. Maximum power 180bhp (gross) at 5,500rpm.
Transmission and chassis: The transmission and the chassis, with independent front suspension, were shared with the LG6 and the same type of coachwork could be fitted to either motor car.
History: W. O. Bentley's first job after joining Lagonda was to refine the existing six-cylinder 4½-litre car, but once this was achieved he designed a magnificent new V12 engine — apart from Rolls-Royce's Phantom III unit, the only such 1930s British design — and an independently sprung chassis to suit it. The engine was actually shown at the 1936 motor show, fitted to an existing LG45 frame, but the car did not go into production until the end of 1937. The engine itself was everything one could have expected from the designer of great Bentleys, and though it was never developed properly (the war saw to that) it was good enough for special Lagondas to finish third and fourth overall at Le Mans in 1939.

The design was at once advanced and behind the times. Each cylinder bank had single-overhead-camshaft valve gear, which was ahead of the times, but there was only a four-bearing crankshaft and rather rudimentary breathing arrangements. The maximum speed of a V12 was at least 100mph, but some cars were fitted with elephantine coachwork, which rather hampered acceleration.

The engine found naval use in the war, but the jigs and tools were destroyed later and the magnificent V12 car and engine were never built again. They were arguably W. O. Bentley's finest products.

Right: Lagonda's vee-12 car was designed by W. O. Bentley, no less. No car needs any other recommendation. It was fast, expensive, and exclusive.

Below: The LG6 of 1938 shared frame and body with the rarer vee-12, and had a 4½-litre six-cylinder Meadows engine.

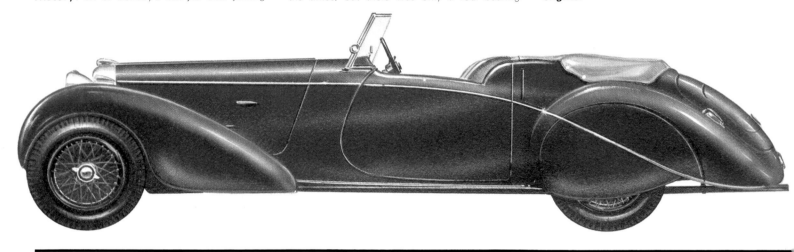

LAGONDA 4½-LITRE

4½-litre models, built from 1933 to 1939 (data for LG45, 1936 model)
Built by: Lagonda Motor Co. Ltd. (later Lagonda Ltd.), Britain.
Engine: Meadows manufactured. Six cylinders, in line, in cast-iron block attached to four-bearing light-alloy crankcase. Bore and stroke 88·5mm by 120·6mm, 4,453cc (3·48in × 4·75in, 271·7 cu.in). Two overhead valves per cylinder, operated by pushrods and rockers from single side-mounted camshaft. Two constant-vacuum SU carburettors. Maximum power never stated by manufacturers, probably about 130bhp at 3,500rpm.
Transmission: Single-dry-plate clutch and separate four-speed manual gearbox with synchromesh on third and top gears. Right-hand gearchange, or optional direct-acting central change. Open propeller shaft to spiral-bevel 'live' rear axle.
Chassis: Separate steel chassis frame, with channel-section side members and tubular and pressed cross bracing. Forged front axle beam. Semi-elliptic leaf spring suspension at front and rear, with controllable Luvax hydraulic dampers. 'Harmonic stabiliser' type of front bumper, as chassis-frame damper. Bishop, cam-and-roller steering. Four-wheel, mechanically operated drum brakes. 19in centre-lock wire wheels. 5·50 × 19in tyres.
Coachwork to choice (not built by Lagonda) in two-seat tourer, four-seat tourer or drop-head, and four-door saloon guise.
Dimensions: Wheelbase 10ft 9in (328cm), tracks (front and rear) 4ft 9·7in (147cm). Overall length 15ft 4in (467cm). Unladen weight, depending on coachwork, from 3,800lb (1,723kg).
History: The first of the 4½-litre Lagondas, the M45, appeared in September 1933, different from, but developed from, the 3-litre car which had been running since 1927. The 4½-litre, with a Meadows six-cylinder engine once used by Invicta, was to carry on in progressively improved form, until the outbreak of World War II. At first, the 4½-litre was a rugged and rather agricultural machine, very simply constructed, in the vintage Bentley tradition. The chassis frame was solid, the suspension firm and the road behaviour in the best British tradition too. The Meadows engine, large and understressed, gave the car a high-geared and adequate performance and was responsive to considerable power tuning and improvement.

The M45 Rapide followed in 1934, with more power, a transmission freewheel and higher gearing. Maximum speed was raised from 95mph to more than the magic 100mph. The company's prospects were then transformed in the summer of 1935, under new owners and with the arrival of W. O. Bentley as technical director. The LG45, a much-refined version of the cars, followed within months; among its improvements were a less robust engine, flexible engine mountings and revised suspension. Tuned M45R models, in the meantime, had unexpectedly won the Le Mans race outright in 1935. In the autumn of 1937, the car grew up even further and shared a completely new chassis with the V12 Lagonda engine which Bentley had rushed through at the behest of his new employers. The LG6, as it was to be called, had independent front suspension by longitudinal torsion bars and used the synchromesh gearbox developed for the recent LG45s and Rapides for 1936 and 1937. The car was faster than almost every other British car, excepting perhaps the latest from Rolls-Royce at Derby and its own V12 cousin. Some of the specially designed coachwork on LG6s was as splendid and dashing as anything found on a Bentley or a Rolls-Royce. This model, however, was not revived after the war, as Lagonda were concentrating on a new design of 2½-litre twin-cam car.

Above and right: Lagonda's 1937 Rapide was a 100mph machine, one of the fastest of all the world's fine cars. Other bodies were offered too.

Above: Lord Howe's L45R 4½-litre Lagonda raced in the Tourist Trophy of 1936, and finished fifth. The previous year a similar car won the Le Mans race.

LAMBORGHINI MIURA AND COUNTACH

Miura models, built from 1966 to 1972 (data for P400S)

Built by: Automobili Ferruccio Lamborghini S.p.A., Italy.

Engine: Twelve cylinders, in 60-degree vee-formation, in seven-bearing light-alloy block. Bore and stroke 82mm by 62mm, 3,929cc (3·23in × 2·44in, 240cu.in). Two detachable light-alloy cylinder heads. Two overhead valves per cylinder, opposed to each other at 70 degrees and operated by inverted-bucket tappets from twin overhead camshafts per bank. Six down-draught twin-choke Weber carburettors. Maximum power 370bhp (DIN) at 7,700rpm. Maximum torque 286lb.ft at 5,500rpm.

Transmission: Transverse, mid-mounted engine ahead of line of rear wheels. Single-dry-plate clutch and gear-driven connection to five-speed, transversely mounted, all-synchromesh gearbox, also ahead of rear wheel line. Spur-gear final-drive unit, with limited-slip differential. Exposed universally joint drive shafts to rear wheels.

Chassis: Pressed and fabricated punt-type steel floor pan/chassis, clothed by light-alloy two-seat coupé body from Bertone. Independent suspension on all four wheels, by coil springs, wishbones and anti-roll bars. Telescopic dampers. Rack-and-pinion steering. Four-wheel, hydraulically operated disc brakes, with vacuum-servo assistance. 7 × 15in centre-lock cast-alloy wheels. GR70VR15 tyres.

Dimensions: Wheelbase 8ft 2·6in (250cm), tracks (front and rear) 4ft 7·8in (141·7cm). Overall length 14ft 3·5in (435·6cm). Unladen weight 2,860lb (1,300kg).

History: Rumour has it that Italian industrialist Ferruccio Lamborghini, who was a fast-car enthusiast, was so unhappy with the reliability of his latest Ferrari that he decided he could do the job better himself. In any case, he hardly needed an excuse, as the market for such super cars was beginning to boom. The very first Lamborghini was built in 1963 and was exhibited at the Turin Show in November 1963. This car, the 350GT, was a rather ugly two-seater coupé with protruding headlamps, but had a shattering performance conferred on it by the brand-new Lamborghini V12 engine. This masterpiece, by Ing. Dallara, whom Lamborghini himself had enticed over from Maserati, was a sculpturally beautiful twin-overhead-camshaft design of 3½-litres. Even though the 350GT was no beauty, it sold well enough from Lamborghini's newly constructed factory at Sant'Agata Bolognese, not very far from the deadly rivals Ferrari (in Maranello) and Maserati (in Modena).

At the end of 1965, however, Lamborghini caused a sensation by showing a single rolling chassis, without a body shell at that stage, in which the splendid V12 engine had been enlarged to four litres, and was transversely mounted in the middle of the car, between the seating position and the rear driven wheels. Few observers thought this was a serious venture, as it looked too complicated and too unusual for a small manufacturer (even one headed by such a shrewd operator as Lamborghini, who had already made two fortunes in business, one by building a special type of small tractor), to contemplate making. Lamborghini himself was perfectly serious, as was his technical chief Gian-Paulo Dallara. By March 1966, at the Geneva motor show, the chassis had been clothed in an incredibly sexy two-seater coupé body by Bertone, one feature of which was headlamps which lay flush (but not hidden) during the day, but were electrically erected for night-time motoring. The car went into production, smoothly and successfully, during 1966, and proved not only that it looked beautiful, but that it was a very fast and stable machine, completely practical in every way for the rich enthusiast who liked to travel far and fast.

The Miura (the name is that of a Spanish fighting bull), was the first practical mid-engined super-car and the very first to go into any sort of series production. Since the whole of the nose,

and the entire tail section panel, could be swung up for inspection and maintenance, and because there was reasonable stowage space in the nose and also in the tail (behind the transmission), it was not the crazy and expensive plaything that the cynics had feared it would become. Even Lamborghini himself was surprised by the demand and several hundred Miuras were made on a modern if very simple assembly line between 1966 and 1972. With 170mph performance, even in its original P400 350bhp guise, the car was fast enough for almost everybody, but the impact of cars like De Tomaso's Mangusta and the latest in front-engined Ferraris made Lamborghini up-engine their car to the P400S, with an astonishing 370bhp from slightly less than four litres. During the six year life of the car, the engine size was never increased (although it is known that it could be stretched to five litres without difficulty), and it was persuaded to give one of the highest-ever specific outputs to date. The 180mph speeds attainable by the last Miuras prove that the power claims were not idle. It was too big and too powerful an engine to operate silently, with the carburettor intakes only inches from the occupants' ears, but the character of the commotion was such that people treated it as part of this powerful car's charm.

Roadholding and braking standards were well up to sports-racing standards, and the pity is that Lamborghini could never be persuaded to race lightened and tuned versions of the Miura, for the car would surely have been successful. To improve on this car required something sensational and this duly arrived in 1971 in the shape of the Lamborghini Countach, still mid-engined, but this time with a fore-and-aft engine layout. This car is even quicker, and has now replaced the Miura as probably the world's fastest road car. The engine size, 3,929cc, has still not been enlarged — what delights might await motorists of the 1980s?

Above right: Lamborghini's Miura was the original mid-engined supercar, with that magnificent transversely-mounted 4-litre vee-12 four-camshaft engine. Chassis design was to current racing sports car standards, and road performance lived up to this.

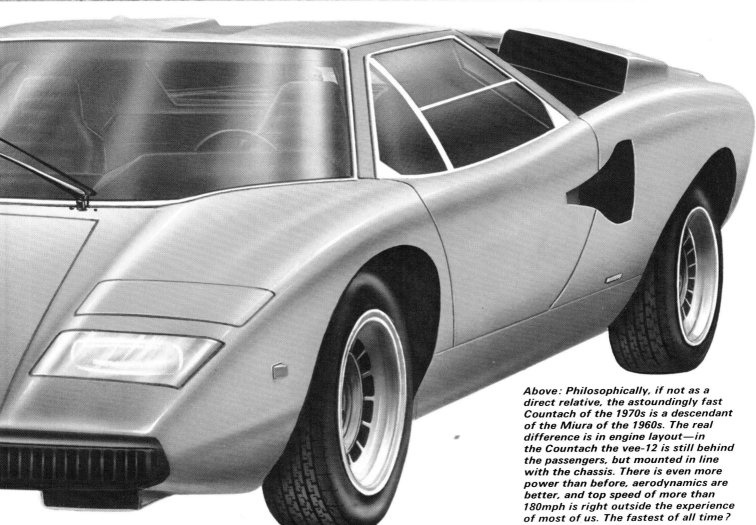

Above: Philosophically, if not as a direct relative, the astoundingly fast Countach of the 1970s is a descendant of the Miura of the 1960s. The real difference is in engine layout—in the Countach the vee-12 is still behind the passengers, but mounted in line with the chassis. There is even more power than before, aerodynamics are better, and top speed of more than 180mph is right outside the experience of most of us. The fastest of all time?

LANCHESTER 8/12HP

8/12hp, built in 1902
Built by: Lanchester Engine Co., Britain.
Engine: Two cylinders, horizontally opposed, in separate cast-iron blocks. Water cooled, although alternative model was air-cooled. Two crankshafts, geared together, above and below the plane of the cylinders. Multiple connecting rods, giving counter-rotating crankshaft movements. Bore and stroke 133·3mm by 144·46mm, 4,032cc (5·25 × 5·69in, 246cu.in). Single overhead valve, with additional feed valve cutting off inlet and exhaust port in turn. Camshaft operating valves via rockers, rollers and cams. Total loss lubrication system. Maximum power about 12bhp at 1,200rpm.
Transmission: Gearbox bolted to base of engine platform. Three forward speeds and reverse, by epicyclic reduction gears. Top gear direct. Short shaft-drive to worm-gear live rear axle.
Chassis: Punt-type chassis frame, with aluminium-sheet side members strengthened by steel channel and angles, and ash wood bolsters as frame to accept the bodywork. Tubular front axle. Front and rear suspension by long cantilever leaf springs. Engine and transmission mounted behind and below the front seats, driving rear wheels. Tiller steering — lever on right of driver. Transmission cone brake. Simple open bodywork, including rear entrance for back seat passengers. Wire wheels. 875 × 105mm pneumatic tyres.
Dimensions: Wheelbase 7ft 10in (239cm), track (front and rear) 4ft 10in (147cm). Overall length 11ft 5in (348cm). Unladen weight 2,436lb (1,105kg).
History: Dr. Frederick Lanchester, assisted by his brother George, designed the first all-British motor car in 1894/95 and had it built up in a small Birmingham workshop. Unlike most other pioneering designs, it was not just a copy of whatever Benz and Panhard were building at the

time. The very first experimental Lanchester was a single-cylinder air-cooled machine, later converted to a twin-cylinder design. The second car, preserved in a London museum, had the first of the two-cylinder, two-crankshaft engines which solved the balance problem in an ingenious though complex way. Design of the first production cars, which were sold either as air-cooled or water-cooled machines to choice, began in 1898.

Lanchester himself was a great innovator — being the first to test disc brakes, for instance, just a year after the first production cars were sold. He made stationary engines and engines for boats before turning to thoughts of cars in 1894. He was also much taken with the pioneering problems of flight and spent much time building glider models.

The Lanchester cars were extraordinarily refined and were developed for years before sales began. Lanchester's first factory was in Sparkbrook, Birmingham and deliveries began in 1900. Cars to the same basic layout, with a flat-twin engine mounted amidships and with the light and rigid composite-material chassis, were sold until 1904, when Lanchester's first four-cylinder car was introduced. A financial crisis overcame the company at the end of 1902, after which it was reconstituted as the Lanchester Motor Co. Ltd. Features of the first Lanchesters which were later adopted by the rest of the industry included the steering, with properly contrived 'Ackermann' geometry, the live-axle drive to rear wheels and easily detachable bodywork. Starting, incidentally, was by a *side*-mounted handle on the driver's side of the car.

Below and bottom: Lanchester's first 8/12hp cars were remarkably advanced, with punt-type frames, under-seat engines, but with tiller-type steering. They were ahead of Mercedes by years.

LANCHESTER 40

Lanchester 40, built from 1919 to 1929
Built by: Lanchester Motor Co. Ltd., Britain.
Engine: Six cylinders, in line, in two three-cylinder cast-iron blocks fixed to aluminium crankcase. Bore and stroke 101·6mm by 127mm, 6,178cc (4·0in × 5·0in, 377cu.in). Non-detachable cylinder head. Two overhead valves per cylinder, operated by rockers from single overhead camshaft. Single Smith carburettor. Maximum power approximately 100bhp.
Transmission: Single-dry-plate clutch and Lanchester three-speed epicyclic gearbox, both in unit with engine. Propeller shaft in torque tube, attached to 'live' rear axle incorporating Lanchester worm-gear and differential.
Chassis: Separate chassis frame, with two principal channel-section side members, braced by tubular cross members. Front axle beam suspended on semi-elliptic leaf springs. Rear suspension by trailing cantilever quarter-elliptic plate springs. Choice of wheelbase lengths depending on coachwork desired. Single transmission foot-operated drum transmission brake and handbrake lever connected to rear wheel drums (pre 1924); four-wheel, hydraulically operated drum brakes, with vacuum-servo assistance (post 1924), no transmission handbrake. 895 × 135 tyres (early models), or 33 × 6½in (later models).
Normally Lanchester-constructed coachwork — steel and light-alloy panels on cast-aluminium and ash framing. Special coachwork to choice.
Dimensions: Wheelbase 11ft 9in or 12ft 6in (358 or 381cm), tracks (front and rear) 4ft 10in (147cm). Length from 15ft 8in (478cm), depending on coachwork and wheelbase. Unladen weight, chassis only, 4,480lb (2,031kg).
History: The Lanchester 40 was a magnificent engineering masterpiece, built to the highest possible standards of workmanship and quality and therefore priced accordingly. It rivalled Rolls-Royce and later Daimler as the finest car in the world for its period. It sold in restricted numbers to the gentry, to royalty and to many foreign potentates. Lanchester had made their name in Edwardian times and the 40, designed by George Lanchester (assisted by his brother Frederick), was spiritually descended from both the pre-war 38hp model and the Sporting Forty. It was big and heavy — up to 5,500lb (2,494kg), with long-wheelbase limousine coachwork — and therefore ponderous and stately. A maximum of

Below: By the start of the Vintage years, Lanchester were building very conventional, but grand and impressive carriages. This three-quarter landaulet, built in 1923, was rated at 40hp, and carried its 12ft 6in wheelbase with great elegance.

65mph was all that a limousine would normally achieve, but it did this with great dignity and refinement. This was exactly what its customers wanted. On sale from 1919 to 1929 (and, in theory, still available until 1931, although replaced by the new 'Straight Eight'), the car made no concessions to cost-saving. The original price of £2,200 was reduced to £1,800 in 1921, but the model was still among the world's most costly cars. The Duke of York, later King George Sixth, preferred his '40' to all other machines.

The Lanchester brothers never trusted others to do their own engineering, which explains why not only the engine, but the complex and effective epicyclic gearbox and the worm-drive axle were also Lanchester made. The four-wheel brakes, adopted in 1924 (because Rolls-Royce were also rumoured to be doing so), were not truly hydraulic, but had servo-assisted mechanical linkages connected to a hydraulic accumulator pressed from the gearbox, which assisted the driver's own efforts.

Above: A smart three-seat coupe with separate luggage boot. Top: A 1926 short chassis tourer, with front brakes.

One 40 was extensively modified, tuned, lightened and rebodied, and in 1921 achieved great things as a racing car at Brooklands. The car was easily capable of beating 100mph and later took a clutch of long-distance endurance records.

LANCIA LAMBDA

Lambda Series 1 to 9, built from 1923 to 1931 (data for Series 1 Lambda)

Built by: Fabbrica Automobili Lancia e Cia., Italy.

Engine: Four cylinders, in 13-degree vee-formation, in three-bearing light-alloy block/crankcase. Bore and stroke 75mm by 120mm, 2,120cc (2·95in × 4·72in, 129·4cu.in). Single detachable cast-iron cylinder head. Two overhead valves per cylinder, operated by rockers and cam followers from single overhead camshaft. Single Zenith carburettor at rear of head, feeding to middle of engine. Maximum power 50bhp at 3,000rpm. Maximum torque 38lb.ft at 2,125rpm.

Transmission: Multiple-dry-plate clutch and three-speed manual gearbox (without synchromesh) both in unit with engine, direct-acting central gearchange. Two-piece open propeller shaft to spiral-bevel 'live' rear axle unit.

Chassis: Separate sheet-steel chassis, really a unitary structure forming frame and basic body structure in one. Independent front suspension by Lancia-type coil springs and sliding pillar linkage, with vertical telescopic dampers. Rear suspension by semi-elliptic leaf springs, with Hartford friction-type dampers. Worm-and-wheel steering. Centre-lock wire wheels. 765 × 105

tyres. Four-wheel drum brakes. Coachwork to choice – tourer, sports, or saloon. Structural boot compartment supplied as part of Lancia unitary-construction chassis structure.

Dimensions: Wheelbase 10ft 2in (310cm), tracks (front and rear) 4ft 4in (132cm), overall length 14ft 4in (437cm). Unladen weight (depending on coachwork) about 2,400lb (1,088kg).

History: Narrow-angle vee-formation engines had been an obsession in Vincenzo Lancia's plans for many years before his Lambda was announced in 1921, but the Lambda will also be remembered for its remarkable, unique, and rigid chassis. The engine, with only 13 degrees between banks (the block casting was actually almost cubic) was very short and stubby, with no attempt to deal with the out of balance dynamic forces. It is interesting to note that later Lambdas used 14-degree engines and final versions a 13-degree 40-minute layout.

The chassis was even more remarkable. It was a skeleton framework of flanged pressed-steel members, riveted together in ship fashion, with cut-outs for doors and for lightening. Cross bracing for these deep side members was provided by scuttle and bulkhead panels, and a

rigid backbone, which included the propeller shaft tunnel. Suspension and steering were hung from strategically placed tubular cross members. Front suspension was independent, by coil springs bearing above and below on to the sliding pillar stub axles—an arrangement used by Lancia for another thirty years. The firm was even forced to invent its own type of hydraulic dampers, integral with the 'king pin' housing.

The Lambda, made in nine series between 1923 and 1931, was at once light, low, and with exceptional roadholding, by any standards. More than 12,000 were made and Lancia's reputation for making 'way out' engineering work was established.

Right: Lancia's famous Lambda model was introduced in 1923 and ran through to 1931. The example shown was a 1928 version, mechanically very similar to the originals, and with that unique type of narrow-angle vee-4 light-alloy engine. The chassis frame was the other Lambda advance—of sheet steel and very deep—really an early example of unit-construction, now universal.

LANCIA APRILIA

Aprilia models, built from 1936 to 1949 (data for 1937 model)

Built by: Fabbrica Automobili Lancia e Cia., Italy.

Engine: Four cylinders, in 18-degree vee-formation, in three-bearing cast-iron block/crankcase. Bore and stroke 72mm by 83mm, 1,352cc (2·83in × 3·27in, 82·5cu.in). Detachable light-alloy cylinder head. Two overhead valves per cylinder, opposed to each other and operated by single overhead rockers and extra pushrods from camshaft. Single-choke carburettor. Maximum power 47bhp at 4,000rpm.

Transmission: Single-dry-plate clutch and four-speed manual gearbox (without synchromesh), both in unit with front-mounted engine. Direct-acting central gearchange. Open propeller shaft to chassis-mounted spiral-bevel final-drive unit.

Chassis: Unitary-construction pressed-steel body/chassis unit, with four-door saloon shell. Independent front suspension by Lancia-type sliding pillar with oil damped coil-spring suspension. Independent rear suspension by transverse leaf spring and swing axles, along with torsion bars. Four-wheel, hydraulically operated drum brakes. Pressed steel disc wheels. 140 × 40 tyres.

Dimensions: Wheelbase 9ft 0·5in (276cm), tracks (front and rear) 4ft 2in (127cm). Overall length 13ft 7·5in (415cm). Unladen weight 1,950lb (884kg).

History: In 1931, to replace the long-running Lambda, the Artena and the Astura were announced, and in 1932 the small-engined Augusta was introduced, with a 1·2-litre narrow-angle V4 engine and hydraulic brakes. Pillarless four-door saloon bodywork was new, as was the chassis-less form of construction. To replace Augusta, Lancia then produced the Aprilia, which sweetly and very effectively bracketed their pre-war and post-war years. The Aprilia carried the Augusta's formula one stage further along, with V4 engine enlarged at first to 1,352cc. The Aprilia stayed true to Lancia traditions with the vertical pillar/coil spring independent front suspension. New, however, was the aerodynamically shaped four-door saloon coachwork, and the structure even nearer to modern concepts of unit construction. Independent rear suspension, by swing axles and transverse leaf spring, was very adventurous for the period, and it all combined to make the little car a particularly nippy and appealing package. Top speed even in standard form was up to

80 mph, quite astonishing at a time when similarly engined British cars might still be struggling for 70mph – and this was really because the engine design was not hide-bound by silly taxation limits and because the car's shape was such a wind-cheater. Fuel consumption, too, was good – 30mpg was easily achieved. The engine capacity was increased to the full 1½-litres in 1939, but the car still exemplified the most advanced type of European-saloon engineering of its day. Production was resumed after the war, with absolutely no changes of signifi-

cance, and thousands more were sold before, in 1949, the model gave way before the arrival of the bigger-engined Aurelia, and shortly after that the new small Appia. Unhappily, the unitary-construction bodies were very prone to premature rusting, so few very good examples now survive. Of its day, the Aprilia was a very competitive little rally and racing saloon, rather in the Cortina image, where a combination of light weight, efficient little engine, and very controllable roadholding and handling made it much faster than might have been expected.

Right: The Lancia Aprilia, announced in 1936, was astonishing advanced for the period. The engine was the 'usual' Lancia type of narrow-angle vee-4, but the four-door saloon shell was sleek and without a separate chassis. It was possibly the first production fast-back apart from the Tatra, and was built in large numbers until 1949.
Below: Side view of the Lancia Aprilia showing off the many advanced features for a car conceived in 1934. The smooth lines show a search for wind-cheating —designers then thought the tail more important than a smooth front—and the low build. Suspension was all-independent, and the handling way ahead of most other European saloon cars.

LANCIA AURELIA

Aurelia model, built from 1950 to 1958 (data for Aurelia GT 2500)
Built by: Fabbrica Automobili Lancia e Cia., Italy.
Engine: Six cylinders, in 60-degree vee-formation, in four-bearing cast-alloy block. Bore and stroke 78mm by 85·5mm, 2,451cc (3·07in × 3·37in, 149·1cu.in). Two detachable light-alloy cylinder heads. Two overhead valves per cylinder, opposed to each other at 52 degrees, longitudinally, in part-spherical combustion chambers and operated by pushrods and rockers from single camshaft mounted in centre of cylinder block 'vee'. Single down-draught twin-choke Weber carburettor. Maximum power 118bhp at 5,000rpm. Maximum torque 134lb.ft at 3,500 rpm.
Transmission: Front-mounted engine and two-piece open propeller shaft to single-dry-plate clutch and four-speed, synchromesh manual gearbox (no synchromesh on first gear), both in unit with chassis-mounted spiral-bevel final-drive unit. Remote-control steering column gearchange. Exposed, universally jointed drive shafts to rear wheels.
Chassis: Box-section and pressed-steel platform chassis frame, with steel and light alloy two-door coupé 2+2 body shell by Pininfarina. Independent front suspension by sliding-pillar Lancia-type coil springs and telescopic hydrau-lic dampers. De Dion rear suspension, with semi-elliptic leaf springs and Panhard rod. Worm-and-sector steering. Four-wheel, hydraulically operated drum brakes, inboard at rear. Bolt-on pressed-steel-disc wheels. 165 × 400mm tyres.
Dimensions: Wheelbase 8ft 8·7in (266cm), front track 4ft 2·4in (128cm), rear track 4ft 3·2in (130cm). Overall length 14ft 4in (437cm). Unladen weight 2,630lb (1,193kg).
History: Lancia's first post-war model, the Aurelia, was delayed until 1950, but was an outstandingly up-to-date layout. As with most Lancias, a V-engine layout was chosen, this time with a conventional 60-degree cylinder bank angle. New and very advanced was the transmission, with clutch, gearbox and final drive all grouped together at the rear. The saloon came first, with 1,754cc, but this was enlarged in stages to nearly 2½ litres. The star of the range, the Aurelia Grand Tourismo coupé, arrived in 1951, at first in 2-litre form. Bracco drove the car into second place overall in the Mille Miglia and the car won its class at Le Mans. The 2½-litre Aurelia GT was announced in the autumn of 1953 and Louis Chiron won a protested victory in the 1954 Monte Carlo Rally. Production of GTs ceased at the end of 1955 although the car was listed for another couple of years, and the last saloons had gone by 1958. In place of the Aurelia was the dramatically-styled Flaminia, which nevertheless used some of the well-proven Aurelia engineering. The GT is generally accepted as being the first of that elusive breed, the 'grand touring' car.

Above: The Aurelia GT's classic lines —in 1950 it was a sensational shape.

LANCIA BETA

Beta models, built from 1972 to date (data for Beta Coupe 2000)

Built by: Fabbrica Automobili Lancia e Cia. (now part of Fiat), Italy.

Engine: Four cylinders, in line, in five-bearing cast-iron block. Engine transversely mounted as part of front-wheel-drive power pack. Bore and stroke 84mm by 90mm, 1,995cc (3·31in × 3·54in, 121·7cu.in). Aluminium rcylinder head. Two overhead valves per cylinder, inclined to each other in part-spherical combustion chamber and operated by twin overhead camshafts. One down-draught Weber or Solex twin-choke carburettor. Maximum power 119bhp (DIN) at 5,500rpm. Maximum torque 128lb.ft at 2,800 rpm.

Transmission: Single-dry-plate clutch and five-speed, all-synchromesh manual gearbox, in unit with, and in line with, transverse engine.

Direct drive from gearbox to spur-gear final-drive unit, mounted behind power pack; engine/gearbox ahead of front wheels. Exposed, universally jointed drive shafts to front wheels.

Chassis: Unitary-construction pressed-steel body/chassis unit, with 2+2 seating layout. Engine and transmission in nose, driving front wheels. All-independent suspension by Mac-Pherson struts, wishbones, anti-roll bars and telescopic dampers. Rack-and-pinion steering, with optional power assistance. Four-wheel hydraulically operated servo-assisted disc brakes. Pressed-steel disc wheels. 175/70HR14in tyres.

Dimensions: Wheelbase 7ft 8·5in (235cm), track (front) 4ft 7·3in (140·5cm), track (rear) 4ft 6·7in (139cm). Overall length 13ft 1·2in (399cm). Unladen weight 2,183lb (990kg).

History: Lancia's second Beta model — the first was built in 1909 — was inspired by Fiat. The giant Torinese company had taken over Lancia in 1969 and had authorised an all new range, using the well-known twin-cam Fiat 125/132 engine. The styling, engineering and unique transverse-engine front-drive package were all to Lancia's credit and the new range was launched in the autumn of 1972, initially as a series of five-door saloons. These were completely different, in every way, from previous Lancias and existing Fiats and they put Lancia firmly back on the road to prosperity. The saloons were soon followed by attractive coupés and spiders (with shortened wheelbases), and later by the HPE, literally a High Performance Estate with saloon wheelbase, coupé front styling, and a unique three-door layout. Last and most exciting of all was an Abarth-developed car, now on sale as the Lancia Monte Carlo. This used the Beta's power pack, but placed it behind the two-seat driving compartment in a very special mid-engined layout. The entire range is available, depending on the model chosen, with 1·3, 1·6 and 2·0-litre engines, all different versions of the same twin-cam unit. All Betas are very refined machines, with advanced suspension, excellent safety characteristics and styling which obviously appeals to many thousands. It is the model range which has put Lancia back in the forefront of 'Classic Car' makers, and carries on a 70-year tradition.

Left: The Lancia Beta saloon, now available with a choice of three Fiat-based twin-cam engine sizes. It is in the Euro-standard mould, with a five-door shell and a wind-cheating profile but other more exciting versions are also sold. The Beta Coupes share the front-wheel-drive, but with a shorter chassis and sleeker styling, as does the Beta Spyder. There is also the Monte Carlo, with mid-mounted engine.

LANCIA STRATOS

Stratos model, built from 1973 to 1976

Built by: Fabbrica Automobili Lancia e Cia. (now part of Fiat), Italy.

Engine: Ferrari manufactured. Six cylinders, in 65-degree vee-formation, in four-bearing light-alloy block, transversely mounted behind seats. Bore and stroke 92·5mm by 60mm, 2,418cc (3·64in × 2·36in, 147·5cu.in). Light-alloy cylinder heads. Two overhead valves per cylinder, inclined to each other in part-spherical combustion chambers and operated by twin overhead camshafts. Three down-draught twin-choke Weber carburettors. Maximum power 190bhp (DIN) at 7,000rpm. Maximum torque 159lb.ft at 4,500rpm.

Four-valve cylinder heads also available for competition purposes, along with fuel injection in some applications.

Transmission: Single-dry-plate clutch and five-speed, all-synchromesh manual gearbox, behind and below the main engine block. Remote-control central gearchange. Direct gearbox shaft to hypoid-bevel final-drive unit. Exposed, universally jointed drive shafts to rear wheels.

Chassis: Fabricated sheet-steel chassis structure, with tubular and other fabricated cross-bracing members. Glassfibre body skin panels, non-load-bearing. Engine/transmission behind driving compartment. Two seats in closed coupé layout. All independent suspension, by coil springs, wishbones, and anti-roll bars. Telescopic dampers. Rack-and-pinion steering. Four-wheel, hydraulically operated disc brakes. 14in bolt-on cast-alloy wheels. 205/70VR14 tyres. Wider wheels optional.

Dimensions: Wheelbase 7ft 1·8in (218cm), track (front) 4ft 8·2in (143cm), track (rear) 4ft 9·5in (146cm). Overall length 12ft 2in (371cm). Unladen weight about 2,160lb (980kg).

History: The Stratos was born out of Lancia's desire to dominate international production car motor sport, and particularly rallying. Cesare Fiorio, at once sales director and competition chief at Lancia, knew that the front-drive Fulvia coupés were no longer competitive and co-operated with Bertone in evolving a very special machine. It was nothing less than a full-blown mid-engined competition car, of which the minimum number (400 in a 12-month period) would be made to ensure approval for Group 4 competition. The first 'show car' by Bertone was a non-runner and was fitted with a Lancia Fulvia V4 engine, but as Lancia and Ferrari were now both controlled by Fiat it seemed reasonable to go the whole way to domination. The 'production' Stratos, therefore, was given a straight transplant, without any need for modification, of the 2·4-litre, four-cam, V6 Ferrari Dino engine and transmission, which was already engineered for mid-mounting. The Stratos, although stubby, low, and wickedly purposeful-looking, was also very strong. It had to be — it was meant to win not only the fastest tarmac rallies, and road races

LANCIA FULVIA COUPE

Fulvia Coupe, built from 1965 to 1976 (data for 1600HF Lusso)

Built by: Fabbrica Automobili Lancia e Cia. (now part of Fiat), Italy.

Engine: Four cylinders, in 13-degree vee-formation, in cast-iron block bolted to three-bearing light-alloy crankcase. Bore and stroke 82mm by 75mm, 1,584cc (3·22in × 2·95in, 96·7cu.in). Single light-alloy detachable-cylinder head, covering both cylinder banks. Twin-overhead camshafts, operating one valve in each cylinder bank. Two overhead valves per cylinder, inclined to each other in part-spherical combustion chambers and operated by rockers, or by rockers and extended tappets as appropriate, from camshafts. Twin horizontal twin-choke Solex carburettors. Maximum power 115bhp (DIN) at 6,200rpm. Maximum torque 112lb.ft at 4,500rpm.

Transmission: Front-wheel-drive power pack, with engine mounted ahead of front wheel drive line and gearbox behind the line. Drive from engine through hollow pinion shaft to gearbox, then back to hypoid-bevel final-drive unit. Single-dry-plate clutch and five-speed, all-synchromesh manual gearbox. Direct-acting central gearchange. Exposed, universally jointed drive shafts to front wheels.

Chassis: Unitary-construction pressed-steel body/chassis unit, with some light alloy skin panels. Closed 2+2 coupé body style. Engineering based on longer-wheelbase Fulvia saloon structure. Independent front suspension by transverse leaf spring, wishbones and anti-roll bar. Rear suspension by tubular 'dead' axle, semi-elliptic leaf springs, Panhard rod and anti-roll bar. Telescopic dampers. Four-wheel hydraulically operated disc brakes, with vacuum-servo assistance. 13in bolt-on light-alloy wheels. 175 × 13in tyres.

Dimensions: Wheelbase 7ft 7·7in (233cm), track (front) 4ft 3·2in (130cm), track (rear) 4ft 2·4in (128cm). Overall length 13ft 0·5in (397cm). Unladen weight 2,000lb (907kg).

History: The Fulvia family was launched in 1963 to replace the long-running Appia small car. Saloons with 1,100cc engines were first, but the first of the chunky and beautiful short-wheelbase coupés was launched in 1965, with the larger 1,216cc engine. Zagato soon developed a bulbous but attractive coupé of his own and the Fulvias began to make their names in competition. The Lancia factory became serious about competitions, which helped to ensure the use of bigger engines, and lightweight construction. The Fulvia became 1,300cc in 1967 and there was a competition 'HF' version, but the last and greatest Fulvia coupé was the 1600HF, first seen in 1968. All used the same twin-cam narrow-angle V4 engine, but in the 1600 this was stretched to its practical limit. The later Fulvias were given a five-speed gearbox (which they shared with the larger Flavia models) and this meant that their performance matched their good looks. There were two versions of the 1600 coupé, the lightweight of which was known as the HF Lusso — the HF meaning High Fidelity, after a club of Lancia enthusiasts who also entered competition cars with the factory's support. Only the arrival of the Stratos and Beta coupés spelt the demise of the Fulvias.

Left: The Fulvia saloons were always dumpy little machines, but the Fulvia Coupe produced from 1965 to 1976 was startling attractive. It had a vee-4 engine, front-wheel-drive, and (in some versions) a five-speed gearbox. Sandro Munari used a 1600HF to win the Monte Carlo Rally in 1972.

to be found in Europe, but also to tackle the rough events like the East African Safari, the Moroccan rally and the RAC rally. After some development problems, speedily solved because the solution could be applied to the small batch of production machines, the Stratos soon began to win, more or less as it pleased. It has to be said that the 'works' machines were usually stronger and more reliable than those supplied to private owners, but this is only to be expected.

The production Stratos disposed of 190bhp, but competition versions usually had 240bhp, and — once the four-valve cylinder heads were homologated — up to 280bhp was available. This, along with the splendid traction and road-holding of the cars, allied with the bravery of factory-hired drivers, made the cars almost unbeatable. Only the Safari (where dust in the engines is a major hazard) has really defeated the arrow-shaped projectile from Turin. The Stratos was never a serious road car, although some wealthy enthusiasts use the cars in this way. Production has now ceased, although the factory continues to campaign the machines.

Left: The Lancia Stratos is a purpose built competition car, of which only a few hundred were made between 1973 and 1976. It could win races, or survive the roughest and toughest rallies, with a combination of very powerful 2·4-litre vee-6 Ferrari engine, and a light but rigid structure. The dramatic style is by Bertone, and the skin is of glass-fibre. The engine is behind the seats and mounted across the car, with the five-speed gearbox in unit with it. 'Works' 24-valve engines produce up to 280bhp; the Stratos has now won three Montes.

LA SALLE

La Salle models, built from 1927 to 1940 (data for 1927 V8 model).
Built by: Cadillac Motor Car Co, United States.
Engine: Eight cylinders, in 90-degree vee-formation, in two cast-iron blocks, with three-bearing light-alloy crankcase. Bore and stroke 79·4mm by 125·4mm, 4,967cc (3·12in × 4·94in, 303cu.in). Two detachable cast-iron cylinder heads. Two side valves per cylinder, operated by single camshaft mounted in centre of crankcase 'vee'. Single up-draught Cadillac carburettor. Maximum power 75bhp (gross) at 3,000rmp.
Transmission: Twin-dry-plate clutch and three-speed manual gearbox (without synchromesh), both in unit with front-mounted engine. Direct-acting central gearchange. Propeller shaft, enclosed in torque tube, driving spiral-bevel 'live' rear axle.
Chassis: Separate pressed-steel chassis frame, with channel-section side members and tubular and channel-section cross members. Forged front axle beam. Front and rear suspension by semi-elliptic leaf springs. Lever-arm hydraulic dampers. Worm-and-sector steering. Four-wheel, mechanically operated drum brakes. Centre-lock wire wheels. 32 × 6·75in tyres.
Dimensions: Wheelbase 10ft 5in (317·5cm), tracks (front and rear) 4ft 8in (142cm). Overall length 15ft 9in (480cm). Unladen weight 4,030lb (1,828kg).
History: La Salle was a marque name 'manufactured' by General Motors, being chosen, like that of the Cadillac, from the ranks of explorers noted in that part of North America. It was a deliberate 'gap-filler', in price and performance, between Buick and Cadillac cars of the mid 1920s. The first model, announced in 1927, used the basis of a Cadillac chassis and new V8 engine, with individually styled bodies, and was a great if conventional success. Since Cadillac were about to expand into low-production V16 products it also gave the Cadillac division a wider selling base. The name only lasted for 13 years. All the modern GM technical innovations — synchromesh, safety glass, chromium plating, hydraulic brakes and the like — were adopted in that time and for a short period the later La Salles shared Oldsmobile straight-eight engines and Oldsmobile and Buick bodies. The marque was finally squeezed out by the cheaper Cadillacs.

Below: The La Salle was a perfect example of the 'manufactured' marque, invented by General Motors as a gap-filler between Buick and Cadillac. This was the original 1928 5-litre model.

LAURIN-KLEMENT 14/16HP

14/16hp Laurin-Klement, built from 1908 to 1912 (data for 1908 model)
Built by: Laurin und Klement A.G., Czechoslovakia (Bohemia before WWI).
Engine: Four cylinders, in line, in cast-iron block, with two-bearing cast-alloy crankcase. Bore and stroke 84mm by 110mm, 2,438cc (3·31in × 4·33in, 148·7cu.in). Non-detachable cast-iron cylinder head. Two side valves per cylinder, with exposed stems and springs, operated by tappets from single camshaft mounted in side of crankcase. Single up-draught carburettor. Maximum power about 16bhp.
Transmission: Cone clutch, in unit with front-mounted engine, and shaft drive to separate three-speed manual gearbox (without synchromesh). Remote-control right-hand gearchange. Open propeller shaft to straight-bevel 'live' rear axle.
Chassis: Separate pressed-steel chassis frame, with pressed cross members. Forged front axle beam. Front and rear suspension by semi-elliptic leaf springs. No dampers. Worm-type steering. Foot-brake, mechanically operating externally contracting drum on transmission behind gearbox. Hand brake operated by cable to drums (externally contracting shoes) at rear wheels. Artillery-style road wheels. 760 × 90mm tyres. Open four-seat coachwork.
Dimensions: Wheelbase 8ft 10in (269cm), tracks (front and rear) 4ft 4in (132cm). Overall length 12ft 7in (383·5cm). Unladen weight (chassis only) 1,900lb (862kg).
History: Laurin-Klement of Bohemia had made their reputation by building fine motor cycles before they turned to making cars in 1906. Thereafter, they concentrated on making brisk little *voiturettes* and soon built up an equal four-wheeler reputation. The first Laurin-Klement car was actually a 6/7hp V-twin, but conventional 14/16hp and 10/12hp four-cylinder models followed in 1908 and 1909. The 14/16hp was neatly designed in detail by Otto Hieronymus, with such features as a single four-cylinder casting for the block (when most foundries could only cope with two-cylinder blocks), and a short wheelbase which allowed the development of taxicabs for Vienna, Paris, Moscow and St. Petersburg. There was also a straight-eight Laurin-Klement, the Type FF, which effectively used two of the 14/16 cylinder blocks on a new crankcase, but very few of these cars were made. The two light four-cylinder cars were superseded in 1912 by new, larger and more powerful cars, still with conventional engines, but in 1913 a pair of Knight sleeve-valve models appeared, and the original *voiturette* strain was lost. The make was merged with Skoda in the 1920s.

Above: The Laurin-Klement was a car for Czechoslovakia to be proud of in the 1900s. The voiturettes sold well.

LEA-FRANCIS

'Hyper' models built from 1928 to 1932
Built by: Lea and Francis Ltd., Britain.
Engine: Meadows manufactured Type 4ED. Four-cylinders, in line, in three-bearing cast-iron block. Bore and stroke 69mm by 100mm, 1,496cc (2·72 × 3·94in, 91·3cu.in). Detachable cast-iron cylinder head. Two overhead valves per cylinder, operated by pushrods and rockers from single camshaft mounted in side of cylinder block. Single Cozette carburettor, bolted direct to No. 8 Cozette supercharger driven from nose of crankshaft. Maximum power 61bhp (net) at 4,100rpm (competition version 79bhp (net) at 4,500rpm).
Transmission: Single-dry-plate clutch and four-speed manual gearbox (without synchromesh), both in unit with front-mounted engine. Remote-control right-hand gearchange. Open propeller shaft to spiral-bevel 'live' rear axle.
Chassis: Separate pressed-steel chassis frame. Channel-section side members, with pressed, fabricated or tubular cross bracing. Forged front axle beam. Semi-elliptic leaf springs at front and rear, with friction-type dampers. Worm-and-wheel steering. Four-wheel, rod-operated drum brakes, with Clayton Dewandre servo assistance. 28in centre-lock wire wheels. 4·50 × 28in tyres. Open two-seat sports bodywork, in standard or lightweight 'Competition' form.
Dimensions: Wheelbase 9ft 3in (282cm), tracks (front and rear) 4ft 2in (127cm). Overall length 13ft 2in (401cm). Unladen weight (TT 2-seater) 2,200lb (998kg).
History: Most Lea-Francis cars of the 1920s were unashamedly 'kit' cars, with proprietary parts. In particular, every car made between 1923 and 1932 with four-cylinder power got its engine from Meadows of Wolverhampton. Lea-Francis, however, married their bought-in parts into a very harmonious whole. Their first sports cars were the L-types, which had evolved into P-types by 1927. These were fine and competitive in

many ways with the contemporary (and locally built) 12/50 Alvis sports cars, but it was the exciting supercharged 'S' type Hyper sports cars which really made their reputation. The Hyper's engine was still made by Meadows, but had Cozette supercharging and rakish lines with a rearwards-inclined radiator shell. For two years, from 1928 to 1930, the factory supported sports car racing and Kaye Don drove a Hyper to first place in the 1928 TT race in Northern Ireland. Racing in Ireland and at Le Mans showed that the Hypers were only just out-paced by the

blown 1750 Alfas. The company, however, was in financial trouble because of the depression and stopped racing. Car manufacture ceased in 1932 and when Lea-Francis was revived in 1938 it was with a new Riley-like engine design.

Below: The 'Hyper' Lea-Francis was the high-point of the Coventry firm's vintage designs. Race-tuned Hypers won the Tourist Trophy in 1928, and showed well at Le Mans. The engine was built by Meadows, with a supercharger.

LEYLAND EIGHT

Leyland Eight, built from 1920 to 1922 (data for one-off 1927 sports car)
Built by: Leyland Motors Ltd., Britain.
Engine: Eight cylinders, in line, in six-bearing light-alloy block. Bore and stroke 89mm by 140mm, 6,967cc (3·50in × 5·5in, 425cu.in). Cast-iron cylinder head. Two overhead valves per cylinder, inclined in part-spherical combustion chambers and operated by short rockers from single overhead camshaft. Leaf valve-return springs. Single Zenith carburettor. Maximum power 200bhp (net) at 2,800rpm.
Transmission: Single-dry-plate clutch and separate four-speed, sliding-gear manual gearbox. Right-hand gearchange. Propeller shaft, enclosed in torque tube, to spiral-bevel 'live' rear axle. Splayed drive shafts, giving positive wheel camber.
Chassis: Separate steel chassis frame, with channel-section side members and tubular and pressed cross braces. Forged front axle beam. Front suspension by semi-elliptic leaf springs. Rear suspension by cantilever quarter-elliptic leaf springs, connected by anti-roll torsion bar. Marles steering. Rear-wheel drum brakes, vacuum-servo assisted; no front brakes. Steel-disc road wheels. 895 × 135 tyres.
Dimensions: Wheelbase 10ft 6in (320cm), tracks (front and rear) 4ft 8·5in (143·5cm). Overall length 16ft 1in (490cm). Unladen weight 3,140lb (1,424kg).
History: Before the 1960s there was, quite literally, only one design of Leyland private car. This was the magnificent Leyland Eight, designed by J. G. Parry Thomas during World War I. Shown for the first time at London's Olympia motor show, it was dropped in little more than two years. Reputedly only 18 cars were built and sold, although when Thomas went off to indulge his passion for motor racing, at Brooklands, he took several spare chassis and other components with him. The Eight was meant to be the best car

in the world, regardless of cost, and was aimed squarely at the Rolls-Royce market. The design was good enough for its purpose, but Leyland themselves never backed Thomas's skills with their facilities. Trucks were more important to them and when post-war financial problems intruded the project was unceremoniously dropped.

The only surviving Leyland Eight is the short-chassis sports car now owned by British Leyland, built up in 1927 from parts held at the Thomson and Taylor workshops in Brooklands. The engine was remarkable for its detail — including leaf spring control of the valves, and eccentric camshaft drive. The live axle was

Above: Not until Leyland took control of Jaguar in 1968 did they build a finer car than the Leyland Eight. It was grand and exclusive—only 18 cars were built in three years—with an advanced 'straight eight' engine.

arranged to give positive road wheel camber to match the steeply cambered roads of the day. The starter motor, incidentally, was fixed to the gearbox. A few engines were enlarged from 7 litres to 7,266cc by means of a 6mm (0·24in) stroke increase. Opinion is that, mechanically at least, the Leyland Eight *was* the best car in the world during its short life.

LINCOLN CONTINENTAL

Continental, built from 1940 to 1948 (data for 1940 model)

Built by: Lincoln Motor Co. (a division of Ford Motor Co.), United States.

Engine: 12-cylinders, in 75-degree vee-formation, in cast-iron block. Bore and stroke 73.0mm by 95.25mm, 4,784cc (2.87in × 3.75in, 292 cu.in). Aluminium cylinder heads. Two side valves per cylinder, operated by hydraulic tappets from single camshaft mounted in centre of cylinder block 'vee'. Single downdraught Holley carburettor. Maximum power 120bhp (gross) at 3,500rpm.

Transmission: Single-dry-plate clutch and three-speed manual gearbox (synchromesh on top and second gears), both in unit with engine. Remote-control steering column gearchange. Propeller shaft in torque tube to spiral-bevel 'live' rear axle. Optional two-speed Columbia 'over-drive' axle, giving 28 per cent higher gearing when in use.

Chassis: Separate steel chassis frame, with channel-section side members and pressed and tubular cross braces. Forged front axle beam. Transverse-leaf suspension with radius arms, at front and rear. Hydraulic lever-arm dampers. Four-wheel hydraulically operated drum brakes. Mechanical hand brake operating on rear wheels. 16in pressed-steel wheels. 7.00 × 16in tyres.

Dimensions: Wheelbase 10ft 5in (317cm), track (front) 4ft 7.5in (141cm), track (rear) 5ft 0.7in (154cm). Overall length 17ft 6in (533cm). Unladen weight (coupé) 3,890lb (1,764kg).

History: Unlike the KV2 and the Lincoln-Zephyr models, the Continental was a very exclusive, high-priced machine for the status conscious. It was the brainchild of none other than Edsel Ford, who was president of his father's Ford Motor Company from 1919 to 1943. Edsel was much more interested in engineering and up-to-the-minute styling than his father (who was much more attracted to the idea of selling millions of cars at the lowest possible price) and it was his decision which led to the formation of a styling department in the corporation at a time

Above and below: In the beginning, the Lincoln 'Continental' name meant much more than it does today. The vee-12-engine was shared with other models but the two-door bodies (coupe or drop head) were sleek and special.

Above and below: Collectors now look on the drop-head cabriolet Lincoln Continental as the most desirable of the range. Edsel Ford inspired the styling, after much study of European trends. From 1940 to 1948, only 5,324 Continentals were built. The chassis was standard vee-12 Lincoln—but the bodies had special fixtures and fittings. The quality rivalled Cadillac —something Ford always wanted. Few other Detroit cars have such an aura.

when such things were still unusual in Detroit. Edsel Ford always regretted that Lincoln's fine name had progressively been down graded since the 1920s, when Ford had bought it, and by the mid 1930s he was determined to do something

about this. The styling studio was set up in 1932 and within a year their first Edsel-inspired efforts were on the road. Commercial pressures meant that Lincoln had to concentrate on the bread-and-butter Zephyrs in the mid and late 1930s, but by 1938 the fashion-conscious Edsel Ford decided to have a very special looking model developed. He was much influenced by the cars being made (at high prices) in Europe, and it was natural that the new car should immediately be known as a 'Continental' — a name which stuck to Lincoln even when the first famous model was discontinued, and which appears on modern products to this day.

Sales, Ford had no doubt, would be restricted, especially as he was prepared to see a £4,000 showroom price, so all his team's efforts were put into the body and fittings. Under the skin,

disappointing to those more interested in engineering than in styling, was the 1939-model Lincoln-Zephyr convertible coupé chassis. The engine, a 75-degree V12 side-valve unit already sold in the Lincoln-Zephyr, owed much to Ford's famous V8 engine and was none the worse for that, even though it was a very simple and cheap engine to make. Aluminium cylinder heads, three-speed gearbox with steering column gearchange and the Columbia two-speed axle were also familiar components. Unfortunately, so was the transverse-leaf suspension insisted on by Henry Ford himself for many years. In spite of the fact that General Motors had adopted independent front suspension years earlier, the elderly Ford was adamant and the Continental was way behind in this respect.

The styling, on the other hand, was not. Although enthusiasts now look on the car as very special, it shared some panels with the Lincoln-Zephyr cars. Prototypes were built in 1939 and the first batch of production cars was delivered early in 1940. All were two-door machines, in coupé or cabriolet form, and at first an exposed rear-mounted spare wheel was a recognition point. Mechanically the car was changed very little over the years, but for 1942 (a short-lived season because of the outbreak of war in America) the Lincoln-Zephyr type of nose was superseded by a modern trend with box-style wings and coffin-type nose. The engine was bored out to a full five litres at the same time, but unreliability caused this change to be reversed in 1946. Very important too was the option of 'Liquimatic' automatic transmission, but it was not a success. Overdrive, to replace the two-speed axle, was much more popular. Post-war production of Continentals was resumed in 1946, but the model's sponsor Edsel Ford had died in 1943, so there was little impetus to develop a successor. The price shot up with post-war inflation, but there was no shortage of buyers. This is proved by looking at sales figures — 5,324 cars were sold in all, but nearly 1,300 of these were sold in January to March 1948, after which the model was discontinued. One reason for the high price was that fittings and furnishings were always individually specified and much of the bodywork was hand-formed by craftsmen — a most unlikely thing for any Detroit-based concern to attempt. Only 404 were made in the 1940 model year, and 1,250 in the 1941 series.

The Continental was to reappear, with similar success and distinction, as the Mark II in the mid 1950s and as the Mark III in the late 1960s. In neither case, however, was it so exclusive, or so sought-after by the well off. Continentals live on, but are no more than super de luxe Fords.

LINCOLN K-SERIES V12s

K-Series cars, built from 1932 to 1939 (data for 1932 V12)

Built by: Lincoln Motor Co, United States.

Engine: 12 cylinders, in 65-degree vee-formation, in two cast-iron blocks, with seven-bearing light-alloy crankcase. Bore and stroke 82·55mm by 114·3mm, 7,340cc (3·25in × 4·5in, 448cu.in). Two detachable cast-iron cylinder heads. Two side valves per cylinder, operated by tappets from single camshaft mounted in top of crankcase. One twin-choke down-draught carburettor.

Transmission: Twin-dry-plate clutch and three-speed, synchromesh manual gearbox (without synchromesh on first gear), both in unit with front-mounted engine. Freewheel mounted in tail of gearbox. Propeller shaft, enclosed in torque tube, driving spiral-bevel 'live' rear axle.

Chassis: Separate pressed-steel chassis frame, with channel-section side members and pressed and tubular cross-bracing. Forged front axle beam. Front and rear suspension by semi-elliptic leaf springs, rear location by torque tube. Lever-arm hydraulic dampers. Worm-and-roller steering. Four-wheel, rod-operated drum brakes, with vacuum-servo assistance. 18in bolt-on wire wheels. 7·50 × 18in tyres. Choice of coachwork, saloon, convertible or limousine.

Dimensions: Wheelbase 12ft 1in (368cm), tracks (front and rear) 5ft (152cm). Overall length 17ft 10in (543·5cm). Unladen weight, depending on coachwork, from 5,800lb (2,630kg).

History: Henry Leland resigned from Cadillac in 1917 and evolved a new car for 1921 which he called the Lincoln. However, the new concern was not financially successful and it was ac-quired by Henry Ford in 1922. Ford himself was happy to let Lincoln carry on making small numbers of exclusive machines for well over ten years before the first 'Ford–Lincoln' (the Zephyr) was designed. The new management carried on building V8 Lincolns for ten years, but in 1932 they announced the splendid and rather exclusive K-Series cars, one of which (the KB) was given a new V12 engine of 7·3 litres. The cars were beautifully made and were impressive rather than attractive to look at. Their quantity-production

Below and right: One of Lincoln's finest cars was the K-Series vee-12, built throughout the depression years. Quality and engineering always came ahead of price, though in later years the styling was recognisably related to cheaper Fords. Below: A 1932 KB sedan with the 7·3-litre side-valve engine. Below right: A 1934 Model K with Dietrich convertible body, 6·8-litres, and a top speed of 100mph.

LINCOLN ZEPHYR

Zephyr, built from 1935 to 1948 (data for 1936 model)

Built by: Lincoln Motor Co (Division of Ford Motor Co), United States.

Engine: 12 cylinders, in 75-degree vee-formation, in four-bearing cast-iron block/crankcase. Bore and stroke 69·8mm by 95·2mm, 4,375cc (2·75in × 3·75in, 267cu.in). Two detachable aluminium cylinder heads. Two side valves per cylinder, operated directly by single camshaft positioned in centre of cylinder block 'vee'. One single-choke down-draught Stromberg carburettor. Maximum power 110bhp (gross) at 3,900rpm.

Transmission: Single-dry-plate clutch and three-speed, synchromesh manual gearbox (without synchromesh on first gear), both in unit with front-mounted engine. Propeller shaft, enclosed in torque tube, driving spiral-bevel 'live' rear axle.

Chassis: Unitary-construction pressed-steel body/chassis unit. Forged front axle beam. Front and rear suspension by transverse leaf spring and radius arms. Lever-arm hydraulic dampers. Four-wheel, cable-operated drum brakes. 16in bolt-on pressed-steel-disc wheels. 7·00 × 16in tyres.

Dimensions: Wheelbase 10ft 2in (310cm), track (front) 4ft 7·2in (140cm), track (rear) 4ft 8·7in (144cm). Overall length 16ft 10·5in (514cm). Unladen weight 3,350lb (1,519kg).

History: By 1935, Ford were in the full flow of their success, having capitalised perfectly on the reliability, performance, and low cost of the V8 car. They now turned their attention to the prestigious Lincoln marque, which had been making no more than about 40 cars every week in the V12 K-Series for some time. In a clever and entirely successful marketing move, a 'new' Lincoln was created with much family resemblance to Ford's current models, and with a new side-valve V12 engine which drew on the Ford V8 for many of its parts and all of its design

precision engineering was obvious, but they were just one of seven 12s on the market in 1932, so sales were low: only just over 2,000 were sold in 1933. Even though the KA, which had been V8 powered, acquired a smaller-edition 6·2-litre V12 in 1933, it had to retail for $2,700 dollars, which put it in the luxury category and out of reach of most impoverished rich Americans. Even so, there was much of interest in the technical details. The chassis and suspension were entirely conventional, but the engine was a mixture of old and new — among its features being a 65-degree angle between banks (60 degrees would have been normal and would have given perfect balance), side valves and detachable cylinder blocks on a light-alloy crankcase. There was synchromesh in the gearbox (all America was fast following GM's 1928 example) and a freewheel feature into the bargain. Surprisingly the brakes were mechanically operated, but they had a vacuum servo to assist the driver.

A new Model K was announced for 1934 to replace both the original KAs and KBs; this had a slightly smaller engine, of 6·8 litres (414cu.in), aluminium cylinder heads and a top speed of about 100mph. There was important restyling a year or two later, but sales gradually died away and the last of this type of V12 was built in 1939. In the meantime the Ford-designed Lincoln Zephyr, much cheaper yet still fast, had begun to sell like hot cakes. As one Lincoln tradition had been destroyed, another was beginning to burgeon.

philosophy. It was a big 4·4-litre design, but it produced only 110bhp. The main innovation was that the car had unitary construction (the first time in a car from the Ford empire); it was also by far the cheapest 12-cylinder car in the world.

Left and below: Designed specifically to fill a gap between Ford V8s and the expensive K-Models, the Lincoln Zephyr had an advanced unit-construction shell, and a simple, new, vee-12 engine based on the Ford V8. Both the saloon and the typically American coupe shown were built in 1937.

That outweighed other carryover points like the transverse-leaf suspension and the wide-ratio three-speed gearbox. The styling, with headlamps recessed in the wings, a six-window shape and a fastback tail with spatted rear wheels, was no more 'modern' than Chrysler's Airflow, but was much more commercially successful. A year later Ford's own styling was brought into line and the two marques shared identical noses and many sheet metal panels.

The V12, at first, was not entirely successful, for the exhaust passages were brought out across the cylinder block from the line of valves in the centre of the 'vee' and there were overheating problems. These were soon overcome, and the Lincoln Zephyr went on to become a very important model in Ford's line-up. The engine, too, became popular with other manufacturers (like Allard and Jensen in Britain), as it was a sure-fire way to enough power and torque to power any self-respecting trials or rally car. A facia-mounted gearchange was adopted in 1938, but it was replaced by a column change in 1940 and there were hydraulic brakes from 1939. Overdrive, a fluid coupling and power windows all became optional before production closed down in 1941. The same model was built between 1945 and 1948.

LOCOMOBILE MODEL H

Model H, built from 1905 to 1909 in 5·7-litre form (data for 1907 model)

Built by: Locomobile Company of America, United States.

Engine: Four cylinders, in line, in two cast-iron blocks, with three-bearing cast manganese-bronze crankcase. Bore and stroke 114·3mm by 139·7mm, 5,734cc (4·5in × 5·5in, 350cu.in). None-detachable cast-iron cylinder heads. Two side valves per cylinder, in T-head layout with exposed valve stems and springs, operated via tappets from two camshafts mounted in sides of crankcase. On up-draught carburettor. Maximum power about 40bhp.

Transmission: Cone clutch, in unit with front-mounted engine, and shaft drive to separate four-speed manual gearbox (without synchromesh). Remote-control right-hand gearchange. Straight-bevel differential in tail of gearbox, and countershaft to sprockets. Final drive to rear wheels by twin side chains.

Chassis: Separate pressed-steel chassis frame, with channel-section side members and tubular and pressed cross bracing. Forged front axle beam. Front and rear suspension by semi-elliptic leaf springs. No dampers. Worm-and-sector steering. Foot and brake, mechanically operating on contracting band on transmission countershaft drum. Hand lever, operating by cable on two internally expanding drums at rear wheels. Wooden artillery-style road wheels with 34 × 4in (front) and 34 × 4½in (rear) tyres. Choice of open or closed four-seat coachwork.

Dimensions: Wheelbase 10ft 0in (305cm).

History: The Locomobile motor car business was founded on steam cars, whose design rights had been purchased from the Stanley brothers. However, they sold back these rights to the Stanleys in 1903, by which time they had designed their first petrol-powered cars. Within a year they had transformed their image, that of makers of cheap steam buggies to one of manufacturers of expensive luxury petrol-powered cars. The definitive range of Locomobiles which developed in 1905 and 1906 had big T-head engines in true North American style and (until 1909), drove through side chains to a forged rear axle beam. The Model H, or 30/35hp type, was typical of the breed and included a long aluminium undertray to keep the engine and transmission free from road filth. The early cars were all four-cylinder machines, but the Famous 48, an eight-litre six-cylinder car, evolved very logically from them. The 48 was actually in production from 1911 to 1929 and, although it was thoroughly out-of-date when finally discontinued, it was always much sought-after and was advertised as 'The Exclusive Car for Exclusive People'. That sort of appeal to North American snobbery worked very well, even at a final price of S9,600. As early as 1905, incidentally, the more modest H had sold for S6,000. When the Famous 48 expired, so did Locomobile, who went out of the automotive business at the beginning of the depression.

Below: Locomobile's big Model H car, with a vast 5·7-litre four cylinder engine, was typical of the North American breed of fast touring car of this period. The style was elegant and dashing, the engine simply engineered, and the price very high—at more than $6,000. This is the last, 1909, version.

LORRAINE-DIETRICH SILENT SIX

Silent Six models, built from 1919 to 1932 (data for 1924 model)

Built by: Société Lorraine des Anciens Etablissements de Dietrich et Cie., France.

Engine: Six cylinders, in line, in cast-iron block, with four-bearing light-alloy crankcase. Bore and stroke 75mm by 130mm, 3,445cc (2·95in × 5·11in, 210cu.in). Non-detachable cast-iron cylinder head. Two overhead valves per cylinder, operated through pushrods and rockers from single camshaft mounted in side of crankcase. One up-draught Zenith carburettor.

Transmission: Twin-dry-plate clutch and three-speed manual gearbox (without synchromesh), both in unit with front-mounted engine. Direct-acting central gearchange. Propeller shaft, enclosed in torque tube, driving spiral-bevel 'live' rear axle.

Chassis: Separate pressed-steel chassis frame, with channel-section side members and pressed cross bracing. Forged front axle beam. Front suspension by semi-elliptic leaf springs. Rear suspension by cantilever semi-elliptic leaf springs, with torque tube location. Friction-type dampers. Worm-and-nut steering. Four-wheel mechanically operated drum brakes, internal-expanding (rear-wheel brakes before 1924 model). Detachable artillery-style road wheels. 820 × 120mm tyres. Choice of two-seat or four-seat, sporting, touring or saloon coachwork.

Dimensions: Wheelbase 10ft 0in or 10ft 9in (305cm or 328cm), tracks (front and rear) 4ft 7in (140cm). Overall length 13ft 0in or 13ft 9in (396cm or 419cm). Unladen weight, depending on coachwork, 2,450lb to 2,580lb (1,111kg to 1,170kg).

History: A Lorraine-Dietrich is a direct descendant of a De Dietrich, as one car evolved from the other in 1905 – from 1928, incidentally, they were simply called Lorraines. Like most Edwardian makers of fine machinery, Lorraine-Dietrich dabbled in motor racing, but after the war, which had been spent in making aero-engines at Argenteuil, they concentrated on fine touring cars. Marius Barbarou, the company's new technical director, produced a new in-line six-cylinder car, the 15CV. Called the Silent Six because of its silky road behaviour, this car was Lorraine's mainstay throughout the vintage years and was made until 1932. Although it was originally meant only as a touring car, a team put up creditable performances at Le Mans in the 1923 24-hour race and for 1924 more specialised models took second and third place behind the winning 3-litre Bentley. Better than this, a Lorraine-Dietrich won the race in 1925 and 1926 (with second and third places also being taken in the latter year). Right at the end of its career, the 15CV in 'Sport' form failed to beat Donald Healey to victory in the 1931 Monte Carlo Rally. The 15CV was replaced by the 20hp four-litre model, but Lorraine's last car was built in 1934, after which the firm concentrated on aero-engined and commercial vehicles.

Below: The Silent Six was originally meant to be a touring car, but fine Le Mans performances meant that these special four-seater racing machines were sent to the 24 Hour race in 1925 and 1926. Each year they won, beating—among others—Bentley. Handling and performance were both ahead of their time, and the cars were very reliable.

LOTUS ELITE (1950s TYPE)

Lotus Elite, built from 1957 to 1963 (data for 1959 car)
Built by: Lotus Cars Ltd., Britain.
Engine: Coventry Climax manufactured. Four cylinders, in line, in three-bearing light-alloy block. Bore and stroke 76·2mm by 66·6mm, 1,216cc (3·0in × 2·62in, 74·2cu.in). Light-alloy cylinder head. Two overhead valves per cylinder, in line in wedge-shaped combustion chamber, operated by inverted-bucket tappets from single overhead camshaft. Single or twin side-draught constant-vacuum SU carburettors to choice. Maximum power with single carburettor 71bhp (net) at 6,100rpm. Maximum torque with single carburettor 77lb.ft at 3,500rpm. Maximum power with twin carburettors 83bhp at 6,300rpm.
Transmission: Single-dry-plate clutch and four-speed, synchromesh manual gearbox (no synchromesh on first gear), both in unit with engine. Remote-control central gearchange. Exposed propeller shaft to chassis-mounted hypoid-bevel differential. Exposed, universally jointed drive shafts to rear wheels.
Chassis: Three main piece glassfibre monocoque, with steel-tube reinforcements. No separate chassis frame. Independent front suspension by coil springs, wishbones and anti-roll bar. Independent rear suspension by Chapman strut and coil springs. Telescopic dampers. Rack-and-pinion steering. Four-wheel, hydraulically operated disc brakes, inboard at rear. 15in centre-lock wire wheels, with 4·90 × 15in tyres.
Dimensions: Wheelbase 7ft 4in (224cm), tracks (front and rear) 3ft 11in (119cm). Overall length 12ft (366cm). Unladen weight 1,200lb (544kg).
History: Colin Chapman had established Lotus's reputation on the race track by 1956, but the Elite coupé, conceived in 1956 and revealed in 1957, was his first true road car. Nearly 1,000 were made between 1959, when full production began, and 1963 when it ceased, but although it was attractive and very functional the Elite was never a profit-maker for the company. In particular the cost of making the bodies became prohibitive, which is one reason why the Elan sports car had a steel chassis.

The Elite's concept was of a glassfibre monocoque — made in three major sections — floor, structural centre section and one-piece outer skin — on to which all mechanical and suspension parts would be mounted. This worked remarkably well, even if there were refinement problems in bolting the axle and engine units to the shell, and it certainly made the whole car very light. The shape was sleek, and the fuel economy therefore very good. Series II cars, produced in the 1960s, incorporated revised rear suspension and other improvements, and late in life Coventry-Climax engines of up to 100bhp were offered.

Perhaps the Elite's biggest disadvantage was that the roof was stressed and a convertible version was therefore impossible. Ventilation was also poor, because door shape did not allow for opening side windows. It is already a collector's piece in many countries.

Below: The Elite, revealed in 1957, was beautiful and technically clever. A unit-construction shell in glass-fibre was unique, the car was very light, and used a Climax engine.

LOTUS SEVEN

Sevens, built from 1957 to date (data for 1977 Seven Twin-Cam)
Built by: Lotus Cars Ltd., Britain and (since early 1970s) Caterham Car Sales Ltd., Britain.
Engine: Four-cylinders, in line, in five-bearing cast-iron block. Bore and stroke 82·55mm by 72·8mm, 1,558cc (3·25in × 2·86in, 95·2cu.in). Light-alloy cylinder head. Two overhead valves per cylinder, inclined in part-spherical combustion chamber and operated by inverted-bucket tappets from twin overhead camshafts. Twin Dell'Orto side-draught dual-choke carburettors. Maximum power 126bhp (DIN) at 6,500rpm. Maximum torque 113lb.ft at 5,500 rpm.
Note: Car also available with Ford pushrod 1,599cc engine, giving 85bhp (net) at 5,500rpm.
Transmission: Single-dry-plate clutch and four-speed, all-synchromesh manual gearbox, both in unit with engine. Remote-control central gearchange. Open propeller shaft to hypoid-bevel 'live' rear axle.
Chassis: Multi-tubular steel chassis, with open two-seater sports bodywork in aluminium and glassfibre panelling. Front mounted engine. Independent front suspension by coil springs and wishbones. Rear suspension by coil springs, radius arms. Telescopic dampers. Rack-and-pinion steering. Disc front brakes and drum rear brakes. 13in pressed-steel wheels. 165×13 tyres.
Dimensions: Wheelbase 7ft 4in (224cm), track (front) 4ft 1in (124cm), track (rear) 4ft 3·5in (131cm). Overall length 11ft 2in (340cm). Unladen weight 1,165lb (528kg).
History: Colin Chapman began his motor industry career by buying and selling used cars. From there he progressed to building specials for sporting trials and sports car racing. Early in the 1950s he started marketing his first 'production' car, the Lotus 6. In 1957, with his reputation established, and a more advanced multi-purpose two-seater sports car in mind, he replaced the Lotus Six by the Lotus Seven. The Seven was everything that most contemporary sports cars were not. It was very light, with very good roadholding, and (depending on the choice of engine) very rapid indeed. It was also supplied as a kit, thereby escaping British purchase tax, and being very cheap. Even so, within the limits of its mass-production suspension and back axle parts, it also rode and handled very well indeed. Although a Seven could be, and mostly was, used on the public road, its real stamping ground was the race track, where it could dominate its engine size class because of light weight and splendid roadholding.

It was not long, however, before Lotus lost interest in the car — the streamlined sports-racers and the single-seaters were much more exciting — but in spite of this, sales continued, and even when Lotus actively neglected the car, when it had reached its fourth series, it was still in demand. Even in the 1970s, twenty years after its concept, it is still a very competitive club-racing car. Weather protection is a bit of a joke and to get in and out with the hood erect is nearly impossible. When Lotus finally decided to drop the car, they disposed of the whole project to Caterham Car Sales in south London, where, albeit in revitalised and ever-popular Series III form, it continues to be manufactured.

Below: This Series 4 Seven had a glass fibre body, all others used light alloy.

LOTUS EUROPA

Lotus Europa, Europa Twin-Cam and Europa Special, built from 1966 to 1975 (data for Europa of 1967)
Built by: Lotus Cars Ltd., Britain.
Engine: Four cylinders, in line, in five-bearing light-alloy block. Bore and stroke 76mm by 81mm, 1,470cc (2·99in × 3·19in, 90·5cu.in). Light-alloy cylinder head, two overhead valves per cylinder, operated by pushrods and rockers from high-mounted camshaft in cylinder block. Single down-draught dual-choke Solex carburettor. Maximum power 78bhp (net) at 6,000 rpm. Maximum torque 76lb.ft at 4,000rpm.
Transmission: Combined clutch/gearbox/axle unit in transaxle, mounted behind mid-positioned engine. Single-dry-plate clutch ahead of axle unit and four-speed, all-synchromesh, all-indirect manual gearbox behind axle unit. Remote linkage to central gearchange. Hypoid-level final-drives. Exposed, universally jointed drive shafts to rear wheels.
Chassis: Separate pressed-steel chassis frame, in backbone 'tuning fork' shape. Engine mounted behind seats, but ahead of rear wheels, longitudinally. Independent front suspension by coil springs and wishbones. Independent rear suspension by coil springs, transverse links and radius arms. Telescopic dampers. Rack-and-pinion steering. Front disc and rear drum brakes. 13in pressed-steel wheels. 155×13in tyres.
Two-seater glassfibre bodywork, coupé construction, bonded to chassis frame (later made detachable).
Dimensions: Wheelbase 7ft 7in (231cm), tracks (front and rear) 4ft 5in (135cm). Overall length 13ft 0·5in (397cm). Unladen weight 1,350lb (613kg).
History: The Elite, expensive to make, was followed by the simpler but very successful front-engined Elan sports car. In 1966, as a complete contrast, Lotus then announced their mid-engined Lotus Europa, which in Europe was the cheapest production Lotus yet sold. Its

concept was a marketing arrangement between Renault and Lotus. Renault would supply Renault 16 engines and transmissions (suitably modified for driving the rear wheels of the Lotus — in the 16 they drove front wheels), Lotus would build the rest of the car, and the first sanction of cars would be sold only through Renault outlets in Europe — hence the car's appropriate name. Within a couple of years Lotus had gained agreement to sell the Europa all over the world. The car carried on the Elan's backbone chassis philosophy, but the mid-engined layout was new. Lotus, with their vast knowledge of mid-engined racing cars, had plenty of experience to call upon, and the Europa's handling was exemplary. It was, incidentally, one of the world's first quantity-production mid-engine cars, and certainly has always had the most renowned road manners.
Originally, the glassfibre body was bonded to the chassis frame on assembly, but for ease of maintenance and repair the mating became a bolt-on affair when the Europa was upgraded to Series II in July 1969. The biggest problem with the car was that it always seemed to be under-engined, but this complaint was stilled in October 1971 when the Europa Twin-Cam was announced, having the Elan's 1,558cc engine with 105bhp. This engine was a Lotus-converted twin-overhead-cam unit, based on the Cortina 1,500cc pushrod engine, and was also in use by Ford at the time in their Escort competition cars. A year later the Twin-Cam became the Special, with 126bhp and a five-speed gearbox. Production ran out in 1975, and the car has been replaced by the mid-engined Esprit.

Below: The Europa was a classic mix of Lotus engineering with a Renault engine at first. The Twin-Cam version pictured arrived in 1971. Bottom: A few Europas have been re-bodied by specialists, without chassis changes.

LOTUS ELITE

Lotus Elite and Eclat (data for Elite)
Built by: Lotus Cars Ltd., Britain.
Engine: Four-cylinders, in line, in five-bearing light-alloy block. Bore and stroke 95·2mm by 69·3mm, 1,973cc (3·75in × 2·73in, 120·5cu.in). Engine inclined at 45 degrees. Light-alloy cylinder head. Four overhead valves per cylinder, operated by twin overhead camshafts. Twin side-draught twin-choke Dell'Orto carburettors. Maximum power 160bhp (DIN) at 6,500rpm. Maximum torque 140lb.ft at 5,000rpm.
Transmission: Single-dry-plate clutch and five-speed, all-synchromesh manual gearbox, both in unit with engine. Remote-control gearchange. Open propeller shaft to chassis-mounted hypoid-bevel differential. Optional Borg Warner automatic transmission on some versions. Exposed, universally jointed drive shafts to rear wheels, doubling as suspension location links.
Chassis: Pressed-steel separate chassis frame forming a 'backbone' construction. Independent front suspension by coil springs and anti-roll bar. Independent rear suspension by coil springs and combined link/radius arm arrangement. Telescopic dampers. Rack-and-pinion steering (optionally power assisted). Four-wheel, hydraulically operated brakes, front discs and rear drums. Glassfibre three-door bodywork.
Dimensions: Wheelbase 8ft 1·7in (248cm), track (front) 4ft 10·5in (149cm), track (rear) 4ft 11in (150cm). Overall length 14ft 7·5in (446cm). Unladen weight 2,550lb (1,156kg).
History: As Lotus entered the 1970s, their founder Colin Chapman decided to move the product further up the social and price scale and gradually to phase out kit-built cars. When the Elan Plus Two became obsolete, he decided to replace it with something altogether more grand. The new Elite, confusingly given the same name as the coupé of the 1950s, was this car. Coded the M50 at Lotus, it was just the first of a whole new family of Lotus cars. Alongside it are the

Right: The Elite of the 1970s had nothing in common with the 1950s car. The modern version has a pressed steel chassis and Lotus' own slant-four twin-cam engine. The glass-fibre body is built from two large pieces. The Eclat is mechanically similar, with fast-back styling.

Eclat (mechanically like the Elite, but with fast-back instead of square-back styling) and the mid-engined Esprit, which effectively replaced the Europa at greatly increased cost. All share the completely Lotus-manufactured Type 907 2-litre 16-valve twin-cam engine (which was also sold to Jensen for use in their Jensen-Healeys until Jensen closed down in 1976). The Elite was designed to meet all existing and projected safety regulations, and in spite of being made with a glassfibre body is very strong and rigid. Lotus, in their Norfolk factory, make most of the motor car, instead of merely assembling proprietary parts. The Elite's backbone steel chassis frame carries on the Lotus tradition established with the 1962 Elan sports car and the all-independent suspension follows racing car lines of wheel location and control. The five-speed gearbox actually uses British Leyland internals. Performance is high — maximum speed being over 120mph — because of the light weight and efficient aerodynamic shape, the fuel consumption is low because of the car's light weight. Styling is mainly the work of Lotus staff, with suggestions from the Ital Design offices, and might be expected to stay unchanged for some years. The cheaper and more simple Eclat uses an Elite chassis, together with nose and centre sections from that car. Only the tail styling is unique.

It is well known that a larger V8 engine could easily be fitted into the Elite's engine bay; performance then would be quite phenomenal.

Left and above: From the rear the Elite looks like a fast estate car, but there is nothing commercial about the engine, which produces 160bhp from only two litres. Lotus build most of the car themselves—a far cry from the 'kit-car' Lotus machines of the 1960s

LOZIER TYPE I 50HP

Type I 50hp, built from 1907 to 1911 (data for 1910 model)

Built by: Lozier Motor Co., United States.

Engine: Six cylinders, in line, in three cast-iron blocks, with four-bearing light-alloy crankcase. Bore and stroke 117·5mm by 139·7mm, 9,089cc (4·62in × 5·5in, 554·6cu.in). Three non-detachable cast-iron cylinder heads. Two side valves per cylinder, in T-head layout with exposed valve stems and springs, operated via tappets from two camshafts mounted in sides of crankcase. Single up-draught carburettor.

Transmission: Multiple-dry-plate clutch, in unit with front-mounted engine, and shaft drive to separate four-speed manual gearbox (without synchromesh) — third gear direct and fourth gear an overdrive. Remote-control right-hand gearchange. Propeller shaft, enclosed in torque tube, driving straight-bevel 'live' rear axle.

Chassis: Separate pressed-steel chassis frame, with channel-section side members and pressed and tubular cross bracing. Forged front axle beam. Front suspension by semi-elliptic leaf springs. Rear suspension by semi-elliptic leaf springs, with transverse 'platform' leaf spring picking up rear of these springs, plus torque tube and radius arm location. Friction-type dampers. Worm-and-sector steering. Foot-operated transmission drum brake. Hand brake on rear wheel drums. Artillery-style road wheels. 36 × 4½in tyres. Choice of coachwork.

Dimensions: Wheelbase 10ft 11in (333cm), tracks (front and rear) 4ft 8in (142cm).

History: Lozier cars, like Pierce-Arrows and Packards, were among the finest American cars of the highest quality in the halcyon days before the outbreak of World War I. Unhappily, like many other firms around them, the social and financial changes which followed this conflict served to kill off many of the bespoke car makers. Lozier was one of the unlucky ones. The original Loziers had 'conventional American' T-head engines and chain drive, but only two years later they adopted shaft drive, and the 'platform' type of leaf spring suspension so beloved of the American designers. The engines had alloy crankcases and paired cast-iron blocks, which made it easy and straightforward to build fours or sixes. The 1907 range was precisely that — a high-quality mixture of components and a 40hp four alongside a 50hp six. Aids to luxury motoring were the chassis-long cast-alloy undertray (which protected the mechanicals from the dust of the era's unmade roads), and, in the case of the Type I, the geared-up fourth speed, which gave an 'overdrive' effect. It was no wonder that the Lozier marque was active in motor sport — in 1910 they won the National Stock car championship, and in 1911 the Vanderbilt Cup, with a second place overall in the Indianapolis 500.

Above: Lozier's Type I was one of North America's finest cars. Only a few were built, and raced successfully.

MARMON 16-CYLINDER

16-cylinder model, built from 1931 to 1933 (data for 1931 model)

Built by: Marmon Motor Car Co, United States.

Engine: 16 cylinders, in 45-degree vee-formation, in five-bearing light-alloy combined blocks and crankcase. Bore and stroke 79·4mm by 101·6mm, 8,049cc (3·12in × 4·00in, 491cu.-in). Two detachable cast-alloy cylinder heads. Fork-and-blade connecting rod layout at big ends. Two overhead valves per cylinder, operated by pushrods and rockers from single camshaft mounted in centre of cylinder block 'vee'. One twin-choke down-draught Stromberg carburettor. Maximum power 200bhp (gross) at 3,400rpm.

Transmission: Single-dry-plate clutch and three-speed synchromesh manual gearbox (without synchromesh on first gear), both in unit with front-mounted engine. Direct-acting central gearchange. Open propeller shaft to hypoid-bevel 'live' rear axle.

Chassis: Separate pressed-steel chassis frame, with channel-section side members and seven pressed cross members. Forged front axle beam. Front and rear suspension by semi-elliptic leaf springs, with torque arm at rear. Lever-arm hydraulic dampers. Cam-and-lever steering. Four-wheel, cable-operated drum brakes. Choice of artillery-style, pressed-steel-disc, or bolt-on wire wheels. 7·0 × 18in tyres. Choice of coachwork — open or saloon type.

Dimensions: Wheelbase 12ft 1in (368cm), tracks (front and rear) 5ft (152cm). Overall length 18ft 2·4in (554·7cm). Unladen weight (depending on coachwork) about 5,300lb (2,403kg).

History: Howard Marmon's first cars, built in 1902, were advanced for the period, with air-cooled V4 engines. Before 1908, he also offered an unsuccessful V8 and a choice between air-cooling and water-cooling on some models. Convention set in after that, with a series of T-headed cars. There was much Marmon success in competitions between 1909 and 1912 — the make winning at Indianapolis in 1911. In vintage years the company produced more and more technically interesting machines, notable for splendid lightweight alloy engines.

Straight sixes were followed by eights, and by 1929 the company was selling more than 20,000 cars a year. This success, and the booming state of the United States economy, encouraged Marmon to produce a glorious 16-cylinder machine, which had to compete for sales with the Cadillac 16 announced more than a year earlier. Marmon's car was magnificently engineered in detail, with an engine almost entirely built of light alloy but which nevertheless weighed more than 930lb (421kg)! Marmon had been quick to adopt Cadillac's new-fangled synchromesh transmission, but made no attempt to do anything fancy with the chassis, which was built on strictly 'traditional American' lines. The hypoid-bevel back axle, developed to get the line of the propeller shaft down, could only help a little and the Marmon was always an imposing sight.

You had to be very rich to buy a Marmon 16, and since the car was launched at the time of the worst of North America's depression (having been designed before the worst struck home), it is not surprising that very few were sold. With a fuel consumption of not much better than 8mpg, and a price of nearly $5,000, it was definitely an indulgence and not a practical piece of transportation. It was the right car at the wrong time. Cadillac could afford to carry a 'white elephant' in their range. Marmon could not, and in spite of dabbling with independently-sprung V12-powered cars for the future, they were forced to close down in 1933. That trade depression, as far as motoring enthusiasts are concerned, has a lot to answer for!

Right: Any 16-cylinder car was for the rich, and the Marmon cost $5,000. The US depression killed this fine car.

MARENDAZ SPECIAL

Marendaz cars, built from 1926 to 1936 (data for 1932 13–70 model)

Built by: D. M. K. Marendaz Ltd. (later Marendaz Special Cars Ltd.), Britain.

Engine: Six cylinders, in line, in four-bearing cast-iron block/crankcase. Bore and stroke 59mm by 114mm, 1,869cc (2·32in × 4·49in, 114cu.in). Detachable cast-iron cylinder head. Two side valves per cylinder, directly operated by single camshaft mounted in side of cylinder block. Single down-draught Amal carburettor.

Transmission: Single-dry-plate clutch, in unit with front-mounted engine, and separate four-speed manual gearbox (without synchromesh). Direct-acting central gearchange. Propeller shaft, enclosed in torque tube, driving spiral-bevel 'live' rear axle.

Chassis: Separate pressed-steel chassis frame, with tubular cross-bracing and channel-section side members. Forged front axle beam. Front suspension by semi-elliptic leaf springs. Rear suspension by cantilever leaf springs. Friction-type adjustable dampers. Bishop cam-gear steering. Four-wheel, hydraulically operated drum brakes. Centre-lock wire wheels. 4·75 × 28in tyres. Open two-seater sports bodywork, with occasional rear seats.

Dimensions: Wheelbase 9ft 9in (297cm), tracks (front and rear) 4ft 2in (127cm). Overall length 13ft 5in (409cm). Unladen weight 2,240lb (1,016kg).

History: Captain D. M. K. Marendaz, a well-known Brooklands racing driver, was first connected with the motor industry through the Marseal car, made in Coventry from 1919 to 1925, mainly from proprietary parts. After this project folded, Marendaz moved to London and there he designed new and much more sporting cars, calling them Marendaz Specials.

The first cars of 1926–7 used simple side-valve Anzani engines and were built in a part of the Bugatti importer's service buildings in Brixton. By 1931 the cars had been further developed, and the six-cylinder 13–70 model appeared with an enlarged engine much-disguised by an engine top cover which looked like a rocker case, but proved on inspection merely to hide a line of sparking plugs, as the valves were side-mounted as before. Later there was a supercharged version, but the final star performer was the 15–90 model of 1935, which

Above: Most Marendaz Specials were sports cars. This 15-90 coupe was made in 1935. Note the exhaust pipes.

used a 2-litre overhead-inlet, side-exhaust, Coventry Climax unit. Production had moved out to the 'Jam Factory' at Maidenhead in 1932 and prices were surprisingly low (as performance was high), but each car was essentially hand-built and the company was not profitable enough. The last Marendaz Special, as rakish and as purposeful as the first, was built in 1936.

MASERATI BORA AND MERAK

Bora V8 model and Merak V6 model, built from 1971 to date (data for Bora of 1972–3)
Built by: Officine Alfieri Maserati SpA, Italy.
Engine: Eight cylinders, in 90-degree V8 formation, in five-bearing light-alloy block. Bore and stroke 93·9mm by 85mm, 4,719cc (3·70in × 3·34in, 290cu.in). Light-alloy cylinder heads. Two overhead valves per cylinder, inclined to each other in part-spherical combustion chambers and operated by inverted-bucket tappets from twin overhead camshafts. Four down-draught twin-choke Weber carburettors. Maximum power 310bhp (DIN) at 6,000rpm. Maximum torque 340lb.ft at 4,200rpm.
Transmission: Mid-mounted engine ahead of final drive and five-speed, all-synchromesh

Below: Recognition points on the vee-6 Merak are the road wheels and the more sloping rear quarters. There is also a very occasional rear seat.

manual gearbox behind final drive. Single-dry-plate clutch, all-indirect gearbox and straight-bevel final drive, all in unit with the engine. Remote-control central gearchange. Exposed, universally jointed drive shafts to rear wheels.
Chassis: Unitary-construction fabricated steel (sheet and tubular) structure, with tubular extensions to support engine and transmission. Engine mid mounted, between two-seat closed passenger cabin and transaxle. All-independent suspension by coil springs, wishbones, anti-roll bars and telescopic dampers. Rack-and-pinion steering. Four-wheel, hydraulically operated disc brakes, with vacuum-servo assistance. 15in bolt-on cast-alloy wheels. 215/70VR15 tyres.
Dimensions: Wheelbase 8ft 6·2in (260cm), track (front) 4ft 9·9in (147cm), track (rear) 4ft 9·1in (145cm). Overall length 14ft 2·4in (433cm). Unladen weight 3,090lb (1,400kg).
History: Maserati were a noted Italian company for many years before they built there first mid-

engined machines. The first Maseratis raced in the 1920s and were usually active in Grand Prix racing thereafter, but the company built their first true touring cars in the 1940s. By the 1950s they were selling cars with productionised versions of their racing six-cylinder units, but they fell into severe financial trouble in 1957, after the entire team of racing sports cars was wiped out in one race in Venezuela. Racing was therefore abandoned and small numbers of exotic, expensive and very fast road cars were sold for a time. The Mexicos and Ghiblis were followed by the Indys, all front-engined cars, but in 1968 Citroën took a controlling interest in the firm and transformed their prospects. It was Citroën, therefore, who should really be credited with the inspiration of the twin mid-engined Maseratis — the Bora and the Merak — which are still made today.

The Bora evolved around a 4·7-litre V8 engine, which Maserati had steadily been refining since the days when it had powered the lusty $4\frac{1}{2}$-litre

Left and below: Both Merak (vee-6 engine) and Bora (vee-8 engine and 4·7-litres) share the same basic chassis. In each case the unit is mid-mounted, behind the seats, with all-independent suspension. The Bora is a strict two-seater; the Merak has a shorter engine, set back, and room for a bit more space in the shape of an upholstered shelf. The Merak (left) has craggy wheels and sloping rear, the Bora a squared-off tail.

two-seat racing sports cars. Mid-engined cars were not new to them (their first rear-engined 'birdcage' racing two-seaters had been used in 1961), although they knew little about the unitary-construction techniques which went with them. The Bora, revealed at Geneva in March 1971, was at once a gamble and a technical triumph. Like other supercars to come from the Modena region (such as the soon to follow Ferrari Boxer and Lamborghini Countach), it followed a predictable trend, with mid-mounted in-line engine, five-speed gearbox and transaxle bolted to it, a wedge-shaped body and room for precisely two passengers and a small amount of their luggage.

The performance — 160mph was a perfectly usable maximum speed — was sensational, and the roadholding and response for experienced and skilful drivers was also superb. Not that the Bora was by any means an excuse for a road-going racing car, not by any means. Air-conditioning and electric windows were standard, along with adjustable pedals and many other creature comforts. Styling was by Giugiaro (Ital Design). Citroën influence, incidentally, was obvious in the fully powered braking circuits, with the zero-travel brake pedal.

To supplement the Bora, Maserati next revealed the Merak, which once again owed its existence to Citroën. The kernel of the Merak was the V6 engine, a Maserati development which the Italian firm could never have afforded to put into production without a contract also to supply it to Citroën for their SM coupé. In effect the V6 engine (3 litres in the Merak but 2·7 litres in the Citroën SM) was developed from the ageing Maserati V8, but was very different in detail. The overhead-camshaft drives, for instance, were taken up the centre of the engine, between one end pair and the centre pair of cylinders. The angle between banks, at 90 degrees, was unusual for a V6, but allowed the V8's production tooling, such as it was, to be used in another application. The Merak itself looked virtually identical to the Bora, except in detail, but because the engine was substantially shorter than the V8, Maserati managed to insert a pair of almost useless 'jump seats' behind the existing front seats. Even with only a 3-litre engine installed, the Merak had a maximum speed of around 140mph, together with much improved operating economy. Maserati struck financial difficulties soon after their agreement with Citroën had been dissolved in 1973 and stopped trading for a time in 1975. With government finance, Alejandro de Tomaso made a take-over bid and restored the factory to activity during the year. Boras and Meraks were still being made at the end of 1976, in developed form, the Bora boasting a full 5-litre engine and the Merak more power than ever before. Some Citroën influence is still present — both cars having the Citroën brakes, the Merak having the SM's gearbox and the Bora having hydraulic adjustment to seats and pedals. The Merak incidentally, has inboard rear brakes (Citroën SM style) while the Bora's are outboard. These two cars are about to be joined by a new front-engined Quattroporte four-door saloon and the future of Maserati seems to be assured.

Left: Maserati's mid-engined machines are classic Italian 'supercars' with enormous performance potential (more than 160mph top speed from 4·7 litres —even the 2·7-litre Merak can nudge 140mph), splendid stability and handling, huge brakes, and a touch of exclusive class. To trim the road holding properly, the back tyres are wider than the fronts. Engine accessibility is good because the whole of the rear section of the body hinges at the rear. Headlamps pop up from recesses for night driving. The famous 'Trident' trade mark is obvious.

MATRA-SIMCA BAGHEERA

Bagheera models, built from 1973 to date (data for original 1973 model)
Built by: Engins Matra, France.
Engine: Simca manufactured. Four cylinders, in line, in five-bearing cast-iron block. Bore and stroke 76·7mm by 70mm, 1,294cc (3·0in × 2·75in, 79·0cu.in). Detachable light-alloy cylinder head. Two overhead valves per cylinder, operated by pushrods and rockers from single camshaft mounted in side of cylinder block. Two down-draught twin-choke Weber carburettors. Maximum power 84bhp (DIN) at 6,000rpm. Maximum torque 78lb.ft at 4,400rpm.
Transmission: Combined engine/transmission/final-drive assembly, driving rear wheels. Transverse engine, ahead of rear wheels. Single-dry-plate clutch and four-speed, all-synchromesh manual gearbox, in line with and in unit with engine. Remote-control central gearchange. Spur-gear drive to spiral-bevel final-drive unit behind engine/transmission. Exposed, universally jointed drive shafts to rear wheels.
Chassis: Separate steel tubular and pressed-steel chassis frame. Independent front suspension, by wishbones, longitudinal torsion bars and anti-roll bar. Independent rear suspension by radius arms, transverse torsion bars and anti-roll bar. Telescopic dampers. Rack-and-pinion steering. Four-wheel, hydraulically operated disc brakes. 13in pressed-steel disc wheels. 155 × 13in (front) and 185 × 13in (rear) tyres. Glassfibre two-door coupé bodywork and three-abreast seating, by Matra.
Dimensions: Wheelbase 8ft 9·3in (237cm), track (front) 4ft 6·3in (138cm), track (rear) 4ft 8·2in (143cm). Overall length 13ft 0·5in (397·5in). Unladen weight 2,117lb (960kg).

History: Matra's main interests are in aerospace, rockets and military equipment, but in 1964 they became interested in motor cars and took over the bankrupt René Bonnet sports car firm. After continuing Djet production for some time (the cars were Renault-based) they switched to the angular styling of the Matra 530, which had a mid-mounted Ford V4 engine. This was no more than an interim model, and after concluding a marketing and engineering agreement with Simca at the beginning of the 1970s they replaced it with a much more advanced car — the Bagheera.

The design of the Bagheera is unique in that it has three-abreast seating and has Matra-designed chassis and bodywork, but the mechanical items are taken from the Simca 1307/Chrysler Alpine models. This eases the spares and maintenance problem considerably. The Simca 1307 has a transverse-engine/front-wheel-drive arrangement and its entire power pack is used in the Bagheera, in this case placed behind the seats and driving the rear wheels. Simca 1100 front suspension and steering components are used at the front. The Bagheera was also marketed in an 'S' version from the autumn of 1975 with the aid of an enlarged 1,442cc Simca engine and in this guise it is capable of about 115mph.

Below: Matra-Simca Bagheera, with mid-mounted Simca engine, and 3 seats.

MERCEDES 60 MODEL

60 models, built from 1903 to 1904 (data for 1903 model)
Built by: Daimler Motoren Gesellschaft, Germany.
Engine: Four cylinders, in line, in two cast-iron blocks, with three-bearing light-alloy crankcase. Bore and stroke 140mm by 151mm, 9,293cc (5·52in × 5·94in, 567cu.in). Non-detachable cylinder heads. Two valves per cylinder: overhead inlet valves, with special Mercédès annular construction, operated by pushrods and rockers, and side exhaust valves; both valves operated from single camshaft in side of crankcase. Single up-draught Mercédès-Simplex carburettor. Maximum power about 65bhp at 1,100rpm.
Transmission: Scroll clutch in unit with front-mounted engine and separate four-speed manual gearbox (without synchromesh) and straight-bevel differential in rear of gear case. Final drive by countershaft from transmission to sprockets. Drive to rear wheels by chains.
Chassis: Separate pressed-steel chassis frame, with channel-section side members and tubular cross bracing. Forged front axle beam. Front and rear suspension by semi-elliptic leaf springs. No dampers. Worm-and-nut steering. Externally contracting drum brake, foot-pedal and mechanically operated, on gearbox counter shaft. Hand lever operating drums on rear wheel hubs. Wooden artillery style wheels. 910 × 90mm tyres (front) and 920 × 120mm tyres (rear). Open two-seat or four-seat bodywork.
Dimensions: Wheelbase 9ft 0·2in (275cm), tracks (front and rear) 4ft 7·5in (141cm). Overall length 12ft 3·5in (375cm). Unladen weight 2,204lb (1,000kg).
History: Emil Jellinek was a wealthy admirer of the German Daimlers and ordered a series of cars to his own requirements at the end of the 19th century. For 1901, he persuaded Daimler's Wilhelm Maybach to design him a completely new type of car, one which is now recognised as the forerunner of modern designs. The chassis, much lower than before, was of pressed steel and the layout and detail represented a complete change from 19th-century practice. These

Mercédès-Simplex cars were progressively developed in racing after 1901, until the Mercédès 60 cars were announced for 1903. The name Mercédès, incidentally, is that of Jellinek's own daughter.

For the infamous 1903 Paris–Madrid race a 90hp car was produced, but it was beaten by the 60s and a fire at Cannstatt destroyed all five special racing cars. For the Gordon Bennett races in Ireland, the factory appealed for owners to return their cars on loan. The American Clarence Gray Dinsmore lent his car, and Camille Jenatzy duly won the race in it, achieving 49·2mph in average speed, and notching up a 66mph maximum speed.

The transmission, with countershaft and chain drive to the rear wheels, was typical of the period, as was the braking system, with foot brake operating on the transmission drum. The engine, with its cast-alloy crankcase and paired cast-iron cylinders, had an integral cylinder head and overhead inlet valves which, admitted mix-

ture through annular slots. The basic design of these cars was so good that the 12·7-litre 90 and the 14-litre 120 models used virtually the same chassis and details, and all used the same robust family of four-cylinder engines. The success of the predecessors of the famous 60 cars caused the name Mercédès to be applied to all private cars built at Cannstatt from 1902. Jellinek himself had been on the board of the company since 1900. By 1908, however, when Mercédès won the Grand Prix, their cars had become even more advanced and with repeat wins in 1914 (with overhead-camshaft engines) they were established as leading makers of really fast cars.

Right and below: Sheer exciting modern engineering in the Mercedes 60. It is hard to believe that this splendid car was built as early as 1903. Most truly modern cars seem to evolved from this brilliant design. A Mercedes 60 won the Gordon Bennett race in 1903.

MAYBACH ZEPPELIN V12

Zeppelin models, built from 1930 to 1939 (data for 1930 model)

Built by: Maybach Motoren Werke GmbH, Germany.

Engine: 12 cylinders, in 60-degree vee-formation, in seven-bearing cast-alloy combined blocks and crankcase. Bore and stroke 86mm by 100mm, 6,922cc (3·39in × 3·94in, 422·4cu.in). Two detachable cast-iron cylinder heads. Two overhead valves per cylinder, operated by push-rods and rockers from single camshaft positioned in centre of cylinder block 'vee'. Two down-draught twin-choke Solex carburettors. Maximum power 150bhp at 2,800rpm.

Transmission: Single-dry-plate clutch and six-speed manual gearbox (without synchromesh), both in unit with front-mounted engine. Six speeds obtained by normal three-speed gearbox, with direct-acting central gearchange, and auxiliary two-speed unit mounted behind gearbox and operated by special vacuum-servo unit (later models had more complex six-speed box with preselection and gearchange on steering column). Propeller shaft, enclosed in torque tube, driving spiral-bevel 'live' rear axle.

Chassis: Separate pressed-steel chassis frame, with channel-section side members and pressed and tubular cross bracing. Forged front axle beam. Front and rear suspension by semi-elliptic leaf springs, with torque tube location at rear. Lever-arm hydraulic dampers. Worm-and-nut steering. Four-wheel, cable-operated drum brakes. Pressed-steel-disc wheels. 32 × 6·75in tyres. Choice of coachwork, closed or semi-sporting.

Dimensions: Wheelbase 12ft (366cm), tracks (front and rear) 4ft 10in (147cm). Overall length 16ft 4·8in (500cm). Unladen weight (for saloon) 6,200lb (2,812kg).

History: Maybachs were between-wars quality cars. Wilhelm Maybach had once worked for Daimler, but along with Count Zeppelin he founded an aero-engine factory in 1907. After World War I, Maybach built a 5·7-litre six-cylinder engine for motor car use, but apart from Spyker there were no takers, so Maybach designed and sold complete cars around this unit. The first Maybachs with the auxiliary two-speed gearboxes appeared in 1926, but the magnificent Zeppelin V12 tried to 'out-Mercedes' Mercedes from the end of 1929. The engine itself was splendid enough, but the Maybach transmission (now with effectively six forward speeds) was unique. The 'overspeed' gear, which acted on each forward ratio, was actuated by a thumb lever on the steering wheel (preselection) and the change came about, with the aid of vacuum assistance, by releasing the accelerator pedal. Later in the decade the transmission was made even more complex and completely preselective, with seven-speed gearboxes known. Along with the vast Grosser Mercedes 770, the V12 Zeppelin was Germany's most exclusive car of the 1930s and it was very expensive.

Below: Along with the Grosser Mercedes the vee-12 6·9-litre Maybach Zeppelin was the type of car chosen by German tycoons and leaders in the 1930s.

MERCEDES-BENZ 'GROSSER' 770

770 models, built from 1938 to 1940 (data for 1939 model)

Built by: Daimler-Benz A.G., Germany.

Engine: Eight cylinders, in line, in cast-iron block, with nine-bearing light-alloy crankcase. Bore and stroke 95mm by 135mm, 7,655cc (3·74in × 5·31in, 467cu.in). Detachable cast-iron cylinder head. Two overhead valves per cylinder, operated by pushrods and rockers from single camshaft mounted in side of crankcase. Single up-draught Mercedes-Benz twin-choke carburettor, with optionally engaged Roots-type supercharger, driven through friction clutch and gearing at nose of crankshaft and engaged by flooring throttle pedal. Maximum power 155bhp (unsupercharged) or 230bhp (supercharged) at 3,500rpm.

Transmission: Single-dry-plate clutch and five-speed, synchromesh manual gearbox (without synchromesh on first gear), both in unit with front-mounted engine. Direct-acting central gearchange. Open propeller shaft to chassis-mounted spiral-bevel final-drive unit. Universally jointed drive shafts enclosed in swinging half-axles.

Chassis: Separate steel chassis frame, made up of oval-section tubes, with tubular side members and tubular and pressed cross-bracing. Independent front suspension by coil springs and wishbones. Independent rear suspension by swing axles, coil springs and radius arms. Lever-arm hydraulic dampers. Worm-type steering. Four-wheel, hydraulically operated drum brakes, with servo assistance. 17in bolt-on steel disc wheels. 8·25 × 17in tyres. Open or closed coachwork, four doors in each case.

Dimensions: Wheelbase 12ft 11·1in (394cm), track (front) 5ft 4in (162·6cm), track (rear) 5ft 6in (167·6cm). Overall length 20ft 6in (625cm). Unladen weight (depending on coachwork and amount of armour-plating) 7,600lb to 8,100lb (3,447kg to 3,673kg).

History: There had been Grosser Mercedes models since 1930, when the first model with its exclusive 7·7-litre engine was announced. These cars were intended for state ceremonial use, and for selected and prestigious private owners. At first the cars had classic chassis with beam axles and leaf springs, but in 1938, the massive Type 770 model was announced. Production was even more restricted — to Adolf Hitler and his party colleagues — and the car's design leaned heavily on the company's newly gained Grand Prix racing expertise. The oval-tube frame, the independent suspensions, and the general lay-out, were all inspired by the W125 racing cars, although there were no common parts. The usual Mercedes 'optional' supercharger feature was present, together with a firm injunction *not* to use it for more than a minute at any one time. The five-speed gearbox, like the massive but conventional engine, was unique to the Grosser model and no other passenger car used the oval-tube type of chassis. There was never any economic reason for building these cars, which were purely prestige models, yet they were magnificently engineered in every way. As most of them carried armour plate and bullet-proof glass they were heavy and ruinously uneconomical. Something less than 5mpg was normal in most conditions!

MERCEDES-BENZ 38/250

36/220 and 38/250 models, built from 1927 to 1933 (data for 1929/30 SS model)

Built by: Daimler-Benz A.G., Germany.

Engine: Six cylinders, in line, in four-bearing light-alloy combined block/crankcase. Bore and stroke 100mm by 150mm, 7,069cc (3·94in × 5·91in, 431·4cu.in). Detachable cast-iron cylinder head. Two overhead valves per cylinder, vertically mounted, but staggered, and operated by fingers from single overhead camshaft. Two up-draught single-choke Mercedes-Benz carburettors, with or without assistance from Roots-type supercharger driven from nose of crankshaft. Maximum power (supercharged) 200bhp at 3,000rpm (140bhp if not supercharged).

Transmission: Multi-dry-plate clutch and four-speed manual gearbox (without synchromesh), both in unit with front-mounted engine. Direct-acting central gearchange. Propeller shaft enclosed in torque tube, driving spiral-bevel 'live rear axle.

Chassis: Separate pressed-steel chassis frame, with channel-section side members and pressed and tubular cross bracing. Forged front axle beam. Front suspension by semi-elliptic leaf springs. Rear suspension by semi-elliptic leaf springs and torque tube. Lever-arm hydraulic dampers or friction-type dampers (depending on customer). Four-wheel, shaft and rod-operated drum brakes (some cars with vacuum-servo assistance). Centre-lock wire wheels. 6·50 × 20 tyres. Two-seat or four-seat open coachwork.

Dimensions: Wheelbase 11ft 4in (345·4cm), tracks (front and rear) 4ft 10in (147·3cm). Overall length 15ft 5in (470cm). Unladen weight 2,800lb (1,270kg).

History: Following the completion of the merger between Mercédès and Benz, in 1926 (the accents on the name were dropped thereafter), the new combine continued to develop a fabulously fast, brutally impressive, starkly attractive and very successful series of supercharged sports cars. These cars are, in the beginning, to the credit of Dr. Ferdinand Porsche, who worked for the company after leaving Austro-Daimler earlier in the 1920s and before leaving to set up his own engineering consultancy business. The origins of a remarkable series of cars lie in the Mercédès (pre-merger, that is) 24/100/140PS of 1924. This car was designed around a vast new six-cylinder unit and the three figures, respectively, referred to the tax horsepower, the unsupercharged peak power output and the supercharged peak power. The blower itself was mounted at the nose of the engine, in an upright position, and could be clutched in or out of engagement (by friction clutches at the front end of the crankshaft) by the driver. Mercedes were at pains to point out to owners that the supercharger should be used only when needed, as it vastly increased the stresses on the engine and on the transmission. The engagement linkage was connected to the throttle pedal. Newer and faster models followed with great industry. First came the 36/220S, with its engine enlarged to 6·8-litres and that 220 referring to supercharged peak horsepower; this then paved the way for the 7-litre 38/250. This last car, in more and yet more developed

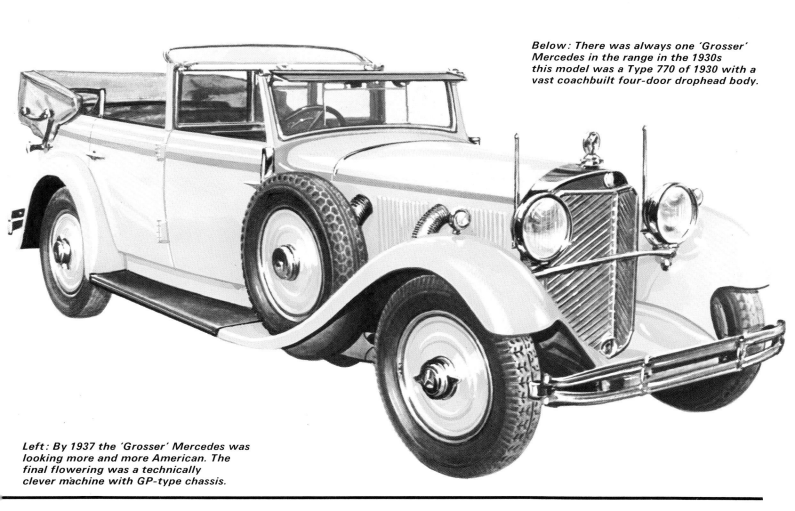

form, was the basis of all the Mercedes sports racing two-seaters of the late 1920s and early 1930s, which culminated in the very rare SSKL cars with their 300bhp and a top speed of more than 145mph in streamlined form. After the Mercédès and Benz merger, the 'basic' 140bhp supercharged car was given a shorter chassis and became the K (K = Kurz). This car was fast, but was not yet nimble enough, so it was re-engineered for an S version to be built alongside it. The S had a new chassis frame, dropped considerably by comparison with the K, and with the engine moved back by about 12in along with a lowered radiator. This car, in German numbering, was the 26/120/180PS, which indicated how the power was being increased. The 1928 cars which, among other things, won the German Grand Prix, were SSs (27/140/200PS), and had 7·1 litres compared with 6·8 litres for the original S. The cars were now becoming very specialised and a series of SSK cars (K = Kurz again, for shortened chassis) were raced with great success. These, in German terms, were

27/170/225PS cars. There was now only one more development to come — the SSKL — which was incredibly expensive to build, very special-ised, much lightened, even more highly tuned, and intended for factory use only. The SSKLs were 27/170/300PS cars — which gives an idea of the engine boost they were asked to withstand from the latest enlarged 'elephant blowers. No doubt Mercedes-Benz could have improved the cars still further, but by then they were com-mitted to a large-scale single-seater racing pro-gramme, with cars being built for the new 750kg Grand Prix formula, and the sports car programme was dropped. Perhaps even more than the much-vaunted Bentleys and Hispano-Suizas, and cer-tainly more so than the bigger Bugattis, the Mercedes supercharged sports cars said every-thing about the magnificence of the vintage era. The cars were, frankly, expensive, fast and exhilarating toys for their rich buyers; with usually more than 200bhp on tap and often only a token four-seater body shell without much weather protection provided, they were hardly

practical every-day machines. Their 'optional' supercharging was a unique way of providing, at one and the same time, a potential race-winning car which could also be cruised around when the pressure was off and which could also be used on the road in its less forceful state. Even if the supercharger could not be used with impunity, the howl emitted when it was in use must have made quite an impact on its oppo-sition. Strangely enough, a weak point with these cars was the brakes, which is hardly surprising when one considers that they were, relatively speaking, faster in their day than a Ferrari or Lamborghini road car is today *and* cable-operated drum brakes were all that could be provided. Such performance, too, was achieved without any pretence to streamlining. Cycle type wings, which did not turn with the front wheels, were the order of the day, and between them was the bluff and legendary vee-shape of the Mercedes radiator, with the equally famous three-pointed star fixed to its apex. Yet this immense per-formance, much feared by any rival met on road or track, was mostly to the credit of Dr. Porsche's splendid engine; the rest of the chassis engineer-ing, although carried out with great care and in high-quality materials, was entirely conven-tional, and was on a par with cars like the W.O. Bentleys and the Hispanos.

MERCEDES-BENZ 300SL

300SL models, built from 1954 to 1963 (data for 1954 model)

Built by: Daimler Benz AG., West Germany.

Engine: Six cylinders, in line, in seven-bearing cast-iron block, installed in car at angle of 45 degrees. Bore and stroke 85mm by 88mm, 2,996cc (3·35in × 3·46in, 182·8cu.in). Detachable light-alloy cylinder head with joint not perpendicular to cylinder bores. Combustion chamber formed in top of piston and top of cylinder block. Two overhead valves per cylinder, staggered (with inlet valves in one line and exhaust valves in other line) and operated by rockers from single overhead camshaft. Dry-sump lubrication. Bosch direct fuel injection. Maximum power 215bhp (net) at 5,800rpm. Maximum torque 228lb.ft at 5,000rpm.

Transmission: Single-dry-plate clutch and four-speed, all-synchromesh manual gearbox, both in unit with engine. Direct-acting central gearchange. Open propeller shaft to chassis-mounted hypoid bevel final drive.

Chassis: Separate multi-tubular spaceframe, with many small-diameter steel tubes linking points of stress. Lightweight aluminium two-seater body shell — coupé with gull-wing doors or open 'roadster' with conventional doors. Independent front suspension by coil springs, wishbones and anti-roll bar. Independent rear suspension by coil springs and swing axles. Telescopic dampers. Steering wheel hinged for access to driving seat and steering by recirculating-ball unit. Four-wheel, hydraulically opera-

Above: Striking comparison between the world-famous gull-wing Mercedes 300SL (on the right), and the mid-engined four-rotor Wankel engined Mercedes C111 Coupe. Both are from the same stable, but the progress made in less than 20 years is obvious. The 300SL engine is front-mounted, on its side; the Wankel is mid-mounted.

ted drum brakes, vacuum-servo assistance. 15in pressed-steel road wheels. 6·70 × 15in tyres.

Dimensions: Wheelbase 7ft 10·5in (240cm), track (front) 4ft 7in (140cm), track (rear) 4ft 9in (145cm). Overall length 15ft (457cm). Unladen weight 3,000lb (1,364kg).

History: Mercedes-Benz began to introduce a new series of passenger cars in 1950 and 1951, among which was a big and impressive six-cylinder 3-litre car, but they made a sensation when re-entering motor sport in 1952 with the futuristic 300SL sports-racing car. The fact that this car won its very first Le Mans race was startling enough, but that Mercedes were proposing to put it into some sort of quantity production was even more astonishing. Apart from the obvious facts that it was at the same time very fast and very attractive, it was also exceedingly complex, mechanically, and was not really designed for quantity production. The heart of the car's performance lay in its engine, which had direct fuel injection on production cars (although the Le Mans winner had used an engine with conventional carburettors), but the main interest was in the structure. Mercedes had gone all the way towards a theoretically perfect multi-tube

'spaceframe' structure, where all tubes were slim and absolutely straight and none had to withstand bending or torsional stresses of any nature. Taken to extremes, this would deny access to the car altogether, so there were inevitable compromises in the region of the passenger compartment. To ease this problem as much as possible, the frame was very deep along the sills and the doors were arranged to hinge along their top edge and open upwards in 'gull-wing' fashion. The car's only failing, more noticeable at very high speeds than at touring speeds, was that Mercedes were then wedded to swing-axle independent rear suspension. This allowed large (driven) rear wheel camber changes and produced serious and possibly dangerous oversteer at times. To handle a 300SL at really high speeds required really good 'racing-driver' reflexes. Far more of the 300SLs were ordered than Mercedes had bargained for and in 1957 they introduced the open-topped 300SL Roadster, which was a little easier to make, and handled better by virtue of its low-pivot swing-axle rear suspension. This model continued to be made at Stuttgart until the early 1960s and a total of 3,250 of both types were eventually sold.

There was no doubt that a suitably-geared 300SL, particularly in the more-streamlined coupé condition, had a very high maximum speed. The original publicity claims were that the car could accelerate from 15mph to no less than 165mph in top gear (which said a lot for the flexibility of the fuel-injected engine), but the higher figure was not attainable by a normally equipped road car. In British tune the cars could certainly beat 130mph, which made them supreme; however, with very high gearing it was possible for something like 150mph to be passed. The 300SL was forecast to start a new trend in sports car design, but even Mercedes themselves did not really want to have to build a spaceframe chassis in quantity and they were not copied by any other serious production-car concern. The multi-tube layout was very expensive and very difficult to build properly, as Mercedes soon found out. Neither did the gull-wing doors find favour elsewhere and when the Roadster 300SL was announced it was seen to have a modified frame with conventionally hinged doors.

The 300SL's descendants, truly, were the W196 Grand Prix car, which had many family resemblances, and the 300SLR sports-racing car (which in unique closed-coupé guise looked astonishingly similar to the 300SL). A car does not have to be a commercial success to be an all-time 'classic'. In looks, in performance and in the sheer exuberance of its complex engineering, the 300SL stood quite apart from any really fast supercar of the 1950s. Not even Ferrari, with exotic V12 engines in more mundane chassis, could match their ambience. The 300SL's engine, in less highly tuned form, was a mainstay of the Mercedes production car range until the end of the 1960s, when it was at last replaced by a new $3\frac{1}{2}$-litre/$4\frac{1}{2}$-litre V8 unit. The direct-injection system in the 300SL is still unique.

Left: The gull-wing Mercedes 300SL, of which about 1,000 were built, is one of two different versions of the car; the later 300SLs were Roadsters, with open sports car bodies and with conventional doors. Both had a multi-tube 'space frame' chassis, fuel injection for their 3-litre engines, and swing-axle rear suspension.

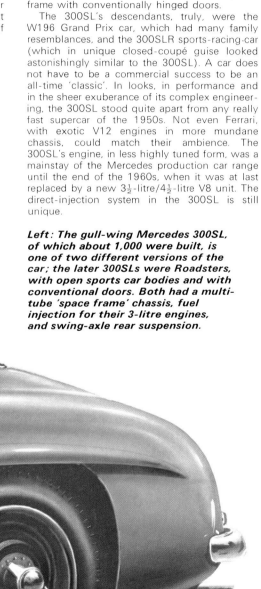

MERCEDES-BENZ 540K

500K, built from 1933 to 1936; 540K, built from 1936 to 1939 (data for 1936 model 540K)

Built by: Daimler-Benz A.G., Germany.

Engine: Eight cylinders, in line, in nine-bearing cast-iron block/crankcase. Bore and stroke 88mm by 111mm, 5,401cc (3·46in × 4·37in, 329·6cu.in). Detachable cast-iron cylinder head. Two overhead valves per cylinder, operated by pushrods and rockers from single camshaft placed in side of cylinder block. Single up-draught Mercedes-Benz carburettor, with optionally engaged Roots-type supercharger, driven through friction clutch and gearing at nose of crankshaft and engaged by flooring throttle pedal. Maximum power 115bhp (unsupercharged) or 180bhp (supercharged) at 3,500rpm.

Transmission: Single-dry-plate clutch and four-speed, synchromesh manual gearbox (without synchromesh on first gear), both in unit with front-mounted engine. Direct-acting central gearchange. Open propeller shaft to chassis-mounted spiral-bevel final drive. Universally jointed drive shafts enclosed in swinging half-axles.

Chassis: Separate pressed-steel box-section chassis frame, with box-section side and cross-bracing. Automatic chassis lubrication. Independent front suspension by coil springs and wishbones. Independent rear suspension by swing axles and double coil springs (one in front, one behind the axle). Lever-arm hydraulic dampers. Worm-type steering. Four-wheel, hydraulically operated drum brakes, with Bosch vacuum-servo assistance. 17in bolt-on wire wheels. 7·00 × 17in tyres.

Variety of coachwork—cabriolet, saloon, sports car and others.

Dimensions: Wheelbase 10ft 9·5in (329cm), track (front) 4ft 11·5in (151cm), track (rear) 4ft 11in (150cm). Overall length 17ft 2·5in (524·5cm). Unladen weight (depending on coachwork) about 5,000lb (2,268kg).

History: The spiritual, and actual, successor to the massive 38/250s was the 500K series, but if one was a true vintage car the 500Ks were typical cars of the 1930s. They still had separate chassis frames, but these were much more rigid than before and they followed the new Mercedes line of all-independent suspension — the rear, as for so many years to come on other models, by swing axles. The 500Ks grew up to become 540Ks (with an engine capacity increase from 5 litres to 5·4 litres) in 1935 and they were built almost unchanged up to the outbreak of war in 1939. Without splendid flagships like the Grosser models in the range, the 540Ks would have carried that title with pride. They were fast, excellently engineered and as intriguing as ever, with that unique-to-Mercedes optional-supercharger feature, and they carried some of the most dramatic and attractive sweeping body lines of the period. The external exhaust pipes, in chromium-plated flexible steel material, the big headlamps, the proud radiator topped by its three-pointed star and the rakish windscreen were all quite unmistakeable.

Below: Instantly recognisable as a Mercedes was the supercharged 5·4-litre 540K model. It was built for four years with a choice of body styles. This cabriolet was good for 106mph.

MERCEDES-BENZ 230SL

230SL, 250SL and 280SL, built from 1963 to 1971 (data for 230SL)

Built by: Daimler-Benz AG., West Germany.

Engine: Six cylinders, in line, in seven-bearing light-alloy block. Bore and stroke 82mm by 72·8mm, 2,306cc (3·23in × 2·87in, 140·7cu.in). Light-alloy cylinder head. Two overhead valves per cylinder, operated by finger-type rockers from single overhead camshaft. Indirect Bosch fuel injection into inlet ports. Maximum power 170bhp (gross) at 5,600rpm. Maximum torque 159lb.ft. at 4,500rpm.

Transmission: Single-dry-plate clutch and four-speed, all-synchromesh manual gearbox, both in unit with engine. Remote-control central gearchange. Open propeller shaft to chassis-mounted hypoid-bevel final drive. Optional four-speed Daimler-Benz automatic transmission, with fluid coupling. Exposed, universally jointed drive shafts to rear wheels.

Chassis: Unitary-construction pressed-steel body/chassis unit, in 2+2 open, convertible, or detachable fixed-head coupé styles. Independent front suspension by coil springs, wishbones and anti-roll bar. Independent rear suspension by low-pivot swing axles, coil springs and central compensating spring. Telescopic dampers. Recirculating-ball steering, optionally power-assisted. Four-wheel, hydraulically operated brakes, front discs and rear drums, vacuum-servo assisted. 14in steel-disc wheels. 185×14in tyres.

Dimensions: Wheelbase 7ft 10in (249cm), tracks (front and rear) 4ft 10·5in (151cm). Overall length 14ft 1·5in (430cm). Unladen weight 2,700lb (1,224kg).

History: Mercedes had had more sales success with the complex and very special 300SLs than they could ever have hoped, but they decided to replace it (and the 190SL) by a rather different car. The individually styled 230SL, announced in March 1963, subscribed to a completely different philosophy. Although it was still very much of a sports car in every way *except* in refinement, it used many more standard parts than its predecessors.

Apart from the all-new pressed-steel body shell, with that distinctive 'pagoda-style' of hardtop, almost all the mechanical components were shared with other Mercedes touring cars. The engine, for instance, already found a home in the 220SE, as a 2·2-litre, while the gearbox was used in several other models. Suspensions were 'standard M-B', and there was no doubt that the car could be made much more cheaply, and speedily, than the desirable old 300SL. It was a car with a great deal of performance and a great degree of refinement. The wide doors had wind-down door glass and with the solid and well-built glass-windowed hardtop in place the car was to all intents and purposes a little two-door saloon. Although it was billed as a 2+2, there was really very little space behind the front seats. In order to keep up with improving performance standards, the 230SL became 250SL (with 2,496cc) for 1967, and 280SL (with 2,778cc) for 1968 onwards; the first was achieved with a stroke increase and the second with a cylinder bore enlargement. The 280SL was finally replaced by the new 350SL in 1971.

Below: The 230SL effectively took the place of the legendary 300SL, and had the distinctive 'pagoda' roof profile. The range continued for nine years in three engine sizes. It was very strong.

MERCER RACEABOUT

Type 35, built from 1911 to 1914 (data for 1911 model)

Built by: Mercer Automobile Co., United States.

Engine: Four cylinders, in line, in two cast-iron blocks, with three-bearing light-alloy crankcase. Bore and stroke 111·1mm by 127mm, 4,925cc (4·37in × 5·0in, 300cu.in). Non-detachable cast-iron cylinder heads. Two side valves per cylinder, inlets on one side of block and exhausts on other side, operated by tappets and interposed fingers from two camshafts mounted in side of crankcase. Single up-draught carburettor. Maximum power about 56bhp at 1,800rpm.

Transmission: Multiple-dry-plate clutch ('wet' clutch from 1912) in unit with front-mounted engine. Shaft-drive to three-speed manual gearbox (without synchromesh). Remote-control right-hand gearchange. Open propeller shaft to straight-bevel 'live' rear axle.

Chassis: Separate pressed-steel chassis frame, with tubular and pressed-steel cross-bracings and channel-section side members. Forged front axle beam. Front and rear suspension by semi-elliptic leaf springs. Friction-type dampers. Worm-type steering. Rear-wheel brakes by hand-lever; transmission drum brake mechanically operated from foot pedal. Artillery-style road wheels. 3½×34in tyres. Open two-seater bodywork, with no weather protection and with 'monocle' windscreen.

Dimensions: Wheelbase 9ft (274cm), tracks (front and rear) 4ft 8in (142cm). Unladen weight 2,300lb (1,043kg).

History: Finlay Porter's stark and purposeful Mercer raceabout has been called the best sports car ever made in North America and it certainly looks the part. In effect it was a fast-car chassis with little more than a radiator, bonnet and cowl and two stark seats. The only form of weather protection for the driver was that splendid 'monocle' windscreen fixed to the steering column. His poor passenger got nothing at all!

Mercer's owners were the Roebling family, engineers who had already built the Brooklyn bridge. The engine was a proprietary unit from Beaver, with a very ordinary T-head layout, but as the car was very light the Raceabout really could motor very fast. It was entirely impractical, but every red-blooded American lusted after one and more than 500 were built in about four years, before a new-design of L-head unit was installed. It was, indeed, an adaptation of a 1910 Mercer Type 30-M racing car and no compromise was made in the transformation. Tragedy struck the company when all three of the Roeblings died before 1918 (one of them went down with the *Titanic*): with them sank the company's fortunes.

There were improved but more civilised Mercers, later, but the last of the original strain died early in the 1920s. The 22/70 which succeeded the Type 35 in 1915 was a good car, faster and more comfortable, but it was by no means as exciting. Perhaps that was a cause for the decline?

Below: The Mercer Raceabout was all about performance, dash, and glamour. Comfort and weather protection came last. The driver got a 'monocle' screen and the passenger nothing at all. The whole car was very simple, with a big 5-litre engine, exposed petrol tank, high gearing, and a strong steel frame. More than 500 were made before 1914.

METALLURGIQUE 60/80HP

60/80hp model, built from 1906 to 1914 (data for 1906 model)

Built by: S.A. L'Auto Métallurgique, Belgium.

Engine: Four cylinders, in line, in two cast-iron blocks, with light-alloy three-bearing crankcase. Bore and stroke 150mm by 140mm, 9,896cc (5·91in × 5·51in, 604cu.in). Fixed cylinder heads. Two valves per cylinder, overhead inlets operated by pushrods and rockers, side valves operated by tappets, all from single camshaft mounted in crankcase (valve stems and pushrods exposed). Single up-draught Sthenos carburettor. Maximum power about 100bhp at 1,400rpm.

Transmission: Expanding shoe clutch, in unit with flywheel on front-mounted engine and shaft to separate four-speed manual gearbox (without synchromesh). Remote-control right-hand gearchange. Open propeller shaft to straight-bevel 'live' rear axle.

Chassis: Separate pressed-steel chassis frame, with channel-section side members and pressed cross bracing. Forged front axle beam. Front and rear suspension by semi-elliptic leaf springs. No dampers. Worm-type steering. Two brake pedals and two transmission brakes — one behind gearbox and one ahead of axle casing, both operated mechanically. Hand brake mechanically operating drums in rear wheel hubs. Centre-lock wire wheels. 935 × 135mm tyres (920 × 120mm on early models).

Dimensions: Wheelbase 9ft 10in (300cm), tracks (front and rear) 4ft 8in (142cm). Overall length 14ft 6in (442cm).

History: Well before they became interested in motor cars, Métallurgique were well-established locomotive and rolling-stock manufacturers at La Sambre in Belgium. Their first car was built in 1898 and within a couple of years they had established a special car-building plant at Marchienne-au-Pont. Shaft drive was adopted

in 1905 and the cars owed much to the ultra-modern Mercédès-designs, which was not surprising as their designer, Ernst Lehmann, was an ex-Daimler man. The cars were splendidly built and fast, and eventually became Belgium's most renowned sporting cars.

The massive 10-litre 60/80 model was immensely powerful (100bhp) and could reach 100mph on what passed for main roads in the period before World War I. The car was very strong and very reliable — as is shown by the fact that one was fitted with a 21-litre Maybach aero-engine in the 1920s and survives to this day in good health. Métallurgique never fell for the

European fashion of building six-cylinder engines, as they did not trust the torsional vibration problems of that layout. All of the classic Edwardian cars were big fours. Every car after 1907 had that well-known vee-fronted radiator, whereas the early cars used a flat-fronted cooler similar to that of the Mercédès cars.

Below: Metallurgique's monstrous 60/80 sports car was one of the very best Edwardian machines, and the pride of Belgium. In layout the 4-cylinder cars had much in common with Mercedes.

163

MG 18/80

18/80 Mk I, Mk II and Mk III (data for 18/80 Mk I)

Built by: MG Car Co. Ltd., Britain.

Engine: Six cylinders, in line, in four-bearing cast-iron block. Bore and stroke 69mm by 110mm, 2,468cc (2·72 × 4·33in, 150·6cu.in). Cast-iron cylinder head. Two overhead valves per cylinder, directly operated by a single overhead camshaft. Twin horizontal constant-vacuum SU carburettors. Maximum power 60bhp at 3,200rpm.

Transmission: Double-plate clutch, with cork inserts, running in oil, and three-speed gearbox without synchromesh, both in unit with engine. Propeller shaft in torque tube to spiral-bevel 'live' rear axle, with ball joint behind gearbox.

Chassis: Channel-section pressed-steel side members, with riveted cross members, in separate chassis frame. Semi-elliptic leaf springs front and rear, helped by Hartford friction-type dampers. Four-wheel, cable-operated drum brakes, with vacuum-servo assistance on Speed Models (all models from late 1930). Fly-off handbrake. 19in centre-lock wire wheels. Two-seat tourer, four-seat tourer, Speed and four-door saloon coachwork all available on same basic mechanical chassis.

Dimensions: Wheelbase 9ft 6in (290cm), tracks (front and rear) 4ft (122cm). Overall length (Speed Mk I) 13ft 8in (417cm). Unladen weight (Speed Mk I) 2,548lb (1,156kg).

History: By 1927, Cecil Kimber was making great efforts to establish MG as a separate *marque* from Morris. All early MGs, of course, had been very closely and obviously based on 'bullnose' and 'flatnose' Cowleys. However, the 18/80 model, first shown to the public at the 1928 Olympia exhibition (at the same time, incidentally, as the M-Type Midget), was a much more specialised car. The engine, in its first form, had been designed by Frank Woollard at Morris Engines (both he and Kimber had worked together some years earlier) for use in the Morris Light Six. The 18/80, which used some 'carry over' parts from the first 14/40 MGs, had a new Kimber-designed chassis frame, but used many standard Morris suspension and axle parts. The engine itself, a fine 2,468cc unit, was advanced in design with a single-overhead-camshaft type of valve operation. As a 'Morris' it had a single carburettor, but for MG Woollard provided a cross-flow cylinder head fed by twin SU carburettors.

The 18/80 title was nearly meaningless; the

Left: An MG 18/80 Mark I saloon of 1930, with four-door saloon body having much in common with current Morris styles. Though the 18/80 was designed by Cecil Kimber, it drew many parts from the Morris Motors group, as William Morris also owned the MG ('Morris Garages') concern. Already familiar on the 18/80 is the now-famous octagonal MG badge, and the distinctive radiator shell. The car had a 2½-litre six-cylinder overhead camshaft engine. With about 60bhp, the car could reach nearly 80mph. Bottom: There were several other bodies—this being a two-seat/dickey.

'18' correctly referred to the British rated horse-power, but as the engine only produced about 60bhp the '80' part was optimistic nonsense. This did not detract from the fact that the car was very smooth and refined and could reach 78mph – a very respectable gait for 1929 – when it first went into production. All MG bodies of the period came from Carbodies in Coventry and right from the start there was a choice of sports, tourer and saloon car coachwork. The saloon cost £555, which was high for depression-struck Britain, but at least the specification was full.

After only a year, and when MG had moved their production lines from Edmond Road Oxford to the old Pavlova leather works at Abingdon, a Mark II version of the 18/80 was produced, although the Mark I car continued to be made. The Mark II, apart from its power train

and basic suspensions, was really another new model, as it had a massively strong chassis frame, widened wheel tracks (up from 4ft to 4ft 4in), larger 14in cable-operated drum brakes and – most important of all – a four-speed gearbox with a remote-control central change-speed lever. As before, there was a full range of alternative coachwork, very closely related to the original bodies. The Mark II chassis was much heavier than the original (at least 300lb, or 136kg), so even though it was more expensive and better equipped, it was also considerably slower. During 1930, a Mark III 'Tigress' version of the Mark II, intended strictly for road racing, was announced, and called the 18/100, but only five such cars were made.

The Mark I Speed Model, announced in September 1930, featured a very smart four-

seater touring body, which was very light as it was merely an ash frame panelled in aluminium (at the tail) or fabric. This car could be guaranteed to exceed 80mph in standard form, and MG were willing to *sell* certificates to their new owners to that effect. Although this was a fine car, it was not cheap at £525, and once MG started to make a lot of their very popular small four-cylinder sports cars the 18/80 range was eclipsed. Mark I cars were discontinued in mid 1931, and the Mark II models during 1933. The 18/80 was really a vintage car being built carefully to obsolete standards after 1930s-motoring was well into its stride. None of its six-cylinder engine features were carried over to new MG models. The engine of the F-Types and K-Types, of course, was a completely different 1,272cc unit from the same stable.

Below: Here is the 18/80 Speed model of 1930, with a very light fabric tourer 4-seater body, guaranteed to beat 80mph. Though small and delicate, the 18/80 was 'vintage' in every way.

Below and right: A smart and purposeful 18/80 Mk II with the stiffened chassis, bigger brakes and four-speed gearbox making it more desirable. It is owned by MG writer Wilson McComb. The 18/80s were the zenith of 'vintage' MGs—later cars followed 1930s trends.

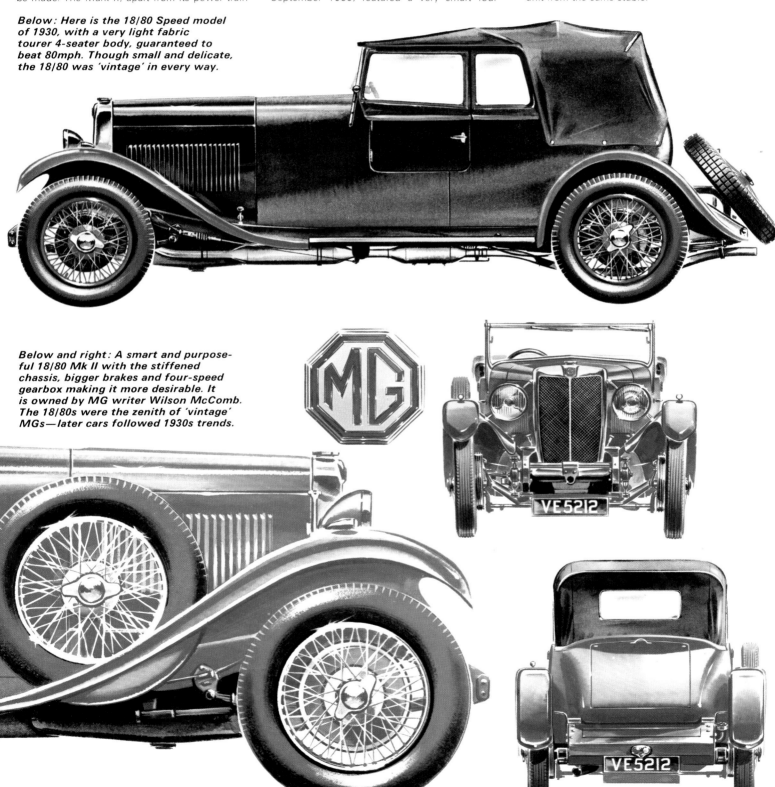

MG M-TYPE MIDGET

M-Type Midget, built from 1929 to 1932
Built by: M.G. Car Co. Ltd., Britain.
Engine: Four cylinders, in line, in two-bearing cast-iron block. Bore and stroke 57mm by 83mm, 847cc (2·24 × 3·27in, 51·8cu.in). Cast-iron cylinder head. Two overhead valves per cylinder, operated by single overhead camshaft. Single SU side-draught carburettor. 5·4:1 compression ratio. Maximum power 20bhp at 4,000rpm (raised to about 27bhp at 4,500rpm after 2,000 cars had been built). Engine (like chassis) derived from that of Morris Minor saloon.
Transmission: Single-dry-plate clutch and three-speed manual gearbox (without synchromesh), both in unit with engine. Optional four-speed gearbox (also without synchromesh) from autumn 1930. Open propeller shaft to spiral-bevel 'live' rear axle.
Chassis: Simple channel-section frame with five pressed cross members. Semi-elliptic leaf springs at front and rear, with Hartford friction-type dampers. Four-wheel, cable-operated drum brakes. 19in wire wheels. 4 × 19in tyres. Original coachwork was light and simple two-seat sports car layout with pointed tail, framed in ash and fabric covered. First cars had rear-hinged doors (changed in 1930), but later versions had metal panels with a folding hood. A closed two-door 'Sportsman's coupé was also

offered as an extremely attractive alternative.
Dimensions: Wheelbase 6ft 6in (198cm), track (front) 3ft 6in (106·7cm), track (rear) 3ft 6in (106·7cm). Overall length 10ft 3in (312cm). Unladen weight 1,120lb (508kg).
History: The very first MGs were built in 1924 and were no more than lightly modified and rebodied 'Bullnose' Morris Cowleys. They were inspired by Cecil Kimber at Morris Garages Ltd. in Oxford, which was owned by William Morris himself. The M.G. Car Co. Ltd. was formally established in 1928, by which time Kimber was already planning to build a tiny new two-seater sports car. Morris, having bought Wolseley Motors of Birmingham, were proposing to announce their new Morris Minor in the autumn and Kimber decided that this car's little chassis and Hispano-inspired overhead-camshaft engine would be an ideal starting point.

Mechanically, therefore, the M-Type MG Midget, announced in 1928, first sold in April 1929 and withdrawn in June 1932 after 3,235 examples had been delivered, was almost pure Morris Minor. To make it a proper MG, the suspension was lowered, the steering column was re-angled and that distinctive MG radiator was added. The initial bodies were simplicity themselves, having a very light plywood and ash frame mainly covered by fabric. The ensemble

was completed by cycle-type wings, a neat little vee-shaped windscreen and a very elementary hood.

Apart from its cheekily attractive lines, the car's main attraction was the price — £175 in Britain — much lower than for almost any other sports car in the world. Performance was good for its size, with a maximum speed of more than 60mph and an average fuel consumption of around 40mpg. The brakes were not very efficient, but the handling and roadholding made up for this.

The press and the first customers loved the car and it was not long before it started to appear in competition, being used equally in sporting trials and on the Brooklands race track. Camshaft changes intended to make the car competitive boosted the power from 20bhp to 27bhp and several factory-backed cars raced with distinction in 1930. The C-Type Montlhéry Midgets, out-and-out competition cars, were derived directly from the M-Type and its racing experiences.

Even with the optional four-speed gearbox and a tuned engine, the M-Type was not quite competitive enough in international racing, although it established the pedigree of all other MGs built before 1950.

Production moved from Oxford to Abingdon in September 1929, where MG sports cars have been assembled ever since.

Above: 1930 Brooklands Double-12 car.
Below: 1930 Le Mans M-Type Midget.

Above: The standard production Midget M-Type, built from 1929 to 1932. This car is a 1930 example, with appropriate 'MG' registration plate found on many such London-sold Midgets in the 1930s. The chassis and engine were developed from the Morris Minor. Note fabric body.

Left and right: M-Type Midgets prepared for competition had tiny and lightweight bodies. This 1930 car averaged 60·23mph for 24 hours at Brooklands, and was the highest-placed of the Team Prize winning cars, driven by C. J. Randall and F. M. Montgomery.

Below: Not much space for the riding mechanic, whose seat was set back. Note bonnet straps and wire mesh screen.

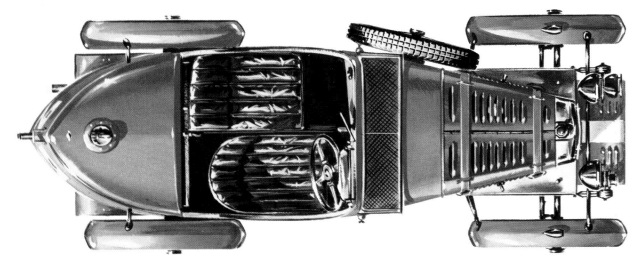

MG MIDGETS

All marks except M-Type – from C-Type of 1931 to TF of 1955 (data for 1946 model TC)
Built by: MG Car Co. Ltd., Britain.
Engine: Four-cylinder, in line, based on three-bearing cast-iron block. Bore and stroke 66·5mm by 90mm, 1,250cc (2·62 × 3·54in, 76·3cu.in). Cast-iron cylinder head. Two overhead valves per cylinder, operated by pushrods and rockers from single side-mounted camshaft. Twin semi-down-draught SU constant-vacuum carburettors. Maximum power 54bhp (net) at 5,200rpm.
Transmission: Single-dry-plate clutch, and four-speed, synchromesh manual gearbox (un-synchronised first gear), both in unit with engine. Remote-control central gearchange. Open propeller shaft to spiral-bevel 'live' rear axle.
Chassis: Separate channel-section steel chassis, with two main longitudinal members, braced by pressed and tubular cross members. Semi-elliptic front and rear springs. Luvax-Girling piston-type dampers. Bishop cam-and-lever steering. Four-wheel, hydraulically operated drum brakes. Fly-off handbrake. 19in centre-lock wire wheels. 4.50 × 19in tyres.
Two-seat open sports bodywork, of steel panels on an ash frame. No alternative coachwork.
Dimensions: Wheelbase 7ft 10in (239cm), tracks (front and rear) 3ft 9in (114cm). Overall length 11ft 7·5in (354cm). Unladen weight 1,736lb (787kg).
History: After the original small MG sports car, the M-Type, had made its mark, there was never any doubt that it would have successors. Even so, nobody could have forecast that there would be a continuous and recognisable strain of MG Midgets in production until 1955, when the last of the TFs was replaced by the first of the MGAs. The MG Midget reborn in 1961 was from a different pedigree – that of the Austin-Healey Sprite. Midgets built between 1931 and 1955 were all designed around the same type of mechanical layout (only the very rare R-Type single-seater racing Midget having an advanced all-independent suspension system) and only two completely different types of engine were used. Up to 1936, developments of the original single-overhead-camshaft M-Type engine were always fitted and thereafter a more conventional pushrod 'four' (1,292cc at first, 1,250cc in maturity, and 1,466cc for the last few thousand TFs) were employed.

Midgets, by definition, were the smallest MGs being built at any particular time and all used four-cylinder engines. Just to confuse matters a

little there was one other MG sports car – the VA – with a four-cylinder engine which was *not* called a Midget. All other MG sports cars of the period were 'sixes' in the Magna/Magnette family. Although MG's type numbers seemed to make no sense at first, as the M-Type was followed in 1931 by the C-Type Montlhéry, the sequence then became more logical. Designation then progressed smoothly through the alphabet (taking in other MG models on the way) – so it is easy to see that a PB was a later model than a J2, and a TD later than a TA.

The basis of all Midgets was a very simple chassis frame, special to that particular model. The two main side members were of channel section in all models up to the TC, while the TD and TF used box section members. Only the TD/TF cars

Above: Perhaps not the copybook way to corner a racing Midget, but at least we get a good view of the front end and the good steering lock! This particular car is a TC, built in large numbers immediately after the Second World War. By then all of MG's design traditions were thoroughly established and the car sold well in export markets. Below: The PA Midget of 1934 was one of the last MGs to be sold with an overhead-cam engine. Like the earlier J2s, the PA retained four cylinders and 847cc; the later PBs grew to 939cc. Separate simple steel chassis frames meant that other body styles were made too—including four-seater tourers.

used independent front suspension (by coil springs and wishbones). All other Midgets used semi-elliptic leaf springs and a beam axle at the front and semi-elliptic leaves with a 'live' axle at the rear. The basic styling of all the cars was the same and all were two-seater open sports cars. Bodies were ash framed, with steel panelling, obviously separate flared front and rear wings, and running boards. On all but the last (and not very successful) model, the TF, the headlamps stood proud of the wings, on brackets at each side of the characteristic MG radiator. The spare wheel was always mounted behind the slab-type petrol tank, and always exposed. All Midgets before the TD had centre-lock wire wheels, but on the TD/TF cars pressed-steel-disc wheels were standard, with the wires optional.

Along the way MG built short series of competition Midgets, which culminated in them building just ten of the supercharged R-Type single-seater racing cars, which had pressed-steel backbone chassis and four-wheel independent suspension by wishbones and torsion bars. The M-Type's successor was the short-lived D-Type of 1932, followed by the J1/J2 cars of 1932 to 1934, and the PA/PB series of 1934/36. These all used the 847cc engine, which was finally enlarged to 939cc in the PB. The TA, announced in 1936, was a larger car with a new chassis and wider wheel tracks. It used a Morris-based ohv engine of 1,292cc. The TA became the TB in 1939, with a much altered and improved 1,250cc engine (which had an enlarged cylinder bore and shorter stroke).

The TB, with widened bodywork, became the post-war TC, which first made exported MGs famous. The TD/TF series, which ran from 1950 to 1955, used a much-altered and shortened-wheelbase version of the YA saloon's chassis frame, but the TC's engine and transmission.

Sales rose persistently: 2,460 J-Types were followed by 2,526 P-Types, 3,003 TAs, 10,000 TCs and no fewer than 29,664 TDs. The competition versions (31 J3/J4, 8 Qs, 10 Rs) were never proper 'production cars'. As with the 44 C-Types, they were all sold with supercharged engines. MG kept to their faith in building 'traditional', simply engineered sports cars for a little too long, as the TF was not as popular as the TD, but their reputation was made once again by the smart new MGA of 1955.

Top: A TC fully modified for circuit racing in Britain, with a roll cage and fat non-standard tyres on 16 inch wheels (a popular modification). Above: The well-known overhead-cam 847cc or 939cc PA/PB engine, with twin-carburettors and three main bearings. Right: The PB Midget of 1935, with a full array of instruments, and much evidence of Cecil Kimber's well-loved octagonal MG emblem.

MG MAGNETTE K-SERIES

K-Type and N-Type Magnettes (data for K3 Magnette)

Built by: MG Car Co. Ltd., Britain.

Engine: Six cylinders, in line, in four-bearing cast-iron block. Bore and stroke 57mm by 71mm, 1,087cc (2·24in × 2·80in, 66·3cu.in). Cast-iron cylinder head. Two overhead valves per cylinder, operated by rockers from single overhead camshaft. Compression ratio 6·2:1. Single SU constant-vacuum carburettor and Powerplus vane-type supercharger. Power output depending on racing state of tune and supercharger boost, but sometimes in excess of 120bhp at 6,500rpm.

Transmission: Four-speed Wilson preselector gearbox, with remote-control, central selector lever. No clutch, as such, drive taken up by first gear transmission bands. Open propeller shaft to straight-cut-bevel 'live' rear axle.

Chassis: Separate steel chassis frame, with channel-section side members and pressed and tubular cross members; underslung at rear. Semi-elliptic leaf springs at front and rear, with Hartford friction dampers. Cam-and-lever steering. Four-wheel, cable-operated drum brakes. Fly-off handbrake. 19in centre-lock wire wheels.

Two-seat open sports bodywork, of light-alloy panelling on ash frame.

Dimensions: Wheelbase 7ft 10·2in (239cm), tracks (front and rear) 4ft (122cm). Overall length 11ft 1in (338cm). Unladen weight 2,030lb (921kg).

History: 'Magnette' was the collective name given by MG to saloons, tourers, and out-and-out sports cars equipped with the Wolseley-based overhead-cam six-cylinder engine and built at Abingdon between 1931 and 1935. A related, but different family of MGs, the Magnas, also used the engine in rather less sporting tune, and with more mundane bodywork. Cecil Kimber of MG decided to capitalise on the success of his tiny M-Type and C-Type Midgets by offering a new and larger range of MGs. It was no coincidence that one version of the six-cylinder engine chosen for exploitation could power new MG racing sports cars in the International Class G (1,100cc) category! The first of the Magnettes, seen at the British Olympia Show in October 1932, was the K1 saloon, a big car for MG with its 9ft wheelbase, and notable for having the popular Wilson-type of preselector gearbox. The short-stroke 1,087cc engine had originally been designed by Wolseley (like MG, personally owned by Lord Nuffield) and was mechanically neat but rather underpowered. MG's own engineers were stuck with the original design at first, but within months had pushed up the maximum power output from 39 to 55bhp, with the aid of a special cross-flow cylinder head and improved carburation.

The K1 was a saloon and the K2s which followed were two-seater sporting cars, but more important to Kimber than either of these was the K3 project, which he had already authorised, and which he intended as a long-distance racing two-seater. The first K3, with a shortened wheelbase and rather ungainly bodywork, competed in the 1933 Monte Carlo Rally with little success, but a team of works-prepared machines tackled the 1933 Mille Miglia with conspicuous success. In spite of having to change no fewer than 157 sparking plugs during the 1,000 miles, Count 'Johnnie' Lurani and

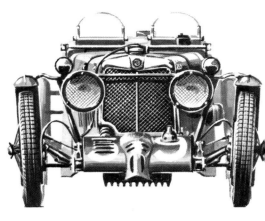

Above and right: Magnettes appeared in many shapes, but the most famous were the supercharged K3s. Among many successes were their class win in the 1933 Mille Miglia (driven by Lurani and Captain George Eyston). The supercharger is hidden behind the bulge on the front apron. The 1,087cc engine was very powerful—over 120bhp in 'sprint' form. More than any other car, the K3 Magnette was 'everyman's racing car'.

Below: K3s were often stripped out for racing car events, like this very purposeful machine in which Norman Black won the Mannin Beg race of 1934.

George Eyston won their class, with another Magnette close behind them. The legendary Tazio Nuvolari capped this by coming to Northern Ireland for the 1933 Tourist Trophy race and winning it outright (on handicap) at 78·6mph. Although the K3, with its very powerful supercharged engine, was essentially a racing machine, a few brave private owners also used their cars on the open road. One K3, modified and yet more modified, achieved lasting fame as a record-breaking special. Coded EX135, it was first of all a specialised Brooklands single-seat version, but as rebuilt and rebodied by Major 'Goldie' Gardner it broke literally hundreds of records. With several types (and even alien makes) of engine installed, EX135 was competitive even up to the day of its retirement in 1952.

After the slow-selling K1 and K2 Magnettes came the more successful KN saloon, but total K-Type sales were only just over 500, of which 34 were the exciting K3 models. More successful, but still in tiny numbers compared with most manufacturers' sales, were the N-Type Magnettes of 1934 to 1936. In these cars the engine was restored to its 'as designed' long-stroke 1,271cc (which, of course, made it obvious that it was really one-and-a-half of the M-Type Midget engine — a straight six' instead of a straight 'four'). At the same time a conventional four-speed gearbox, without synchromesh, was specified, the wheelbase was shortened to eight feet and a range of attractive new bodywork (two-seat, four-seat and a smooth 'Airline' coupé among them) was offered. The cars were less specialised, but easier to work on and also cheaper to buy. The moral of the story was that although MG's reputation had been cemented by its racing record, the majority of its customers were not really interested in having to work repeatedly on their temperamental machines. When Lord Nuffield finally sold MG, his personal possession, to the Nuffield Group, his vast business, the new owners decreed that the next generation of MGs should be even simpler. The last of the Magnettes was sold near the end of 1936 and that was the last overhead-camshaft MG to be sold until 1958 when the MGA Twin-Cam was born.

Above: Pure racing cars were almost non-existent in Britain in the 1930s. Any suitable sports car was modified as a substitute. This K3, originally a two-seater sports car, became a sleek single-seater racing car in 1934 and was used by Hugh Hamilton, and—later—by Reg Parnell. In final form this particular car gained independent front suspension.

Left: Details of Norman Black's 1934 K3 are typical of MG sports and racing cars of the period. All had the famous radiator, and MG 'octagon' badge, and all shared the same style of compact square-rigged body. Simple frames, friction-type shock absorbers, centre lock wire wheels, louvred bonnets and security straps were normal wear.

MORGAN PLUS-FOUR AND PLUS-EIGHT

Morgan Plus-Four and Plus-Eight, built from 1950 to date (data for 1954 Plus-Four)
Built by: Morgan Motor Co. Ltd., Britain.
Engine: Triumph manufactured. Four cylinders, in line, in three-bearing cast-iron block. Bore and stroke 83mm by 92mm, 1,991cc (3·27in × 3·62in, 121·5cu.in). Cast-iron cylinder head. Two overhead valves per cylinder operated by pushrods and rockers from single camshaft mounted in side of cylinder block. Twin semi-downdraught constant-vacuum SU carburettors. Maximum power 90bhp (net) at 4,800rpm. Maximum torque 130lb.ft at 2,600rpm.
Transmission: Single-dry-plate clutch in unit with engine. Moss four-speed, synchromesh manual gearbox (no synchromesh on first gear) mounted separately. Direct-acting central gearchange. Open propeller shaft to hypoid-bevel 'live' rear axle.
Chassis: Separate steel chassis frame, with Z-section boxed side members and tubular and pressed cross-bracing members. Independent front suspension by sliding pillars and coil springs, with telescopic dampers. Rear suspension by semi-elliptic leaf springs, with lever-type hydraulic dampers. Worm-and-nut steering. Four-wheel hydraulically operated drum brakes (later models had front discs). Fly-off handbrake. 16in pressed steel-disc road wheels (optional centre-lock wire wheels). 5·25 × 16in tyres. Morgan-built two-seat sports, two-seat DH coupé or four-seat tourer coachwork to choice.
Dimensions: Wheelbase 8ft (244cm), tracks (front and rear) 3ft 11in. (119cm). Overall length 11ft 8in (356cm). Unladen weight 1,900lb (862kg).
History: The present-day Morgan has, fairly accurately, been described as the only vintage car still in production. Like all *bon mots* this tends to be an exaggeration, but there is no doubt that the philosophy of Morgan design is entrenched in the 1930s. Although the engines, the performance and the details receive regular attention, the chassis, ride, roadholding, body style and construction are old designs with old-fashioned results. The modern Plus Eight Morgan, with its 155bhp Rover-made 3½-litre engine and five-speed gearbox, is good for nearly 130mph with acceleration to match. Weather protection, noise-suppression and refinement do not match this, however.

Morgan machines have been built in the same Malvern Link factory, under the direction of the Morgan family, since Edwardian times. Up to 1936, however, every Morgan was a three-wheeler, with a single, driven, rear wheel — and three-wheeler production carried on into the early 1950s. In 1936, the first four-wheel Morgan, the four-seat 4/4, was revealed in a form which would be very familiar to present-day Morgan buyers. The sliding-pillar independent suspension used today was on that first 4/4, but it had been on the 1910 three-wheeler too! The Z-section side members of the chassis frame are still a feature, and the bodies, erected by Morgan themselves, were of simple steel foldings on an ash wood frame. Engines of the first 4/4s were side-valve Fords. Other pre-war 4/4 engines used were overhead-inlet, side-exhaust Coventry Climax 1100s and overhead-valve-converted Standard Ten engines of 1,267cc. After the war, the Standard unit was used for a time, but when Standard decided to follow a 'one-model' (or rather a 'one-engine') policy, Morgan had to think again. Because of their links with Standard they decided to upgrade the 4/4 by fitting the big and heavy Standard Vanguard unit of 2,088cc, along with a proprietary Moss gearbox.

The Plus-Four, as the new two-seat car was named, arrived in 1950, and soon made a name for itself in competition. Compared with the little 4/4 the new car was very much faster and more rugged. Even so, once Triumph had developed their TR2 sports car, it made sense for Morgan to use the tuned-up 2-litre engine. This, then, was the definitive Plus-Four, a car lighter and more accelerative than either the Triumph TR2 or the Austin-Healey 100. During the life

of the car, Morgan made few concessions to modernisation, although they improved the body style with a cowled nose and a sleeker tail. Disc front brakes were standardised late in the 1950s and when Triumph increased their TR engine size to 2,138cc Morgan followed them. For a time, too, they offered a 'Competition' model with Lawrence-tune TR engine and light-alloy body panels. In the meantime, from 1955, the 4/4 was re-introduced as a Series II, powered by Ford's side-valve 1,172cc engine and matching gearbox. The 4/4 continues to this day, uprated regularly with the latest Ford engines — overhead-valve units being adopted in 1960.

With Triumph dropping the four-cylinder engine completely in 1967, it was clearly only a matter of time before supplies to Morgan ran out. From the autumn of 1968, then, it was no surprise to see that the Plus-Four was equipped with the 1,600cc Ford Cortina engine, and that the exciting Plus-Eight was added to the range. This car is powered by the ex-Buick Rover 3½-litre V8 engine. When Rover introduced a manual gearbox for their engine, this replaced the old Moss gearbox, but it has itself been dropped in favour of the 'new' Rover 3500 five-speed box. Many features of the Plus-Four are evident in the Plus-Eight models. To take account of the greatly increased performance

since the first Vanguard engine was fitted in 1950 (there is more than twice the power nowadays) the wheel tracks have been increased and fatter tyres and wider wheel rims introduced, along with better and more powerful brakes. Interior appointments have been improved, but the cockpit's size is little larger than it was a quarter of a century ago. More important than anything — the car's character has been maintained. Orders exceed the ten-per-week production capability and waiting lists stretch ahead for years

Below: This Plus Four coupe was built in 1950—one of the first with the Standard Vanguard engine—but the same basic style is produced today. Each Morgan has a Z-section chassis frame, a hand-beaten body shell of steel or light-alloy panels on an ash framework, very hard suspension, and a neat but close-coupled cockpit. One model always evolved from the last, though the latest Plus Eight has little in common, mechanically, with the Plus Four. Over the years there have been two-seaters, sports and coupe, and a four-seater tourer, but Morgan never offered a hardtop version.

Above: Today's Morgan is the very fast 3½-litre vee-eight engined Plus Eight. The engine and gearbox are from Rover, but the rest is pure Morgan, built now to the standards and tastes of yester-year. Along with the 4/4, only about ten cars a week are built and sold.

Below right: Chris Lawrence and Richard Shepherd-Barron used this Triumph TR3 engined Plus Four to win the 2-litre class at Le Mans in 1962, beating Porsche and several other very special sports racing cars.

MINERVA TYPE AL

AL straight-eight models, built from 1929 to 1937 (data for 1929 model)
Built by: Minerva Motors S.A., Belgium.
Engine: Eight cylinders, in line, in cast-iron block, with nine-bearing light-alloy crankcase. Bore and stroke 90mm by 130mm, 6,616cc (3·54in × 5·12in, 403·7cu.in). Detachable cast-iron cylinder head. Knight double-sleeve-valve breathing arrangements, with concentric sleeves moving up and down inside cylinder walls in eccentric motion, actuated by connecting rods from operating shaft in side of crankcase. One twin-choke Zenith carburettor.
Transmission: Multiple-dry-plate clutch and four-speed manual gearbox (without synchromesh), both in unit with front-mounted engine. Remote-control right-hand gearchange. Two-piece propeller shaft — front section open, rear section enclosed in torque tube — driving spiral-bevel 'live' rear axle.
Chassis: Separate pressed-steel chassis frame, with channel-section side members and pressed and tubular cross-bracing. Forged front axle beam. Front suspension by semi-elliptic leaf springs. Rear suspension by semi-elliptic leaf springs and torque tube, with transverse radius arm location. Friction-type dampers. Bijur automatic chassis lubrication. Worm-and-lever steering. Four-wheel, mechanically operated drum brakes, with Dewandre operation. Separate shoes in rear drums, for operation by handbrake. Centre-lock wire wheels. 6·75 × 33in tyres. Open or closed coachwork to choice.
Dimensions: Wheelbase 12ft 9·5in (390cm), tracks (front and rear) 4ft 9in (145cm). Overall length 17ft (518cm). Unladen weight, depending on coachwork, from 3,800lb (1,723kg).
History: Belgium's greatest car manufacturing concern rose from humble beginnings as a bicycle maker in 1897, the factory having been opened by Sylvain de Jong. Manufacture of

Above: The Type AL Minerva had a straight-eight engine of 6·6-litres with Knight sleeve valve operation. It was a pinnacle of 1930s design, last made in 1937.

proprietary motor cycles followed this, then the company made its own motor cycles in 1900 and finally progressed to cars in 1902. Bigger and ever faster Minervas followed, with the obligatory prestige firm's interest in motor sport; the famous Knight sleeve-valve engines were adopted in 1909. Every subsequent Minerva was so equipped. After World War I, the fours and sixes got bigger, better and more costly, but the biggest and best cars were the straight-eights launched in 1929. The 6·6-litre AL model was a vast affair, but unfortunately came at the wrong time economically, and even the smaller related six did not help much. The straight-eight car was nicely engineered, without much regard to cost, and the vibration-free eight-cylinder layout

allied to the silence of Knight sleeve-valve operation made it a most sybaritic machine. Dimensions, including an overall length of 17ft and a weight of more than 3,800lb (1,723kg), tell us that this was a petrol-guzzling beauty for the rich and the famous. Alas! there were few of these in the early 1930s and although the car was listed until 1937 it sold very slowly. Minerva disappeared from the scene completely in 1938.

MORRIS 'BULLNOSE'

Morris Oxford and Cowley models, built from 1913 to 1926 (data for 1920s Cowley)
Built by: Morris Motors Ltd., Britain.
Engine: Four cylinders, in line, in three-bearing cast-iron block. Bore and stroke 69·5mm by 102mm, 1,548cc (2·74in × 4·02in, 94·5cu.in). Cast-iron cylinder head. Two side valves per cylinder, directly operated by cylinder-block mounted camshaft. One Smith carburettor. Maximum power 26bhp (gross) at 2,800rpm.
Transmission: Double-plate clutch, cork lined, running in oil, and three-speed, sliding-pinion manual gearbox (without synchromesh), both unit with engine. Direct-acting central gearchange. Propeller shaft in torque tube, connected to spiral-bevel 'live' rear axle.
Chassis: Separate steel chassis frame, with channel-section side members and tubular and pressed-steel cross bracings. Forged front axle beam. Front suspension by semi-elliptic leaf springs. Rear suspension by three-quarter-elliptic leaf springs. Dampers not standard until 1925. Gabriel snubbers optional (standard from 1925). Worm-and-wheel steering. Foot operated rear drum brakes; no front brakes until 1926, when they became optional. Artillery-style road wheels.
Morris-built coachwork, several styles from two-seat-with-dickey tourer to closed four-door saloon.
Dimensions: Wheelbase 8ft 6in (259cm), tracks (front and rear) 4ft (122cm). Unladen weight (depending on coachwork and options fitted), from 1,750lb (794kg).
History: The 'Bullnose' Morris was the British equivalent of the Model T Ford — with one important exception. Whereas Ford made sure that he built as much of his car as possible, William Morris made sure that he purchased as many 'bought out' components as he could. That way he cut down on the capital cost of selling his cars and could make more cars from a small factory in Cowley, near Oxford. The first

Above: The 'Bullnose' Morris, surely the British equivalent of the Model T Ford. In the 1920s it outsold any other British or European car. This saloon model was built in 1924. There were two engines, and many optional bodies.

'Bullnose' (so called, retrospectively, because of the shape of its distinctive radiator) was delivered in 1913 and the last — more than 150,000 examples later — in 1926. Even then it was not finished, as the then-new 'flatnose' Morris was a development of the same chassis and mechanicals. Before World War I, the cars had British White-and-Poppe engines, during it Continental Motors engines from the United States were used and from 1919 they were fitted with power plants produced by Morris Engines in Coventry.
The two basically different models (only in terms of engine size and fittings — the chassis were always the same) were the 11·9hp Cowley and the 13·9hp Oxford, but there were many sub-derivatives. Like Henry Ford in North America, Morris cut his prices aggressively and every time

he did so, sales rocketed. Like Ford, too, he held on to one basic model for far too long, but recovered quicker after a change of heart. The 'Bullnose' cars were lovable, reliable and cheap (the cheapest tourer's price fell from £465 in 1920 to a mere £162·50 in 1925), but they were never sporting. The British public, however, merely wanted cheap transportation. Morris gave it to them. At one time in the 1920s he held more than half of the entire British market.

MORS TYPE Z 60HP

Type Z 60hp Paris-Vienna car, built in 1902
Built by: Société d'Electricité et d'Automobiles Mors, France.
Engine: Four cylinders, in line, in light-alloy block, with three-bearing light alloy crankcase. Bore and stroke 140mm by 150mm, 9,236cc 5·52in × 5·91in, 563·6cu.in). Two detachable cast-iron cylinder heads. Automatic (atmospheric) inlet valves, and side exhaust valves — exhaust valves operated by single camshaft mounted in side of crankcase. Single up-draught Mors carburettor. Maximum power 60bhp.
Transmission: Cone clutch, in unit with front-mounted engine, and shaft drive to separate three-speed manual gearbox (without synchromesh). Remote-control right-hand gearchange. Double straight-bevel differential integral with gearbox. Countershaft with sprockets. Final drive by chain to rear wheels.
Chassis: Separate chassis frame, with wooden side members, reinforced by steel flitch plates, and fabricated and tubular-steel cross bracing. Forged front axle beam. Front and rear suspension by semi-elliptic leaf springs. Friction-type dampers. Worm-type steering. Externally contracting transmission drum brake, operated by foot pedal. Rear wheel drum brakes, operated by hand lever. Artillery-style road wheels. 875 × 105mm tyres (front) and 920 × 120mm tyres (rear). Open two-seater racing bodywork.
Dimensions: Wheelbase 7ft 11·6in (243cm). Overall length 10ft 9in (328cm). Unladen weight, approximately 2,204lb (1,000kg).
History: Emile Mors was originally an electrical engineer, but began making cars in 1895. The racing cars, designed by Brasier, challenged the might of Panhard at once, winning Paris-St Malo and Paris-Bordeaux in 1899 in their first year. Other big wins fell to the team in 1900 and 1901 and for 1902 the company built six of the mag-

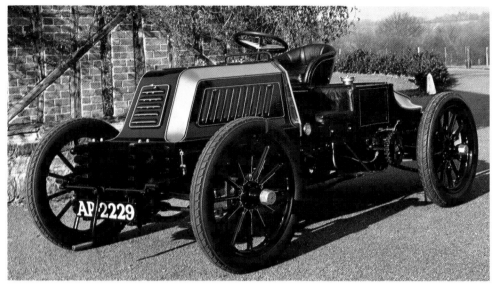

nificent 60hp racing cars, to comply with the 1,000kg limit for the Paris-Vienna race. Although the cars did not win this race, one of them was used by the brave Gabriel to win the Paris-Bordeaux section of that infamous Paris-Madrid road race. The Mors was in every way a 'car of the year' when built, and was only ever eclipsed by the Sixty Mercédès. It was absolutely typical of the big-engined long-distance racing cars of the period, with final drive by exposed chain, a slow-revving 9·2-litre engine, high-seated driver and riding mechanic and no weather protection of any nature. It was capable of more than 70mph and indeed another Mors took the Land Speed Record at 77mph around this time. Little of the machinery was protected from the choking

Above: Nothing could be more purposeful than this Type Z Mors built in 1902 for long-distance town-to-town racing. It relied on a huge engine (9·2-litres) and a light chassis for its high performance. Final drive was by chain, and maximum speed more than 70mph—on awful roads!

dust — the workings of the clutch and the chain drive being plainly visible. Braking, by comparison with performance, was virtually non-existent, and it was usual for both foot brake *and* hand brake to be applied together to get maximum retardation.

NACIONAL PESCARA

Eight-cylinder models, built from 1929 to 1932 (data for 1930 model)
Built by: Fabrica Nacional de Automóviles, Spain.
Engine: Eight cylinders, in line, in nine-bearing light-alloy combined block and crankcase. Bore and stroke 70mm by 90mm, 2,771cc (2·76in × 3·54in, 169cu.in). Detachable light-alloy cylinder head. Two overhead valves per cylinder, operated by bucket-type tappets from single overhead camshaft. Single carburettor. Maximum power 80bhp.
Transmission: Single-dry-plate clutch and three speed manual gearbox (without synchromesh), both in unit with front-mounted engine. Direct-acting central gearchange. Open propeller shaft to hypoid-bevel 'live' rear axle.
Chassis: Separate pressed-steel chassis frame, with channel-section side members and tubular and pressed cross bracings. Forged front axle beam. Semi-elliptic leaf springs for front and rear suspension, with lever-arm hydraulic dampers. Ross steering gear. Four-wheel, hydraulically operated drum brakes. Pressed-steel-disc wheels. Open touring or saloon car coachwork.
Dimensions: Wheelbase 9ft 10in (300cm). Unladen weight (with saloon car coachwork) 2,550lb (1,156kg).
History: Once Hispano-Suiza had moved most of their activities to France, this left Spain without a domestic motor industry. In an attempt to reestablish this, the Spanish government backed the Marquis Raoul de Pescara in a new project, based in Barcelona, and the strange but exciting Nacional Pescara was born in 1929. Its designer was an Italian, Edmond Moglia, and the plan was that there would be two models, with related engines. The car which actually got into small-scale production was the straight-eight 2·8-litre machine, which mixed European and North American ideas with great skills. The disc wheels, styling, hydraulic brakes and three-speed gearbox were all pure-Detroit in their origins. A

development of this car was to have been a straight-ten-cylinder machine, in normal and supercharged form, of 3·9 litres, something never tackled by any other car maker and an idea which, understandably enough, did not get beyond the drawing board. The revolution in Spain in 1931 meant that government assistance was thereafter withdrawn and the company speedily collapsed. A few cars raced with some success until 1935.

Above: Rare shot of a very rare car. The Nacional Pescara was Spanish and backed by that country's government, but was too expensive to sell fast. This lightweight 'eight' raced at Shelsley Walsh in 1931. A 'ten' was proposed, but was never completed. 1932 saw the last made.

NAPIER-RAILTON

Napier-Railton Brooklands car – used from 1933 to 1937
Built by: Thomson and Taylor Ltd., Britain.
Engine: Napier 'Lion' aero-engine, 12 cylinders (three banks of four set in 'W' formation) in individual forged steel barrels. Bore and stroke 139·7mm by 130·2mm, 23,970cc (5·5in × 5·72in, 1,463cu.in). 60 degrees between cylinder banks, central bank vertical. Light-alloy crankcase. Four-throw crankshaft, with three connecting rods to each crank pin. Three light-alloy cylinder heads. Four overhead valves per cylinder, operated by twin overhead camshafts per bank. Napier carburettors. Maximum power 502bhp at 2,200rpm.
Transmission: Single-dry-plate clutch and three-speed manual gearbox, without synchromesh, separated by exposed coupling. Left-hand gearchange position. Open propeller shaft to ENV straight-bevel 'live' rear axle.
Chassis: Separate steel chassis frame, with channel-section side members, and pressed-steel cross members. Beam front axle. Front suspension by semi-elliptic leaf springs. Rear suspension by twin cantilevered semi-elliptic leaf springs at each side of chassis. Hartford friction type dampers. Foot-operated rear brake drums, no front brakes. Drum handbrake on transmission, behind gearbox. Centre lock wire-spoke wheels, various sizes depending on race or function. Tyres up to 35 × 6in.

Gurney Nutting coachwork, in light alloy, on lightweight metal frame. Offset single-seat accommodation. No weather protection.
Dimensions: Wheelbase 10ft 10in (330cm), tracks (front and rear) 5ft (152cm). Overall length 15ft 6in (472cm). Unladen weight 3,400lb (1,542kg).
History: When British fur-broker John Cobb decided to have a car built for Brooklands track racing and for long-distance record attempts, he did not do it by halves. The one-off Napier-Railton was the biggest, the fastest, the most out-of-the-ordinary in every way. Cobb did not mind – he only wanted a functional machine. The Napier-Railton, designed for him by Reid Railton at Thomson & Taylor's workshops inside Brooklands, used a redundant 1920s type of Napier Lion aero-engine. This, for other uses, could be supercharged and otherwise boosted. For the car, it was almost unburstable in 500bhp form. The car was never intended for road racing, so it had no rear brakes; neither was handling, as opposed to stability, considered important. It had no reverse gear, so for events which required this a crude sort of electric motor, with friction drive to a rear wheel, was devised. The car's maximum speed was over 180mph and its propensity for destroying tyres on poor surfaces was enormous. Built in 1933, it became the Brooklands lap record holder almost at once, and finally in 1935 it left that record at 143·44

mph – a figure which was never beaten. Between 1933 and 1936, many long-distance endurance records were taken, at speeds up to 169mph and over durations of up to 24 hours. It also won the prestigious BRDC 500 twice – in 1935 and again in 1937 – before John Cobb retired it, to concentrate on the Land Speed Record with another Napier-engined car.

After World War II, the old car achieved fame by being used as a 'record car' in the film *Pandora and the Flying Dutchman* and in the 1950s it was used with great distinction as a mobile test bed for G.Q. parachutes. Later still, at the end of the 1950s, it was acquired by the Hon. Patrick Lindsay, who restored it and even raced it on modern motor-racing circuits before its lack of front-wheel brakes caused it to be banned. It is now owned by Mr Bob Roberts and is occasionally exhibited.

The Napier-Railton was the largest-engined car ever to race in Britain, but sadly its absolute capabilities were never fully known as tyre companies could never provide covers to cope with its speed.

Right: The unique Napier-Railton, the fastest-ever car at Brooklands. It had a vast W12 24-litre Napier Lion engine, twin rear leaf springs at each side, and took many distance records.

NAPIER 40/50

Napier 40/50, built from 1919 to 1924)
Built by: D. Napier and Son Ltd., Britain.
Engine: Six cylinders, in line, in seven-bearing light-alloy block/crankcase, with shrunk-in cast-iron cylinder liners. Bore and stroke 102mm by 127mm, 6,177cc (4·0 × 5·0in, 377cu.in). Light-alloy cylinder head. Two overhead valves per cylinder, operated directly by a single overhead camshaft. Single constant-vacuum Napier-SU carburettor. Maximum power 82bhp at 2,000rpm.
Transmission: Single-dry-plate clutch, in unit with engine, and four-speed manual gearbox separated from clutch by girder casting and two flexible couplings. Direct-acting central gearchange. Propeller shaft in torque tube to spiral-bevel 'live' rear axle.
Chassis: Separate steel chassis with channel-section side members and five supporting cross members. Forged front axle beam. Front suspension by semi-elliptic leaf springs. Rear suspension by cantilever semi-elliptic leaf springs; anti-roll device on nose of torque tube. Worm-and-sector steering. Foot-operated drum brake on transmission and hand-operated drums on rear wheels (late models – 1924 – had four-wheel foot brakes). Centre-lock wire wheels (sometimes disc covered). 895×135mm beaded-edge tyres. Coachwork usually by Cunard, a subsidiary of Napier – many choices including limousines, cabriolets, sedancas, coupés and touring bodies.
Dimensions: Wheelbase 11ft 5in or 12ft (348 or 366cm), tracks (front and rear) 4ft 8in (142cm). Overall length from 15ft (457cm). Unladen weight (chassis only) 2,800lb (1,270kg).
History: Before World War I, Napier were one of the greatest of the British thoroughbred building companies. From 1919 to 1924, with the 40/50 model, they tried to beat Rolls-Royce once again. They failed – gallantly. Although their all-new engine was very advanced and effective, the rest of the chassis was Edwardian in concept. 40/50 prices were always very high and most of the bodies were supplied by Cunard, whom Napier had taken over earlier. The car, splendid and dignified though it was, could not quite match the Silver Ghost in all-round excellence, particularly as the bespoke coachbuilders were rarely allowed to ply their craft. By then, in any case, Napier were very famous for their powerful and effective aero-engines and were inclined to specialise in that direction

in the future. Their original enthusiastic chief, Selwyn Edge, had left the company in 1913. Incidentally, there was also a 40/50 in pre-war days, but this had a side-valve engine and different chassis.

Maximum speed of up to 70mph was clearly superior to that of the Rolls-Royce, but the suspension was hard and set more to provide stability than comfort. The engine itself, designed by A. J. Rowledge, who was also responsible for the W-formation 'Lion' aero-engine, was very advanced and effective, being light in weight wherever possible, with a single overhead camshaft and intriguing details. One interesting point is that engine roughness at low speeds was

cured by having a special low-compression piston in the rear cylinder (number 6) piston only!

In addition to normal models, there was a 'Colonial' version (of which 17 were built), with increased ground clearance provided by special chassis side members and suspension parts. All up weight of the normal British limousines could be more than 5,200lb (2,358kg), which helps to explain the high price and petrol consumption. The last of the 40/50s was built in 1924, after four-wheel braking had been adopted. Only 187 of the hoped-for 500 were ever made. Strikes and very high prices had much to do with this.

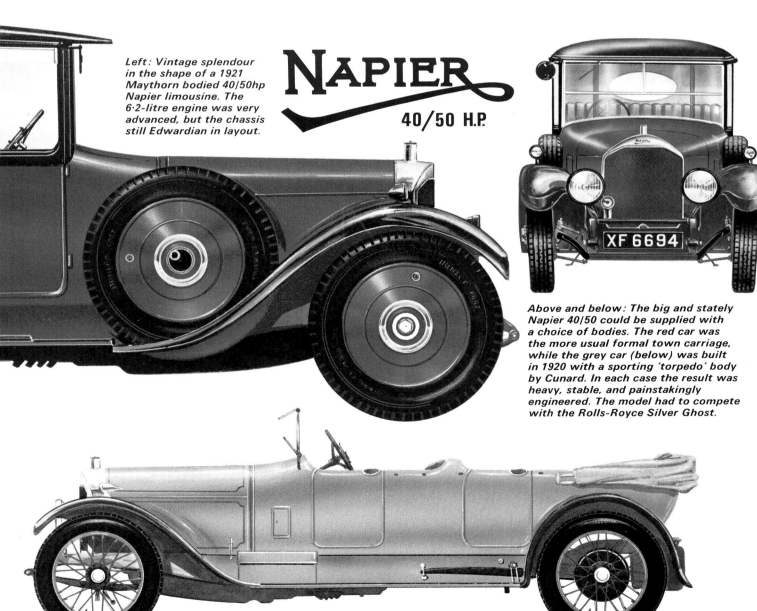

Left: Vintage splendour in the shape of a 1921 Maythorn bodied 40/50hp Napier limousine. The 6·2-litre engine was very advanced, but the chassis still Edwardian in layout.

NAPIER
40/50 H.P.

Above and below: The big and stately Napier 40/50 could be supplied with a choice of bodies. The red car was the more usual formal town carriage, while the grey car (below) was built in 1920 with a sporting 'torpedo' body by Cunard. In each case the result was heavy, stable, and painstakingly engineered. The model had to compete with the Rolls-Royce Silver Ghost.

NSU Ro80

Ro80s Mk I, Mk II and Mk III, built from 1967 to date (data for Mk I)

Built by: NSU-Werke AG (since 1969, VW-Audi-NSU AG), West Germany.

Engine: Wankel-type rotary engine. Two rotors in two-chamber light-alloy housing. Engine displacement 995cc (60·7cu.in) per revolution, equivalent to 1,990cc (121.4cu.in) for four-stroke piston engine. Two-bearing eccentric crankshaft. No valves and no camshafts — ports covered and uncovered once each revolution. Three-sided trochoidal rotor forms own combustion chamber, therefore three explosions per engine revolution. Two horizontal Solex carburettors. Maximum power 115bhp (DIN) at 5,500rpm. Maximum torque 117lb.ft at 4,500rpm.

Transmission: Semi-automatic Fichtel and Sachs transmission with torque converter and three-speed, all-synchromesh manual gearbox, both in unit with engine. Direct-acting central gearchange, with clutch actuated by microswitch in gearchange knob. Front-wheel-drive power pack, with torque converter and engine ahead of front-wheel line and gearbox behind it. Exposed, universally jointed drive shafts to front wheels.

Chassis: Unitary-construction pressed-steel body/chassis unit, four-door saloon. Engine/transmission pack in nose, driving front wheels. Independent front suspension by MacPherson struts (with built-in dampers) and anti-roll bar. Independent rear suspension by coil springs, trailing arms and telescopic dampers. Power-assisted rack-and-pinion steering. Four-wheel hydraulically operated disc brakes, inboard mounted at front, with vacuum-servo assistance. 14in pressed-steel disc road wheels and 175× 14in tyres.

Dimensions: Wheelbase 9ft 4·6in (286cm), track (front) 4ft 10·3in (148cm), track (rear) 4ft 8·5in (143cm). Overall length 15ft 8·2in (478cm). Unladen weight 2,670lb (1,211kg).

History: Felix Wankel spent years developing his rotary engine concept and eventually sold his ideas to NSU in West Germany. Their first pilot-production machine was the single-rotor Wankel

Spider, merely a sighting shot to test commercial possibilities. The Ro80, with its 115bhp twin-rotor engine, was a much more ambitious project. Even without the revolutionary engine, the Ro80 would have been quite a car. In road manners, in response and in engineering, it is a simpler equivalent of the big Citroëns; the Wankel engine merely makes it technically more interesting. There was never any doubt about the engine's power potential, but NSU had many problems in achieving reliability. Tip-seal wear, now cured, was an early bugbear, and most motor traders did not like the car's complexities. The semi-automatic transmission was necessary to damp down the engine's rough low-speed characteristics. When going properly, however, an Ro80 is a delightful machine. There is no limit to the engine's revs, apart from considera-

Above: NSU's Ro80 was the world's first Wankel-engined saloon car, and could reach 110mph. The twin-rotor engine was rated as a 2-litre.

tions of wear, and it is one of those rare cars which seems to get quieter as speeds rise. The front-wheel-drive system is very effective, the aerodynamics good and high-speed cruising very restful.

Mazda in Japan have sold many more Wankel engines than NSU have, but the Ro80 is unquestionably the most sensuous of the breed. NSU also produced a piston-engined derivative of the chassis — the K70 (later made as the VW K70) — but the Ro80 has not been further developed since the early 1970s. Production continues, but at a very low rate.

OLDSMOBILE TORONADO

Toronados, built from 1965 to date (data for 1976 model)

Built by: Oldsmobile Division of General Motors, United States.

Engine: Eight cylinders, in 90-degree vee-formation, in five-bearing cast-iron block. Bore and stroke 104·8mm by 108·0mm, 7,450cc (4·125in × 4.25in, 455cu.in). Detachable cast-iron cylinder heads. Two overhead valves per cylinder, operated by pushrods and rockers from single camshaft mounted in base of cylinder-block 'vee'. Down-draught four-choke Rochester carburettor. Maximum power 218bhp (DIN) at 3,600rpm. Maximum torque 370lb.ft at 2,400rpm.

Transmission: Front-wheel-drive power pack. Engine longitudinally mounted above line of front wheels, gearbox behind line. Engine drives through torque converter and chain to three-speed automatic gearbox, connected direct to hypoid-bevel final drive. Remote steering-column gearchange control. Exposed, universally jointed drive shafts to front wheels.

Chassis: Separate box-section steel chassis frame, with box and pressed cross braces. Independent front suspension by wishbones, longitudinal torsion bars and anti-roll bar. Rear suspension by 'dead' beam axle and semi-elliptic leaf spring. Telescopic dampers. Power-assisted recirculating-ball steering. Vacuum-servo four-wheel, hydraulically operated brakes front discs and rear drums, with vacuum-servo assistance. 15in pressed-steel wheels. JR78× 15in tyres.

Dimensions: Wheelbase 10ft 2in (310cm), tracks (front and rear) 5ft 3·5in (161·5cm). Overall length 18ft 11·5in (578cm). Unladen weight 4,763lb (2,160kg).

History: Oldsmobile, bought by General Motors in 1909 five years after Ransom Olds had left his original company to found Reo, was the technical leader at GM for many years. Almost every mechanical innovation in post-war years was marketed by Oldsmobile first and shared out to other divisions later. Of these the most sensational, and the most courageous, was the front-wheel-drive Toronado of 1965 — the first front-drive North American car for very many years. Even the mechanical layout, using many well-proven conventional-drive components, was unique. A conventional 7-litre Oldsmobile V8 unit was mounted more or less in a standard position, but the Hydramatic automatic transmission was placed alongside and below the engine itself. The torque converter was bolted to the rear of the crankshaft as usual, but drove across to the transmission by a two-inch wide rubber-damped multi-link chain. The transmission was bolted direct to the final-drive unit, itself chassis mounted, and the wheels were then driven by exposed drive shafts. Other features, like the perimeter-type chassis frame, power-assisted everything, and long/wide/low Detroit styling, were normal, even though the 'dead' rear suspension was a departure. Oldsmobile intended this smart car as a 'personal machine' — and as a direct competitor for Ford's grown-up Thunderbirds. It was therefore marketed in two-door form, as a coupé or as a convertible, but no four-door saloon or estate car variants were ever sold. Within a year it was joined by a Cadillac Eldorado — mechanically similar but visually changed.

Over the years the concept has remained unchanged, though it has not been taken up by

other North American car makers. Engines grew bigger and more powerful in the late 1960s and front wheel disc brakes were adopted, but recently the onset of emission control has emasculated the engines. In almost all respects except detail, the Toronado and the Cadillac Eldorado are now twin cars. GM's enterprise has been worthy and the cars are technically exciting, but they will probably never be replaced by new front-drive designs.

OLDSMOBILE 'CURVED DASH'

Curved Dash single-cylinder car, built from 1901 to 1906 (data for 1901 model)
Built by: Olds Motor Works, United States.
Engine: Single cylinder in horizontally mounted cast-iron block. Bore and stroke 113·4mm by 151·2mm, 1,565cc (4·46in × 5·95in, 95·5cu.in). Cast-iron cylinder head. Two overhead valves, operated via rocking levers from single camshaft running longitudinally along the side of the cylinder barrel. Single carburettor. Maximum power about 4bhp at 500rpm.
Transmission: Engine and transmission unit mounted together, installed under seats. Engine to left of centre of car and transmission to right of centre. No separate clutch. Two-speed epicyclic gearbox, with friction bands doubling as clutch. Remote-control right-hand gearchange. Final drive from transmission to 'live' rear axle by chain.
Chassis: Separate reinforced wooden chassis frame, with springs acting as frame stiffening members. Forged front axle beam. Front and rear suspension by very long semi-elliptic leaf springs, effectively front and rear cantilever springs, with centre part acting as chassis stiffening. Auxiliary full-elliptic front spring. No dampers. Tiller steering by levers and cranks. One transmission brake. No brakes in rear wheel hubs. Artillery-style or wire-spoke wheels. 26 × 3in tyres. Variety of open coachwork, or very light commercial vehicle bodywork.
Dimensions: Wheelbase 5ft 7in (170cm), tracks (front and rear) 4ft 7in (140cm). Overall length 8ft 2in (249cm). Unladen weight 700lb (317kg).
History: Ransom Olds built his first experimental car in 1891, in the family business's machine shop. The little company sold stationary gasoline engines, which made it prosperous, and by 1896 his first practical 'gas-buggy' was a familiar sight in Lancing. Car manufacture was seriously considered in 1899, when S. L. Smith put in nearly $200,000 dollars, to which Olds himself added only $400, and became President/General Manager. The prototype car was saved

from a disastrous company fire which destroyed all the drawings, so replicas could be made from that prototype and production cars, priced at only $650, went on sale in 1901. The Curved Dash (so named after the profile of the bodywork in front of the passengers' legs) was a frail little thing, where the longitudinal leaf springs doubled as auxiliary chassis members, but it was reliable and wildly successful. Oldsmobile lay claim to it being the world's first true mass-production car — a claim backed up by 2,100 sales in 1902 and 5,000 in 1904. It had but a single-cylinder engine under the seats and an epicyclic transmission alongside that (as did the first Fords sold a couple of years later), but it could beat 20mph and record more than 30mpg, which was good by any standards in those pioneering days. Engines and transmissions,

Above: Like the Model T Ford, the 'curved dash' Oldsmobile is now part of North American folklore. Its name comes from the shape of the cowl in front of the passengers' feet. The engine was under the seats, and final drive was by chain. Tiller steering featured on this 1903 example, and the springs were really part of the frame.

incidentally, were subcontracted to the Dodge brothers, who were already a force to be reckoned with in the area. Olds himself then clashed with Smith over future policy and left his foundling model in 1904, to found the Reo organisation. Bigger and more luxurious Oldsmobiles followed the Curved Dash, which was not at all what Olds himself had suggested.

Left: The mechanically complex Oldsmobile Toronado, announced in 1965, has front-wheel-drive and automatic transmission under the engine. The layout is unique, but styling is just like most other recent Detroit cars.

O.M. SIX-CYLINDER CARS

Six-cylinder cars, built from 1925 to 1930 (data for 1925 model)

Built by: SA Officine Meccaniche (later O.M. Fabbrica Bresciana di Automobili), Italy.

Engine: Six cylinders, in line, in cast-iron block, attached to four-bearing light-alloy crankcase. Bore and stroke 65mm by 100mm, 1,991cc (2·56in × 3·94in, 121·5cu.in). Detachable cast-iron cylinder head. Two side valves per cylinder, directly operated by camshaft in crankcase. Single side-draught Zenith carburettor. Maximum power about 45bhp.

Transmission: Single-dry-plate clutch and four-speed manual gearbox (with sliding pinions and no synchromesh), both in unit with front-mounted engine. Direct-acting central gearchange. Propeller shaft, enclosed in torque tube, to spiral-bevel 'live' rear axle.

Chassis: Separate steel chassis frame, with channel and box-section side members and pressed, fabricated and tubular cross members. Forged front axle beam. Semi-elliptic leaf springs at front and rear, with friction-type dampers. Four-wheel, cable-operated drum brakes. Worm-and-sector steering. Centre-lock wire wheels. 765×105mm beaded-edge tyres.

Touring, sporting or saloon car coachwork by O.M.

Dimensions: Wheelbase 10ft 2in (310cm), tracks (front and rear) 4ft 5·5in (136cm). Overall length, depending on coachwork, from 14ft (427cm). Unladen weight (chassis only) 1,800lb (816kg).

History: The pedigree of the vintage O.M. cars was established by the Züst concern in Edwardian times. Züst cars were sold from Brescia from 1907, but by before 1914 they had been taken over by the Officine Meccaniche, which was a vast heavy-engineering enterprise. After World War I, O.M. decided to make cars under their own name and elected to build them at the Züst works in Brescia. Early products were unashamedly rebadged Züsts, but the first four-cylinder O.M.s followed very quickly. The O.M. four, with

Below left: Built in 1927, this open tourer was typical of many vintage styles of body fitted to the classic six-cylinder O.M.s built between 1925 and 1930. Their chassis engineering was always entirely conventional, but the side-valve engines were efficient and light in weight. Below right: Even in 1925, when bodies still tended to be high off the ground, O.M.'s own 'Superba' style of full five-seater tourer was rakish and purposeful. O.M. stood for Officine Meccaniche, and the production of cars was only a diversion from the heavy engineering works which filled the factories. But there was nothing ponderous about the light-alloy six-cylinder engine, as racing wins proved. O.M. only built trucks from 1930.

PACKARD TWIN-SIX

Twin-Six, built from 1915 to 1923 (data for 1920 model)

Built by: Packard Motor Car Co., United States.

Engine: 12 cylinders, in 60-degree vee-formation, in two cast-iron blocks, with three-bearing light-alloy crankcase. Bore and stroke 76·2mm by 127mm, 6,950cc (3·0in × 5·0in, 424cu.in). Detachable cast-iron cylinder heads (integral heads in original production design). Two side valves per cylinder, operated by tappets from single camshaft mounted in top of crankcase. Single up-draught Packard carburettor. Maximum power 85bhp.

Transmission: Multiple-dry-plate clutch and three-speed manual gearbox (without synchromesh), both in unit with front-mounted engine. Direct-acting central gearchange. Open propeller shaft to spiral-bevel 'live' rear axle.

Chassis: Separate pressed-steel chassis frame, with channel-section side members and pressed and tubular cross bracing. Forged front axle beam. Front and rear suspension by semi-elliptic leaf springs. Worm-and-nut steering. Rear-wheel drum brakes, mechanically operated from foot pedal. Artillery-style road wheels, with fixed centres but detachable rims. 33 × 5in tyres.

Dimensions: Wheelbase 11ft 4in (345cm), tracks (front and rear) 4ft 8in (142cm). Unladen weight depending on chosen coachwork, 3,910lb to 4,415lb (1,773kg to 2,002kg).

History: The Packard brothers bought a Winton car in 1898 and decided they could improve on it and the result was the 1899 Packard car. The single-cylinder 12hp soon led to bigger and better fours and sixes and before 1910 Packard was established as one of North America's finest cars. However, for 1915, while the rest of the industry was still debating the merits of six or eight cylinders as the best for a luxury car, Packard (with a car designed by Henry Joy) jumped straight to a 12-cylinder machine, the Twin Six, which was the world's first such machine. The engine was neatly designed, with all the porting concentrated in the centre of the vee (which meant that exhaust pipes were led out behind the centre of the engine, over the transmission), and it had fixed cylinder heads. Left-hand-drive was a novelty, but this was later abandoned. It was Packard's only model from 1916 to 1920, when it was joined by a new six, and it was finally dropped in 1923.

A total of 35,046 Twin Six cars were made and Packard's reputation as a premium manufacturer was completely sealed. The cars, with their noble radiators and excellent equipment, were spirited competitors for Cadillac and any of the exotic imported makes.

Below: Packard's Twin-Six model of 1915, the world's first production vee-12. It was built until 1923.

its bore and stroke dimensions of 65mm and 100mm, established the general design principles around which the first and only six-cylinder O.M.s were to be built from 1925 to 1930.

Looked at in engineering terms, the 'Superba' six-cylinder cars were not technically outstanding, but were always carefully built and the O.M. foundries knew all about thin-wall castings years before this became a fashionable phrase in North America. One feature of the engines, which helped when the inevitable

super-tuning took place, was that the intermediate crankcase bearings were water-cooled.

The four-cylinder O.M.s were raced with great success in the early 1920s and much of this experience rubbed off on the sixes. Right from the start, the six was committed to competition – with two cars finishing equal fourth at Le Mans in 1925 (the performance being repeated in 1926). 1926 was another good year for the six, which, in spite of its side-valve layout, was remarkably tunable. Successes included

wins in the Tripoli Grand Prix and in the San Sebastian 12-hour race and a 15,000-kilometre endurance record at Monza. Even this was beaten in 1927, when the cars took a 1—2—3 placing in the first Mille Miglia race.

Low chassis models were introduced in 1928 and these were often fitted with enlarged supercharged units. By 1930, O.M. were less interested in cars and more involved in commercial vehicles, so the O.M. line of sporting cars was discontinued, never to return.

PACKARD EIGHTS

Eight-cylinder cars, built from 1923 to 1942 (data for 1930 Speedster)
Built by: Packard Motor Car Co., United States.
Engine: Eight cylinders, in line, in cast-iron block, attached to nine-bearing light-alloy crankcase. Bore and stroke 88·9mm by 127mm, 6,306cc (3·5in × 5·0in, 384·8cu.in). Detachable cylinder head. Two side valves per cylinder, operated by tappets and rocker levers from single crankcase-mounted camshaft. Single up-draught Detroit Lubricator carburettor. Maximum power 145bhp (gross) at 3,200rpm.
Transmission: Single-dry-plate clutch and four-speed manual gearbox (without synchromesh), both in unit with front-mounted engine. Direct acting central gearchange. Open propeller shaft to spiral-bevel 'live' rear axle.
Chassis: Separate pressed-steel chassis frame, with channel-section side members and fabricated and tubular cross bracings. Bijur automatic chassis lubrication. Forged front axle beam. Semi-elliptic leaf springs at front and rear, with lever-type hydraulic dampers. Four-wheel, rod, shaft and cable-operated drum brakes. Wire-spoke, artillery-style or steel-disc wheels available to choice (exclusively wire disc on Speedster cars). 7·00 × 19in tyres.
Two-seater coachwork with dickey.
Dimensions: Wheelbase 11ft 8·5in (357cm), track (front) 4ft 9·5in (146cm), track (rear) 4ft 11in (150cm). Overall length 16ft 9in (510cm). Unladen weight 3,900lb (1,769kg).
History: Packard's Single Eight was revealed in 1923 as the successor to the Twin Six and the new engine served as a backbone of Packard production until the end of the 1930s. Only in

1932, with the arrival of another exclusive (and expensive) 12-cylinder Packard, and in 1935, when the Type 120 8-cylinder engine replaced the famous unit as a modern eight, was it out of the limelight. Mechanical development in these years was steady and patient and, unlike other firms in the American industry, Packard had to pay little heed to the disasters of the depression. By the 1930s the company was a market leader, with about 50 per cent of the 'prestige car' business. At the beginning of the 1930s, the Type 734 Speedster was a very rare model, with only about 150 examples built

in 1930. Four-speed gearboxes were new to Packard in that year and they were given synchromesh gears in 1932. In 1933 came the addition of servo-assisted brakes and down-draught carburation. For 1937, every Packard had independent front suspension and hydraulic brakes. The pedigree was finally lost in 1939 when an entirely new straight-eight, with no light-alloy in its structure, was announced.

Below: There were Packard Eights for nearly 20 years. This Super Eight Roadster was built in 1933.

PANHARD DYNA 54 AND 24C/24CT SERIES

Dyna 54, announced 1953, replaced by 24C/24CT in 1963, dropped in 1967 (data for 1953 Dyna 54)

Built by: Sociétés des Etablissements Panhard et Levassor (latterly owned by Citroën), France.

Engine: Two cylinders, horizontally opposed, in light-alloy cylinder barrels, attached to two-bearing light-alloy crankcase. Bore and stroke 85mm by 75mm, 850cc (3·35in × 2·95in, 51·9 cu.in). Non-detachable cylinder heads. Two overhead valves per cylinder, operated by pushrods and rockers from single crankcase-mounted camshaft; valve closure controlled by torsion-bar springs. Single down-draught Zenith carburettor. Maximum power 40bhp at 4,000rpm.

Transmission: Single-dry-plate clutch and four-speed manual gearbox (overdriven top gear), both mounted in unit with engine (in transaxle) for front-wheel-drive. Remote-control steering column gearchange. Engine and clutch ahead of line of wheels, gearbox behind it. Exposed, universally jointed drive shafts to front wheels.

Chassis: Unitary-construction four-door saloon structure, mainly constructed of light-alloy pressings. Subframes carrying power pack at front and suspension at rear. Independent front suspension by twin transverse leaf springs. Rear suspension by tubular 'dead' axle, pivoted to chassis at centre, with radius arms and transverse torsion bars. Auxiliary rubber springs for heavy load conditions. Lever-type hydraulic dampers. Rack-and-pinion steering. Four-wheel hydraulically operated drum brakes. 16in pressed-steel-disc wheels (fixed spiders but detachable rims). 145 × 400mm tyres.

Dimensions: Wheelbase 8ft 5in (256·5cm),

tracks (front and rear) 4ft 3in (129cm). Overall length 15ft 0·4in (458cm). Unladen weight 1,450lb (657·6kg).

History: World War II was a great watershed in the fortunes of Panhard, who took on the ingenious design established by Gregoire and marketed it as the first of the Dyna series. In this guise the car had a 610cc, air-cooled flat-twin engine and a structure made up substantially of light-alloy castings (as opposed to pressings, which would have been thought conventional). In 1953, after the original model had been made by the thousand, Panhard revealed their Dyna 54

Above and right: Two generations of Dyna Panhard. In 1961 the Tigre model won the Monte Carlo Rally (on handicap). The Citroen-styled 24CT (right) was made after 1963, but died in 1967.

model, which was a thoroughly reworked derivative of the original theme. The air-cooled flat-twin engine (now of 850cc) was retained, along with front-wheel drive and transverse-leaf front suspension, all subframe-mounted to the body. Rear suspension, too, was unconventional rather than advanced, with a kinked tubular axle

PANHARD 1895 MODEL

Front-engined twin-cylinder car, introduced 1895

Built by: Panhard et Levassor, France.

Engine: Two cylinders, in line and vertically mounted, in two cast-iron blocks, with two-bearing light-alloy crankcase. Engine size (Phönix-type engine) 2,400cc (146cu.in). Non-detachable cylinder heads. Two valves per cylinder, automatic (atmospheric) overhead inlet valve and side exhaust valve, the latter operated by tappets from camshaft mounted in side of crankcase. Maybach spray-type carburettor.

Transmission: Cone clutch, in unit with front-mounted engine, and shaft drive to separate four-speed manual gearbox (without synchromesh). Straight-bevel differential in tail of box (early single-cylinder cars had completely exposed gears). Countershaft to sprockets. Final drive to rear axle by side chains.

Chassis: Separate chassis frame, with wooden side members and steel flitch plates. Forged front axle beam. Front and rear suspension by full-elliptic leaf springs. No dampers. Simple tiller steering. Foot brake, mechanically operated, on externally contracting bands on transmission drum. Handbrake on band brakes on rear wheel drums. Also crank handle and jacks to apply spoon brake to rear tyres. Fixed wooden artillery-style wheels. Solid tyres 31½in diameter (front) and 42in diameter (rear). Two-seat and four-seat open bodywork.

Dimensions: Wheelbase 5ft 6in (168cm), tracks (front and rear) 4ft 6in (137cm). Unladen weight about 1,650lb (748kg).

History: Louis-René Panhard (born in 1841) worked for the Perin firm, who made woodworking machinery. Here he met Emile Levassor. Panhard became a business partner, then, in 1886 (following Perin's death), he and Levassor became joint proprietors. One of Levassor's friends gained patent rights to build Daimler-type cars in France and the stage was set for the two friends to become motor industry pioneers. Their first car, with V-twin Daimler engine amidships, ran successfully in 1891, but after trying other rear-engined layouts the partners evolved a new car layout, revolutionary at the time,

but soon to be acknowledged as the classic. The 'Panhard system' involved a front-mounted engine, a gearbox in line behind it and drive to the rear wheels. Originally, however, the final drive was by chain, from a gearbox countershaft and the transmission was not actually a gear 'box' as the gears were completely exposed to rain, mud and general road filth, which did them no good at all. The gearchange worked through a quadrant, which meant that missing out any intermediate gears was not possible. It was a crude car at first, but one which was rapidly improved. Tyres were of solid rubber for some years, but a float feed carburettor was adopted by 1895, enclosed gears in the same year, wheel instead of tiller steering in 1898 and a front-mounted radiator in 1899.

Above: Panhard's early cars were the most significant of all in the 1890s, establishing the front engine layout.

That first car used a Daimler engine, but four-cylinder water-cooled engines were raced in 1896 and offered for sale from 1898. By 1900, the Panhard was in every way the archetype of the modern medium-sized car and the company prospered mightily. One car was awarded equal first place in the world's first motoring competition — the 1894 Paris-Rouen Trial — alongside a Peugeot and a year later Levassor himself won the 732-mile Paris-Bordeaux race (really the world's first motor race). This trip took 48hr 48 minutes, and the exhausted proprietor averaged 15mph without stops for rest!

beam hinged to a subframe at its centre and sprung on grouped torsion bars and trailing arms. The big four-door body shell, however, was now made almost entirely of light-alloy pressings and although roomy it was not very heavy; it was also surprisingly streamlined.

This range was a great success, its high gearing suiting it to French *routes nationales*, and the mechanical power pack soon found its way into lighter and more sporting machines. Panhard themselves produced faster versions culminating in the 60bhp PL17 Tigre model. The bodyshell was made of steel pressings after 1958, which made it cheaper but rather heavier, and generous handicapping made the cars obvious winners in the 1961 Monte Carlo Rally, which they duly became. In the meantime, Citroën had taken a financial interest in Panhard in 1955 and by the mid 1960s the company was integrated with its 'big brother'.

In 1963, the PL17 was supplemented (but not immediately killed) by the Citroën-styled 24C and 24CT cars. The 'C' was a two-door saloon, and the 'CT' a shorter-wheelbase coupé. The shape was attractive, if typically French, and the engineering under the skins was substantially unchanged, except for all-synchromesh gears, and (eventually) four-wheel disc brakes on the 24CT. With a gross power output of 60bhp, the car could reach 90mph. Citroën had urgent plans for the Panhard factories, however, and closed down production of these individually made cars in 1967.

PEERLESS V8

Peerless V8, built from 1915 to 1929 (data for 1919 model)
Built by: Peerless Motor Car Co., United States.
Engine: Eight cylinders, in 90-degree vee-formation, in two cast-iron blocks, with three-bearing light-alloy crankcase. Bore and stroke 82·55mm by 127mm, 5,438cc (3·25in × 5·0in, 332cu.in). Non-detachable cast-iron cylinder heads. Two side valves per cylinder, operated by tappets from single camshaft mounted in centre of crankcase 'vee'. One twin-choke Ball carburettor. Maximum power 80bhp at 2,700rpm.
Transmission: Multiple-dry-plate clutch and three-speed manual gearbox (without synchromesh), both in unit with front-mounted engine. Direct-acting central gearchange. Open propeller shaft to spiral-bevel 'live' rear axle.
Chassis: Separate pressed-steel chassis frame, with channel-section side members and pressed cross bracing; additional tubular tension rods for extra beam strength. Forged front axle beam. Front suspension by semi-elliptic leaf springs. Rear suspension by semi-elliptic leaf springs and transverse leaf 'platform' spring connected to these springs. Lever arm hydraulic dampers. Worm-type steering. Rear wheel brakes only — separate mechanically operated foot and hand systems — one externally contracting and one internal expanding set of shoes. Centre lock wire wheels. 34 × 5½in tyres.
Choice of coachwork, open or closed.
Dimensions: Wheelbase 10ft 5in (317·5cm), tracks (front and rear) 4ft 8in (142cm).
History: In its heyday, the Peerless car was 'One of the Three Ps' — a prestige title indicating the magnificent trio of Packard, Pierce-Arrow and Peerless. They made their first car in 1900, but first sprung to fame with a converted Gordon-Bennett racing car, christened Green Dragon and raced all over the United States by Barney Oldfield. The company's first six-cylinder car came along in 1907, but they really made the news in 1915 by announcing a brand-new V8-engined car only months after Cadillac had astonished the public with their own. The glamorous V8 did much for Peerless in the years immediately after World War I. Bodies, however,

gradually fell further and further behind the prevailing fashion and by the end of the vintage years the Peerless name was no longer at the front of the prestige race. Their peak year was probably in 1923, when they sold about 5,000 cars, but sales declined steadily thereafter. The rugged and powerful old V8 engine, with its fixed-head origins firmly in the industry's 'growing-up' period, no longer had customer appeal by 1929, when it was ditched in favour of a Continental design. The last of the Peerless cars was built in 1931, the marque being killed off by the North American depression.

Above: Peerless by name, and with a splendid chassis and engine, this vee-eight car was too exclusive and too costly to sell to many. With Packard and Pierce-Arrow, Peerless was one of the most prestigious American cars for some years. This smooth tourer is an early 1920s style, modern then, but hardly altered as the decade moved on. About 5,000 vee-8 Peerlesses were sold in this year, 1923, at their peak, but the fixed-head engine had lost its sales appeal by 1929 and the depression.

PEGASO Z102

Z102 cars, built from 1951 to 1958 (data for 1951 Z102)
Built by: Empresa Nacional de Autocamiones SA., Spain.
Engine: Eight cylinders, in 90-degree vee-formation, in five-bearing light-alloy block/crankcase. Bore and stroke 75mm by 70mm, 2,474cc (2·95in × 2·75in, 151cu.in). Two detachable light-alloy cylinder heads. Two overhead valves per cylinder, opposed to each other at 90 degrees in part-spherical combustion chambers and operated by twin overhead camshafts per cylinder head. Dry-sump lubrication. Single down-draught twin-choke Weber carburettor. Maximum power 140bhp at 6,000rpm. Maximum torque 135lb.ft at 3,900rpm.
Alternative engines, either with higher-compression heads and twin Weber carburettors, or bored-out to 2·8 litres and with original carburation, were available.
Transmission: Single-dry-plate clutch, in unit with front-mounted engine. Open propeller shaft to five-speed manual gearbox (without synchromesh), in unit with spiral-bevel final drive. Remote-control central gearchange.

Chassis: Unitary-construction pressed-steel and light-alloy body/chassis structure. Independent front suspension by wishbones and longitudinal torsion bars. De Dion rear suspension, with transverse torsion bars, radius arms, and sideways slide-block location. Telescopic dampers. Four-wheel hydraulically operated drum brakes, inboard at rear. 16in centre-lock wire wheels. 6·00 × 16in tyres.
Dimensions: Wheelbase 7ft 8in (234cm), track (front) 4ft 4in (132cm), track (rear) 4ft 2·7in (128·8cm). Overall length 13ft 4in (406cm). Unladen weight 2,160lb (980kg).
History: The only post-war Spanish car to achieve international 'super car' fame in the 1950s was the Pegaso, designed by Wilfredo Ricart (ex-Alfa Romeo) and built in a factory once occupied by Hispano-Suiza. The Z102 was first shown in 1951 and was a thoroughly exotic and modern design, obviously meant for small-scale production at high cost. The company was government-backed and had already made its name with unitary-construction coaches of more than 9-litres.
The original car had a 2½-litre V8 engine, with

four overhead camshafts, dry-sump lubrication, a five-speed gearbox in unit with the back axle and de Dion rear suspension. Later developments, also at a very low rate of production, were the Z102B (with 2·8-litres and 210bhp), the Z102SS (with 3·2-litres and up to 280bhp) and finally the Z103 series (which had a rather different overhead-valve engine of 4·0, 4·5 or 4·7-litres). The cars were supplied with a bewildering variety of engine tunes, including a few with superchargers, and one or two sprint records were taken in 1953. The cars were strikingly styled in the Italian-coupé manner. When Ricart retired in 1958, car production ceased; only about 125 Pegasos were made in all.

Below: Just about every Pegaso Z102 coupe was hand-built. Both these 1953 models have Touring of Milan body styles, but differ considerably in tail treatment. Hidden away is the unique Spanish twin-cam vee-8 engine, in this case of 2·8-litre capacity, along with a five-speed gearbox, and advanced De Dion rear suspension.

PEUGEOT QUADRILETTE

Quadrilette models, built from 1921 to 1924 (data for Type 161 model of 1921)
Built by: S.A. des Automobiles et Cycles Peugeot, France.
Engine: Four cylinders, in line, in two-bearing cast-iron block. Bore and stroke 50mm by 85mm, 668cc (1·97in × 3·35in, 40·8cu.in). Fixed cast-iron cylinder head. Two side valves per cylinder, operated by tappets from single camshaft side-mounted in cylinder block. Single side-draught Zenith carburettor. Maximum power 9·5bhp (net) at 2,000rpm.
Transmission: Multi-plate clutch, running in oil, in unit with front-mounted engine; propeller shaft, enclosed in torque tube, driving three-speed manual gearbox (without synchromesh) in unit with underslung-worm-drive rear axle, without differential. Remote control, quadrant-type, right-hand gearchange.
Chassis: Pressed-steel punt-type platform chassis, with boxed side members and sheet metal floor pan. Tubular front axle beam. Front suspension by transverse leaf spring and radius arms. Rear suspension by trailing quarter-elliptic leaf springs and torque tube. No dampers. No front brakes. Hand brake on right-hand brake drum, and foot brake on left-hand brake drum. Centre-lock wire wheels. 650 × 65mm tyres.
Open two-seater (tandem seating) bodywork by Peugeot.
Dimensions: Wheelbase 7ft 6·7in (230·4cm), track (front) 3ft 0·5in (92·6cm), track (rear) 2ft 5·5in (75cm). Overall length 9ft 9in (297cm). Unladen weight 840lb (381kg).
History: After World War I, Peugeot decided to replace the Bébé with an even more extraordinary minimum-market car. This one would

be so small and so narrow that it would be necessary for the two passengers (there was certainly not enough space for more) to be carried in tandem, one behind the other. The rear track was so narrow, at 2ft 6in (76·2cm) that a differential was not necessary. In one form or another the Quadrilette, as it was originally known, was in production throughout the 1920s, at first with a 668cc engine, then with 719cc and finally with a 950cc unit. The chassis became

Above: Peugeot's Quadrilette succeeds the legendary 'Bébé' (see above right) in Peugeot history, but was a similar type of machine. It really was a lot smaller than it looked at first glance —there are only two seats in this 1921 tourer, set in tandem fashion. The rear track measured a mere 29·5in and the whole car weighed 840lb. Right: Boat tail style was sweet.

PEUGEOT BÉBÉ

Bébé model built from 1912 to 1919 (data for 1912 model)

Built by: S.A. des Automobiles et Cycles Peugeot, France.

Engine: Four cylinders, in line, in two-bearing cast-iron block/crankcase. Bore and stroke 55mm by 90mm, 855cc (2·16in × 3·54in, 52·2cu.in). Fixed cylinder head. Two side valves per cylinder, inlets on one side of block and exhausts on other side operated by two camshafts, side-mounted in block. Single Claudel-Hobson carburettor.

Transmission: Leather-cone clutch in unit with front-mounted engine. Shaft to forward end of two concentric propeller shafts, leading to straight bevel 'live' rear axle. Selection of each ratio by sliding dog clutch at forward end of propeller shafts; reverse by separate gear train, through special lever and Bowden cable. Remote-control right-hand gearchange.

Chassis: Separate pressed-steel chassis frame, with channel-section side members and pressed, fabricated and tubular cross members. Forged front axle beam. Front suspension by semi-elliptic leaf springs. Rear suspension by reversed quarter-elliptic leaf springs. Friction-type dampers. Rear wheel drum brakes, operated by foot pedal or by hand lever. Centre lock wire wheels. 550 × 65 tyres.

Dimensions: Wheelbase 6ft (183cm), tracks (front and rear) 3ft 5in (104cm). Overall length 8ft 4·5in (255cm). Unladen weight (chassis only) 730lb (331kg).

History: The Peugeot family first became interested in wheeled vehicles (cycles) in 1885 and built their first steam-powered car four years later. The first five petrol-engined Peugeots were sold in 1891 and a separate company took over car manufacture from Peugeot's interests in 1897. There were very large and very tiny cars at first and some were very successful racing, but in 1911 Ettore Bugatti was asked to produce a modern small car, which went into production as the Peugeot Bébé.

This was really Peugeot's Austin Seven or 'people's car'; it was an enormous success and

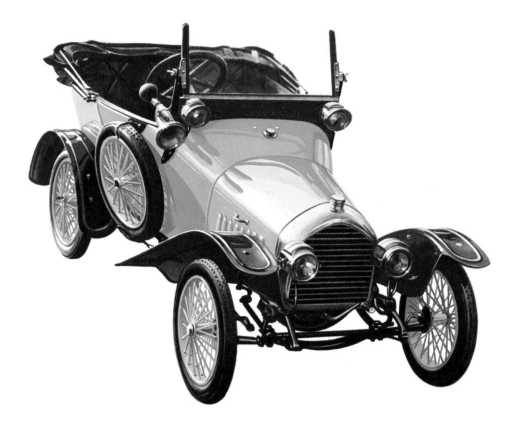

sold in large numbers up to the 1920s, when it was finally replaced by the Quadrilette. By Bugatti's already developing standards, the Bébé was a very simple machine, whose most intriguing mechanical feature was the transmission, which included twin concentric propeller shafts meshing with two rows of teeth on the crown wheel — gear selection being via sliding dog at the front of the shafts. The Bébé was so small and narrow that it was necessary to

Above: Built by Peugeot from 1912 to 1919, but designed by Ettore Bugatti, the Bébé model was marginal motoring at its best. The car was narrow—the passenger's seat is set well back.

place the passenger's seat partly behind the line of the driver's seat, to allow him space to operate the controls. The wheel, incidentally, was on the right, even for the left-hand-driving French.

more conventional over the years: the passenger space was improved and front brakes were added for 1929. To cope with the increased weight the back-axle ratio eventually had to be lowered to 7·25:1, which must have made motoring a very busy-sounding business. The engine's cylinder head was integral at first, but detachable for the 950cc version. Other quirks were that the gearbox was in unit with the final drive and that the gearchange was in the form of a quadrant, rather

than the usual 'gate'. As with all normal-sized vintage cars, that change was on the right, outside the narrow bodywork. In the original tourer, the driver's door was on the left, while the passenger's door was on the right.

The car was first shown to the public in 1919, although it did not get into production until April 1921. The Quadrilette as such — Types 161 and 172 — was renamed the 5CV car in 1924, but this retained most of the original car's engineering.

Side-by-side seating was soon available on the Type 161E (E = élargi, or enlarged). Its principal attractions, in war-torn France, were its low first price (9,400 francs in 1921) and the astonishing promise of low petrol consumption due to low weight and almost negligible performance. Without Peugeot's good name behind it, it would have been dismissed as just another cyclecar, but many thousands were sold to forge its reputation and eventually its legend.

PIERCE-ARROW 66HP

66hp, built from 1910 to 1918 (data for 13·5-litre model)

Built by: Pierce-Arrow Motor Car Co., United States.

Engine: Six cylinders, in line, in three cast-iron blocks, with seven-bearing light-alloy crankcase. Bore and stroke 127mm by 177·8mm, 13,514cc (5·0in×7·0in, 825cu.in). Three non-detachable cylinder heads. Two side valves per cylinder, in T-head layout, operated by tappets from two camshafts mounted in crankcase. Single up-draught carburettor. Maximum power 80bhp at 1,200rpm.

Transmission: Cone clutch, in unit with front-mounted engine, and shaft to separate four-speed manual gearbox (without synchro-mesh). Remote-control right-hand gearchange. Open propeller shaft to straight-bevel 'live' rear axle.

Chassis: Separate pressed-steel chassis frame, with channel-section side members and tubular and pressed-steel cross bracing; separate sub-frame for engine and gearbox. Tubular front axle beam. Front and rear suspension by semi-elliptic leaf springs. Worm-and-sleeve steering. Rear-wheel drum brakes — hand and foot brakes on same drums by separate pairs of shoes. Mechanically operated foot brake on externally contracting shoes, mechanically operated hand brake on internally expanding shoes. Artillery-type road wheels with detachable rims. 38 × 5½in tyres. Open two-seater bodywork.

Dimensions: Wheelbase 12ft 4in (376cm). Unladen weight 4,750lb (2,154kg).

History: Of all the prestige cars built in North America, the Pierce-Arrows stayed in favour longer than most. The original cars were humble little Pierces, but the first of the big Pierce Great Arrows followed in 1904. Power and engine size now began to increase inexorably over the years, which was a good thing as the body panels were eventually cast (not pressed) from light alloy — a distinctive feature which persisted until the beginning of the 1920s. The first six-cylinder engine was used in the 1906 Glidden Tour and the Pierce-Arrow name adopted in 1909. By then the smallest engine was a 5·7-litre and the largest a 10·6-litre of 66hp. This archaic machine

was uprated to 11·7 litres in 1910 and finally to 13·5 litres in 1912, by which time it rode on a huge 12ft 3in wheelbase. The 66 is therefore (along with the less-known Fageol) America's largest-ever car and in ten years of production only 1,638 examples were made. Interestingly enough, many found their way to Minneapolis, where the Fire Chief had found that a most satisfactory fire engine could be created from a Model 66. The last 66 of all was built in 1918, after a year in which no fewer than 300 of these fabulous (in every sense of the word) cars had been built. Even Pierce-Arrow had no way of

Above: One of the earliest Pierce-Arrow 66hp cars with a 10·6 litre 'six'. The final versions, in 1912, had no less than 13·5 litres. Many Model 66 cars became fire-engines later!

following that, as the market for very-large engines had almost gone. A 66 could look quite ordinary, or splendidly purposeful, depending on the coachwork chosen, but the sheer size of its vast engine, with six separately cast cylinders, could never be overlooked.

PIERCE-ARROW STRAIGHT EIGHT

Pierce-Arrow Eight, built from 1928 to 1938 (data for 1930 6·3-litre)

Built by: Pierce-Arrow Motor Car Co., United States.

Engine: Eight cylinders, in line, in cast-iron block, with nine-bearing light-alloy crankcase. Bore and stroke 88·9mm by 127mm 6,318cc (3·5in × 5·0in, 386cu.in). Detachable cast-iron cylinder head. Two side valves per cylinder, operated by tappets from camshaft in crankcase. Single up-draught Stromberg carburettor. Maximum power 125bhp at 3,000rpm.

Transmission: Single-dry-plate clutch and four-speed manual gearbox (without synchro-mesh), both in unit with front-mounted engine. Direct-acting central gearchange. Open propeller shaft to spiral-bevel 'live' rear axle.

Chassis: Separate pressed-steel chassis frame, with pressed and tubular cross bracing. Forged front axle beam. Front and rear suspension by semi-elliptic leaf springs. Lever-arm hydraulic dampers. Worm-and-ball-tooth steering. Four-wheel, mechanically operated drum brakes. Bolt-on disc wheels.

Dimensions: Wheelbase 12ft 0in (366cm). Track (front) 4ft 10in (147cm), track (rear) 5ft 1·5in (156cm).

History: After the gargantuan Model 66, Pierce-Arrow had to make more modest cars for a time and even though North America was prosperous during the 1920s, sales began to slide rather ominously. Like other rivals in the business, the company decided that an eight-cylinder engine could be their salvation and in 1928 they duly launched the Group A and Group B straight-eights which were to carry them through the 1930s. In the meantime, the com-

pany's shareholders had voted to merge their company with Studebaker of South bend, Indiana, which was duly accomplished in 1928. For four years, until the V12 Pierce-Arrow car was ready as a new flagship, the straight-eight cars did their best to keep the company afloat. The car itself was excellent — and sales of 8,000 in 1929 confirmed this. Even in 1930, when expensive cars were a drug on the market, 7,000 were delivered. Most were delivered with factory-built bodies, in many styles, and all but a few were discreet and unadorned.

For years, of course, there was no company badging in the nose — a possible client was not thought to need that sort of ostentation to bolster up his standing in the community. In spite of the fact that Studebaker sold off Pierce-Arrow to a group of businessmen in 1933 and in spite of the announcement of the outstandingly modern Model 1601 car with the straight-eight engine, nothing seemed to go right for the cars,

Above and right: Details of the Straight-Eight Pierce-Arrow and the car itself. It was an exclusive and costly product, made in good numbers in spite of the American depression. This car dates from 1929.

and sales continued to slide. Prices were too high and appeal too limited for the straitened times of 1930s North America, but Pierce-Arrow could not readily adjust without losing their cars' character altogether. The last was made in 1938, less than ten years after the new engine design and model range had been launched. It was another nail in the coffin of American car individuality. It is no more than coincidence that Studebaker also announced a straight-eight when they annexed Pierce-Arrow — the engines were of different designs, but with obvious modern similarities.

PIERCE-ARROW V12

V12 models, built from 1931 to 1938 (data for 1934 model)

Built by: Pierce-Arrow Motor Car Co., United States.

Engine: Twelve-cylinders, in 80-degree vee-formation, in two cast-iron blocks, with seven-bearing light-alloy crankcase. Bore and stroke 88·9mm by 101·6mm, 7,568cc (3·5in×4·0in, 462cu.in). Two detachable cast-iron cylinder heads. Two side valves per cylinder, operated by hydraulic tappets from single camshaft mounted in top of crankcase. Two single-choke down-draught Stromberg carburettors. Maximum power 175bhp (gross) at 3,600rpm. Maximum torque 350lb.ft at 1,500rpm.

Transmission: Twin-dry-plate clutch and three speed, synchromesh manual gearbox (without synchromesh on first gear), both in unit with front-mounted engine. Freewheel built in to tail of gearbox. Direct-acting central gear-change. Open propeller shaft to hypoid-bevel 'live' rear axle.

Chassis: Separate pressed-steel chassis frame, with box-section side members and channel-section and tubular cross bracing. Forged front axle beam. Front and rear suspension by semi-elliptic leaf springs. Lever-arm hydraulic dampers. Cam-and-roller steering. Four-wheel cable-operated drum brakes, with friction-type servo assistance. 17in artillery-style or steel-disc road wheels. 7·50 × 17in tyres. Choice of open-touring or closed bodywork.

Dimensions: Wheelbase 11ft 7in, 12ft 0in or 12ft 3in (353cm, 366cm or 373cm). Track (front) 4ft 11in (150cm), track (rear) 5ft 1·5in (156cm). Unladen weight, depending on coach-work or chassis length, from 5,150lb to 5,530lb (2,236kg to 2,508kg).

History: Even though sales of the expensive, grand and exclusive Pierce-Arrow cars continued to fall during the worst of the depression, the company felt that it had to join in the current North American craze of supplying a V12 engine for its top models. Announced at the end of 1931, there were two versions — 5·5-litre and 7-litre — of a unit built in classic vintage style with separate cylinder blocks on a light-alloy crankcase. To boost performance, the engines grew to 7 litres and 7·6 litres respectively, a year later. Sales totalled 2,692 (all Pierce-Arrows) in 1932 and only 1,740 by 1934. Even the beautifully styled Silver Arrow show car, as sleek as any North American car even of the late 1930s and priced at $10,000, could do little for the company, which was fighting for its life against the big battalions.

Ab Jenkins broke many endurance records in specially prepared Pierce-Arrows and a consortium of Buffalo businessmen took over the company in 1933, but no really new models were forthcoming and the once-proud company slid into insolvency in 1938.

Below: One of several competing American vee-12s was marketed by Pierce-Arrow in the 1930s. This car was a 1934 model, after the company takeover. There were no more mechanical changes to 1938.

PORSCHE 356

Porsche 356 cars, built from 1948 to 1965 (data for 1960-type S90)

Built by: Dr. Ing.h.c. F. Porsche KG., West Germany.

Engine: Four cylinders, horizontally opposed, in three-bearing, light-alloy block/crankcase, air cooled. Bore and stroke 82·5mm by 74mm, 1,582cc (3·25in × 2·91in, 96·5cu.in). Two light-alloy cylinder heads. Two overhead valves per cylinder, operated by pushrods and rockers from single camshaft, centrally mounted in crankcase. Two downdraught Zenith carburettors. Maximum power 90bhp (net) at 5,500rpm. Maximum torque 89lb.ft at 4,300rpm.

Transmission: Single-dry-plate clutch, and four-speed, all-synchromesh manual gearbox, both in unit with rear-mounted engine. Engine behind line of rear wheels and gearbox ahead of it. Remote-control central gearchange. Spiral-bevel final drive, and exposed, universally jointed drive shafts to rear wheels.

Chassis: Pressed-steel punt-type chassis frame, topped by pressed-steel and light-alloy-panelled coupé or convertible bodyshells. Independent VW-type front suspension by trailing arms, transverse torsion bars and anti-roll bar. Independent rear suspension by swinging half-axles, radius arms and transverse torsion bars. Telescopic dampers. Worm-and-roller steering. Four-wheel, hydraulically operated drum brakes. 15in pressed-steel-disc wheels. 5·60 × 15in tyres.

Dimensions: Wheelbase 6ft 10·7in (210cm), track (front) 4ft 3·4in (130·5cm), track (rear) 4ft 2·1in (127cm). Overall length 13ft 1·9in (401cm). Unladen weight 1,985lb (900kg).

History: Dr. Porsche had been in the centre of motor car development since Edwardian times, but it was son Ferry who laid out the bare bones of the Porsche car project after World War II. Using VW Beetle mechanical equipment — engines, transmissions and suspensions — Porsche built their very first car in 1948 and this had the engine ahead of the rear wheel line. However, all production cars reverted to the familiar VW-style layout, with the air-cooled flat-four engine overhanging the rear wheels.

Type 356, incidentally, indicates that this was the 356th project undertaken by the Porsche design office since its formation in 1930. Early Porsches were 1100s, with very nearly standard

VW engines, but they very rapidly found success in motor racing and proved to be surprisingly strong rally cars.

Production was well under way by 1950, when steel-bodied cars were phased in at the new Zuffenhausen works, to replace the original light-alloy. Enlargement began in 1951 when the 1,286cc car was announced, 1,488cc Porsches were revealed in 1951 and the first 1,582cc car followed in 1955. This engine, developed from its original 60bhp output to 95bhp in 1965, was standardised for the last ten years of the 356's life. In all this time there was only one significant restyling operation — in 1959 when headlamps and bumpers were raised, the

Above: Only an expert can tell the age and pedigree of a Porsche 356 from a picture. This is a 1951 Cabriolet—note the divided screen and flush-fitting headlamps. Engines and 1100cc to 2000cc were supplied, and the last of all 356s was built in 1964.

windscreen enlarged and trim updated. The Porsche's shape was always aerodynamically efficient, and the last of the Super 90s was good for 115mph, with excellent petrol economy. Although the 356 carried on until 1965, it was effectively replaced by the 911 series, which went into series production in 1964.

PORSCHE 917

917 model, built for racing from 1969 to 1971 (data for 1971 5-litre)

Built by: Dr. Ing.h.c. F. Porsche KG, West Germany.

Engine: Twelve cylinders, horizontally opposed, in detachable finned light-alloy cylinder barrels, with eight-bearing magnesium crankcase. Air cooled. Bore and stroke 86·8mm by 70·4mm, 4,998cc (3·42in × 2·77in, 305cu.in). Detachable aluminium cylinder heads. Two overhead valves per cylinder, inclined to each other in part-spherical combustion chambers and operated inverted-bucket tappets from twin overhead camshafts per bank. Bosche fuel injection. Power drive take-off from gears at centre of crankshaft, through drive shaft in base of crankcase. Dry-sump lubrication. Maximum power 630bhp (DIN) at 8,300rpm. Maximum torque 425lb.ft at 6,400rpm.

Transmission: Mid-mounted engine, driving through gearbox, behind line of back wheels, in transaxle. Triple-dry-plate clutch, and four-speed or five-speed all-synchromesh gearbox (depending on application). Spiral-bevel final drive with limited-slip differential. Exposed, universally-jointed drive shafts to rear wheels.

Chassis: Separate multi-tubular aluminium frame. Engine and transmission mounted behind seats. All independent suspension, front by coil springs, wishbones and anti-roll bar, rear by coil springs, lower wishbones, radius arms and anti-roll bar. Telescopic dampers. Rack-and-pinion steering. Four-wheel, hydraulically operated disc brakes. 15in cast-magnesium road wheels

of varying widths (depending on application). Tyre size according to requirements. Glassfibre two-seat racing bodywork by Porsche, short or long tail, open or closed, according to requirement.

Dimensions: Wheelbase 7ft 6in (230cm), track (front — with 12in rims) 5ft 1·7in (156cm), track (rear — with 17in rims) 5ft 2·7in (158cm). Overall length (917K short tail) 13ft 7·6in (416cm). Unladen weight 1,763lb (800kg).

Above: Porsche 917s came in many shapes, but all shared the same flat-12 engine with more than 630bhp. For years they were fast and unbeatable.

History: The Type 917 sports-racing car was designed specifically to meet a new category, which allowed 5-litre cars to be raced as long as 25 identical examples had been made. This, the authorities thought, would get rid of

PORSCHE 911

Porsche 911 and 912 models, built from 1963 to date (data for 1976 3-litre Turbo)

Built by: Dr. Ing.h.c. F. Porsche KG., West Germany.

Engine: Six cylinders, horizontally opposed, in detachable finned light-alloy barrels, with two-piece, eight-bearing magnesium crankcase. Air cooled. Bore and stroke 95mm by 70·4mm, 2,994cc (3·74in × 2·77in, 182·7cu.in). Detachable light-alloy cylinder heads. Two overhead valves per cylinder, inclined to each other in part-spherical combustion chambers and operated by rockers from single overhead camshafts; Bosch fuel injection and KKK turbocharger. Dry-sump lubrication. Maximum power 260bhp (DIN) at 5,500rpm. Maximum torque 253lb.ft at 4,000rpm.

Transmission: Single-dry-plate clutch and four-speed, all-synchromesh manual gearbox, in transaxle assembly. Engine behind line of rear wheels, gearbox ahead of it. Remote-control central gearchange. Hypoid-bevel final drive. Exposed universally jointed drive shafts to rear wheels.

Chassis: Unitary-construction pressed-steel body-chassis unit. Rear-mounted engine/transmission, engine overhung to rear of car. All-independent suspension, front by lower wishbones, torsion bars and anti-roll bar, rear by semi-trailing links, transverse torsion bars and anti-roll bar. Telescopic dampers. Rack-and-pinion steering. Four-wheel hydraulically operated disc brakes. 15in forged aluminium-alloy road wheels. 205×15in front tyres, 225×15in rear tyres.

Dimensions: Wheelbase 7ft 5in (226cm), track (front) 4ft 8·5in (143cm), track (rear) 5ft 1in (155cm). Overall length 14ft 2in (432cm). Unladen weight 2,700lb (1,224kg).

History: To replace the legendary Type 356 family, Porsche embarked on an entirely new design. Although no old component was carried forward, the design philosophy was not changed — the car still had a rear-mounted, horizontally opposed, air-cooled engine, a 2+2 seating arrangement and a sleek closed coupé body style. In the case of the 911, the engine was a flat-six, with a single overhead camshaft per bank, and there was a five-speed or four-speed gearbox according to the model. Although the 911 was

Above: Announced in 1963, the Porsche 911 sells strongly in the late 1970s. Engines have been enlarged from 2-litre to 3-litre over the years. The basic two-door fastback always looks good.

in a different, higher, price class than the 356, once this had been drawn a 912 model was sold with the 1,582cc Super 90's flat-four unit installed. Even in this guise the car could clock up 120mph, but 130 was quite normal for the sixes. The 911 was launched as a 2-litre in 1963, and was in production by the following summer. The 911S was a highly tuned version with 160bhp, and was immediately successful in endurance racing and rallying. Over the years the car was further developed: the 2-litre engine became 2·2-litres in 1969, 2·4-litres in 1971, and 2·7-litres in 1973. Carreras have been 3·0-litres since 1975.

Also introduced in the model's 13-year life span has been the removable-roof 'Targa' body style, and the semi-automatic 'Sportomatic' transmission, but the most sensational development of all has been the 3-litre Turbo. This

installation, proved first in prototype racing, has an exhaust-gas-driven turbocharger to boost the inlet mixture, is very tractable, and endows the car with a maximum speed of more than 160mph. Even with twice as much power as the original 911 had, the Porsche Turbo's handling is probably safer and more predictable than ever and the aerodynamic aids (including the large engine-lid spoiler) make it very stable at high speeds. All 911s have an impressive reliability record, and recent versions use galvanised structural panels, a five-year guarantee being offered accordingly.

specialised racing cars. They were wrong. Porsche developed the 917 (using 8-cyl 908 parts in the flat-12 engine) in less than a year and announced the car with a line-up of 25 examples standing in the factory ready for inspection! Only very few of these were ever sold, most being used by the factory or loaned out to sponsored teams. The car was the ultimate expression of Porsche's air-cooled lightweight two-seater racing car philosophy.

Although it had a poor 1969 season, it was well-nigh invincible thereafter.

The 917 used the most powerful automotive air-cooled engine of all time and was one of the most rapid two-seaters ever built. 'Works' cars were run by the JW Automotive team from Britain in 1970 and 1971, winning the world sports car championship very easily from Ferrari. When the rules were again changed, banning 5-litre cars (the 917 had originally been

Above: The low and stubby short-tail 917s were aerodynamically very stable on all tracks. Most were closed coupes.

4·5 litres, but got its enlarged engine after the first year), some cars were converted to open sports cars and when turbocharged they could boast outputs of at least 1,000bhp. They, without doubt, are the most powerful racing cars ever built.

RENAULT GRAND PRIX CARS

Grand Prix Renaults of 1906, 1907 and 1908 (data for 1906 model)
Built by: Renault Frères Billancourt, France.
Engine: Four cylinders, in line, in two cast-iron blocks, with light-alloy crankcase. Bore and stroke 166mm by 150mm, 12,975cc (6·54in × 5·91in, 791·7cu.in). Two fixed cylinder heads. Two side valves per cylinder, exposed at side of cylinder blocks and directly operated by single camshaft mounted in crankcase. Single Renault carburettor. Maximum power 105bhp at 1,200rpm.
Transmission: Leather-cone clutch, in unit with front-mounted engine and shaft drive to separate three-speed manual gearbox (without synchromesh). Remote-control right-hand gearchange. Open propeller shaft to straight-bevel final drive, without differential.
Chassis: Separate pressed-steel chassis frame, with channel-section side members and tubular cross members. Forged front axle beam. Front suspension by semi-elliptic leaf springs. Rear axle location. Rear suspension by semi-elliptic leaf springs (with torque arm between axle casing and chassis frame in gearbox area in 1907 version). Lever-arm hydraulic dampers. Hand brake to drums on rear wheels, foot brake to transmission drum behind gearbox. Wooden artillery-type wheels, with detachable rims only. 870 × 90 (front) or 870 × 120 (rear) tyres. Open two-seater bodywork.
Dimensions: Wheelbase 9ft 6·2in (290cm), tracks (front and rear) 4ft 5·2in (135cm). Overall length 14ft 1·8in (431cm). Unladen weight 2,183lb (990kg).
History: In the good old days when motor racing was not so tightly wrapped around with rules and regulations, it was much simpler for any interested manufacturer to build a competitive machine. At the beginning of the twentieth century, with motoring still in its infancy, the sport was still easy to understand. When the French decided to organise the very first Grand Prix in 1906, the only regulation applying to the cars was that they should weigh no more than 1,000kg (2,205lb) unladen. Renault had been active in motor sport from the start (Marcel Renault himself being the team's star driver), but when Renault was killed in a Paris–Madrid crash in 1903 the factory abruptly withdrew its support. In 1904, however, they built a machine for an American customer, with an enlarged version of the Paris–Madrid engine, and by 1905 they were tempted to return to the sport, with further-developed versions of this engine and its transmission in a new chassis. For 1906, for the Grand Prix to be held at Le Mans, a team of new cars was built up; this represented modern thinking about that sort of car. The chassis, of course, was simple in the extreme, with handling and braking taking a back seat to sheer power and (hopefully) strength. The nucleus of Renault's GP effort was a yet further developed version of the 1903 Paris–Madrid engine, which got its power and formidable torque from 13 litres, rather than from any particularly advanced breathing capability.

It was a big, slow-revving, four-cylinder unit, with vast 6·5in pistons, and peak power of 105bhp produced at a mere 1,200rpm. It was a trend-setter in some ways, because, like every other Renault ever made, it had shaft drive. Most fast cars of the period were faithful to chain drive, which was very vulnerable to damage from dust and from the atrocious roads used, even for racing, in those days. The three-speed gearbox, right-hand gearchange and stark two-seater body were all normal to the period. The Renault was noted for its very sleek sloping nose and for its water radiators carried behind the engine and immediately in front of the passengers. A riding mechanic was compulsory and necessary, to look after the car and to deal with the inevitable punctures. In this respect, the car was originally built with non-detachable wire-spoke wheels, but after practice a set of artillery wheels was substituted, with detachable rear rims. Other oddities were that the rear axle had no differential and that the cars (three were built) were painted bright red (national colours not then being compulsory). In 1906, only one of the three cars finished, but it won the race outright, driven by Ferenc Szisz. Its maximum speed was about 100mph and it averaged 63mph for the gruelling 769 miles. A year later, with identical but newly built cars, Szisz's car took second place, ham-

pered by a fuel-restriction formula, six minutes behind Nazzaro's Fiat.

For 1908, with new restrictions on piston area limiting the four-cylinder bore to 155mm, Renault modified the engines with a longer (160mm) stroke. Breathing and other improvements allowed the unit to peak at 2,000rpm, and maximum power was very slightly improved. The cars were still completely competitive, but tyre troubles robbed Szisz of another high placing and his team-mates were neither as experienced nor as brave.

The cars are now legendary, because they were the first of that long and continuing strain of machinery which culminated in the ultra-specialised single-seaters of today. Yet the Grand Prix car of the early 1900s was very closely related to a big fast touring car and some of the less-specialised machines were often converted for ordinary road use after their racing career was over. Looking at those narrow tyres, the complete lack of weather protection and the terrible state of the roads used, one has to marvel at the cars and the drivers who tackled the early races. The Renault, by its consistent running and fine appearance, is a splendid and significant member of that rare breed of Titans. We must be thankful that one has survived, and that Renault themselves now cherish it.

Right: Colourful detail of the world's first successful Grand Prix car. The 1906 Renault, however, was a development of a 1904 machine, and the engine was new for the 1903 Paris-Madrid road race. Radiators mounted behind the engine were a feature of all Renaults —racing or production cars—built up to 1928. Tyre changes because of punctures were inevitable on the bad roads of the day, and the Renault's detachable Michelin rims helped to cut down the time needed for this. In spite of the car's mechanical crudity, it could exceed 100mph, though the brakes were almost non-existent. There were two seats because a mechanic travelled with the driver.

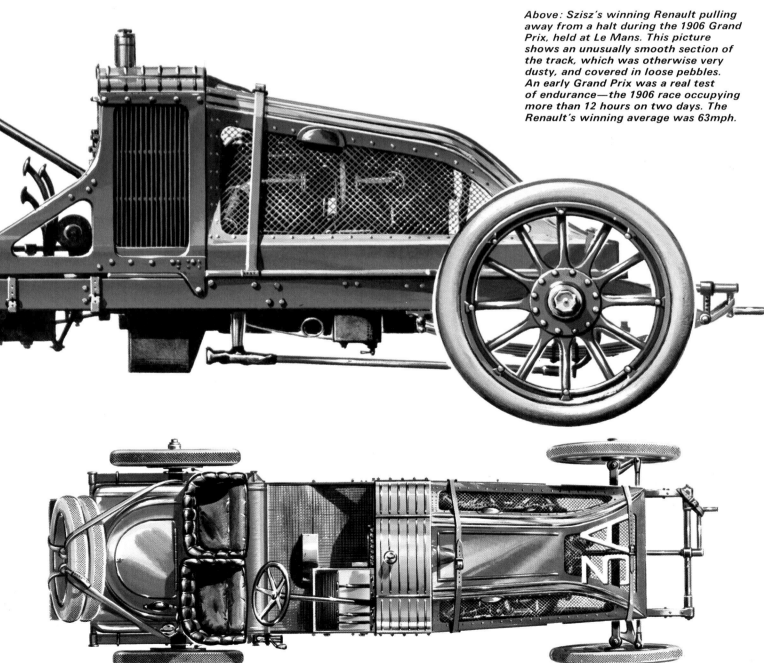

Above: Szisz's winning Renault pulling away from a halt during the 1906 Grand Prix, held at Le Mans. This picture shows an unusually smooth section of the track, which was otherwise very dusty, and covered in loose pebbles. An early Grand Prix was a real test of endurance—the 1906 race occupying more than 12 hours on two days. The Renault's winning average was 63mph.

RENAULT REINASTELLA

Reinastella, built from 1928 to 1934 (data for 1929 model)

Built by: S.A. des Usines Renault, France.

Engine: Eight cylinders, in line, in cast-iron block, with five-bearing light-alloy crankcase. Bore and stroke 90mm by 140mm, 7,125cc (3·54in × 5·52in, 434·8cu.in). Detachable cast-iron cylinder head. Two side valves per cylinder, operated directly by single camshaft positioned in side of crankcase. One twin-choke Solex carburettor.

Transmission: Twin-dry-plate clutch and three-speed manual gearbox (later models with synchromesh on top and second gears), both in unit with front-mounted engine. Propeller shaft, enclosed in torque tube, driving spiral-bevel 'live' rear axle. Direct-acting central gearchange.

Chassis: Separate pressed-steel chassis frame, with channel-section side members and tubular and pressed cross bracings. Forged front axle beam. Front suspension by semi-elliptic leaf

springs. Rear suspension by transverse leaf spring, allied to diagonal cantilever leaf springs. Lever-arm hydraulic dampers. Four-wheel drum brakes, operated by shafts and rods and assisted by gearbox-driven mechanical servo. Pressed-steel disc wheels. 16 × 50 tyres.

Closed saloon or limousine coachwork.

Dimensions: Wheelbase 12ft 2in (371cm), tracks (front and rear) 4ft 11in (150cm). Overall length 16ft 9·2in (511cm). Unladen weight 5,950lb (2,700kg).

History: After years of building cars of all sizes with radiators behind the engine, Louis Renault, against his better judgement, was persuaded that everyone else in the industry was correct and that radiators should be in the nose of the car. The first model to be announced, and a worthy successor to the 9-litre machine of earlier vintage years, was the Reinastella. Graced with a straight-eight engine of 7·1 litres (Renault's first eight) and a series of magnificent and dignified

designs of coachwork, the Reinastella was the French 'Head of State' car. It had a French fiscal rating of no less than 41cv, which meant that few could afford it — just as intended by Renault. Apart from the transverse-leaf rear suspension, the chassis was conventional. The car could sweep along in great style at more than 80mph, and the sporting version with its four-speed gearbox, was good for nearly 100mph. The Reinasport was much influenced by Detroit thinking in its dashboard and controls layout. It was the star of Renault's firmament until 1934, when it and the Primastella were replaced by Viva and Nervastella Grand Sport models, with smaller (85mm bore) engines having light-alloy cylinder blocks.

Below: Renault's Reinastella was a true 'flagship', the first Renault to have a front-mounted radiator. It had a splendid 7-litre 8-cylinder engine.

RENAULT ALPINE

Alpines 1955 to date (data for 1600S model of 1970)

Built by: Automobiles Alpine srl., France.

Engine: Renault-manufactured, four cylinders, in line, in five-bearing light-alloy block. Bore and stroke 77mm by 84mm, 1,565cc (3·03in × 3·31in, 95·5cu.in). Light-alloy cylinder head. Two overhead valves per cylinder, operated by pushrods and rockers from single camshaft, high-mounted in cylinder block. One twin-choke Weber carburettor. Maximum power 138bhp (gross) at 6,000rpm. Maximum torque 106lb.ft at 5,000rpm.

Transmission: Engine mounted longitudinally behind line of rear wheels, driving through gearbox, ahead of rear wheels, and transaxle. Single-dry-plate clutch and five-speed, all-synchromesh manual gearbox. Central, remote-control gearchange. Drive forward over final drive to gearbox, then back to hypoid-bevel final drive. Exposed universally jointed drive shafts to rear wheels.

Chassis: Separate tubular backbone chassis frame, with square-section and circular-section built-up frames supporting suspensions and power pack. Independent front suspension by coil springs, wishbones and anti-roll bar. Independent rear suspension by swinging half axles, coil springs, radius arms and anti-roll bar. Telescopic dampers. Rack-and-pinion steering. Four-wheel disc brakes, with optional vacuum servo. Cast-alloy, 15in road wheels. 145 × 15in, or 165 × 13in tyres.

Two-door, two-seat, closed glassfibre bodywork by Alpine.

Dimensions: Wheelbase 6ft 10·6in (210cm),

track (front) 4ft 3in (129·5cm), track (rear) 4ft 2·2in (127·5cm). Overall length 12ft 7·5in (385cm). Unladen weight 1,400lb (635kg).

History: Jean Redélé worked in the family Renault dealership when young, and started competition motoring in the not-very-sporting 4CV saloon model. From this he progressed to building a glassfibre special using mainly 4CV parts — the very first Alpine-Renault sports car. From very small beginnings, this dumpy little machine was built in limited quantities; it was given a larger engine and refined and it gradually built up a loyal clientele. The breakthrough came in 1961, when the A108 Tour de France machine was introduced, visually very similar to the cars to be made for the next fifteen years, with a steel backbone chassis and steel platform floor, with the Renault Dauphine 956cc engine. Development thereafter was rapid, with first an 1,108cc and later a 1,255cc engine.

Alpines were very successful class and 'Index' performers on the race track and in smooth-road rallies, but it was not until the light-alloy Renault 16 unit was made available that outright victories became possible. From the end of the 1960s, the cars were also strengthened, until by the early 1970s they could win rallies through the Alps, in the dust and sand of Morocco, and continue to shine on the race tracks. As a production car, the Alpine was only a compromise, for its very lightweight and flexible glassfibre body shell and tail-out handling was strictly competition-inspired. The company is now financially controlled by Renault, the French giant, and operates that company's official competition programme.

Right: Alpine-Renaults are really rally cars which can be used on the road. With a tubular chassis, light glass-fibre bodies, and powerful modified Renault engines, the A110 was an outright winner for years. This was Pat Carlsson's Monte example.

RENAULT 4CV

4CV, built from 1946 to 1961 (data for 1948 '760' model)

Built by: Régie Nationale des Usines Renault, France.

Engine: Four cylinders, in line, in three-bearing cast-iron block. Bore and stroke 55mm by 80mm, 760cc (2·16 × 3·15in, 46·4cu.in) Detachable cast-iron cylinder head. Two overhead valves per cylinder, operated by pushrods and rockers from single camshaft positioned in side of cylinder block. Down-draught single-choke Solex carburettor. Maximum power 19bhp at 4,000rpm.

Transmission: Single-dry-plate clutch and three-speed, all-synchromesh manual gearbox, in transaxle in unit with rear-mounted engine. Engine and clutch behind line of rear wheels, and gearbox ahead of the line. Remote-control central gearchange. Spiral-bevel final-drive unit and exposed, universally jointed drive shafts to rear wheels.

Chassis: Combined unitary-construction pressed-steel body/chassis unit. Engine/transmission pack mounted in tail. Independent front suspension by coil springs and wishbones. Independent rear suspension by swinging half shafts and coil springs. Telescopic dampers. Rack-and-pinion steering. Four-wheel hydraulically operated drum brakes. 15in pressed-steel-disc wheels (with fixed spiders and detachable rims). 4·75 × 15in tyres.

Right: The stubby but effective 4CV was the car which restored Renault's fortunes after World War II, which had resulted in severe damage to their factories, and to the arrest of Louis Renault himself. The 4CV (this is a 1959 model with 747cc) was the first rear-engined Renault, was very popular, and sold over a million examples. It cost very little, and was mechanically simple—just the thing for war-impoverished France. Factory cars raced and rallied with honour, and the Alpine-Renault evolved from this design. The Dauphine followed.

Dimensions: Wheelbase 6ft 10·5in (210cm), tracks (front and rear) 3ft 11in (119cm). Overall length 11ft 10in (361cm). Unladen weight 1,330lb (603kg).

History: During the war years and during German occupation, Renault secretly developed the ugly but cheekily successful rear-engined 4CV model. The company was nationalised in 1944, as soon as France had been liberated and Renault himself imprisoned as a collaborator. The 4CV, with its simple and rugged layout and minimal four-door four-seat layout, was put into production in 1946–7 and ran through until supplanted by the sleek Dauphine in 1956, finally being dropped in 1961, when more than a million had been sold. In the main, the cars were strictly utilitarian, but sporting versions with as much as 38bhp were sold and at least one car raced with honour at Le Mans. The 4CV's mechanical components were eagerly snapped up by France's 'special' builders and cars like the Alpine-Renault could not have been born without the existence of the little 4CV. The rear-engine theme established by the 4CV was carried on by the Dauphines and Renault 8s, but the real successor to the 4CV was the Renault 4, announced in 1961, with front engine and front-wheel drive. This set an entire new trend, to which all modern Renaults have conformed.

RILEY SPORTS CARS

Riley Nines, Lynx, Imp, MPH and Sprites, built in the 1930s (data for 1936/7 Sprite two-seater)

Built by: Riley (Coventry) Ltd., Britain.

Engine: Four cylinders, in line, in three-bearing cast-iron block. Bore and stroke 69mm by 100mm, 1,496cc (2·72in × 3·94in, 91·3cu.in). Detachable cast-iron cylinder head. Two overhead valves per cylinder, inclined to each other at 90 degrees in hemispherical combustion chamber and operated by pushrods and rockers from two high-mounted camshafts in cylinder block; one cam for inlet valves mounted in 'inlet' side of block, one in 'exhaust' side for exhaust valves. Twin horizontal constant-vacuum SU carburettors. Maximum power 60bhp at 5,000 rpm.

Transmission: Wilson-type preselector epicyclic gearbox with four forward speeds. No clutch, drive taken up by gear friction band as it is engaged. Gearbox in unit with engine. Pre-selector quadrant control on right side of

steering column, under steering wheel. Propeller shaft enclosed in torque to be fixed to spiral-bevel 'live' rear axle.

Chassis: Separate pressed-steel chassis frame, with box and channel-section side members and pressed and tubular cross bracing. Forged front axle beam. Semi-elliptic front and rear springs, with friction-type dampers. Worm-and-wheel steering. Four-wheel rod and cable-operated drum brakes. 19in centre-lock wire wheels. 5·00 × 19in tyres.

Two-seat open sports coachwork by Riley, with optional cowled or 'traditional' front.

Dimensions: Wheelbase 8ft 1·5in (248cm), tracks (front and rear) 4ft (122cm). Overall length 12ft 4in (376cm). Unladen weight 2,210lb (1,002kg).

History: The true pedigree of Riley's famous sports cars of the late 1920s and the 1930s was established by the new family of engines with the still-unique twin-high-camshaft arrangement and inclined valves in the hemi-headed cylinder

Above and below: Riley's Sprite of 1936 saw the first tentative breakaway from 'classic' styling, with the option of a cowl radiator. The Sprite used a modified MPH chassis, and a 1½-litre 4-cylinder engine. A pre-selector gear change was standard. Helped by this the Sprite was a successful rally car.

ROCHET-SCHNEIDER 20/22

20/22 model built from 1903 to 1907 (data for 1903 model)

Built by: S.A. des Etablissements Rochet-Schneider, France.

Engine: Four cylinders, in line, in two cast-iron blocks with three-bearing light-alloy crankcase. Bore and stroke 100mm by 150mm, 4,712cc (3·94in × 5·91in, 287·5cu.in). Fixed cast-iron cylinder head. Two side valves per cylinder, in 'T-head' layout: inlet valves on one side of cylinder blocks, exhaust valves on the other side, with exposed stems; operated by tappets from two camshafts mounted in crankcase. Single up-draught carburettor.

Transmission: Cone clutch, in unit with front-mounted engine, and shaft drive to separate four-speed manual gearbox (without synchromesh). Remote-control right-hand gearchange. Straight-bevel final drive in tail of gearbox and countershaft output to chain sprockets. Final drive to rear wheels by chain.

Chassis: Separate wooden chassis frame, stiffened by flanged steel flitch plates. Engine mounted to main frame in separate steel sub-frame. Forged front axle beam. Front suspension by semi-elliptic leaf springs. Rear suspension by semi-elliptic leaf springs. No dampers. Worm-type steering. Two brakes, water-cooled external-contracting drums, on each side of gearbox on countershaft. Drum hand brake on off-side rear wheel. All brakes cable operated. Artillery-type

road wheels. Open two-seat or four-seat touring coachwork.

Dimensions: Wheelbase 7ft 8·5in (235cm), tracks (front and rear) 4ft 5in (135cm). Overall length 11ft 5in (348cm). Unladen weight 2,250lb (1,020kg).

History: The Schneider name crops up twice in French motoring history. Théophile Schneider first of all set up the Rochet-Schneider car-making business in Lyons in 1894, when he was content to sell copies of other successful and innovative designs, but from 1910 he branched out into a new breed of car at Besançon (the Th. Schneider). Rochet-Schneiders, undoubtedly, were the most famous of all cars built in Lyons. The first cars were copies of the contemporary Benz, while from 1901 the company produced two front-engined cars — a 7hp twin and a 12hp four — based on the Panhard pattern. However, at the end of 1902, Schneider had got down to some individual designs, three of which were revealed at the Paris Salon.

The new cars, which replaced old copies, were a 6½hp single, a 10hp twin and a 16hp four, known in Britain as the 20/22. This last owed a lot to the latest in Mercédès thinking, but retained an armoured wood chassis (steel flitch plates giving much rigidity), yet it could reach nearly 60mph. The water-cooled drum brakes were novel, although chain-drive was the norm for cars of this period. The cars were the sensa-

tion of the Salon and in the next few years the range was expanded upwards in a consistently engineered fashion. British imports, at first, were in the hands of Captain Deasy (who later got involved in the Siddeley-Deasy car).

Whereas other makes had turned to motor racing for publicity (and many suffered humiliation and financial embarrassment in the process), Rochet-Schneider preferred hill-climbs and reliability trials. By 1906 there were 16hp, 18/22, 30hp, 30/35 and 40/50 models, and within a year a couple of new big six-cylinder machines (30/40 and 45/60) had been added. However, in spite of a wide range, cars were only being sold at the rate of about 250 machines a year, so the bankruptcy of 1907 was not unexpected. This was the cue for Schneider himself to leave and to start again in Besançon; when the company was reformed in 1909 its principal asset was the acquisition of the Zenith carburettor company. The last Rochet–Schneider car was made in 1932.

Right: The Rochet-Schneider was one of two cars sponsored by Théophile Schneider, and was the most famous of all cars built at Lyons in France. The 20/22 shown was actually a 16hp, with a wooden chassis and water-cooled drum brakes. The engine was in the nose, and the gearbox under the floor of the car.

heads. The first engine was called the 'Nine' and was produced in 1927, with 1,087cc; this was followed by a 1,458cc six in 1932 and a big and lusty 1,496cc four in 1934. The famous Freddie Dixon 'Brooklands' Rileys achieved their first miracles with much-tuned 'Nines', but later became ferociously fast projectiles, with 2-litre versions of the six. This engine, with its water-cooled crankshaft bearing, was also the basis of the ERA racing-engine design, where in super-charged form the very best 2-litres produced well over 300bhp! Nevertheless, the 1½-litre four was the most useful, commercially and was to be a Riley production engine until the mid 1950s.

From 1933, the trio of really shapely Rileys consisted of the Imps (with 'Nine' engines), the very rare MPHs (with the six), and the Sprites (which used the 1½-litre four). MPHs were very fast and very exotic and they bore a strong resemblance to the 8C Alfas *and* to the Triumph Dolomite prototypes (not surprising, as Donald Healey was connected with both Riley and Triumph at the critical time), but they were too expensive. Only about 15 were built. The Sprite, in effect, used the MPH body and chassis with a new engine installation. The preselector gearbox was a popular proprietary fitment in British 1930s cars, being strong and versatile if heavy. In the days when gearboxes had no synchromesh it was a great advance and was very suitable for

Above: The 1934 Riley Imp, so obviously related to the later Sprite, had a tuned Riley Nine engine of 1,087cc. Imps were tiny and pretty, with sleek lines.

driving tests and other forms of motor sport. The Sprite was offered by Riley with alternative noses — the one style with a traditional (but sloping) exposed radiator, and the other with the radiator cowled by a semi-streamlined panel. With no fuss from its very practical engine, the 1½-litre Sprite could beat 85mph for £425, which made it a very good bargain. Production ran out in 1938 when Riley were purchased by Lord Nuffield.

ROLLS-ROYCE THREE-CYLINDER CAR

Rolls-Royce three-cylinder car, built in 1905, only six made
Built by: Royce Ltd., Britain

Engine: Three cylinders, in line, in separate cast-iron blocks, fixed to four-bearing aluminium crankcase. Bore and stroke 101·6mm by 127mm, 3,089cc (4·0in×5·0in, 188·5cu.in). Non-detachable cylinder heads. Two valves per cylinder, overhead inlet valve completely exposed, and operated by pushrod and rocker, exhaust valve at side, directly operated from crankcase-mounted camshaft. Single up-draught Royce carburettor. Maximum power 15bhp, but rotating speed not quoted.

Transmission: Internal cone clutch, leather lined, and separate three-speed manual gearbox, without synchromesh. Right-hand quadrant gearchange. Open propeller shaft to straight-bevel 'live' rear axle.

Chassis: Separate steel chassis frame, with channel-section side members and channel-section cross braces. Forged front axle beam. Front suspension by 'semi-elliptic leaf springs. Rear suspension by semi-elliptic leaf springs, with additional transverse leaf spring, and radius rods. No dampers. Foot-operated brake bands

on drum mounted at tail of gearbox. Hand-operated drum brakes in rear wheel hubs. Non-detachable artillery-type road wheels. 810 × 90 tyres. Several choices of coachwork, all with exposed driving seat.

Dimensions: Wheelbase 8ft 7in (262cm), tracks (front and rear) 4ft (122cm). Overall length, depending on coachwork, about 12ft 4in (376cm). Unladen weight, chassis only, 1,600lb (726kg).

History: Henry Royce, a manufacturer of electrical items in Manchester, started designing his first car in 1903. Charles Rolls, a motor trader from the same city, tried one of the three prototypes in May 1904. The result was that they became partners and decided to market a whole family of cars with the same basic cylinder dimensions, in two-cylinder, three-cylinder, four-cylinder and six-cylinder form. The 'three', unlike the others, was unique because it had its cylinders individually cast. Even for Royce, already a stickler for high quality, the 'three' presented problems of balance and carburation. In size and performance it was not as economical as the little 'twin', and not as impressive as the 'four' or the 'six'. This probably explains why

only six were made, all in 1905 (although Rolls-Royce's production in that first year was very restricted indeed).

Apart from the engine, the rest of the design was conventional for the period, built without regard to cost-saving and already with a distinctive and very elegant Greek-style radiator. Like other cars of the time, the suspension was primitive, except that Royce cradled his longitudinal semi-elliptic leaf springs on a transverse leaf spring to improve the ride and also fitted radius arms to improve axle location. It seems certain that it was Rolls, whose garage already sold three-cylinder Panhards, who asked for this particular Rolls-Royce to be designed and manufactured. As a design itself, or as a commercially-successful model, the Rolls-Royce 'three' is not significant. Along with the rest of this original and very short-lived family, it was responsible for the beginning of a dynasty. Without these cars, exclusively supplied to Rolls in Manchester, there would have been no Silver Ghost and without the Ghost there would have been no 'Best Car in the World'. One car of the six built survives, beautifully restored, in private hands in Scotland.

Above: The only surviving 3-cylinder Rolls-Royce, of six built in 1905. This model was one of a family, all having engines of the same basic cylinder dimensions. Note the radiator shell.

Left: In spite of its modest engine, the three-cylinder car had a large and impressive open touring body. The driver had little weather protection, and his gear lever was on the right, tucked away behind the spare wheel rim. To give a soft ride there was a transverse 'helper' leaf spring. This was one of the few Rolls-Royce cars built by Royce in Manchester.
Below: The radiator badge used on these cars. As yet there was no 'RR'.

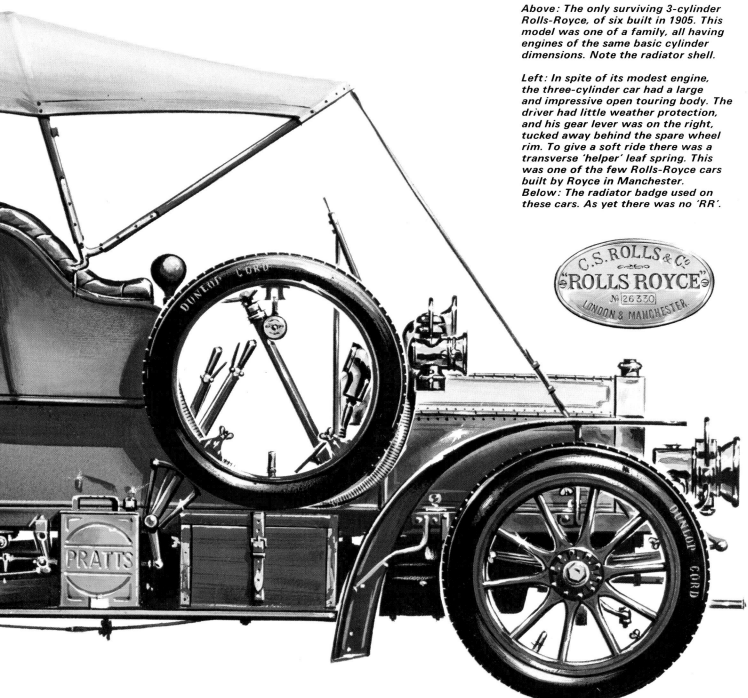

ROLLS-ROYCE SILVER GHOST

Silver Ghosts, built from 1906 to 1925 (data for 1907 model)
Built by: Rolls-Royce Ltd., Britain.
Engine: Six cylinders, in line, in two groups of three cast-iron blocks, bolted to seven-bearing light-alloy crankcase. Bore and stroke 114·3mm by 114·3mm, 7,036cc (4·5in × 4·5in, 429cu.in). Non-detachable cylinder heads. Two side valves per cylinder, with springs and shafts exposed, operated by rockers and anti-friction rollers from single crankcase-mounted camshaft. Single Rolls-Royce/Krebs two-jet carburettor. Power and torque figures never quoted by Rolls-Royce.
Transmission: Cone clutch, in unit with engine, and separately mounted four-speed manual gearbox (without synchromesh). Right-hand gearchange. Open propeller shaft to straight-bevel 'live' rear axle.
Chassis: Separate pressed-steel chassis frame, with channel-section side members and tubular and pressed cross braces. Forged front axle beam. Front suspension by semi-elliptic front springs. Rear suspension of 'platform' type by

semi-elliptic leaf springs, with rear extremities attached to single transverse leaf spring bolted centrally to the chassis frame. From 1908, Rolls-Royce friction-type dampers. Worm-and-nut steering. Foot-operated contracting-shoe brake acting on propeller shaft drum behind gearbox. Hand-operated expanding shoe brake in rear-wheel drums. Non-detachable artillery-type wood-spoke wheels. 875 × 105 front tyres and 875 × 120 rear tyres.
Dimensions: Wheelbase 11ft 3·5in, or 11ft 11·5in (344cm or 364cm), tracks (front and rear) 4ft 8in (142cm). Overall length, depending on coachwork, from 15ft 3·8in (467cm). Unladen weight (chassis only), from about 2,464lb (1,117kg).
History: Strictly speaking there has only ever been one 'Silver Ghost' — the car built up by Rolls-Royce on the thirteenth chassis, with a silver-painted touring body and silver-plated fittings, and given that name by them in 1907. A more conventional title would be the '40/50', which denotes the engine type and power rating,

but as this could be confused with later Phantoms it is never used.

The Ghost was conceived by Henry Royce in 1905 as a complete redesign of the six-cylinder Thirty which the company had been making for a short time. While the Thirty had suffered from all manner of technical problems in its engine, mainly concerned with the vibration characteristics of a long six, the Ghost was almost immediately very reliable; it was magnificently built and rightly became a legend in its own lifetime. Around 8,000 Ghosts were built in total, between 1907 and 1926, of which just over 1,700 were built by Rolls-Royce of America at Springfield, Massachusetts. In spite of the fact that the car was no more than technically up-to-

Below left: The very Silver Ghost, built in 1907, and now owned by Rolls-Royce, has silver-plated fittings.
Below right: A more typical four-seater 40/50 'Ghost' with timeless and elegant styling. About 8,000 were made.

ROLLS-ROYCE TWENTY

Twenty model, built from 1922 to 1929 (data for 1922 model)
Built by: Rolls-Royce Ltd., Britain.
Engine: Six cylinders, in line, in cast-iron block, with seven-bearing cast-iron crankcase. Bore and stroke 76·2mm by 114·3mm, 3,127cc (3·0in × 4·5in, 190·8cu.in). Detachable cast-iron cylinder head. Two overhead valves per cylinder,

operated by pushrods and rockers from single crankcase-mounted camshaft. Single two-jet Rolls-Royce carburettor, with separate starting carburettor. 53bhp (net) at 3,000rpm.
Transmission: Single-dry-plate clutch and three speed gearbox (no synchromesh), both in unit with engine. Direct-acting central gearchange (right-hand change when four-speed

box introduced in 1925). Open propeller shaft to spiral-bevel 'live' rear axle.
Chassis: Separate pressed-steel chassis frame, with channel-section side members and pressed and tubular cross bracing. Forged front axle beam. Semi-elliptic leaf springs at front and rear. Friction-type dampers (hydraulic dampers at front — 1926 on — and rear — 1928 on). Worm-

date when announced and well behind the times when dropped, it always seemed to perform better and in a more refined manner, than any of its contemporaries and it was with this car that the 'best car in the world' reputation was established. While the engineering, in many cases, was matched by concerns like Napier and Lanchester, the workmanship and the care taken in building were peerless.

The car was available with a variety of splendidly-built bodies – Rolls-Royce never built their own bodies at this point in their development – and a really well-equipped and kitted-out limousine of the type purchased by the gentry could weigh as much as 5,000lb (2,268kg). There were two wheelbase lengths, the shorter of which measured 11ft 3·5in, and a long, low, and exquisitely rivetted bonnet panel leading back from the Rolls-Royce radiator, whose shape was becoming famous, and which was scarcely to need change in the next seventy years.

The engine, although conventionally laid out, with side valves, was meticulously detailed, even to the extent of having rocking levers between the camshaft and the valve stems themselves. It had a very sturdy crankshaft, which defied the onset of torsional vibrations, and ran very silently indeed at all times. Despite the deliberately conventional design, and none better than Royce realised how it was slipping back in the 1920s, there were significant improvements over the years. The engine itself was 'stroked' to 7,428cc in 1909. The original gearbox had an 'overdrive' fourth gear at first, but three speeds were used between 1909 and 1913, after which a direct-top arrangement was restored. The platform-type of rear suspension soon gave way to normal semi-elliptic springs, and to cantilevers from 1912.

The straight-bevel axle, not silent enough for Royce, was replaced by a spiral-bevel design in 1923. A Lanchester-type engine torsional damper was added from 1911. Dynamo current generation was adopted from 1919. The foot-brake operated on a transmission drum at first, but on rear wheel drums from 1913. Four-wheel brakes arrived in 1924, along with the unique RR-type of transmission-driven servo. Hartford dampers were standardised in 1924. Wire wheels became optional in 1909, and were standardised in 1913.

At no time was the Silver Ghost a design leader, but at all times it was the best built and most carefully tested car in the world. It was never ostentatious, but always most obviously dignified. It was very expensive to buy, and was invariably tended by a full-time chauffeur with a heated motor-house and workshop at his disposal. It was the best, for the best, and expected the best treatment. It would have to be replaced by a supreme design – and the Phantom 1 was that design.

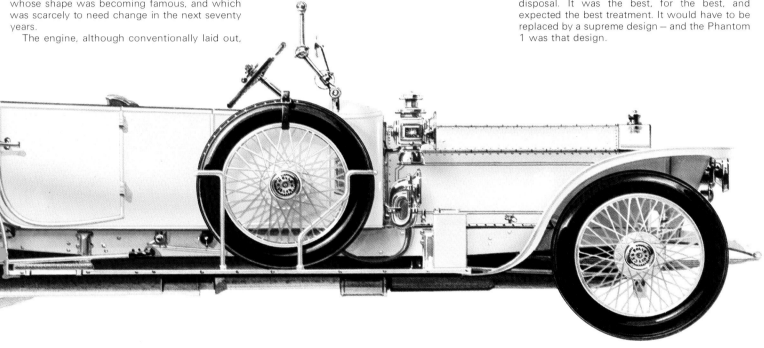

and-nut steering. Rear-wheel, mechanically operated drum brakes (four-wheel brakes from 1925 on). 32in centre-lock wire wheels. 4·5 × 32in tyres.
Dimensions: Wheelbase 10ft 9in (327·6cm), tracks (front and rear) 4ft 6in (137cm) Overall length 14ft 10in (452cm). Unladen weight (chassis only) 2,305lb (1,045kg).
History: The Twenty was conceived before World War I, but not released until 1922 and was much the smallest Rolls-Royce model for some years. If the Silver Ghost was the first true production Rolls, then the Twenty was the second. In a way it was even built down to a price, with a three-speed gearbox and a simple but beautifully-built six-cylinder engine, which inspired that of the later Phantoms. The engine

and its bare bones, left their mark on all Rolls-Royce sixes until the 1950s and the cylinder centre spacings were unchanged for more than thirty years. The Twenty was meant to be an owner-driver's car at a time when virtually every Ghost was chauffeur driven. It was thought most un-Rolls-like to have a three-speed gearbox with central change, so in 1925 this component

was changed to conform with customer preference. The Twenty (as also its successors the 20/25 and 25/30 models), was never a fast car, nor even a very large car, but it was built rigidly to the best standard the Derby concern could achieve. A total of 2,940 Twenties were built up to 1929, followed by 3,827 20/25s and 1,201 25/30s.

Left: People called the Twenty a 'small' Rolls-Royce, but it was still an exclusive and large car. This sleek four-seater touring car was built in 1923. Few owners of the period actually drove their Twenties—a whole genre of chauffeurs enjoyed this privilege.

Right: A recognition point for the Twenty was the horizontally-slatted radiator shell. This car was bodied in 1923 by the Grosvenor Carriage Co. The famous 'Spirit of Ecstacy' mascot has not yet been fitted. Special bodies took several months to be constructed.

ROLLS-ROYCE SILVER WRAITH

Silver Wraith models, built from 1947 to 1959 (data for 1947 model)

Built by: Rolls-Royce Ltd., Britain.

Engine: Six cylinders, in line, in seven-bearing cast-iron block/crankcase. Bore and stroke 88·9mm by 114·3mm, 4,257cc (3·5in × 4·5in, 259·8cu.in). Detachable aluminium cylinder head. Two valves per cylinder, overhead inlet and side exhaust, in so-called 'F-Head' layout; exhaust valve directly operated and inlet valve operated by pushrod and rocker, from single side-mounted camshaft. Single down-draught twin-choke Stromberg carburettor (downdraught Zenith on long-wheelbase models). Power and torque figures never quoted by Rolls-Royce.

Transmission: Single-dry-plate clutch and four-speed, synchromesh manual gearbox (no synchromesh on first gear), both in unit with engine. Remote-control right-hand gearchange. Two-piece open propeller shaft to hypoid-bevel 'live' rear axle.

Chassis: Separate pressed-steel chassis frame. Channel-section side members, with pressed-cruciform members and pressed and tubular cross bracing. Independent front suspension by coil springs and wishbones, with cross-coupled hydraulic lever arm dampers. Rear suspension by semi-elliptic leaf springs and controllable lever arm hydraulic dampers. Cam-and-roller steering. Four-wheel drum brakes, hydraulically operated at front, mechanically operated at rear, and assisted by gearbox-driven mechanical servo. 17in pressed-steel-disc wheels. 6·50 × 17in tyres (7·50 × 16in tyres on long-wheelbase versions).

Dimensions: Wheelbase 10ft 7in or 11ft 1in (322·5cm or 337·8cm), track (front) 4ft 10in (147·3cm), track (rear — short wheelbase) 5ft (152·4cm), track (rear — long wheelbase) 5ft 4in (162·6cm). Overall length 16ft 8in or 17ft 2in (508cm or 523cm). Unladen weight, depending on coachwork, from 4,700lb (2,131kg).

History: The Silver Wraith was purely a post-war model, but it stemmed from the pedigree of both the 1939-model Wraith and the Mark V Bentley. The pre-war Wraith was a much-modernised 25/30, but with a new welded-construction chassis and independent front suspension like that of the Phantom III. After the war, the Silver Wraith took on the mantle of the company's most expensive model (and was export-only for some time), along with the exposed-spring front suspension and a newly developed engine. This unit, of overhead-inlet, side-exhaust layout, was also shared with the new Bentley models and with the Silver Dawn, which followed, and was the final derivative of the 1920s-type Twenty design. In this guise it displaced 4,257cc, but before the end of its life it was to be bored out twice more — to 4,566cc and finally to 4,887cc. The Wraith was important because it was the only Rolls-Royce model supplied to coachbuilders in chassis form specifically for their attention. Post-war Bentleys and the Silver Dawn had a standard steel saloon

Above: Traditionally British lines of a 1950s Silver Wraith with coachbuilt body by Hooper; this was a Touring Limousine. Right: In 1954 Park Ward produced a less-formal Silver Wraith, which could be owner or chauffeur-driven.

body shell (although chassis were also supplied to coachbuilders to special order). The Silver Wraith was in production for twelve years, during which automatic transmission, power-assisted steering and many other improvements were standardised. Even though disc brakes were fitted by many British manufacturers in the late 1950s, they were never offered on the Wraith, which continued to use the famous transmission-driven servo for its drums. When the all-new Rolls-Royce V8 engine was launched in 1959, it was fitted to the Phantom V chassis, which replaced that of the Wraith and continuity with the 1920s was finally lost.

ROLLS-ROYCE PHANTOMS I AND II

Phantom I model, built from 1925 to 1929 (data for 1925 model)

Built by: Rolls-Royce Ltd., Britain.

Engine: Six cylinders, in line, in two groups of three cast-iron blocks, with seven-bearing light-alloy crankcase. Bore and stroke 107·9mm by 139·7mm, 7,668cc (4·25in × 5·5in, 467·9cu.in). One-piece detachable cast-iron cylinder head. Two overhead valves per cylinder, operated by pushrods and rockers from single crankcase-mounted camshaft. Single twin-jet Rolls-Royce carburettor, with separate starting carburettor on top of induction manifold. Power and torque figures never quoted by Rolls-Royce.

Transmission: Single-dry-plate clutch, in unit with engine. Separate four-speed manual gearbox, with remote-control right-hand gearchange. Propeller shaft, in torque tube, to spiral-bevel 'live' rear axle.

Chassis: Separate pressed-steel chassis frame, with channel-section side members and pressed, fabricated and tubular cross bracing. Forged front axle beam. Front suspension by semi-elliptic leaf springs. Rear suspension by canti-lever leaf springs. Adjustable friction-type dampers (lever arm hydraulic dampers from 1926 — front — and 1927 — rear). Worm-and-nut steering. Four-wheel rod and cable-operated drum brakes, with Rolls-Royce servo-assistance (motor driven from tail of transmission). 33in centre lock wire wheels (disc covers often specified). 5 × 33in tyres.

Dimensions: Wheelbase 12ft or 12ft 6·5in (366cm or 382cm). Short wheelbase tracks (front) 4ft 9in (144·7cm), (rear) 4ft 8in (142cm). Overall length, 15ft 10·2in or 16ft 4·7in (483cm or 499·6cm). Unladen weight, depending on coachwork, up to 6,500lb (2,948kg).

History: The New Phantom, as the Phantom I was called until it was replaced in 1929, was really only the third new production Rolls-Royce in more than 20 years — after the Silver Ghost

and the Twenty. It was a direct replacement for the Ghost and retained that car's chassis, complete with Edwardian suspension design. The engine, however, was much modified, being an amalgam of the best of the Ghost (having two three-cylinder blocks on a common crankcase), and of the much more modern and sleek Twenty layouts. There was no single part of the Twenty in the Phantom's engine, but many of the details were visually similar. One great advance (not a pioneering invention — Hispano-Suiza had seen to that) was the mechanical servo-motor assistance for the four-wheel brakes. The motor itself, a small disc-clutch device mounted to the side of the gearbox, used the momentum of the car to help brake actuation through friction in the discs. This was marvellously effective and refined, and was used by Rolls-Royce for a

Above: The elegance of a Phantom II hides the real advances in mechanical design compared with the Phantom I.

complete generation before they came to trust the normal vacuum-type of servo assistance.

Phantom I cars were built in Britain and (from Springfield) in the United States — a total of almost 3,500 being sold. The price in Britain was £1,850 for the chassis alone and it was a lucky and parsimonious customer who got his complete car for less than £2,600. As always, Rolls attempted to build the best possible car, as refined and as dignified as any other in the world, and they succeeded in this. They gave a full three-year-guarantee (much more extensive than for the Ghost) and the car's construction

made this quite practical. Rolls-Royce never built bodies themselves, but Phantoms were finished off in many guises — sporting, touring, or as limousines, by the cream of coachbuilders in Britain and North America. Standards of workmanship were very high and quality control second to none. The car, however, badly needed a new chassis and suspensions, which could only be supplied by a re-design.

In 1929 the New Phantom became the Phantom II. This was achieved by giving the car a new chassis frame with better controlled (semi-elliptic) springs all round; hydraulic damping had already been adopted for later New Phantoms. The engine was given more power, with an aluminium cylinder head and revised manifolding, while the transmission was simplified, with the gearbox now in unit with the engine. Strangely enough, this advance was to be reversed for the Phantom III in 1935. The axle was quietened by having hypoid-bevel gearing and the propeller shaft was now of the exposed type. Other and later improvements included centralised chassis lubrication and the gradual adoption of synchromesh gearing. Even so, the general design began to fall behind that of the

Above: The Phantom I of 1925 replaced the Silver Ghost, but kept that car's chassis and all its Edwardian mechanical items. This actual car was supplied to Lord Montagu, and has a splendid five-seater touring body.

prestigious continental rivals, particularly in performance and general silence and refinement. The car, however, was still splendidly built of the very best materials and was retired in 1935 in favour of the more advanced Phantom III.

ROLLS-ROYCE PHANTOM III

Phantom III models, built from 1935 to 1939
Built by: Rolls-Royce Ltd., Britain.
Engine: Twelve cylinders, in 60-degree vee-formation, in seven-bearing light-alloy block/crankcase. Bore and stroke 82·5mm by 114·3mm, 7,338cc (3·25in × 4·5in, 447·7cu.in). Two detachable light-alloy cylinder heads. Two overhead valves per cylinder, operated by pushrods, rockers and hydraulic tappets from single camshaft mounted in centre of cylinder block 'vee'. Single down-draught twin-choke carburettor. Power and torque figures never quoted by Rolls-Royce.

Transmission: Single-dry-plate clutch, in unit with engine. Separate four-speed, synchromesh manual gearbox (no synchromesh on first gear). Remote-control right-hand gearchange. Open propeller shaft to hypoid-bevel 'live' rear axle.

Chassis: Separate pressed-steel chassis frame, with box-section side members and pressed cruciform, fabricated and tubular cross bracing. Independent front suspension by wishbones and coil springs in oil-filled casing, also containing adjustable hydraulic lever arm dampers. Rear suspension by semi-elliptic leaf springs and anti-roll bar. Hydraulic lever arm dampers. Cam-and-roller steering. Four-wheel, cable-operated brakes, with servo-assistance by motor driven from back of gearbox. Centralised chassis lubrication. 18in centre-lock wire wheels. 7·00 × 18in tyres.
Coachwork not supplied by Rolls-Royce. Several approved specialist coachbuilders and a multitude of styles.

Dimensions: Wheelbase 11ft 10in (361cm), track (front) 5ft 3in (160cm), track (rear) 5ft 1in (155cm). Overall length (depending on coachwork) 16ft 10in (513cm). Unladen weight from 5,400lb (2,449kg).

History: Under Sir Henry Royce, Rolls-Royce had stuck too long to the successful traditions of the Ghosts and Phantoms. By the time of his death, in 1933, it was already obvious that the next new 'big' Rolls would have to jump forward by a complete generation. The new car, conceived before Royce died, but not revealed until the end of 1935, was a magnificent piece of engineering in all respects. At a stroke, it seemed, Rolls-Royce could once again claim to be making 'The best car in the world'. Logically enough, the new car was called a Phantom III, but there was no part of the old Phantom car carried forward. In that the new design had a separate chassis and was still clothed by the same exclusive band of coachbuilders, there was some family resemblance (and of course the radiator design was not changed), but that was all. The new car's two great innovations were that it had independent front suspension, and that it had a very advanced V12 engine. Neither was altogether unexpected. Independent suspension was well established in North America and becoming fashionable in Europe, while Rolls-Royce themselves (with aero-engines) were already noted for their V12 designs.

The engine itself was new from end to end, except that the bore and stroke were the same as the smaller six-cylinder Rolls-Royce. It leaned heavily on the R-Type and Merlin aero-engine experience, with light-alloy castings and wet liners, but the hydraulically operated tappets were a British innovation, inspired from Detroit. It is interesting to know that Rolls-Royce had been experimenting with new engines for many years; the most promising alternative had been a straight-eight. A V8 had also been considered, but rejected as it was neither exclusive enough, nor smooth enough to satisfy the perfectionist engineers. The new V12, although never officially given a power output by the discreet management, was nevertheless man enough to propel cars weighing up to 6,000lb (2,721kg) at more than 90mph. Fuel consumption, on the other hand, rarely amounted to better than about 10mpg, but to a Rolls-Royce owner this was not something for him to worry about. In 1935, when announced, the Phantom III cost more than

£2,500 with the cheapest of the RR-approved bodies, which made it easily the most expensive of all British cars. Only hand-built machines like the best of Hispano-Suiza, or the virtually unobtainable Grosser Mercedes, were as costly.

It has to be said that the car was not necessarily the fastest, nor even the grandest, of all, but it had a combination of virtues quite unmatched by any other make and model of car at the time. The suspension, in fact, was very advanced for the period and exceptionally so for an enormous

Above: By 1939 a typical Phantom III had become even more impressive and dignified than at first. This splendid machine had an H. J. Mulliner-built four-door body with twin side-mounted spare wheels. The Phantom III was a massive car—about 17 feet long—but the body shape usually disguised this. A complete car could cost between £2,700 and £3,000 depending on details. Most have been lovingly preserved.

Above left: 'Maharajah' drop head styling and a very appropriate number plate for this silver-plated Phantom III. Cost was, literally, no object.

Above: An owner-driver Phantom III, by the Barker coachbuilders. This was built in 1936, but the same style was shown at Olympia in 1935 as a 'non-runner'.

prestige car. It was based on a General Motors design and Rolls-Royce paid royalties for the privilege of using it. The chassis, certainly, was very stiff and the handling was better than almost any other large saloon in the world. Even so, it was as an ultra-dignified town carriage that the Phantom III sold so well and the company notched up an impressive list of titled customers.

British coachbuilders produced a variety of sumptuous bodies for the chassis, some of them surprisingly sporting, but the car was most often seen as an ultra-sophisticated town carriage or limousine. Very few Phantom IIIs were driven by their first owners, which must have been a source of great joy to their chauffeurs. There was a vast amount of space in the rear seat area where the titled or moneyed owner would normally recline and much work went into making the ride first class.

In spite of its price and in spite of the work that had gone into the design, the V12 engine was not immune from lubrication problems. The hydraulic tappets, in particular, demanded absolutely clean and well-filtered oil to work properly, which was a source of worry to second and subsequent owners. The Phantom III went out of production at the end of 1939, with the outbreak of war, and would have been much too expensive to re-introduce in 1945/46. It was, and is, the most exclusive of all pre-war pro-duction-line' Rolls-Royce cars, a total of 710 being built in about four years.

ROLLS-ROYCE SILVER SHADOW AND CAMARGUE

Rolls-Royce Silver Shadow four-door, four-door long-wheelbase, and coachbuilt two-door Corniche, built from 1965 to date (data for 1966 Shadow)

Built by: Rolls-Royce Ltd. (since 1971, Rolls-Royce Motors Ltd.), Britain.

Engine: Eight cylinders, in 90-degree vee-formation, in five-bearing cast-alloy cylinder block. Bore and stroke 104·4mm by 91·4mm, 6,230cc (4·1in × 3·6in, 380cu.in). Two light-alloy cylinder heads. Two overhead valves per cylinder, inclined in wedge combustion chambers and operated by pushrods, hydraulic tappets and rockers, from single camshaft mounted in cylinder block 'vee'. Two side-draught constant-vacuum SU carburettors. Neither power nor torque figures quoted by Rolls-Royce.

Transmission: General Motors/Rolls-Royce four-speed automatic transmission, with torque converter. Steering-column gearchange. No manual transmission option. One-piece open propeller shaft to subframe-mounted hypoid-bevel final-drive unit. Exposed, universally jointed drive shafts to rear wheels.

Chassis: Unitary-construction pressed-steel four-door saloon body/chassis unit. Front and rear suspensions mounted on pressed-steel subframes, attached to main shell. Independent front suspension by wishbones, coil springs and anti-roll bar. Independent rear suspension by semi-trailing wishbones and coil springs. Telescopic dampers and self-levelling controls. Power-assisted recirculating-ball steering. Four-wheel disc brakes with multiple hydraulic circuits. 15in pressed-steel-disc wheels. 8·45 × 15in tyres.

Dimensions: Wheelbase 9ft 11·5in (304cm), tracks (front and rear) 4ft 9·5in (146cm). Overall length 16ft 11·5in (417cm). Unladen weight 4,636lb (2,100kg).

History: After nearly ten years development of systems and components, Rolls-Royce announced their new Silver Shadow in 1965. Apart from the 6·2-litre light-alloy V8 engine and the four-speed automatic transmission, carried over from the superseded Silver Cloud model, the Shadow was an all-new concept. No previous Rolls had used a unitary-construction body shell, and none had offered independent rear suspension, let alone a complex but effective self-levelling control system. Four-wheel disc brakes were new, as was the safety-conscious duplicated hydraulic circuitry which went with them. Every effort had gone into eliminating extraneous noises from the cabin and the suspensions were most carefully mounted on insulated sub-frames. There was also the Bentley T-Series, identical with the Shadow

Above left: The Silver Shadow in 1974 guise, with flared wheel arches and radial-ply tyres. Recent versions have an air dam under the bumper and many hidden mechanical improvements.
Above: Mulliner/Park Ward's special drophead car of 1966 became the faster Corniche of 1971. There is also a two-door closed coupe version of this body. The underframe and mechanicals are as for the Shadow, but power is boosted.

except for its radiator and badging. This 'badge engineering' was no stigma and both cars continue to this day. Although the Shadow has been in production for more than ten years, it is still mechanically abreast of the times. The styling was always meant to be 'timeless' and it remains so, but it is now very familiar. Production has crept up over the years — the factory at Crewe can now make more than 4,000 cars in a year, every one of which is sold before completion.

Coachbuilders had a hard time making special bodies for the Shadow. Only Mulliner-Park Ward (owned by Rolls-Royce) were supplied with rolling underbody units. Only 50 of the James Young two-door saloon were made, these being converted from complete four-door cars. The Mulliner cars — a two door coupé and a two-door convertible — were announced in 1966. In 1971, the Mulliner cars were updated and re-named Corniches, becoming official members of the Rolls-Royce Shadow family. In the late 1960s, too, a longer-wheelbase Shadow (with or without division) had been announced, although this was never badged as a Bentley. Over the years many mechanical improvements have unobtrusively been phased in. A new three-speed automatic transmission arrived in 1968 and in 1970 the engine was enlarged, by lengthening the stroke, to 6,750cc. Major suspension revisions and flared wheel arches to accommodate fatter tyres were phased in in 1974 and in 1976 a further facia revision was incorporated. Shadow II was announced in 1977. Now, as then, Rolls-Royce like to think of their car as 'The Best Car in the World'.

ROLLS-ROYCE CAMARGUE
Camargue Coupé, introduced in 1975
Built by: Rolls-Royce Motors Ltd., Britain.
Specification as for Rolls-Royce Silver Shadow, except for engine with single Solex carburettor. Special two-door light-alloy closed four-seater coachwork by Mulliner-Park Ward.
Dimensions: Wheelbase 10ft (305cm), track (front) 5ft (152cm), track (rear) 4ft 11·5in (151cm). Overall length 16ft 11·5in (417cm). Unladen weight 5,175lb (2,347kg).
History: The Camargue, quite simply, is the most expensive production car in the world. Rolls-Royce conceived it that way. The Camargue, in Britain, is double the price of a Silver Shadow saloon. It is based on the same chassis and power train as the Silver Shadow, except that further work has taken place on the engine to reduce emissions. A feature is the automatic air-conditioning, standard to every Camargue, claimed to be the most advanced in the world. The bodies are painstakingly made by Mulliner-Park Ward in North London, at the rate of just one car every week, and the waiting list stretches into years. Styling was by Pininfarina, to a Rolls-Royce brief, and the classic radiator shell has been retained. Even so, for all that money, it is more difficult to get into the rear seats than the Shadow and the performance is in no way improved. On exclusiveness alone, however, the Camargue is extremely desirable. Almost every example built is earmarked for an export market.

Left: The Camargue, introduced in 1975 is probably the world's most exclusive car. Not more than 100 are built in a year; there is a long waiting list.

205

ROLLS-ROYCE PHANTOM IV

Phantom IVs, built from 1950 to 1956
Built by: Rolls-Royce Ltd., Britain.
Engine: Eight cylinders, in line, in nine-bearing cast-iron combined block/crankcase. Bore and stroke 88·9mm by 114·3mm, 5,675cc (3·5in × 4·5in, 346·3cu.in). Detachable cast aluminium cylinder head. Two valves per cylinder, in overhead inlet and side exhaust layout; inlet valves operated by pushrods and rockers, exhaust valves operated by tappets, both from single camshaft mounted in side of crankcase Twin-choke down-draught Stromberg carburettor. Power output and torque figures never quoted by Rolls-Royce.
Transmission: Single-dry-plate clutch and four-speed, synchromesh manual gearbox (without synchromesh on first gear), both in unit with front-mounted engine. Remote-control right-hand gearchange. Open propeller shaft to hypoid-bevel 'live' rear axle.
Chassis: Separate pressed-steel chassis frame, with box-section and channel-section side members, pressed-steel box-section cruciform and pressed and tubular cross bracings. Independent front suspension by coil springs, wishbones and anti-roll bar. Rear suspension by semi-elliptic leaf springs. Lever-arm hydraulic dampers, adjustable at rear. Cam-and-roller steering. Four-wheel drum brakes, hydraulic at front, mechanical at rear, with servo assistance from friction servo mounted on transmission. 17in pressed-steel disc wheels. 7·00 × 17in tyres. Ceremonial four-door limousine coachwork by specialist coachbuilders.
Dimensions: Wheelbase 12ft 1in (368cm), track (front) 4ft 10·5in (148·6cm), track (rear) 5ft 3in (160cm). Overall length 19ft 1·5in (583cm). Unladen weight not quoted — approximately 5,000lb (2,268kg).
History: Apart from the original hand-built cars of 1903, the Phantom IV is undoubtedly the most exclusive Rolls-Royce of all time. It was conceived purely for use by Royalty and Heads of State and in six years no more than 16 examples were made. In its parentage the Phantom IV

owes nothing at all to the obsolete Phantom III, which disappeared with the arrival of World War II, but is related to the Silver Wraith and to the military machinery which Rolls-Royce were then developing. The Silver Wraith had appeared in 1947, with chassis and mechanicals developed from the Mark VI Bentley. The Phantom IV followed similar lines; but had a longer wheelbase to accommodate a longer engine. This was a

superbly 'civilianised' version of the B-range straight-eight used in considerable quantity by the British Army in military vehicles and it shared its cylinder dimensions, valve gear, and other family 'trademarks' with the Bentley Mk VI/Rolls-Royce Silver Dawn six-cylinder cars. The transmission — with that superb right-hand gearchange — the wide back axle and the suspensions were all shared with the Silver Wraith, but the

---

ROVER GAS TURBINE CARS

Rover T1 (JET 1), T2, T3, T4 and Rover-BRM (data for T3)
Built by: Rover Co. Ltd., Britain.
Engine: 2S/100 automotive gas turbine unit, having single-stage centrifugal compressor rotor, driven by axial-flow compressor turbine. Single-stage axial-flow power turbine rotor, not physically connected to compressor turbine shaft. Compressor shaft runs up to 52,000rpm. Minimum self-sustaining speed 20,000rpm. No valves or camshafts. Continuous gas flow and continuous combustion. Simple heat exchange transfers heat from exhaust gases to inlet air. Maximum power 110bhp at 52,000 compressor shaft rpm.
Transmission: No clutch and no multi-ratio gearbox. Overall three-stage reduction gearing between power turbine rotor and drive shafts — 28·92 to 1. Power turbine shaft directly connected to simple forward/reverse control and directly connected to spiral-bevel final-drive unit. Four-wheel drive from transmission unit, directly to rear wheels by exposed, universally jointed drive shafts and via two-piece propeller shaft to spiral-bevel front final drive, then by exposed, universally jointed drive shafts to front wheels. Remote-control central gearchange.
Chassis: Unitary-construction body/chassis unit, coupé style, with pressed steel structural 'chassis' members, light-alloy honeycomb and light-alloy sheet, topped by glassfibre body shell and skin panels. Mid-mounted gas-turbine unit, immediately behind seats. Independent front suspension by fixed-length drive shafts, upper wishbones, coil springs and anti-roll bar. Rear suspension by De Dion system, with fixed-length drive shafts, radius arms and coil springs. Telescopic dampers. Rack-and-pinion steering.

Four-wheel, hydraulically operated disc brakes, inboard-mounted. 15in pressed-steel disc wheels. 5·90 × 15in tyres.
Dimensions: Wheelbase 7ft 10in (239cm), tracks (front and rear) 4ft 0·5in (123cm). Overall length 12ft 5·7in (380cm). Unladen weight 2,085lb (911kg).
History: Rover's interest in gas turbines stems from 1940, when they were asked to help in developing the earliest Whittle jet engines for aeroplane use. After 1945, a small team began developing private car and industrial turbine units. At first it was thought that the typical gas turbine problems of high construction costs and poor fuel (paraffin/kerosene) consumption could be solved, but 20 years of work showed this to be a vain hope. In that time, however, Rover built a series of more and more practical gas-turbine cars and sold hundreds of marine and auxiliary-use aviation units. After the formation of British Leyland in 1968, work was also directed to making turbine-powered trucks practical, but this work also was abandoned in the mid 1970s.
Rover's first turbine car was 'JET 1', com-

Left: Rover's first purpose-built gas turbine car, T3, dates from 1956, and has a rear-mounted engine and four-wheel-drive. Apart from high paraffin consumption, it was an excellent car.

pleted and demonstrated in 1950. In effect this was a Rover 75 car with converted sports-car type of bodywork, and a front-mounted turbine. This car, in spite of its shape, achieved 150mph in officially timed test runs. Next was T2, a Rover 90 saloon with front-mounted engine. T3, however, was an all-new and very practical

12ft 1in wheelbase allowed a number of splendidly proportioned ceremonial limousines to be built, usually by Park Ward or by H. J. Mulliner. Attention to detail is shown in the road wheels, fixed by no fewer than ten nuts each, in the controllable damper settings and in the intricacies of the mechanical-servo assistance for the brakes. The best of Rolls-Royces, whenever built, should always be like that. No price

was ever quoted, as no private individual ever bought one, and in purely practical terms the Phantom IV can only have been a nuisance to Rolls-Royce at Crewe. It was dropped in 1956 and a successor — the V8 engined Phantom V — did not arrive until 1959. The V, and its descendant the VI, were allowed out on general sale, but in recent years they have been built at a rate of only about 50 cars every year.

Above left: A ceremonial Phantom IV carries Harold Wilson (then British Prime Minister) to talks in Salisbury, Rhodesia.
Above: A Phantom V owned by H.M. Queen Elizabeth II. It is easily recognisable by its high roof and bigger-than-standard glass area, and is directly descended from the very rare Phantom IVs, but had a vee-8 compared with a straight-eight engine.

Above: Rover and BRM combined in 1963 to build a racing sports car. This was used at Le Mans with great success, then stylishly re-bodied for the 1965 race. Driven by Graham Hill and Jackie Stewart, it averaged 98·2mph and took tenth place. The intakes by the doors are for the engine, behind the seats.

design, with mid-mounted gas turbine engine, four-wheel-drive, and de Dion rear suspension. Ideas from this car eventually found their way into the new Rover 2000 car of a few years later. The last road car was T4, based on prototype Rover 2000 body/chassis units, but with a front-mounted turbine engine and front-wheel-drive.

This car was first shown in 1961. Last of all the turbine cars was the Rover-BRM racing two-seater, which combined Rover expertise with a widened BRM grand prix car chassis. The car raced twice at Le Mans. In 1963 it was driven by Graham Hill and Richie Ginther in a non-competitive 'demonstration', averaging 107·84

mph for the 24 hours. In 1965, with a much sleeker body shell and a radically new type of revolving heat exchanger, it was driven by Graham Hill and Jackie Stewart into 10th place at 98·2mph. Development work on private-car turbine units was abandoned in 1965, but every Rover prototype except T2 survives.

SAAB 93, 95 AND 96

Saab 93 model, introduced 1955, replaced by 95 and 96 in 1960 (data for 93)

Built by: Svenska Aeroplan Aktiebolaget, Sweden.

Engine: Three cylinders, in line, in four-bearing cast-iron block. Two-stroke operation, using petroil mixture for fuel and lubrication. Bore and stroke 66mm by 72·9mm, 748cc (2·60in × 2·87in, 45·6cu.in). Detachable light-alloy cylinder head. No valves or camshaft, porting and transfer porting all contained in cylinder block. Single down-draught Solex carburettor. Maximum power 38bhp at 5,000rpm. Maximum torque 52lb.ft at 2,000rpm.

Transmission: Single-dry-plate clutch and three-speed, synchromesh manual gearbox (no synchromesh on first gear), in front-wheel-drive power pack. Engine ahead of front wheel line and gearbox behind that line. Steering column gearchange. Freewheel standardised, capable of being locked out of action, giving solid drive. Exposed, universally jointed drive shafts to front wheels.

Chassis: Pressed-steel, unitary-construction body/chassis unit, sold only as a two-door saloon in fastback style. Independent front suspension by coil springs, wishbones and anti-roll bar. Rear suspension by 'dead' beam axle, coil springs and radius arms. Telescopic dampers. Four-wheel, hydraulically operated drum brakes. 15in pressed-steel-disc wheels. 5·00 × 15in tyres.

Dimensions: Wheelbase 8ft 2in (249cm), tracks (front and rear) 4ft (122cm). Overall length 13ft 1·1in (399cm). Unladen weight, approximately 1,800lb (816kg).

History: Saab (the name is an abbreviation of the legal title), Sweden's noted aeroplane manufacturers designed and tested their first car during World War II (in which Sweden was neutral) and unveiled it as the Saab 92 in 1947. The number, 92, as with later model numbers, merely indicates the new car's project number within the company. The 92 set the style for future Saabs, having a two-stroke engine of DKW-type and front-wheel drive with a freewheel. The 92, however, had torsion-bar suspension, which was dropped when the time came for a change. The body had obviously been shown to a wind-tunnel, for it was more aerodynamic than beautiful, while being immensely strong and functional.

The Saab 93, announced in 1955, was a natural successor to the 92 in every way. The suspension was simplified to use coil springs and the body restyled to become rather less bizarre, but the general principles were retained. Whereas the 92 had used a twin-cylinder engine, the 93 had a three-cylinder 748cc engine, with more power and sweeter torque characteristics. There was also a GT version of the 93, much tuned and reputedly capable of more than 90mph. This was eminently suitable for high-speed rallying, where the Saabs were already making quite a name for themselves. The combination of tuneability, front-wheel drive, a smooth underside, and the talents of a large and incredibly brave driver called Eric Carlsson, was irresistible. Sales were never very high, not in the same league as Ford or VW for instance, but they continued to increase. By 1960, with the 93 about to be replaced, home sales totalled nearly

SALMSON

Grand Sport, GSC and Grand Prix cars, built from 1923 to 1930 (data for 1923 GS model)

Built by: Société des Moteurs Salmson, France.

Engine: Four-cylinders, in line, in cast-iron block, with two-bearing light-alloy crankcase. Bore and stroke 62mm by 90mm, 1,087cc (2·44in × 3·54in, 66·3cu.in). Detachable cast-iron cylinder head. Two overhead valves per cylinder, opposed to each other at 60 degrees in part-spherical combustion chambers and operated by inverted-bucket tappets from twin overhead camshafts. Single side-draught Solex carburettor. Maximum power 36bhp.

Transmission: Cone clutch and three-speed manual gearbox (without synchromesh), both in unit with front-mounted engine. Direct-acting central gearchange. Propeller shaft, enclosed in torque tube, driving straight-bevel final drive, without differential.

Chassis: Separate pressed-steel chassis frame, with channel-section side members and tubular cross bracing. Forged front axle beam. Front suspension by semi-elliptic leaf springs. Rear suspension by trailing quarter-elliptic leaf springs and radius arms tied to torque tube. Friction-type dampers. Rear wheel brakes only, in drums, cable operated. Centre-lock wire wheels. 720 × 120mm tyres.

Dimensions: Wheelbase 8ft 6in (259cm), tracks (front and rear) 3ft 6in (106·7cm). Overall length 10ft (305cm).

History: The Salmson pedigree dates from 1919, but as the first two years were spent in building GN cycle cars under licence, the first true Salmson cars arrived in 1921. Although the marque continued in production near Paris until the 1950s, its most noted period was in the 1920s, when Salmson race cars with 1,100cc four-cylinder engines performed valiantly in many guises and especially in *Voiturette* events. The height of Salmson's career was in 1927, when Salmson cars took second and third places in the Le Mans 24-hour race. The twin-cam touring and sports cars, introduced in 1922, ran only to 1930 and about 2,700 were built in all. The cars were noted as being *the* first production twin-cams, with neat but otherwise conventional mechanical layouts. The vogue for small French sports cars (Amilcar was another such make) disappeared suddenly towards the end of the 1920s, particularly when much cheaper rivals from MG and others came on to the scene. A small number of these were 'Service de Course' special machines, sold to agents and racing drivers specifically to show the flag and to contest the less-important events.

Below: The Salmson was a French car of the 1920s—a true 'vintage' sports car with small engine and lightweight construction. This is a 1925 Grand Sport model, with the 1,087cc twin-cam engine. Like the Amilcar, Salmsons could be toured or raced with success.

Below left: The Saab pedigree was established in 1947 when the Saab 92 model, shown here, was announced. It had front-wheel-drive and a twin-cylinder two-stroke engine. Below right: By 1958 the Saab had become the 93B, with three-cylinder 748cc engine. A notable feature was a freewheel in the transmission, and the aircraft-inspired aerodynamics in the shape.

14,000, while more than 11,000 of them were exported.

In 1960, the 93 gave way to the 95 and 96 — an estate and saloon respectively — which were restyled and further improved, but were faithful to the original concept. With the passing of time, the two-stroke engine became unpopular, mainly on the grounds of pollution from its exhaust system and because it was none too powerful unless tuned to inflexible limits. The

Saab 96 was therefore given a transplant of the German 1·5-litre V4 engine, and has only recently been discontinued. There have also been rare coupé versions of the cars, but the two-door saloons have provided interesting and instantly recognisable motoring for hundreds of thousands of Saab customers throughout the world. Britain and the United States, incidentally, have been two of the most popular export markets.

SERPOLLET

Flat-four steam cars, built from 1900 to 1903 (data for 1900 6hp model)

Built by: Gardner Serpollet, France.

Engine: Four cylinders, horizontally opposed, with cast-iron cylinders, lying parallel to the ground and to the chassis side-members, around light-alloy crankcase. Bore and stroke 65mm by 72mm, 956cc (2·56in × 2·83in, 58·3cu.in). Steam generator, heated by paraffin burners, under rear seats, engine under floor ahead of steam generator. Side-mounted valves, operated by cams with variable action. Maximum power 6bhp.

Transmission: No clutch and no variable-ratio gearbox. Drive from end of crankshaft to rear axle by exposed chain to differential and 'live' axle layout.

Chassis: Separate wrought-iron chassis frame, with channel-section side members and pressed cross members. Forged front axle beam. Front and rear suspension by semi-elliptic leaf springs. No dampers. Direct link-and-lever steering. Rod-operated foot brake, by contracting band, on differential gear on rear axle. Hand brake rod-operated on contracting bands on rear wheel hub drums. Fixed artillery-style road wheels.

Dimensions: Unladen weight 2,205lb (1,000 kg).

History: Léon Serpollet was a steam-car pioneer, with several notable engineering advances to his name including the multi-tube flash boiler of 1888. The first Serpollets sold were heavy and slow tricycles with flat-twin engines, but four-wheelers were sold from 1891. Coke was supplanted by paraffin as fuel in the 1890s and the major turning point came in 1898 when Serpollet was joined by the wealthy American Frank Gardner, which allowed a factory to be set up on a quantity-production basis. A series of flat-four steam-engined cars was on the market in 1900 — 6hp, 9hp and 12hp

types, all with the same basic layout and details. The engine was under the passenger floor in the classic 'steam-car' position, and the transmission (without clutch or normal gearbox) was simplicity itself. This range of cars stood up well for itself in the market place, but Serpollet's achievement in taking the world's Land Speed Record at 75·06mph in a big-engined steamer in 1902 gave them much valuable publicity. The original designs were replaced by new flat-fours in 1903 and by further improved cars in 1904, in which a feature was engines which could be

run in neutral (which was not possible on the first cars, whose engines were always connected to the axle by the drive chain). Serpollet himself died in 1907 and the famous cars died with him. They were never revived.

Below: By the beginning of the Edwardian era, Serpollets looked conventional but stuck to steam engines to the end.

SHEFFIELD-SIMPLEX 45HP

45hp model, built from 1908 to 1912 (data for original 1908 model)
Built by: Sheffield-Simplex Motor Works Ltd., Britain.
Engine: Six-cylinders, in line, in three cast-iron blocks, with light-alloy crankcase. Bore and stroke 114·3mm by 114·3mm, 7,037cc (4·5in × 4·5in, 429·4cu.in). Fixed cast-iron cylinder heads. Two side valves per cylinder, exposed on left-hand side of cylinder block and operated directly by single camshaft mounted in side of crankcase. Craven carburettor. Maximum power about 45bhp.
Transmission: Multiple-dry-plate (45) clutch, in unit with front-mounted engine, and propeller shaft, enclosed in torque tube, connected to two-speed manual gearbox (without synchromesh) mounted in unit with straight bevel 'live' rear axle. Remote-control right-hand gearchange.
Chassis: Separate pressed-steel chassis frame, with channel-section side members and tubular cross bracing. Forged front axle beam. Front and rear suspension by semi-elliptic leaf springs. No

dampers. Worm-and-nut steering. Rear-wheel drum brakes, operated by foot pedal or by hand lever mounted outside bodywork on right. Clutch withdrawal mechanism also operated by same pedal. Centre-lock wire wheels. 875 × 105mm tyres (front) and 880 × 120mm tyres (rear).
Open four/five seater coachwork.
Dimensions: Wheelbase 10ft 8·5in (326·4cm), tracks (front and rear), 4ft 8in (142cm). Overall length 14ft 4in (437cm). Unladen weight (chassis only) 2,350lb (1,066kg).
History: The ancestor of these Yorkshire-built cars was the Brotherhood-Crocker of 1904, a Mercédès-like chain-driven machine. This was renamed Sheffield-Simplex in 1907. In 1908 it was replaced by three new models, two being 14/20 and 20/30hp copies of existing Renaults, while the new 45hp machine was all-new and very individual. The car, with its big and flexible 7-litre six was in the luxury class and was meant to be driven without changing gear. The two-speed transmission was in unit with the back axle case, and bottom gear was meant only for emer-

gencies. Other quirks were that one opened the throttle by moving the pedal sideways (instead of pushing it down) and that the same floor pedal first operated the clutch withdrawal fork and then, when pushed further, operated the brakes. This made smooth progress a delicately learned business. The makers had a change of heart in 1911 about flexibility, when they gave the car a three-speed transmission, still in unit with the axle. Unsprung weight was considerable, but at the speeds such cars habitually achieved this posed few problems. The 45hp car was replaced by the more conventional 30hp in 1912, and the last Sheffield-Simplex car of all was built in 1922.

Below: One of several very grand and stately cars sold in Britain in Edwardian times, the Sheffield-Simplex 45hp model was vast yet mechanically simple. The 7-litre engine drove through a two-speed gearbox on the back axle, but it was really meant as a 'one-speed' motor car. This is a 1912 model.

SINGER NINE

Nine sports, built from 1932 to 1937 (data for 1935 Special Speed Le Mans model)
Built by: Singer Motors Ltd, Britain.
Engine: Four cylinders, in line, in two-bearing cast-iron block/crankcase. Bore and stroke 60mm by 86mm, 972cc (2·36in × 3·38in, 59·3cu.in). Detachable cast-iron cylinder head. Two overhead valves per cylinder, operated by fingers from single overhead camshaft. Two horizontal constant-vacuum SU carburettors. Maximum power 41bhp at 5,500rpm.
Transmission: Single-dry-plate clutch and four-speed manual gearbox (without synchromesh), both in unit with front-mounted engine. Remote-control central gearchange. Open propeller shaft to spiral-bevel 'live' rear axle.
Chassis: Separate pressed-steel chassis frame, with channel-section side members and tubular and pressed cross bracing. Forged front axle beam. Front and rear suspension by semi-elliptic leaf springs. Friction-type dampers. Worm-and-nut steering. Four-wheel, hydraulically operated drum brakes, 18in centre-lock wire wheels. 4·50 × 18in tyres.
Open two-seater sports car bodywork.
Dimensions: Wheelbase 7ft 7in (231cm), tracks (front and rear) 3ft 9in (114cm). Overall length 11ft 9in (358cm). Unladen weight 1,766lb (801kg).
History: Singer production started in 1905

and the Coventry-based company expanded rapidly in Edwardian and Vintage times. By the middle 1920s, Singer's British production was only outstripped by the two giants – Austin and Morris. To keep up their position, Singer continued to widen their model range and there is no doubt that this later led them into financial problems. A cornerstone of their 1930s model range was the little two-bearing overhead-cam four-cylinder engine. First sold in 1927, cars with this engine became more popular as the Depression made its effect. There were sporting Singer Juniors from 1928, but the first proper Singer Nine sports car arrived in July 1932. With its hydraulic brakes and revvy 972cc, it gave as much performance as any equivalent MG and found a lot of custom. In the next three years Singer developed their sports car further, first naming it the Le Mans, and later still (for 1935) the Le Mans Speed Special. With more than 40bhp from less than a litre, it was an efficient little engine (one which was also adopted by HRG for their 1100 model) and it had the chunky good looks expected of any popular-price 1930s sports car. The twin exposed spare wheels, double-hump facia outlines, sprung Bluemels-type steering wheel, remote gearchange with stubby lever, slab tank and centre-lock wire wheels were all absolutely typical – and apart from the radiator design it might just as well have

been an MG Midget. Nor was it only good looks, for the Speed Special was good for more than 70mph in standard trim. Singer went in for motor sport too – with great success in sporting trials and rallies, but rather less in motor racing. One well-publicised crash in the 1935 Tourist Trophy, where three ultra-light team cars crashed with broken steering at the same corner, did nothing for their reputation, which was a pity. The Singer Nine Le Mans was the equal of any MG, PA or PB, but MG had more glamour. As a strain, the Le Mans disappeared in 1937, and with it, most of Singer's sporting pretensions.

Right: In the 1930s there were many successful British sports cars. The Singer Nine sold well in competition with J-Type and P-Type MG Midgets. Between 1932 and 1937 there were several versions, but all shared the same overhead cam 972cc engine, which was very tuneable in spite of a two-bearing crank. The 'Le Mans' model name followed successful showings in the French 24 Hour race, and this example was built in 1935 at the height of the range's fame. This was an occasional four-seater, but two-seat versions were sold, and the factory raced ultra-light cars.

SIMPLEX 50HP

Simplex 50hp, built from 1907 to 1914 (data for 1907 model)
Built by: Simplex Automobile Co. Inc., United States.
Engine: Four cylinders, in line, two cast-iron blocks, with three-bearing light-alloy crankcase. Bore and stroke 146·1mm by 146·1mm, 9,797cc (5·75in×5·75in, 598cu.in). Non-detachable cast-iron cylinder heads. Two side valves per cylinder, in T-head layout with exposed valve stems and springs, operated by tappets from two camshafts, each in separate cast tunnel on outside of crankcase. One up-draught carburettor.
Transmission: Cone clutch, in unit with front-mounted engine, separate four-speed manual gearbox (without synchromesh). Remote-control right-hand gearchange. Straight-bevel differential in tail of gearbox and countershaft to sprockets. Final drive to rear wheels by twin side chains.
Chassis: Separate pressed-steel chassis frame,

with channel-section side members and pressed and tubular cross bracing. Forged front axle beam. Front and rear suspension by semi-elliptic leaf springs. Friction-type dampers. Worm-and-sector steering. Foot brake, mechanically operated, by contracting bands on gearbox countershaft drums. Hand brake, mechanically operated, on rear wheel drums. Fixed artillery-style road wheels. 35 × 5in tyres.
Choice of coachwork, open or closed touring or saloon.
Dimensions: Wheelbase 10ft 6in (320cm), tracks (front and rear) 4ft 8in (142cm). Unladen weight, depending on coachwork, from 3,750lb (1,701kg).
History: The Simplex car evolved from the Smith and Mabley motor agents in New York. At first they sold Mercédès, Panhard and Renault cars, but in 1904 they began to build a Smith and Mabley Simplex car, first of 18hp and later of 30hp. The company went out of business in 1907, but the moribund concern was acquired

by Herman Broesel, who had a vast new 9·8-litre 50hp car designed and called it – simply – a Simplex. The company was only to live for ten years, but the original chain-drive 50 was always part of the range. It was a big, expensive ($4,500 for the chassis alone) and exclusive car, with bodies from prestigious coachbuilders. The mechanical layout was typical of the period, but the engine had a lot of potential, as stripped models proved time and time again on the American race tracks. By 1911, there was a shaft-driven 38hp model being built alongside the 50 and in 1912, the massive 75 (still with chain drive) was introduced as a faster version of the 50 model.

A change of company ownership in 1914 spelt the end for the classic Simplex car and the big 50 disappeared. No more Simplexes were built after 1917. There were two types of radiator fitted to these cars – one a conventional Mercédès-type flat unit and the other a sharply pointed vee radiator.

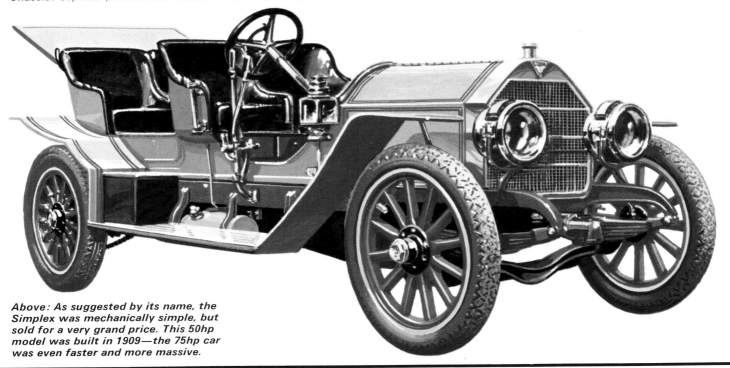

Above: As suggested by its name, the Simplex was mechanically simple, but sold for a very grand price. This 50hp model was built in 1909—the 75hp car was even faster and more massive.

S.P.A.

S.P.A. cars, built from 1906 to 1926 (data for 1921 30–40hp model)

Built by: Società Ligure Piemontese Automobili, Italy.

Engine: Six cylinders, in line, in three-bearing light-alloy block/crankcase. Bore and stroke 85mm by 130mm, 4,426cc (3·35in × 5·12in, 270·1cu.in). Detachable cast-iron cylinder head. Four overhead valves per cylinder, opposed to each other in pairs and operated by twin overhead camshafts. One twin-choke up-draught S.P.A. carburettor.

Transmission: Multiple-dry-plate clutch, in unit with front-mounted engine, and separate four-speed manual gearbox (without synchromesh). Remote-control right-hand gearchange. Propeller shaft, enclosed in torque tube, driving spiral-bevel 'live' rear axle.

Chassis: Separate pressed-steel chassis frame, with channel-section side members and tubular cross-bracing. Forged front axle beam. Front suspension by semi-elliptic leaf springs. Rear suspension by cantilever leaf springs and anti-roll joint at nose of torque tube. No dampers. Four-wheel, mechanically operated drum brakes. Bolt-on artillery-style or wire wheels. 895 × 135mm tyres.

Dimensions: Wheelbase 12ft (366cm), tracks (front and rear) 4ft 9in (145cm). Overall length depending on coachwork, from 16ft (487·7cm).

History: Matteo Ceirano's product was always a modern and well built sporting car in the Italian traditions. Before World War I there were several four-cylinder and six-cylinder machines and after the war there were two models – the Type 23 (which was an updated 1914 16/20 model) and the much more exciting Type 24. This was the splendid 30–40hp, 4·4-litre car; it had thoroughly advanced light-alloy engine, which included a light-alloy block and four-valves per cylinder, operated by two gear-driven overhead camshafts. The company even found a way of building anti-roll qualities into the torque tube mounting. Naturally enough the 30–40 was very expensive – £1,750 complete in Britain – and sold only in small numbers. This twin-cam, incidentally, should not be confused with the original post-war 4·4-litre unit, which had side valves and was related to the Type 23 four. S.P.A. were taken over by Fiat in 1925 and production ceased almost immediately.

Below: S.P.A.s were always big and expensive—this 1922 30-40hp was no exception. The engine was advanced, with four valves per cylinder and two overhead camshafts. 1925 saw the last.

STANLEY STEAM CARS

Steam models, built from 1897 to 1907 (data for 1907 EX model)

Built by: Stanley Manufacturing Co. (later Stanley Motor Carriage Co.), United States.

Engine: Two cylinders, horizontally positioned in parallel, in cast-iron casings. Bore and stroke 76·2mm by 101·6mm, 926cc (3·0in × 4·0in, 56·5cu.in). Stevenson's Link valve-gear motion, and double-acting porting. Vertical fire-tube boiler, with 450 18in tubes. Normal steam working pressure 380lb per sq.in. Furnace heated by kerosene. Power output 10bhp at 380lb per sq.in steam pressure, rising to 28bhp at 650lb per sq.in.

Transmission: By spur gear from engine crankshaft to toothed ring on differential gear of 'live' rear axle. No reverse gear, except by reversing valve motion.

Chassis: Wooden chassis frame supporting body. Tubular front axle, linked to 'live' rear axle by light tubular steel underframe. Fully elliptic leaf springs at front and rear. No dampers. Worm-and-wheel steering. Foot-operated contracting-band brake on differential housing. Hand-operated internally expanding drums on rear wheels. Emergency braking by reversing valve motion and admitting steam. Wood-spoked artillery wheels. 30 × 3in tyres.

Dimensions: Wheelbase 7ft 6in (229cm), tracks (front and rear) 4ft 8in (142cm), overall length 10ft 3in (312cm). Unladen weight 1,400lb (635kg).

History: In the earliest days of motoring, steam engines were immeasurably more reliable and powerful than petrol engines. Their disadvantages were – then as now – that engine auxiliaries (furnace, condenser and other details) were more complex than the engine itself. Water consumption was always a big problem and the more efficient little units had intricate plumbing. The first-ever Stanley runabout was a frail little thing completed by F. E. Stanley in 1897. He was joined by his brother in 1899. By then only four cars had been sold, but hundreds of orders received. To fulfil the promise, the business was sold to Locomobile.

A feature of all Stanleys of the period was the light tubular underframe connecting both axles together. Bodies had their own chassis frame (of wood) and also carried the steam engine and works. The frames were separated by elliptical leaf springs (a transverse spring on the early Stanleys). The first two-cylinder car had its engine positioned vertically under the seats, with the valve-motion open to attack by dust and

SPYKER 18HP

18hp model, built from 1909 to 1916 (data for 1911 model)
Built by: De Industrieele Maatschappij Trompenburg, Holland.

Engine: Four cylinders, in line, in cast-iron block, with three-bearing light-alloy crankcase. Bore and stroke 90mm by 110mm, 2,799cc (3·54in × 4·33in, 170·8cu.in). Cast-iron cylinder head. Two side valves per cylinder, in 'T-head' formation, operated by rockers from two transverse camshafts, in cylinder block, between cylinders 1/2 and 3/4. Single up-draught Zenith carburettor.

Transmission: Multiple-dry-plate clutch, in unit with front-mounted engine, and shaft drive to separate four-speed manual gearbox (without synchromesh). Remote-control right-hand gearchange. Propeller shaft, enclosed in torque tube, driving straight-bevel 'live' rear axle.

Chassis: Separate pressed-steel chassis frame, with channel-section side members and pressed cross bracing. Forged front axle beam. Front suspension by semi-elliptic leaf springs. Rear suspension by three-quarter-elliptic leaf springs, with torque-tube and radius-arm location. No dampers. Worm-type steering. Transmission-drum brake behind gearbox, operated by foot pedal. Rear wheel drum brakes operated by hand lever. Artillery-style road wheels. 875 × 105mm tyres.

Dimensions: Wheelbase 10ft 0in (305cm), tracks (front and rear) 4ft 5·5in (136cm). Overall length 13ft 9·5in (420cm). Unladen

weight (chassis only) 1,800lb (816kg).

History: The Spijkers (a simpler spelling was used for the cars) began as Hilversum coachbuilders, took out a Benz agency in 1895 and began making their own cars from 1900. Conventional machines were followed by the unsuccessful 'circular' four-cylinder engines and what is generally accepted to be the world's first six-cylinder car. Spykers were carefully enclosed and streamlined underneath, which earned the marque the 'Dustless' nickname. Technically, the most interesting Spyker feature between 1909 and 1916 was the range of engines – from 12hp to 40hp by 1911 – which included transverse camshafts in their layout. These were

Above: This 1911 18hp Spyker was used by Queen Wilhelmina. Later models had a vee-profiled radiator.

housed between pairs of cylinders, above the crankshaft and operated the valves through rockers. Spectacular internal derangements were known with this system, but Spijker persisted with it until World War I caused them to close down production. One of the car's distinctive external features was the circular radiator, which became vee-fronted in 1914. Spykers, without doubt, were Holland's leading make, and were the make of car chosen by Queen Wilhelmina in 1911.

---

mud. The boiler, placed behind the engine, was simple, but with the drawback that the water level had to be constantly watched. Surprisingly, condensers (to improve water consumption) were optional extras.

Locomobile had lost faith in steam cars by 1903 and they sold back the rights to the Stanley brothers, who celebrated this by producing the

EX model in 1904. This was so successful that it remained in production until 1909. There were no fundamental changes, although the tubular frame was now sprung on fully elliptic leaf springs all round and the burner was redesigned to run on high-grade kerosene. Boiler and furnace were moved up front, under the 'bonnet', and the two-cylinder engine was horizontally

placed under the floor, with its crankshaft directly geared to the back axle. Cruising speed was about 30mph, but, with judicious over-pressurising of the steam engine, up to 50mph was possible. The range between stops for water, because of a big tank, was now 40 to 50 miles.

Stanley steam cars, in progressively improved form, were made until 1927.

Far left: The Stanley steamer belongs to North American folklore, like the Curved Dash Oldsmobile and the Model T Ford. This beautiful Model EX was one of the last made. Note the high frame and full elliptic springs.

Above: Not only the engine, but the layout of Stanley steam cars was unusual. Axles were connected by a frame and the body had a separate frame, with the two-cylinder engine under the floor, geared to the axle.

SQUIRE

Squire cars, built from 1934 to 1936 (data for 1934 1½-litre)

Built by: Squire Car Manufacturing Co Ltd, Britain.

Engine: Anzani manufactured. Four cylinders, in line, in cast-iron block, with four-bearing light-alloy crankcase. Bore and stroke 69mm by 100mm, 1,496cc (2·72in × 3·94in, 91·3cu.in). Detachable light-alloy cylinder head. Two overhead valves per cylinder, opposed to each other at 90 degrees in hemispherical combustion chambers and operated by steel tappets from twin overhead camshafts. One horizontal constant-vacuum SU carburettor and Roots-type supercharger. Maximum power 110bhp (gross) at 5,000rpm.

Transmission: No separate clutch. Separate Wilson-type preselector gearbox, with clutch take-up by gear friction bands. Remote-control central gearchange. Open propeller shaft to spiral-bevel 'live' rear axle.

Chassis: Separate pressed-steel chassis frame, with channel-section side members, tubular and pressed cross-bracing and pressed cruciform. Forged front axle beam. Front and rear suspension by semi-elliptic leaf springs and lever-arm hydraulic dampers. Marles Weller steering. Four-wheel, hydraulically operated drum brakes. 18in centre-lock wire wheels. 5·00 × 18in tyres (short chassis); 5·25 × 18in tyres for long chassis.

Dimensions: Wheelbase 8ft 6in or 10ft 3in (259cm or 312·5cm), tracks (front and rear) 4ft 6in (137cm). Overall length 13ft or 14ft 9in (396cm or 450cm). Unladen weight (chassis only) 1,680lb or 1,740lb (762kg or 789kg).

History: The Squire sports car, as a commercial proposition, was doomed right from the start. It was one man's dream of his ideal machine, to be sold in small numbers to the public. Nothing was allowed to interfere with this dream, certainly not the questions of costs and profits. The car itself was one of the most exciting-looking and best detailed of all the British post-vintage thoroughbreds. Its two most impressive features in 1934, when it was announced, were the sleek and lovely looks (this was at a time when many body designers were still reluctant to consider sweeping lines on a sports car) and its unique twin-camshaft supercharged engine.

Adrian Squire had cherished the ambition of building his own sports cars since he had been at school. An engineering apprenticeship was followed by spells of work with Bentley at Cricklewood and with MG at Abingdon, before the 21-year-old Squire moved in to a cottage on Remenham Hill, near Henley. There a small garage and filling station was established, and

later he also acquired showrooms in Henley-on-Thames. Design on the Squire car began in 1933 and the manufacturing company was founded in January 1934 with capital of only £6,000.

Squire were too small to make much of their own cars, so they contracted to buy engines from British Anzani, gearboxes from ENV (of the preselector Wilson type) and axles from the same source. The engine was unique in Britain in that it was a supercharged twin-cam unit. Its origins were in a special car raced by Archie Frazer-Nash in 1927/28, but the supercharging was Squire's own idea. It was a very powerful unit, but not at all refined or quiet, as the camshaft drive was by a train of gears with considerable backlash, and valve clearances were always very high. The chassis itself was conventional enough, but rather more rigid than was usual, with a stout cruciform member behind the gearbox. Suspension was entirely 'British conventional', as Squire's own aspirations had not yet experienced the latest European independent suspensions. Such was the flexibility (and small scale) of Squire's operations, that they built the first three

cars with overslung rear frames and the remainder with underslung frames.

The most immediately striking aspect of the Squire, apart from its engine noise, was the styling. The general layout was conventional enough — there were only two seats and the usual 'build-up' weather protection — but the vee-profile radiator was swept back to make the nose distinctly rakish and both front and rear wings were well swept with delicately profiled skirts. The very first car, bodied by Vanden Plas, looked reminiscent of a Bugatti from some angles and of an Aston Martin from a few others, but was unmistakeably a Squire. In the manner of the 1930s, a great proportion of the body was taken over by mechanical components, but on the first car there was even an enclosed tail for the spare wheel and big petrol tank.

There was no doubt that it was going to be an expensive car — at £1,220 complete with body it rivalled a 3½-litre Bentley — but, with a 100mph maximum speed, individual craftsmanship in the construction and the promise of exclusivity, Squire was confident enough. The tragedy was

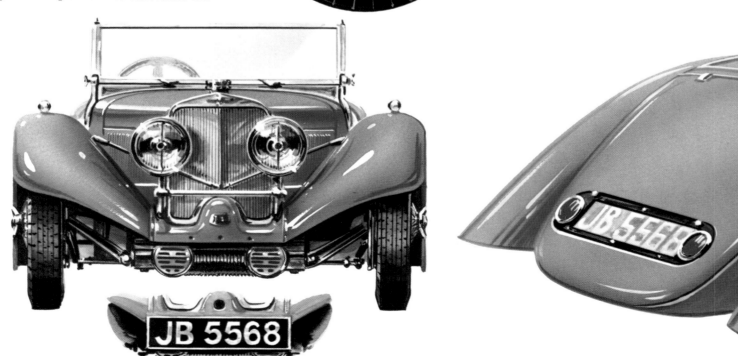

that although hundreds of enquiries were received after the car's first showing, they were not backed by firm orders. Within two years that part of Squire's activities had failed financially and it is a sad commentary that of only seven cars built, no less than four of them were first owned by Squire themselves, or by Squire directors.

Even though the asking price was slashed in 1935 to less than £1,000, there was no demand for this elegant but costly device. By then, unfortunately, SS had released the SS100 two-seater and had rendered most other people's prices obsolete. The company had to be wound up; all the spare parts were sold off and Squire himself moved to Staines where he rejoined W.O. Bentley at Lagonda. Then, during the war, Squire worked for the Bristol Aeroplane Company and was tragically killed in an air-raid. Val Zethrin, of Kent, bought up a lot of parts and managed to assemble two more Squires before the war, but total production of all Squires, including the single-seater which raced at Brooklands, was no more than nine. All but the single-seater survive to this day.

Above: Built in 1935, the unique Squire 'featherweight' had an eye to competitions, and not to elegance. It used the short chassis, and super-tuned twin-cam Anzani engine.

Above: The 1½-litre supercharged Squire was one man's dream car—made in tiny numbers (nine in all) by Adrian Squire's little company near Henley-on-Thames. Almost everything was bought out, including the elegant and rakish bodies. This beautiful two-seater style was by Vanden Plas.

STEYR TYPE XII

Type XII, built from 1925 to 1928 (data for 1925 model)
Built by: Steyr-Werke A.G., Austria.
Engine: Six cylinders, in line, in cast-iron block, with light-alloy crankcase. Bore and stroke 60mm by 88mm, 1,493cc (2·36 × 3·46in, 91·1cu.in). Detachable cast-iron cylinder head. Two overhead valves per cylinder, operated by single overhead camshaft. Single up-draught Pallas carburettor. Maximum power 36bhp at 4,000rpm.
Transmission: Multiple-dry-plate clutch and four-speed manual gearbox (without synchromesh), both in unit with front-mounted engine. Direct-acting central gearchange. Two piece propeller shaft, front section open then rear section enclosed in tube, driving chassis-mounted spiral-bevel final drive. Universally jointed drive shafts, enclosed in swinging half-axles to rear wheels.
Chassis: Separate steel chassis frame, with channel-section side members and channel and tubular cross bracing. Forged front axle beam. Front suspension by semi-elliptic leaf springs. Independent rear suspension by transverse leaf spring and swinging half-axles, with radius arms. No dampers. Worm-and-nut steering. Four-wheel, rod-operated drum brakes. Steel-disc road wheels. 775 × 145 tyres. Open or closed bodywork.
Dimensions: Wheelbase 9ft 10in (300cm), tracks (front and rear) 4ft 2·5in (128cm). Overall length 13ft 5·5in (410cm). Unladen weight 2,350lb (1,066kg).
History: As an armaments-producing factory in Austria, Steyr had to look for new outlets in 1919 and they chose to produce private cars. Their first machine, called the Waffenauto, was designed by Hans Ledwinka (who later became famous with Tatra in Czechoslovakia) and appeared in 1920, but Ledwinka left the company in 1921. His new design, for a cheap and simple machine, went with him, and became the first Tatra. This led to thoughts of joint technical ventures with Tatra, but nothing formal became

Above: Steyr's Type XII model had a sturdy 1·5-litre six-cylinder engine —and a beam front axle allied to independent rear suspension.

Right: Without its unique chassis layout, the Steyr Type XII would have been a typical vintage car. No other car in the world had a swinging-axle rear allied to conventional front end. Both cars shown were 1926 models, the 'saloon' being based on the Torpedo.

of this. Ledwinka's hand, however, was obvious in the Type XII of 1925, which must surely be the only car ever built with a beam front axle and independent *rear* suspension. The car itself, apart from the suspension, was conventional and neatly designed, with a fine overhead-camshaft engine. The rear end, with swing axles and a transverse leaf spring, was a simple way of achieving independence, but as anybody who bought a Triumph Herald knows this layout can bring roadholding problems. Steyr, however, were never large-volume car producers (1,000 cars a year was their average) and they were more interested in fighting Mercédès in the luxury car market, so the intriguing Type 12 only lasted for three years.

STUDEBAKER AVANTI

Avantis, built 1962–3, then 1965–72, with Chevrolet engines (data for R-1 1962 model)
Built by: The Studebaker Corporation, United States.
Engine: Eight cylinders, in 90-degree vee-formation, in five-bearing cast-iron block/crankcase. Bore and stroke 90·4mm by 92·1mm, 4,736cc (3·56in × 3·63in, 289cu.in). Two detachable cast-iron cylinder heads. Two overhead valves per cylinder, operated by pushrods and rockers from single camshaft mounted in centre of cylinder block 'vee'. Single down-draught four-choke Carter carburettor. Power output never officially quoted, probably about 250bhp (gross) at 5,000rpm.
R2 model had Paxton supercharger and Carter four-choke carburettor and produced approximately 315bhp (gross) at 5,000rpm.
Transmission: Single-dry-plate clutch, with three-speed all-synchromesh manual gearbox, both in unit with front-mounted engine. Direct-acting central gearchange. Optional four-speed manual gearbox, or three-speed Borg Warner automatic gearbox with torque converter. Open propeller shaft to hypoid-bevel 'live' rear axle with optional limited-slip differential.
Chassis: Separate pressed-steel chassis frame, with box-section side members and pressed-steel cross bracing. Independent front suspension by coil springs, wishbones and anti-roll bar. Rear suspension by semi-elliptic leaf springs, Panhard rod and anti-roll bar. Telescopic dampers. Power-assisted worm and roller steering. 15in pressed-steel-disc wheels. 7·75 × 15in tyres.
Dimensions: Wheelbase 9ft 1in (277cm), track (front) 4ft 9·4in (146cm), track (rear) 4ft 8·6in (144cm). Overall length 16ft 0·5in (489cm).

Above: Only the date of build—1967 —tells us that this Avanti was not made by Studebaker. The company failed in 1963, and the car was re-born in 1965 with a Chevrolet vee-8 engine.

Unladen weight 3,307lb (1,500kg).
History: The sleek and startlingly beautiful Avanti, with its glassfibre body, was Studebaker's last desperate attempt to find themselves a prestige product, following the disappearance of the Packard marque name in 1957. Under the new model's skin was conventional Studebaker engineering (although a supercharged engine was to be an option), but the skin itself was Raymond Loewy's creativity at its best. In the

usual Detroit manner there were several engine and transmission options, but the Dunlop-licensed front disc brakes were a distinct rarity by North American standards. In looks the Avanti predated other American cars by years, but this did not save Studebaker, who were in deep financial trouble. Within a year of its announcement, all Avanti production had closed down.

In 1965, however, a group of enthusiastic businessmen bought body tools and machine tooling special to the Avanti at the liquidation auction and set up in business, still in South Bend Indiana, to make Avanti IIs with Chevrolet engines. Small-scale production was successfully carried on for some years, but the last of these specials has now been sold.

Above: Studebaker's Avanti was a last attempt to put a fast prestige model in the line-up. The glass-fibre body was styled by Raymond Leowy, and there was an optional supercharged vee-8 engine. In America in 1962, the Avanti had disc brakes which were a rarity. Original cars had 4·7-litres.

STUTZ BEARCAT

Bearcat, built from 1914 to 1917 in original design (data for 1914 model)

Built by: The Stutz Motor Car Co of America, United States.

Engine: Wisconsin manufactured. Four cylinders, in line, in cast-iron block, with three-bearing light-alloy crankcase. Bore and stroke 120·6mm by 139·7mm, 6,388cc (4·75in × 5·5in, 390cu.in). Non-detachable cylinder head. Two side valves per cylinder, in T-head layout. Single up-draught carburettor. Maximum power about 60bhp at 1,500rpm.

Transmission: Cone clutch, in unit with front-mounted engine, and shaft drive to three-speed manual gearbox (without synchromesh), in unit with straight-bevel 'live' rear axle. Remote-control right-hand gearchange.

Chassis: Separate pressed-steel chassis frame, with tubular and pressed cross bracing. Forged front axle beam. Front and rear suspension by semi-elliptic leaf springs. Optional friction-type dampers. Worm-type steering. Rear-brakes only. Choice of artillery-style wheels with detachable rims, or centre-lock wire wheels.

History: Harry C. Stutz's famous Bearcat sports car was also one of the very first cars his Indianapolis-based company ever designed. His first products were racing cars, from 1911 onwards, but the Stutz Motor Car Co. was founded in 1913 and announced the Bearcat for 1914 production. The racing Stutz cars helped pave

the way for the Bearcat, but this had also been obviously developed with an eye to the Mercer Raceabout, which it resembled visually and whose market it sought to invade. Like the Raceabout, the Bearcat was a big-engined rough-and-ready sports car, of the type where hairy-chested behaviour and performance was thought all-important. There were two seats, but no doors and certainly no windscreen. The driver had a 'monocle' screen to protect him from the flys and debris, but the passenger had nothing at all. The uncompromising bonnet hid a big and conventional 6·4-litre engine and really the only novel fitting in the chassis was the three-speed gearbox: this found itself in unit with the back axle, which had been a Stutz-built speciality for several years.

One reason behind the car's fame was that a team of racing cars, the White Squadron, performed well in 1915. These cars had special sixteen-valve overhead camshaft engines of 4·8-litres, and were far from standard, but this did not deter the customers. Cannonball Baker also used a Bearcat to break the Atlantic-Pacific record by 1916 — by an astonishing margin and without any mechanical problems.

Right: The stark and purposeful Stutz Bearcat of 1914, with that distinctive monocle windscreen for the driver. The engine was a 6·4-litre.

STUTZ VERTICAL EIGHT

Vertical Eights, built from 1926 to 1935 (data for 1928 Model BB Black Hawk)

Built by: The Stutz Motor Car Co. of America, United States.

Engine: Eight cylinders, in line, in nine-bearing cast-iron block/crankcase. Bore and stroke 82·55mm by 114·3mm, 4,894cc (3·25in × 4·5in, 298cu.in). Detachable cast-iron cylinder head. Two overhead valves per cylinder, operated by inverted pistons attached to valve shafts, from single overhead camshaft. Up-draught twin-choke Zenith carburettor. Maximum power 115bhp at 3,600rpm. Maximum torque 238lb.ft at 1,600rpm.

Transmission: Single-dry-plate clutch and three-speed manual gearbox (without synchromesh), both in unit with front-mounted engine. Direct-acting central gearchange. Open propeller shaft to underslung-worm-drive rear axle.

Chassis: Separate pressed-steel chassis frame, with channel-section side members and channel

and tubular cross bracing. Forged front axle beam. Semi-elliptic leaf springs at front and rear. Hydraulic dampers. Four-wheel hydraulically operated drum brakes. Transmission drum handbrake. 32in centre-lock wire wheels. 6·20 × 32in tyres.

Open two-seater sports car bodywork.

Dimensions: Wheelbase 10ft 11in (333cm), track (front) 4ft 10·5in (148·6cm), track (rear) 4ft 8·4in (143cm). Overall length 16ft (488cm). Unladen weight 3,600lb (1,633kg).

History: The original Bearcat had been closely linked with motor sport, but when road racing disappeared from the American scene its attractions, too, faded. By 1925 Stutz were in trouble. To pull out of this, Charles Schwab, the new owner of Stutz, enticed Fred Moskovics away from Marmon to become Stutz's president. Under his leadership the famous Vertical Eight Stutz cars were conceived. In one form or another they ran from 1926 to 1935, but the

single-cam cars were probably most famous as the Black Hawk sports cars. Cars of this type raced at Le Mans in 1928 and proved to be as fast as the victorious Bentleys, while in 1929 supercharged versions could achieve no more than fifth place. A much modified Stutz Eight raced at Indianapolis in 1930 and finished a creditable tenth overall. After 1931 the cars were renamed SV16s, because by then the even more exciting DV32 models had been introduced. Stutz eights looked typical of late-vintage North American cars, but were distinguished under the skin by straight-eight engines and the under-slung-worm-drive back axle.

Below and right: The Stutz Vertical Eight (so named because of the type of engine used) was built for ten years. Both the cars shown were built in 1929. The most famous derivatives were the fast sports 'Black Hawks'.

STUTZ DV32

DV32 models, built from 1931 to 1935 (data for 1931 model)
Built by: The Stutz Motor Car Co. of America, United States.
Engine: Eight cylinders, in line, in nine-bearing cast-iron block/crankcase. Bore and stroke 85·72mm by 114·3mm, 5,277cc (3·37in × 4·5in, 322cu.in). Detachable cast-iron cylinder head. Four overhead valves per cylinder, opposed to each other and operated by inverted pistons attached to valve stems from twin overhead camshafts. Up-draught twin-choke Schebler carburettor. Maximum power 156bhp (gross) at 3,900rpm. Maximum torque 300lb.ft at 2,400rpm.
Transmission: Single-dry-plate clutch and four-speed manual gearbox, both in unit with front-mounted engine. Direct-acting central gearchange. Open propeller shaft to underslung-worm-drive 'live' rear axle.
Chassis: Separate pressed-steel chassis frame, with channel-section side members and channel and tubular cross bracing. Forged front axle beam. Semi-elliptic leaf springs at front and rear. Hydraulic dampers. Four-wheel, hydraulically operated drum brakes. Transmission drum hand-brake. 18in bolt-on wire wheels. 7·00 × 18in tyres. Variety of coachwork — open or closed styles.
Dimensions: Wheelbase 11ft 2·5in to 12ft 1in (342cm to 368cm), track (front) 4ft 10·5in

(148·6cm), track (rear) 4ft 8·4in (143cm). Overall length from 16ft (488cm). Unladen weight from 3,900lb (1,769kg).
History: At a time when the opposition was busy introducing cars with V12 or even V16 engines, Stutz already knew that they had one of the very best chassis in the North American motor industry. Their engineering standards were high and because they lacked the resources — in men or in money — to produce a brand-new 'vee'

engine to meet the competition, they elected to produce a splendidly conceived twin-cam version of the Vertical Eight engine, with no less than four valves per cylinder. This, of course, explains the new model's title of DV32. Apart from updated bodies to match the new engineering — which, incidentally, endowed the car with at least a 100mph maximum speed in open 'speed model' form — the car was mechanically much as before. The snag, a very important one in

SUNBEAM ALPINE AND TIGER

Alpines I, II, III, IV and V, Tigers I and II 1959 to 1968 (data for Tiger I)
Built by: Rootes Ltd., Britain
Engine: Ford-of-Detroit manufactured. Eight cylinders, in 90-degree vee-formation, in five-bearing cast-iron block. Bore and stroke 96·5mm by 73·0mm, 4,261cc (3·80in × 2·87in, 260cu.in). Two cast-iron cylinder heads. Two overhead valves per cylinder, operated by pushrods and rockers from single camshaft mounted in centre of cylinder block 'vee'. One down-draught twin-choke Ford carburettor. Maximum power 164bhp (gross) at 4,400rpm. Maximum torque 258lb.ft at 2,200rpm.
Transmission: Single-dry-plate clutch and four-speed, all-synchromesh manual gearbox,

both in unit with engine. Remote-control central gearchange. Open propeller shaft to hypoid-bevel 'live' rear axle.
Chassis: Unitary-construction pressed-steel two-seat sports car body/chassis unit, heavily modified by Jensen from Sunbeam Alpine shell. Independent front suspension by coil springs, wishbones and anti-roll bar. Rear suspension by semi-elliptic leaf springs and Panhard rod. Telescopic dampers. Rack-and-pinion steering. Four-wheel, hydraulically operated brakes, front discs and rear drums, vacuum-servo assisted. 13in pressed-steel-disc wheels. 5·90 × 13in tyres. Optional bolt-on steel hardtop.
Dimensions: Wheelbase 7ft 2in (218cm), track (front) 4ft 3·7in (131cm), track (rear) 4ft 0·5in

(123cm). Overall length 12ft 11·2in (394cm). Unladen weight 2,640lb (1,197kg).
History: In the early 1950s, Rootes produced a stylish two-seater car, based on a Sunbeam-Talbot saloon, called the Sunbeam Alpine. This was too heavy and cumbersome to be very popular, although it did have some competition successes. In 1959, a new Sunbeam Alpine appeared, this being based on the short-wheel-base Hillman Husky floorpan and fitted with Sunbeam Rapier engine and transmission. The fashionable finned body was Rootes' own work. In a complex commercial deal involving Rootes having an engine like that of the Armstrong-Siddeley Sapphire for their big Humbers, the Alpine was originally assembled by Armstrong-

Depression-hit North America, was that the DV32 retailed for nearly $5,000. In spite of being a bravely marketed car of undoubted merit, there were simply not enough customers to keep this sort of model afloat and Stutz, unlike Cadillac, did not have the backing of luckier and more viable partners. Even though the transmission reverted to three-speed (customer preference) in 1932, and the price was cut by $1,000, it meant a slow and lingering death for Stutz.

Two versions of the most illustrious of all Stutz sports cars—the DV32 'Super Bearcat' models. Left: A close-coupled four-seater tourer on the specially shortened 116in wheelbase. Right: A two-seater with a chunky but purposeful body and many obvious but typical North American accessories. Both date from the 1933 range of body styles marketed by Stutz. Not only did the DV32 have a straight-eight engine, but it had twin overhead camshafts and it boasted four-valves per cylinder—an unheard-of sophistication in North American cars. Thus there were 32 valves which explains the car's model title. Maximum power from the 5·3-litre engine was more than 150bhp, and maximum speeds were in excess of 100mph.

Below left: The Rootes Alpine had a sleek body style hiding more humble mechanical parts. The floor was from the Hillman Husky, and the power train from the Rapier. The 1959/64 version had more pronounced tail fins. Later cars had an all-synchromesh gearbox. This final version, the 1,725cc Series V, could beat 100mph. The last was built in 1968.
Below right: The Sunbeam Tiger was Rootes' answer to the AC Cobra, and had a similar Ford vee-8 engine squeezed into the modified Alpine body shell. The Tiger II of 1967 had 4·7 litres and 200bhp.

Siddeley in Coventry. At first the car had a 1½-litre engine, but this was soon enlarged to 1·6 litres. That was the Alpine II. Alpine III came along in the early 1960s, with more refinement and a smart new steel hardtop, but within a year this was superseded by Alpine IV which had its rear fins cropped. In the meantime, Rootes' North American importers looked at the AC Cobra, liked what they saw and engineered a similar prototype transplant of their own. The Sunbeam Tiger, announced in the spring of 1964, was really a Sunbeam Alpine with a 4·2-litre Ford V8, a Borg-Warner four-speed gearbox and a heavy-duty back axle installed, together with many other modifications to keep the engine cool and

to make the handling satisfactory and the traction sound. Pressed Steel produced the bodies (as they did for the Alpine), then Jensen made all the Tiger changes and carried out final assembly on Rootes' behalf. Soon after this, Alpine IV became Alpine V, the engine being enlarged to 1,725cc to match the already specified all-synchromesh gearbox. Both cars were smart and sold well, but unhappily they did not make profits for Rootes. Soon after Chrysler took a financial stake in Rootes they brought political pressure to bear and the rival Ford V8 engine was dropped. This was a shame, as Tiger II, announced for 1967, had been much fiercer with its more powerful 4,727cc (289cu.in) V8 engine. The Alpine V was discontinued in 1968.

SUNBEAM 3-LITRE COUPE DE L'AUTO

3-litre, built from 1911 to 1913 (data for 1912 type)

Built by: Sunbeam Motor Car Co. Ltd., Britain.

Engine: Four cylinders, in line, in cast-iron cylinder block, bolted to five-bearing light-alloy crankcase. Bore and stroke 80mm by 149mm, 2,996cc (3·15in × 5·87in, 182·8cu.in). Non-detachable cylinder head. Two side valves per cylinder, completely exposed and directly operated by crankcase-mounted camshaft. Single up-draught Claudel-Hobson carburettor. Maximum power 74bhp at 2,600rpm.

Transmission: Leather-faced cone clutch, in unit with engine, and separate four-speed manual gearbox (without synchromesh). Right-hand gearchange. Open propeller shaft to straight-bevel 'live' rear axle.

Chassis: Separate pressed-steel chassis frame, with channel-section side members and tubular and pressed cross bracing. Forged front axle beam. Semi-elliptic leaf springs front and rear, with Triou friction-type dampers. Worm-and-sector steering. Foot-operated drum brake, on transmission behind the gearbox. Hand-operated brake on rear-wheel-mounted drums. Detachable steel artillery-type road wheels. 815 × 105 (front) and 815 × 120 (rear) Michelin tyres. Open racing type two-seater bodywork, in light alloy. No weather protection and, normally, no wings.

Dimensions: Wheelbase 8ft 11in (272cm), tracks (front and rear) 4ft 6in (137cm), overall length 14ft (427cm). Unladen weight 2,030lb (921kg).

History: The Coupe de l'Auto Sunbeam was developed particularly for a series of races in France and was Louis Coatalen's first real triumph as a designer of very fast cars. Coatalen had worked for Hillman in Coventry before joining Sunbeam in Wolverhampton, and had already designed noted road cars before being encouraged to turn the 12—16 series of 1910 into a competition car. The Coupe de l'Auto was awarded for a race for *voiturette* machines, restricted to a minimum weight of 1,764lb (800kg) and with a stroke/bore ratio not more than 2:1. The maximum stroke allowed, too, was 156mm. These restrictions came about because of the freak machines built by French manufacturers a few years previously.

Sunbeams were actually raced in three successive events, between 1911 and 1913, although they would once again have been used in 1914 if the event had not been cancelled because of the outbreak of war. Their basis, at first, was a perfectly standard 12-16 production car chassis, with the addition of friction-type dampers and a modified version of that car's engine. Twin overhead camshafts had not yet been 're-invented' by Peugeot, so Coatalen thought it normal to use side valves like the production engine. However the 'racer' used a monobloc cylinder casting, whereas production cars had twin pairs, and the stroke was lengthened to 149mm to take full advantage of the regulations. Incidentally, it may be more than coincidence that W. O. Bentley's first 3-litre car also used identical dimensions a few years later. Another change from the production chassis was that the racing car used a straight-bevel final drive, whereas production cars had used a worm drive. In 1911 form, the four-speed gearbox had an 'overdrive' top gear ratio, although this was changed to give revised ratios and a direct top gear for the following year.

The 1911 cars, which looked rather ungainly because of the angular coachwork lines and the vestigial wings fitted to satisfy the scrutineers, were not a success. For 1912, though, everything was to be different. Coatalen had learnt much from that first race and, although the 1912 event was not scheduled until the end of June, he sent much revised cars to the circuit near Dieppe in February for practice and training. The new cars were much sleeker and more striking, as well as rather more powerful than in the year before. Although a touring-car gearbox was still used, it had closer ratios in this racing application.

The cars' maximum speed was around 90mph, which was very creditable, although Coatalen had hoped for 100mph. Five cars were taken to the race, one of them a spare. In the event, over this very gruelling two-day course, three of the four cars survived to win the *voiturette* section of the race outright (Grand Prix machines could also enter). Rigal drove the winning car, averaging 65·3mph, which compared well with the best Grand Prix car (Peugeot) speed of 68·45mph.

In 1913, the same cars were improved, and used once more, with the important (but disastrously wrong) innovation of having axles without differentials. Power was increased to about 87bhp and maximum speed was increased to between 95 and 100mph. Three cars were entered and the 1913 race was held at Boulogne. In that year, success was not as sweeping, but Guinness' car took third place overall behind two of the Peugeots. The cars also raced at Brooklands in 1912 and 1913. Touring 12-16s were improved noticeably because of the racing experience, and by 1914 sporting models with Coupe de l'Auto details were on sale, but in rather detuned form. As Sixteens these cars were also adopted by the British army as staff cars for the 1914—18 conflict — made by Rover in Coventry on Sunbeam's behalf, as the firm was too busy building aero-engines. In post-war days the cars carried on until 1924, before finally being replaced by more modern 'vintage' designs.

The Sunbeams, like the Peugeots with which they were contemporary, proved for the first time that it was often wiser to get more performance by improving engine efficiency than by increasing engine size and Coatalen's careful attention to roadholding and reliability was also significant. Sunbeam's great successes with Grand Prix cars in the 1920s stems from this experience.

Right and below: In almost every way the Coupe de l'Auto *Sunbeams were typical of pre-Great War voiturettes. Illustrated are the three versions raced by the factory. Car '17' is the original 1911 version, with a rather humped body, as driven at Boulogne by T. Richards without success. Car '4' is the 1913 car, with a revised body and much lower seating, while Car '3' is the famous 1912 car which (driven by Victor Rigal) won the Coupe de l'Auto race at Dieppe at 65·3mph.*

Above: Rear view of the victorious 1912 3-litre Sunbeam shows the simple construction, and the exposed back axle. Half-elliptic leaf springs were used and the exhaust pipe swept up high to the tail. The car weighed about 2,000lb but could reach more than 90mph. Two people were carried.

Above and right: There was no attempt at streamlining, even by using a radiator cowl, in 1912. A single splash guard protected the driver from the worst of the stones and road water—the passenger had no such luck. There were no front brakes, and the tyre treads were almost smooth.

TATRA

Type 77, built from 1934 to 1937

Built by: Ringhoffer-Tatra-Werke AG, Czechoslovakia

Engine: Eight cylinders, in 90-degree vee-formation, in three-bearing cast-iron block/crankcase, cylinder block with fins and air-cooling. Bore and stroke 75mm by 84mm, 2,970cc (2·95 × 3·31in, 181·2cu.in). Two detachable cylinder heads. Two overhead valves per cylinder, and operated by pushrods and rockers from single camshaft mounted in centre of cylinder-block 'vee'. Single down-draught Zenith carburettor. Dry-sump lubrication. Maximum power 60bhp at 3,500rpm.

Transmission: Single-dry-plate clutch and four-speed manual gearbox (without synchromesh), both in transaxle and in unit with rear-mounted engine. Clutch behind line of rear wheels and gearbox ahead of that line. Remote-control central gearchange. Spiral-bevel differential. Exposed, universally jointed drive shafts to rear wheels.

Chassis: Tubular-section steel backbone chassis frame, with full-width four-door saloon body shell fixed to it. Independent front suspension by transverse leaf spring and control links. Rear suspension by transverse leaf spring and swinging half axles. Four-wheel, hydraulically operated drum brakes. Pressed-steel-disc wheels. 16 × 45 tyres.

Dimensions: Wheelbase 10ft 4in (315cm), tracks (front and rear) 4ft 3in (129·5cm). Overall length 16ft 11in (515·6cm). Unladen weight 3,700lb (1·678kg).

History: The first Tatras were built in 1923, having succeeded the Nesselsdorf cars built before that time. All Tatras have been built in Koprivnice in Czechoslovakia, but as this town was called Nesselsdorf and was in Austria, before and during World War I, the connection becomes a little more clear. Tatra's distinguished designer was Hans Ledwinka, who had started his career with Nesselsdorf at the end of the 19th century. He had, however, left that concern tó join Steyr during the war, and only returned to the renamed town to design the first true Tatra of 1923. Right from the start, Ledwinka's cars exhibited their pedigree and his personal likes in motor car design. The first Type 11 used an air-cooled 'vee' engine and swing-axle rear suspension. Even though its engine was at the front, these traits were to be continued forward

for generation after generation. The backbone chassis frame, similarly, was a Ledwinka trademark. Things progressed in logical fashion until the 1930s, when Tatra startled the entire motor car world by announcing the brand-new Type 77 machine. Not only was it a vee-engined air-cooled car, with backbone chassis and swing-axle suspension, but the engine was at the rear, overhung behind the line of the back wheels, and the full-width body was streamlined in a more successful style than that of Chrysler's Airflow, which had preceded it. The Type 77 was the first of a whole family of Tatras, traces of which can still be seen in modern examples built in Czechoslovakia for the Communist party leaders who are the only Czechs able to run them.

The backbone chassis tube was forked at its rear and embraced an air-cooled 90-degree V8

engine. The power pack, unusually for its time, but familiarly today, had the engine behind the line of the transaxle and the gearbox ahead of it, so that the gear linkage could pass through the backbone tube to a lever between the front seats. The rear suspension, as in so many subsequent rear-engine designs, featured a massively wide transverse leaf spring clamped to the top of the axle case and fixed to hub carriers at each side; along with the fixed length half-shafts this gave the car swing-axle rear suspension. The Type 77 was a big car in every way. It was as long from bumper to bumper as a Rolls-Royce of the 1970s and weighed about 3,700lb (1,678kg) without passengers, so its engine had to work hard to give it a respectable performance. Maximum speed was of the order of 85mph (or more than 90mph when an enlarged 3,400cc engine was fitted).

TALBOT ROESCH SERIES

Talbot 14/45, 65, 70, 75, 90, 95, 105 and 110 models, built from 1926 to 1937 (data for 1931 '105' model)

Built by: Clement Talbot Ltd., Britain.

Engine: Six cylinders, in line, in seven-bearing cast-iron block. Bore and stroke 75mm by 112mm, 2,969cc (2·95in × 4·41in, 181·1cu.in). Detachable cast-iron cylinder head. Two overhead valves per cylinder, 'staggered in line' and operated by pushrods and rockers, from single side-mounted camshaft. Single up-draught Zenith carburettor. Compression ratio 6·7:1. Maximum power 100bhp at 4,500rpm.

Transmission: Single-dry-plate clutch and four-speed manual gearbox (without synchromesh), both in unit with engine (from late 1932, preselector four-speed gearbox was standardised). Right-hand gearchange. Propeller shaft, in torque tube, to spiral-bevel 'live' rear axle.

Chassis: Separate pressed-steel chassis frame. Channel-section side members and pressed and tubular cross bracing. Forged front axle beam. Semi-elliptic leaf springs at front and rear, with piston-type hydraulic dampers. Worm-and-nut steering. Four-wheel, rod and cable-operated drum brakes. 29in centre-lock wire-wheels. 5·5 × 29in tyres.

Rolling chassis constructed by Talbot. Coachwork to choice — four-seat tourer, sports or saloon — by Darracq (commercially linked to Talbot) or specialist coachbuilders.

Dimensions: Wheelbase 9ft 6in (290cm), tracks (front and rear) 4ft 7·5in (141cm). Overall length (depending on coachwork) about 14ft 9in (450cm). Unladen weight (chassis only) 2,050lb (930kg).

History: Talbot cars were made in West London, at Barlby Road, from 1904, but it was not until just after World War I that the company became part of the French–English Sunbeam–Talbot–Darracq combine, whose guiding light was Luios Coatalen. Georges Roesch, Swiss-born, had learned his craft as a motor car designer in France, later moving to Britain, where he became chief engineer of the Talbot concern in 1916. After a short period with Sunbeam, in Wolverhampton, and at the French Talbot concern in Paris, he returned to London in 1925. The British Talbot company was struggling, with almost non-existent sales and a poor but honest design. Roesch's job was to revitalise both.

His first new design, dubbed the 14/45, was launched in the autumn of 1926 and established the pedigree which was to be unbroken for a decade. The chassis, like all subsequent Roesch chassis, was conventional enough, and not outstanding in any department, but the six-cylinder engine was superb. At first it had only four main bearings and 1,665cc, but successive redesigns eventually gave it a seven-bearing crankshaft and 3,377cc (in the 110). The engine was

brilliantly conventional, with very light and efficient valve gear and only ever a single carburettor. Even so the best (racing) version version of the 110 engine developed more than 160bhp and allowed a Talbot to reach nearly 140mph at Brooklands. Talbots raced and rallied with distinction between 1930 and 1934, being noted for their refinement and reliability as much as for their great pace. In an era where supercharging was very fashionable in motor sport, Talbots never even used multiple carburettors. This was Roesch's policy and undoubtedly held the cars back from outright victories, but the publicity spin-off was obvious. Talbot (along with Sunbeam) were taken over by the Rootes group in 1935, and the Roesch pedigree was speedily lost as the existing models were progressively 'Humberised'. The last Roesch-Talbot being prepared would have established a new pedigree, with all-independent suspension, but the Barlby Road factory was, by 1935, ill equipped to build modern designs. Roesch also designed a magnificent straight-eight 'Sunbeam' engine for Rootes, based on the 110 six, but this did not go into production.

Right: Georges Roesch's brilliantly integrated design served Talbot from 1926 to 1937, in different guises. The 105s were famous as race or rally cars. This is a 1931 Offord tourer body.

Handling was not very good — a combination of the heavy rear engine and the swing-axle suspension did not help· — but there was an astonishing amount of space by conventional standards. The absence of a normal chassis frame was a great advance, of course, and the full width styling did the rest.

During the 1930s the Type 77 family was steadily improved and expanded. After the Type 77A came the Type 87, in which the engine became 2,970cc again, but with a lot of weight taken out of the car, and power output boosted to about 75bhp, maximum speeds of up to 100mph were claimed. A sister car, the Type 97, with the same basic body but with a new horizontally opposed four-cylinder 1,760cc engine, produced only 40bhp. After the German occupation in 1939, private car manufacture was

discouraged, and the factory was turned over to truck production, although there were Type 87 models on sale until 1941. Tatra's factories were nationalised by the Communist Czech state in 1945 and the Type 87 rear-engined car was put back into production. The engine pedigree of the Type 77/87/97 family was lost in 1948 when the Tatraplan 600 appeared, but even this car was based on the same structure and chassis engineering. Production was transferred to Mlada Boleslav from Koprivnice, to make way for expanded truck production, and sales of cars continued to be restricted to Czechoslovakia and her immediate friendly neighbours. There was even a gap between 1954 and 1957 when no private cars were made at all, but the new Type 603, which still subscribed to the well-known Ledwinka layout was then introduced, with a

Above: The rear-engined Type 77 Tatra, one of the most famous designs ever to come from Hans Ledwinka's drawing board. It was made in restricted numbers in Czechoslovakia, yet contained many advanced features. The engine was an air-cooled vee-8 at the rear, the style of body full-width, and there was all-independent suspension from a tubular steel backbone chassis frame. The wind-cheating qualities were good, but the car was heavy and handled rather badly.

2,472cc rear-mounted air-cooled V8 engine. This car, in much restyled and much modernised form, is now known as the T613, and survives with a 3·4-litre engine. A classic, if unconventional strain.

THOMAS-FLYER

K-6-70 models, built from 1907 to 1912 (data for 1908 New York-Paris racing car)

Built by: E. R. Thomas Motor Co., United States.

Engine: Four cylinders, in line, in four separate cast-iron blocks, with three-bearing light-alloy crankcase. Bore and stroke 146·1mm by 139·7mm, 9,362cc (5·75in × 5·5in, 571cu.in). Non-detachable cast-iron cylinder heads. Two side valves per cylinder, in T-head layout with valve stems and springs exposed, operated by two camshafts mounted in sides of crankcase. Single up-draught carburettor. Maximum power 72bhp.

Transmission: Triple-dry-plate clutch, in unit with front-mounted engine, and separate four-speed manual gearbox (without synchromesh). Remote-control right-hand gearchange. Straight-bevel differential, in tail of gearbox, and countershaft drive to exposed sprockets. Final drive to rear axle by side chains.

Chassis: Separate pressed-steel chassis frame, with channel-section side members and pressed cross bracing. Forged front axle beam. Front and rear suspension by semi-elliptic leaf springs. Friction-type dampers (on New York-Paris race car). Worm-type steering. Mechanically operated foot brake by externally contracting bands on drums fixed to transmission countershaft each side of gearbox. Mechanically operated hand brake by externally contracting bands on rear wheel drums. Fixed artillery-style wheels. 36 × 4in tyres (front) and 36 × 5in tyres (rear).

Dimensions: Wheelbase 11ft 8in (356cm), tracks (front and rear) 4ft 8in (142cm).

History: Edwin Ross Thomas was a businessman, previously interested in railways, bicycles and motor cycles, although he never learned to drive a car. The first Thomas car was built in 1902 and the name changed to Thomas-Flyer in 1905. By that year the range included four big chain-drive cars, 40hp and 50hp fours and a 60hp six, all in the best North American engineering traditions, with individually cast cylinders on an alloy crankcase, a T-head layout and fixed cylinder heads. Prices ranged from $3,000 to $7,000 — which put the cars in the Peerless/Packard bracket.

The company's high spot was in winning the New York-Paris race in 1908 — the longest race ever promoted then and now. A K-6-70 model driven by George Schuster (the company's chief road tester) took 170 days to complete 13,341 miles — and that car is preserved in Harrah's Collection in the United States. The car was quite typical of Thomas-Flyer engineering at the time, except that shaft-drive cars were already being offered. The famous victory, however, meant that the K-6-70 model was retained, complete with chain drive, until 1912, by which time its engine had been enlarged to 12·8-litres.

Left: There were Thomas cars from 1902 and Thomas-Flyers from 1905. At first they all featured chain drive, and big T-head pattern engines, but from 1908 conventional shaft drive was also used. The 1909 model shown had everything a wealthy North American enthusiast could need, including fine styling, a strong chassis, ample ground clearance and good effortless performance. The Thomas-Flyer which won the mammoth 170-day New York to Paris road race of 1908 (a distance of 13,341 miles) was a factory-developed version of the standard product, and was driven by the company's chief tester. This historic car has been restored, and is in Harrah's collection, in America.

TRIUMPH DOLOMITE (1930s TYPE)

Dolomites, built from 1936 to 1939, in four-cylinder and six-cylinder form (data for 1939 Dolomite Roadster)

Built by: Triumph Motor Co. Ltd., Britain.

Engine: Six cylinders, in line, in four-bearing cast-iron block. Bore and stroke 65mm by 100mm, 1,991cc (2·56in × 3·94in, 121·5cu.in). Cast-iron cylinder head. Two overhead valves per cylinder, operated by pushrods and rockers from single camshaft mounted in side of cylinder block. Three horizontal constant-vacuum SU carburettors. Maximum power 75bhp at 4,500 rpm.

Transmission: Single-dry-plate clutch and four-speed, synchromesh manual gearbox (no synchromesh on first gear), both in unit with engine. Remote control central gearchange. Open propeller shaft to spiral-bevel 'live' rear axle.

Chassis: Separate pressed-steel chassis frame, with channel-section side members (underslung at rear), tubular and braced cross members and central cruciform. Forged front axle beam. Semi-elliptic leaf springs at front and rear. Hydraulic piston-type dampers. Worm-and-nut steering. Four-wheel, hydraulically operated drum brakes. 17in centre-lock wire wheels. 5·50 × 17in tyres.

Dimensions: Wheelbase 9ft 8in (295cm), tracks (front and rear) 4ft 4·5in (133cm). Overall length 15ft 3in (465cm). Unladen weight 3,150lb (1,428kg).

Triumph-supplied coachwork, three-abreast seating, with separate two-seat dickey seat. Folding hood. Saloon and drophead coachwork on same chassis with less power, still called Dolomites.

History: The story of the Dolomites begins with the Glorias, announced in 1933. These used a new chassis, but licence-built Coventry Climax inlet-over-exhaust engines. Donald Healey became Triumph's technical director soon afterwards, and developed an all-Triumph overhead-valve engine, which had many similarities to the Climax units. The Dolomites, announced in 1936, effectively replaced the Glorias, had synchromesh gearboxes and were available in four-cylinder (1,232cc) and six-cylinder (1,991cc) guise — the six having a longer wheelbase. Bodywork was all Triumph designed, by Walter Belgrove, and special coachbuilt versions were also available. Donald Healey was a great sporting person, and wanted a special rally car in this range. The Dolomite Roadster, therefore, appeared in 1938 and effectively was an ordinary Dolomite (four or six), with the same Jumbo-style nose, but with a graceful sloping tail in which a couple of dickey seats were hidden. The Roadster was a good looker and a great success, although a bit pricey, and helped Triumph forge a good sporting name. The company, overall, was not financially healthy and closed down in 1939 while the Roadster was still selling well. The car was never revived after World War II, although the 1800 Roadster carried on its dickey-seated traditions.

Below and right: Triumph's Dolomite Roadster was made in 1938/39, but its influence was felt at Standard-Triumph post war too. It was an excellent rally and concours car, the last of a line of Healey-designed touring cars.

TRACTA

Tractas, built from 1926 to 1934 (data for 1930 model)

Built by: S.A. des Automobiles Tracta, France.

Engine: S.C.A.P. built. Four cylinders, in line, in three-bearing cast-iron combined block/crank-case. Bore and stroke 67mm by 105mm, 1,498cc (2·64in × 4·13in, 91·4cu.in). Detachable cast-iron cylinder head. Two overhead valves per cylinder, operated by pushrods and rockers from single camshaft positioned in side of crankcase. Two side-draught RAG carburettors.

Transmission: Front-wheel-drive: engine behind gearbox and gearbox behind line of final drive and front wheels. Single-dry-plate clutch, four-speed manual gearbox (without synchromesh) and spiral-bevel final drive unit, all in unit. Remote-control facia-position gearchange. Universally jointed drive shafts to front wheels.

Chassis: Separate pressed-steel chassis frame, with channel-section side members and pressed and tubular cross-members. Independent front suspension by coil springs and vertical pillar location. Light 'dead' rear axle beam, with reversed quarter-elliptic leaf springs. Lever-arm hydraulic dampers. Four-wheel, cable-operated drum brakes, inboard at front, at each side of final drive unit. 29in centre-lock wire wheels. 5 × 29in tyres.
Open or coupé body styles.

Dimensions: Wheelbase 8ft 6in (259cm), widest track (front) 4ft 3in (129·5cm). Overall length 13ft 3in (404cm). Unladen weight 2,075lb (941kg).

History: Once designers had worked out how to make driven wheels able to be steered, they turned their hands to front-wheel-drive cars. Up until the 1920s, however, only conventionally laid-out cars sold well. In France several designers elected to build front-drive machines, but only one, the Tracta, was successful. Designed by J. A. Grégoire, the Tracta sports car used a Citroën-type (or should we call the Citroën a Tracta-type?) layout, where the final drive was at the front, a gearbox behind it and the engine behind that. This, almost incidentally, gave ideal weight distribution and helped to improve the handling. Grégoire cut corners by adopting a Lancia-style independent front suspension, but with drive shafts and inboard brakes, and located the rear suspension beam by reversed quarter-elliptic springs copied from Bugatti. The wheels were given a pronounced crab track. The original car had 1,100cc (and could be Cozette-supercharged to order), but by 1929 the car had grown up to 1½-litres and there was a 1,600cc saloon. Grégoire even tried six-cylinder (Continental or Hotchkiss manufacture) engines, but the last Tracta was made in 1934.

Below: J. A. Grégoire's Tracta sports cars had front wheel drive, later copied by Citroen. They sold for 8 years.

TRIUMPH TR SPORTS CARS

**TR2, TR3, TR3A, TR4, TR4A, TR5 and TR6
(data for TR3A)**

Built by: Standard-Triumph Motor Co. Ltd., Britain – later British Leyland Motor Corporation Ltd., Britain.

Engine: Four cylinders, in line, in three-bearing cast-iron block. Bore and stroke 83mm by 92mm, 1,991cc (3·27in × 3·62in, 121·5cu.in). Cast-iron cylinder head. Two overhead valves per cylinder, operated by pushrods and rockers from single side-mounted camshaft. Twin semi-down-draught constant-vacuum SU carburettors. Maximum power 100bhp (net) at 5,000rpm. Maximum torque 118lb.ft at 3,000rpm.

Transmission: Single-dry-plate clutch and four-speed, synchromesh manual gearbox (no synchromesh on first gear), with optional Laycock overdrive, all in unit with engine. Remote-control central gearchange. Open propeller shaft to hypoid-bevel 'live' rear axle.

Chassis: Separate steel chassis frame, with box-section side members, box and tubular cross bracing and cruciform centre section. Independent front suspension by coil springs and wishbones with telescopic dampers. Rear suspension by semi-elliptic leaf springs and lever-type hydraulic dampers. Worm-and-peg steering. Four-wheel, hydraulically operated brakes, front discs and rear drums. 15in pressed-steel-disc wheels or centre-lock wire spoke wheels. 5·50 × 15in tyres. Open two-seat pressed-steel sports car bodywork, with optional steel hardtop.

Dimensions: Wheelbase 7ft 4in (224cm), track (front) 3ft 9in (114cm), track (rear) 3ft 10in (117cm). Overall length 12ft 7in (384cm). Unladen weight 2,170lb (984kg).

History: Triumph were taken over by the Standard company in 1945. Several minor attempts were made to sell successful pre-war Triumphs in the 1940s, but it was the inspired improvisation which produced the TR2 that really provided the spark. The TR sports car was requested by managing director Sir John Black as a small-production car to compete with MG and Morgan, but using many standard parts. The prototype even used a much-modified pre-war Standard Nine chassis frame, which

made it certain that the roadholding would be poor; development soon eradicated the problems, however. The TR2's design started in 1952, the car was on sale by summer 1953 and by the end of 1954 it was an acknowledged success. The formula, apart from low cost and simplicity, was to use the understressed Vanguard engine, tuned and modified (and sleeved down below the important 2-litre competition class limit), with modified versions of the Vanguard's gearbox and back axle behind it. The chassis frame was, in production form, quite new, but front suspension was from the quaintly styled Mayflower saloon. The Laycock overdrive was an important option, and before long this was arranged to operate on top, third *and* second gears. The TR2 was fast – it could nudge 110mph – and recorded more than 30mpg in everyday use. It was also very rugged and reliable, which made it an ideal prospect for European-style rallying. Private

owners also found that the engine could be persuaded to give more than 120bhp and found the TR2 a worthy club-race car. The factory also raced, for publicity purposes and to prove engineering developments such as the Girling disc brakes tried successfully at Le Mans in 1955.

The TR2 became the TR3 in 1955, with more power, and a year later that car was equipped with front-wheel disc brakes – the first British car to be so offered. For 1958, the TR3 became the TR3A, with yet more power (100bhp instead of the TR2's original 90bhp), with a revised front style, better trim and more standard fittings. The doors now had outside handles and with the hardtop the car was a cheekily effective little GT car. Before the last of the TR3As was sold in 1962 a total of 83,500 examples had been built and the United States market in particular had taken the car to its heart. MG, for all their traditions, feared the TRs very much and did

Below: Perhaps the most 'classic' of all Triumph TRs—the TR3A built from 1957 to 1962. This was the improved version of the TR2, with front-wheel disc brakes, and a 100bhp engine. It was the most popular British rally car of the 1950s, winning many events.

everything they could to surpass them. After the TR3A, changes came thick and fast. In 1961 the TR4 arrived, really an improved TR3 chassis, with modern wind-up-window body by Michelotti. Less than four years later the TR4A was revealed, using TR4 mechanicals and the same basic body, but with a new all-independent suspension chassis (rear coil spring suspension was like that of the luxurious Triumph 2000 saloon).

That was the last of the 'traditional' four-cylinder engined TRs, for the TR5 of 1967 was really a TR4A in chassis and body with the relatively new fuel-injected six-cylinder 2,498cc engine, also developed for Triumph 2000 saloon use. The last of the changes to the still-recognisable strain came at the beginning of the 1969 year, when the Karmann-styled bodyshell, adapted from that of the TR5, was announced as the TR6. The TR6, then taking on the mantle of almost a 'vintage style' British sports car, ran more or less unchanged until 1976, when it was finally phased out from the North American market. The last examples had been sold in Britain and Europe a year earlier. By now the TR6 had been superseded by the all-new TR7 which carried over absolutely none of the traditional features. The TR's attraction, whether in 1955, 1965 or 1975, was that it was a determinedly simple machine, refined enough for its purpose, but nevertheless a man's car. Well over a quarter million of all types produced — TR2 to TR6 — confirm that the formula was right.

Left: Spiritual ancestor of the TR2, but with little common engineering, was the TRX prototype of 1950. Only three were built (two are still in use) with this smooth two-seater touring body. The chassis and engine were Standard Vanguard, and there was electro-hydraulic operation of seats, hood, and headlamp covers. The body shell was of double-skinned alloy. Unfortunately the car was quite heavy, and could only reach about 80mph.

Bottom right: Latest in the line is the fixed-head coupe TR7, with its engine taken from the Dolomite saloon range. The TR7 is aimed particularly at the North American market, and fittings like the 'safety' bumpers are obvious on this example.

Above: One of the very first Triumph TR2s, built in the autumn of 1953. The driver is Ken Richardson, who had much to do with the car's development and its (later) competition programme. The TR2 was simple, strong, and offered remarkable value for money. Only 8,628 TR2s were built, but well over a quarter million TRs have been sold.

Below: By 1967 the Triumph TR series had already been given one new body shell and an all-independent chassis. Then came this version, the TR5, with a 2½-litre six-cylinder engine, with fuel injection (first on a British production car), and 150bhp. It could reach 120mph, was restyled for 1969, and became the long-running TR6.

TURCAT-MÉRY 14HP

14hp models, built from 1912 to 1914 (data for 1912 model)

Built by: Automobiles Turcat-Méry S.A., France.

Engine: Four-cylinders, in line, in cast-iron block, with three-bearing light-alloy crankcase. Bore and stroke 80mm by 130mm, 2,610cc (3·15in × 5·12in, 159·3cu.in). Non-detachable cast-iron cylinder head. Two side valves per cylinder, operated directly from single camshaft mounted in side of crankcase. Single horizontal Turcat-Méry carburettor.

Transmission: Cone clutch, in unit with front-mounted engine, and shaft drive to separate four-speed manual gearbox (without synchromesh). Remote-control right-hand gearchange. Open propeller shaft to straight-bevel 'live' rear axle.

Chassis: Separate pressed-steel chassis frame, with channel-section side members, tension tie rods under frame for extra strength and tubular cross bracing. Forged front axle beam. Front and rear suspension by semi-elliptic leaf springs. Worm-type steering. Rear wheel drum brakes, operated by foot pedal. Artillery-style road wheels. 875 × 105mm tyres.

Choice of open touring or closed coachwork.

Dimensions: Wheelbase 10ft 1in or 10ft 7·5in (307cm or 324cm), tracks (front and rear) 4ft 5in (135cm). Unladen weight (chassis only), 1,900lb or 2,000lb (862kg or 907kg).

History: This company was founded by Leon Turcat and brother-in-law Simon Méry after they had tested Panhards and Peugeots in the 1890s. The first cars, built in Marseilles, were sold in 1898, but the two shortly signed an agreement with De Dietrich to design cars for that firm. Subsequently, parallel types were marketed by both firms — both having 12·8-litre monsters in the 1904 Gordon-Bennett trials. Later Turcat-Mérys became more conventional, but even so it was one of these cars which won the very first Monte Carlo Rally of 1911. In the last three years before World War I, an entire range of cars from 14hp to 35hp was marketed, with a family of related side-valve engines. Even the massive 6-litre 35 was a big four. The 14hp, with 2·6-litres, was the smallest and the cars were expensive and aimed at the upper-class market. In this period the Turcat-Mérys were ruggedly handsome, with elegant and recognisable radiators and with styling that would not disgrace the later vintage years. This, however, was Turcat's high period, for the firm declined in the 1920s and stopped making cars altogether in 1928.

Right: A typical pre-World War One Turcat-Mery tourer, with an impressive full four-seater body. Most cars of this type, made in France, Belgium, or even in North America, were built to a pattern—the high and stately styling, massive lamps, impressive fold-down hood, big and solid artillery-style road wheels, and no-nonsense chassis could all be seen on competing motor cars. From 1911 there was a big range of Turcats—from 14hp to 35hp.

UNIC 12/14 TAXI

12/14 model, built from 1908 to 1928 (data for 1910 model)

Built by: Sté. des Anciens Ets. Georges Richard (later S.A. des Automobiles Unic), France.

Engine: Four cylinders, in line, in cast-iron block, with three-bearing light-alloy crankcase. Bore and stroke 75mm by 110mm, 1,944cc (2·95in × 4·33in, 118·6cu.in); stroke increased to 120mm and capacity to 2,121cc (4·72in and 129·4cu.in) from 1912. Integral cast-iron cylinder head. Two side valves per cylinder, in T-head formation with exposed valve stems and springs, operated by tappets from crankcase-mounted camshafts. Single up-draught Unic carburettor. Maximum power about 15bhp at 1,500rpm.

Transmission: Cone clutch, in unit with front-mounted engine, and shaft drive to separate three-speed manual gearbox (without synchromesh). Remote-control right-hand gearchange. Open propeller shaft to straight-bevel 'live' rear axle.

Chassis: Separate pressed-steel chassis frame, with channel-section side members and channel-section cross bracing. Forged front axle beam. Front and rear suspension by semi-elliptic leaf springs. Optional lever-arm hydraulic dampers. Worm-and-sector steering. Rear wheel drum brakes operated by foot pedal. Transmission drum brake, externally contracting, operated by hand lever. Artillery-style wheels. 810 × 90mm tyres.

Taxi-cab bodywork, with no front doors.

Dimensions: Wheelbase 8ft 10·3in (270cm), tracks (front and rear) 4ft 5in (135cm). Overall length 12ft 2·1in (371cm). Unladen weight (chassis only) 1,455lb (660kg).

History: The marque name derives from Georges Richard's desire to make only a single model of car from his new factory, but this resolve lasted less than a year. Richard had left the Richard-Brasier business in 1905, after a policy clash, and set up again nearby. Unic products were never famous for their performance, or for their looks, but the 12/14 model, which was never sold as a private car, is now legendary as the famous London taxi for more than a generation. The taxi was simple and rugged, having that mandatory tiny turning circle, and seemed to be mechanically indestructible. All the time that the taxi was being made, other private cars were being sold, but in general they were undistinguished and Unic became more interested in selling commercial vehicles (they are now a subsidiary of Fiat). Modern taxi drivers, and enthusiasts, should look closely at the Unic, to see the spartan conditions in which the drivers had to operate. They had no doors to keep them warm, and certainly no heater, although the fare-paying passengers were somewhat better off.

Right: The legendary Unic 12/14 model, only ever sold as a taxicab, and a well known sight on London streets for a generation. The driver was exposed, but the 'fare' was comfortable. Below: In 1909, Unic also built private cars with similar basic layout, like this tourer.

VOISIN 18CV TYPE C1

18CV model, built from 1919 to 1926 (data for 1919 model)

Built by: S.A. des Aeroplanes G. Voisin, France.

Engine: Four cylinders, in line, in cast-iron block, with five-bearing light-alloy crankcase. Bore and stroke 95mm by 140mm, 3,969cc (3·74in × 5·51in, 242·2cu.in). Detachable cast-iron cylinder head. Knight sleeve-valve breathing, with sleeves moving up and down, and in eccentric motion, inside cylinder walls. Sleeves operated from shaft and connecting rod linkages, shaft located in side of crankcase. Single side-draught Zenith carburettor.

Transmission: Single-dry-plate clutch and four-speed manual gearbox (without synchromesh), both in unit with front-mounted engine. Remote-control right-hand gearchange. Propeller shaft, enclosed in torque tube, driving spiral-bevel 'live' rear axle.

Chassis: Separate pressed-steel chassis frame, with channel-section side members and pressed-steel and tubular cross bracing. Forged front axle beam. Front suspension by semi-elliptic leaf springs, rear suspension by cantilever semi-elliptic leaf springs, torque tube and radius arms. No dampers. Worm-and-nut steering. Rear wheel drum brakes, with two pairs of shoes — one pair operated by hand-lever, and one pair by foot pedal — with mechanical linkage. Bolt-on disc wheels. 880 × 120mm tyres. Open or closed coachwork to choice.

Dimensions: Wheelbase 11ft 6in (350·5cm), tracks (front and rear) 4ft 8in (142cm). Overall length 14ft 10in (452cm). Unladen weight 3,950lb (1,791kg).

History: Gabriel Voisin was first of all famous for his aircraft. He was a pioneer and claims to have invented a *practical* aeroplane before the Wright brothers had properly developed their own. With mass-production of aeroplanes looming after the end of World War I, he turned to making cars. A licence to build a Citroën model was taken up and the Voisin C1 car was launched. This was notable for its Knight sleeve-valve engine of nearly four litres, but was otherwise conventional in design. The torque-tube transmission and the lack of front brakes were both typical of the period. It was a strong, silent and very refined car, and later versions could achieve up to 80mph. Voisin himself was so impressed by the sleeve-valve layout that he made sure that every other Voisin car made until 1939, when manufacture closed down, was so equipped. The C1 was by no means Voisin's only early design — it was joined shortly by the little 1¼-litre C4 on the one hand and the very rare V12 car in 1921 on the other. Later there were straight sixes, and revived V12s, but fortunately nothing came of his proposal to build a straight-12 in 1936 (which was really two sixes, one behind the other).

Because they all used Knight sleeve-valve engines, the Voisin cars were always more silent and refined than their competition. Sports car buyers were still of a breed which expected fast cars to be rough and noisy, so the Voisin's well-behaved 4-litre four-cylinder engine came as a very pleasant surprise. One of the hallmarks of the early cars was the distinctive vee-formed radiator shell — as proud and as easily-recognised as the massive prow of a real 'W.O.' Bentley, or as notable as that of the classic Rolls-Royce or Hispano-Suiza. Voisin's engine's were both more powerful and more spirited than one usually expected of a sleeve-valve unit (not all were as under-state as those sold by Daimler of Great Britain by any means). This was due to the liberal use of light-alloy in engine construction.

By the time Voisin cars came to be raced, they had been given four-wheel brakes. Voisins romped home one-two-three in the French Touring Grand Prix in July 1922, the winning car averaging 66·9mph and accomplishing no less than 16·6 miles per gallon. However, not even the excellence of the sleeve-valve fours allowed them to last for ever — some engine vibration was still present — and the 4·5-litre straight six introduced in 1927 took over from the famous old 18CV car.

Right: All Voisin cars made between 1919 and 1939 (when production ceased) had Knight sleeve-valve engines. The 18CV model, built until 1926, was a heavy but excellent vintage sports car with masses of torque from its four-litre engine. Like the Bentleys and Vauxhalls of its day, the Voisin was long on strength and power, but short on agility. This is a 1923 example.

VOLVO P1800

P1800, 1800S, 1800E and 1800ES, built from 1960 to 1973 (data for 1800S)

Built by: AB Volvo, Sweden.

Engine: Four cylinders, in line, in five-bearing cast-iron block. Bore and stroke 84·1mm by 80mm, 1,778cc (3·31in × 3·15in, 108·6cu.in). Cast-iron cylinder head. Two overhead valves per cylinder, operated by pushrods and rockers from single side-mounted camshaft. Twin semi-down-draught constant-vacuum SU carburettors. Maximum power 100bhp (net) at 5,800rpm. Maximum torque 110lb.ft at 4,000rpm.

Transmission: Single-dry-plate clutch and four-speed, all-synchromesh manual gearbox, with electrically operated overdrive, all in unit with engine. Remote-control, central gearchange. Open propeller shaft to hypoid-bevel 'live' rear axle.

Chassis: Unitary-construction pressed-steel body chassis unit, in closed two-seat coupé form. Bodies built by Pressed Steel in Britain. Car assembled by Jensen, but from mid 1960s assembled by Volvo in Sweden. Independent front suspension by coil springs, wishbones and anti-roll bar. Rear suspension by coil springs, radius arms and Panhard rod. Cam-and-roller steering. Front disc brakes, and rear drums. 15in bolt-on pressed-steel-disc wheels. 165 × 15in tyres.

Dimensions: Wheelbase 8ft 0·5in (245cm), tracks (front and rear) 4ft 3·8in (132cm). Overall length 14ft 5·3in (440cm). Unladen weight 2,500lb (1,140kg).

History: The Volvo 1800 sports coupé made its name all over the world as the car chosen by 'The Saint' in that well known TV series based on the Leslie Charteris novels. It was a strikingly styled closed two-seater (shaped by Volvo without outside assistance) and used a complete power train from the Amazon' range of saloons which had already established Volvo's reputation for rugged, reliable and no nonsense motoring. At the end of the 1950s Volvo were short of factory space, and made a unique agreement in Britain. Pressed Steel would build the body shells, while Jensen would assemble the cars from components supplied from Sweden. The arrangement worked well for a few years, until Volvo decided to upgrade the car, improve the quality, and make it themselves. P1800s were Jensen-built, while

1800S cars were built in Sweden. The 1800 engine was enlarged to a full two litres in 1968, but from 1969 this engine was given Bosch petrol injection and developed up to 125bhp. In 1971 Volvo jumped on the three-door bandwagon by giving the car an estate car shape with a vast opening rear window. This, as the 1800ES, carried on into 1973, when it was finally discontinued. There has been no sporting-car successor from Volvo, who appear to be completely wedded to heavy safety-car engineering for the late 1970s.

Above: Almost identical views of two versions of the 1800, showing how the basic styling was unchanged for more than ten years. Top: The 1966 1800S with twin carburettor engine and 1800cc. Above: The 1970 1800E with fuel injection and 2-litres.
Above right and right: Two views of the original Jensen-assembled P1800. In the 1970s Volvo made a square-back 'estate' 1800ES.

VAUXHALL 30/98

30/98 models, built from 1919 to 1927, E and OE Types (data for 1927 OE type)

Built by: Vauxhall Motors Ltd., Britain.

Engine: Four cylinders, in line, in five-bearing cast-alloy block/crankcase. Bore and stroke 98mm by 140mm, 4,224cc (3·86in × 5·5in, 257·7cu.in). Detachable light-alloy cylinder head. Two overhead valves per cylinder, operated by pushrods and rockers. Single up-draught Zenith carburettor. Maximum power 120bhp (gross) at 3,500rpm.

Transmission: Multi-dry-plate clutch, in unit with engine. Four-speed, synchromesh manual gearbox. Remote-control right-hand gearchange. Open propeller shaft with channel torque stay and sliding-block rear universal to spiral-bevel 'live' rear axle.

Chassis: Separate pressed-steel chassis frame, with rolled-steel subframe to support engine and gearbox. Channel-section side members, with pressed and tubular cross bracing. Forged front axle beam. Semi-elliptic leaf springs at front and rear, with Hartford friction-type dampers. Worm-and-nut steering. Hydraulically operated drum brakes (1927 model only) on front and on transmission, hand-operated brakes on rear. Centre-lock wire wheels. 820 × 120 beaded edge tyres. Coachwork normally supplied by Vauxhall, of four-seat open-touring type. Chassis very rarely supplied to outside coachbuilders for closed styles to be erected.

Dimensions: Wheelbase 9ft 9in (297cm), tracks (front and rear) 4ft 8in (142cm). Overall length 13ft 7in (414cm). Unladen weight 3,360lb (1,524kg).

History: Vauxhall began making cars in 1904, but these were of no great distinction until L. H. Pomeroy became chief engineer. He loved to develop competition machinery and his great forte was in engine design, the cars which won the British 2,000 miles trial proving this in no uncertain manner. In 1910 the first sporting Vauxhalls were prepared for the 'Prince Henry' German trials and following success in that event a series of cars called 'Prince Henry' were sold for around £600 each. There were also Coupe de l'Auto single seaters in 1911/1913 and even a Grand Prix Vauxhall in 1914. The very first 30/98, the prototype of a classic vintage series, was built in 1913, as a better and faster derivative of the 'Prince Henry', but its story really belongs to the vintage years. The 30/98 had a larger engine (4,525cc) than the Prince Henry Vauxhall, which was no longer as rapid as the opposition, and right from the start was guaranteed to be capable of 100mph in stripped racing form. This, in effect, made it the Jaguar E-type of Edwardian days as it was so much quicker than almost all its rivals. The price was however so high (£900 for the chassis alone) that it found few takers in 1914.

The origins of the 30/98 model name are obscure, but possibly the 30 denoted power developed at 1,000rpm (a figure important to the RAC for taxation purposes), and 98 referred to the claimed maximum output at around 3,000rpm. Production of the car, with its simple but effective side-valve engine, got under way properly in 1919 and the car was properly called the E as it had followed Bs, Cs, and D-type cars designed before the war. It was a fast and heavy car, with good roadholding for its day and very impressive performance. The snag was that the price was still very high — £1,670 in the beginning, but down to £1,300 in 1921, which still put it up among the elite like the 3-litre Bentley, which was always one of its principal rivals. About 270 of these cars were made before the car was redesigned in 1922.

The main change for the new series of car was that the engine was converted to overhead-valve operation, which probably explains why the model name became OE (O = overhead-valve engine). By this time, Pomeroy had left the company, but as Ricardo was an engine consultant to the company he was able to advise on the new layout. The new engine produced about 115bhp at 3,300rpm and was notable, among other things, for having dura-lumin connecting rod stampings — a material which had come into use in World War I aero-engines. Surprisingly enough the OE had no front-wheel brakes when announced, which left it technically behind Bentley in the middle of its life. The car also had a spiral-bevel axle, instead of the previous straight bevel, and a stiffened chassis frame. By now the 30/98 was a very fast car (considerably more so than the 3-litre Bentley, as its supporters never tired of recalling)

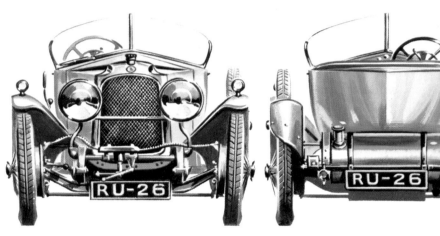

Above and right: Vauxhall's 30/98 sports car, especially the later OE model, was a match for the 4½-litre Bentleys of the day. The car shown was built in 1924, with a pretty boat-tailed four-seater body called a Wensum, and the overhead valve 4·2-litre engine produced about 115bhp. Only the last (1927) models had front wheel brakes. Like all the best vintage cars, the 30/98 was strong but simple, fast and reliable.

Left: The famous 'Prince Henry' Vauxhall, designed to compete in the well-known German trials, was the real ancestor of the 30/98. The Prince Henry, however, was a true Edwardian car, the 30/98 really a vintage car.

Below: Full four-seater OE 30/98 of 1924, with polished aluminium panels.

because of the excellent power output, and also because of the relatively light weight (about 3,000lb — 1,360kg), but it was never one of Vauxhall's biggest-selling models. By 1925, indeed, and the time of the company's take over by General Motors, it was only truly in batch production as demand called for new stocks. In 1926, however, the finest and best of all OEs were announced, and made in small numbers. For £950 (chassis alone) the customer could now have yet more power — about 120bhp — but could control it with four-wheel brakes. The fronts and the transmission drum brake were hydraulically operated (a very early hydraulic application) while the rear brakes were cable operated from the hand lever. By then, however, the 30/98's biggest problem was becoming its age as a design (it was still noticeably 'Edwardian' in its outlook and its proportions) and the fact that it had a 'big four' engine which made its delightful presence very obvious. At the price asked it was having to compete with more sophisticated six-cylinder models from Sunbeam and Bentley. The last OE model was built in 1927, making a total of 312 of that variant. 586 30/98s were made, in all, between 1919 and 1927, and a goodly proportion survive to this day. It is sad to say that Vauxhall never again made such a fine car, as General Motors policy was to turn Vauxhall into a mass-production combine.

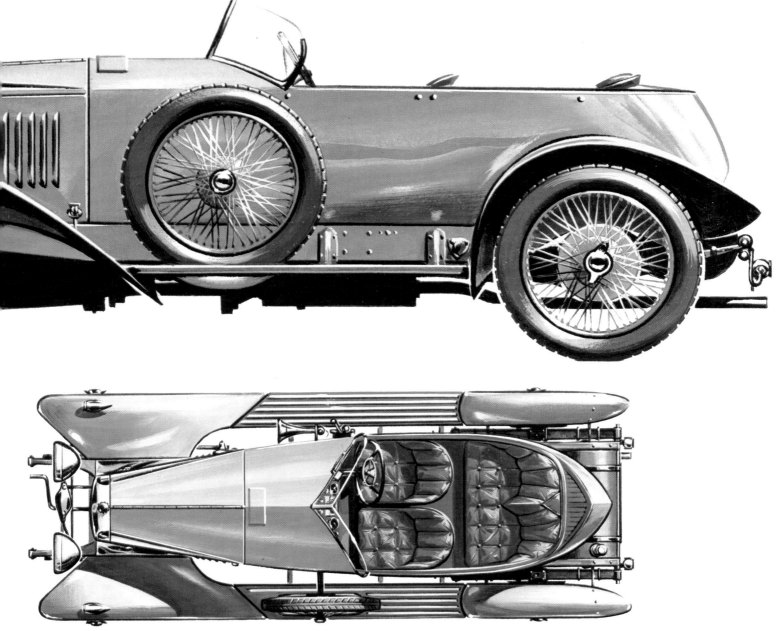

VW BEETLE

Beetles, built in various forms from 1939 to date (data for 1950s-type 1200)
Built by: Volkswagenwerk GmbH, West Germany.
Engine: Four cylinders, horizontally opposed in separate light-alloy cylinder barrels, with three-bearing light-alloy crankcase. Air cooled with vertical cooling fan driven from crankshaft. Bore and stroke 77mm by 64mm, 1,192cc (3·04in × 2·52in, 72·7cu.in). Two light-alloy cylinder heads. Two overhead valves per cylinder, operated by pushrods and rockers from single camshaft, centrally mounted in crankcase. Single down-draught Solex carburettor. Maximum power 36bhp (gross) at 3,700rpm. Maximum torque 56lb.ft at 2,000rpm.
Transmission: Single-dry-plate clutch and four-speed, synchromesh manual gearbox (without synchromesh on first gear), both in unit with rear-mounted flat-four engine. Engine behind line of rear wheels and gearbox ahead of it. Remote-control central gearchange. Spiral-bevel final drive and exposed, universally jointed drive shafts to rear wheels.
Chassis: Pressed-steel punt-type platform chassis frame, topped by bolted-on pressed-steel two-door saloon or convertible coachwork, all built by VW. Independent front suspension by trailing arms and transverse torsion bars. Independent rear suspension by swinging half-axles, radius arms, and transverse torsion bars. Telescopic dampers. Worm-and-roller steering. Four-wheel, hydraulically operated drum brakes. 15in bolt-on pressed-steel-disc wheels. 5·60 × 15in tyres.
Dimensions: Wheelbase 7ft 10·5in (240cm), track (front) 4ft 3in (130cm), track (rear) 4ft 2in (127cm). Overall length 13ft 4in (406cm). Unladen weight 1,610lb (731kg).
History: By every logical consideration, the VW Beetle should never have succeeded. It was uncompromisingly original, the victim of politics and a ruinous world war, and it was rejected as war reparations by the so-called sophisticated car-makers. Yet the Germans persevered with it, put it haltingly into production at the end of 1945 and made an enormous success of it. To date — it is still being built not only in Germany but in several other countries — getting on for 20 *million* have been sold — which makes the Beetle the best-selling car of all time. Only the Model T Ford could approach it and that now lags around five million behind. The VW has never officially been called a 'Beetle', but was given that nickname soon after its public debut at the end of the 1930s. The general layout of the car goes even further into history than is generally realised. At first it was the private brainchild of Dr Ferdinand Porsche, who set up his own design studios in Stuttgart at the beginning of the 1930s. For Zundapp (a five-cylinder radial engined car) and for NSU (a flat-four) he designed rear-engined prototypes, but neither could afford to tool up for mass production. In 1934 Porsche was directed by the Nazi government to design a 'people's car'. The first three prototypes, similar in many ways to the NSU designs, were built by Porsche in his own workshops, and were ready in 1936. A series of 30 pre-production cars were built on his behalf by Mercedes-Benz in 1937 and by 1938 the final version was ready. Foundations for the new factory at Wolsburg were laid in 1938; but for the preparations for war the production cars would have been ready in 1939/40.

Military machines, using VW mechanicals, were built in the 1940s, but in 1945 the factory had been bombed and was nearly derelict, and private-car production had still not really begun. However, under the direction of the occupying powers (the British in this part of Germany) the cars began to be built; the first 1,785 examples were made before the end of 1945. At first they had 1,131cc engines, un-synchronised transmission and cable brakes, but they were remarkably cheap, reliable and popular in car-starved Germany. In spite of every possibly

practical and financial obstacle, sales continued to rise. By the end of the 1940s the factory was already being expanded and VW was well on its way to being a formidable German car maker, with the dedicated Nordhoff in charge of the business. Exports, world-wide, began at the start of the 1950s, and with this came the gradual refinement of the early crude machine. Technically, everything was against the Beetle's success: the roadholding was always poor, performance very restricted, styling was a non-event and passenger/luggage space was restricted. On the other hand, air-cooling meant that the Beetle could be used anywhere in the world and the car's impressive quality and reliability record soon made it an essential for the developing countries.

VW stayed faithful to the machine for far too long — they were a one-product company until the beginning of the 1960s — but this meant that they could concentrate every effort on the Beetle's progressive improvement. Engines were enlarged to 1,192cc in the 1950s, but it was the end of the 1960s which saw the engine pushed up first to 1300, then 1500, and finally to 1600. Hydraulic brakes, Porsche-type synchromesh and very high standards of construction were developed, but nothing was ever done about the living space and very little about the roadholding. Automatic transmission became optional at the end of the 1960s and for a long time Beetles were being built with three or four different engine sizes as options. As the car slipped more and more behind the times, it was given coil-spring front suspension and major restyling, but when VW began to announce their new water-cooled cars — Passat, Golf and Polo — in the 1970s, it became clear that the Beetle would be allowed to die. Interestingly enough, it has outlived all the cars developed from it — notably the VW1500/1600 range and the rather different 411/412 cars. Sales will continue from overseas factories long after German production has ceased — only one plant is still building Beetles in Germany today. It is the classic case of reliability and ruggedness succeeding against all fashion. Like the Model T Ford, it had no obvious close rivals and benefited strongly because of that.

Above: By 1953 the VW Beetle only differed visually from pre-war cars by having a small rear window. The squat shape, conceived by Dr. Porsche, is basically unchanged in modern times.

Above: Love it or hate it, nobody can ignore the Beetle. Styling may be old-fashioned, but detail construction is always sound. Reliability is a legend. The 20 millionth car is due.

Above: Even by 1970, the Beetle looked almost the same as ever. Under the skin was the platform chassis, the torsion bar independent suspension, the rear engine, air-cooled, and a high standard of workmanship. Equipment was sparse, and there wasn't much room, but there were long queues of customers. Beetles loved a rugged life-style, and seemed to last for ever, even if performance was lacking, and roadholding limited. In this model the engine had grown to 1,493cc, and automatic transmission was optional. Front disc brakes had also been added.

WHITE MODEL O 20HP

White Model 0, built from 1909 to 1911 (data for 1908 model)

Built by: The White Co., United States.

Engine: Two-cylinder steam engine, with compound operation, cylinders mounted vertically in nose of car and carried in two-bearing crankcase. High-pressure cylinder bore and stroke 63·5mm by 76·2mm and low pressure cylinder 108·0mm by 76·2mm; total capacity 1,777cc (2·5in × 3·0in and 4·25in × 3·0in; total capacity 108·4cu.in). Joy valve motion, with piston valves operated by levers from cranks attached to crankcase, steam admission at side of chambers. Variable steam-admission cut-off by rocking member. Steam-generator, paraffin powered, under front seats. Maximum power approximately 20bhp.

Transmission: No clutch and no normal gearbox. Drive by open propeller shaft direct from rear engine crankshaft to straight-bevel 'live' rear axle. Two-speed gearbox in unit with final-drive, providing 'normal and emergency low' ratios. Emergency-low ratio not normally required. Remote-control right-hand gearchange.

Chassis: Separate pressed-steel chassis frame, with channel-section side members and pressed and tubular cross bracing. Forged front axle beam. Front and rear suspension by semi-elliptic leaf springs. No dampers. Worm-type steering. Foot and hand brakes mechanically operating on rear-wheel drums, foot brake by externally contracting bands. Artillery-style road wheels. 840 × 90mm tyres. Open four-seat coachwork.

Dimensions: Wheelbase 8ft 8in (264cm), tracks (front and rear) 4ft 8in (142cm). Overall length 12ft 0in (366cm).

History: Although manufacture of White steam cars covered a span of only ten years (1901 to 1911), only one other American 'steamer' enjoyed a longer production run. The 'classic' Whites, with their front-mounted compound engines and shaft drive, appeared in 1903 and formed the pattern for a range of cars built until 1911, when the company turned to conventional petrol-powered machines. Frames, at first, were of armoured wood, but conventional channel-section chassis were adopted later; even so the larger 40hp Model M, announced alongside the Model 0 in 1908, retained its wooden frame. At first the Stephenson-link valve gear system was employed and the nominal '15hp' cars could achieve 50mph. They relied to a great extent on the steam engine's ability to develop its maximum torque from zero revolutions and a two-speed 'emergency' gearbox was fitted in the rear axle only so that the car could pull away up very steep hills.

Apart from its engine, a White steamer looked completely conventional: the engine itself lived under the bonnet where a petrol engine would be found, the fuel was carried in a tank at the rear and the only stranger was the semi-flash boiler, which lived under the seats in the middle of the car. Stanley steamers performed well in early Glidden tours and with success in North American racing events. More powerful Whites – a 20hp Model L and a 30hp Model K – arrived in 1907, but in the autumn of 1908 these were replaced by the 20hp model 0 and 40hp Model M, in which the engine's valve gear had radically been re-designed. The Joy valve gear layout was adopted in place of the previous Stephenson system, which meant that the power units both looked, and were, much simpler and more elegant-looking than before. These were fine cars, but the snag was that the market for steam cars was contracting rapidly. The public was too impatient to get into a car in the morning, start up the burner and wait until steam was raised; they wanted to reach the car, swing it into life and drive away. This, and not the question of unreliability, finally killed off the steamers and White were no luckier than the rest.

Right: By the end of their production run, the White steam cars looked entirely conventional, though they hid steam engines under that compact little bonnet. White steam cars were built for only ten years. Although they were silent and powerful, it took too long to fire them up from cold.

WILLYS JEEP

Jeeps, built from 1942 onwards (data for 1942 military model)

Built by: Willys-Overland Co., United States.

Engine: Four cylinders, in line, in three-bearing cast-iron combined block/crankcase. Bore and stroke 79·4mm by 111·1mm, 2,199cc (3·12in × 4·37in, 134·2cu.in). Detachable cast-iron cylinder head. Two side valves per cylinder, operated, by tappets, from single camshaft mounted in side of cylinder block. One single-choke down-draught Carter carburettor. Maximum power 60bhp (gross) at 3,600rpm. Maximum torque 105lb.ft at 2,000rpm.

Transmission: Four-wheel-drive layout, with normal and emergency-low speed ranges. Single-dry-plate clutch and three-speed, synchromesh manual gearbox (without synchromesh on first gear), along with two-speed-range transfer box, all in line and in unit with front-mounted engine. Three direct-acting gearchanges, in centre of car. Optional front-wheel drive (can be locked in or out of action by one gear lever). Open propeller shaft from transfer box to front and rear hypoid-bevel 'live' axles.

Chassis: Separate pressed-steel chassis frame, with box-section side members and pressed-steel cross bracings. Live front and rear axle beams. Front and rear suspension by semi-elliptic leaf springs. Telescopic hydraulic dampers. Cam-and-lever steering. Four-wheel, hydraulically operated drum brakes, in wheel hubs. Cable-operated hand brake, acting on internally expanding shoes in transmission drum behind transfer gearbox. Pressed-steel bolt-on disc wheels. 6·00 × 16in tyres. Open four-seat bodywork, cross-country type, with canvas hood.

Dimensions: Wheelbase 6ft 8in (203cm), tracks (front and rear) 4ft 0in (122cm). Overall length 11ft 1in (333cm). Unladen weight 2,315lb (1,050kg).

History: Until the beginning of World War II, Willys had led a largely unspectacular and often unsuccessful existence in Toledo. Indeed, as recently as 1933–1936 the company had been struggling through receivership with unpopular and dull cars. In 1939, however, Joe Frazer became president and general manager, and in 1942 he made sure that Willys got a contract to produce probably the most famous utility vehicle of all time – the four-wheel-drive Jeep. This machine was built against a US Army require-ment for a general purpose (G.P.) vehicle for its forces, and although Bantam claim to have built the first such car it was Willys and Ford who reaped the benefit and produced many thousands of them. The 'Jeep' name was a natural bowdler-isation of 'G.P.', and Frazer was astute enough to register it as a Willys trade-mark, which survives to this day. Hundreds of thousands of military Jeeps were made and civilian versions are still in production. The Jeep, along with the British Land-Rover, which followed its layout closely, is probably the most universally exported and most universally appreciated, working machine in the world. The design was simple, rugged, and obvious. The 2·2-litre, four-cylinder engine had been used by Willys cars of the 1930s and there was a rugged three-speed gearbox with transfer gearing, a choice of upper or lower sets of ratios and the option of driven

Above and right: Two views of the legendary Willys Jeep. The vehicle's name was originally 'G P'—or 'General Purpose'—but was quickly modified. A Jeep could go anywhere, and do most things. It was simple, rugged and had excellent (four-wheel-drive) traction. Millions have now been made in military and civilian form.

front-wheels or free-wheeling front wheels. The chassis had boxed main members, the tyres were 'chunkies' and the bodywork was rudimentary almost to a fault. It was meant to – and could – tackle almost anything, and during the war the Allied forces used their Jeeps as indiscriminately as they used bicycles. The Jeep might not have won the war, but victory would have been that much less attainable without it.

WINTON MK XVI

Mk XVI model, introduced 1908
Built by: Winton Motor Carriage Co., United States.
Engine: Six cylinders, in line, in three cast-iron blocks, with four-bearing light-alloy crankcase. Bore and stroke 114·3mm by 127mm, 7,819cc (4·5in × 5·0in, 477·1cu.in). Non-detachable cast-iron cylinder heads. Two side valves per cylinder, operated by tappets from single camshaft mounted in side of crankcase. Single twin-choke Winton carburettor.
Transmission: Multi-disc clutch running in oil, in unit with front-mounted engine. Four-speed manual gearbox (without synchromesh), with third gear direct, and fourth gear and over-drive. Remote-control right-hand gearchange. Engine sump, clutch and gearbox all shared oil from same cast-alloy sump. Propeller shaft, enclosed in torque tube, driving straight-bevel 'live' rear axle.
Chassis: Separate pressed-steel chassis frame, with channel-section side members and pressed and tubular cross-bracing. Forged front axle beam. Front suspension by semi-elliptic leaf springs. Rear suspension by semi-elliptic springs, with location by torque tube and radius arms. Friction lever-type dampers. Worm-type steering. Hand brake and foot brakes both operating mechanically on drums at rear wheel hubs — foot

brakes by externally contracting bands, hand brake by internally expanding shoes. Artillery-style road wheels. 870 × 100mm tyres (front) and 880 × 120mm tyres (rear).
Choice of coachwork.
Dimensions: Wheelbase 10ft 0in (305cm), tracks (front and rear) 4ft 8·5in (143.5cm). Overall length 15ft 0in (457cm).
History: One of *the* very first American cars to be sold to a private customer was a Winton, built by Alexander Winton, a Scotsman, in 1897. This car had a horizontal single-cylinder engine and a two-speed transmission and one mark of respect was that an early sale of a replica was to the Packard brothers. Wintons took part in the first Gordon Bennett races in 1900 with massive 3·8-litre single-cylinder cars. Winton, like other early companies, ran through various mechanical layouts, including an enormous 17-litre, eight-cylinder car driven by Alexander Winton himself in 1903 races. By 1905 the production cars had settled down with conventional in-line four-cylinder engines and gearboxes, though the building rate was very low as each car was essentially hand-built. This, if Winton had only known it, was the beginning of the end for his firm, as no attempt was ever made to streamline these methods. The 16/20, 24/30 and 40/50 cars sold for between $1,800 and $3,500 —

probably not expensive enough to make profits and not as expensive as the more exotic North American rivals. By 1906, production was concentrated on the 5·8-litre Model K, soon followed by the Type XIV. In 1908, however, Winton took another splendid step away from economic reality by announcing their six-cylinder Mk XVI car — or Six-Teen-Six model, as they liked to call it in their advertising. That the company was becoming less and less in touch with the mainstream of North American motor engineering was proved in future years, when such way-out features as a compressed-air starter, and on-board equipment for pumping up tyres, were provided. This, however, was the end of Alexander Winton's pioneering design, for the cars gradually became more and more conventional. The Six-Teen-Six, and its 9½-litre development of 1909, was the peak of mechanical endeavour, so much so that the cars were carried on, basically unchanged, until the last of the Wintons was built in 1924. The company then concentrated on marine diesel engines, and is now a subsidiary of the giant General Motors.

Right: Winton's Six-Teen-Six was built without a thought to car-buying fashion —it looked splendid and handled like a thoroughbred. This is a 1911 model.

WOLSELEY HORNET SPECIAL

Wolseley Hornet Specials, built from 1932 to 1934
Built by: Wolseley Motors (1927) Ltd., Britain.
Engine: Six cylinders, in line, in four-bearing cast-iron block. Bore and stroke 57mm by 83mm, 1,271cc (2·24in × 3·27in, 77·5cu.in). Cast-iron cylinder head. Two overhead valves per cylinder, operated by single overhead camshaft. Twin side-draught constant-vacuum SU carburettors. Power output not quoted. Maximum rpm about 5,000.
Transmission: Single-dry-plate clutch and four-speed manual gearbox, without synchromesh, but in unit with engine. Remote-control central gearchange. Open propeller shaft to spiral-bevel 'live' rear axle.
Chassis: Separate pressed-steel chassis frame, with channel-section double-drop side members and minimal pressed-section cross members. Forged front axle beam. Semi-elliptic leaf springs at front and rear, with hydraulic lever arm dampers. Worm-and-wheel steering. Four-wheel hydraulically-operated drum brakes. 18in centre-lock wire wheels. 4·75 × 18in tyres. Supplied as rolling chassis to specialist coachbuilders.
Dimensions: Wheelbase 7ft 6·5in (230cm), track (front) 3ft 9in (114cm), track (rear) 3ft 6in (107cm). Overall length (depending on coachwork) from 11ft 5·2in (348cm). Unladen weight (chassis only) 1,316lb (597kg).
History: The Hornet Special is a much-maligned motor car. When in production, in the early 1930s, it got itself a bad name because of the flashy bodywork fitted by firms which Wolseley could not control. This was their own fault, as the Hornet Special was sold purely as a rolling chassis. It must not be confused with Hornet saloons completely made by Wolseley in Birmingham. The Special's chassis was too flimsy, which made roadholding not as good as — say — that of an MG Magna with which it had to compete. The engine, although genealogically related to that of the six-cylinder MGs, was not as well developed, and not nearly as powerful. In particular it needed good cylinder-head breathing. The camshaft drive, note, was conventional in this version, by chain, whereas in the MG it was by vertical shaft incorporating the dynamo armature. MG and Wolseley were both personally owned by Sir William Morris at the time and eventually MG record-breaking experience with cross-flow cylinder heads led to this type being fitted to Hornet Specials.

Hornet Specials were rarely used in racing, as their engine size was well below the 1½-litre class limit, but coachbuilders like Eustace Watkins and Swallow could produce some very purposeful sports-car bodies. Cars could have two-seat or four-seat layouts to choice. Along with the cross-flow cylinder head, 1934 models also had synchromesh added to top and third gears, while the chassis frame had cross-bracing added in the shape of a distorted cruciform. Finally, in 1935, the Hornet Special's engine was enlarged to 1,604cc (once again, quite unsuitable for serious competition), with a larger bore *and* stroke of 61·5mm by 90mm (2·42in × 3·54in, 97·9cu.in). In this form it boasted 50bhp at 4,500rpm and was lively though rather under-geared. After 1935, with Nuffield rationalisation progressing apace, the Hornet Special was discontinued and MG was the group's only future sports car.

Right: Every Hornet Special had a coachbuilt body, as Wolseley only sold a rolling chassis. Swallow, who later evolved the SS car, built this four-seater in 1932. Hidden away is the double-drop chassis frame, and the six cylinder engine which was related to MG units of the day. At the time, the bodies were sometimes thought to be flashy.

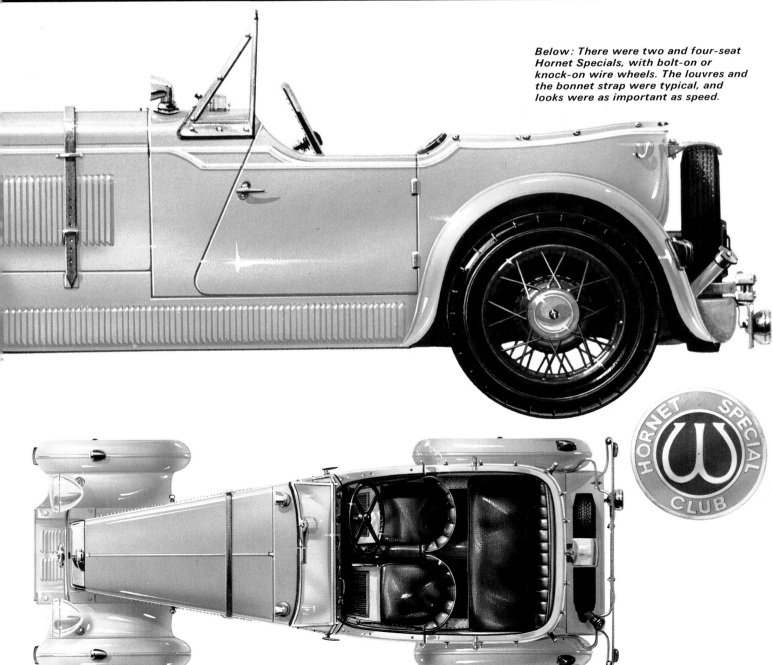

Below: There were two and four-seat Hornet Specials, with bolt-on or knock-on wire wheels. The louvres and the bonnet strap were typical, and looks were as important as speed.

241

WOLSELEY 'HORIZONTAL-ENGINED' MODELS

Wolseley single, twin and four-cylinder cars, built from 1900 to 1905 (data for 1902 10hp)

Built by: Wolseley Tool and Motor Car Co. Ltd., Britain.

Engine: Two cylinders, parallel to each other, in two-bearing cast-iron block, horizontally positioned under the forward floor. Bore and stroke 114·3mm by 127mm, 2,606cc (4·5in × 5·0in, 159cu.in). Cast-iron cylinder head. Two valves per cylinder; automatic (atmospheric) inlet valve and side exhaust valve operated by single cylinder-block mounted camshaft. Leaf-spring return pressure for exhaust valve. Single Wolseley carburettor. Maximum power 10bhp at 700rpm.

Transmission: Leather-faced cone clutch and Renolds chain drive from clutch to separately mounted gearbox. Sliding-pinion gears, giving four forward speeds; differential and countershaft inside gearbox and final drive by side chain on exposed sprockets to rear wheels.

Chassis: Separate steel chassis frame, with channel-section side members and pressed-steel cross members. Forged front axle beam. Semi-elliptic leaf springs at front and rear. No dampers. Tiller steering at first, but wheel steering by 1902. Steering by worm and wheel. Footbrake operating on gearbox countershaft-mounted drum. Handbrake (early series) acting on rear wheel rims (later series) or in drums in rear wheel hubs. Wooden artillery road wheels.
Coachwork to choice — ash framing and hand-beaten steel panels.

Dimensions: Wheelbase 7ft (213cm), track (front) 4ft (122cm), track (rear) 4ft 1·2in (125cm). Overall length (with four-seat tonneau body) 10ft 9·8in (330cm).

History: The Wolseleys built between 1900 and 1905 are historically important because they were really the first *wholly British* machines in any sort of quantity-production. Daimler were selling cars which were mainly Benz copies and Lanchesters were hand-built in very small numbers. The very first Wolseley (a tricycle) was built in 1896 and the second (also a tri-car) followed in 1897/98. These two cars, like all the later horizontal-engined models, were designed by Herbert Austin, General Manager of the Wolseley company. Their story comes to an end when Austin's career at Wolseley ends. In effect, his directors wanted to adopt vertical engines and Austin refused to design such things. The result was that he left the company, formed his own Austin concern — then introduced a series of vertical engined Austins! His first four-wheel Wolseley voiturette was built in 1899 and examples competed in the Automobile Club's 1,000 Miles Trial of 1900. Its performance was such that the company decided to go into production with it. That first car, a single-cylinder machine, was speedily followed by others — twins or horizontal in-line fours — between 1900 and 1905. A total of 327 cars were sold in 1901 and 800 in 1903. This made Wolseley the most prolific of all British makes, a lead which they retained until the outbreak of World War I.

Features of the layout were that the single-cylinder $4\frac{1}{2}$hp engine was placed under the toe-board, with the axis of the cylinder pointing forward and the head, therefore, being at the front of the unit. Whereas the prototype slipped its primary drive belt (from engine flywheel to separately mounted gearbox) the production car had a conventional cone clutch between crankshaft and belt pulley. The gearbox, mounted amidships, had a countershaft with the final drive teeth attached to it, and drive to the rear wheels was by chain. The 1,000 Miles Trial car had had tiller steering, but this was replaced by conventional wheel steering in 1901. Within months the first production Wolseley was joined by the 10hp twin-cylinder model, which effectively had double the original engine, but mounted essentially in the same place in a rather longer and more capacious chassis. Between 1900 and 1904 the single's power output was pushed up to 6hp, while the twin was consequently urged to give 12hp. Between 1902 and 1904 there was also a more expensive horizontal-engined 'four', with a horizontally opposed layout, which also shared the same cylinder dimensions. This engine, for obvious reasons, had two primary chain drives

to the gearbox, one on each end of the engine's crankshaft, and therefore two clutches. A feature common to many other cars of the period was the 'automatic' or 'atmospheric' inlet valve, opened by suction within the cylinder during the appropriate stroke. This was not at all efficient and one reason for the cars' improvements in power in later years was that a mechanically operated inlet valve was specified. Austin was a great believer in motor sport for publicity purposes (at least, he was at this time — later he changed his tune somewhat) and caused a whole series of vast horizontally engined race cars to be built for the Paris–Madrid, Circuit des Ardennes,

and Gordon Bennett events. Called Beetles these machines never enjoyed much success.

Once the Wolseley directors had decided they preferred vertical engines (and inexorable motoring fashion all over the world suggested that they should), there was no future for the original range of cars at Wolseley. The company had already been building Siddeleys, on behalf of J. D. Siddeley, which had vertical engines, and these were satisfactory. The last 'horizontal' Wolseley was built in 1906, but it left behind a legacy of well-proven design details and a company which was already renowned in the British motor industry.

Left and right: In 1904 the single-cylinder 6hp Wolseley looked like this with its engine under the floor, and final drive by chain. There was no windscreen. Wheels were fixed.

Left and right: From 1900 to 1905 the horizontal-engined Wolseleys grew up steadily. The first cars were singles with 4½hp, but by 1905 there were twins and four-cylinder machines. This 10hp twin was built in 1902. The Wolseley-built body is a 'tonneau' and the mechanical layout is typical of the range. Below right: Entrance to rear seats was from the back.

Glossary of Terms

Most items mentioned in the specifications will be familiar to motoring readers, but the following explanations might help

Artillery-style wheels Often shaped from hard wood, these have a few large-section spokes and look like the wheels used on field guns.

Automatic inlet valves Such valves open automatically when the piston sucks air past them and are held closed by compression in the combustion chamber. They have no mechanical connection to camshafts.

Backbone chassis A frame in which the main load-carrying members run down the centre of the car from front to rear

Band brake Where the friction materials are on the outside of the brake -drum and clamp down on to it to apply stopping force

Cantilever spring An elliptic spring where the axle or suspension member is attached to one end, and the main body of the spring is clamped to the frame

Cone clutch Where the drive from engine to gearbox is taken up by a friction clutch shaped like a segment of a cone, mating with a similarly profiled flywheel face

Dry clutch A clutch without lubrication, and where asbestos-based friction materials are used

Dry sump Where the pan under the engine is positively drained by a scavenge pump to a separate oil tank and where a pressure pump returns oil to the lubrication system

Flitch plate Strengthening steel plates — plain or angle-section — for frames made of wood

Gull-wing doors Doors hinged at their top edges rather than front or rear edges. Often gull-wing shaped in profile

Hypoid-bevel final drive A type of final drive where the drive pinion is not directly aligned to the axis of the crown wheel. This gives more silent running and allows the propeller shaft line to be lowered

'Live' axle An axle basically tubular in shape, inside which axle shafts revolve (a 'dead' axle refers to a rear axle which has no drive components of any sort — as with a front-wheel-drive car)

Monobloc Refers to a casting in one unit. Applied particularly to cylinder blocks cast with all cylinders in one unit, or cast integrally with crankcases

Monocle windscreen A circular section windscreen, carried on the steering column, giving protection only to the driver

Monocoque Derived from the French language and literally meaning a structure with one shell, but more generally applied to unitary-construction pressed-steel welded body shells

Punt-type frame A chassis frame with welded-up pressed-steel floor, vaguely resembling a punt, in which most of the stresses are taken

Siamesed When two features — cylinders or inlet ports — are merged together to become one

Sliding pillar A type of suspension where the wheel stub axle is fixed to a pillar which slides up and down a pillar

Space frame A chassis frame with many small-section tubes, welded up in straight lines from stress point to stress point, in three dimensions

Spiral bevel A type of final drive where the drive pinion is directly aligned to the crown wheel axis, but where the teeth are cut in spiral fashion to cut down on noise

T-head North American slang, for side valve engines with one set of valves on one side of the combustion chamber, and one set of valves on the other side. With the piston near the bottom of its stroke, the gaseous space is sectioned like a 'T'

Torque tube A tube fixed firmly to the rear axle and universally jointed at its front end to the car's structure. This takes all torque and driving stresses from the rest of the suspension members and from the propeller shaft

Transaxle General term for front-drive or mid/rear-engine-transmission, where engine, gearbox and final drive are grouped together. Or (in front engined cars) where gearbox and final drive are grouped together at the rear

Unitary construction More strictly this should be 'chassisless', where the structural frame, and the bodywork are all welded-up together when built, and where a separate stress-bearing frame is not present

'Wet' liner Where the engine cylinder liner is not part of the block casting, but is directly in contact with the cooling water

Index

All figures in bold type
refer to items mentioned
in captions.

A

AC (Autocarriers Ltd) co.,
   Britain, 8, 10, 43
   AC 289, 11
   AC 428, 11
   Ace, 8, 10–11
   Ace-Bristol, 10
   Aceca, 10–11
   Acedes, 8
   Aero, 8
   Cobra 260/289/427, 10–11,
      221
   Daytona Cobra 289, 10–11
   Ford Cobra, 11
   Greyhound, 10
   Magna, 8
   Montlhéry 16/40, 8–9
   Shelby American Cobra, 11
   Six 2-litre, 8–9
Adler (Heinrich Kleyer) co., 12
   Trumpf Eight, 12
   Trumpf Six, 12
   1935 Trumpf Junior, 12
AFN (Frazer Nash) co., 39, 108
Ainsworth, Harry, 120–1
Akar, Emil, 19
Albert I, King of the Belgians,
   88
Aldington, H. J. and family,
   42, 108
Alfa Romeo co., Italy, 80, 98,
   143
   B-type, 14
   Giulia GT, 15
   Giulietta, 15
   Montreal, 14
   Monza, 14
   P2 Grand Prix, 14
   RL (Romeo L) series, 12, 13
   RLN, 12, 13
   RLS, 12, 13
   RLSS, 12, 13
   RLT, 12, 13
   Spider Corsa, 14, 15
   Sprint GT, 15
   Sprint Veloce, 15
   Type 33, 14
   8C series, 14
   1500, 14
   1750, 14
   2000, 14
   2300 B-type, 14
   2300 Monza, 14
   2600, 14
   2900, 14
Alfonso XIII, King of Spain, 114
Allard co., Britain, 147
   J/J1/J2R/J2X, 15
   K, 15
   L, 15
   M, 15

P, 15
Palm Beach, 15
Alvis co., Britain
   F-series, 17
   FA/FB/FD/FE 4-cyl., 16
   Grey Lady, 17
   SA/SC, 16
   Supersports, 16
   TA14/TA21, 17
   TB14, 17
   TC21, 17
   TC21/100, 17
   TD21, 17
   TE/TE21, 16, 17
   TF21, 17
   TG/TJ, 16
   10/30, 16, 17
   10/30 Supersports, 16
   11/40, 16
   12/40, 16
   12/50, 16
   12/60, 16
Amilcar co., France, 208
   C-series, 18–19
   E, 19
   G, 19
   J, 19
   L, 19
   M, 19
   Surbaissé, 19
Amon, Chris, 107
Ansaldo co., Italy
   Type 4A, 17
   Type 4CS, 17
Anzani engines, 108, 153,
   214–5
Appleyard, Ian, 126
Aquila co., Italy
   Italiana, 20
Arkus-Duntov racing specials,
   55
Armstrong Siddeley co., Britain
   Sapphire, 20, 220
   Special, 20
Armstrong Whitworth co., 20
Ascari, Antonio, 12
Aston-Martin co., Britain
   DB2, 21, 22
   DB2/4, 21
   DB3, 21
   DB4/DB4GT, 22–3
   DB5, 22–3
   DB6, 22–3
   DB6 Mark II, 23
   DBR1, 22
   DBR2, 22
   DBS, 23
   International, 21
   Le Mans, 21
   Mark II, 21
   Ulster, 21
   2-litre, 21
Auburn co., U.S. 70, 71
   M12/160, 28
   Speedster, 24–5, 28
   Straight-Eight series, 24–5
   V12, 28
   851 Speedster, 24–5

851 Supercharged, 24–5
   see also Cord
Audi co., 118, 178
Austin co., Britain
   A30, 27
   Bantam, 27
   Big Seven, 26–7
   Mini, 30, 44–5
   Seven, 26–7, 96, 111, 185
   Twenty, 26
   Top Hat saloon, 26
Austin, Sir Herbert, 26, 27, 242
Austin-Healey co., Britain,
   15, 16
   Sprite, 115, 168
   100, 28, 172
   100-6 models, 28–9
   100 Sebring, 29
   3000 models, 28–9
Austrian Alpine Tour (1911), 29
Austro-Daimler co., 158
   AD617, 26
   ADM models, 26–7
   ADMI, ADMII, ADMIII, 26–7
   ADR, 27
   ADV17/60PS, 26
   Prince Henry, 26, 29
   16/25 PS, 27
   22/80 PS, 27
Auto Métallurgique co.,
   Belgium, 163
Autocarriers Ltd. see AC
Automobile Club 1000 Miles
   Trial (1900), 242

B

Baker, Cannonball, 218
Ballot co., France
   HS 26, 31
   RH Series Eight, 30–1
   2LS, 30
   2LT, 30–1
   2LTS, 31
Barbarou, Marius, 148
Barnato, Woolf, 32
Bayerische Motoren Werke
   A.G. see BMW
Beaver engines, 163
Belgrove, Walter, 226
Benjafield, Dr., 31
Bennett, Gordon, 230
Benoist, Robert, 79
Bentley co., Britain, 22, 148,
   159, 232, 234–5
   Mark V, 34, 200
   Mark VI, 34, 206
   Peregrine, 34
   Silent Sports, 34
   Speed, 30–1
   Speed-Six, 32–3
   Standard, 30–1
   T-series, 204
   3-litre, 30–1, 234
   3½-litre, 34–5, 214
   4¼-litre, 34–5, 234

6½-litre, 32–3
   8-litre, 32
   Engines, 8, 21, 132
Benz co., Germany, 136, 242
   1880's Tricycle car, 36
   Engines, 59, 77
   see also Daimler, Mercedes
Berliet co., France
   80hp model, 36
Bertelli designs, 21
Bertone designs, 14, 15, 134,
   140
Bignan co., France
   12hp and variants, 37, 54
Birkigt, Marc, 114, 116, 117
Bizzarrini designs, 124
Black, Sir John, 228
Blackburne engine, 108, 122
Blue Flame engine, 55, 57
Blythe Bros. of Canterbury,
   58–9
BMW co., West Germany,
   10, 108, 110
   Batmobile, 40
   Dixi (Austin Seven), 27
   Frazer-Nash, 39
   Mini, 37, 40
   Six-Cylinder coupés, 37,
      40–1
   315, 38
   319, 38
   326, 37, 42, 43
   327, 42
   328, 37, 38, 42, 43
   501 series, 37, 38
   507, 37, 38
   1600 saloon, 40
   1800 saloon, 40
   2000 saloon, 40
   Engines: 37, 38
Bollée cars, 77
   "Bond, James", 23
Bonnet, René, 156
Borghese, Prince Scipio, 125
Boulanger, M., 65
Bow, Clara, 124
Bracco, driver, 139
Brasier co., France, 230
   24hp, 42
Brescia race (1921), 46
Bristol co., Britain, 39, 215
   400–407, 42–3
   450, 43
   Engines: 10, 110
British Grand Prix (1926), 79
   (1927), 16
British Leyland co., 206, 228
   Mini-cars:
   Clubman, 44
   Cooper, 44–5
   Cooper S, 44–5
   Cooper 970S, 45
   Cooper 1071S, 45
   Cooper 1275S, 45
   Moke, 45
   Riley, 44–5
   Sprint, 44–5
   Wolseley, 44–5

850, 44–5
   1000, 44
   1275GT, 44
Broadley, Eric, 107
Brotherhood-Crocker car, 210
Brown, David see David
   Brown Industries
Bruce, Hon. Victor, 8
Buehrig, Gordon, 24, 70, 71
Bugatti co., Italy, 15, 153,
   159, 227
   13 Brescia, 46–7, 72
   30 series, 48
   40 series, 48
   41 Royale/Golden Bugatti,
      47, 48, 49
   49, 48
   49 Weymann, 48
   50 series, 48
   57, 49
   57SC, 49
Burney, Sir Dennistoun, 72

C

Cadillac co., U.S., 12, 16, 98,
   142, 145, 146, 152, 180,
   183, 220
   Black Bess, 53
   Eldorado, 52, 53, 178
   Great Six, 52
   V12, 50–1, 52
   V16, 52
   V63, 51
   50 series, 51
   51 V8, 50–1, 68
   314, 51
   Engines: 15, 28, 142
Cappa, Giulio Cesare, 20, 125
Carlsson, Eric, 208
Carlsson, Pat, 192
Cattaneo, Giustino, 124
Ceirano, Matteo, 125, 212
Chadwick Great Six, 52–3, 178
Chaigneau-Brasier cars, 42
Chapman, Colin, 149, 151
Chapron, Henri, 121
Chapuis-Dornier engine, 111
Charteris, Leslie, 232
Chenard et Walcker co.,
   France
   Torpille, 55
   3-litre, 54–5
Chevrolet co., U.S., 60
   Camaro, 54
   Classic Six, 56
   Corvette, 54
   International Six, 56
   Masters, 57
   Pontiac Firebird, 54
   Standard, 57
   Stingray, 54
   Stovebolt Six, 56
   Engines, 55, 57, 124, 216
Chiron, Louis, 139
Chitty-Bang-Bang, 58–9

Chrysler co., U.S., *12, 15*
Airflow, **56–7**, *147, 224*
Airstream, *56*
Alpine, *156*
De Soto, *60*
Imperial Six, *60*
Maxwell, *60*
Plymouth Superbird, *62*
70–72, **60–1**
300, **62–3**
Engines, *42, 62, 73, 88, 89, 130, 131*
Cisitalia co., Italy
Type 202, *63*
1100, **63**
Citroën co., France, *19, 154–5, 178, 182, 227, 232*
A, **62–3**
Ami 6, *65*
B2, *62*
Big Six, *64–5*
Clover Leaf, *62*
CX, *66*
DS series, *65,* **66–7**
Dyane, *65*
ID series, **66**
Safari Estate, *66*
SM, **66–7**
Traction Avant, *12,* **64–5**
2CV, **65**
5CV, *62*
7CV, *64*
7S, *64*
11CV, **64**
15CV, **64**
Clément-Bayard co., France
Clément, *68*
Clément-Bayard 30, **68**
Clément-Gladiator, *68*
Clément-Panhard, *68*
Clément-Stirling, *68*
Clément-Talbot, *68*
Clyno co., Britain
Eight, *69*
10hp, **69**
Coatalen, Louis, *222*
Cobb, John, *176*
Cole V8 car, **68**
Colombo engine, *88, 90, 94*
Cooper, Gary, *87*
Coppa Acerbo (1924), *12*
Cord cars: L-29, *70–1*
Model 810, *24,* **70–1**
Model 812, **70–1**
Sportsman, *71*
Westchester, *71*
Cosworth engine, *106*
Cottin et Desgouttes co.,
France
Sans Secousse, *72*
Coupe de l'Auto (1911, 1912, 1913), *222*
Coupes des Voiturettes (1906, 1908), *78*
Coventry-Climax engine, *69, 122, 149, 153, 172*
Crossley co., Britain
Crossley-Burney, *72*
Cunningham co., U.S., **62**
C-series, **73**
Cushman, Leon, *16*

D

Daimler co., Germany and Britain, *50, 136, 156, 157, 158, 160, 162, 163, 182, 233, 242*
Corsica, *75*
Double Six, **74**
Phönix, *73*
Sleeve-Valve models, **74–5**
4hp, **73**
see also Mercedes
Dallara, Gian-Paulo, *134*
Darracq co., France, *224*
6·5hp, **76**
Datsun co., Japan
"Austin Seven", *27*
Fairlady, *76*
240Z, **76**
260Z, *76*
280Z, *76*
David Brown Industries, *21, 22*
Davis, "Sammy", *31*
Daytona World Championship (1965), *107*
Deasey, Captain, *194*
De Dietrich co., France, *146, 148, 230*
Lorraine, *77, 148*
24/28hp, **77**
De Dion, Bouton co., France
Single Cylinder, **77**
Engines, *51, 77, 78*
Suspension, *16, 43, 70, 73, 77, 83, 90, 110, 118, 139, 207*
Delage co., France
Colonial, *78*

D1 series, **78–9**
D8 series, **80–1**
Grand Prix, *79, 122*
Sedanca, *81*
Sporting, *78*
Supersports, *78*
Delahaye co., France, *80, 81*
Competition cars, *83*
Coupe des Alpes, *82–3*
Superluxe, *82–3*
135 Sports/Saloon, **82–3**
175S, *83*
235, *83*
Delaunay-Belleville co.,
France, *53, 84*
Sixes, **84–5**
Torpedo de luxe, *85*
Type H/HA, **84–5**
Type HB, **84–5**
Dempsey, Jack, *124*
De Tomaso co., Italy, *134*
Deauville, *86*
GTS, *86*
Mangusta, *86, 134*
Pampero, *86*
Pantera, **86**
Vallelunga, *86*
Dinsmore, Clarence Gray, *156*
Dixon, Freddie, *195*
DKW engine, *208*
Doble Steam Car, **86**
Dobson, Arthur, *82*
Don, Kaye, *143*
Duesenberg co., U.S.
Eight, *87*
J, **87**
Model A, **87**
SJ, **87**
SSJ, *87*
Engines, *52*
Dunn, W. M., *16*
Dusio, Pietro, *63*

E

Earl, Harley, *55*
Earls Court Motor-Show (1948), *110*
East African Safari (1971), *76*
Eberhorst, Eberan von, *130*
Edge, Selwyn, *8, 176*
Elizabeth II, Queen, *207*
England, Gordon, *26*
Excelsior co., Belgium
Adex, **88**
Adex B, *88*
Adex, C, *88*
Albert Premier, **88**
Expo 67, Montreal, *14*
Eyston, George, *171*

F

Facel co., France
Facel Vega HK500, **89**
Facel II, **89**
Facellia, *89*
FVS, *89*
Fall, Tony, *76*
Ferguson Formula car, *131*
Ferrari co., Italy, *10, 12, 73, 98, 134, 159, 161, 189*
America, **92**
Berlinetta, **88–9**
Berlinetta Boxer, **94–5**
Boxer, **94–5**
Daytona, *94–5*
Dino, **92–3**, *95*
Europa, *92*
Grand Prix, *90–1, 92*
Inter, *92*
Lusso, *89*
Mexico, *90*
Mille Miglia, *90*
Superamerica, *92*
Superfast, *92–3*
125, *90*
166, *92*
195, *92*
206GT Dino, **92–3**
212 Inter, *92*
246GT Dino, **92–3**
250 Europa, *90*
250GT, **88–9**, *94*
250GT Berlinetta, **88–9**
250GT Lusso, *89*
250GT 2+2, **93**
250GTO, *89*
275GTB, *89, 94*
275S, *90*
308GTB, *92*
330GT 2+2, **93**
330P, *91*
340/375 Sports, **90–1**
340 Mexico, *90*
340 Mille Miglia, *90*
342 America, *92*
365GT 2+2, *92–3*

365GT/BB, **94–5**, *155*
365GTB4 Daytona, **94–5**
375 America, **92**
375 Plus, *90*
375S, **90–1**
410 Plus, *90*
410 Superamerica, *92*
410 Superfast, *92–3*
500 Superfast, *92–3*
512 GT/BB, *94*
Fiat co., Italy, *17, 20, 92, 140, 141, 212, 230*
Balilla, *96*
Berlinetta aerodinamica, *96*
Campagnola Cross-country, *98*
Spider Lusso, *97*
Topolino, **96–7**
8-V, **98–9**
126, *44*
500 Topolino, **96–7**
508 Balilla, **96–7**
508S Balilla, **96–7**
514, *96*
600, *96*
1100 saloon, *98*
Fiedler, Dr., *39, 108, 110*
Fiorio, Cesare, *140*
Fivet engine, *8*
Ford co., U.S., *208, 238*
Capri, *40*
Cortina, *138*
Edsel, *145*
Escort RS1600, *105,* **106**
Galaxie, 11, **102–3**
GT40, **106–7**
Mirage, *107*
Model A, *56,* **98**, *99*
Model B, *98*
Model C, *98*
Model K, *98*
Model N, *98*
Model T, *26, 56, 96, 98, 99, 238,* **100–1**, *174*
Mustang, *54,* **104–5**
Phaeton, *101*
Runabout, *101*
Thunderbird, *55,* **102–3**, *178*
Tourer, *101*
V-8 1930's, *99*
Zephyr, *10*
Engines, *10, 11, 15, 86, 145, 146, 150, 172, 220*
Foster, Captain, *47*
Franklin co., U.S.
Air-Cooled Model IIB Six, **107**
V12, *107*
Franz Ferdinand, Archduke, *112*
Frazer, Joe, *238*
Frazer-Nash co., Britain, *38, 39, 43*
Boulogne, *108*
Chain Gang, **108**
Continental, *110*
Fast Roadster, *110*
High Speed, *110*
Le Mans Replica, **110**
Le Mans Replica Mk II, *110*
TT Replica, **108**
French Grand Prix (1906), *68, 190*
(1908), *156*
(1912), *88*
(1922), *233*
(1936), *83*

G

Gable, Clark, *87*
Gallop, Clive, *58–9*
Gardner, Frank, *209; see also* Serpollet
Gardner, Major "Goldie", *171*
Gas turbine engine, *207*
Geneva Motor Show (1966), *134*
George V, King, *75*
George VI, King, *137*
German Grand Prix (1928), *159*
Ghia co., *86, 98*
Ginther, Richie, *207*
Gladiator, *68; see also* Clément
Glidden Tour (1906), *186*
GN cars, **110–1**
Gobron-Brillié 100mph Car, **112**
Godfrey, H. R., *111*
"Goldfinger" (film), *23*
Gonzales, driver, *91*
Gordon Bennett Race (1903), *156, 240*
(1904), *42, 230*
Gough-Meadows engine, *108*
Graf und Stift co., Austria
SP5, *112*
SP8, *112*
SR4, *112*
VK, *112*
28/32hp, *112*

Grant, Gerry, *10*
Grégoire co., France, *37, 182*
Triple Berlina, *113*
16/24, **113**
Guinness, driver, *222*
Gurney, Dan, *10*
Guy 20hp cars, **113**
Guy, Sidney, *113*

H

Haig, Betty, *39*
Halford, engineer, *118*
Hall, Eddie, *34*
Harrah Collection, *226*
Harvey, driver, *16*
Healey co., Britain
Abbott, *115*
Alvis-Healey, *115*
Duncan, *115*
Elliott, *115*
Nash-Healey, *115*
Silverstone, **115**
Tickford, *115*
Warwick, *115*
Healey, Geoff, *29, 115*
Hearst, William Randolph, *124*
Henry, Ernest, *30*
Heynes engine, *126*
Hieronymus, Otto, *142*
Higham Special car, *59*
Hill, Graham, *207*
Hispano-Suiza co., Spain and France, *31, 52, 80, 83, 88, 159, 175, 184, 200, 202, 233*
Alphonso, *114*
Boulogne, *116*
H6B, **116–7**
H6C, *116–7*
Sport, *116*
V12, **116–7**
Hitler, Adolf, *158*
Horch co., Germany
Grand Prix, *118*
Straight Eight, *118*
Trabant, *118*
Type 450, *118*
Type 850, **118**
Type 951, *118*
V8, *118*
V12, *118*
33/80PS, *118*
Hotchkiss co., France, *227*
Grand Sport, **120**
Six-Cylinder, **120–1**
Howe, Lord, *133*
HRG co., Britain
Aerodynamic, *118*
1½-litre, **118**
1100, *118*
1500, **118**
Hughes, Howard, *86*
Hurlock bros., *8*

I

Iacocca, Lee, *104*
Indy engine, *73*
Indianapolis 500 Race (1911), *152*
(1930), *218*
Invicta co., Britain, *132*
Black Prince, *122*
1½-litre, *122*
2½-litre, *122*
3-litre, *122*
4½-litre A/NLC/S, **122**
100mph, *122*
Iso co., Italy
Fidia, *124*
Grifo, **124**
Isetta bubble, *40, 124*
Lele, *124*
Rivolta, *124*
Isotta Fraschini co., Italy
Super Spinto, *124*
Tipo 8 series, **124**
Itala co., Italy, *20*
12·9-litre, **125**
61 models, *125*
Italian 2-litre GT Championship (1954), *98*

J

Jaguar co., Britain, *15, 38, 39, 73, 83, 143*
C-type, *126*
D-type, *73, 91,* **126**, *128*
E-type, *76, 127,* **128–9**, *234*
Mark VII saloon, *127*
SS1, *126*
SS90, **126**

SS100, **126**
V12, **128**
XJ6, *128*
XJ-S, *128*
XK120, *39, 83, 126,* **127**, *128*
XK140, **127**
XK150, **127**
XKE, *128–9*
Jano, Vittorio, *12, 14*
JAP engine, *110*
Jeeps, *131, 238*
Jellinek, Emil, *156*
Jenatzy, Camille, *156*
Jenkins, Ab, *24, 87, 187*
Jensen co., Britain, *232*
FF models, **130–1**
Jensen-Healey co., *115, 151*
John, T. G., *16*
Jong, Sylvain de, *174*
Jowett co., Britain
Javelin, *130*
Jupiter, *130*
Joy, Henry, *180*
JW Automotive, *107*

K

Kimber, Cecil, *164, 166, 170*
Kissel co., U.S.
Goldbug Speedster, **131**
Kissel Kar, *131*
6-38, *131*
6-45, *131*
6-55, **131**
Kleyer, Heinrich, *12*
Knight engine, *174*
Knight, Charles Y., *74*

L

La Cuadra car, *114*
Lagonda co., Britain, *22*
LG45 Rapide, *132*
LG6, *132*
V12, **132–3**
4½-litre, **132–3**
Lamborghini co., Italy
Countach, *95,* **134–5**, *155*
Miura, *94,* **134–5**
350GT, *134*
Lampredi engine, *88, 90, 92*
Lamy, Joseph, *19*
Lanchester co., Britain, *74, 242*
Sporting, *40, 136*
Straight Eight, *136*
8/12hp, **136**
38hp, *136*
40, **136–7**
Engines, *199*
Lancia co., Italy, *227*
Appia, *138*
Aprilia, **138**
Artena, *138*
Astura, *138*
Augusta, *138*
Aurelia, *138,* **139**
Beta, **140**
Beta Coupé 2000, **140**, *141*
Beta Spyder, *140*
Flaminia, *139*
Flavia, *141*
Fulvia-Coupé, *140,* **141**
Fulvia HF, *141*
Fulvia HF Lusso, *141*
Fulvia 1600HF/Lusso, *141*
GT 2500, **139**
HPE, *140*
Lambda 1–9, **138–9**
Monte Carlo, *140*
Stratos, *92,* **140**, *141*
Land-Rover, *131, 238*
Land speed record (1902), *209*
(1904), *112*
La Salle V8 cars, *50,* **142**
Laurin und Klement co.,
Czechoslovakia
Laurin-Klement 14-16hp, **142**
Lawrence engine, *172*
Lawrence, Chris, *173*
Lawson, Harry, *73*
Lea and Francis co., Britain
Hyper, **143**
L-types, *143*
P-types, *143*
S-types, *143*
Ledwinka, Hans, *216, 224–5*
Lehmann, Ernst, *163*
Leland, Henry M., *50, 98, 146*
Le Mans Race (1923), *148*
(1924), *30, 148*
(1925), *148, 181*
(1926), *31, 148, 181*
(1927), *30–1*
(1928), *16, 218*
(1929), *32, 218*
(1930), *32, 166*
(1935), *83, 132*

(1937), *119*
(1938), *83*
(1939), *132*
(1949), *21, 110*
(1950), *130*
(1951), *126, 130, 139*
(1952), *130*
(1953), *43, 126*
(1954), *43, 91, 126*
(1955), *127, 228*
(1956), *127*
(1957), *127*
(1962), *173*
(1965), *107*
(1967), *107*
(1968), *107*
(1969), *107*
Leyland Eight car, **143**
Liberty engine, *59*
Ligier, Guy, *66–7*
Lincoln co., U.S.
  Continental, **144–5**
  K-series V12, **146–7**
  Zephyr, *56*, 144, **146–7**
  Engines, *28*
Lindsay, Hon. Patrick, *176*
Locomobile co., U.S.
  Famous 48, *148*
  Model H, *148*
Loewy, Raymond, *216–7*
Lord, Sir Leonard, *174*
Lorraine-Dietrich Silent Six
  car, **148**; *see also* De
  Dietrich
Lory, Albert, *78, 79*
Lotus co., Britain
  Eclat, **151**
  Elan, *150*
  Elite (1950's type), **149**
  Elite, **150, 151**
  Esprit, *150*
  Europa, **150**
  Europa Special, **150**
  Europa Twin-cam, **150**
  Seven, **149**
  Seven Twin-cam, *149*
  Six, *149*
  Engines, *106*
Low, A. M., *113*
Lozier co., U.S.
  Type 1 50hp, **152**
Lurani, Count "Johnnie", *170*
Lycoming engines, *24, 28, 70,
  131*
Lyle, Oliver, *122*
Lyons, William, *26, 38, 126–7*

M

McComb, Wilson, *165*
Macklin, Noel, *122*
McLaren, Bruce, *107*
Maigret police car, *64*
Makinen, Timo, *29*
Marendaz Special car, **153**
Marmon co., U.S.,
  16-cylinder, **152**
  Engines, *28, 52*
Marseal car, *153*
Maserati co., Italy, *86, 98, 134*
  Bora series, *66*, **154–5**
  Merak series, *66*, **154–5**
  Quattroporte saloon, *155*
  Engines, *66*
Matra co., France
  Matra 530, **156**
  Matra-Simca Bagheera, **156**
Maybach co., Germany, *52*
  Zeppelin V12, **157**
  Engines, *58, 59*
Mays, Raymond, *46*
Meadows engine, *108, 118,
  122, 132, 143*
Mercedes (Daimler-Benz), *36,
  65, 136, 157, 163, 182,
  194, 211, 236*
  Grosser, *202*
  Grosser 770, **158**, *162*
  38/250, *158*
  60 model, **156**, *175*
  230SL, **162**
  250SL, **162**
  280SL, **162**
  300SL, *160*
  500K, **162**
  540K, **162**
Mercer co., U.S., *85*
  Raceabout *35*, **163**, *218*
  22/70, *163*
  30-M, *163*
Mercury engine, *15*
Metallurgique 60/80hp car, *163*
MG co., Britain, *21, 28, 29,
  208, 214, 228*
  C Montlhéry Midget, *115
  166, 168, 169, 170*
  D Midget, *169*
  EX135, *171*
  F Midget, *165*
  J1/2/3/4 Midgets, *169, 210*

K Midget, *165*
KN saloon, *171*
M Midget, *164*, **166–7**, *168,
  170, 171*
Magna, *168, 170, 240*
Magnette K, **170–1**
Magnette N, **170–1**
MGA, *169*
MGA Twin-cam, *171*
Midgets, *166–7*, **168–9**
PA/PB Midget, *169, 210*
Q Midget, *169*
R Midget, *168, 169*
TA/TB/TC/TD/TF Midgets,
  168, 169
VA Midget, *168*
YA saloon, *169*
14/40, *164*
18/80, **164–5**
18/80 Mk II, *165*
18/100 Mk III Tigress, *165*
Mille Miglia Race (1927), *181*
  (1933), *170*
  (1947), *63*
  (1951), *139*
  (1953), *90*
Miller, Harry, *70*
Minerva co., Belgium, *88*
  Type AL, *174*
Mini *see* British Leyland
Moglia, Edmund, *175*
Montagu of Beaulieu, Lord,
  201
Monte Carlo Rally (1911), *230*
  (1924), *37*
  (1926), *8, 9*
  (1927), *19*
  (1931), *122, 148*
  (1932), *120, 122*
  (1933), *120, 170*
  (1934), *120*
  (1936), *99*
  (1937), *83*
  (1939), *120*
  (1950), *120*
  (1952), *15*
  (1954), *139*
  (1961), *182*
Montgomery, Field-Marshal,
  167
Monza Race (1924), *58*
  (1926), *181*
Morel, André, *17*
Morgan co., Britain
  Competition, *172*
  Plus Four, **172**
  Plus Eight, **172**
  3-wheeler, *172*
  4/4 4-wheeler, *172*
  4/4 series II, *172*
Morris co., Britain, *69*
  Bullnose Cowley, *9*, *166*,
  174
  Bullnose Oxford, **174**
  Light Six, *164*
  Morris-Minor, *69, 166–7*
Morris, William *see* Nuffield
Mors co., France
  Type Z 60hp, **175**
Moskovics, Fred, *218*
Moss, Stirling, *23*
Moulton, Alex, *44*
Moyet, Edmond, *19*
Munari, Sandro, *141*
Mussolini, Benito, *14, 96*
Mustang engine, *10*

N

Nacional Pescara car, *175*
Napier co., Britain, *8, 50, 84–5*
  Napier-Railton, **176**
  40/50, **176**
Nazzaro, driver, *190*
Nesselsdorf co., Austria, *224*
New York–Paris Race (1908),
  226
Nicholas II, Czar, *85*
Northway engine, *68*
NSU co., West Germany, *96,
  178*
  Ro80 MK I, II, III, **178**
Nuffield, Lord, *170–1, 174,
  195, 242*
Nutting, Gurney, *33, 81, 176*
Nuvolari, Tazio, *63, 171*

O

Offenhauser engine, *73*
Officine Meccaniche co., Italy
  see OM
Oldfield, Barney, *183*
Olds, Oldsmobile co., U.S., *52*
  Curved Dash, *179, 213*
  Toronado, *178*
  Engines, *142*
Olympia Motor Show (1919),

30
  (1928), *164*
  (1932), *170*
OM co., Italy
  Four-cylinder, *180–1*
  Six-cylinder, *180–1*
  Superba, *180*
Österreichische Daimler
  Motoren co., *see* Austro-
  Daimler
Otto, Nikolaus, *36*
Owen, Owen Wyn, *59*

P

Packard co., U.S., *52, 152,
  183, 226, 230*
  Single Eight, **181**
  Super Eight Roadster, **181**
  Twin Six, **180**, *181*
  Type 734 Speedster, **181**
  12-cylinder, *181*
  1899 original, *180*
Panamerica Race, Mexico
  (1951), *90,91*
Panhard et Levassor co.,
  France, *73, 76, 89, 136,
  194, 196, 211*
  Dyna 54, **182**
  Tigre, *182*
  Twin-cylinder, **182**
  24C/24CT series, **182**
Paris Motor Show (1919), *116*
  (1933), *82*
Paris–Bordeaux Race
  (1895), *182*
  (1899), *175*
Paris–Madrid Race
  (1902), *175*
  (1903), *156, 190*
Paris–Rouen Trials (1894), *182*
Paris–St Malo Race (1899),
  175
Paris–Vienna Race (1902), *175*
Parry Thomas, J. G., *59, 143*
Peerless co., U.S.
  Green Dragon, *183*
  V8, **183**
Pegaso Z102/3 cars, **184**
Peking–Paris Race (1907), *125*
Peugeot co., France, *30, 67,
  76, 230*
  Bébé, *184, 185*
  Grand Prix, *222*
  Quadrilette, **184, 185**
  5CV, *185*
Pescara, Raoul, Marquis de, *175*
Pierce-Arrow co., U.S., *52,
  152, 183*
  Fageol, *186*
  Silver Arrow, *187*
  Straight Eight, **186**
  V12, **187**
  66hp, **186**
Plas, Vanden, *33*
Pomeroy, Laurence, *74, 234*
Porsche co., Germany, *26, 63,
  110, 173*
  356, **189**
  911, **189**
  912, **189**
  917, **188**
Porter, Finlay, *163*
Portwine, John, *8*
Prince Henry Tour (1910), *29*
Procter, Peter, *104*
Purdy, driver, *16*

R

Rabe, Karl, *27*
RAC Rally (1965), *29*
  (1972), *76*
Railton *see* Napier
Randall, C. J., *167*
Redélé, Jean, *192*
Renault co., France, *62, 77,
  136, 150, 211*
  A108 Tour de France, *192*
  Alpine, **192**, *193*
  Dauphine, *193*
  Grand Prix, **190**
  Nervastella, *192*
  Primastella, *192*
  Reinasport, *192*
  Reinastella, **192**
  Viva, *192*
  4CV, *192, 193*
Rheims 12-hour Race (1954),
  43, 126
  (1955), *43*
Ricardo, engineer, *234*
Ricart, Wilfredo, *184*
Richard, Georges, *42, 230*
Richards, T., *222*
Richardson, Ken, *229*
Rigal, Victor, *222*
Rigolly, driver, *112*

Riley co., Britain
  Brooklands, *195*
  Imp, **194–5**
  Lynx, *194*
  MPH, **194–5**
  Mini, *44–5*
  Nines, **194–5**
  Engines, *115, 143, 194–5*
Ringhoffer Tatra co. *see* Tatra
Roberts, Bob, *176*
Robins, engineer, *118*
Rochet-Schneider co., France
  18/22, *194*
  20/22, **194**
  30/35, *194*
  30/40, *194*
  40/50, *194*
  45/60, *194*
Roebling family, *163*
Roesch, Georges, *224*
Rohr, Hans Gustav, *12*
Rolls-Royce co., Britain, *34,
  52, 67, 74, 80, 83, 84,
  85, 86, 87, 136, 137,
  143, 176, 224, 233*
  Camargue, **205**
  Corniche, **204–5**
  Phantom I, *198*, **200–1**
  Phantom II, *47, 198*, **200–1**
  Phantom III, *132, 200, 201*,
  202–3, *206*
  Phantom IV, *206*
  Phantom V, *200, 207*
  Silver Cloud, *204*
  Silver Dawn, *200, 206*
  Silver Ghost, *176, 177, 196*,
  198–9, *200, 202*
  Silver Shadow, **204–5**
  Silver Wraith, **200–1**, *206*
  Three cylinder, **196–7**
  Twenty, *34*, **198–9**, *200*
  20/25, *199*
  25/30, *199*
  40/50, *75*
Romeo co. *see* Alfa Romeo
Rootes co., Britain, *220, 224*
Rosengart co., France, *12*
  "Austin Seven", *27*
Rover co., Britain, *222*
  Gas Turbine, **206–7**
  Rover-BRM, **207**
  T1 (Jet 1), **206**
  T2, **206–7**
  T3, **206–7**
  T4, **207**
  75, *206*
  90, *206*
  2000, *207*
  Engines, *172–3, 206–7*
Royce co. *see* Rolls-Royce

S

SAAB co., Sweden
  92, *208*
  93, *208*
  95, *208*
  96, *208*
"Saint", the, *232*
Salmson co., France
  Grand Prix, **208**
  Grand Sport, **208**
  GSC, **208**
San Sebastian 12-hour Race
  (1926), *181*
Savannah Grand Prix (1908),
  53
Sayer, Malcolm, *126*
Schneider, Theophile, *194*
Schuster, George, *226*
Schwab, Charles, *218*
Seaman, Dick, *79*
Serpollet Steam Cars, **209**
Sheffield-Simplex co., Britain
  14/20hp, **210**
  20/30hp, *210*
  45hp, **210**
Shelby, Carroll, *10, 11, 104,
  107*
Shepherd-Barron, Richard, *172*
Siddeley cars, *243*
Siddeley-Deasy co., Britain,
  20, 194
Silver, C. T., *131*
Simca co., France, *63, 96, 156*
Simplex co., U.S.
  38hp, *211*
  50hp, *211*
Singer co., Britain
  Nine, **210**
  Special Speed Le Mans, **210**
  Engines, *118*
Sitges Voiturette Race (1909,
  1910), *114*
Sivocci, driver, *12*
Smith cousins, *69*
Smith S. L., *179*
Società Ligure Piemontese co.,
  see SPA
SPA co., Italy

30–40hp, *212*
Spa 24-hour Event (1949), *21*
Spyker (Spijker) co., Holland,
  157
  6-cylinder, *213*
  12–40hp, *213*
  18hp, **213**
Squire co., Britain
  1½-litre, **214**
Standard-Triumph co. *see*
  Triumph
Standard Vanguard engine, *229*
Stanley co., U.S.
  Steam Cars, **212**
Stewart, Jackie, *207*
Steyr co., Austria, *27, 224*
  Steyr Type XII, **216**
  Waffenauto, *216*
Stuck, Hans, *27*
Studebaker co., U.S., *186*
  Avanti, **216–7**
  Avanti II, *217*
  R-I, *216*
Stutz co., U.S.
  Bearcat, **218–9**
  Black Hawk, *218*
  DV32, *218*, **220–1**
  SV16, *218*
  Vertical Eight, *218*
Sunbeam/Rootes co., Britain
  Alpine I–V, **220–1**
  Coupe de l'Auto, **222–3**
  Sixteen, *222*
  Tiger I–II, **220–1**
  Touring 12–16 series, *222*
  3-litre, **222–3**
  12–16 series, *222*
  Engines, *220–1, 224*
Svenska Aeroplan Aktiebolaget,
  Sweden *see* SAAB
Swedish Rally (1968), *45*
Szisz, Ferenc, *190*

T

Talbot co., Britain, *68*
  Roesch series, **224–5**
  14/45, *224*
  65, *224*
  70, *224*
  75, *224*
  90, *224*
  95, *224*
  105, *224*
  110, *224*
Targa Bologna (1908), *36*
Targa Florio (1923), *12*
Taruffi, Piero, *63*
Tatra co., Czechoslovakia, *216*
  Tatraplan 600, *225*
  Type 77/87/97, **224–5**
  Type 603, *225*
  T613, *225*
Thomas co., U.S.
  Thomas-Flyer, **226**
  K-6-70, *226*
Tojeiro, John, *10*
Tour de France (1964), *104*
Tourist Trophy Race (1906), *36*
  (1922), *30*
  (1928), *16, 27, 143*
  (1931), *108*
  (1932), *108*
  (1934), *108*
  (1936), *133*
Touté, designer, *54*
Tracta Sports Cars, **227**
Trépardoux, designer, *77*
Trevoux, designer, *120*
Tripoli Grand Prix (1926), *181*
Triumph co., Britain, *15, 195*
  Dolomite Four, **226**
  Dolomite Gloria, *226*
  Dolomite Roadster, **226–7**
  Dolomite Six, **226**
  Dolomite 2000, *229*
  Triumph Herald, *229*
  TR series, **228–9**
  TR2, *172*, **228–9**
  TR3, *172*, **228–9**
  TR3A, **228–9**
  TR4, **228–9**
  TR5, **228–9**
  TR6, **228–9**
  TR7, *229*
  TRX, *229*
Turcat-Méry co., France
  14hp, **230**
  Tourer, *230*
Turin Motor Show (1963), *134*

U

Unic co., France
  12/14 Taxi, **230**
U.S. National Stock Car
  Championship (1910),
  152

Utah Trials (1935), *87*

V

Valentino, Rudolph, *124*
Vanderbilt Cup (1908), *53*
  (1911), *152*
Vauxhall co., Britain, *232*
  Coupe de l'Auto, *234*
  Grand Prix, *234*
  Prince Henry, *234*
  Type B/C/D, *234*
  Type E, **234–5**
  Type OE, **234–5**
  30/98, **234–5**
Voisin co., France
  12V, *232*
  18CV Type C1, **232–3**
  18CV Type C4, *232*
Volkswagen co., Germany, *208*
  Beetle, *188*, **236–7**
  Golf, *236*
  Passat, *236*
  Polo, *236*
  411/412, *236*
  1500/1600, *236*
Volvo co., Sweden
  Amazon, *232*
  P1800, **232**
  1800E, **232**
  1800ES, **232**
  1800S, *232*

W

Waite, Arthur, *27*
Wankel engine, *160, 178*
Watkins, Eustace, *240*
Watson, W. G., *122*

Weller, John, *8*
White co., U.S.
  Model K 30hp, *238*
  Model L 20hp, *238*
  Model M 40hp, *238*
  Model O 20hp, **238**
White and Poppe engine, *174*
Whittle jet engines, *206*
Wilhelmina, Queen of Holland, *213*
Willys-Overland co., U.S.
  Jeep, **238**
Wilson, Harold, *207*
Winton co., U.S., *180*
  Mk XVI, **240–1**
  Six-Teen-Six, **240–1**
  Type XIV, *240*
  3 8-litre, *240*
  5 8-litre Model K, *240*
  9½-litre, *240*
  16/20, *240*
  17-litre, *240*
  24/30, *240*
  40/50, *240*
Wisconsin engine, *218*
Wolseley co., Britain, *166, 170*
  Horizontal-Engined, **242–3**
  Hornet Special, **249–1**
  Minis, *44–5*
  Tricycle cars, *242*
Woollard, Frank, *164*
World GT Championship
  (1964), *11*
Wright brothers, *232*
Wyer, John, *107*

Z

Zborowski, Count Louis, *58*
Zeppelin, Count, *157*
Zethrin, Val, *215*
Zundapp car, *236*

Picture Credits

Artwork Credits

PRINTED IN BELGIUM

Vincenzo Trucco winning the 1908 Targa Florio by 14 minutes in an Isotta Fraschini.